Principles of

MACROECONOMICS

Max Gillman

University of Missouri, St. Louis

An Evolutionary Approach

Kendall Hunt
publishing company

Credit for FRED charts throughout:
"FRED" charts (c) Federal Reserve Bank of St. Louis. 2017. All rights reserved. All "FRED(r)" charts reprinted by permission.
http://research.stlouisfed.org/fred2/

Cover image © Shutterstock, Inc.

Kendall Hunt
publishing company

www.kendallhunt.com
Send all inquiries to:
4050 Westmark Drive
Dubuque, IA 52004-1840

ISBN 978-1-5249-1675-6

Published in the United States of America

CONTENTS

Approach of the Book

0.1 Approach of the Book

History, facts and analytic tools combine to create modern macroeconomics. The history shapes the policy imperatives of the time. Facts are used to understand the history and current issues. The analysis drives understanding beyond intuitive capability. The book uses graphs throughout to present the facts of the economy in an historical context. It also uses graphs as the main analytical devise, as based on the underlying models being used.

The urgency of solving national economic, or "macroeconomic", problems, the capability to explain facts, and the expression of policy prescriptions in a rigorous way have merged the "environmental" policy forces with the "genetic" coding of our analytic tools. As in the evolution theory of natural selection, there is a selection of the best traits, while other traits become anachronisms. Through policy dilemmas, a body of facts, and analytic techniques, the less useful Macroeconomic principles become obsolete while the more useful principles flourish. In comparison to Microeconomics, Macroeconomic is the "newer" branch of Economics and its principles have taken new form as they evolve over time.

The evolving nature can make Macroeconomics confusing. Any one era of "Macroeconomics" can be taught as the absolute truth at the cost of discrediting the way in which the consensus "truth" of Macroeconomics principles continues to change. As a result, books on Macroeconomics differ greatly in what they choose to emphasize, unlike Microeconomics books that have an older, firmer, more established basis.

This book gives due respect to how Macroeconomic principles gradually arose and how they continue to be considered today. This necessarily involves a careful look at the *consensus dichotomy* that exists in Macroeconomics. This dichotomy is that Macroeconomics can include as "principles" either the Keynesian approach, or the Neoclassical approach. Many books try to merge these together in a wide variety of ways, with each book's mixture being unique.

This book presents each approach as being unique and albeit often seemingly contradictory to the other approach in its policy prescriptions. The need to include both approaches is that each still dominates a major segment of economic analysis and policy advice as seen in international discourse: in newspapers, in multi-media, news and internet content outlets, and in political election debates. Therefore each of the two major opposing approaches are presented and critiqued in order to understand the different consensus views of the principles of Macroeconomics.

The two main branches of the macroeconomics that have emerged as dominant over time result in often suggest diametrically different policies: the Keynesian emphasis is on useful government intervention within a market environment and the Neoclassical emphasis is on market analysis with government intervention for when there is a break-down of the market mechanism. The dichotomy is not mutually exclusive and it overlaps in various ways, but with different policy prescriptions and different tools of analysis for each of the Keynesian and Neoclassical approaches.

The two branches both have evolved from the Classical lineage of competitive market analysis (as does Marxian analysis to which this book makes reference). The most clear bifurcation point into the two major lineages took place during the economic Great Depression that was experienced internationally in the 1930s. Today these same two lineages continue to dominate strikingly different, alternative, versions of macroeconomic analysis and policy prescriptions.

The common ancestor of Classical economics has meant that both Neoclassical and new Keynesian economics build on often common elements: the foundation of microeconomics. In particular,

Macroeconomics has come to be viewed as extending microeconomics concepts such as supply and demand to the entire economy. We call this entire economy the *aggregate economy*, in that it is measured as the sum of economic activity.

Macroeconomics then gets its name because it is applying Microeconomic principles to the sum of the whole economy's activity. Although a ubiquitous basis for Macroeconomics, sometimes this is called a "Microfoundations approach" to Macroeconomics.[1] Microeconomics develops theory and application of how individual consumers and firms together create supply and demand for particular goods. Macroeconomics in turn looks at ways to sum together all of the markets and analyze a type of *aggregate supply and demand* for all of the economic activity.

0.2 Relation of the Book to Reference Texts

A paradigm shift in macroeconomics has left research and graduate education using the general equilibrium model with capital accumulation of Frank Ramsey (1928) as the basis of both Neoclassical and New-Keynesian models, while undergraduate texts do not include the Ramsey model's of aggregate supply and aggregate demand (AS - AD). In contrast, they use AS - AD as derived from generations of Keynesian models: the Cross, IS-LM, Stagflation theory, and the Phillips Curve. Unfortunately none of these Keynesian models imply an internally consistent theory of AS - AD: they are just "The Stories We Tell: A Reconsideration of AS/AD Analysis", as David Colander put it.[2]

The Ramsey (1928) model does deliver an internally consistent AS - AD analysis and one that can simply tell both the story of real business cycles and the Solow story of long term growth. It may be surprising that all of the below-mentioned texts fail to derive aggregate supply and aggregate demand for output (AS - AD) in a way consistent with our "work-horse" Ramsey (1928) model that lies at the foundation of most graduate level Macroeconomics courses. The main difference of this book to the rest is that it presents the Ramsey AS - AD analysis using a relative price of output, this being the real price of goods relative to leisure. This Ramsey approach underlies modern Economics research, both New-Keynesian and Neoclassical, but is lacking in nearly all current undergraduate macroeconomics textbooks.[3]

Keynesian themed approaches to aggregate supply and aggregate demand are surprising in their diversity of deriving AS - AD from Keynesian foundations. Most common is that instead of using relative prices for supply and demand as in microeconomics they use nominal prices for AS - AD analysis. The resulting failure to derive AS - AD from the Keynesian analysis in a consensus fashion has led to numerous unique derivations of what could well be the basic concept of Macroeconomics: aggregate supply and aggregate demand as graphed against its relative price.

For example Goodwin, Nelson and Harris's (2009, 2nd edition, Routledge) *Macroeconomics in Context* derives the AS - AD from the Keynesian Cross and explains oil price shocks and stagflation by making the inflation rate the price of output in the AS - AD graphs. In contrast, but using the same conceptual approach, Mankiw omits the Keynesian Cross that dates back at least to Samuelson's *Economics* (1951, 2nd edition, McGraw-Hill), but explains stagflation using the nominal price level as the price on the AS - AD diagram. No Keynesian consensus exists on what is the price of AS - AD or how it can be rigorously derived.

A focus on a few of the most popular principles textbooks now in use, with a discussion of comparative content, provides a view of how this book *Principles of Macroeconomics: An Evolutionary Approach* (PMEA) fits within this mix. Many other texts exist. But a focus on Mankiw is apt as it is an international best-seller, with exceptionally high quality writing, and a standard of the economics profession. The following comparison

[1]Kosnik (2015) writes that in "general research foci of economists over the last fifty years," . . . "the 'microfoundations' of macroeconomic papers appears to be increasing." See Kosnik, Lea-Rachel, 2015, "What have economists been doing for the last 50 years? A text analysis of published academic research from 1960–2010," *Economics—The Open-Access*, vol. 9, pages 1–38.

[2]David Colander, 1995, Journal of Economic Perspectives, 9 (3, Summer): 169–188.

[3]See Gillman (2011) *Advanced Modern Macroeconomics*, Pearson Financial Times Press, for the full mathematical derivation of the Ramsey AS - AD model.

in the rest of this section is not essential to read for understanding the PMEA text. Perhaps only teachers themselves would find it of interest.[4]

0.2.1 Mankiw

N. Gregory Mankiw's (2015, 7th edition) *Principles of Macroeconomics* is reputedly one of the most popular textbooks. It is very well-written, has excellent coverage and deserves its best-seller status. It begins with a review of microeconomics in its first nine chapters. Chapter 1 of PMEA covers key micro concepts used subsequently.

Mankiw's text starts a study of national income accounts in Chapter 10. This compares to coverage in Chapter 2.3.2 of PMEA. Mankiw's Chapter 11 shows how to compute price indices in a simple two-good economy, which then are used to determine the inflation rate. This compares to discussion of price indices in Chapter 2.3.3 in PMEA.

Mankiw presents the production function in Chapter 12. He uses it to discuss growth without any supply and demand analysis. In comparison, PMEA's Chapters 1 and 2 present production functions, while PMEA Chapter 9 presents a fuller development of Solow growth theory. This includes its presentation using aggregate supply and demand.

Mankiw introduces aggregate supply and demand graphs in Chapters 20, with an implicitly nominal price of output that leads to a presentation of the Keynesian "oil shock" theory of cost-push inflation and stagnation. This puts forth a non-monetary, Keynesian, approach to inflation and oil price shocks that does not relate to the money supply. PMEA discusses these Keynesian inflation theories in Chapter 6. There PMEA provides an alternative way to view aggregate supply and demand using relative prices. And PMEA presents the alternative monetary basis of the 1970's oil shocks that occurred after the world gold standard (Bretton Woods) ended.

Mankiw discusses the monetary system in Chapter 16 and the money supply cause of inflation in Chapter 17. PMEA presents in Chapter 5 the monetary system along with supply and demand for money and the quantity theory of inflation being caused by money supply. Mankiw adds in money demand that he links to an aggregate demand analysis in Chapter 21, again using the nominal price of goods rather than a relative price.

In contrast, PMEA sets out the Ramsey (1928) -based aggregate supply and demand (AS – AD) analysis in Part III of the book. Chapter 8 presents the basics of AS – AD analysis in the "Ramsey World" using the relative price of goods output, as in Microeconomics, along with a close link to labor market supply and demand as consistent with modern day labor theory. Mankiw's Chapters 20 and 21 have no link between its output supply and demand and modern labor market theory.

Mankiw presents a Chapter 15 on "unemployment" in which he describes aspects of the labor market without use of supply and demand in the labor market except for a graph on the minimum wage. PMEA covers the special case of a labor market with a fixed wage rate in Chapter 8.5. PMEA first sets out the general Ramsey labor market with supply and demand as dependent on the price of labor relative to goods. PMEA shows changes in employment through its real business cycle analysis in Chapter 8.

PMEA Chapters 7 and 8 analyze business cycles first in the capital market in Fisher's two-period framework of Chapter 7, and then in the full Ramsey economy in goods, labor and capital markets in Chapter 8. PMEA explains changes in both employment and investment through supply and demand changes over the business cycle. Mankiw alternatively considers what are called "short-run" changes in aggregate demand for goods output in the Chapters 21 and 22.

Mankiw characterizes normal business cycles in Chapter 20.1 by the "Fact 1: Economic Fluctuations are Irregular and Unpredictable". This contrasts with the real business cycle theory that dominates Neoclassical Macroeconomics by its ability to explain many of the "stylized facts" of normal business cycles. PMEA introduces real business cycle facts in Chapter 4.4.1 with an in-depth analysis in Chapter 8.

[4]There are many principles textbooks in Macroeconomics that can be used as references for additional reading. Some focus on the evolution of Macroeconomics as does this book, such as De Vroey's 2016 *A History of Macroeconomics from Keynes to Lucas and Beyond*. Numerous other alternative macroeconomic principles books have been written and widely used.

Mankiw's Chapter 13 is on savings and investment. It uses supply and demand graphs to show policies. In PMEA, Chapter 7 covers both the Keynesian IS-LM savings theory and the Neoclassical Fisherian two-period savings and investment approaches. Mankiw's Chapter 14 presents finance theory including the present value discounting of capital. PMEA emphasizes the role of banking in Chapter 3, capital market risk measures in Chapters 4, Sections 4.3 and 4.4, banking more broadly in Chapter 5, banking in crisis periods in Chapters 6.5 and 6.6 and Irving Fisher's present discounted value in Chapter 7.5. PMEA includes a Ramsey World banking productivity led crisis in Chapter 8.6. PMEA turns to banking regulation in Chapter 10.6 and banking is found throughout the last Chapter 11.

Mankiw's Chapter 22 is devoted to the theory and evidence of the Phillips curve, with a cost-push AS – AD theory and a nominal price of output. PMEA Chapter 6 presents the Phillips curve theory and evidence and compares it to the debt-deflation theory of Neoclassical economics. Chapter 6 also provides new Phillips curve evidence for during the Great Depression and the Great Recession as well as during the 1960's. Chapter 6 shows a link between deflation and asset market crashes, as a possible explanation for Phillips curve evidence, to contrast with the Mankiw Chapter 22 approach that Phillips curves are caused by cost-push inflation.

Mankiw discusses major economic crises with "boxes" such as in Chapter 20 "In the News" on "The Social Influence of Economic Downturns". PMEA takes on major economic crises as a major theme of the book. PMEA Chapter 3 describes how Keynesian Economics arose from "Depression Era Economics", as Samuelson's (1951) textbook describes it. PMEA Chapter 3 describes the Keynesian Cross analysis as the crisis based economics that Keynes began, while contrasting that to the Neoclassical Debt-Deflation crisis that focuses on asset market crashes and banking.

PMEA continues description of crisis analysis in Chapter 4 as it is presented in real business cycle theory, an aspect not found in Mankiw. PMEA Chapter 5 includes how crisis policy can cause interest rate effects related to the Neoclassical Debt-Deflation theory. PMEA Chapter 6 presents the Phillips curve analysis as viewed not only in terms of the "expectations theory" but also relative to crisis experience. Mankiw instead offers an oil price theory of the economic crisis called "stagflation", which he argues explains Phillips curves evidence during the Vietnam war period. PMEA presents the alternative Debt-Deflation theory using Phillips curve evidence; PMEA shows the correlation of these Phillips curve episodes to stock market crashes and booms, and corresponding finance sector crashes and booms (Chapters 6 and 11).

PMEA Chapter 6 describes how the turning point of the Great Depression coincided with major bank reform, especially the establishment of federal deposit insurance with the FDIC; Mankiw's Chapter 16 (p.337) describes bank runs including during the Great Depression. PMEA Chapter 7 shows how the IS-LM analysis assumes special assumptions based on the Great Depression; it shows how to reproduce the only graph in Keynes's (1936) *General Theory* using Fisher's two period analysis. This is a capital market graph that leads to the familiar IS curve, which Keynes used to characterize "excess savings" during the Great Depression.

While Mankiw has no description of the Keynesian Cross or the Keynesian IS-LM analysis and how these were used to justify "stabilization policy", Mankiw's Chapter 23-1 provides a general discussion on "stabilization policy". PMEA Chapter 4.4 describes how the stabilization policy concept arose, and how real business cycle theory offers business cycles as normal, regular, changes that are likely to be impossible to eliminate, although social insurance policy (Chapter 10) can ameliorate the detrimental effects. PMEA Parts II and III endeavor to explain both these normal business cycles and more extreme economic crises. PMEA Part IV on Policy presents Chapters 10 and 11 for a broad macroeconomic perspective on government action in general and during the Great Recession in particular.

PMEA Chapter 8.6 shows the modern AS – AD graphical explanation of a bank-led crisis such as the Great Recession. It does this by extending the Ramsey economy to include financial intermediation and a crash in bank productivity that in turn lead to an asset market crash. This represents analytically key elements of the experience during the Great Depression and Great Recession. And this is formally presented using only graphs: of aggregate supply and demand in the goods, labor and capital markets.

Mankiw Chapters 9, 18 and 19 discuss international trade and aspects of international economic analysis. Mankiw's Chapter 19 switches to supply and demand for "loanable funds", instead of savings and investment, while his Chapter 18 presents a historical graph of US investment and savings. PMEA omits international trade, real exchange rates and net capital accounts; instead it only includes in Chapter 7.6 how net exports affects the domestic savings rate in national income accounting and in historical data on the US personal savings rate and the investment rate. PMEA leaves trade analysis to more a advanced treatment, such as the two-agent Neoclassical Ramsey economy in Gillman (2011), *Advanced Modern Macroeconomics*); Chapters 3, 6, and 14.

0.2.2 Barro

Robert J. Barro's 1997 5th edition of *Macroeconomics* takes a similar approach to PMEA. It uses advanced equations unlike PMEA but lacks the PMEA AS – AD graphs as derived from the Ramsey model. Yet it still takes the same "representative agent economy" approach as does PMEA. Barro's textbook was one of the first renown Macroeconomics text to describe the Neoclassical view in this way, although other texts have included various representative agent elements of Neoclassical Economics.

Barro's first four editions, starting in 1984, were published by John Wiley and Sons. Barro's fifth edition in 1997 was published by MIT Press. Barro switched publishers again for his updated version that he renamed Macroeconomics: a Modern Approach, published in 2008 by Thomson/Southwestern. Barro (2008) is at a more advanced level than Barro (1997). Not found in Barro's excellent textbooks is the Ramsey (1928) representative agent's AS – AD analysis, as derived originally in Gillman (2011) and as used in PMEA.

Barro's textbooks and PMEA share in common a methodologically consistent approach based around the Ramsey representative agent economy. This approach is taken at higher levels by Obstfeld and Rogoff (1996, first edition), by Ljungqvist and Sargent (2000, first edition) and Stokey and Lucas with Prescott (1989). But most undergraduate texts instead offer some Neoclassical elements plus a mix of Keynesian IS-LM, Keynesian Cross and Phillips Curves that is used in turn to "derive" AS – AD analysis, despite much criticism of the invalidity of the resulting AS – AD analysis such as by Colander (1995).[5] PMEA instead offers both Neoclassical and Keynesian analyses within historical context such that the demonstrated weaknesses of each are made clear from the unifying microfoundations perspective.

0.2.3 Other Textbooks

Blanchard's six editions of *Macroeconomics* with Pearson Prentice-Hall began in 1997, with the 6th in 2013. Here is a standard Keynesian approach but with neoclassical elements of technological progress and Solow (1956) growth included. This derives AS – AD from IS-LM analysis despite ongoing criticism of this. Mankiw (2014) instead, as described above, completely drops IS-LM analysis and proceeds to derive AS – AD in a yet different Keynesian-themed way. Both Blanchard and Mankiw use a nominal price of aggregate output.

Hall and Taylor's (1991, third edition, Norton; now in its fifth 1997 edition) *Macroeconomics* derives AS – AD from a combination of the Keynesian Cross and IS-LM. It ends up with the same AS – AD and nominal price of output found in Mankiw's (2015) *Principles of Macroeconomics*. But in comparison Mankiw (2015) uses the Keynesian Phillips Curve to derive AS – AD, a different attempt to derive an internally consistent AS – AD within a Keynesian approach.

Abel and Bernanke's *Macroeconomics* (2001 fourth edition, Addison Wesley Longman) derives AS – AD from IS-LM and uses the nominal price of output for the price in the AS – AD framework. They include an "exact" graphing of AS – AD from IS-LM, another derivation of Keynesian AS – AD that is based on a nominal price of output, not the real price. Their approach to AS – AD is different from, and apparently inconsistent with, the Ramsey approach that is used in real business cycle and growth theory, despite their book including large sections on real business cycles and growth. Abel and Bernanke is now in its 2013 eighth edition with Pearson Prentice-Hall.

[5]Colander, David. 1995. "The Stories We Tell: A Reconsideration of AS/AD Analysis." Journal of Economic Perspectives, 9(3): 169–188. DOI: 10.1257/jep.9.3.169.

Gordon's *Macroeconomics* (2000, eighth edition, Addison Wesley Longman) has an elaborate derivation of AS - AD from IS-LM. It is now in its 2011 12th edition, published by Pearson Prentice-Hall. It is similar in approach to Blanchard (1997), Hall and Taylor (1997), and Abel and Bernanke (2013). These authors are unquestionably among the most extremely well-respected, esteemed, economists of our generation. None of them present AS - AD from the now-pervasive Ramsey (1928) "work-horse" model as does PMEA.

0.3 Outline of Book's Content

The book studies Macroeconomics from the 1930's Great Depression though to the 2008–2010 Great Recession and its aftermath. It examines how policies have arisen and evolved from such tumultuous periods. It shows how analysis has tried to explain both these crisis periods and in a related way the more normal periods.

Part I of the book sets out how Macroeconomics was developed originally from Microeconomics. Part II presents the early divergence of Macroeconomics from Microeconomics. Part III continues the development of Macroeconomics's focus on the aggregate comovement of economic variables both in normal business fluctuations and in economic crises, and with a focus on inflation. Part IV presents the study of business cycles, growth and government policy during the Great Recession.

Each chapter follows a set structure, starting with an Introduction followed by a Who Made it Happen section that provides historical context. Then the main sections on Facts and Theory are presented. These are followed by an Application section, an Appendix, a chapter Summary, a Glossary and Questions at the end of each chapter.

Questions include assignment of the Federal Reserve Bank of St. Louis *Econlowdown* "Course" modules, for every chapter. These cover a range of basic, complementary, topics relative to each text chapter. The modules are found online and completed online, with free access after registration.

Part I is called Microeconomic to Macroeconomic Foundations. Its Chapter 1, "Micro Principles used in Macro", sets out Microeconomic principles that form the basis of the Macroeconomics presented in the subsequent text. Facts concern translating common aspects of the economy into the language, or "jargon", of microeconomics. The theory emphasis is on the principles of supply and demand in terms of their schedule, or functional relationship, between price and quantity. This includes description of how production and utility give rise to supply and demand relationships and how supply and demand can shift from one *equilibrium* to another. An Application explores the microeconomics of the US automobile industry, the role of the real price of gasoline and possible effects of government policy such as the prohibition of oil exports since 1973 (lifted in December 2015). The Appendix focuses on graphing data in simple relations used in macroeconomics, and includes a relation of graphs of production and utility to the biological basis of population growth.

Chapter 2 on "Aggregate Income and Production" starts with a Who Made it Happen section that describes the economists behind the accounting foundations of economics and the distinction between nominal and real economic variables. Facts include some key accounting foundations of macroeconomics. Theory includes the production function for national output, the representative agent of the economy and the circular flow of the economy. An Application covers "real" versus "nominal" output accounts and the Appendix shows how real and nominal interest rates differ.

Chapter 3 is "Macro Divergence from Micro". It provides a description of the US Great Depression and describes how economists viewed the crisis at the time. Both Neoclassical and Keynesian theories of a solution to the Great Depression are described. The Keynesian theory is illustrated in detail using national income and product accounting concepts and graphs; its simple graphical presentation has coincided with an enduring popularity of this approach. The idea here is that government spending can increase output during a depression or recession. The Application shows how to use the Keynesian "Cross" to illustrate the Great Depression and the Appendix shows how Keynes based his original business cycle theory on Marshall's microeconomic theory of the firm.

Part II is called Aggregate Comovement and Crises. It starts with Chapter 4 on "Business Cycles, Crises and Growth". First the chapter introduces the contrasting perspectives on aggregate data comovements between the monetary theory of Milton Friedman and the real theory of Edward Prescott and Fynn Kydland. Exploring real business cycle theory, the chapter then focuses on how data series of the economy, from the national income and product accounts, actually move in conjunction with each other over time. There are regular cycles in different series and also trends that the data follow over time. The real theory of business cycles, economic growth and crises is emphasized, with an Application made to financial data. The Appendix shows main aspects of the US economy's post World War II "structural transformation" of producing less non-durable goods relative to more services.

Chapter 5 is "Money, Banking and Policy", and it picks up some of the monetary directions emphasized by Milton Friedman. After an historical overview of US monetary policy, it presents the institutional facts about public and private bank money. This includes the structure of the US Federal Reserve System and its Monetary Aggregate definitions, as well as aspects of financial markets and different interest rates. The theory of the demand for money is presented, along with the theory of how money supply creation can cause inflation. Liquidity effects are described with an Application on historical US real interest rates, and an Appendix with postwar data on US money supply, inflation, debt and deficits.

Chapter 6 on "Crisis Periods and Inflation" presents a US history of economic crises and the relation of inflation to the crisis periods. The 1970's inflation was explained by alternative hypotheses of Keynesian oil shocks and Neoclassical money supply growth, which the chapter investigates. A modified Keynesian view of aggregate supply and demand is presented to illustrate the oil shock hypothesis, while being consistent with Neoclassical analysis of supply and demand. The chapter then focuses on the "Phillips curve" relation between inflation and unemployment rates from both a Keynesian and Neoclassical view. An Application presents evidence indicating how the Great Depression along with its strongly negative inflation rate appears to have been ended once the bank sector was reformed with the 1933 Banking Act, while an Appendix details the numerous US banking Acts of the 1930's and in the Great Recession.

Chapter 7 on "Savings, Investment and Interest" starts with a brief overview of the history of allowing interest on savings, which gave rise to "capitalism". It then outlines how a savings and investment theory based on supply and demand for capital was developed by Keynes (1936) after that developed by Fisher (1896, 1907, 1930). The Keynes approach requires assumptions that are detailed in order to present the *IS-LM* analysis, still a foundation of modern Keynesian economics. Fisher's analysis provides a more general interest rate theory based on consumption-smoothing over time, the bedrock of Neoclassical analysis. It graphs the optimization-derived supply and demand for capital. An Application follows that shows how to determine the present discounted value of future income using the interest rate as a discount factor. The Appendix supplies more detailed data on the personal savings rate and investment, with a use of National Income accounting to put these different series on a comparable basis.

Part III on Cycles and Growth starts with Chapter 8 on "AS – AD and Business Cycles". This chapter sets out the Ramsey (1928) analysis in supply and demand terms, with historical perspective going back to Keynes. The Ramsey approach extends Fisher's (1896) and forms the basis of modern Macroeconomic analysis, both Neoclassical and (New-) Keynesian. It graphically illustrates the markets for the output of goods and the inputs of labor and capital. The goods market is what we call AS – AD for the aggregate supply and demand for output. The analysis is matched to the stylized facts presented so as to offer an explanation of real business cycles. An Application uses a fixed wage rate to illustrate a crisis-like recession, as in Keynesian analysis. The Appendix uses a decline in the productivity of the bank sector to graphically represent an alternative Neoclassical explanation of a crisis-like recession.

Chapter 9 is "AS – AD and Growth". It provides the context of steady economy growth becoming a fact of the modern experience once the Industrial Revolution took hold and persevered. Solow (1956) explained the basic facts of the growth experience using the Ramsey production approach plus the assumption of steady technological progress. The chapter shows graphically in goods, labor and capital markets how Ramsey's model yields steady economic growth by adding the assumption that "total factor productivity" rises each period at a steady rate. An Application shows how additional growth facts can be explained by assuming a trend in the time endowment. An Appendix shows the growth facts in AS – AD graphs when the growth rate of the economy is instead explained endogenously within a Ramsey economy as supplemented with human capital investment, using the Lucas (1988) "Mechanics of Economic Growth" article.[6]

---

[6]This Lucas article is the third most cited of all papers on REPEC: see https://ideas.repec.org/top/top.item.nbcites.html

Part IV is on Policy. Chapter 10 is called "Policy as Social Insurance". First an historical introduction to modern "social insurance policy" is provided, along with selected key historical persons of this discourse. The analysis continues with a comparison of the Keynesian consumption function and the Friedman-Ramsey consumption function in terms of the implications for income distribution. The idea of consumption smoothing in the aggregate economy is put forth as an ultimate goal of government policy. Achieving this "social insurance" policy that can include efficient income redistribution is discussed in terms of monetary and fiscal policy, as well as banking policy, the three main policies that also dominated the policy discussion during the 1930's Great Depression, the Vietnam War era, and the recent Great Recession. An Application is made to the US Federal Deposit Insurance Corporation and an Appendix covers a discussion of public finance theory, public goods and social insurance.

Chapter 11, called the "Great Recession and Lost Decade", focuses on the Great Recession of 2008–2010 and the following years. It presents facts about government action, capital markets and banking. It proposes theory in order to consolidate a view of the effect of government action on capital markets. An Application makes recommendations on how to end low growth as in the "lost decade" era that followed the beginning of the 2007 downturn, which then became the Great Recession, and the subsequent far-below normal economic growth period. An Appendix spells out some of the details of the banking laws and government policy regarding banks during the Great Recession.

PART I

Microeconomic to Macroeconomic Foundations

1 Micro Principles Used in Macro

1.1 Introduction

The Microeconomic foundations of Macroeconomics today is the predominant approach to postulating Macroeconomic theory and application. This micro approach was not always viewed in a consensus fashion as being the case, in particular that Macroeconomics was formed out of Microeconomic theory. But it will be seen in the Chapters ahead that this theme runs through both Neoclassical Macroeconomics and Keynesian Economics.

The so-called "Micro-foundations" even appear firmly in recent "New-Keynesian" economics, which is a recent name being in a fashion similar to how Classical Economics became called Neoclassical Economics. This makes learning, or re-learning, a limited set of microeconomic foundations very useful for framing the subsequent body of thought that comprises Macroeconomics. And the microfoundation is the focus throughout the book.

Micro-foundations help us answer current policy questions such as:

"Why did the US Federal Reserve Bank System pay approximately $1.2 billion a year in 2016 on average to each of ten private US banks?"

"What caused the 1930's Great Depression and its Lost Decade and why has the 2008–2010 Great Recession been followed by a similar Lost Decade of low real output growth?"

"How do paying for wars as part of 'fiscal policy' and printing US Federal Reserve currency as part of 'monetary policy' interact and lead to a so-called inflation tax that tends to reduce productivity and growth?"

To answer such questions, the microeconomics are developed and its role is revealed in the foundation of Classical, Neoclassical, Keynesian, Monetarist and New Keynesian Macroeconomic theory and policy.

1.2 Who Made it Happen

Supply and demand as the gradually forming foundation stone of economics is well-described in George Stigler's (1965) *Essays in the History of Economics.*[1] He chronologically and conceptually describes how value theory evolved from the Classical economic supply dictum towards the Neoclassical supply and demand view. This description of how value was believed to be determined in the market became known as "price theory". Price theory is the established foundation of modern microeconomics, and forms the basis of the theory of competition and monopoly.

Stigler (1965) details how the labor theory of value differed from the cost of production theory of value, which together formed competing elements of the Classical theory of value. This stated that price was determined only by the supply side factors in terms of the cost of production, with agreement on including labor cost and disagreement on how to include capital cost.[2] This Classical theory of value was presented within Adam Smith's 1776 *Wealth of Nations* and developed in Robert Thomas Malthus's (1798) *An Essay on the Principle of Population*, David Ricardo's (1821) *On The Principles Of Political Economy And Taxation* and John Stuart Mill's (1848) *Principles of Political Economy.*[3] Karl Marx's (1867) *The Capital* (Das Kapital) economic theory was an offshoot of the labor theory of value, as was Henry George's (1879) *Progress and Poverty* and

[1] 1965, The University of Chicago Press, Chicago.

[2] Chapter 6, first published in 1952, as "The Ricardian Theory of Value and Distribution"; reprinted in 1965, ibid above footnote.

[3] See also Frank H. Knight's 1937 "The Ricardian Theory of Production and Distribution" reprinted in Knight (1956) *On the History and Method of Economics*, The University of Chicago Press, Chicago.

George Bernard Shaw's (1889) joint advocation of socialism based on levying property taxes on land, which now is a familiar aspect of Western democracies such as the USA.[4]

Gradually utility theory was brought into play in terms of how scarcity relative to the demand for the goods at a particular place and time could make the price of the goods greater than its cost of production. This started prominently with Jeremy Bentham's utilitarian theory within his 1789 *Introduction to the Principles of Morals and Legislation.* Utility theory as the basis of demand theory became embodied mathematically through a calculus based description of how diminishing marginal utility for a good implies the theory of demand for that good. Stigler (1965)[5] states that the "fundamental principle of marginal utility" was first expressed by Gossen (1854) in a largely ignored book, and then prominently advanced in the 1870's by Jevons (1871), Menger (1871) and Walras (1874). Edgeworth's (1881) *Mathematical Psychics* added *indifference curves* that had slopes equal to the ratio of marginal utilities (of two goods) along with *tangencies* to the production function (or what is called the "production possibilities curve"). This Edgeworth graph formed the full underlying basis for the equilibrium of demand and supply where the demand curve crossed the supply curve.

With diminishing marginal utility as the basis for the downward sloping demand curve, so came the theory of marginal productivity that formed the basis for upward sloping supply curves. Starting with Wood's two essays (1888–1889; 1889, "The Theory of Wages") and J.B. Clark's (1889) "Possibility of a Scientific Law of Wages", the theory was put forth that the marginal product of factor inputs diminished as the factor's use was increased in the production process. This then formed the basis for a diminishing marginal product of each labor and capital as the inputs increased. As output levels became higher and demanded more inputs for more output, the marginal product of factors became lower, and a rising marginal cost resulted. The supply curve became the marginal cost curve and because marginal cost rose as output levels rose, so the supply curve was upward sloping.

Through the process of adding downward sloping demand curves to upward sloping supply curves the basis of Neoclassical Economics and its equilibrium theory of price was established. Neoclassical Economics was promulgated most prominently by Alfred Marshall's eight editions of Principles of Economics from 1890 to 1920. Integral to Neoclassical Economics, a theory of industrial organization arose as part of the equilibrium that established prices.

Marshall's (1890–1920) Neoclassical economics included the organization of industry with description of both competition and monopoly. Dating back to Smith's (1776) *Wealth of Nations*, the theory of perfect competition arose more formally in 1871 in Jevon's *Theory of Political Economy* that also devised marginal utility theory; it was defined further in Edgeworth's (1881) *Mathematical Psychics*, in Clark's (1899) *The Distribution of Wealth*, and in Frank Knight's (1921) *Risk, Uncertainty and Profit.* This saw the result of zero profit as the perfect competition equilibrium.

In contrast, ideas of profit during competition arose in Edward Chamberlain's (1933) *The Theory of Monopolistic Competition* and Joan Robinson's (1933) *The Economics of Imperfect Competition.* These theories developed into what today is called "monopolistic competition". This allows any firm some degree of monopoly power in its every day pricing. Monopolistic competition with "mark-up" profits has become part of what is now known as modern New Keynesian economics. Here every firm has some degree of monopoly power and so all prices potentially reflect a "monopoly markup".

The Neoclassical economic theory of competition has no monopoly profit. If a monopoly does exist in Neoclassical economics it can charge a higher price called monopoly rents. Neoclassical economics makes monopoly pricing the exception rather than the rule, as opposed to Keynesian economics in which on-going

[4]Shaw (1989) writes in *Fabian Essays in Socialism* (section III.1.17) that "The land, as it is required, will, therefore, be honestly purchased; and the purchase money, or the interest thereon, will be procured, like the capital, by taxing rent. Of course this will be at bottom an act of expropriation just as much as the collection of Income Tax to-day is an act of expropriation. As such, it will be denounced by the landlords as merely a committing of the newest sin the oldest kind of way. In effect, they will be compelled at each purchase to buy out one of their body and present his land to the municipality, thereby distributing the loss fairly over their whole class, instead of placing it on one man who is no more responsible than the rest. But they will be compelled to do this in a manner that will satisfy the moral sense of the ordinary citizen as effectively as that of the skilled economist."

[5]Chapters 5, first published as a journal article in 1950, "The Development of Utility Theory".

profit along with aspects of competition typically is the rule of relative price determination. Stigler (1965) lamented that monopolistic competition was not a well-defined equilibrium.[6]

1.3 Facts

Every *industry* is defined by the existence of some number of private companies that produce a particular *product*. These companies can include any number of organizational structures such as large corporations with limited liability structures or privately held small businesses with partnership structures and unlimited liability. Regardless of the legal form of organization we can call these companies *firms* that produce our industrial output. Products are the output of the firms.

The firms in each industry interact with some number of households by selling products to them at a particular price. We can call the households that buy the products the *consumers* of the products. The price is determined freely by each firm (unless subject to special government regulation). Therefore the firms and households interact as the firms supply goods at a certain price to the consumers who in turn purchase those goods at the given prices.

A *market* for a good can be defined generally as the selling and buying by firms and consumers of a good in a certain place and over a certain time period. The market could be for all cars sold and bought in the US over a particular calendar year. The price that is determined by the interaction of the supply and purchasing of the goods similarly can be taken on average over a certain place and over a certain time period.

The market can be further delimited by specifying a type of car manufacturer or a specific car name of that manufacturer, and the average price for the given period. Or the market can be more broadly defined, such as grouping cars within the transportation industry. Therefore a market can be said to be the buying and selling of a particular product, however defined, by firms and consumers over a particular time period at a particular average price.

Data on the amount sold and bought of any particular product and on its average price generally is limited in terms of particular places and time periods. Finding such data allows for analysis of a particular market. Organizing that data in a certain way can enable us to determine how much of a particular product is sold and bought at any one particular price during some given time period. This leads to the formulation of the *supply* and *demand* for the product, which summarizes data about a particular market in a certain way.

We can call the selling by firms as the *supply* of the firms of a particular product for a particular price. And we think of buying by consumers of products as the *demand* for a particular product at a particular price. More broadly the supply and demand by firms and consumers respectively can be determined across an array of different prices if the time period for which data exists is sufficiently long.

The determination of supply and demand empirically typically involves analysis of the data that we call *econometrics*. Through econometrics supply and demand curves can be *estimated*. The result found is that firms supply more of any particular product when the price is higher and that consumers buy more of any particular product when the price is lower.

Markets can be dominated by a small number of firms. Conversely markets can also be dominated by a small amount of consumers. Market domination by either a small number of firms or consumers is sometimes correlated with the ability of either to influence significantly the determination of the price.

Typically, with large numbers of firms and consumers, neither sellers nor buyers can individually influence the price. The inability of the firm or consumer to influence significantly the price is how we define *competitive markets*. When a seller can influence significantly the price of the product we say this seller has *monopoly power*.

When a buyer can influence significantly the price of the product we say this buyer has *monopsony power*. With monopoly power the market is not readily defined as competitive as the monopoly would tend to push the price above the competitive price. Similarly, a monopsony would tend to drive the price down below the

[6]Stigler (1965), Chapter 8, originally published in 1957 as "Perfect Competition, Historically Considered", considers monopolistic competition to be unrealistic as an equilibrium concept and he considers its theory to have been "defeated" by the more standard use of the perfect competition framework; however monopolistic competition still lives on as a systematic markup that makes a key element in modern Keynesian theory today.

competitive price, such as when one company employs almost all of the employed people in a small, isolated, town and pays relatively low *wage rates*.

A monopoly tends to get naturally eliminated by new sellers entering the market. When a new product is created, the firm naturally has a type of monopoly. As other firms enter the market by starting to sell the same product, then the monopoly power of the original firm is eroded.

Sometimes governments intervene using *anti-trust laws* to regulate, or to fix, the prices that industries can charge. However economists often criticize such regulation as providing monopoly rents to industry unless the regulation is with respect to a public good such as water supply for which there can be a so-called natural monopoly. Markets overall tend towards competition but some economists argue that markets always have some degree of monopolistic elements.

When *profit* exists for some firms within a generally competitive market, this means that these firms are selling the product for a price that more than covers their *average cost per unit of product* that is sold. With a price per unit sold higher than average cost per unit, the firm's total profit is positive. Profit equals the difference between average price and average cost as multiplied by the number of units of the product that are sold during that period.

For firms selling the product for a price equal to its cost on average, there will be no profit. For firms selling the product for a price less than cost on average, then the firm will make a negative profit, or a *loss*, during the period. Profit depends on when average cost exceeds or is less than the price.

Every firm has a certain amount of *equity capital*. This is the amount of money that the firm is worth in terms of its assets minus its liabilities. When a firm continually makes a loss, its equity capital can be reduced until it is *insolvent*, which means its liabilities exceed its assets and it has a negative equity value.

Insolvent firms have to start making profit to stay in the market as an active producer or they must close down. Firms can therefore enter or exit a market. When the total firm output of a particular product increases, then the industry is expanding.

Industry expansion can happen through more production by the existing firms or by new firm entry into the market. Conversely, when the total firm output decreases of a particular product, then the industry is contracting either through the same existing firms producing less or through firms exiting the market. Any one industry can go through expansion and contraction over time.

Firms and markets that continually increase output over time cause that market to grow in terms of its output. The growth could be in only the quantity of output, with falling prices. Then the value of the output may not grow over time. If the quantity increases and the price either rises or does not fall sufficiently far then the value of the market for the product grows over time. In this way an industry can obtain sustained growth over time.

1.4 Theory

1.4.1 Market Equilibrium

Microeconomic theory is about the *equilibrium* price and quantity sold in a particular market and about the supply and demand forces that determine the equilibrium. Equilibrium in a market is defined as when the quantity supplied of the product, which we call *goods*, is equal to the quantity demanded of the good at a particular price. This price is called the equilibrium price.

The corresponding quantity is called the equilibrium quantity both sold and bought. Since the quantity sold equals the quantity bought we say that the market *clears* at the equilibrium price. Market clearing is defined as there being no *excess supply* of goods or demand of goods at the equilibrium price. Here excess means simply that either more goods are demanded or supplied at the price.

The *supply schedule* by the industry producing the good is upward sloping with respect to the price per unit of the good when represented on a graph. At a higher price, the quantity supplied of goods in the industry is higher. At a lower price the quantity supplied of goods in the industry is lower.

The *demand schedule* by the consumers buying the good is downward sloping with respect to the price per unit of good when represented on a graph. At a higher price, the quantity of goods demanded by the consumers is lower. At a lower price, the quantity of goods demanded by the consumers is higher.

Any individual seller of goods or buyer of goods in a competitive economy has no influence over price. They take the price as given and the seller sets it equal to its *marginal cost* of producing goods. The marginal cost is the cost increase from producing one more unit of goods.

While marginal cost at first can fall as the number of goods produced increases (due to the existence of fixed costs), after a certain point the marginal cost begins rising as the number of goods that are produced increases. The part of the marginal cost schedule that is rising with the quantity of goods is the supply schedule of the typical competitive firm.

The firm gets the *marginal benefit* of the revenue from selling a unit of the good at the market price. Therefore the price is the marginal benefit to the firm of selling the output. The firm is in equilibrium when it sets its marginal cost of producing equal to the marginal benefit of selling the good. This equilibrium therefore occurs where the given market price equals the marginal cost of producing.

Any individual buyer of goods purchases the quantity of goods where the given price of the good is equal to the marginal benefit from consuming that additional unit of goods. The marginal benefit of the consumer is equal to the value of the *marginal utility* that the consumer derives from the good. The consumer has a certain *utility function* by which all goods are valued internally to the consumer. Based on the increase in the utility that results from consuming an additional good, the consumer decides to purchase the quantity of goods at the point at which the value of the increase in utility from one more good is equal to the price.

The price of a good to a consumer is the *marginal cost* of an additional unit of the good. By choosing a quantity of goods at which the price equals the marginal benefit of the good, the consumer is setting marginal cost equal to marginal benefit, in a similar fashion to the firm. Both firm and the consumer in equilibrium set the marginal cost equal to the marginal benefit. In doing so the firm has an upward sloping supply schedule. In contrast, the consumer has a downward sloping demand schedule.

The consumer's demand schedule is equal to the value of the marginal utility that is derived by buying the good. This marginal utility diminishes as more goods are bought. This decreasing rate of increase in the utility from buying a good is called *diminishing marginal utility*.

As the consumer buys more goods, each additional good consumed results in a smaller increase in utility. The higher the quantity of goods purchased, the lower is the value of the marginal utility. If the market price is relatively low, then the consumer achieves equilibrium by purchasing a large amount of goods so that the marginal utility is relatively low. Then the price equals the value of marginal utility, or marginal benefit at a high quantity of goods demanded by the buyer. If the price is high, the consumer buys a small amount of goods at which point the marginal utility for an additional good is high.

Aggregation occurs in the microeconomic theory of the firm and the consumer in terms of supply and demand. All of the firm's marginal cost supply curves are summed up (horizontally when graphing) to yield the industry supply curve. The aggregate is then the summing up of the firms' supply schedules into an industry supply schedule, of the total quantity of goods offered at each price.

All of the consumers' demand schedules are also summed up (horizontally when graphing). This gives a total demand schedule for a certain good, of the total quantity of goods demanded at each price. The aggregate industry supply schedule is upward sloping and the aggregate industry demand schedule is downward sloping. The equilibrium market price, which each individual firm and individual consumer take as given in a competition setting, is determined where the upward sloping industry supply curve *intersects* the downward sloping industry demand curve.

At the equilibrium price, the total industry quantity of goods supplied and demanded is given. As the total quantity supplied equals that demanded, the industry market for the good *clears*. There is zero excess supply of the good and zero excess demand for the good at the equilibrium price.

Industrial Organization

In a competitive market, we say that there is zero profit for the marginal firm just barely existing in the market at the given equilibrium price. Other firms can earn some profit because they have lower average costs than the marginal firm. For the marginal firm just existing in the market, the marginal cost equals the price, and also average cost per unit of output equal the marginal cost. For the firm earning some profit, average cost per unit of output is lower than the price and the marginal cost.

Often the abstraction is made of a *representative firm* (see A. Marshall, *Principles of Economics*, 1920). By saying that this is what the average firm looks like, the idea is that the single firm's marginal and average cost can be used to represent the entire industry.

The representative firm approach allows for a concept of zero profit in the industry. This occurs when in equilibrium the representative firm has its marginal cost equal to price, and in turn marginal cost equals average cost so that there is no profit. This is called the *perfect competition* model that we often use.

For a market in which there is monopoly power, the representative firm sets marginal cost equal to *marginal revenue*. Marginal revenue is just the price of the good in a competitive market. The competitive firm cannot influence price, so the given price is the marginal revenue.

A monopoly is defined by it being able to push up the price above marginal cost. The monopoly dominates the supply of the good. Therefore it knows that if it produces more, the price of the good will fall. Knowing that its production influences the price in this way, the monopoly produces less than in the competitive equilibrium so as to not push down the price. Instead it produces less output, and so keeps the price from falling down to its marginal cost.

The knowledge of how price affects output enables the monopolist to calculate its own private marginal revenue schedule. This shows the increase in total revenue from selling one more unit of the good. Since price goes down when it produces more, the monopoly's marginal revenue is actually less than the market price of a competitive demand schedule at every level of output.

So the monopoly still sets marginal benefit to marginal cost, but here the marginal benefit is not the market price. Instead the marginal benefit is its actual marginal revenue that takes into account that its additional output lowers the market price below the competitive equilibrium demand schedule at any given level of output. The monopoly produces less than the competitive industry by setting marginal revenue equal to marginal cost in its equilibrium.

The price charged by the monopoly is above its marginal cost, at its equilibrium, since its marginal revenue which equals marginal cost is less than the market price at its equilibrium. So the monopoly earns profit. The representative competitive firm in perfect competition earns no profit in contrast. This shows that the difference in output and pricing by a monopoly relative to a competitive industry is that the monopoly can influence the price of output in the market, by its own quantity of output, whereas the competitive firm cannot influence the price of output in the market no matter what is its own quantity of output.

Firm Production Functions and Production Possibility Curves

Much of microeconomic theory is given assuming perfect competition. It only uses monopoly for a market that is particularly affected by one. Either type of firm is said to produce output using inputs to a *production function*. This function is a representation of how *inputs* of labor and capital are turned into the output of goods that are purchased by consumers. By adding more of one or more of the inputs, additional output is created.

In a two-dimensional graph, we draw how output rises as one of the inputs to production is increased, implicitly assuming that the other inputs are held constant. Figure 1.1 graphs the variable input into the production function on the horizontal axis and the output from the production process on the vertical axis. The production function shows that output rises as the quantity of inputs increase, but output rises at a decreasing rate. This rise in output at a decreasing rate is known as a *diminishing marginal product* from an increase in the input. It is a widely used characteristic of production functions.

Another two-dimensional graphical representation of production functions is to abstract from the inputs and just focus on the output. The idea is to assume just two outputs, such as in the example with political undertones of assuming there are just two goods, guns and butter. More guns are produced at the cost of less butter. Or more butter is produced at the cost of less guns.

The trade-off between guns and butter, or any two outputs, is called a *production possibility curve (PPC)*. It shows the trade-off between possible outputs, assuming a constant amount of inputs. Figure 1.2 shows the production possibility curve for guns and butter. More butter can be made with the set amount of inputs if less guns are produced.

The useful feature of the production possibility curve is it shows the rate of trade-off in producing guns versus butter under assumptions of perfect competition. The actual quantity of guns produced versus butter

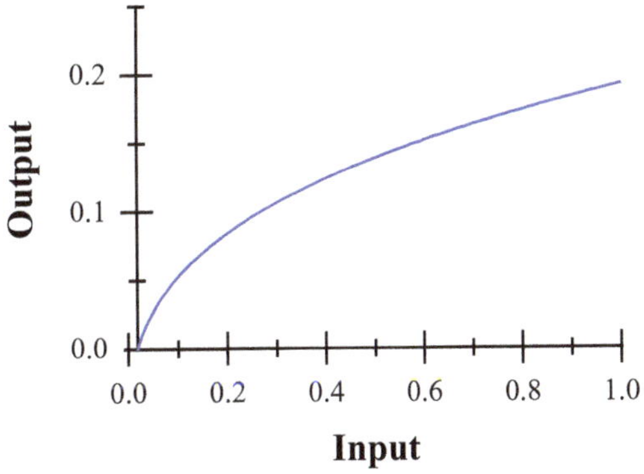

Figure 1.1 Production Function that transforms Inputs into Output

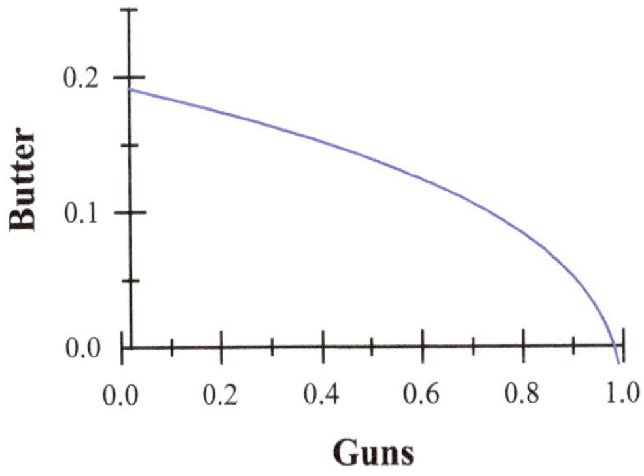

Figure 1.2 Production Possibility Curve

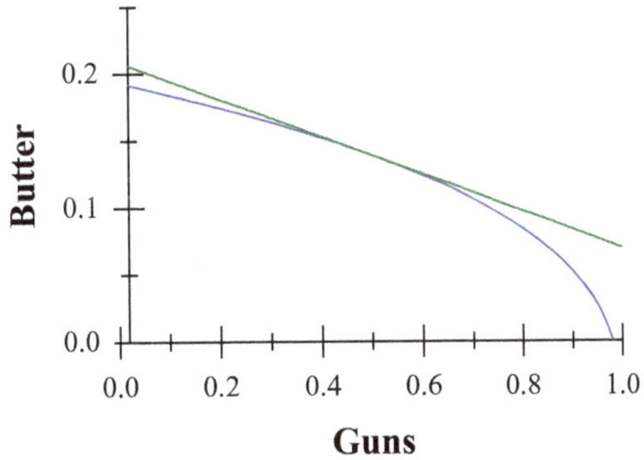

Figure 1.3 Production Possibility Curve and Budget Constraint

produced occurs at the equilibrium at which the marginal change in guns for a given change in butter is equal to the relative price of Guns for Butter.

Figure 1.3 graphs the Green budget constraint whereby income is used to buy either guns or butter at the price of Guns relative to the amount of Butter that has to be given up to buy one Gun. This is a "real" price without any trace of currency units, or money, such as the US Dollar; rather the real price is in terms of how much Butter is given up to get one Gun. The slope of the Green budget line is equal to this relative price of Guns to Butter. And it is tangent to the production possibility curve at one place, the equilibrium that determines how much of each Butter and Guns that will be supplied in the competitive market equilibrium.

The production possibility curve therefore can be used to show the how the equilibrium quantity produced in two markets relates to the relative price of the goods. This implicitly assumes that there are only two goods in the particular, constructed, *market economy*. Note that more gun production requires increasingly less butter production, or more butter production conversely requires increasingly less gun production.

The two-good economy is a simple abstraction from reality. Macroeconomic analysis also makes use of such an *economy-wide* representation, of the entire output of the economy. The PPC curve is often combined, in microeconomics and macroeconomics, with a related abstraction that is called the consumer indifference curve.

1.4.2 Indifference & Production Curves

The relative price ratio of two goods, in an economy with only two goods, is determined in general by where the consumer trade-off in buying the goods just equals the firm trade-off in producing the goods. Just as a representative firm is used for the PPC, here a *representative consumer* is used to determine the utility trade-off between the two goods.

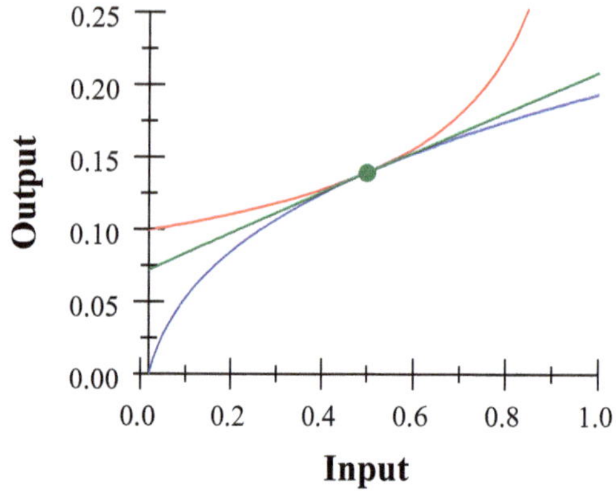

Figure 1.4 General Equilibrium Production Function (Blue) and Utility Level Expressed as Indifference Curve (Red)

The representative consumer trade-off shows how many guns need to be given up to get one more unit of butter, while holding the consumer's total utility constant. This is called an *indifference curve* because everywhere on this schedule, when graphed, the consumer has the same utility. So every bundle of goods, although different, along a curve with the same utility implies that the consumer is indifferent between any one of the bundles.

The actual consumer choice of the goods bundles is determined by where the relative price ratio equals the particular trade-off between say guns and butter as given in the consumer's indifference curve. This is the same way the firm chooses, where the relative trade-off equals the relative price ratio. This is because the relative prices give a trade-off of how much of one good you need to give up to buy another good, which both consumers and firms use to find equilibrium in perfect competition.

The final equilibrium is found where the firm's production possibility curve is tangent to the consumer's indifference curve (IC). This tangency point occurs where the two curves just touch, but do not intersect. The relative price in equilibrium in turn is tangent to each the production possibility curve and the indifference curve at this tangency point. So all three, the PPC, the indifference curve (IC), and the market price ratio line, have the same *slopes* at the equilibrium point.

The equilibrium of the production possibility curve shows the equilibrium quantity and prices of the two goods, say guns and butter. This corresponds to the equilibrium within each the guns and the butter market. The equilibrium gun price clears the supply and demand for guns, and the equilibrium butter price clears the supply and demand for butter, and the ratio of these prices is also the equilibrium slope of the PPC and the indifference curve.

The equilibrium given by the tangency of the PPC and the indifference curve also is consistent with the equilibrium in each of the two respective markets, say for guns and butter. This means that the PPC and indifference curve (IC) is a general representation of the abstract two-good economy. The supply and demand for guns and the supply and demand for butter are the individual markets that comprise this total economy. The individual market representation is one view of the economy that is perfectly consistent and implicit within the more general view of the PPC and the indifference curve.

Further, rather than guns and butter, the PPC can be turned around by considering how much on one input, like labor time or capital goods, needs to be supplied by the consumer to produce a certain output from the firm. And as in Figure 1.4, the PPC (in Blue) can then be reversed so that more goods result when more of the input is used. Thus the PPC becomes a *production function*. The indifference curve (in Red) shows the consumer is indifferent to giving up more of the input as long as increasingly more of the output is received per unit of input. And the budget constraint (in Green) has a slope equal to the price of the input relative to the price of the output.

Relative Prices

Microeconomics always poses the price of a good in terms of it being a price relative to the price of another good. This means that all prices in Microeconomics are *relative prices*. Often the relative price nature of the price given in supply and demand schedules is ignored in practice.

The reasoning for ignoring the relative price nature of equilibrium prices in supply and demand analysis is that we can consider the price of say guns relative to some other good like a dollar. Then we say it cost 100 dollars per gun. That means we have to give up 100 dollars to get one gun so it is a type of relative price.

The problem is that there is no money in a pure microeconomic economy. There is only the possibility of trading one good for so many of another good. Introducing money is not the common practice until we bring money into the analysis in Macroeconomics.

The second approach to ignoring the relative price nature of any particular good in a supply and demand schedule is to consider the second good as a basket of all of the other goods in the economy. In general, there can be more than two goods in an economy. Two goods are chosen for a production possibility curve because it can be graphed in two dimensions. In general there can be any finite number of goods produced and consumed in an economy.

Taking the relative price of any particular good to be giving up so many of the baskets of goods for one unit of say guns is an appropriate Microeconomic analysis. It still is in terms of a relative price whereby so many goods of one sort (a basket) are given up for another sort (a gun). Often the next step is to *normalize* the quantity of the basket of goods to some commonly understood quantity.

If this normalization then ends up being the quantity of dollars again, money again enters the analysis. This can happen even though dollars are not real quantities but rather are what we call a nominal quantity. This immediately takes us into the Macroeconomic distinction about monetary concepts, which is not part of Microeconomics.

The proper Microeconomic price is always a relative price. Thinking of this as relative to a basket of goods is correct. It takes money and *nominal* considerations out of the analysis and keeps it in real terms, which is how all of Microeconomics is formulated. When considering a production function and inputs, instead of two outputs in the PPC curve, then the relative price is in units of the amount of input (say time or capital) that has to be given up for a unit of output.

Supply and Demand Graphs

Using the production function of Figure 1.4, its slope at any one level of input gives the "marginal product of the input". This is the addition to output say from one additional unit of input being used in the production process. The neoclassical theory of income distribution determines that factors get paid their marginal products. For labor this is the real wage, for capital the real interest rental price.

The marginal product rises as the input amount rises. But it rises at a decreasing rate, so that there is a diminishing marginal product of the input as it increases in quantity. Since the price of inputs is their marginal product, and this falls as the input increases, the demand curve for the inputs falls as the quantity rises, when graphed with the relative price on the vertical axis and the quantity on the horizontal axis. This means that the demand for both labor and capital is a downward sloping curve graphed in a (price, quantity) graph.

A similar logic determines that the demand for goods is downward sloping. The consumer has a diminishing marginal utility and so for higher quantities is willing to "demand" these higher quantities only if the price per unit is lower. The graph of the demand for goods is based on the value of the marginal utility; since this value decreases as the quantity consumed rises, the price falls along the demand curve as the quantity rises.[7]

Supply is upward sloping because the marginal cost of supplying an input rises as the quantity increases. The supply price equals the marginal cost. So the supply of inputs is an upward sloping function of the price of inputs. Similarly, the marginal cost of producing a good rises as the quantity produced rises; the supply price equals the marginal cost of production; so the supply of a good is an upward sloping function of the price.

[7]For any given equilibrium, the demand price equals the ratio of marginal utilities between any two goods, and this ratio is known as the marginal rate of substitution between the two goods.

Demand slopes downward both for input demand by firms and for output demand by consumers, and supply slopes upward both for input supply by consumers and output supply by firms. Figure 1.4.2 shows a typical "market" that consists of the competitive equilibrium supply and demand for a quantity with the equilibrium relative price occurring at the intersection of the two curves:

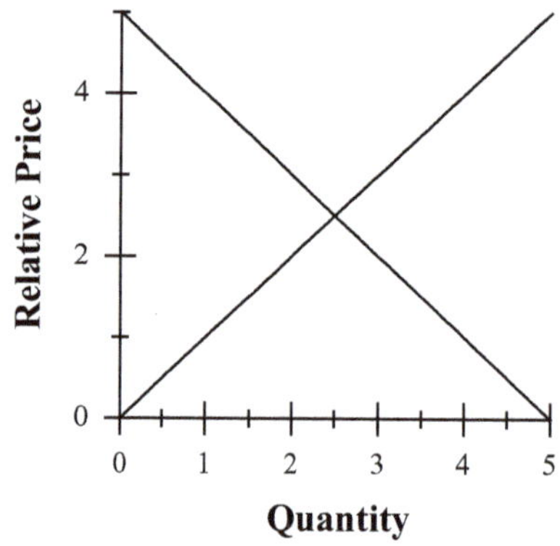

Fixed Prices and Excess Supply or Demand

When a price is fixed by some outside force to the markets, which we call an *exogenous factor*, then this price can only coincide with the actual market equilibrium price by happenstance. In general, we expect the fixed price to be either above the normal equilibrium price, or to be below it.

If a price is fixed exogenously above the equilibrium price, then this fixed price becomes the lowest that the price can be, or what is called in Microeconomics a *minimum price, or price floor.* For example the minimum wage rate in the US can be above the normal market equilibrium wage. If it is above the equilibrium wage, then at that fixed price more labor will be supplied than is demanded. This is called an *excess supply* at the fixed price.

Markets do not clear when more of the quantity is supplied at the fixed price than is demanded at the fixed price. Only the amount demanded gets employed in this case. Some mechanism (such as unions) determines which individuals end up being employed and which are unemployed as part of the excess supply of labor. This mechanism rations out the jobs to firms demanding labor.

For a fixed price below the normal equilibrium, we think of this as a maximum price that can be charged. It is below the market price, so these are typically called *price ceilings.* A well-known example is the rent control in New York City.

Some apartments cannot charge a market price but instead are regulated by the government and forced to charge some below-market rent. This makes for an excess demand for apartments at the rent-controlled prices. Only so many are supplied at this low price, so those lucky enough to get the excess demanded apartments do so through some sort of *rationing* devise. The rationing is an arbitrary way to distribute rent-controlled apartments that can depend on "connections", political influence, or other ways in which markets are *distorted* because market prices are not allowed to be freely determined.

1.4.3 Comparative Statics

A comparative static exercise is to assume that some exogenous factor that influences markets changes and then to see how this change affects for example supply and demand for any particular good. For example, Microeconomics at times assumes the real total income of the consumer is constant, when studying the market for a particular good. Then the income is allowed say to increase.

The question for analysis might then be how does the change in income affect the supply and demand for a particular good. If demand for a good rises when income rises, for every price of the good, then demand is said to "shift out". This shift out in demand means that more of the good is demanded for any given price than previously as a result of the consumer having higher income.

The *comparative static* exercise then is to determine the new equilibrium price and quantity both supplied and demanded given that the consumer's income is now higher. This analysis is performed graphically by shifting out the downward sloping demand, with a set supply curve. The new price and quantity must now be higher since the new demand curve intersects the original supply curve at a higher point along the supply curve at which both the quantity produced and its marginal cost is higher.

Marginal cost equals price. The new equilibrium price is higher as a result of the demand curve shifting out. The shift out in demand involves what is termed a *movement upwards* along the supply to a new high quantity supplied relative to the original equilibrium.

Similarly, the industry's supply of a particular good might be said to depend exogenously on the total output of the economy. If this output is then assumed to increase, then it can be assumed that this shifts out the supply of goods, so that a greater quantity of goods is supplied at every given price. The analysis may assume that demand is not affected by output. Then the shift out in supply is the only result.

The comparative static exercise in this second example is to determine the new equilibrium price and quantity with the supply curve shifted out. Since demand is assumed to be unchanged, a shifted-out supply curve will intersect the downward sloping demand curve at a higher quantity of output and at a lower price. The value of the marginal utility of the consumer will be lower with a higher quantity of goods and so the price will be lower. This shift out in supply gives a new equilibrium which involves what is termed a *movement downwards* along the demand curve relative to the original equilibrium.

Both supply and demand might shift at once, for example if income equals total output and both increase. Then the new equilibrium has to be determined by the way in which each the supply and demand curves shift. This assumes that the exogenous factor that is changed affects both supply and demand.

Shifting supply and demand curves as a result of an exogenous change is a way to do comparative static analysis of the movement from one equilibrium to a new one, given the change in the exogenous factor and how it affects the market. This shifting of supply and demand is perhaps the most common way to conduct comparative static analyses of markets. Comparative statics can also be conducted using the more general production possibility curves and the utility indifference curves.

1.5 Application: US Auto Industrial Decline

An application of Microeconomic principles is to consider why US produced cars have had an increasingly smaller share of the world market for automobiles. In particular the Japanese Toyota share of worldwide automobile production was the largest in the world for three years from 2012–2014, having outstripped US automobile producer General Motors (GM). This is true even though, in the US, GM purchased automobiles still leads with Toyota having a somewhat smaller domestic share than both GM and Ford. For the first half of 2015, Volkswagon took the world lead from Toyota and GM with the most number of automobiles sold worldwide.

World demand for Japanese automobiles includes those purchased in the US. US demand for Japanese cars did not begin in earnest until the 1970's. And in the 1970's there was little if any Japanese production of cars in the US, so Japanese purchased cars in the US were imported. Over time, to avoid the risks associated with fluctuating exchange rates on currencies (so-called exchange rate risk) and to avoid implicit US trade quotas on imports of Japanese cars (a so-called "voluntary restraint agreement"), Japanese manufacturers of cars opened plants in the US. These still count as Japanese cars in the sense that they are owned by Japanese registered companies, but they are American produced.

The question is why did the 1970's see the beginning of a significant demand for Japanese cars from US consumers, a demand which has not abated since. And why has Toyota continued to grow world market share until it finally took the lead in 2012? Or in particular, why have Japanese cars increased their world market share steadily over many decades, including up until now, relative to the US owned car industry.[8]

One well-known answer is fuel efficiency, and in recent years the answer has also been quality. Japanese cars on average are smaller and more fuel efficient that US manufacturer's cars such as General Motors, or GM.

[8]For example it is reported that from its introduction in 1966, the Toyota Corolla by 1974 was the best selling car in the world.

The huge manufacturing capacity of Toyota has also seen it introduce increasingly high quality and safer cars. But can a Microeconomist studying the automobile market go further in the analysis than this?

What if there were something *distorting* this world automobile market such that the type of manufacturing design is affected over long periods of time? This is the proposition here. In particular, US oil industry regulation has caused a long-term bias downwards in the US price for domestic gasoline as opposed to the world price faced in most other developed countries.

Starting in August 15, 1971, the US placed price controls on many goods, including US oil. The Federal Energy Administration created multitiered oil, with lower or "old" and higher or "new" oil. Old oil was defined as "oil produced from domestic wells not exceeding the 1972 rate of output from these wells".[9] Old oil had its price set at $5.25 a barrel, while for example the imported oil as of March 1975 was already up to $13.28.

With US refineries buying up oil to produce gasoline, some could buy the artificially low priced "old" oil and some bought the new oil at higher prices. This distorted the whole oil refining industry pricing. So then the FEA established the "Old Crude Oil Entitlement Program" in order to try to allocate an equal share of the old oil to each refinery.

The program meant that the US price of crude oil for refining into gasoline was kept below the world price of crude oil using in refining for gasoline. Therefore the US price of gasoline was held below the world price. This program of oil regulation was not fully ended until 1981 when President Reagan rescinded the regulation.

Therefore for the entire decade of the 1972–1981 the US automobile manufacturing industry produced cars geared for a significantly lower price of gasoline. US consumers had less incentive to use less gasoline than worldwide consumers. The demand for large, relatively fuel inefficient, US cars continued to flourish famously in the 1970's and into the 1980's.

One part of the early 1970's regulation that lived on was a prohibition of crude oil exports from the US. That continued until December 18, 2015, when a bill lifting the ban was finally signed into law.[10] Thus there has been nearly zero export of the domestic US oil production since President Ford imposed the oil export ban in 1975 (with an exception to allow US oil to go to Canada for consumption after 1985). With almost all US-produced oil having to be used in the US, this artificially captures that market for US oil refiners, leading to a greater domestic supply than would be otherwise possible if exports had been allowed. This continues to keep the US gas price below world prices.

For example World Bank data shows the US Dollar price per liter of gasoline historically across countries. In 2014 the US price was 0.76; in Japan was almost twice that at 1.38; in Germany it was more than twice the US rate at 1.80; and similarly in the UK it was 1.92. In 2010, it was 0.76 in the US per liter and 1.60 in Japan.[11]

Such relatively low US gas prices have existed since the 1970's. Note that taxes also affect these prices but taxes do not explain the bulk of the large discrepancies. For example, including taxes, here are the US Dollar per gallon gasoline prices on May 11, 2015 for Belgium, France, Germany, Italy, Netherlands, the UK and the US, respectively: 6.15, 6.08, 6.28, 6.83, 6.96, 6.75, and 3.06 for the US. The US price is half that of these European Continent countries, according to the US Department of Energy.[12]

A large part of the discrepancy between US gasoline prices and those of other countries can be attributed to the particular national tax on gasoline. In the UK, where they call gas for automobiles "petrol", the tax on petrol has been above 50% of the petrol price since 1952, in some years rising above 80% of the price.[13] In contrast the US has had an 18.4 cent tax per gallon since 1993. However US states also impose taxes now currently ranging around 50 cents per gallon. Even with recent low gasoline prices of say $2.50, the combined federal and state taxes of about 68 cents is just more than a fourth of the total gas price.

Therefore a part of the big price differential between US and world gasoline prices comes from tax rate differentials. But the other reasons remain in terms of the regulatory effect on gasoline prices of multitier oil

---

[9]"Oil Price Controls- A Counterproductive Effort," H. Helbling and J Turley, Federal Reserve Bank of St. Louis, November, 1975.

[10]See Brian Wingfield, 2015, "U.S. Reverses Decades of Oil-Export Limits With Obama's Backing", Bloomberg, Deccember 18; http://www.bloomberg.com/news/articles/2015-12-18/house-votes-to-repeal-u-s-oil-export-limits-senate-vote-next

[11]http://data.worldbank.org/indicator/EP.PMP.SGAS.CD/countries

[12]http://www.eia.gov/beta/international/prices/gasolinewithtax.cfm

[13]https://www.theaa.com/public_affairs/reports/Petrol_Prices_1896_todate_gallons.pdf

regulations from 1972–1981 and the prohibition of oil exports. It can be summarized as saying that from this combination of tax and regulation policy, the US gas price has been kept substantially below the world gas price.

The US average price of gasoline including taxes actually declined for many years in *real terms* and only began an upward trend since 2001; or some would put the rise in oil prices as starting in 1997 when China legally took control of Hong Kong from the UK, more fully entered world capital markets and significantly began importing oil for its growing economy. A US Department of Energy Graph reproduced in Figure 1.5, shows the *nominal*, or current dollar gas price, and the *constant dollar, or real,* US gas price since 1929. In US 2013 constant dollars the real price fell until the 1970s and returned to a low level from 1985 to 2001, after which it rose significantly.[14]

While Figure 1.5 shows the actual dollar price of US gas, the same trend can be seen using the All Gas component of the CPI index. Using the Federal Reserve Economic Data (FRED), Figure 1.6 shows the All

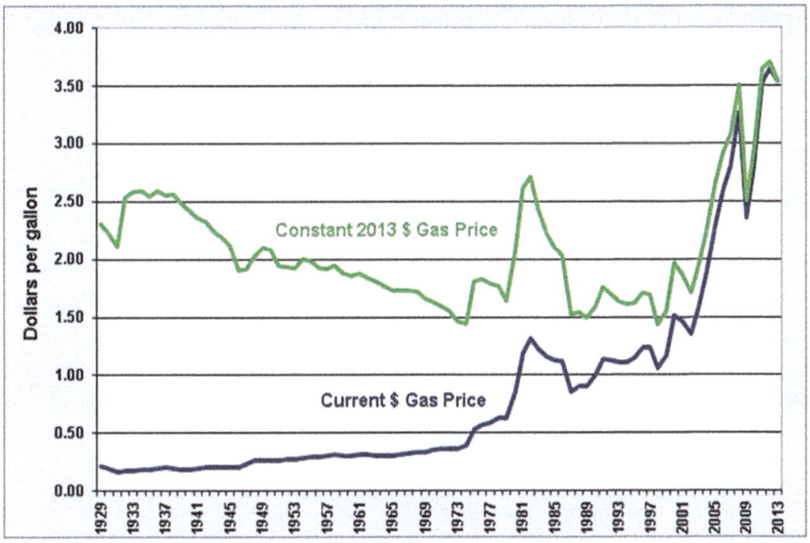

Figure 1.5 US Gasoline Prices: Actual & Constant 2013 Prices, 1929–2014

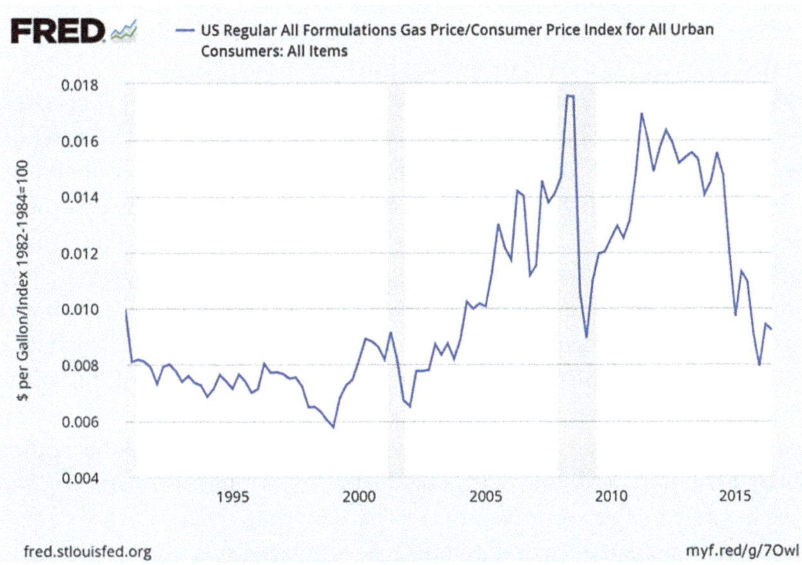

Figure 1.6 US Gasoline Index divided by All Items CPI, 1990:4–2016:3

[14]http://energy.gov/eere/vehicles/fact-835-august-25-average-historical-annual-gasoline-pump-price-1929–2013

Gas component of the CPI put in real terms by dividing by the All Items CPI index, on a quarterly basis from 1990:4 to 2016:3. Recent real gas prices have been as low as in the early 1990's, and below what they were in the 1930's, having fallen significantly since 2013.

The long-standing subsidization of the US gas price through the myriad oil regulations and low tax rates has created a US industry that designed and built automobiles mainly geared to a nearly half-price rate of gasoline as compared to Germany and Japan. Naturally, the design in the US would prove inefficient compared to that in Germany and Japan in terms of fuel efficiency. This gasoline price discrepancy resulting from US policy can therefore be attributed as a primary culprit in the relative worldwide decline of the US automobile industry.

Having low gasoline prices is good for consumers. But if policy is causing this low price it can lead to distortions in industrial production and even less competitiveness on a global scale for a US industry such as automobiles. Our US industry overall may be steadily moving more towards services output instead of manufacturing output. And the decline of US automobile manufacturing may also be related to that long term trend in the structural transformation of US output, which is more of a macroeconomic issue.

1.6 Appendix: Graphing Data and Equations

1.6.1 Sourcing and Graphing US Data from Fred

One of the most popular data sources for economists in the US is provided by the Federal Reserve Bank of St. Louis. It is called by the acronym of Fred and found at the website http://research.stlouisfed.org/fred2/. This acronym stands for Federal Reserve Economic Data.

If you type Fred into Google it will appear as the first result. Fred allows you to search for any data series. Fred has mostly US data but also various amounts of international data as well.

Fred also provides a graph of the data series that you select. You can alter the settings of the graph and re-draw it automatically. For example, the beginning date and ending date of the series can be changed, and Fred will re-graph the results. There are many other ways you can alter the data series including combining multiple data series together.

All of the graphs can be "exported", or downloaded, as a common jpeg file, a pdf file, or within Powerpoint and saved using a .bmp format as in this book. The graphs can be altered so that more than one data series is shown on each graph, by going to "Edit Graph", to "customize data", and using the "add" data series. Each data series that is graphed can be edited in terms of color, data frequency (monthly, quarterly, annual; if available), and the type of graphed line such as a solid or dashed line.

Also the particular series can be expressed in levels or in *percentage change*. For example the CPI index can be graphed by itself as a series. Then the same data can be expressed as the "percentage change from a year ago", using the "Edit data series" opening tab, and then going to "units" and changing them from the initially displayed "Index" to "percentage change from a year ago". This gives the CPI measurement of the US inflation rate. It is available back to 1913, one of the longer data series available on Fred.

The St. Louis Fed also puts up on the Fred website a historical source of various documents in "Fraser" (https://fraser.stlouisfed.org/). This stands for the Federal Reserve Archival System for Economic Research (FRASER). It was instituted in 2004 and provides a mix of historical material, such as statements and speeches by past Federal Reserve Chairmen, historical data series starting back in 1914, the minutes of the Federal Open Market Committee that decides the Federal Reserve policy.

Figure 1.7 shows a FRED graph of the percentage change in US real (constant dollar) output (Gross Domestic Product) from 1929 to 2014. FRED allows you to select whether to put this as an ever rising series, or as the percent change in each data point as compared to the last data point (here a year is a data point as the data is annual), or as the percent change in each data point as compared to a year before. With annual data, the latter two categories, percent change and percentage change from a year ago, are the same. With quarterly data, the "percentage change" choice shows how the particular value of real GDP in some quarter changed compared to the preceding quarter; "percentage change from year ago" with quarterly data shows how much the particular real GDP in a quarter changed compared to the same quarter one year ago.

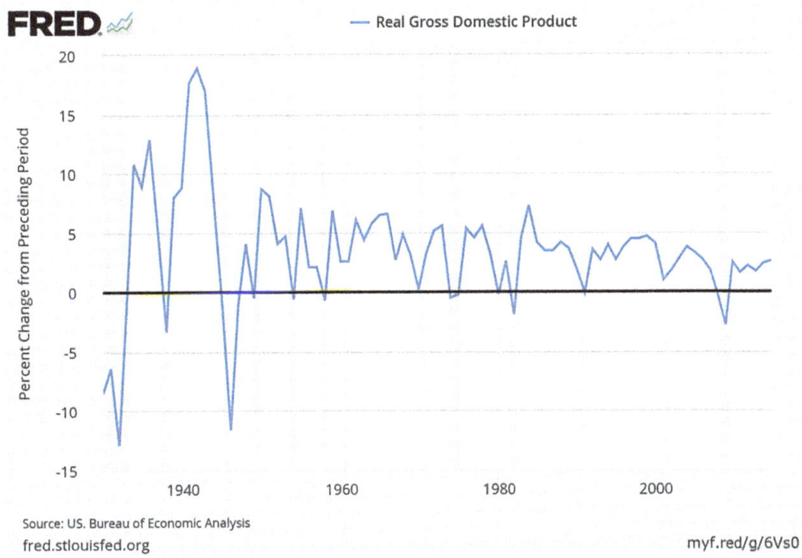

Figure 1.7 US Real GDP Percentage Change, 1929 to 2014

1.6.2 Graphing Lines and Curves

Here we graph a variable x against y. We typically call the horizontal *axis* the x axis and the vertical axis the y axis. That is why we chose x and y here for the axis labels. They also could be for example the quantity of cars on the x axis and the relative price of cars on the y axis. If so then the upward sloping line would be a supply curve. The solid line in Figure 1.8 is the graph of $y = 2x$.

As the variable x increases, so does the variable y along the graphed line. The slope of the line is actually two, or 2.0, despite the appearance of how the graph is drawn. The graph may appear to have a slope less than one if you do not look at the values of the x and y on the axes. But in fact the graph shows that as the x variable rises by 1, the y variable rises by 2 along the graphed line. This can be seen by the fact that when $x = 5$, the graph shows that $y = 10$.

The slope of the line is defined by the change in the vertical variable y, over the change in the horizontal variable x. This is often termed the rise over run. Since it is a straight line, the rise in y is 2 for every increase in x by 1. So the slope is a constant $2/1 = 2$ for all values of x and y.

Suppose that the slope of a new line is higher at every point than the $y = 2x$ line. Then the graph of this line would appear as a pivoting upwards from the origin (where $x = y = 0$) relative to the original line. This is illustrated by the dashed line in the graph. This dashed line is $y = 3x$ and it has a slope of 3 rather than 2, and so is steeper than the original solid line.

Note that supply and demand typically make the y axis the relative price of the good and make the x axis the quantity of the good. The axes can be reversed as long as the definitions of the axes are made clear. It is simply a common convention to plot supply and demand with the relative price on the vertical axis and the quantity on the horizontal axis.

1.6.3 Line with a Positive Vertical Axis Intercept

Here we again graph a variable x against y. We again call the horizontal *axis* the x axis and the vertical axis the y axis. For consumption and income, the vertical axis could be consumption and the horizontal axis income. Consider $y = a + bx$. Let $a = 0$ and $b = 1$. This is graphed in Figure 1.9 as the black line, with a slope of 1.

Now let $a = 0.15$ and still keep $b = 1$, so $y = 0.15 + x$. Then the line shifts up relative to the y axis as in Figure 1.9 in the purple line. Now thirdly, let $a = 0.15$ and change b to 0.6 instead of 1.0, so $y = 0.15 + 0.6x$. Then the new blue line has the same y axis intercept (where $x = 0$) but it has a lesser slope and so intersects the black line.

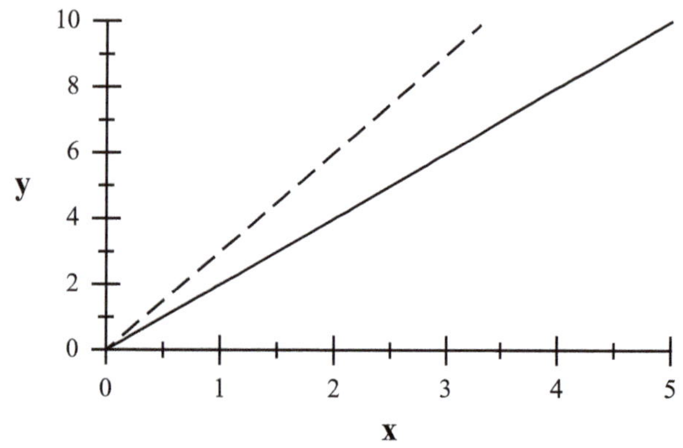

Figure 1.8 Understanding Graph Slopes

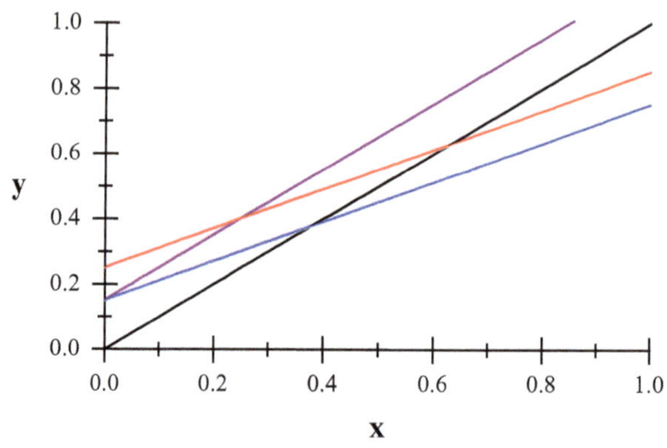

Figure 1.9 Changing the Vertical Axis Intercept and/or Slope

Increasing a shifts any one of these three lines up vertically while keeping the slope the same. Decreasing the slope parameter b causes any one of these three lines to pivot down from their y axis intercept, and so have a lesser slope. Finally consider increasing a in the blue line. Say $a = 0.25$, while $b = 0.6$, so that $y = 0.25 + 0.6x$. This is graphed in the Figure 1.9 as the red line, which is parallel to the blue line since they both have the same slope.

1.6.4 Production Function or Utility Function

A typical production function shows how output rises with the increase in its input. Using a two-dimensional graph, with a vertical and horizontal axis, the vertical axis is typically the quantity of output and the horizontal axis is the quantity of the input. The standard production function uses two inputs: labor and capital.

In a two-dimensional graph of the production function, one input is assumed to be held constant. The standard shape of such a production function is a rising curve from the origin (where there is zero input and zero output). The rise in the curve diminishes as the input increases (called concave to the origin). Figure 1.10 illustrates the output with the labor input variable and capital held fixed.

A utility function that depends on two items that yield utility, such as good x and good z, has the same two-dimensional shape as the production function. Utility rises as the item consumed goes up, but utility rises at a decreasing rate (making it concave to the origin). Figure 1.11 illustrates a utility function depending upon good x, with good z held constant.

An alternative is to graph the two inputs as the axes on the graph and hold output constant. This latter is called an "isoquant": the same quantity of output, produced with different combinations of the two inputs. The graphical shape of an isoquant is a "hyberbola". Figure 1.12 graphs the isoquant of the production function with output constant and labor and capital variable.

The utility level can also be held constant while the goods that enter utility x and z can be variable. The graph of the constant utility curve is the exact analogue of the production isoquant curve. The constant utility level graph is called an indifference curve because utility is the same (so consumer is indifferent to alternatives). Figure x graphs a given, constant, utility indifference curve.

1.6.5 Biological Basis of Production and Utility

George Stigler's 1966 *The Theory of Price* textbook (his Figures 7.1, 7.2) describes the property of a diminishing marginal product by using an S-shaped production function as in Figure 1.14. The output rises at an increasing rate up until the "inflection point" along the curve which occurs at an input level of about 130. This means the marginal product rises until the inflection point. After the inflection point in the curve, output thereafter rises at an ever decreasing rate, with a marginal product that diminishes in tandem with the slope of the curve. The limit of the curve is where the slope and marginal product are zero.

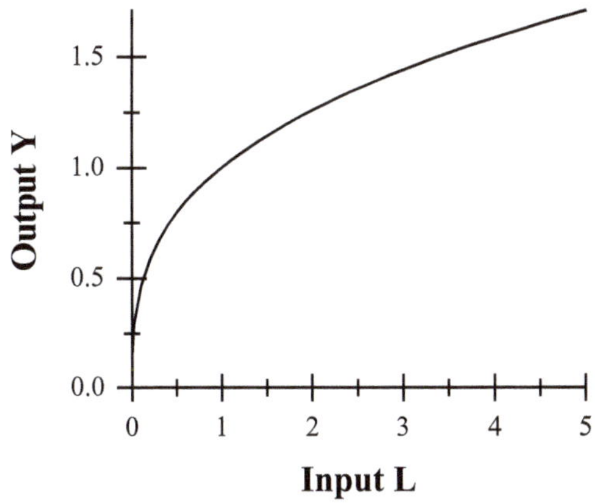

Figure 1.10 2-Dimensional Production Function of Output Y & Input L

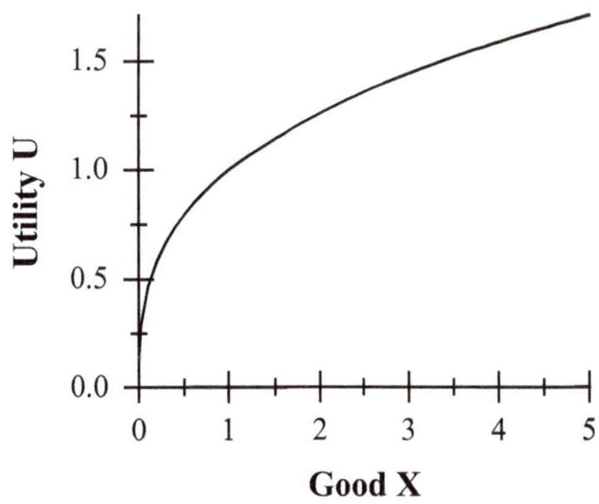

Figure 1.11 Two-Dimensional Utility Function of Consumed Item x

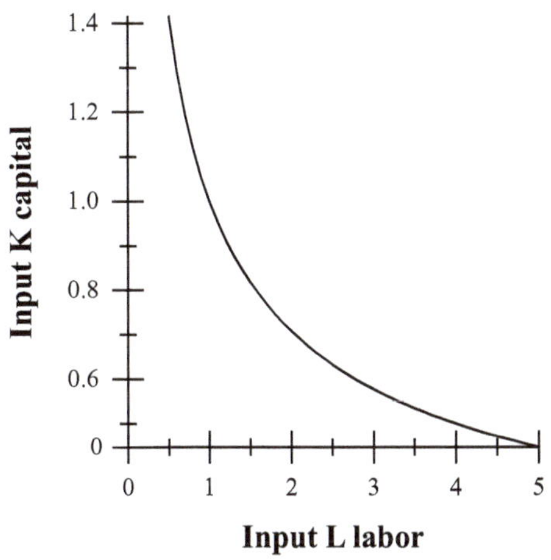

Figure 1.12 Two-Dimensional Isoquant with Constant Output and Two Variable Inputs L and K

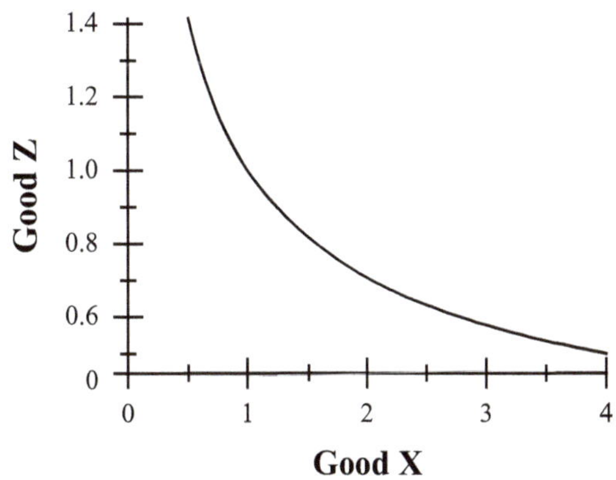

Figure 1.13 Utility Indifference Curve with Constant Utility

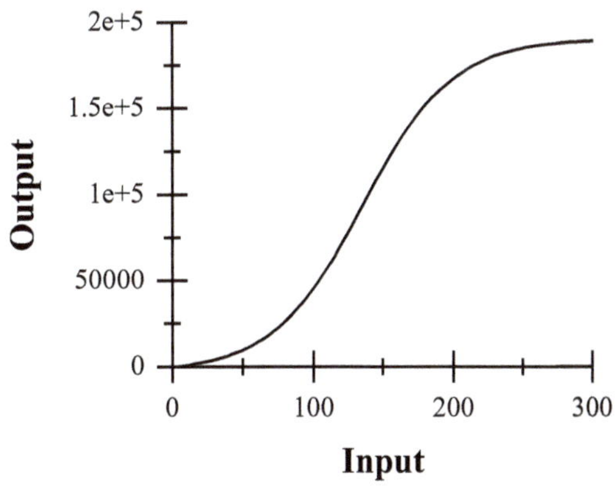

Figure 1.14 Population Growth Curve

The demand for the input comes from the part after the inflection point where the marginal product is diminishing, and this is the part that is drawn in a downward sloping demand curve. Before the inflection point, where the marginal product is increasing the demand curve is upward sloping. But no producer would stay at that point since employing more of the input yields a still increasing increase in output and for the same price per input the producer could produce more. This makes the effective part of the demand curve and production function only the part after the inflection point, or in the positive input range of Figure 1.15.

Figure 1.14, with "time" interpreted to be the input on the horizontal axis, and "population" as the output on the vertical axis, actually has long been used to represent the growth of a population over time, in general, and of people living in the United States as well, as studied for example by Pearl and Reed (1920).[15] Thus the basic structure for the production function of a firm, and in exactly in a similar way for the utility function of the consumer, have strong similarities to the growth of a any population over time.[16]

Robert Thomas Malthus's 1798 *An Essay on the Principle of Population* hypothesized that only the first half of Figure 1.14 would hold, and that instead of an inflection point, population would keep on growing at an increasing rate forever.[17] Therefore the importance of the inflection point is that it starts the beginning of a declining rate of growth in the population, as seems to match current world population studies.[18]

Charles Darwin solved the puzzle of Malthus's seemingly impossible ever-increasing rate of population growth. Darwin suggested that the population would necessarily mutate so as to preserve properties advantageous for surviving and discard properties disadvantageous for surviving. This gave rise to the theory of natural selection in the evolution of species.

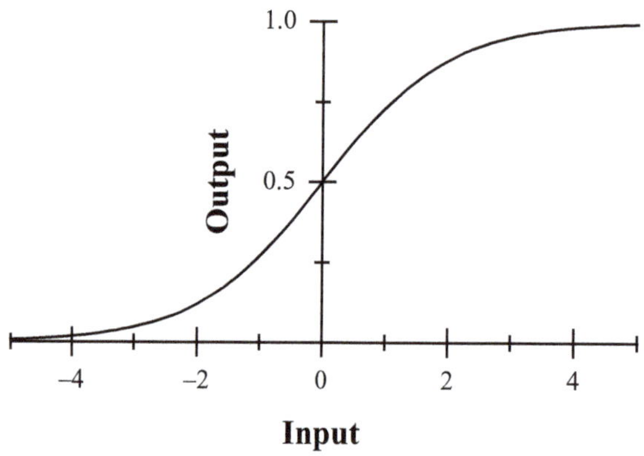

Figure 1.15 Population Growth Curve Centered at 0

[15]Pearl R, Reed LJ.,1920, "On the Rate of Growth of the Population of the United States since 1790 and Its Mathematical Representation." Proc. Natl. Acad. Sci. USA, 6(6, June): 275–288.

[16]"S-shaped growth curve: A pattern of growth in which, in a new environment, the population density of an organism increases slowly initially, in a positive acceleration phase; then increases rapidly, approaching an exponential growth rate as in the J-shaped curve; but then declines in a negative acceleration phase until at zero growth rate the population stabilizes. This decline reflects increasing environmental resistance which becomes proportionately more important at higher population densities. This type of population growth is termed density-dependent, since growth rate depends on the numbers present in the population. The point of stabilization, or zero growth rate, is termed the saturation value (symbolized by K) or carrying capacity of the environment for that organism. K represents the upper asymptote of the sigmoidal or S-shaped curve produced when changing population numbers are plotted over time. It is usually summarized mathematically by the logistic equation" as at http://oxfordindex.oup.com/view/10.1093/oi/authority.20110803100526356

[17]R.T.Malthus, 1798, An Essay on the Principle of Population As It Affects the Future Improvement of Society, with Remarks on the Speculations of Mr. Goodwin, M. Condorcet and Other Writers (1st ed.). London: J. Johnson in St Paul's Church-yard; last (6th) edition appeared 1826.

[18]See for example an online resource at North Dakota State University: https://www.ndsu.edu/pubweb/novozhil/Teaching/484%20 Data/1.pdf

> "In October 1838, that is, fifteen months after I had begun my systematic inquiry, I happened to read for amusement Malthus on Population, and being well prepared to appreciate the struggle for existence which everywhere goes on from long- continued observation of the habits of animals and plants, it at once struck me that under these circumstances favorable variations would tend to be preserved, and unfavorable ones to be destroyed. The results of this would be the formation of a new species. Here, then I had at last got a theory by which to work". Charles Darwin (1876),[19]

This same feature is captured in Economics by its focus on the part of the population curve during which the rate of population growth is ever decreasing, as indubitably results from a scarcity of resources. It follows that new species of products could then arise as substitutes with higher productivity or utility. The result is downward sloping demand curves for any given good by consumers and for a given input by producers. So it might be suggested that the revised "Darwin-Malthusian" economic theory recognizes the impact of scarcity as in diminishing marginal products and diminishing marginal utilities.[20]

1.7 Summary

The chapter sets out facts, theory and application on the use of microeconomics in macroeconomics. It introduces the common concepts from microeconomics that are used in macroeconomics. These include consumers, firms, industries and markets.

Industrial organization is discussed. This includes competition, monopoly pricing and profits. Supply, demand, market prices and wage rates are discussed. Some concepts of finance are also mentioned.

The theory puts forth the concept of equilibrium in markets. This equilibrium involves the quantity of goods produced and their pricing. Equilibrium is different in each competitive and monopolistic markets. In both however marginal cost is set equal to marginal benefit at which point the market price is determined.

Methods of microeconomics that are used in constructing macroeconomics include production possibility curves that macroeconomics typically puts in terms of production functions. Consumer preference for one good relative to another is discussed in terms of utility and indifference curves. And prices in markets are seen in terms of being relative prices of one good for another, rather than absolute prices in terms of money.

Market clearing occurs when the quantity supplied equals the quantity demand at the equilibrium price. Excess supply or demand for a good can happen when prices are forced to be above or below their natural market equilibrium levels. Examples are rent ceilings and the minimum wage. An application is presented which looks at the US automobile industry over time. An Appendix discusses population biology and its relation to diminishing marginal product and utility.

1.8 Glossary of Italic Words

aggregation: adding together a group using some means of making each member of the group likewise so that they can be added.

anti-trust laws: government laws that prohibit monopoly or monopsony.

average cost per unit of product: the total cost of output divided by the quantity of output.

budget constraint: the amount of real income that can be used for purchasing goods in a given period.

clears: characteristic of a market when the quantity demanded equals the quantity supplied at a particular equilibrium price.

comparative statics: comparing one equilibrium to another equilibrium, usually where one exogenous factor to the economy has changed.

competitive market: where each consumer and firm has no influence individually over the market price by means of their demand of and supply for the good respectively; some firms may have lower costs than others and thereby earn profit.

---

[19]The Autobiography of Charles Darwin, written in 1876 by Charles Darwin; edited by his son Francis Darwin and published 1887, John Murray, Albemarle Street, London. See also https://www.blackwellpublishing.com/ridley/tutorials/The_rise_of_evolutionary_biology12.asp

[20]See for example http://web1.cnre.vt.edu/lsg/3104/Overpop.%20FINAL/Poverty4.html

concave to the origin: a curve drawn from the origin in the graph has a slope that gets flatter, the further out the curve goes along the horizontal axis.
constant dollar, or real: in dollars that take out the inflationary effect on prices; real dollars is another term for constant dollars.
constant dollar valuation: determining the value of a good in terms of prices that hold in one given year, as a way to take out inflation from the valuation of the good.
consumers: households who optimize their choice of which goods and how many to consume based on their budget constraints.
demand schedule: A schedule of prices and quantities which shows how many goods the aggregate number of consumers in a particular market will buy at each given price, when that price was the equilibrium price; can be graphed.
diminishing marginal utility: the marginal utility of a particular good becomes less as the quantity of goods consumed increases.
distorted: a feature of markets when they are taxed, subsidized or regulated such that the normal equilibrium price does not hold.
econometrics: the economic statistical methodology for estimating how economic variables relate to each other.
economy-wide: all of the industries of the microeconomy that make up a particular aggregate economy.
endogenous: an event that occurs which is explained as an outcome of the actions taking place within a model economy.
endowment: a quantity of any factor of production with which typically the consumer is given exogenously.
equilibrium: when the forces of supply and demand are at rest in that there is no incentive for the price to be raised or lowered.
equity capital: the net worth or residual value of a firm found by subtracting liabilities from assets.
estimated: a relation that results from econometric analysis of data in which variables are related to each other in a certain fashion.
excess supply: the quantity of goods that are supplied in excess of what is demand at a particular market price.
exogenous: an event that occurs by assumption rather than being explained within the model economy.
firms: companies of any particular legal organization that produce and supply goods to the market-place.
goods: a product of firms that consumers want to purchase.
government regulation: Restrictions to free trade that any branch of government is able to impose upon the market economy.
indifference curve: a schedule that can be graphed which shows the combination of any two goods for which the consumer has the same level of utility.
industry: a grouping of firms producing a similar product, or output.
inputs: the factors of production such as labor and capital that enter a firm's production function for output.
insolvent: a firm with liabilities greater than assets is characterized in this way.
intersects: where two lines or curves cross.
loss: occurs when current period revenues are less that current period costs, and profit is negative.
marginal benefit: the increase in benefits resulting from a one unit increase in a good.
marginal cost: the change in total cost in producing a good due the production of one more unit of that good.
marginal revenue: the increase in revenue from a one unit increase in the quantity of goods sold.
marginal utility: the change in the consumer utility of consuming goods when one additional good is consumed.
market: a grouping in which goods are supplied and demanded.
market clearing: a part of an equilibrium in which the equilibrium price makes the quantity demanded exactly equal to the quantity supplied.
market economy: an economy in which resources are largely allocated according to buying and selling freely in all of its markets.
market entry and exit: firms begin producing a good in a market when they enter the market, and stop producing a good in a market when they exit.
market supply and demand: the supply and demand for goods within a particular market.
minimum price, or price floor: a fixed price imposed exogenously on a market whereby the price is set above the equilibrium price in the market, causing an excess supply of the quantity at the fixed price.
model economy: a simplistic representation of an economy that abstract from certain details.
monopoly power: the ability of a firm to influence the price of a good in a market in which the firm is supplying goods.
monopsony power: occurs when only one buyer of the product exists such that buyer can push the price below its competitive equilibrium value.
movement upwards, movement downwards: along a given graphed line, a movement upwards along the line means that the point of interest goes from a lower position on the line to a higher position along the same line; conversely for a movement downwards.
nominal: any valuation that is given in monetary terms rather than in terms of goods.

perfect competition: firms and consumers sell and buy goods in a market in which firms and consumers cannot individually affect the market price and in which all firms have the same cost structure so that there is zero profit earned in the market.
price ceilings: a minimum price imposed upon a market usually by the government that is below the natural equilibrium price in the case that it is an effective ceiling that changes the equilibrium.
price floors: a maximum price imposed upon a market usually by the government that is above the natural equilibrium price in the case that it is an effective floor that changes the equilibrium.
product: a good that is produced as output of a firm.
production function: a means by which a firm turns inputs of factors such as labor and capital into output of a good.
production possibility curve (PPC): a schedule that can be graphed that shows the combinations of two goods that can possibly be produced given a certain endowment of the factors of production such as labor and capital.
profit: total revenue minus total cost.
rationing: the allocation of goods that takes place outside of market allocation through pricing; this typically involves non-economic behavior such as political favor or influence.
real terms: any valuation that is given in terms of goods, rather than in terms of money.
relative prices: the statement of how many units of one good must be given up in order to purchase one unit of another good.
representative firm: a producer that is thought of as the average within a group of firms
representative consumer: a household that is thought of as the average within a group of households.
slopes: the change in the vertical axis quantity as a result of a unit change in the horizontal quantity, along a particular line or curve; rise over run is one definition that means the vertical axis amount divided by the horizontal axis amount at the given point; a line with a slope of one that starts at the origin is a line that makes a 45 degree angle.
supply schedule: a schedule of prices and quantities which shows how many goods the aggregate number of firms in a particular market will sell at each given price, when that price is the equilibrium price; can be graphed.
tangent to: when two curves, of which one may be a line but not both just "touch" and share a single point without having an intersection at this point of tangency.
utility function: a representation of how different goods give benefits to the consumer.
wage rates: the rental rate of labor supplied for working at a firm.

1.9 Questions

1. What is a market and how does it function?
2. What slopes do the supply and demand functions have when graphed against the relative price (vertical axis) and the quantity of output (horizontal axis)?
3. How are supply and demand related to the firm's production function and the consumer's utility function?
4. How does an increasing marginal cost and diminishing marginal utility relate to supply and demand for a good?
5. Use supply and demand to explain the problem of the US automobile industrial decline.
6. How are comparative static exercises shown using supply and demand?
7. How is the equilibrium determined and defined in any given market?
8. What is the difference between a competitive and a monopolistic market?
9. Provide an explanation for the relative shrinkage worldwide of the US automobile industry.
10. Graph two lines in the same graph: $y = 4 + 3x$ and $y = 4 + x$.
11. Graph a production function, a utility function, an isoquant and an indifference curve.
12. How might the theory of population growth relate to the theory of diminishing marginal utility or diminishing marginal product?
13. Complete the Federal Reserve Bank of St. Louis EconLowdown Course Module "Supply and Demand".

2 Aggregate Output & Income

2.1 Introduction

The national income and product accounts of the USA (NIPA) are officially gathered by the Bureau of Economic Analysis of the Department of Commerce. There are two sides to the macroeconomic ledger: the total value of output on one side and the total value of income earned while producing the output on the other side of the ledger. By definition these form an accounting identity. The two sides of the ledger are mathematically equal to the same amount. This amount we call either our total macroeconomic, or aggregate, output, or equivalently since they are identical in value, our total macroeconomic, or aggregate, income.

The process of producing the output and earning the income involves all of the agents of the economy. The firms produce the output using the inputs of labor and capital. The households, or what we call the consumers, provide the labor and capital that the firms use as inputs. Households also buy the goods that firms sell. We can represent the average household and firm by a "representative agent economy."

The value of the total consumer purchases from the firms is the value of the aggregate output. The income earned on labor and capital is roughly equal to the value of the aggregate income. The government also takes a wedge out of the output and so do net exports. These agents, the firms, households, government, and exporters all interact in what is often called a *circular flow*. This flow of resources is described within two-sides of the national economy accounting ledger.

As this evolution of the flow and its basic accounting occurred, it coincided with the evolution of the analysis of what we call a *production function, whereby the factor inputs come together to produce the aggregate output* of the economy. At the same time, the analysis of the flow of inputs into the role of producing output through a production function was itself a result of evolutionary history. Land was originally considered the third factor that was an input to production, along with the other two labor and capital inputs.

Land was considered a separate input during the time when most economies were largely agricultural. As the *structural transformation of economies* occurred towards more manufacturing and less agriculture, as a percent of economic output, land eventually became considered just a part of the capital that is required to produce output. So the controversy of whether to include land as a separate factor largely drew to an end over time, as agriculture shrunk relative to other sectors in developed economies. This left only labor and capital being the main factors of production in late-classical and neoclassical analysis, with land value being included in the capital needed to produce output.

2.2 Who Made it Happen

The individuals perhaps most responsible for the accounting foundations of Macroeconomics were Simon Kuznets (USA), Richard Stone (United Kingdom) and Irving Fisher (USA). Kuznets and Stone won Nobel prizes for their national economic accounting work (in 1971 and 1984 respectively; Fisher died before the Nobel Prize in Economics was established in 1969). Both Kuznets and Stone did their work while working for government or private agencies responsible for economic statistics. And the Nobel prize and research for both Kuznets and Stone emphasized that the accounting of national income and output formed the basis necessary in order to begin to organize our thinking on what causes the economic growth of nations.[1]

Irving Fisher separated out the so-called "nominal" factors from the real factors in several related ways that bridged the Classical "dichotomy" between the real side of the economy and the nominal side of the economy. Rather than viewing them as completely separate, as in the Classical economics tradition, Fisher showed how to measure the key nominal aspect, which is the inflation rate, by constructing an index number of the aggregate price level for the US. We exam the two most popular price indices here.

Fisher, a renown economist of the 20th century, measured the inflation rate in the USA as the rate of change in the aggregate price index, from one year to the next for example. He also showed how the market interest rates reflect the inflation rate implicitly (this Chapter, Appendix).[2] At the same time, convergence began towards a standard form for the aggregate production function of the economy known as Cobb-Douglas production.[3] Its characteristic of diminishing marginal products of inputs gave rise to downward sloping demand schedules for capital and labor inputs and an upward sloping cost schedule that constituted the supply of output.

2.3 Facts

2.3.1 An Aggregate Economy

An economy in macroeconomics can be defined as a collection of all of the individual markets that exist in a certain well-defined geographic area. This area can be a particular country or the entire world. The former is a national economy; the latter is a global economy.

Any particular economy that is well-defined can be analyzed in macroeconomics. For example, the economies of each of two countries can be analyzed together and this will show how the two economies together determine the supply and demand in the combined market. This international market can be considered a part of Macroeconomics or can be analyzed separately in a sub-discipline such as *international trade.*

When an economy is taken to be the aggregate of all industry within a particular country, then this is thought of as the national economy. It the economy does not engage in any trade with any economy outside of its own economy, then this can be thought of as a *closed* economy, meaning closed to trade.

An economy engaging in trade with some other economy can be thought of as an *open* economy, since some of its output leaves the economy and output from other economies many enter the economy. Such an open economy that engages in trade can have either a higher value of its imports as compared to the value of its exports, or a higher value of its exports as compared to the value of its imports. The former case is said to be that of a net importer, while the latter is said to be that of a net exporter.

---

[1]Richard Stone describes his contribution autobiographically as "I remained in the Ministry about nine months, in the section responsible for shipping and oil statistics. Then, in the summer of 1940, I was transferred to the Central Economic Information Service of the Offices of the War Cabinet, where James Meade was preparing the groundwork for a survey of the country's economic and financial situation and wanted somebody to help with the statistical side. By December 1940, Meade and I had completed a set of estimates which we showed to Keynes, who was then a member of the Chancellor's Consultative Council at the Treasury, and through his advocacy they were published as the second part of a White Paper entitled, An Analysis of the Sources of War Finance and an Estimate of the National Income and Expenditure in 1938 and 1940 which accompanied the budget of 1941. Our estimates consisted of three tables relating to the national income and expenditure, personal income, expenditure and saving, and the net amount of funds required by, and available from, private sources for government purposes. They hardly amounted to a set of national accounts but they were a beginning. In constructing the accounts, we made use of residual estimation. The balancing of the accounts, therefore, threw little light on the accuracy of the entries. But the sources for the first two tables were largely independent of those for the third, and the fact that for 1940 the sum of the first two residuals was not very different from the third, encouraged us to think that the results were not grossly inaccurate." http://www.nobelprize.org/nobel_prizes/economic-sciences/laureates/1984/stone-bio.html. Kuznets in his Economics Nobel prize Lecture describes his accounting work as laying the foundation for economic growth theory; see: http://www.nobelprize.org/nobel_prizes/economic-sciences/laureates/1971/kuznets-lecture.html

[2]In addition Fisher showed how the aggregate money supply of the economy is related to the aggregate price level is his Equation of Exchange (Chapter 5), how inflation and unemployment were related in what is now known as Phillips curve relations (covered in Chapter 6) and how to use the interest rate as a discount factor for measuring the present value of future income (Chapter 7).

[3]Cobb, C. W.; Douglas, P. H. (1928). "A Theory of Production". American Economic Review 18, Supplement, pp. 139–165.

Net exports are positive for a country with a greater value of exports than its value of imports. Another way to look at a net importer is to say that its value of net exports is negative. This means the economy is a net importer.

2.3.2 National Output & Income Accounting

The national output is a typical way to define a country's macroeconomic economy. National output is defined as the value of the production of the economy. Some goods are counted in national output calculations and some are not. Both private sector and government sector output is included.

A distinction of what is counted in national output and what is not is made on the basis of whether the good is a *final good and service* versus being an *intermediate good and service.* Goods themselves are considered whether they are an actual good that is consumed or whether they are services. Each final good and service is counted in national output.

The intermediate goods are not counted in national output. The reason is that part of the cost of the final goods and services is the intermediate goods and services that are bought in order to produce the final goods and services. Counting the value of both intermediate and final goods and services production would result in a type of double counting since the intermediate good and service would be counted once as an intermediate good and service and twice when being part of the cost of producing the final good and service, and therefore part of the price of the final good and service.

The economy-wide national output is defined in many specific ways by the accounting agencies of the US government. In particular the US Bureau of Economic Analysis, of the US Department of Commerce, keeps national product and income accounts. These are called by the acronym NIPA for the National Income and Product Accounts.

The NIPA definitions of output include Gross Domestic Product, or GDP, and Gross National Product, or GNP. The difference in the two is the amount of output by US residents or US companies that is produced outside of the US, such as by US citizens living abroad or US companies located abroad. GNP includes this plus GDP.

In contrast, GDP includes only the value of the goods and services produced within the US. This GDP includes the value of positive net exports since some of the output produced within the US is exported. Likewise GDP can include positive net imports, if imports exceed exports, since the net imports are paid for by output produced within the US.

GDP consists of four main categories:

There are four main kinds of expenditure on GDP that we call the components of GDP.

1. Personal consumption expenditure on goods (durable and non-durable) and services;
2. gross private domestic investment (fixed investment plus inventories) for non-residential (structures, equipment, intellectual property products) and residential;
3. exports minus imports; and
4. government consumption expenditure and gross investment (Federal and State and Local) for Defense and Non-Defense.

Figure 2.1 shows these US contributions in current dollar GDP terms quarterly for 2012:1 to 2014:3. Out of 16 trillion US dollars in total GDP in 2012.1, 11 trillion was for personal consumption expenditure. This is about 69% of GDP. Private gross domestic investment was 2.4 trillion, or 15% of GDP. Imports exceeded exports so net exports were *in magnitude* 0.6/16 or about 3.75%. And government expenditure on consumption and investment was (3.1) /16 or about 19% of GDP. This gives $69 + 15 - 3.75 + 19 = 99.25$, with the 0.75 remainder due to approximation.

Gross Domestic Product

[Billions of dollars] Seasonally adjusted at annual rates

Bureau of Economic Analysis

Last Revised on: December 23, 2014 - Next Release Date January 30, 2015

Line		2012				2013				2014		
		I	II	III	IV	I	II	III	IV	I	II	III
1	**Gross domestic product**	15956.5	16094.7	16268.9	16332.5	16502.4	16619.2	16872.3	17078.3	17044	17328.2	17599.8
2	**Personal cons. Expend.**	10959.7	11030.6	11119.8	11222.6	11351.1	11414.3	11518.7	11653.3	11728.5	11870.7	12002
3	Goods	3709.6	3717.2	3751.9	3788.8	3832.2	3821	3865.3	3886.1	3890.6	3964.5	4011.5
4	Durable goods	1177.3	1179.4	1195.4	1216.1	1237.8	1245.4	1252.4	1261.5	1262.3	1298.4	1320.2
5	Nondurable goods	2532.3	2537.8	2556.5	2572.8	2594.4	2575.6	2612.9	2624.6	2628.4	2666.1	2691.3
6	Services	7250.1	7313.3	7367.9	7433.8	7518.9	7593.2	7653.4	7767.2	7837.8	7906.2	7990.4
7	**Gross private dom. Invest.**	2445.4	2489.3	2500.4	2481.5	2543.3	2594.6	2708.9	2745.2	2714.4	2843.6	2905.1
8	Fixed investment	2364.3	2397.1	2424.7	2471	2499.1	2543.8	2598.1	2654.6	2674.3	2743.4	2810.6
9	Nonresidential	1942	1968.8	1978.3	1998.7	2010.3	2026.9	2060.2	2118.7	2134.6	2191.2	2244.3
10	Structures	437	452.5	452.2	445.9	435.4	448.5	463	481.7	487.9	504.4	513.3
11	Equipment	894.9	897.1	901.4	922.8	933.1	937	948.8	980	979.5	1008.6	1038.2
12	Intellectual property prod.	610.1	619.2	624.7	630	641.8	641.4	648.4	657	667.2	678.2	692.7
13	Residential	422.3	428.3	446.4	472.3	488.9	516.9	538	535.9	539.7	552.2	566.4
14	Change in private inventories	81.1	92.2	75.7	10.4	44.2	50.8	110.7	90.5	40.1	100.3	94.5
15	**Net exports of gds +serv.**	-614.8	-588.5	-541.7	-528.2	-528	-532	-509.9	-462.9	-538	-549.2	-516.5
16	Exports	2162.4	2192.5	2203.2	2218.5	2219.4	2236.4	2268.4	2324.6	2284.7	2344.3	2366.5
17	Goods	1510.1	1530.7	1538.5	1529.2	1528.4	1543.2	1565.7	1614	1575.3	1623.3	1645
18	Services	652.3	661.8	664.7	689.3	691	693.2	702.7	710.7	709.5	721.1	721.4
19	Imports	2777.1	2781.1	2745	2746.7	2747.4	2768.4	2778.3	2787.5	2822.7	2893.5	2883
20	Goods	2327.2	2326.2	2287.7	2283.1	2288.6	2302.2	2308.6	2309.7	2341.5	2405.6	2393.7
21	Services	449.9	454.9	457.3	463.6	458.8	466.3	469.7	477.8	481.2	487.9	489.3
22	**Govt cons.expend.+ invest**	3166.2	3163.3	3190.5	3156.6	3135.9	3142.4	3154.7	3142.7	3139.1	3163.1	3209.3
23	Federal	1291.4	1290	1314.3	1269.9	1241.9	1234.1	1233.9	1216.2	1208.1	1210.5	1241.3
24	National defense	818.6	817.1	840.9	795.4	775.1	772.2	774.9	757.5	749.9	754.6	784
25	Nondefense	472.8	472.9	473.4	474.4	466.8	461.9	459	458.7	458.2	455.9	457.3
26	State and local	1874.8	1873.3	1876.2	1886.8	1894	1908.3	1920.7	1926.5	1931	1952.6	1968

Figure 2.1 GDP Expenditure, Quarterly 2012.1–2014.3

Quality is not accounted for in national output and income accounting. The value of the national output of goods and services is simply the market value of the final goods and services. There may be a large increase in quality due to technological advance in the value of national output from one year to the next, but this is not accounted for.

For example, GDP and GNP are often converted into *index numbers* that show by how much the value of output changes on a period by period basis. The length of the period is typically annual, or quarterly, and sometimes monthly data is available. Within the change in output as determined by the index number for the output, there is no measure of quality change. This is known as the "index number problem" of not being able to reflect quality change in any systematic way.

Quality change is rather immeasurable by its nature. This is because one good gets replaced typically by the same type of good, only one with a higher degree of quality in terms of the dimensions of the product that are consumed. For automobiles, the quality changes in terms of fuel economy, ride smoothness, break-down frequency, even the technological breakthroughs that occur in tire production.

A Corolla is still called a Corolla, but each model change results in quality differences, usually an increase in quality overall. But NIPA simple counts that market value of the product and does not take into account the quality change.

If quality change were taken into account, then the annual growth of real GDP each year would be substantially higher. This would be akin to accounting for all of the increase in our *knowledge base* or what we call our *human capital*, once this knowledge goes from "software into hardware" within the particular good.[4] Counting all of our human capital would greatly increase the total value of our GDP and GNP but human capital is only counted in terms of the value added seen within the product.

[4]Steve Jobs in 1980 makes a presentation on the Apple computer in which he says that the next generation computer has within its hardware the software of the last generation computer. As he defines software and its role, he says "Yesterday's software is today's hardware"(at minute 17:41). He also compares computers to automobiles. See https://www.youtube.com/watch?v=0lvMgMrNDlg

National Income

The national income of an economy is computed by what is earned by the various forms of participants in the economy. There are various definitions of national income in the NIPA. One is Gross Domestic Income, or GDI. A related one is called National Income. We will focus on GDI.

GDI stands for Gross Domestic Income and is defined as the total income earned within an economy. Part of the GDI is what households earn as wages and salaries for their labor time. This is called the "compensation of employees."

Entrepreneurs contribute time and capital and as a result earn positive or negative profit. Corporations own capital and earn the difference between their revenue and cost. Both the entrepreneur and corporate profit is termed in NIPA accounting the "net operating surplus". Households or firms that own capital may earn interest and rent by lending this capital out, and this also counts as part of GDI.

Note that a "capital consumption adjustment" is made to components of net operating surplus in order to subtract from net operating surplus the current value of the depreciated capital stock. This capital depreciation is accounted for separately. It is the next main category of income.[5]

A major category is what gets used up in net income from replacing capital that is already in place. Companies need to maintain their capital stock and so part of the national income that is "earned" is used to maintain this depreciating capital over time. The annual coverage of depreciating or obsolete capital adds a positive component to annual total national income (once subtracted from other sources of income and then gathered together as one entity). It is called the "consumption of fixed capital."

The government also earns revenue in the form of tax revenue net of any subsidy expenditure. Adding together all of the sources of income from each of the economic participants gives a measure of national income. The total national income earned by participants in an economy is equal to the total output produced when the definitions of each "national income" and "total output" such as GDP are carefully defined.

GDI consists of four main categories

The Bureau of Economic Analysis defines Gross Domestic Income (GDI) as "the sum of all incomes earned and costs incurred in production." GDI is in four categories and consists of the sum of income earned

1. by labor: Compensation of employees;
2. by governments: Taxes on production and imports less subsidies; and
3. by entrepreneurs: Net operating surplus;
4. by the private and government sectors: Consumption of fixed capital.

Figure 2.2 shows the current dollar GDI for 2012:1 to 2014:3. The GDI and GDP do not add up exactly because they are calculated differently and so the difference is called a statistical discrepancy, given as an Addendum at the end of the table. They should add up to the exact same total. The compensation of employees is about 8.5/16.2 or 52% of GDI, net operating surplus about 25%, fixed capital consumption about 2.5/16, or 16%, and taxes about 1.1/16 or 7%, for a total of 99% which would be 100% if approximations are not used.

Equality of GDP and GDI within NIPA

GDP and GDI are almost exactly equal. The definitions of GDP and GDI are such that they add up to the same amount, up to what we call a statistical discrepancy. This means they are essentially equal except for accounting errors. Most economists do not study the statistical discrepancy although exceptions exist.

---

[5]The capital consumption adjustment adds the difference between the value of the capital depreciation that has already been recorded in income accounts (the historic cost basis called "book value", or the "capital consumption allowance") and the current cost value of the capital depreciation (called the "consumption of fixed capital"). This means the adjustment subtracts the current value of depreciation as adjusted to exclude what was already subtracted from accounts previously.

Gross Domestic Income by Type of Income

[Billions of dollars] Seasonally adjusted at annual rates

Bureau of Economic Analysis

Last Revised on: December 23, 2014 - Next Release Date January 30, 2015

Line		2012				2013				2014		
		I	II	III	IV	I	II	III	IV	I	II	III
1	**Gross domestic income**	16175.6	16276.3	16403.5	16633.8	16752.7	16909.3	17060	17197.8	17221.5	17481.7	17743.5
2	**Compensation of employees, paid**	8531.1	8552.8	8585.2	8790.6	8742.8	8835.4	8880.5	8955.9	9104.7	9168.7	9247.8
3	Wages and salaries	6869.1	6886.1	6911.4	7095.6	7042.5	7120	7154.3	7217.5	7348.3	7400.9	7467.6
4	To persons	6854.8	6871	6896.3	7080.8	7027.4	7104.2	7138.6	7201.7	7333	7384.9	7451.5
5	To the rest of the world	14.3	15.2	15	14.7	15	15.7	15.7	15.8	15.4	16.1	16
6	Supplements to wages and salaries	1662.1	1666.6	1673.9	1695.1	1700.3	1715.4	1726.2	1738.3	1756.4	1767.8	1780.3
7	**Taxes on production and imports**	1129.5	1132	1127.7	1138.9	1154.8	1152.2	1167.1	1175.7	1184.5	1197.9	1212.4
8	**Less: Subsidies 1**	57.9	58	56.8	59.4	60	61.1	60.6	58.9	57.7	57.5	57.4
9	**Net operating surplus**	4073.2	4127.8	4206.5	4205.4	4329.7	4370.1	4432.7	4454.7	4291.2	4450.3	4590.2
10	Private enterprises	4097.1	4152.3	4231.9	4232.7	4357.5	4399.8	4462.8	4485.7	4322.2	4483.9	4626.6
11	Net interest + misc payments, dom.industry	665.6	639.1	677.2	649.1	686.3	646.2	663.1	682.8	684.5	632.3	650.7
12	Business current transfer payments (net)	119.2	110.8	102	94.6	115.1	122.3	118.4	126.6	119.2	123	182.4
13	Proprietors' income w/ inventory + capit.cons	1226.4	1256.1	1266.1	1292.3	1327.8	1330	1345.9	1342.7	1351	1381	1386.4
14	Rental income of persons w/ capit.cons.	516.6	526.5	537.1	551.7	575	590.8	604.2	613.3	622.9	635.4	646.7
15	Corporate profits w/ inventory +capit.cons.	1569.3	1619.8	1649.6	1645.1	1653.3	1710.5	1731.1	1720.3	1544.6	1712.2	1760.3
16	Taxes on corporate income	451.3	473.5	440.6	453.8	474.9	459.2	467.5	495.4	562.3	608	602.5
17	Profits after tax w/ inventory +capit.cons.	1118.1	1146.3	1209	1191.3	1178.4	1251.3	1263.6	1224.9	982.3	1104.3	1157.8
18	Net dividends	598	605.5	641.6	876.1	697.5	936.5	816.6	856.1	740.4	714.2	709.9
19	Undistributed profit w/ invent. +capit.cons.	520.1	540.8	567.4	315.2	480.9	314.8	446.9	368.8	241.9	390.1	447.9
20	Current surplus of government enterprises 1	-23.9	-24.5	-25.4	-27.3	-27.8	-29.6	-30.1	-31	-31.1	-33.6	-36.3
21	**Consumption of fixed capital**	2499.7	2521.7	2540.9	2558.4	2585.4	2612.7	2640.2	2670.5	2698.7	2722.3	2750.4
22	Private	2008.2	2026.6	2042.9	2059.2	2083.9	2108.2	2132.5	2158.7	2183.5	2203.8	2228.6
23	Government	491.5	495.1	498	499.2	501.5	504.5	507.8	511.8	515.2	518.5	521.8
24	**Addendum:**											
25	Statistical discrepancy	-219.1	-181.7	-134.6	-301.3	-250.3	-290.2	-187.6	-119.5	-177.5	-153.5	-143.7

Legend / Footnotes:

1. Prior to 1959, subsidies (line 8) and the current surplus of government enterprises (line 20) are not shown separately; subsidies are presented net of the current surplus

Figure 2.2 GDI by Category of Receipts, Quarterly 2012.1–2014.3

The equality of the measure of national output with the measure of national income provides the basis for the concept of a flow of expenditure funds that circulates from producers or sellers to consumers or buyers. At the same time the income flows between the firms and households in terms of factor payments. This gives rise to what is called a circular flow between output and income within an economy.

Value Added Accounting of Output

While GDP and GDI are equal, GDP perhaps can more easily be thought of in another way in an accounting sense. GDP can be constructed by industry whereby it shows the *value-added* to national output caused by each industry. Figure 2.3 shows the value added by industry for the US in 2012–2014.

The largest US industry is the financial intermediary industry that we call Finance, Insurance, Real Estate and Leasing. This stands at 20.1% of GDP in 2014. Manufacturing comes in at 12% of GDP and Professional and Business Services also has a 12% share. Government exceeds this somewhat at a 13% share.

2.3.3 Nominal Vs. Real; Inflation & Price Indices

So far we have presented national income and product accounts in current dollars. Economists and newspapers speak of the value of items in terms of nominal or real values. The nominal value is its current dollar value. More generally, a nominal value is in terms of any currency units.

A real value in contrast takes into account that the currency unit itself may have changed in value. Usually these changes are always downwards. Within any economy, the national currency is generally believed to be worth less after a year for example whenever there is a positive *inflation rate* over that year.

Inflation is defined as a general price level rise. Or it might be understood as the average rise in all of the prices in an economy. Inflation is measured by some price index. The most well-known example is the Consumer Price Index, or CPI.

Value Added by Industry as a Percentage of Gross Domestic Product

[Percent]

Bureau of Economic Analysis

Release Date: November 13, 2014

Line		2012				2013				2014	
		I	II	III	IV	I	II	III	IV	I	II
1	**Gross domestic product**	100	100	100	100	100	100	100	100	100	100
2	**Private industries**	86.3	86.4	86.5	86.5	86.6	86.7	86.9	87	86.9	87.1
3	Agriculture, forestry, fishing, and hunting	1.2	1.2	1.2	1.2	1.4	1.4	1.4	1.3	1.2	1.3
4	Mining	2.6	2.5	2.5	2.5	2.5	2.6	2.7	2.6	2.7	2.7
5	Utilities	1.6	1.6	1.7	1.6	1.7	1.7	1.6	1.6	1.7	1.7
6	Construction	3.6	3.6	3.6	3.6	3.7	3.7	3.7	3.7	3.7	3.7
7	Manufacturing	12.4	12.4	12.4	12.2	12.2	12	12	12.2	12	12
8	Durable goods	6.5	6.6	6.5	6.5	6.5	6.5	6.5	6.5	6.5	6.5
9	Nondurable goods	5.9	5.8	5.9	5.7	5.7	5.5	5.5	5.7	5.5	5.5
10	Wholesale trade	6	6	6	6	5.9	5.9	6	6	5.9	6
11	Retail trade	5.8	5.8	5.8	5.8	5.8	5.8	5.8	5.8	5.8	5.8
12	Transportation and warehousing	2.9	2.9	2.9	2.8	2.9	2.9	2.8	2.9	2.9	2.9
13	Information	4.6	4.7	4.6	4.5	4.6	4.6	4.6	4.7	4.7	4.6
14	Finance, insurance, real estate, rental, and leasing	19.6	19.9	20	20.2	20	20.2	20.2	20.2	20.1	20.1
15	Finance and insurance	6.6	6.9	7.1	7.2	7.1	7.2	7.2	7.3	7.1	7.2
16	Real estate and rental and leasing	12.9	12.9	13	12.9	13	12.9	13	13	13	13
17	Professional and business services	11.9	11.8	11.8	12	11.7	11.8	11.9	11.8	12	12
18	Professional, scientific, and technical services	7	7	6.9	7	6.8	6.9	6.9	6.9	7	7
19	Management of companies and enterprises	1.9	1.8	1.9	2	1.9	1.9	1.9	1.9	2	2
20	Administrative and waste management services	3	3	3	3	3	3	3	3	3	3.1
21	Educational services, health care, and social assistance	8.3	8.2	8.2	8.3	8.3	8.3	8.2	8.2	8.3	8.2
22	Educational services	1.1	1.1	1.1	1.1	1.1	1.1	1.1	1.1	1.1	1.1
23	Health care and social assistance	7.1	7.1	7.1	7.2	7.2	7.2	7.1	7.1	7.1	7.1
24	Arts, entertainment, recreation, accommodation, and food services	3.7	3.7	3.7	3.7	3.7	3.7	3.7	3.7	3.7	3.8
25	Arts, entertainment, and recreation	1	1	1	1	1	1	1	1	1	1
26	Accommodation and food services	2.7	2.7	2.7	2.7	2.7	2.7	2.7	2.7	2.7	2.8
27	Other services, except government	2.2	2.2	2.2	2.2	2.2	2.2	2.2	2.2	2.2	2.2
28	**Government**	13.7	13.6	13.5	13.5	13.4	13.3	13.1	13	13.1	12.9
29	Federal	4.5	4.5	4.4	4.4	4.3	4.2	4.1	4.1	4.1	4.1
30	State and local	9.2	9.1	9.1	9.1	9.1	9.1	9	8.9	8.9	8.9
31	**Addenda:**										
32	Private goods-producing industries [1]	19.9	19.7	19.7	19.5	19.8	19.7	19.8	19.8	19.6	19.8
33	Private services-producing industries [2]	66.4	66.7	66.8	67	66.8	67	67.1	67.2	67.3	67.3

Legend / Footnotes:

1. Consists of agriculture, forestry, fishing, and hunting; mining; construction; and manufacturing.

2. Consists of utilities; wholesale trade; retail trade; transportation and warehousing; information; finance, insurance, real estate, rental, and leasing; professional and business

Note. Detail may not add to total due to rounding.

Figure 2.3 US GDP by Industry, 2012–2014

Price levels in an economy can go up for a variety of reasons. If they rise only because the quality of the product has risen, then this would not lead to a reduction in the value of a currency. One would simply pay more because one is getting more. Price is higher in this case because quality is higher.

If the price level rises when there is no quality change, within a competitive economy, we think of this as a monetary change in prices caused by the circulation of more money within the economy. Such a monetary increase that causes prices to rise is what price indices are designed to measure as what we call inflation.

Another reason a price index could rise is because monopoly power increased and pushed up prices. This is not a common reason cited for increases for example in the CPI. Rather the CPI is most typically thought to measure inflation as caused by monetary causes.

The use of the CPI index is broad. The CPI is computed by taking a given basket of goods and seeing how the same basket of goods is priced year after year. The idea is that the same basket of goods will only change in price if there is a monetary influence. The index is keyed to some base year such as 2009, in which the index is normalized so as to have a value of 100.

Price indices such as the CPI can include a Toyota Corolla in its basket of goods for the economy. The CPI then would not make a distinction between a price increase for example due to a quality increase as opposed to a price increase due to more money in circulation. This is a problem with using price indices, already mentioned above as the index number problem of quality measurement.

Given the caveats of using a price index like the CPI, the real value of an item is found by measuring the nominal value of that item over time and then *deflating* the cost of the item by dividing by the CPI index. Dividing a nominal price of any good by the CPI gives the value of the index in real terms as it factors out any price increase due to inflation.

The idea of turning a nominal series of data over time into a real one, in *constant dollar terms*, is to eliminate the effect of the changing value of the currency within the economy. The science of nominal to real conversion is not exact as there are many real factors that can affect even the average aggregate price level such as the CPI. Disregarding these factors, the price indices are thought to approximate the change in the value of the currency unit and so thought to be a good device for converting nominal values to real values.

Consumer Price Index and its Measured Inflation Rate

Using the past quantities for the consumption basket is how the Consumer Price Index is constructed. The CPI enables the construction of a historical picture of the US inflation rate. Figure 2.4 shows the index itself and Figure 2.5 the inflation rate based on the CPI.

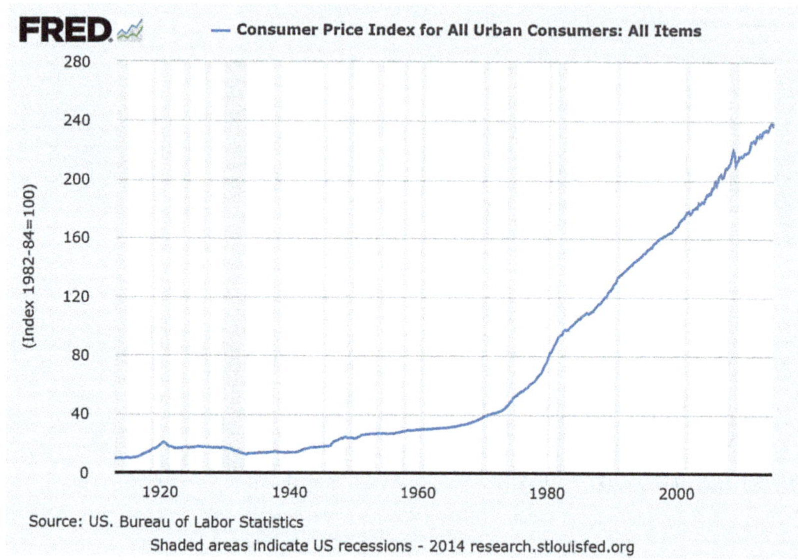

Figure 2.4 CPI, Monthly, 1913–2014, All Urban Consumers, All Items

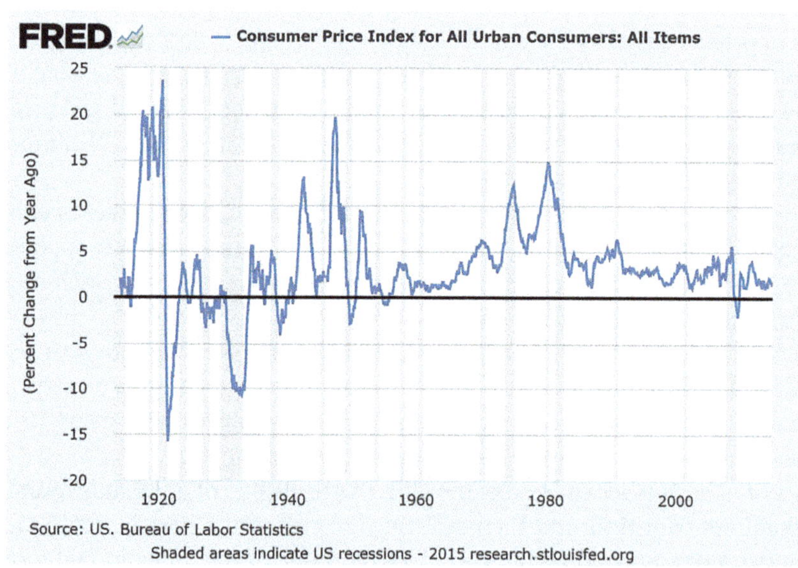

Figure 2.5 Percent Change in CPI, All Urban Consumers, 1913–2014

In Figure 2.4, the Consumer Price Index, Monthly, 1913–2014, for All Urban Consumers, and All Items, has the advantage of a long time series going back until 1913:1 and here ending in 2014:11. It goes from a value of 10 in January 1913 to a value of 33 in March 1967, a 3¼ fold increase in 54 years. It then rises from 33 to 236 in November 2014, a 7 fold increase in 47 years, more than double the multiple in the first 54 years.

In monetary history, we learn how in 1971–73 the *Bretton Woods gold standard* for international monetary arrangements after WWII was ended which required that US currency was partially backed by gold. After that point, US dollars could be printed by the US Treasury without gold backing and used to finance government expenditure. Freshly printed money can be used to finance government expenditure, such as during the Vietnam War. Much evidence exists which shows that the growth in the supply of money is correlated with the rate of change in the price level measure.

The inflation rate is computed from a price index such as the CPI by taking the percentage change in the CPI from the previous period. For example, with 1984 the *base year* in which the CPI equals 100, then if the index rises to 105 in 1985, the annual rate of inflation is (105–100)/100 which equals 0.05. Putting the inflation rate in percentage terms is found by multiplying by 100. This gives (0.05)*100 which equals 5%.

The annual rate of inflation is the most common reported measure. This can be computed from monthly, quarterly, or annual data for the CPI. Figure 2.5 shows the annual rate of inflation using the monthly CPI index from Figure 2.5 for the years 1913–2014. It shows the high inflation during World War I, WWII and the Vietnam War era.

Figure 2.5 also shows volatile inflation periods in the late 1910s, a sharp deflation in 1920–21, and then a more prolonged deflation during the Great Depression of the 1930s. Since the 1980s, the inflation rate has been mainly positive and below 5%. There appears to be some slight deflation in the 2008–2010 recession.

Comparison of GDP Deflator and CPI

A similar price index for the US is called the *GDP Deflator*. It gives an alternative measure of the US inflation rate. Figure 2.6 shows the inflation rate for the US from 1930 to 2014 on an annual basis using the GDP deflator index (Red) versus the CPI index (Blue). They move together fairly closely for most of the period.

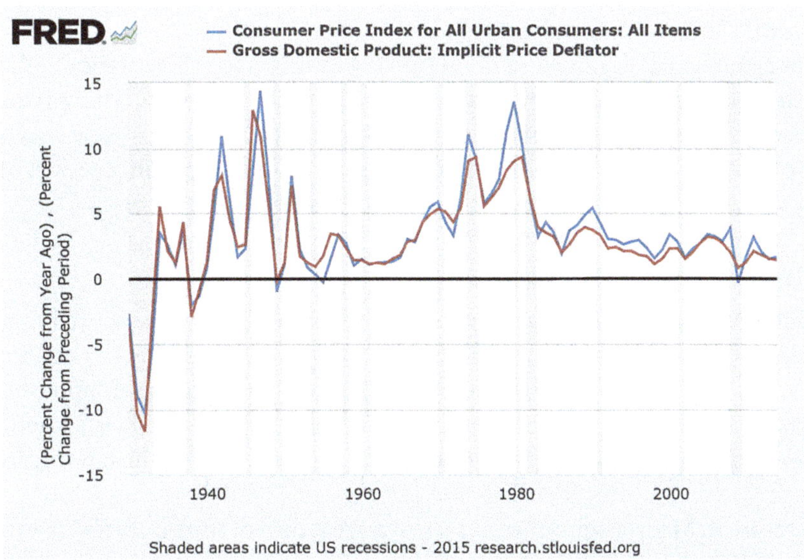

Figure 2.6 Comparison of Inflation Rate Computed Using GDP Deflator (Red) and CPI index (Blue), US 1930–2014, annual basis

2.4 Theory

2.4.1 Output Production

Economists think of the national aggregate economy in terms of it being produced with an aggregate production function. Here we will say that real aggregate output is denoted by y. This y stands for several concepts at once.

First the notation y assumes that there exists this composite real output good that we simply call output. It can be thought of as the basket of all of the goods and services that the economy produces. Second, whatever the number of y that there are in economy in turn indicates the quantity of this composite basket of output. We simply call y the "output" of the economy.

If y grows over time in terms of quantity, then the economy experiences *economic growth.* If the y fluctuates over time, we say that the economy experiences *business cycles.* If the economic output y is unchanged over time, we might say that the economy is *stagnant.*

The idea that output is a function means that certain *inputs* go into the production function, and that this aggregate output y comes out as the output of the production process. The inputs to the aggregate output production function are called the *factor inputs.* These are typically the economy's aggregate labor and capital.

Factor Inputs into Production

Labor is taken to mean the aggregate quantity of labor hours employed in a given period, which could be for example hours in a day, in a week, or hours worked per year. Capital is meant to encompass financial capital as it is used to buy plants, equipment, land and any other type of investment that is used in the production process. Typically we therefore think of this as *physical capital* rather than financial capital in general, as this capital becomes a physical piece of machinery for example. The physical capital is said to incur *depreciation* when it wears out or becomes increasingly obsolete over time. Financial capital in contrast does not experience such physical depreciation.

Qualifications about the nature of our inputs are many. Land used to be considered a factor of production, and so an input into the production process, while now land is simply seen as part of the capital requirement in producing output. Land value is simply included in the capital quantity unless land in particular is being focused on in some separate way such as in agrarian economies engaging mainly in agriculture.

Financial capital is considered a type of capital that is used in production for the financial intermediation sector. There the industry needs labor and capital for example in the production of financial intermediation services such as loans. But it also needs financial capital in the form of deposits. The financial output gives back the deposits in the form of insurance payouts, pensions payouts, loan payouts, with coverage in its fees for the labor and physical capital components used.

Another significant extension of the use and definitions of inputs is to replace labor with the *human capital* content attached to that labor. In this view, *raw labor* is input into the production process along with its corresponding extension through the human capital attached to that labor. This view sees aggregate output y produced by two forms of capital: human and physical capital. This is an advanced form of the production function used mainly in macroeconomic growth theory and business cycle theory.

Functional Form for Production Function

The most conventional way to represent the aggregate production function is to say that output is a function of labor and capital inputs. This is written symbolically as $y = f(l,k)$, where l is the quantity of labor used and k is the quantity of capital used. If we wanted to include how the output and inputs change over time, we add time subscripts for example. Writing the production function as $y_t = f(l_t, k_t)$ means that the output at some time t, where t could be the year 2015 for example, is produced using the labor l_t and capital k_t that is inputted at time t.

The traditional literature in Macroeconomics has spent a great deal of time in evolving towards a common usage for the production function. What we have consensus on is that a function such as $y = f(l,k)$ should show that the two inputs *complement* each other in that using more of one input, holding the other constant, yields more output. And increasing say labor while holding capital constant increases the *productivity of the*

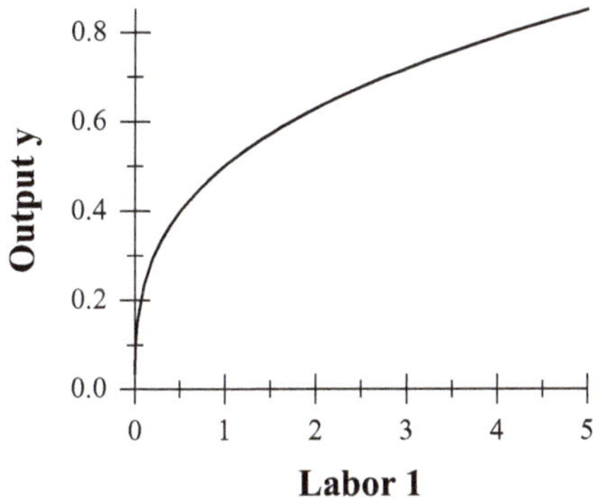

Figure 2.7 Production Function of Output: variable Labor, fixed Capital

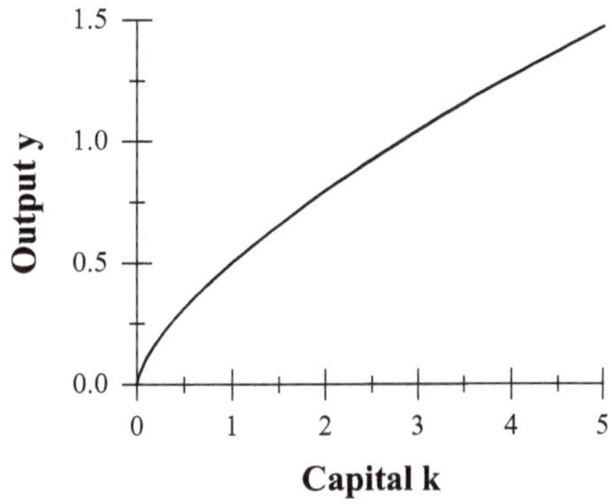

Figure 2.8 Production Function of Output: variable Capital, fixed Labor

input capital since more output now results for the same capital input. So labor complements capital in that increases in labor make capital more productive. Complementarity is originally a microeconomic principle, now here applied to macroeconomics.

The most standard functional form is one with factor input complementarity and also *diminishing marginal product* of each input labor and capital. Adding one more unit of labor increases output, so that the increase in output is positive. But if output goes up by less with each additional increase in a unit of labor input, then the increase in output is diminishing with each additional unit of one of the inputs.

The so-named "Cobb-Douglas" production function is the most common specification of a production function.[6] It can be graphed with either labor or capital on the horizontal axis and output y on the vertical axis. The curve is *concave from the origin*, because it exhibits a diminishing marginal product. As more of the input is added, output rises, but by less with each additional input.

Figures 2.7 and 2.8 show Cobb-Douglas production functions in each the labor and the capital dimensions.[7]

Factor Input Demand Schedules

We call the labor and capital markets the *input markets, or factor input markets.* A diminishing marginal product of labor within the production function causes the demand for labor and the demand for capital to be downward sloping. This is because a higher quantity of labor demanded by the firm comes with a lower value of the marginal product of the higher quantity of labor. So the firm will only demand this higher quantity of labor in the given market if the equilibrium price of labor, such as the wage rate, is low enough.

The demand for factors comes from the firm side. The supply of labor comes from the consumer side in the form of "renting out" labor time by working for wages and salaries. The supply of capital comes from the consumer side by "renting out" capital saved for example as bank deposits in a savings account.

The consumer savings is often intermediated into investment by financial intermediaries who try to make sure the savers get paid back the original savings plus an extra amount for being willing to lend it out rather than consume it. By saving financial capital and lending it out through financial intermediaries or even directly, the consumer supplies capital and receives back the capital plus *interest income* or *dividend income* from lending it out.

2.4.2 Representative Agent Economy

What we call the *representative agent* economy is one that is characterized with a single production function representing all of the firms in the economy that supply output. In addition the representative agent is also

[6]The power exponents attached to each labor and capital are individually between zero and one, and together they add up to one. For example, $y = Al^{0.33}k^{0.67}$ is a Cobb-Douglas production function, where A is just a so-called "productivity" parameter, a number, greater than zero.

[7]Here $y = 0.5l^{0.33}k^{0.67}$.

the single average consumer represented with a utility function over the output (and leisure) that generates the source of all output demand in the economy. The single representative agent is aggregated into one so that the single agent combines both consumer and firm functions.

The representative agent economy is thought of as the "Robinson Crusoe" economy after a novel by that name in which a single occupant of an island must both produce and consume all of the output of the island economy. The representative firm emerges when Robinson Crusoe is producing. The representative consumer emerges when Robinson Crusoe is consuming.

The representative agent economy has a *unique equilibrium* on the firm side and on the consumer side, for each the output market and for the input markets. On the firm side, the marginal cost of supplying one more unit of output equals the marginal benefit the firm receives in terms of the equilibrium price that would be charged for the output in a market economy. On the consumer side, the marginal cost of producing or buying the unit of output just equals the value of the marginal utility of consuming that output. This means the firm's marginal cost of output supply equals the consumer's marginal benefit of consuming that output in equilibrium.

In the input markets similar margins guide the equilibrium. The consumer's marginal cost of supplying each labor and capital, respectively, equals the firm's value of the marginal product of demanding each labor and capital, respectively. Marginal benefit equals marginal cost for both representative firm and consumer, in both input and output markets.

The competitive equilibrium price for output and inputs exists only when there is a full market economy, rather than an island with a single representative. Therefore the representative agent world is an abstraction that includes a large economy with many agents each having an average production function and utility function. They use the competitive price system to decide their allocations. With a large economy, the price system is how each firm and consumer decides on the optimal allocation so that overall marginal benefit equaling marginal cost emerges across the entire economy.

The Robinson Crusoe economy does not have the explicit prices of a market economy. But Robinson Crusoe is guided by the same marginal costs and marginal benefits as in a competitive equilibrium environment. This makes the allocation in equilibrium the same as in an economy with explicit prices. This is a result that makes the Robinson Crusoe representative agent economy a useful, simple, model of the entire economy.

Equality of Real Output and Income

The macroeconomic model says that utility of the consumer is maximized subject to the production technology of the economy, in a Robinson Crusoe world. Within a market economy with explicit relative prices, we say that the consumer maximizes utility by buying the firm's output as constrained by the real income earned by the consumer. The firm in turn uses its real income from purchases to buy the inputs of labor and capital, as constrained by the production technology.

With a *binding budget constraint*, the consumer's total real income is fully spent on real output. Part of the consumer expenditure can include not just consumption of current output but also savings that is invested into current capital investment by firms. This savings enables the consumer to have more future income than if there were no savings.

The *disposable income* of the consumer is defined as that left after paying taxes and deciding how much to save. This disposable income is then spent on current consumption. The total income includes the savings supplied ultimately to firms for investment and the net tax payments made to the government.

The sum of consumption by consumers, investment by firms, spending and investing by the government, and any net exports of output gives a full accounting for total output in the economy. We call this GDP as shown above. The conventional symbolic representation of total output is to put it in nominal terms even though we use real values in our primary macroeconomic models.

Therefore, assume that the nominal value of consumption is denoted by C, of investment is denoted by I, of government spending and its consumption is denoted by G, and of net exports is denoted by NX. Then we have that

$$C + I + G + NX = Py,$$

where P is currency unit price of a unit of output and y the real quantity of output.

To state this fully in nominal terms, in some currency unit, define nominal output Y as $Py = Y$. So the accounting of output in purely nominal terms is then

$$C + I + G + NX = Y.$$

In real terms we would divide all variables by the price level of output P, and could then represent the real values in lower cases letters (except government) as $c + i + (G/P) + nx = y$.

All income is used to purchase consumption, make savings, pay taxes and buy any net imports. Therefore all the sources of national income, in particular GDI in an accounting sense, add up to the output in our macroeconomic model. In particular, total aggregate income can be written approximately as wage income plus capital rental income plus net taxes. This equivalence between the value of aggregate output and total income can be stated in real or nominal terms.

The sum of the four GDI components can be formulated in a similar equation as is used for GDP. Using notation in real terms, we have that wages w times labor l, or wl (for wage and salary compensation), plus depreciation of capital (fixed capital consumption) at the rate δ times the capital stock k, or δk, plus the after-depreciation return on capital (net operating surplus) at the rate $(r - \delta)$ times the capital stock k, or $(r - \delta)k$, plus net taxes τ, gives total income GDI:

$$wl + (r - \delta)\, k + \delta\, k + \tau = wl + rk + \tau = GDI.$$

Government Budget in NIPA

The equality of GDP and GDI gives us that $c + i + (G/P) + nx = wl + rk + \tau$. Now assume that the government spending is exactly financed by taxes collected. This would be what we call running a *balanced government budget.*

With a balanced government budget, symbolically, this would be that $(G/P) = \tau$. As a result we can see that consumption, investment and net exports exactly equal the wage and rental income from labor and capital: $c + i + nx = wl + rk$. This is when the representative agent also runs a balanced budget: aggregate expenditure equals aggregate income.

A *government deficit* in its budget is possible if it borrows by issuing US Treasury debt and selling it to the public. If $(G/P) > \tau$, then government spending is greater than tax revenue. Then the government must borrow money by issuing and selling more debt.

2.4.3 Circular Flow

The equivalence relation between output and income underlies the circular flow that exists in the model representation of the aggregate economy. There are two main sets of markets. These are known as the output, or product, market and the input market.

In the output market, firms sell products to consumers. These consumers as households pay for the products. This creates a two-way flow of goods going from firms to consumers and expenditure of real income going in return from consumers to firms.

In the input market, firms buy or rent labor and capital from the consumers. The consumers as households supply labor and capital to the firms. This creates a two-way flow of income payments from firms going to households who supply factor inputs used to produce output.

The input and output markets create what is called a circular flow. With the input market at the top of the circle, the output market at the bottom of the circle, firms say on the lefthandside of the circle and consumers on the righthandside of the circle, the flow of the economy can be illustrated as a circular flow. This is shown in Figure 2.9.

The government and financial institutions are *intermediaries* that can be put inside the circle and so generate addition sub-flows. These show the payment of taxes by firms and consumers to the government and the provision of payments (and services) from the government to firms and consumers as households.

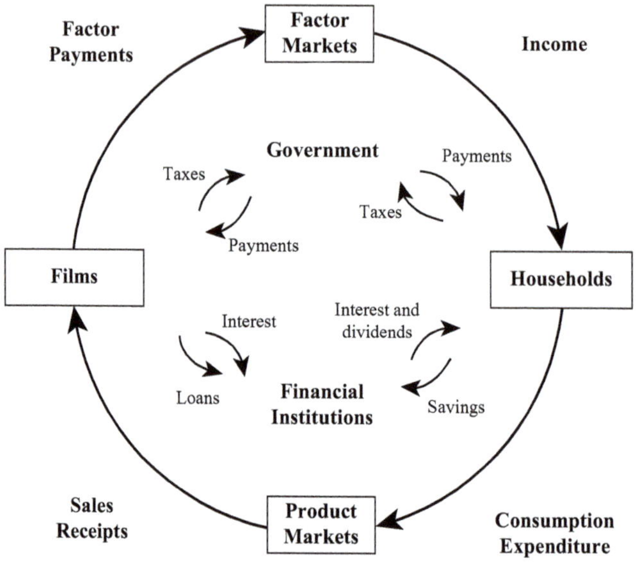

Figure 2.9 Circular Flow of Aggregate Economy

The financial intermediaries show how savings of the consumers goes to banks. In turn the interest and dividends are income sent back from the bank to the consumers. The bank gives the savings to the firms in the form of loans, and then the bank receives back from the firms the interest and dividends that it passes on to consumers minus the banking cost of operation. Note that Table 2.3 shows the importance of financial intermediation as it is the largest industry in the US currently.

2.4.4 Classical Dichotomy: Nominal & Real Economy

The pure theory of microeconomic exchange was set out by Walras (1874)[8] in which there is no money. All prices of goods are relative to the amount of other goods that would have to be given up in order to exchange for a particular good. The Walrasian "auctioneer" allowed all of these exchanges to happen centrally without cost of the need for a means of exchange. In this way the nominal, or monetary aspects, of the economy were not necessary to express the equilibrium of each and every market in the economy. This was the full statement of the Neoclassical equilibrium with both supply and demand determining value. But it remained consistent with the Classical dichotomy in which the monetary side does not affect the real side of the economy; Walras's economy was the real side.

The influence of money was thought in Classical Economics to merely put prices of goods in terms of a unit of exchange like the US dollar without affecting the equilibrium of the real side of the economy. Discussion existed throughout the history of economy thought of how inflation could distort the economy, but this was not integrated into Neoclassical Economics formally until later. In particular Irving Fisher and Milton Friedman are well known for bringing to bear the effect of inflation on the economy.

The idea that the monetary side does not affect the real side was called the Classical dichotomy and then became known in Neoclassical Economics as perfect "money neutrality". Money neutrality existed if the existence and use of money did not affect the real equilibrium of goods. However modern monetary economists starting with Bailey (1956) showed that inflation acted as a tax that distorted the real economy in a way similar to any other tax.

Money neutrality never holds when inflation acts as a distortionary tax. This lack of money neutrality, and the lack of a perfect dichotomy between the real and monetary sides of the economy has become ingrained in modern monetary theory in the Neoclassical tradition. The "New-Keynesian" modern approach follows Keynes's (1930) theory of price, typically does not include money in the economy, and focuses on the effects

[8]Elements of Pure Political Economy, first edition, Lausanne: Carbay (second edition 1926).

of monetary policy. Analysis of monetary policy without money in the model does give rise to certain problems in the New-Keynesian analysis.

2.5 Application: US GDP Growth

The growth rate of real output can be computed using an index for real GDP. The real GDP index is available in Fred data banks. A real GDP index can be computed by dividing a nominal GDP time series of data by a price index such as the CPI or the GDP deflator.

Consider the growth rate of GDP in both constant dollars (real terms) and in current dollar (nominal terms) to see if there is much difference. Figure 2.10 shows the growth rate of real GDP for the US from 1929–2013. This is the percentage change in a real GDP index on an annual basis. Each data point shows how GDP was growing at each point in time, relative to one year ago. This means the growth rate is given on an *annual basis.*

Except for the early period up to WWII and the few years afterwards, the peaks in Figure 2.10 average around 5% since 1948, while the troughs are near 0%. This means that for postwar US the real GDP has gone up and down between around 5 and 0 percent for nearly a century. And the average growth rate during the entire period is roughly seen to be around 2.5%.

Now consider the growth of GDP in nominal terms. This gives the rate of change of GDP in current dollar terms. Figure 2.11 shows the annual growth rate in nominal GDP since 1929. This differs from the real GDP growth rate by generally being higher after WWII. During the Great Depression in the early 1930s the growth rate of nominal GDP is lower than that of real GDP. Both of these differences are due to the US inflation rate.

The inflation rate was positive for nearly all of post WWII, and therefore made the nominal GDP higher than the real, which adjusts for inflation. Inflation was negative in the early 1930s, at around -10%, thereby making nominal GDP growth less than real GDP growth during this period. The difference in the two GDP graphs is the rate of price change of nominal prices, as given by the inflation rate.

During *WWII* the nominal GDP growth rate peaks near 30%, instead of 20% as in Figure 2.10. This is because US inflation was around 10% then. In the post-WWII period, nominal GDP growth rises to above 10% during the Vietnam war period when the US inflation rate was particularly high. Real GDP growth was much lower, to the extent that the 1970s is called a period of *stagflation,* as characterized by relatively high inflation and low real GDP growth.

Inflation is why the nominal and real figures can differ. And it is why economists, as well as newspapers and TV reports, focus on the growth rate in *real* GDP. This is considered generally as the most representative

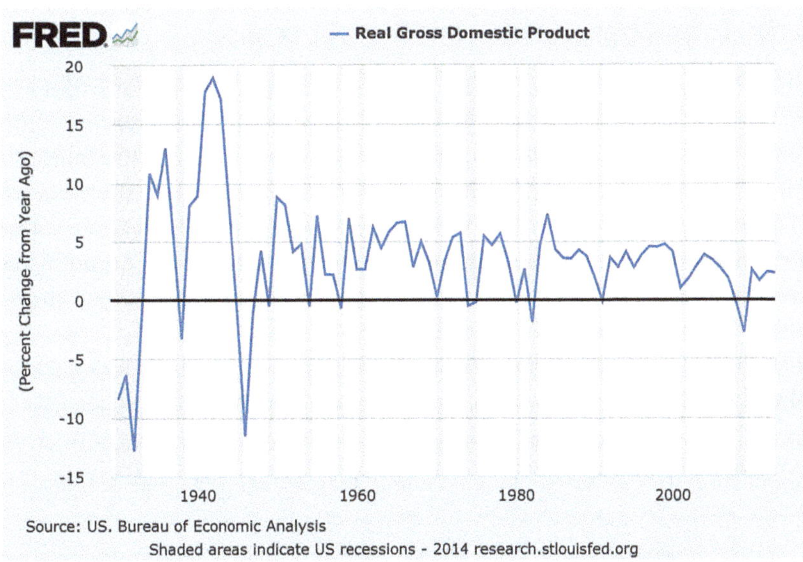

Figure 2.10 Percentage Change in US Real GDP, 1929–2013

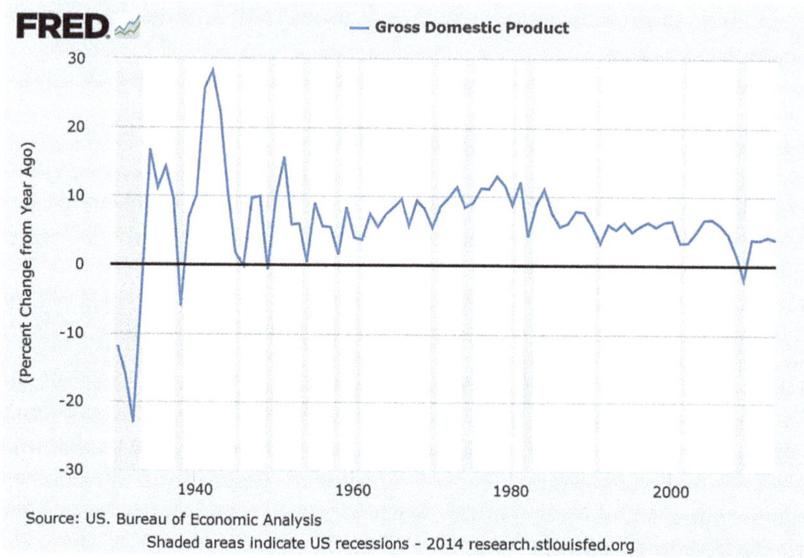

Figure 2.11 Percentage Change in US Nominal GDP, 1929–2013

single data measure of economic growth. Focus is also on the current inflation rate, as economists view this in terms of a tax on currency usage that should not be too high.

A further historical example with this data can be given by considering particular numbers for the average real GDP growth, average nominal GDP growth and average inflation rate over the entire period. Say the historical average inflation rate over the period was 3%, and that the average nominal current dollar GDP growth over the period was 5.5%. This would give an average real GDP of 5.5% minus 3%, or 2.5%.

One way to say this is in terms of the depreciation of the currency unit that is caused by inflation. Inflation means that all prices go up so each dollar is worth less. If annual inflation is 3%, the dollar buys 3% less this year than last year.

Then "net of the 3% depreciation of the US dollar", the real GDP is the nominal average growth of 5.5% minus the depreciation of the dollar of 3% (average inflation). This gives a "net of (currency) depreciation" rate of real growth of GDP output of 2.5%.

2.6 Appendix: Nominal vs Real Interest

An important addition to the theory of the relative price of money is that not only does the real interest rate affect money, but so does the inflation rate. Irving Fisher again emerges since he apparently first put together the theory on *nominal interest rates.* The nominal rates are simply defined as the market rates.

The real rate of interest is computed using Irving Fisher's concept of how the nominal interest rates are formed. His 1930 *Theory of Interest*[9] states that the nominal rate equals the real rate of interest plus the expected inflation rate. This is called the Fisher equation of interest rates. If the nominal/market interest rates include the inflation rate, then the money being borrowed and lent takes into account the natural depreciation in the currency unit of the money as a result of inflation.

Inflation means that the money cannot buy as much at the end of the period as it could in the beginning. If the inflation is 10%, then 10% less can be bought with the currency since the aggregate price level has risen by 10%. If money is lent out, the return then needs to cover the inflation rate and provide some real return. This is the Fisher equation of interest.

[9] http://www.econlib.org/library/YPDBooks/Fisher/fshToI.html

With R denoting the nominal, market, rate of interest, and π^e the expected inflation rate at the time of the loan, then r is the real interest rate as computed as a residual of $R - \pi^e$. This gives the Fisher equation symbolically as

$$R = \pi^e + r.$$

2.7 Summary

The chapter presents facts, theory and application of the national income and product accounts of a country. It discusses the concepts of aggregate output and income, lays out categories in official national income and product accounts, and introduces nominal versus real variables.

Price indices are used to measure inflation. The Consumer price index is the most well-known measure of prices. And the inflation rate is measured as the rate of change in the price index.

The production function for aggregate output is introduced. Aggregate inputs of labor and capital are used to produce output. This creates income flows back to the factor inputs. And income equals output in both accounting terms and in economic analysis terms.

The government also has a budget for expenditure. It uses taxes in part to finance expenditure. And the government spending is a part of both national income and product accounting and economic analysis.

The circular flow of the economy includes the government along with the representative consumer and firm. It shows how expenditures to firms from households are equal to income received by households from firms for factor payments. Intermediaries in the economic flow of resources include financial institutions.

2.8 Glossary of Italic Words

annual basis: the computation of a time series of data that gives the level of the data for the year ending at the particular data point under consideration; monthly, quarterly, or annual data can be presented on an annual basis.

balanced government budget: government expenditure equals government revenue.

base year: the normalized year of a data series, typically stated as 100.

binding budget constraint: a budget that limits effectively the amount of spending such that the total spending is equal to the income from all sources.

Bretton Woods gold standard: established in 1944 as articles of the International Monetary Fund as a system of fixed exchange rates between countries, with the US as anchor via its commitment to fix the US dollar price of gold at $35 an ounce; the US gold reserves of foreign national central banks were convertible to US dollar currency at this rate.

business cycles: fluctuations in the level of real GDP, with downswings known as recessions or contractions and upswings known as expansions.

capital: a stock of an item of value.

closed economy: an economy that does not engage in trade with any other economy.

complement: in factors of production, an increase in one factor causes the productivity of the other factor to increase.

concave from the origin: a mathematical description of the shape of a graph that is a curve starting in the origin, whereby the curve rises initially at a relatively fast rate at the origin and then rises at an increasing lesser rate as the horizontal axis variable is increased; the slope of the line becomes less at every increase in the horizontal axis variable.

constant dollar terms: a calculation of the value of an item whereby the effect of inflation in the general price level of aggregate output is effectively removed; a base year is chosen such that the constant dollar calculation is in terms of prices relative to the base year.

deflation: a negative rate of inflation in the general aggregate price index.

depreciation: a decrease of value in any form of capital due to a variety of reasons such as "wear and tear".

diminishing marginal product: the increase in output caused by an increase in a given input becomes an increasingly smaller increase in output, as the input continues to be increased.

disposable income: the income left to spend after taxes are paid; a secondary definition is for example after taxes are paid and savings are set aside.

dividend income: profit paid out by firms to those owning the firm, according to their share of the company as bought for example through a market for the shares, or stock market.

economic growth: a positive rate of change in national, aggregate, real GDP or real GDI.
factor inputs: material used in the production of output generally grouped into classifications of labor and capital.
final good and service: an output of firms that is directly consumed by households, as opposed to being an intermediate product that is consumed in the process of producing output that is directly consumed by households.
government deficit: government expenditure exceeds government revenue.
human capital: a conceptualization of the stock of knowledge within each individual that is useful for producing output.
in magnitude: a number can be positive or negative by the same amount, say positive 5 or negative 5, and so have the same value (of 5) if the sign is ignored.
index numbers: a series of numbers usually associated with a data series that represents the data at each point in time as relative to the previous period of time, but does not necessarily give the correct magnitude of the data at any point in time as it has been normalized by dividing through all of the data points by some magnitude, such as by the current value of GDP at the base year of say 2009.
inflation rate: the rate of change in the index of the aggregate price level such as the CPI index, given on an annual basis often but which may be given on any particular basis.
input markets: the supply and demand for factors used in production such as labor and capital
interest income: the income earned from renting out capital.
intermediate good and service: a product used in the production of a final good and service that is consumed by households.
intermediaries: an agent that acts as a conduit from one agent to another, such as financial intermediaries.
international trade: the buying and selling of goods and services between nations.
knowledge base: the stock of accumulated information.
labor: time provided for a firm that helps the firm produce its output and that is typically paid for, but can be volunteered.
open economy: an economy engaging in trade with another economy, such as international trade.
percentage change: the change of a value between two points in time, as divided by the value at the earlier of the two points in time.
physical capital: capital taking a form that is used as a factor of production in producing output such as manufacturing plants and equipment, but not including financial capital.
productivity of the input: the amount of output produced divided by the total amount of the input used for a given period of time.
quality change: an increase in the usage value of a product despite the product remaining in a similar form.
raw labor: the least skilled labor that has not been augmented by increases in knowledge known as human capital.
representative agent: a way to view a large group of actors, or agents, in an economy, in terms of a single one that has characteristics of the average of the group.
stagflation: a period of time over which the inflation rate is relatively high and the real output growth rate low.
stagnant: an economy that does not appear to be either experiencing economic growth or sustained contraction.
unique equilibrium: a place within a model where the forces of the model naturally are at rest, such that there is only one such place.
value added: an increase in the value of the product that is created through the production process as compared to the value of the inputs that are used up in the production process.

2.9 Questions

1. What is the national output of an economy?
2. How is economic growth measured typically?
3. What is the difference between GDP and GDI?
4. How do industries add value to the production of goods and services?
5. Explain the difference between nominal and real values.
6. What is an example of an index that can be used to calculate inflation and how is inflation calculated from the index?
7. What is a production function?

8. What are factors of production that are used as inputs in the production process?
9. How are factor input demand schedules related to the marginal product of the factor?
10. How does a representative agent economy represent an entire aggregate economy?
11. Provide a symbolic representation for how the components of GDP add up to total GDP.
12. What happens in order to make a government deficit equal to zero?
13. Describe the circular flow within a model economy.
14. What is an online source for data series of the US economy?
15. What does US experience indicate was the difference between real and nominal GDP growth during the last century?
16. Complete the Federal Reserve Bank of St. Louis EconLowdown Course Module "GDP and Pizza".

3 Macro Divergence from Micro

3.1 Introduction

Up until the 1930s, the federal government was responsible for a relatively minor share of total economic output in the US. The economic, social and political upheavals of the 1930s, including the Great Depression, saw the rise of a gradually extended role for government. At the same time the macroeconomic analysis became more distinct from Microeconomics, with a role for the government emphasized.

3.2 Who Made it Happen

In Keynes's 1930 *Treatise on Money*, he argued that there was excess, unused, savings that was not being invested by the economy's production sector. Rather than focusing on fixing the crash of the bank financial intermediation sector, which created a barrier to the intermediation of savings from the individual saver to the individual producer, Keynes argued that the government should simply take the unused savings and do the investment itself. Since the savings was sitting around unused, direct expenditure of the savings on investment would increase the output and employment of an economy.

Keynes (1930) states explicitly that he is departing from Irving Fisher's (1922) expression of the price level in terms of the money supply, as part of the quantity theory of money. Instead Keynes (1930) sets out to determine the aggregate price level in terms of the microeconomics of Marshall (1920), with no association to the money stock. In doing this, Keynes (1930) apparently wanted to follow his teacher Alfred Marshall who developed the theory of the price of output under competition conditions.

Keynes postulates the aggregate level of prices from the microeconomic theory of the value of goods, or price theory. As an extension of Marshall (1920, Principles of Economics), Keynes in his 1930 Treatise of money said that the price of aggregate output can be considered to be based in cost theory, as the sum of average cost plus profit. The Marshallian competitive price simultaneously equals its marginal cost of production, as well as average cost plus profit; Keynes focuses on the latter. The Marshallian price theory is the still-current microeconomic theory of the firm's price of output under competition.

Arising from the Keynesian conception of aggregate output's price determination, Keynesian economics arose gradually. Keynes (1930) used his new theory of price to describe *business cycles*, with an emphasis more on the market's failure to invest available savings. Keynes (1936) emphasized how the government could increase aggregate economic output by taking savings that were not invested by the private sector and then do the investment itself. The idea was that the government needed to step in, take action, and do the investment instead of the private sector. This government investment is now simply called government spending and the nature of such spending is part of what we term *fiscal policy.*[1]

Keynes (1936) used a theory of consumption to help justify the idea of government spending. He postulated that for low income people consumption is a larger share of income than for high income people. Statistical foundations for such a relation between consumption and output goes back to early empirical studies of the so-called "consumption function". Engel's (1857) study of data on consumption and income led to the formation of Engel's law: "The poorer a family, the greater the proportion of its total expenditure that

[1]See Gillman, Max, 2002, "Keynes's Treatise : aggregate price theory for modern analysis?," The European Journal of the History of Economic Thought, vol. 9(3), pages 430–451.

must be devoted to the provision of food".[2] Keynes's (1936) use of this consumption function suggested that government spending could redistribute income from high income classes to low income classes, and raise the level of aggregate output.Neoclassical Economics emphasized the private sector's health. It focused on private banking, credit problems and the US Federal Reserve Bank during the Great Depression. For example Irving Fisher's 1932 *Booms and Depressions: Some First Principles*, and his 1933 "Debt-Deflation Theory of the Great Depression" focuses on how private investment can be revitalized.[3] Fisher (1932), like Keynes (1930), also frames his Neoclassical approach most broadly as being one describing *business cycles*.[4] Fisher (1933) emphasized that these cycles are usually normal but by inadvertent government action, such as through the US Federal Reserve System, a downturn in the economy could be unnecessarily severe. One focus was on fixing the action of the US Federal Reserve System, which was a type of *monetary policy*, since the Federal Reserve Bank controls the money supply. Neoclassical economics at the time, including Fisher's proposals, could also be viewed as emphasizing *banking policy.* This was also related in part to the Federal Reserve System's policy, since they regulated how the private bank sector operated through their *macroprudential* policy.

3.3 Facts

3.3.1 The Great Depression

The Great Depression of the 1930s occurred internationally and in the US. This deep, prolonged recessionary period was called a depression because of its severity. It arguably transformed what was at the time called Economics into two main strands that became known as Microeconomics and Macroeconomics.

The arising of a separate economics dealing with the aggregate economy apparently emerged from the extreme focus that the economic crisis imposed upon economists of the day. Statistics of the aggregate economy show that the market economy was in danger of collapse. Along with fear of the collapse of the market economy, there was fear of the collapse of democracy itself. During this period extreme political forms that were different from democracy arose more strongly, in particular, fascism and communism.

For a view in terms of real GDP, Figure 3.1 shows the US Real Gross Domestic Product (GDP), in constant 2009 dollars, on an annual basis from 1929 to 1939. The trough in annual real GDP is in 1933, and the trough in quarterly nominal GNP (the only related quarterly data in the Fred data base) occurs in the first three months of 1933. The *National Bureau of Economic Research (NBER) "Business Cycle Reference Dates"* dates March 1933 as the trough of the Great Depression (http://www.nber.org/cycles.html). In this figure and the following ones, the shaded area from August 1929 to March 1933 marks the NBER definition of the time period of the Great Depression.

In capital markets, the Dow Jones Industrial Average Stock Index (DJIA) rose above 360 in August 1929.[5] In October 1929, it later hit its Depression Low of 41.22 on July 8, 1932, about one-ninth the level of its peak. After rising and then falling again, the DJIA started rising ever upwards after March 1933 and never again reached the Depression era low. The DJIA stood at 17769 on July 29, 2015.

In the labor market, equally striking was the change in the *unemployment rate.* Figure 3.2 shows the US unemployment rate from April 1, 1929 to June 1, 1942. Although real GDP recovered to above 1929 levels in 1936, unemployment still remained high at 15% in January 1936, after having peaked at 25% in 1933. It fell once again to the near-0 level of August 1929 only in June 1942, as wartime spending began to increase dramatically.

[2] See Stigler, George, "The Early History of Empirical Studies of Consumer Behavior, 1954, Journal of Political Economy, Vol. 42, April; reprinted as Chapter 7, in G. Stigler, *Essays in the History of Economics*, 1965, University of Chicago Press, Chicago; see page 203 for quote from Engel.

[3] "As will be seen, the main conclusion of this book is that depressions are, for the most part, preventable and that their prevention requires a definite policy in which the Federal Reserve System must play an important role. This problem is of even greater importance than the problems of our old national banking system which led, after two generations of delay, first to the Aldrich Report and then to the establishment of the Federal Reserve System" (Fisher, 1932, p. viii.).

[4] "The vast field of "business cycles" is one on which I had scarcely ever entered before, and I had never attempted to analyze it as a whole" (Fisher, 1932, ibid, p.vii).

[5] See for details for example see http://www3.nd.edu/jstiver/FIN462/US%20Market%20Crashes.pdf

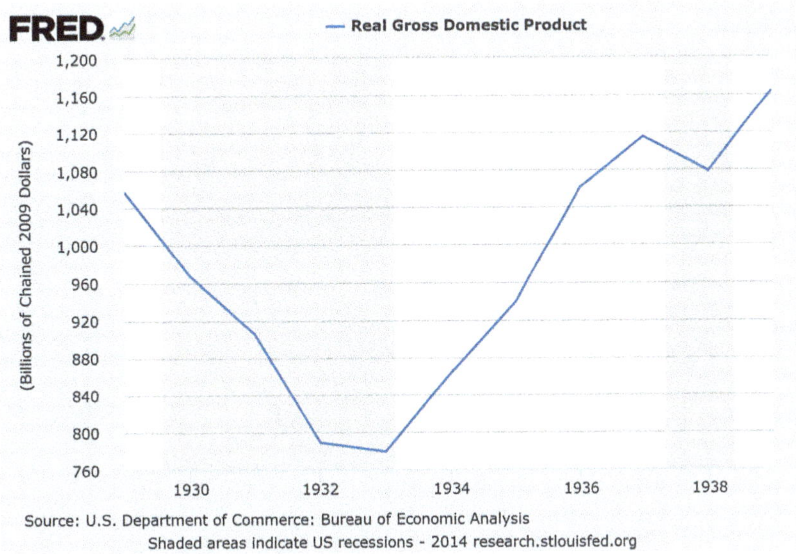

Figure 3.1 US Real *GDP* in the 1930s

Figure 3.2 US Unemployment Rate, 1929–1942

Meanwhile the US *CPI inflation rate*, from January 1923 to January 1939 is shown in Figure 3.3 on an annual basis, using monthly data. The point of March 1933 shows an inflation rate of −10%, a strong deflation. From March 1933 to November 1933, the inflation rate rises by 10 percentage points to a rate of 0.0%. This is an increase of the inflation rate level by 10% in just eight months. This is even more dramatic than the fall in the inflation rate from April 1930, when it was 0.6%, to June 1931 when it was −10.1%. This drop took more than a year and was of similar magnitude to the rise in the inflation rate after March 1933. But the increase from March to November, 1933, took place in three-fourths of the time period of the April 1930 to June 1931 fall in the inflation rate.

Another revealing fact was that private bank deposits as a share of the US money supply dramatically rose starting in March 1933. A chart available on Fred shows the ratio of US currency (dollars) relative to the sum of *currency and bank deposits*. If it rises, then deposits fall relative to currency holding: people take money out of the banks. If it falls, then currency is getting deposited back into the banks, who can then lend it out.

Figure 3.4 shows that the currency to deposit ratio rose dramatically starting at the end of 1930, meaning people began withdrawing deposits from banks, until it peaked at 17.27% in March 1933. The ratio then fell

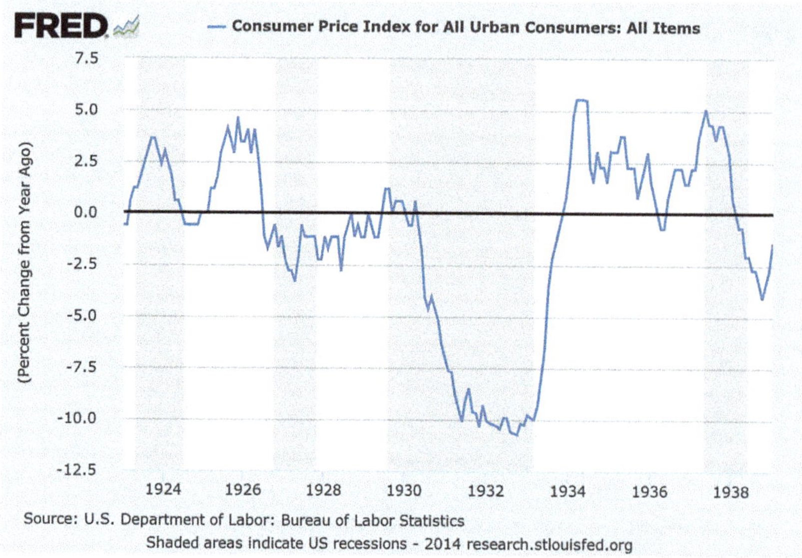

Figure 3.3 Percentage Change in US Consumer Price Index, 1923–1939

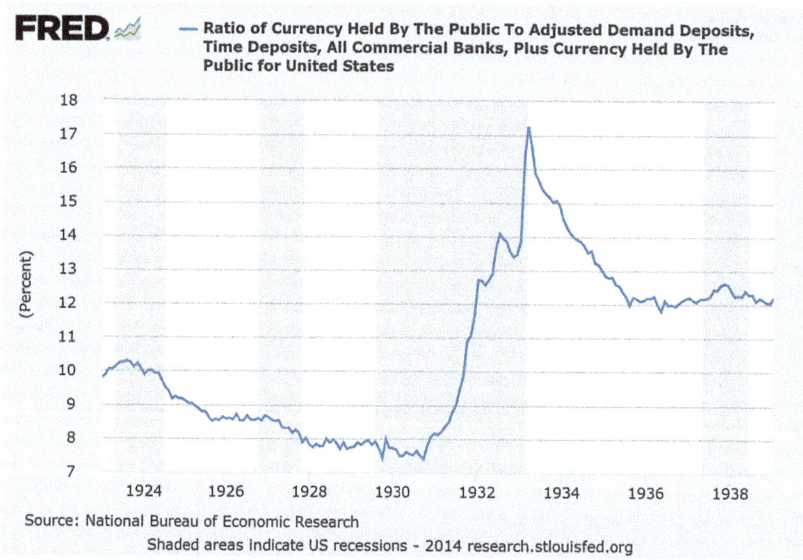

Figure 3.4 US Currency to Demand Deposit Ratio, 1923–1939

quickly as people began putting their money back in banks as deposits, and it stabilized around at around 12%, after August 1935. This jump down in March also coincides with the turning point of the Great Depression, this being the date during which it is thought that the Great Depression ended.

3.3.2 Government Spending including Defense

There was very negligible federal government expenditure during the Great Depression other than Defense. Including state and local government expenditure the *share of GDP* of all government spending was 9% in 1929. Figure 3.5 shows the total government expenditure as a share of GDP. This share rose to 16% during the Great Depression and then drastically increased starting around 1940. This 1940 jump can be seen to be a result of the WWII military expense.

Federal Government defense spending as a share of GDP rose from around 2% in 1940 to over 40% by 1944. Figure 3.6 shows US defense as a share of GDP historically starting in 1900. The WWII share was twice

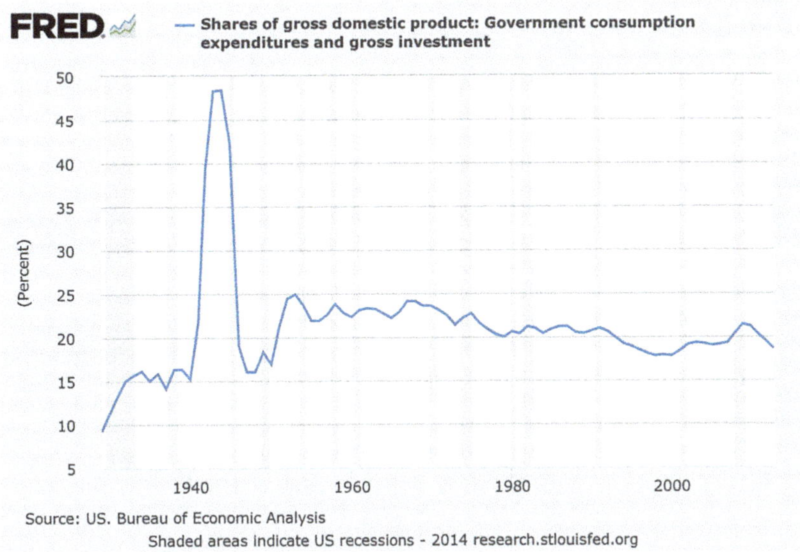

Figure 3.5 US Total Government Expenditure as a Share of GDP

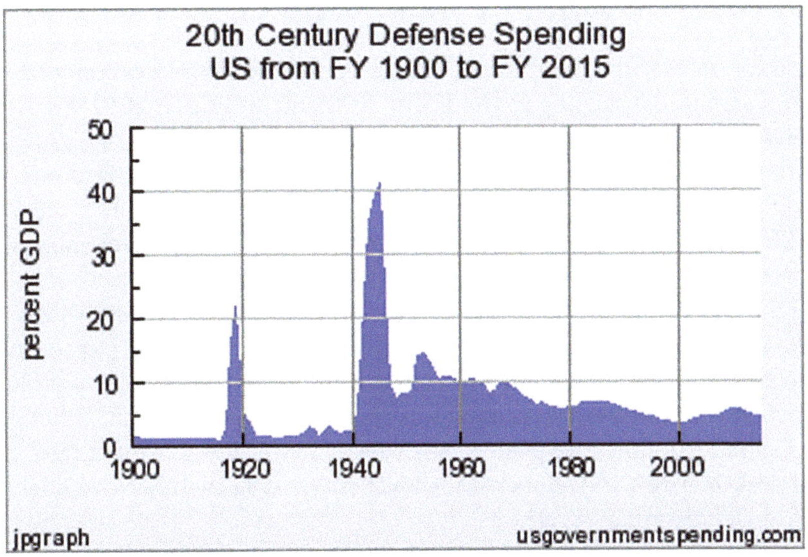

Figure 3.6 US Defense Spending as Share of GDP, 1900–2013

as high at its peak than the WWI share. The Korean War showed a large share near 15%, and since then the defense share has fallen steadily.

For example, Figure 3.7 shows that from 1999 to 2014, US defense as a share of GDP fluctuated between 4% and 5.6%. By comparison the defense share of GDP in the lead-up to WWII and during it were extreme in historical perspective. This suggests that government can influence overall employment, albeit for a wartime economy. However since 2000 Defense accounts for a relatively small share of the total federal government share of GDP that has trended down from 25% in 1953 to 18% in 2015. Note that the non-defense government share of GDP has fluctuated between 13% and 16% from 1967 to 2015.[6]

[6]Milton Friedman has written that government spending as a share of GDP should trend down over time; in private correspondence.

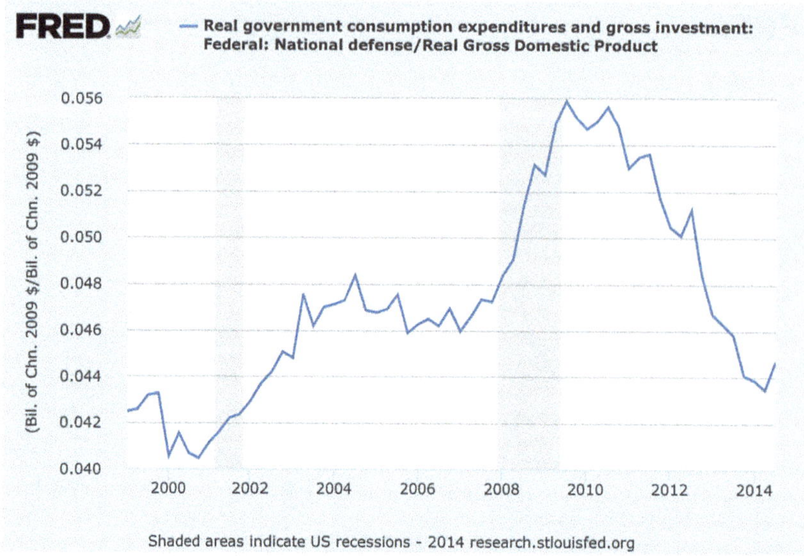

Figure 3.7 US Real Defense as Share of GDP, 1999–2014

3.3.3 The Great Recession of 2008–2010

With similarities and contrasts to the Great Depression, a worldwide deep recession took place recently, with it officially (by NBER standards) starting in the US in 2008 and ending in 2010. Figure 3.8 shows the US growth rate of real GDP with a sharp downturn starting in 2008 and a negative 4% growth rate in the depth of the recession in the fourth quarter of 2008, using quarterly data at an annualized rate. In comparison the 2001 dated recession had a peak decline somewhat above a 0% annualized growth rate in the third quarter of 2001. While the 26% drop in real GDP during the Great Depression, was much more severe than in 2008, the 2008 decrease was much more severe than all other postwar recessions.

Figure 3.9 shows the US growth rate of real GDP since 1929 on an annual basis, with a −2.7% growth rate of real GDP in 2008. This 2008–2010 recession is the most severe since the Great Depression, but mainly it has been difficult because the recovery showed a lower than average low growth rate for a prolonged period.

The unemployment rate in the Great Recession was been prolonged and high, although below that of the Great Depression. Figure 3.10 shows the post-WWII US Civilian Unemployment rate. Using monthly data at an annual rate, it peaked at 10% in October 2009, less than in 1982 (with a November peak of 10.8%) but far less than the Great Depression 25% rate.

The stock market crashed in the Great Recession but has recovered and inflation has been low. This stands in contrast to the prolonged stock market crash and the prolonged negative inflation (a 10% deflation) of the Great Depression. However one other marked feature of the Great Recession is the precipitous drop in the labor force participation rate.

Figure 3.11 shows the US postwar Civilian *Labor force participation rate.* This peaked above 67% in April 2000, declined somewhat following the 2001 recession, and fell by three points steadily starting in 2009. With a continual decline, it stood at 62.6% in June 2015, a level not seen since November 1977.

Non-participation means that workers leave the workforce completely, with them choosing not to participate in the job market. While comparable data is not available for the Great Depression, the data shows a strong postwar upwards trend in the participation rate, with a now reversed trend downwards just as apparent. Explaining this downward participation rate trend is a subject of controversy.

Figure 3.12 graphs US Census Bureau Home Ownership Rates (Table 14) from 1965 to 2015. The rise and fall in the labor force participation rate and the home ownership move together broadly, both rising to the high 60's percent in the early 2000's and then falling back to the low 60's percent in 2015. For US Home Ownership, after a level of about 64% from 1985 to 1995, it rose to 69% in 2004, and fell back to 63.7% in 2015. Houses are typically the biggest wealth asset of households.

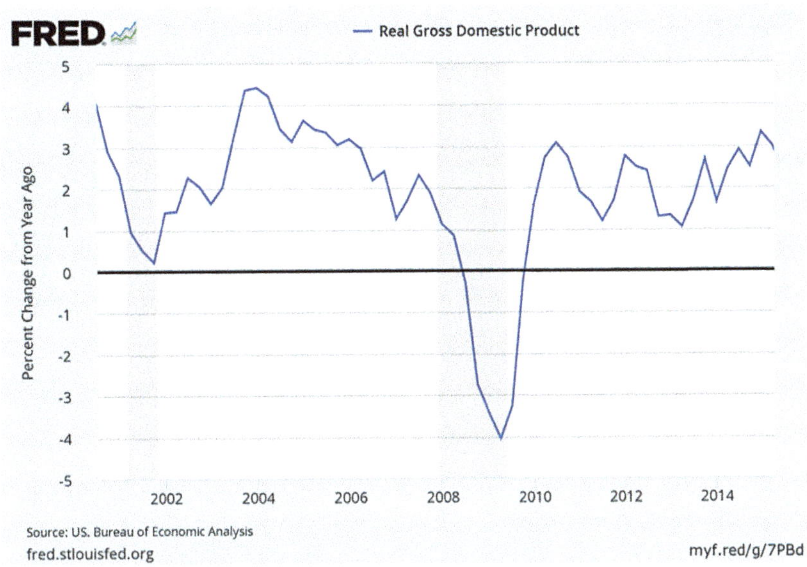

Figure 3.8 Post 2000 Real GDP Growth Rate, Quarterly, at Annualized Rate

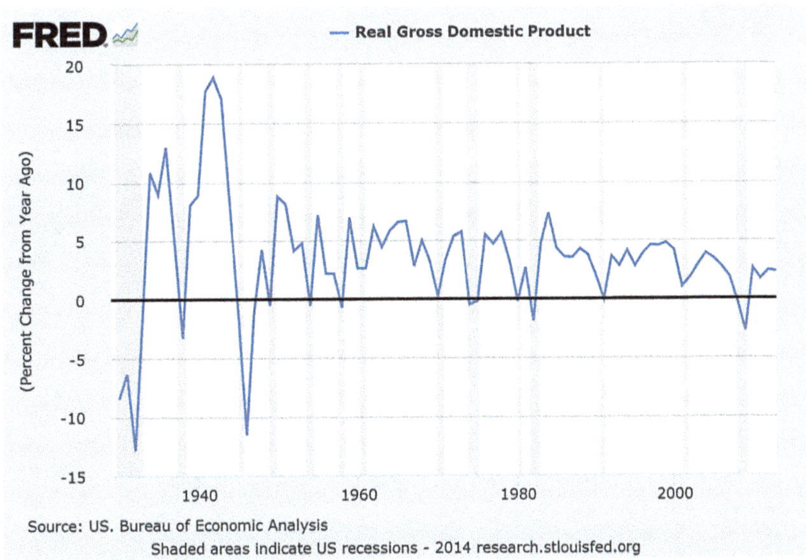

Figure 3.9 Historical Growth Rate of US Real GDP, 1929–2013

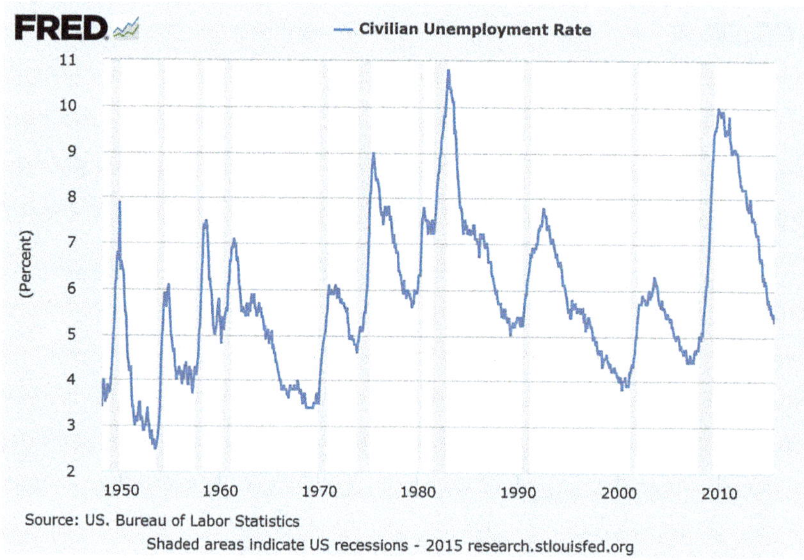

Figure 3.10 US Civilian Unemployment Rate, Post WWII

Figure 3.11 US Postwar Civilian Labor Force Participation Rate

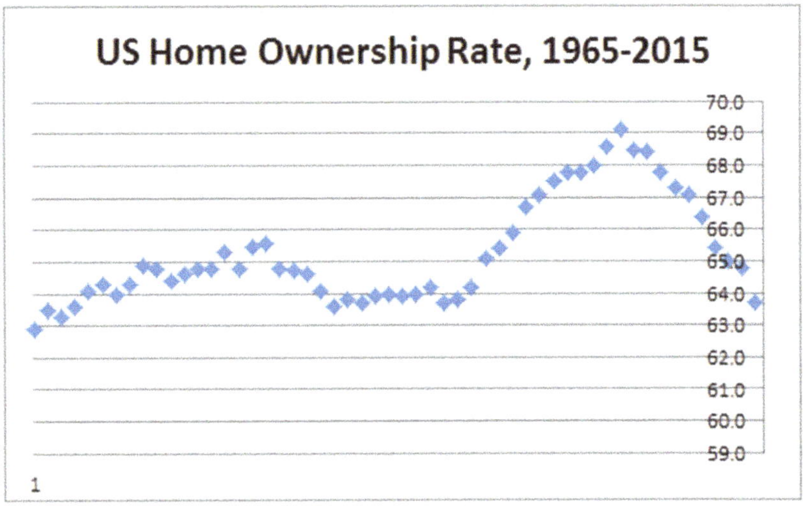

Figure 3.12 US Census Bureau Home Ownership Rates for the US, on an Annual Basis; Reported Quarterly

3.4 Theory

3.4.1 Neoclassical Approaches

Neoclassical economists were defined at the time of the Great Depression by using the supply and demand analysis of microeconomics, as developed in the 1870s (Jevons, Walras, Menger), in trying to describe the entire economy. American economist Irving Fisher developed the analysis of savings and consumption over time. Added to his body of work on interest rates, money supply policy, and on the value of capital, he was the major American voice during the 1920s preceding the Great Depression.

Irving Fisher

Fisher analyzed the Great Depression in terms of supply and demand in his so-called *debt-deflation" theory*, as described in his 1932 book *Booms and Depressions* and his 1933 summary article "The Debt-Deflation Theory of the Great Depression".[7] He considers *business cycles* to be a response to shocks that create dynamic movement around the "ideal equilibrium". There are no set cycles as there are many forces that combine to make each cycle unique. He allows that the entire economy may be in a time of "over" or "under" production of output. And some of these swings in the business cycle can be extreme such that an abnormal crisis occurs.

Looking at the US 1873 depression and the Great Depression of the 1930s, Fisher finds that over-indebtedness precedes the depression and general price deflation occurs during the depression. As a result of over-indebtedness, default and liquidation of debts then occurs with a host of crescendoing factors: selling at distressed prices, fewer bank loans and more currency holding combined with less bank deposits, falling general price level, fall in aggregate profits and company net worth, reductions in output, employment and trade, greater loss of confidence and prolonged keeping of money outside of banks that causes the *velocity of money in circulation* to decrease. Fisher argues that these factors combine to cause abnormally severe recessions that we call depressions.

Fisher finds that the real interest rate rises as a result of the price level deflation and lower money velocity. Here the reduced rate of growth of the money supply is emphasized by Fisher as causing the deflation. This deflation makes existing debt repayment harder, since the real debt burden is higher. This results because making the same dollar amount repayment each month, when the general price level is falling, means the

[7]Fisher, Irving (1933), "The Debt-Deflation Theory of Great Depressions", *Econometrica*, October, pp. 337–357; at https://fraser.stlouisfed.org/docs/meltzer/fisdeb33.pdf Also see: *Booms and Depressions*, Irving Fisher, 1932; at https://fraser.stlouisfed.org/docs/publications/books/booms_fisher.pdf

debtor is making higher *real repayments.* Another way to phrase it is that the *real interest rate* is higher than when the debt was taken on, as a result of the deflation.

Fisher argues that the way out of a severe debt-deflation type of depression is to "reflate" the price level. He stresses that the primary way to reverse the sequence of events is to increase the money supply so the deflation does not cycle ever downwards. And he argues that this is exactly what President Roosevelt accomplished with a series of legislative and executive actions starting in March 1933. Fisher argues this was the turning point but it would not have happened without the *"reflation" policy.*

Fisher argues that the banking collapse was the key to the Great Depression. Its ending resulted from the resuscitation of the bank system by various banking Acts starting in March 1933 (see Figure 3.9 in this regard). Fisher says that just printing fresh central bank (Federal Reserve Bank) money would be an "artificial" reflation that would not work by itself. And Fisher further argues that the Federal Reserve Banks could have averted the Great Depression in the first place with prudential regulation in the beginning after the stock market crash.

Fisher says that too much lending originally leads to over-indebtedness. He stresses that reflation can stop any fall in asset values from becoming extreme by making debt repayment not unusually difficult because of deflation. He equates resorting to pure *laissez-faire policy* as allowing unlimited bankruptcies. Instead Fisher recommends "medication" in the form of reflation primarily coming from banks making more loans again, rather than only from the government printing money. But explicit in Fisher's remedy is that the government must prudentially regulate or reorganize the bank sector.

Fisher was ahead of his time. His point of view was taken very seriously in the US Great Recession of 2008 to 2010. Remedial legislation was enacted that reformed and subsidized the bank sector and that avoided deflation. The result was exactly that real interest rates did not rise in the Great Recession. Private banks were rescued through a wide variety of measures including restructure through prudential government regulation. And combined with this the Federal Reserve did print a great deal of new currency.

Friedrich Hayek

Hayek was known for a broad category of social, political and economic theory and application. His 1929 book, *Monetary Theory and The Trade Cycle,* complements Fisher's perspective. Hayek argues just before the Great Depression that the real interest rate can be lowered below its free-market level by the government. The government does this by persistently printing more money that drives down the real rate of interest in the short term with higher inflation a threat looming for later. The lower real interest rate causes "over-indebtedness" in Fisher's terms. Hayek argues that the credit upswing and cycle occurs because of both private and government action to inflate the money supply through greater indebtedness of both private firms and the government.

Hayek focuses on the private banking system mainly and how credit is expanded when the bank system as a whole increases lending, through the collective action of each of the private banks. He includes discussion of a "pyramid of credit" that is based on insufficient fundamental future ability to repay the debt. He suggests that a general contraction, or recession, can result when the debt load is too heavy to be repaid.

In short he blames a type of natural over-investment, and its coincident high level of credit as the reason the cycle can collapse downwards. And astutely he notes that the Central Bank needs to replenish bank reserves when necessary. Hayek's necessary replenishment of private bank reserves did not happen sufficiently during the Great Depression until the bank Acts starting in 1933.

Hayek argues that such high levels of credit should have been avoided in the first place by rising real rates of interest for example for loans by private banks from the Central Bank. Hayek calls the business cycle by its alternate name at the time, Trade Cycle, and says that both monetary factors and non-monetary factors can contribute to a credit boom, and downwards cycle. And with a focus on banking, he stresses that somehow the private banking activity needs to be kept reasonably stable.

Hayek's 1931 book, *Prices and Production*, reiterates his previous theory and reviews a great body of monetary, classical and neoclassical literature. The emphasis stays on the banking system and on how the general price level can cause inflation or deflation that affects the real rate of interest. This is the so-called *liquidity or illiquidity effect of unexpected inflation*, or deflation, on real interest rates.

Milton Friedman

Hayek in the 1950s became a colleague of Milton Friedman at the University of Chicago, and cofounded the Mont Pelerin Society with Friedman, although their views on monetary theory and business cycles may have diverged. Friedman focused on monetary theory through the supply and demand for real money. He argues that the US depressions were largely influenced by poor money and banking policy.[8]

Friedman built largely on Fisher's theory of savings and consumption in formulating his *permanent income hypothesis of consumption*, which is still popular today as it emerges also within the now mainstream Ramsey (1928) optimization model that we cover starting in Chapter 8. Using optimization theory, Friedman's consumption theory followed Fisher by saying that the consumer wants to optimally smooth consumption over time. This made current consumption a fraction of *permanent income.* Permanent income can be thought of as the expected average income stream over the entire future horizon. The idea here is that current income may be temporarily low or high and does not as directly affect current consumption as does the expected permanent income stream.[9]

Friedman also extended Fisher's monetary theory known as the quantity theory of money, including a focus on the velocity of money.[10] And Friedman also was known as was Fisher for advocating aggregate price level stability. Friedman advocated accomplishing price stability, as did others, through a steady growth rate in the money supply.[11]

Fisher, Hayek and Friedman all lacked proposals for strong government intervention to raise consumption and output during periods such as the Great Depression, except for in the area of money and banking policy. They did not focus on the government increasing investment, but rather on the private bank sector being able to once again resume its role in making loans that became new investment. This body of neoclassical theory therefore emphasized private banking and governmental central banking rather than government intervention in terms of expenditure unrelated to banking.

3.4.2 Keynesian Economics

In contrast to this, the Great Depression brought about new economic theory that became known as Keynesian. This was advocated after the Depression and in modern times. A revival in Keynesian-based discourse came during and after the Great Recession. This Keynesian theory is named after John Maynard Keynes. In broad summation, this theory favors the Macroeconomic policy of greater government spending and private market intervention in order to end recession or depression. It argues that monetary policy is less important and has always lacked a focus on banking policy, until recently.

Before the Great Depression J. M. Keynes was known for his work recommending changing the terms of the 1919 Versailles Treaty that ended WWI and demanded war "reparations" from the losing Central powers, especially Germany, to victorious nations. Keynes (1919, *A Revision of the Treaty*) predicted this would bankrupt Central nations and cause further world economic disruption. He recommended canceling the war payments for damage done during the war. In fact, Germany made more than a third of the payments but soon fell into a deep *hyperinflation*, with inflation rates rising to 41% per day, and 322% per month.[12] Keynes' predictions of the economic crisis war reparations would cause were prescient.

In 1923, Keynes then published his *Tract on Monetary* reform. This was based closely on the monetary theory of Irving Fisher. It advocated *stabilizing the price level* as did Fisher. This was consistent with other *Neoclassical economic theory* that was dominant at the time.

---

[8]A Monetary History of the United States, 1867–1960 by Friedman, M. and Schwartz, A.J., published by Princeton University Press in 1963.

[9]M. Friedman, 1957, *A Theory of the Consumption Function*, NBER no. 63, Princeton NJ; Princeton University Press.

[10]For example, the book by Friedman and Schwartz, 1982, *Monetary Trends in the United States and the United Kingdom: Their Relation to Income, Prices, and Interest Rates, 1867–1975*, NBER.

[11]For example, in M Friedman, *A Program for Monetary Stability*. New York: Fordham University Press, 1960.

[12]http://www.econlib.org/library/Enc/Hyperinflation.html

Keynes broke from this tradition during the Great Depression with the publication of his 1930 *Treatise on Money*. This book presented a theory of the business cycle. It goes on to argue that stronger direct government intervention than monetary policy could positively reverse a cyclic downturn and end a recession.

Keynes based this theory on a different theory of the aggregate price level than is found in Fisher's quantity theory of money. Instead Keynes argues that the price level of aggregate output could be considered to be based in cost theory, as in the microeconomic theory of the firm, rather than based in monetary theory. This amounted to a novel theory of the determination of the aggregate output price level.

Keynes' (1930) new approach to the aggregate price level marks a major break for Keynes relative to his past work. Keynes' (1930) theory of the aggregate price level is as in the microeconomics of Marshall (1920), with no association to the money stock. In particular, Keynes said that the price of aggregate output was equal to the *average cost* (*AC*) of aggregate output plus the per-unit profit from producing the aggregate output.

In Marshallian Neoclassical economic theory, the price of a good in any market equals its average cost plus profit. This price also at the same time equals its *marginal cost* (*MC*) of production. This is still the foundation of the microeconomic theory of the firm's price for any one good (with profit equal to zero in perfect competitive equilibrium). Keynes' innovation was applying this Marshallian theory of the price to the aggregate economy.

Keynes (1930) left aside the marginal cost part of Marshall's price theory, by which price equals marginal cost. Instead Keynes took the other equivalent part of Marshall's price theory whereby the price of aggregate output is equal to the *average cost plus profit* per unit of aggregate output. Price equaling average cost plus profit became the basis for Keynes aggregate theory.

Keynes (1930) proceeds then to turn this price theory into a theory of business cycles with profit, savings and investment playing a key role. Within this business cycle theory, Keynes argued that profit was determined by the difference between investment and savings. With more profit, Keynes argued the economy could turn back towards expansion.

In the face of a dearth of private sector investment, which Hayek and Fisher focused on as well, Keynes argued that increased government expenditure could act as new economic investment in place of the banking sector's role in facilitation such new investment. The idea was that this direct federal government investment would then raise national output and income. Using a focus on savings and investment, this proactive role of government became the most enduring part of the theory.[13]

Keynes's (1936) book, *The General Theory of Employment, Interest, and Money,* further detailed elements of Keynes theory of how increased government expenditure could increase output. In Macroeconomic textbooks, Keynes's (1930,1936) price, business cycle, and policy theories evolved into what became known as the *Keynesian Cross analysis*, starting in the 1950s and persisting until now. This analysis included a role for consumption such that there could be a *multiplier effect from government spending.*[14]

Aggregate Output Theory with Government Spending

It is now rather a curiosity that Keynes' (1930) price theory argues that aggregate profit is defined as aggregate investment minus savings. This definition of profit in Macroeconomics is rejected now in a consensus fashion. Such particulars of Keynes' (1930) theory are not used today.

However Keynes (1930, 1936) stated that firms would expand when making profit and contract when making losses, which makes sense to a wide array of economists. And further his main argument was that when private investment was insufficient, the government should step in and make investment for the private economy by using *unused, excess savings.* This intervention would take the form of increased government spending designed to *stimulate the economy.*

---

[13]For details on this business cycle theory, see the first Appendix at the end of this Chapter.

[14]These ideas are furthered in a restatement of Keynes in terms of what is called *IS-LM theory,* which is covered in the text in Chapter 7.4.

The foundation of excess savings also became a largely unused part of the theory.[15] Instead of a focus on savings alone, the focus shifted also to consumption. The idea of an aggregate *consumption function* endures to this day, and Keynes (1936) made use of this concept to argue for increased government spending to cause increased consumption.

Earlier, Fisher had analyzed consumption and savings theory based on current and future income using neoclassical general equilibrium theory. Keynes instead postulates consumption simply as a function of current income and does not use the optimization theory that is the foundation of neoclassical economics. This led Keynes to a theory of how government spending can cause greater consumption and aggregate output.

Keynesian Consumption Theory

Keynes' (1936) theory of consumption has evolved to a simple form that appears consistent with his original concept. The simple form of the aggregate *consumption function* is that it has three features: 1) consumption depends in a *linear fashion* on output, 2) consumption has a certain positive level even when output is zero, and 3) the rise in consumption is always less than proportional to the rise in output.

The assumptions about the consumption function imply a unique form. Using nominal notation and so ignoring inflation differences that distinguish nominal from real, denote aggregate consumption by C. *Let* a and b be some positive *parameters*, with the key assumption that b is positive but less than one: $0 < b < 1$. Denoting total (nominal) aggregate output by Y, *the consumption function follows as:*

$$C = a + bY.$$

Figure 3.13 graphs the C function, with C on the vertical axis and Y on the horizontal axis. It assumes that $a = 0.15$ and $b = 0.6$. The graph is a line starting from a vertical axis intercept of 0.15, where output is zero.

When output rises, consumption also rises. But consumption rises by less in proportion to the rise in output. This is because the parameter $b < 1$. If $b = 1$, and a were close to zero, then consumption would rise at the same rate as does output.

Note that the parameter b shows how much consumption C will increase *at the margin* when income Y goes up. So the change in C divided by the change in Y is equal to b for a small amount of a change in Y. This marginal effect of Y on C causes the parameter b to be called the "*marginal propensity to consume*".

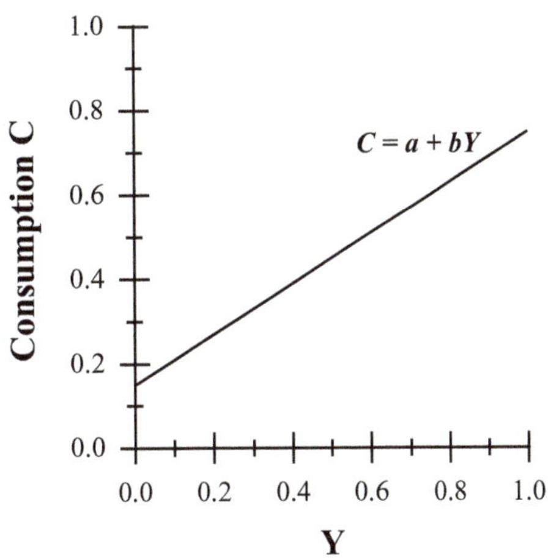

Figure 3.13 Keynesian Consumption Function, $C = a + bY$

[15]For a modern exception, see L. Summers blog, "The Age of Secular Stagnation": "Excess savings tend to drive interest rates down . . . Secular stagnation occurs when neutral real interest rates are sufficiently low . . . At that point, desired levels of saving exceed desired levels of investment." http://larrysummers.com/2016/02/17/the-age-of-secular-stagnation/

3.4.3 National Accounting & Keynesian Cross

Now consider adding together the aggregate consumption and the aggregate investment. Denote this investment again by I. Assume a) zero government expenditure, and b) zero net exports as in a closed (no international trade) economy. Then adding these together gives the entire GDP under the assumptions that $G = NX = 0$. In other words the sum of consumption and investment is total output.

We can write the aggregate of consumption and output, with not government expenditure and net exports, symbolically as

$$\mathrm{C + I = Y.}$$

At the same time we know from out national income and product accounting that total GDP output equals the total income GDI. This gives us a line that can be graphed as

$$\mathrm{Y = GDI.}$$

The Keynesian Cross can be graphed simply by graphing the two lines, of $C + I = Y$ and $Y = GDI$.

One key additional assumption is that investment is independent of output.[16] This goes against strong empirical correlation between current output and investment. However, it is convenient here for expositing Keynes's theory of how government spending can increase output. So we will assume investment is constant, contrary to empirical evidence.

For example let investment equal a constant amount such as $d > 0$, where d is just a parameter like the ones a, and b; the only restriction is that d is positive or equal to zero. With constant investment, and the consumption function $C = a + bY$, the sum of consumption and investment is the line $C + I = (a + d) + bY$. Therefore graphically adding investment to consumption just shifts up the line, keeping the slope the same.

Figure 3.14 shows in the blue line the combined $C + I$. It shows a shift upwards, by the amount d, relative to the C line. The example, in Figure 3.14, assumes that $d = 0.1$, while $a = 0.15$ and $b = 0.6$. So that $C + I = (0.15 + 0.1) + (0.6)\ Y$.

We can now add the line that $Y = GDI$. Since aggregate output and income are equal, and since $C + I = Y$, we can add this as an identity showing that output equals income. If we graph it, we include output Y as an additional vertical axis variable, and GDI as an additional horizontal axis variable. By adding this line, we are adding what is called a *45 degree line*, since its slope is one, and the angle of the line from the origin is 45 degrees. Figure 3.15 combines the three lines of $C = a + bY$, $C + I = Y$, and $Y = GDI$.

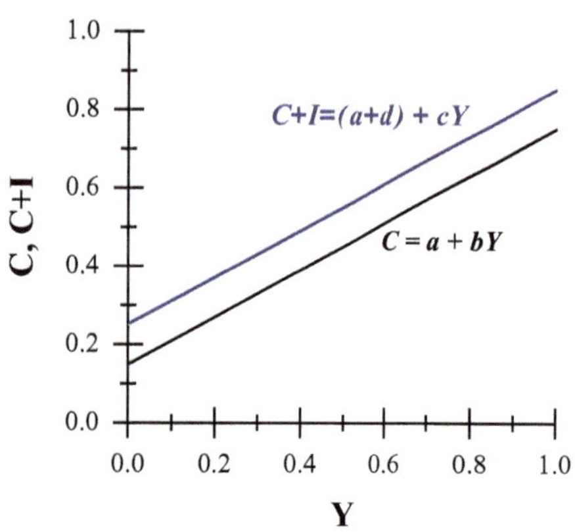

Figure 3.14 Adding Investment to the Consumption Function: $C + I$

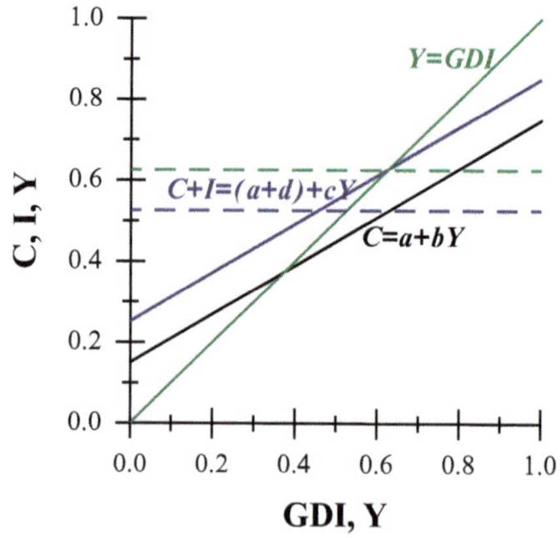

Figure 3.15 Adding in the TC 45% line, with the C and $C + I$ Lines

[16]This was the view of some of Keynes's followers such as Hansen (1953); the idea is to think of long term maintenance of the capital stock that may not depend on current output (Hansen, Alvin H., 1953, A Guide to Keynes. New York: McGraw-Hill Book).

In Figure 3.15, the intersection of the $C + I = Y$ and the $Y = GDI$ lines gives the equilibrium in the economy. This is in the sense that we can read off the equilibrium amount of consumption, investment and output from the vertical axis. The equilibrium output level is given by $Y = 0.625$, as in the green dashed line.

To find this amount using the equations, we need only that $C + I = Y$, where we substitute in the equation for consumption in terms of income ($C = a + bY$) and we substitute in the values of the parameters: $a = 0.15$, $b = 0.6$, $d = 0.10$. Then $C + I = (0.15) + (0.6)\ Y + 0.1$. And since $C + I = Y$, we can say that $(0.15) + (0.6)\ Y + 0.1 = Y$. Then we subtract $(0.6)Y$ from both sides of the last equation and get that $(0.15 + 0.1) = Y - (0.6)Y = (0.4)Y$. Last we solve for Y by dividing both sides of the last equation by 0.4 and we get the solution for Y:

$$\frac{(0.5 + 0.1)}{0.4} = 0.625 = Y.$$

This is also the amount of income, GDI.

Knowing $Y = 0.625$, consumption can be found using the consumption function: $C = 0.15 + 0.6(0.625) = 0.525$. This is given as the dashed blue line in Figure 3.15. The vertical difference between the green and blue dashed lines is the constant investment of $I = 0.10$.

Multiplier and Government Spending

A key idea of using the so-called Keynesian Cross is to show the effect of government spending on output. It depends closely on the nature of the equation for the consumption function. For example, if we used $C = \hat{b}Y$, a version of consumption advocated by Milton Friedman which has zero as the vertical axis intercept ($a = 0$), we could not graph this with an equilibrium existing in this diagram, in the sense that $C = \hat{b}Y$ would not have an intersection with $Y = GDI$, except at the origin; there would be no "cross". So the consumption function and indeed the whole "Cross" graph is Keynesian in nature.

The consumption function form with $a > 0$ and $b < 1$ allows for a so-called *multiplier effect of government spending*. This multiplier arises because when we add any type of new investment, then output and consumption both rise. If the multiplier is greater than one, then the increase in the output is greater than the increase in the investment.

To see this, increase I from 0.10 to 0.20. The new output is found from equation as $\frac{(0.15 + 0.2)}{0.4} = 0.875 = Y$.

The output level rises from 0.625 to 0.875, or by 0.25, while the increase in investment was only by 0.1 ($0.20 - 0.10 = 0.10$) So the investment increase has seen a *multiplier increase* by a factor of 2.5 times the original amount of the increase in investment of 0.10.

Where does the 2.5 multiplier come from? Directly from the *marginal propensity to consume* which here is $b = 0.6$. In particular the multiplier of 0.10 in the expression for output $\left(\frac{(0.15 + 0.2)}{0.4} = 0.875 = Y\right)$ is the term $\frac{1}{0.4}$ This factor multiplies the increase in investment of 0.10. Now $\frac{1}{0.4}$ is just the term equal to one divided by the quantity of one minus the marginal propensity to consume, or $\frac{1}{1-b}$. With $b = 0.6$, $\frac{1}{1-b} = \frac{1}{0.4} = 2.5$ This multiplier is just an artifice of solving for output Y from the two equations of $C + I = Y$, and $C = a + bY$, with I constant.

Government enters by making the assumption that government spending is like additional new investment in the economy. So if federal government non-defense spending is near zero as it was before the Great Depression, then we can think of $G = 0$ now going up to some new amount such as $G = 0.10$. This increase in G above zero makes the accounting identity now $C + I + G = Y = GDI$. And since G is just a constant, like investment, it shifts up the $C + I$ line along the 45 degree line to a new equilibrium with a higher output.

The idea behind set of logic whereby government spending is new investment comes from Keynes who suggested there was "excess savings" during the Great Depression that was not being used. So the government should step in and get the savings from the private sector and spend it. With a multiplier above one, which holds for all $b < 0$ with the Keynesian consumption function, such government spending increase would raise output by more than the government spent. This was an attractive idea in the time of a Great Depression.[17]

Example with Positive Government Spending

Take an example in which we let government be a constant amount: $G = e = 0.05$. Then $C + I + G$ is shown by the purple line in Figure 4.9. Here $C + I + G = (a + d + e) + bY$.

In Figure 3.16 with originally there being zero government spending so that $G = 0$, we will call this aggregate output level "*GDP1*", which is equal to just $C + I$ and given by the blue line. Now with what we call *GDP2*, where we add the new government expenditure of $G = 0.05$, then $GDP2 = C + I + G$. Figure 3.16 shows that the new equilibrium output is given at the intersection of the purple line and the 45 degree green line. This is an increase from the output level at the previous equilibrium at the intersection of the blue and green lines.

In Figure 3.16, the output is $GDP1 = 0.625$ and the new equilibrium output is $GDP2 = Y = 0.75$. This is an increase in output of $\frac{0.05}{0.4} = 0.125$, which is the government spending amount (0.05) times the multiplier of 2.5. Or using the solution for total output, $\frac{(0.15 + 0.1) + 0.05}{0.4} = 0.75 = Y$.

Taxes to Finance Government Spending

Government spending can be included in the Cross model. However this addition brings up the issue of how the spending is financed. In national income accounting we include taxes, but did not in the above Cross analysis. Even if we assume the taxes will only be raised at some time in the future, the correctly expected

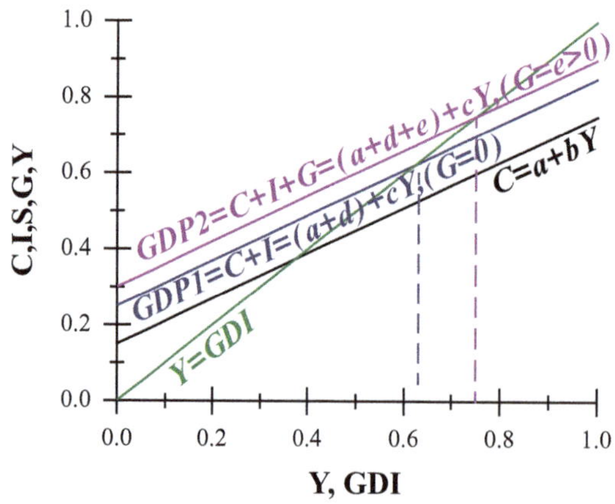

Figure 3.16 Adding in an increase in G to $C + I$, to get $C + I + G$, where G does not depend on Y

[17]In terms of Keynes's (1930) Treatise, there was "excess" savings over investment, firms were suffering a loss, and so firms were contracting in size, producing less output and employing fewer employees. Government spending would reverse the recession/depression.

future taxes would decrease output below that given by the *multiplier* assumptions. Also disincentive effects on output that usually occur from taxation would additionally lower output.

Suppose when government spending was increased that taxes were increased by the same amount so as to finance the spending. This would be a *balanced budget increase in spending.* It may not be optimal in the middle of a Great Depression (as President Hoover found out when he signed exactly such legislation in 1932).[18] In fact, within our analysis the result is clear. Output would not increase at all.

For example let taxes rise by an amount T, whereby $T = G$, and G is the increase in spending as in the Great Depression. We call $T = G$ the "government budget constraint" and it is a balanced budget. Now *GDP* is $C + I - T$, before factoring in the increase in government spending. Once we do add the new spending, we get that $C + I - T + G = Y$. Since $G = T$, the increase in spending, G, is cancelled out exactly by the increase in taxes, T, so that aggregate output would not change.

The whole idea of the Keynesian Cross model is that payment for the spending is simply not included in the logic. For example if the government issues new debt and borrows to cover its deficit spending, the idea is that the economy would not consider the new debt as a future tax burden that would inhibit current consumption or investment. The Neoclassical *Ricardian theory of the government debt,* in contrast argues like David Ricardo in the 1800s that government debt must eventually be paid off.

Ricardian debt theory suggests that the future taxation required by additional government borrowing will be considered as a liability by consumers and firms. As a consequence, this liability arguably will decrease consumption and investment even in the present time. The "multiplier" on government spending would accordingly then be less or even negative.

3.4.4 Stabilization Policy Arises

Paul Samuelson (1951) bases his Cross analysis just as above. And this is the form common in most macroeconomic textbooks to this day, a mark of Samuelson's influence. Samuelson (1951) includes how Investment minus Savings occurs but he does not explicitly call $I - S$ profit as does Keynes (1930,1936). Modern textbooks usually leave out any discussion at all about I being different from S, since most of our equilibrium analysis has that savings always equals investment (except for the cost of intermediating the savings from consumers to firms through banks, for example, or when there is international capital trade).

Samuelson goes on to describe the Great Depression in his Chapter 13 with the aggregate "cross" analysis. He says that the actual output during the Depression was below the hypothetical level of the "*full employment output*". This full employment output level is supposedly the level achieved over time if the economy keeps growing at its previous historic full employment rate such as during the 1920's expansion.

Samuelson argues that federal government spending can enable the economy to close the "gap" between the full employment level of output and the level during the Depression. He uses the Keynesian Cross analysis above to show this. And this gap is now known as the *output gap.*

Therefore the idea of the Cross, in current macroeconomic textbooks, avoids the original motivation of profit equaling $I - S$, and instead just shows how an increase in G lifts the economy. Textbooks currently use notions of national income accounting and often use the Cross to discuss aggregate supply and aggregate demand just as did Samuelson as far back as 1951. But this is the tenuous nature of the Cross: it does not derive the consumption or investment functions, or aggregate supply and demand functions, from optimization as in modern analysis. And the output gap has continually been redefined over time as Keynesian analysis is updated. And taxes in modern analysis have a serious effect in reducing output.

Samuelson also presents the notion of how taxes to finance spending can reduce output, but he offers that the net effect of spending can still be positive. And we are left then with the theory that recessions, or Great Depressions, can be eliminated by government spending: Any kind of government spending. If true, then we always could always stay at the "full employment level" and have no business cycles of expansions and recessions. This view of perspicacious government spending has become known as *stabilization policy.*

[18]This was the Revenue Act of 1932.

3.5 Application: Analysis of Depression

Keynes idea was that one way to get the economy back up to its previous position is to increase government spending. If the economy has already gone down to a lower *C* and a lower *I* (and so a lower *Y*), as in the Great Depression, then a Keynesian answer for this would be to bring the economy out of the recession by spending money G. This can be illustrated by using years to mark the level of GDP.

Say in 1929, output is equal to 0.75, so that GDP in 1929 is $Y_{1929} = 0.75$. Then the stock market crash occurs, firms cannot repay loans, the bank sector collapses, and investment falls. In addition, as workers get paid less and capital owners earn less, consumption also falls. So say the 1933 output is now $Y_{1933} = 0.056$, a reduction of output by 25% as actually occurred in the Great Depression ($\frac{0.56 - 0.75}{0.75} = -0.25$ a 25% fall in real output).

Illustrate $Y_{1929} = \mathrm{C} + \mathrm{I} = 0.75$ in Figure 3.17 by the purple line. This falls to $Y_{1933} = C + I = 0.56$ as illustrated by the blue line. Here *C* and *I* both fall from their 1929 level to the assumed 1933 level of 0.56 (so that the output decrease is 25%). We assume that in 1929 $a = 0.18$, and $d = 0.10$. And in 1929 these consumption and investment parameters, respectively, each fall by about 25% to $a = 0.135$ and $d = 0.089$.

With a multiplier of 2.5, assume that government spending of $G = 0.076$ occurs. Then the output increase from the new government spending is found as 0.076 times the multiplier of 2.5. This equals $\frac{0.076}{0.4} = 0.19$ Adding this to the depression output level of 0.56 gives an output level of 0.75, the same as before the Depression started, back in 1929.

Now assuming we are in 1933, one Macroeconomic policy answer at the national level for getting out of the Great Depression could be to increase Federal government spending, as Keynes (1930, 1936) proposed. Now assume that we increase government spending from the assumed 0 amount in 1929 to an amount in 1933 equal to the drop in output, divided by the multiplier of 2.5. Here we are assuming that although consumption fell, the "multiplier" remains at 2.5, since the coefficient in the consumption function, *b*, is unchanged at 0.6.

Then the amount of government spending in 1933 would be (0.75–0.56) /2.5 = 0.076. And as a consequence of $G_{1933} = 0.076$, an increase from $G_{1929} = 0$, the hypothetical output (Y^{*}_{1933}) would rise back up to the level of output that existed in 1929 of $Y^{*}_{1933} = Y_{1929} = 0.75$. In other words, the government spending would immediately get us out of the Depression and return us to the 1929 level of real output.

Figure 3.18 illustrates this hypothetical increase in output by calling it GDP*1933. The dotted Black line coincides with the Purple *GDP* 1929 line. Thus the government spending increase from 0 to 0.05 shifts up the GDP 1933 line to the *GDP**1933 line, where it intersects with *GDI* at 0.75.

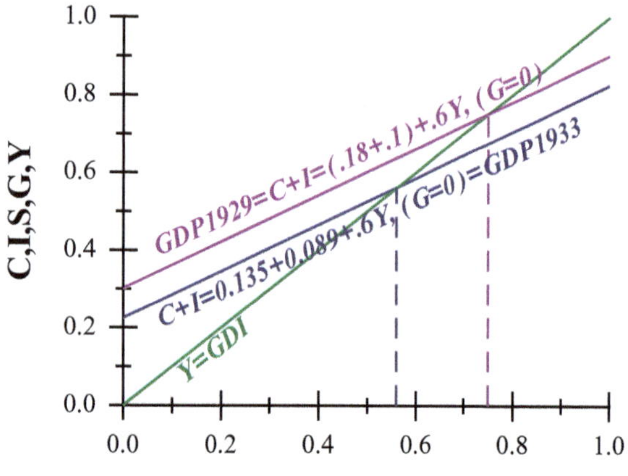

Figure 3.17 Add *G* to *C* + *I*, to get *C* + *I* + *G*

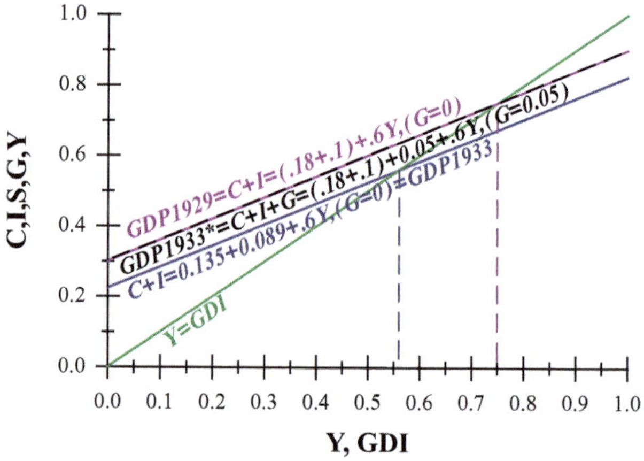

Figure 3.18 How an Increase in *G* Can End Great Depression

3.6 Appendix: Keynes' Price Theory

Keynes started with the price of a unit of aggregate output, call this price P, and said it is equal to average cost plus profit. Then he made an argument and ensuing (first) assumption that aggregate profit is equal to aggregate investment, call it I, minus aggregate savings, call it S. So profit was the difference between aggregate Investment and Savings, or $I - S$. Keynes then constructed a business cycle theory by arguing that firms expand when profit, which he claimed was $I - S$, was positive and firms contracted when $I - S$ was negative.

The definition of profit as $I - S$ was promulgated by Keynes (1930) and it is not found in Marshall (1920) or in any part of modern macroeconomics. While Keynes (1936) dropped emphasis on this definition of profit, he defended the definition in a series of footnotes in his famous *General Theory* (see Gillman, 2002, European Journal of the History of Economic Thought, for details). Second, the General Theory instead offered just one graph: it was of the capital market with supply (savings) and demand (investment), with an increase in income causing a fall in the interest rate. This led to the rise of "$IS - LM$" analysis; in Chapter 7 we cover both this $IS - LM$ analysis and the actual Keynes (1936) graph using Fisher's Neoclassical analysis.

3.6.1 Keynes' Version of Marshall's Price

To get aggregate output on a per-unit-of output basis, divide total profit by total output of goods, and we get the average profit per good. Denote total real output by y. Then $(I - S)/y$ is the profit per unit of output as in Keynes (1930). Now denote by AC the average cost. Then the aggregate price theory is that

$$P = AC + (I - S) / y.$$

Multiply the price per unit of aggregate output P by the total real output of the economy, and still calling it y, we get the Py which Keynes calls Total Revenue (received by companies producing output). Denote Total Revenue by TR. Multiply average cost of output by the quantity of output, and get the total cost of output, $(AC) * y$. Denote Total Cost by TC, so $TC = (AC)\, y$.

Multiply the price equation above through by y, and substitute in for Total Revenue and Total Cost. This gives that total revenue equals total cost plus profit. In an accounting sense, this is true (but profit is not $I - S$):

$$TR = TC + (I - S)$$

Keynes' (1930) next big assumption is that total revenue equals aggregate nominal consumption plus aggregate investment. Denoting C for consumption, this gives that

$$TR = C + I.$$

It then follows from these assumptions that Total Cost TC is equal to consumption C plus savings S:

$$C + I = TR = TC + I - S;$$

subtracting I from both sides of the above equation, $C + I = TC + I - S$, and solving for total cost gives that $TC = C + S$. Further, subtracting Total Cost TC from Total Revenue TR gives the "profit" $I - S$:

$$TR - TC = (C + I) - (C + S) = I - S.$$

The profit definition led to Keynes' (1930) theory of the business cycle. When $I > S$, profit was positive, firms expanded output, and the economy's aggregate output expanded. When $I < S$, profit was negative, firms contracted output, and the economy contracted. The stationary equilibrium was with zero profit and $TR = TC$.

Once the Keynes (1930) price and business cycle theory was combined with Keynes' (1936) theory of the consumption function, a more tangible, theoretical, perspective became possible. It became known as the Keynesian Cross. However the original theory was based on whether investment exceeded or was less than investment. The Cross theory today typically avoids comparing savings and investment.

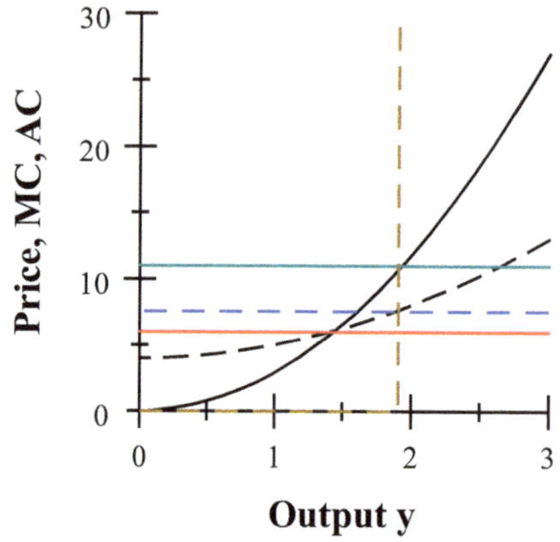

Figure 3.19 Marshall's (1920) Microeconomic Theory of Price

3.6.2 Marshallian Theory of Competitive Equilibrium

Figure 3.19 graphically illustrates the Marshallian theory of the competitive equilibrium price. The solid black curve is the marginal cost *MC*. The dashed black curve is the average cost *AC*. Two possible prices are shows at 6 (red horizontal line) and at 12 (green horizontal line).

If the price is equal to 6 as in the red line, then the price equals the marginal cost and it also equals the average cost. This means the profit is zero, and output *y* is about 1.4. However if the price is 12, then the price still equals the marginal cost, while at the same time output is higher at 1.9.

At this higher price of 12, there now is a profit per unit of output. Per unit profit is equal to the difference between the average cost of 7.5 (horizontal blue dashed line) when producing 1.9 units of output and the price of 12. Per unit profit here is about 4.5. The profit per unit is shown as the vertical segment of the dashed brown line between the prices of 12 and 7.5. Note: the AC and MC curves should intersect where MC is at a minimum.

3.7 Summary

Neoclassical theory emphasized business cycles and how they occur through the bank system creating credit. Neoclassical economists emphasize that stabilizing inflation is key to avoiding severe recessions that can become depressions if significant deflation is allowed. This stabilizing of the price level comes from a combination of prudential banking regulation and government monetary policy. The Great Depression ushered in theory that challenged the limited role of government in Neoclassical theory.

Unemployment during the Great Depression rose to 25% and only fell down to near zero once the spending by the US on Defense during *WWII* accelerated. Government spending was the key to Keynes' proposal of how to raise output during a business cycle recession. Keynes constructed a theory of the price level different from microeconomic Marshallian (1920) theory so as to describe how a business cycle operated.

From this alternate price theory, Keynesian economics developed the Cross analysis which emphasizes how direct government spending is a key to ending a recession. The Keynesian stabilization policy has government spending act as private investment that brings the economy back up to its "full employment level of output".

The increase in output from an increase in government spending would be "multiplied" by a factor based on the consumption function's "marginal propensity to consume", which is given above as b. The higher would be the government spending multiplier, the higher would be the subsequent increase in aggregate output from an increase in G. The multiplier is higher with a lower b, because consumption C would be lower, and savings would be higher.

The original Keynes idea is that excess savings, whereby $S - I > 0$, exists during a recession such that the government could "utilize" it and turn it into active spending. The current usage of the Cross theory finds recourse in the national income accounting theory whereby output is equal to income. It turns this accounting identity into a theory of how government spending can increase output. It invokes a *multiplier theory* and ignores taxes used to finance the new government expenditure.

To end depressions, or moderate recessions, Keynesian policy emphasizes government spending while Neoclassical policy emphasizes banking and monetary policy. These divergent views are a broad scope statement of the different perspectives as they occurred historically and are often discussed today. But the contrasting positions are often today much more nuanced. Modern macroeconomics sees government spending and even bank policy often in terms of social insurance for when the markets cannot supply this insurance.

A convergence of these perspectives is possible such as through a *social insurance function* of government. This has roots in classical and neoclassical economics. Keynes' theory of additional government spending also can be seen from the view of supplying government insurance. This is because additional government spending during a recession often is in the form of explicit social insurance programs that increase spending when the incomes fall. Well-known examples are unemployment insurance benefits, income support payments, and medical and old age benefit support.

Macroeconomic US policy during the US 2008–2010 Great Recession was often called Keynesian for its increase in government spending. However it is argued that much of this Great Recession spending was used to rescue the US bank system. Such a banking focus was also a focus of the neoclassical economists.

Today bank insurance has been spread internationally across the globe and much of the worldwide policy reaction to the Great Recession involved bank policy that further insured the soundness of the banking system. This bank policy combined with monetary policy resulted in stable inflation in the Great Recession worldwide as opposed to the strong deflation seen in the Great Depression. The relative price stability accomplished during the Great Recession is what Fisher (1932, 1933) stressed was missing during the Great Depression and provoked him to postulate his debt-deflation theory of crises. It appears that depressions are, for the most part, preventable and that their prevention requires a definite policy in which the Federal Reserve System must play an important role.

3.8 Glossary of Italic Words

45 degree line: a line with a vertical axis intercept of zero and a slope of one.

a priori: looking at variables in the beginning of the period before shocks for example occur.

average cost: the total cost of producing the output divided by the quantity of the output gives the average cost per unit of the output.

average cost plus profit: adding the average cost per unit of output plus the profit made per unit of output gives the market price of a unit of output in microeconomic theory.

balanced budget increase in spending: this occurs when new government spending is at the same time financed by new tax revenue equal in amount to the amount of new government spending.

business cycles: expansion and contraction of GDP output, employment, and investment in an economy that continually reoccurs over long periods of time.

consumption function: the formulation of how consumption depends on other macroeconomic variables, such as current or permanent income.

consumption smoothing across time: having a stable amount of consumption each year despite the occurrence of temporary income increases or decreases.

currency and bank deposits: the notes of the Federal Reserve Bank that we call dollars are government money, or currency, while bank deposits are held in private banks and thought of as private money since these deposits can be used to buy goods such as with a check or debit card; together currency in circulation and bank deposits comprise the definition of the *M1 monetary aggregate* of the Federal Reserve System.

CPI inflation rate: the rate of aggregate price level increase as defined by using the rate of change in the Consumer Price Index.

debt-deflation" theory: I. Fisher's conceptualization of how an economic depression occurs through high debt accumulation that begins to default, causing ultimate general price deflation that makes paying off existing debt even more difficult.

ex post: end of the period values of variables, after all shocks have occurred.

FRED graphs: Federal Reserve of St. Louis Economic Database graphs of data over time.

hyperinflation: an extremely high rate of inflation often defined as more than 50% per month.
labor force: number of the population that is working in the *market economy* or actively seeking such work.
labor force participation rate: share of labor force in the total population.
laissez-faire policy: a government policy of minimal intervention in markets, with the idea that normal market forces should work such that the economy remains relatively stable.
liquidity or illiquidity effect of unexpected inflation: When a temporary increase in the government money supply temporarily drives down the real interest rate: liquidity effect; a temporary decrease in government money supply drives up the real interest rate: illiquidity; these effects can be persistent if accelerated or decelerated changes in the money supply growth rate occur.
linear fashion: on a graph a linear equation is a straight line; movement along the line anywhere involves a constant slope, a characteristic of any line going through two given points along it.
M1 monetary aggregate: currency in circulation plus demand deposits (current accounts) in private banks.
macroprudential: considered regulation of economy-wide effects of the private market, especially the bank sector.
marginal cost: the change in total cost from a one unit change in output.
marginal propensity to consume: the change in consumption from a one unit increase in output.
market economy: that part of the economy that explicitly reports sales, income, and pays taxes; in contrast the underground, shadow, or non-market, economy includes enterprises evading taxes, but also legal activities such as child raising.
multiplier: any multiplicative factor that affects a variable.
multiplier effect from government spending: the magnitude of the increase in output relative to the magnitude of the increase in government spending; this multiplier is one for example if output rises by the same amount that government spending rises; this multiplier is zero for example if output does not increase when government spending increases.
multiplier increase: the magnitude of the increase in output relative to the magnitude of the increase in government spending.
multiplier theory: the idea that government spending increases can cause output increases as based both on the magnitude of the marginal propensity to consume and the lack of fully offsetting taxes.
National Bureau of Economic Research (NBER) "Business Cycle Reference Dates": these are dates on a quarterly basis of when a recession starts and ends as judged by a variety of macroeconomic indicators by the NBER; the NBER recessions are indicated by grey-shaded areas in *FRED graphs*.[19]
Neoclassical economic theory: economics arising out of the discovery of marginal utility theory which forms the basis of demand and is combined with the theory of supply to give equilibrium prices and quantities within markets for consumers and firms.
output gap: defined sometimes as the amount of output in the economy when the economy is at full employment minus the output of the economy when it is at less than full employment; this assumes there is some level of output that we can determine to be the full employment level of output of an economy.
parameters: a simple number that can be positive or negative; is in contrast to a variable that is a function of other variables, such as consumption being a function of output.
permanent income: the expected average income over the full future horizon.
permanent income hypothesis of consumption: consumption depends on permanent income rather than current income, so that temporary shocks to current income only affect current consumption to the degree the shocks affect the expected permanent income stream.
real interest rates: interest rates in the market are in nominal terms; to get the real interest rate *a priori* the expected inflation rate is subtracted from the nominal interest rate; the real interest rate *ex post* is the nominal interest rate minus the reported inflation rate that actually occurred during the period.
real repayments: the amount that is repaid in real terms, after adjusting the nominal payments for inflation.
reflation policy: a government policy that explicitly tries to increase the inflation rate after the rate has fallen, perhaps even so far that deflation has occurred.
Ricardian theory of the government debt: the government must eventually repay all debt through its expected current and future stream of taxes.
share of GDP: percent of GDP by any particular category of GDP.

---

[19]"The NBER does not define a recession in terms of two consecutive quarters of decline in real GDP. Rather, a recession is a significant decline in economic activity spread across the economy, lasting more than a few months, normally visible in real GDP, real income, employment, industrial production, and wholesale-retail sales. For more information, see the latest announcement from the NBER's Business Cycle Dating Committee, dated 9/20/10.": from http://www.nber.org/cycles.html

social insurance function: the government or possibly the private sector provides a means to offset bad times with pay-outs of income received during good times, such that it acts as an insurance program against the event of a bad time, such as a recession.

social insurance policy: an explicit attempt to run an insurance program typically by the government so as to cover risk that the private markets typically cannot insure against, such as a recession.

stabilization policy: the attempt by the government to smooth out or eliminate business cycle movements in the aggregate economy.

stabilizing the price level: the attempt by the government to smooth out or eliminate fluctuations in the aggregate price level, creating zero inflation; often this is alternatively interpreted as keeping the inflation rate stable at some low rate that may be different from zero.

stimulate the economy: an attempt by the government to increase aggregate output through government policy such as government spending, or through monetary policy, or even banking policy.

stock market crash: a large reduction in the asset value of an aggregate of the publicly traded companies, such as the Dow Jones Industrial group.

unemployment rate: percent of the *labor force* that is unemployed.

unused, excess savings: savings that is somehow sitting around in storage rather than being invested; this is a concept that in neoclassical economics can only happen if the real interest rate is fixed at some above-market level, which many economists believe is not possible.

velocity of money in circulation: defined as the value of output divided by the money stock, this is also thought of in terms of how much real money is demanded; velocity is known to increase as the inflation rate increases since holding money is more costly because of the implicit taxation on currency from inflation.

3.9 Questions

1. How did the US unemployment rate change from the beginning of the Great Depression to the beginning of *WWII?*
2. How did US government spending on Defense as a percent of *GDP* evolve from the beginning of the Great Depression to the end of *WWII?*
3. What was the Neoclassical view of the Great Depression at the time as seen in the writings of Fisher and Hayek?
4. What was the Neoclassical remedy for the Great Depression at the time it occurred?
5. Keynes (1930) focused on government spending as a way out of the Great Depression. How did Keynes start from a Microeconomic perspective to build a theory of the aggregate Price Level?
6. What is the Neoclassical, Marshallian (1920), theory of the price?
7. How did Keynes' (1930) theory of the price level define aggregate Profit?
8. What was Keynes' (1930) theory of the aggregate Consumption Function?
9. What is the "Keynesian Cross" theory and how does government spending affect output in this theory?
10. How does the parameter b in the consumption function determine the "multiplier" of government spending, and the increase in output caused by government spending?
11. What was Friedman's view of the consumption function?
12. How can *consumption smoothing across time* imply that the government should engage in optimal *social insurance policy*?
13. Complete the Federal Reserve Bank of St. Louis EconLowdown Course Module "The Great Depression 1".
14. Complete the Federal Reserve Bank of St. Louis EconLowdown Course Module "The Great Depression 2".

PART II

Comovement & Crises

4 Business Cycles, Crises & Growth

4.1 Introduction

The Great Depression gave rise to new evidence and theory about severe business downturns. Depressions tend to be crisis type situations. Comparing more "normal" business cycles with severe ones can help characterize each and see key differences between them. Knowing the differences is key for policy responses. The business cycle and crisis theory also is used in formulating growth theory and policy.

4.2 Who Made it Happen

Friedman and Schwartz (1964) argued that business cycles and economic crises were caused by errant monetary policy. The monetary hypothesis influenced the economics consensus heavily as it was based on an exhaustive study of US history with a focus on the Great Depression. But what may have been key for crises such as the Great Depression ended up not holding up as the consensus explanation for normal business cycles.

Kydland and Prescott (1982) instead described how random shocks to the economy's aggregate productivity trend could give a good description of correlations of economic variables over the average post World War II US business cycle. The idea of having increasing technological progress followed by periods of decreasing technological progress, or even technological regress became a popular and well-tested theory. It was shown through numerous iterations that it could explain many of the business cycle correlations. Making shocks to productivity the basis for generating business cycle facts from an otherwise standard neoclassical economy became well-known as *real business cycle theory* (RBC).

4.3 Facts

4.3.1 Cycles and Growth Trends

What we have come to view as a business cycle includes deeper depressions as a sub-category of business cycles. In general we view business cycles as a comovement of various aggregate macroeconomic variables. In particular, real GDP growth, the unemployment rate, and investment and consumption changes are all central variables that are used in describing business cycles.

A central way economists describe cycles and growth trends are through so-called *stylized facts.* These facts are general, broad, characterizations that we can make in studying cycles and trends. The most well-known stylized fact of a business cycle is that real GDP grows at a faster and positive rate during an expansion, or *boom*, in the economy and that it grows at a slower and often negative rate during a contraction of activity, or *recession.*

A related stylized fact of growth is that the economy tends to grow at a somewhat steady rate over long periods of time. The half century of post-1959 US data up until 2009 shows a high average growth rate in real GDP of 3.5%. Looking back further in history, the industrial revolution of the 18th century started a trend upwards in the growth rate itself. It initially hovered around zero in the agricultural economies of Europe during the 1700's and started upwards towards its present trend after technical change brought about gradually increasing use of *physical capital* and *human capital.*

We can see stylized facts using a variety of data sources. At the same time we introduce terminology related to how data series tend to move together or not. We also use the term *trend* for the long term average of a series, or the long term movement upwards or downwards in a data series.

Real GDP

Real GDP growth rises in expansions and falls in recessions. This is a central stylized business cycle fact. It can be seen clearly in the Figure 3.9. The graph shows the annual growth rate of real GDP since 1929 and how it fluctuates in a repeated cyclic fashion. These cycles coincide with NBER dated recessions (grey-areas of graphs) and expansions.

Figure 3.9 also allows us to eyeball the data to see that it has some average "trend" growth rate of approximately 2% to 3%. This average real GDP growth rate is one of the most elemental "trends" of the economy. A trend of between 2 to 3% since 1929 indicates that on average real GDP is rising steadily upwards, despite having many swings below and above that average.

Figure 4.1 illustrates what the real GDP growth rate looks like when a trend, or average, rate is subtracted from the real GDP growth rate series. In particular, by subtracting 2.61 from every growth rate data point, the graph becomes centered at a zero that is actually the 2.61% growth rate. The graph shows how business cycles fluctuate around this 2.61%.

Figure 4.1 shows that every grey-shaded area that the NBER classifies as a business cycle recession is characterized by real GDP growth that is below the 2.61% trend (which is zero in the Figure). In contrast, the non-*detrended* graph in Figure 3.9 does not show below zero real GDP growth in every NBER recession as some NBER recessions actually have a positive growth rate. This highlights that business cycles are classified generally with respect to how the economy is doing relative to its average, or trend, rate of growth.

An important note about Figure 4.1 is that after the last NBER recession of 2008–2010, the economy has remained below the 2.61% trend growth rate, unlike all previous expansions dating back to 1933. This gives rise to discussion about how the current economy is still under-performing. Rather that rising quickly back above the trend, the last recession has been followed by a below-trend growth rate in real GDP. With a higher trend rate of growth, say the 3.5% experienced from 1959 to 2009, the recent recovery appears even more anemic as it is even further below the trend growth rate.

Business Cycle Terminology

Business cycles formally are "dated" by the National Bureau of Economic Research (NBER). NBER says only that it looks at a full set of comovements in macroeconomic variables in dating business cycles. Therefore it is the convention that a business cycle is defined by how a set of macroeconomics variables comove, either with each other or with real GDP growth.

If a variable moves up in expansions and down in contractions, then we term this to be *procyclic*. Real GDP growth is pro-cyclic for example. If a variable moves down in expansions and up in contractions, then

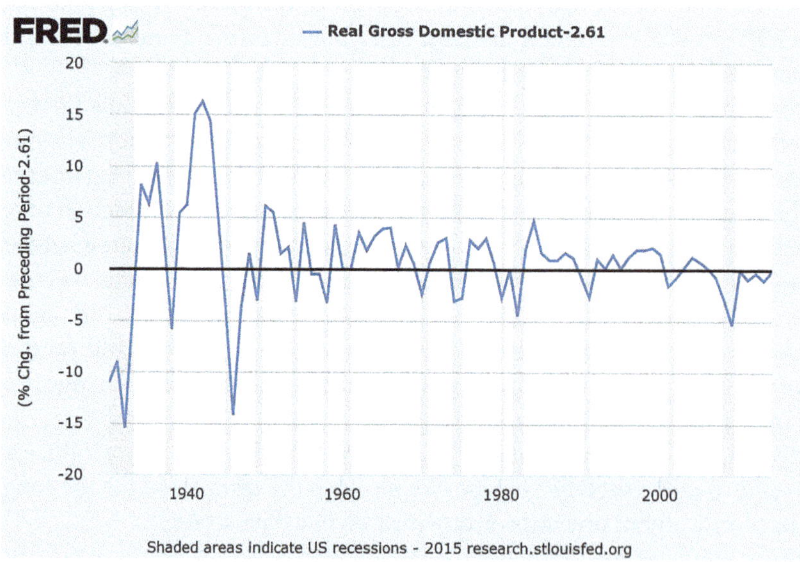

Figure 4.1 Real GDP Growth minus a 2.61% trend

we term it to be *countercyclic*. If a variable has no marked tendency to move either up or down with business cycle, then we term this to be *acyclic*.

For example, the biggest two private sector components of GDP are consumption, called Personal Consumption Expenditure in national income accounts (NIPA), and second investment, called Gross Private Domestic Investment in NIPA. These are both pro-cyclic in that they tend to rise with the real GDP growth rate, and fall when the real GDP growth rate falls.

4.3.2 Consumption and Investment

Figure 4.3.2 shows in blue the annual growth rate of real Personal Consumption Expenditure in the US from 1929 to 2014. In green is the annual growth rate of real GDP. The real Consumption and real Output growth series move together very closely and overlap for much of the post-WWII period. Consumption is pro-cyclic since its growth rate moves up and down in close correlation with real GDP growth.

The growth rate of real Gross Private Domestic Investment is also graphed in Figure 4.2, in red. It comoves with real Consumption and real GDP growth, but with much greater variability than both. It is pro-cyclic because it is also highly correlated with real GDP growth. It is more *volatile* than either of the other series because the investment growth rate rises by more in expansions and falls by more in recessions.

Consider a focus on the trend rate of growth of these series. If we graph postwar real consumption and GDP growth, and subtract 3.5%, the series are detrended and fluctuate around the new zero value of the new graph. Figure 4.3 shows the real consumption growth and real output growth rates, minus a trend amount of growth equal to 3.5%.

Striking is how closely real consumption growth and real GDP growth move together. Output growth tends to fluctuate a bit more in the Figure. Post 1959, the correlation between the two series is 0.89 (for comparison, 1.00 is a 100% correlation which would mean the two series move one-for-one with each other).

4.3.3 Shares of GDP

As a stylized fact, output tends to rise and fall by more than consumption over the business cycle. Therefore the additional stylized fact follows that consumption as a share of output, which is the ratio of consumption to GDP, as denoted by C/Y, falls in an expansion. This may be intuitively confusing since consumption itself is very procyclic. But since consumption takes a smaller share of GDP in the expansion, as savings gets turned into more investment, C/Y falls in an expansion.

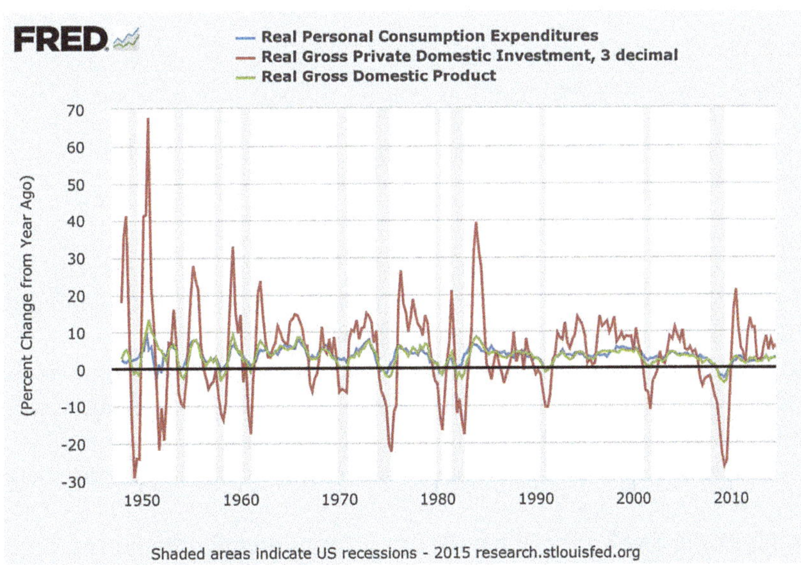

Figure 4.2 US Growth Rate of Real: Personal Consumption Expenditure (Blue), Gross Private Investment (Red), and Gross Domestic Product (Green), 1947–2014

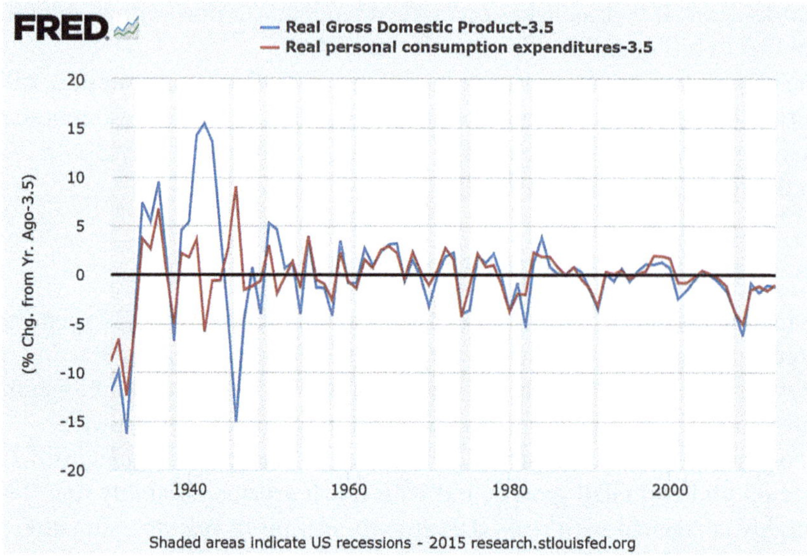

Figure 4.3 US 1930–2014, Growth Rate of Both Real Personal Consumption Expenditure (Red) and Real GDP (Blue) Minus 3.5% (trend growth rate)

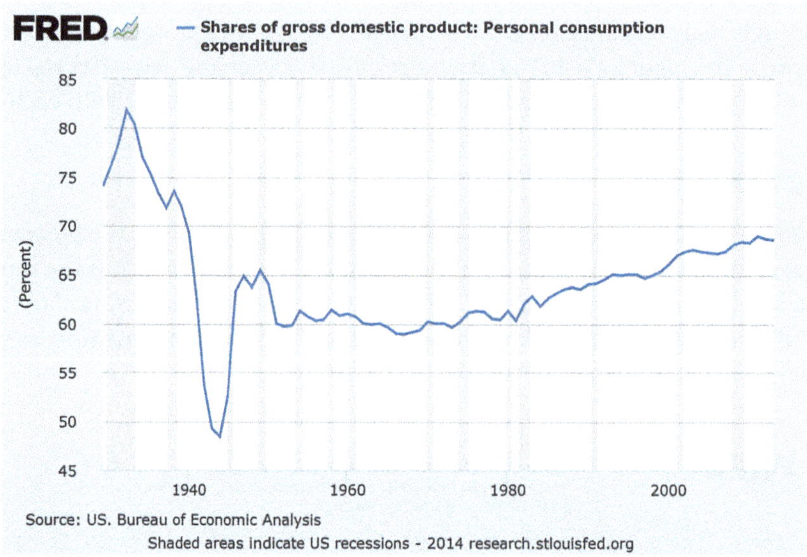

Figure 4.4 US Consumption Expenditure as a Share of GDP, 1929–2014

Figure 4.4 shows that from 1946 until the early 1980's C/Y was indeed countercyclic. Starting in the 1980's a trend upwards developed as well for C/Y. Relative to this upward trend, C/Y tended to rise less strongly during expansions and rose more strongly during recessions.

Investment is the next main share of GDP, with this share post WWII tending to be between 15 to 20%. For investment, it is a stylized fact that investment as a share of GDP rises in an expansion and falls in a recession. This share, denoted here by I/Y , is thereby procyclic. Figure 4.5 shows by casual observation that I/Y is regularly, strongly, procyclic, with troughs (low points) occurring during the grey-shaded NBER dated recessions.

Therefore the stylized facts that both real personal consumption growth and real investment growth are procyclic are then further delineated with the coincident observations about their respective shares in GDP. Because investment growth is more procyclic than GDP and consumption growth slightly less procyclic than

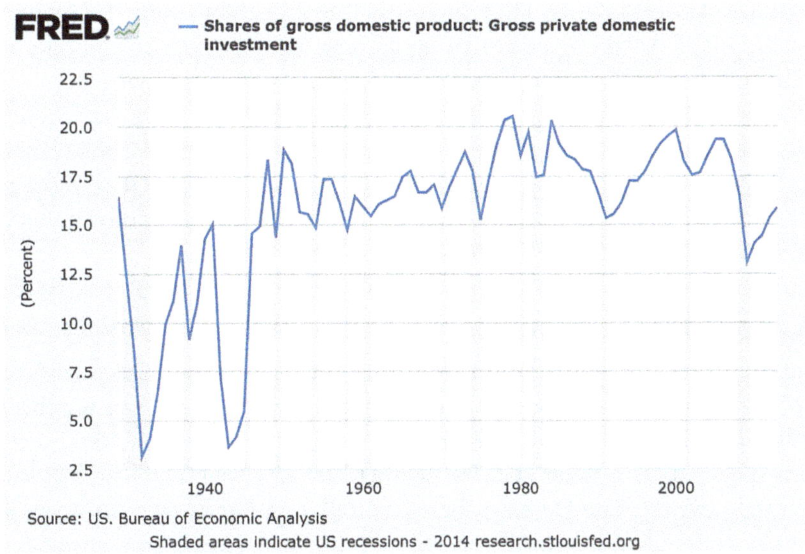

Figure 4.5 US Gross Private Domestic Investment as a Share of GDP, 1929–2014

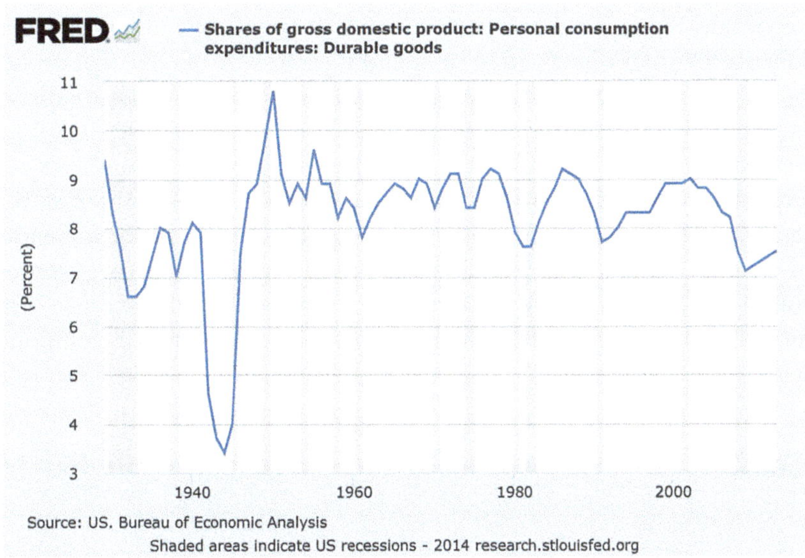

Figure 4.6 US Personal Consumption Expenditures on Durable Goods, as share of GDP, 1929–2013

GDP, their shares of GDP, being C/Y and I/Y, move in opposite directions over the business cycle. Compared to real GDP growth, C/Y is countercyclic; I/Y is procyclic.

Consumer Non-durables and Durables

Consumption is the largest share of GDP, now at about two-thirds. Consumption expenditure is actually a combination of elements that are both consumption-like and investment-like. In detail, real personal consumption growth is made up of three primary components: non-durable goods, services, and durable goods. Real non-durable goods and services are similar to what we think of as consumption. Accordingly this consumption component has a share of GDP that tends to be countercyclic.

In contrast, the durable goods component of consumption captures household investment. Just like firm investment, Figure 4.6 shows that this durable goods component as a share of GDP is very procyclic, rising in expansions and falling in contractions. Therefore investment both by firms and by households, as shares of GDP, are procyclic. This is driven by both firm and consumer "investment" accelerating in expansions faster than total GDP and decelerating in recessions more than does total GDP.

The procyclic durable goods component of consumption, as a share of GDP, has been between 7 to 9% of GDP since the 1950's. The bulk of the 66% share of total consumption in GDP is made up of the non-durable goods and services. Therefore taking both the durable goods as a share of GDP and the non-durable goods and services as a share of GDP, consumption as a share of GDP is dominated in movement by the non-durable goods and services. This makes the total *C/Y* somewhat countercyclic.

Government Expenditure

Government expenditure tends to accelerate in recessions and decelerate in expansions. Figure 4.7 shows the rate of growth of real total government expenditure, minus a 3.5% trend. The graph shows several peaks occurring during the NBER grey-shaded recession times, and troughs (low points) during expansion times.

Total government spending as a share of GDP, denoted by *G/Y*, overall is slightly countercyclic, rising in recessions as we might expect. The Defense share of GDP is rather acyclic, showing little variation over the business cycle and a generally downward trend (see Figure 3.6). However, Figure 4.8 shows that Federal Nondefense Government spending as a share of GDP is countercyclic, tending to rise in recessions and fall in expansions. Figure 4.9 shows that state and local government expenditure as a share of GDP is also countercyclic, rising in recessions and falling in expansions. Both of these non-defense countercyclical shares are as expected in that government programs often provide relatively more assistance when times are bad.

In terms of its magnitude, Figure 4.8 shows that Federal Nondefense spending as a share of GDP is a small level near 3%. And Figure 4.9 shows State and Local spending as a share of GDP is at a much higher level that is now close to 12%. Given the steady trend downwards that was found in defense expenditure as a share of GDP, this indicates that most of the rise in government spending as a share of GDP from the 1940's to the 1970's is from state and local sources rather than from the federal level, after which the shares become more stable.

If government expenditure is acting as social insurance, it is interesting to note that this is dominated by state and local action rather than federal. This shows how important state and local spending is during recessions as a source of income that acts is an insurance fashion. Total Non-defense government spending as a share of GDP is around 15%, so this can be an important source of "social insurance". Together these three shares, *C/Y*, *I/Y* and *G/Y*, make up most of GDP with net exports a small fourth component.

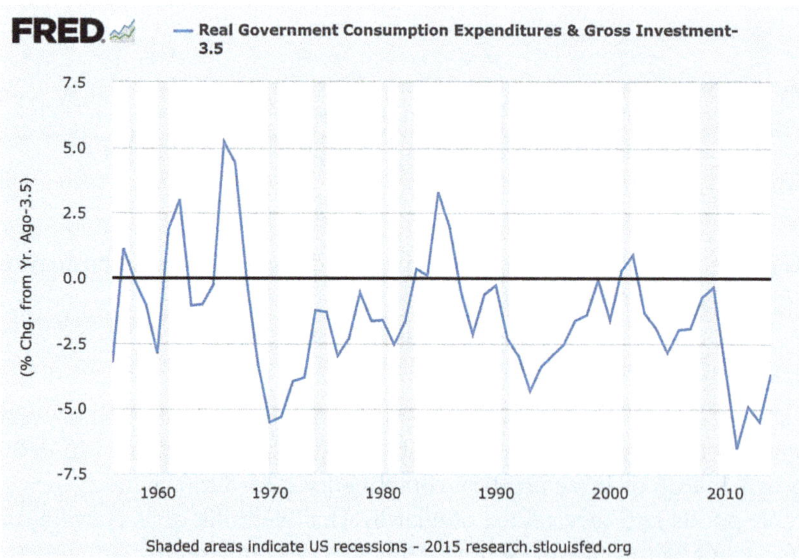

Figure 4.7 US 1956–2014 Growth Rate of Real Government Consumption and Gross Investment Minus 3.5% (growth trend)

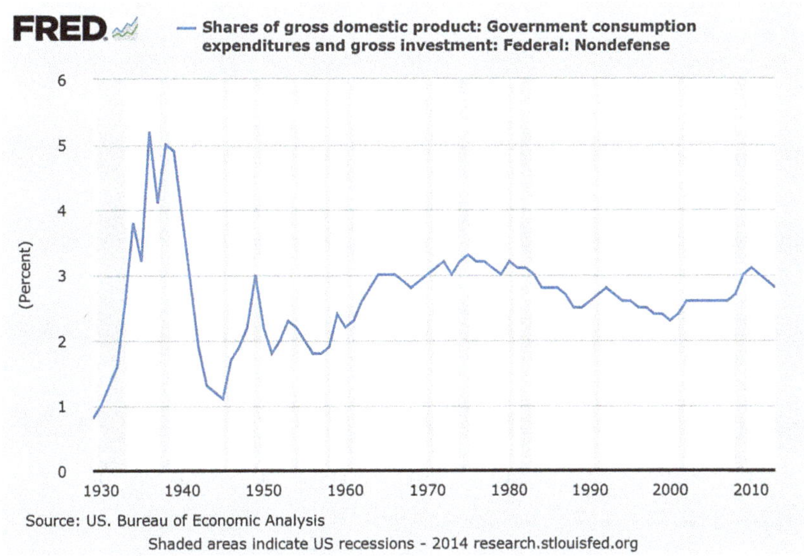

Figure 4.8 US Federal Non-Defense Consumption Expenditure and Gross Investment, Share of GDP, 1929–2013

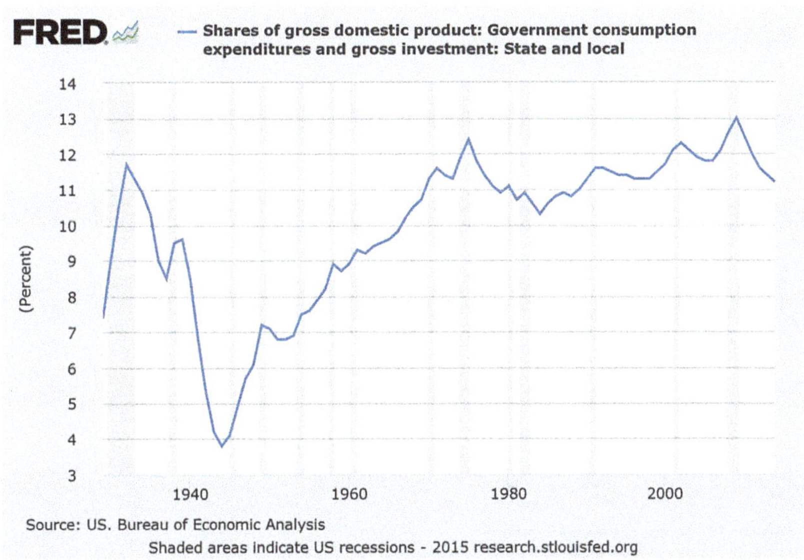

Figure 4.9 Government Consumption and Gross Investment at the State and Local level, as a share of *GDP*, US 1929–2014

4.3.4 Shares of GDI

Switching from GDP components to income components, it makes sense that Compensation of Employees as a share of GDI is strongly procyclic. Similarly, the Net Operating Surplus of Private Enterprise as a share of GDI tends to peak during expansions, and bottom out during recessions. This makes both of these potentially reliable indicators of where in the business cycle the economy may be.

Figure 4.10 shows that the Compensation of Employees takes the lion's share of GDI, at a level above 50% since 1929; and this is a procyclic share as it fluctuates up and down in tandem with real GDP. Figure 4.11 shows the Net Operating Surplus share of GDI at around half of the former, at a level of 25% recently, with the share being procyclic in a somewhat *leading fashion*. The latter share tends to start falling before a full recession ensues, which is the sense in which we could call it leading the cycle. Corporate profits are a component

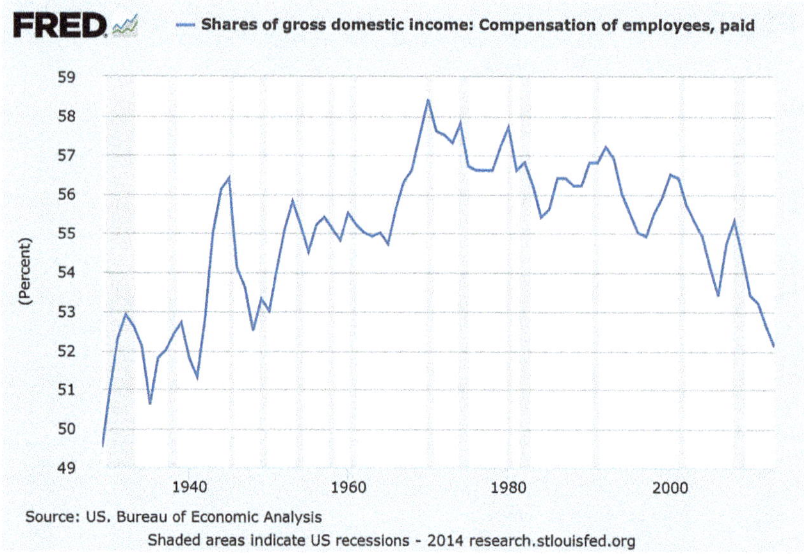

Figure 4.10 US Compensation of Employees as a Share of GDI, 1929–2013

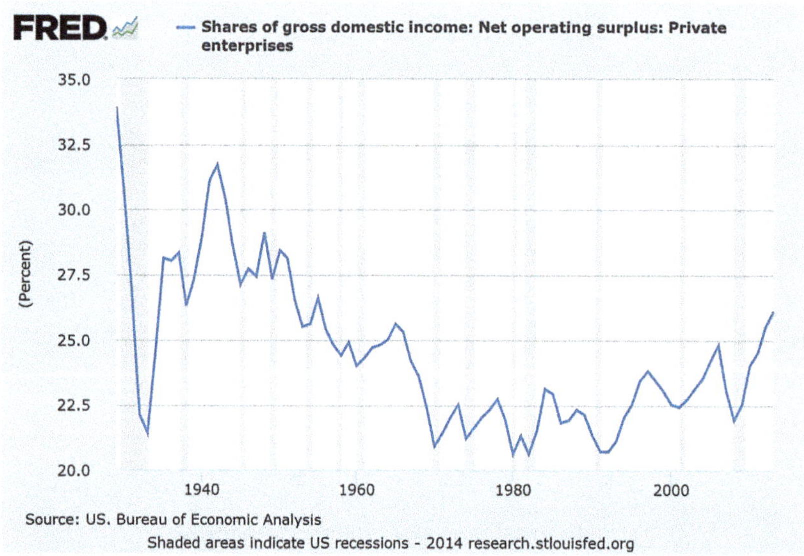

Figure 4.11 US Net Operating Surplus Private Enterprise, as a Share of GDI, 1929–2013

of net operating surplus and their share of GDI, with a level at around 5%, moves in a similar fashion to that of net operating surplus.

The Consumption of Fixed Capital is also a big share of GDI. This is a category that includes capital *depreciation*. Figure 4.12 shows that this share was at a level recently near 15%; and its share rises in recessions, in a countercyclic fashion. This is the capital that gets "used up" or "consumed" at a faster rate than GDP falls when there is recession. When firms have to *scrap their capital* as they shrink their output or go out of business, the capital gets *liquidated* and sold off piecemeal. Intuitively, this capital consumption could well happen at a faster rate than real GDI and GDP fall, as businesses contract or fail.

The wage compensation, net operating surplus and consumption of fixed capital make up more than 90% of GDI. The remainder is government net taxes, which is now around 7%. This then covers all of the NIPA components of GDI and how the behave over the business cycle as a share of GDI.

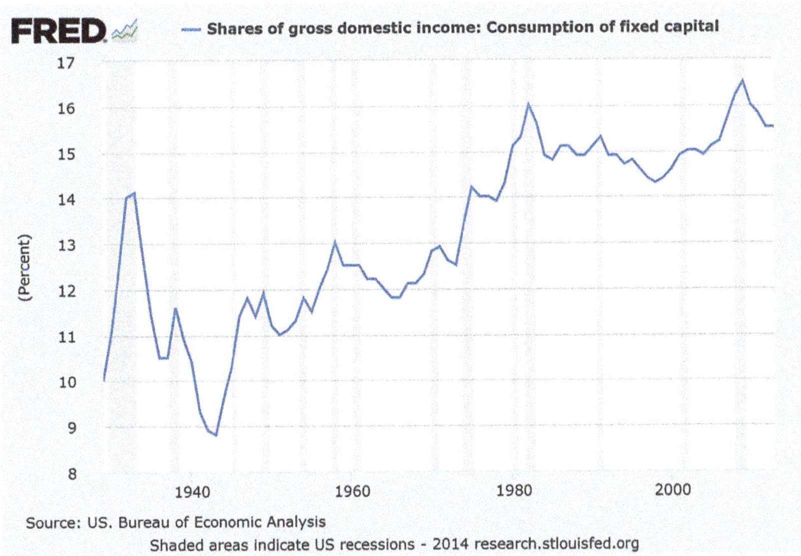

Figure 4.12 US Consumption of Fixed Capital, as a Share of GDI, 1929–2013

4.4 Theory

Business cycle and trend evidence show systemic cycles and strong growth trends in real output and its components. This suggests that business cycles are not subject to being eliminated by any perspicacious government policy. They exist and economists try to explain why they exist and how the government can help ameliorate the effects of downturns. This government policy is often characterized as providing insurance against recessions.

Two different types of recessions are apparent. Crisis recessions are one, and more normal business cycles are the others. The crises are themselves of two types: i) a severe depression as in the 1930s and ii) the "lost decade" type with prolonged unemployment and a long slow growth period such as the period starting with the 2008-2010 Great Recession. These types of crises appear exaggerated in impact relative to more usual business cycles. Banking crises featured strongly during both the Great Depression and the Great Recession.

Banking crises were largely absent in recessions since the Depression, until the Great Recession. Economists accordingly try to explain crisis-type recessions or depressions in terms of the function of the banking sector. This does not concern economists typically when studying more normal business cycles.

Economists also try to explain growth trends and formulate policy that leads to stronger growth in real GDP. The strong growth post-WWII was notched downwards during the 2008–2010 Great Recession. Economists discuss the possibility that the economy moved to a lower growth rate path for real GDP. Such low growth periods called "lost decades" also characterized Japan in the 1990s. Others characterize these shifts in GDP growth rate paths, as well as crisis recessions and lost decades, as being due to *rare events* such as bank crises or wars.

Normal growth in the economy has been explained by rising productivity. The productivity increase is widely attributed to what is called *technological progress*. Efforts exist in determining exactly what causes this technological change, with focus on candidates such as intangible capital, human capital, innovation and research and development.

Policy also can affect growth. For example, higher tax rates have been found to lower economic growth, both in theory and in *empirical research*. Determining the best policy for high growth remains a key focus by economists.

4.4.1 Real Business Cycle Theory

The traditional idea of RBC theory is based on explaining historical averages of business cycle experience, possibly including crises experience. This research finds that it is not changes in monetary policy causing the

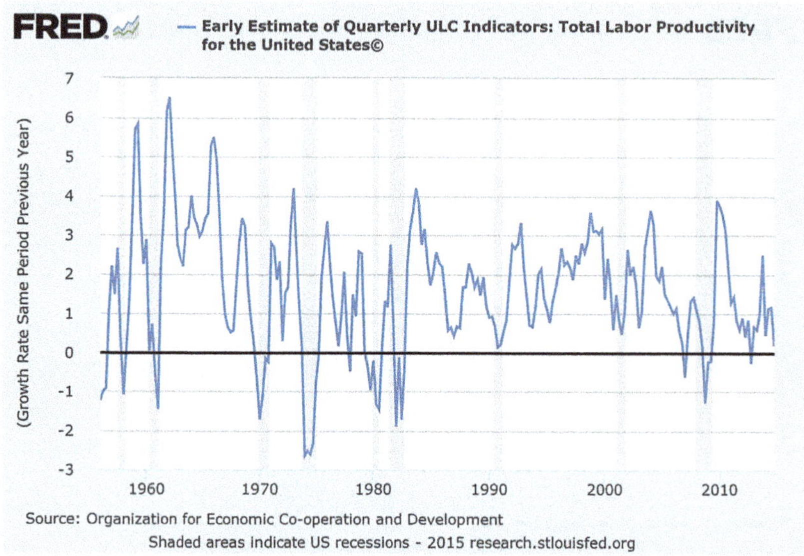

Figure 4.13 US Labor Productivity 1955–2014

historic succession of business cycles but rather it is changes in real productivity advances. This simple but potent productivity concept relegated an emphasis on money and banking to a different role: Money and banking appear to remain essential in understanding the crises of the Great Depression and the Great Recession.

Figure 4.13 graphs the annual rate of change for US labor productivity, on a quarterly basis. Labor productivity is defined as aggregate output divided by total labor hours. The graph shows its rate of change. Decreases in the Figure's productivity growth rate appear to align well with NBER dated recessions. In some recessions, productivity grew at lower rates, with some of these recessionary periods showing negative growth rates in productivity.

The basis of the RBC theory is to focus on the production function for output. In Chapter 2 we set out the production function for real output y as a function $f(.)$ of the inputs of labor hours l and of capital k. This gave that $y = f(l,k)$ in symbolic terms. We can now specify how productivity in real business cycle theory is included. Consider specifying an example of the production function $f(.)$. Let $y = Al^{0.33}k^{0.67}$, an example of the *Cobb-Douglas production function.* This gives a normal shaped *isoquant*, which in turn is a graph of how labor and capital inputs can be combined in order to give the same level of output.[1]

The productivity factor in $y = Al^{0.33}k^{0.67}$ is the parameter A. This is some constant. If it increases then any set combination of labor and capital inputs ends up giving more output. This is why A is thought of as the productivity indicator of the inputs, both labor and capital. The A parameter indicates both the productivity of labor and the productivity of capital. In contrast, labor productivity is typically considered as only the productivity of labor, and not of capital.

Total Factor Productivity

Labor productivity is found by dividing output by the labor input. This measure can be affected by variation in the capital stock as is normal over the business cycle. A more comprehensive measure of productivity is called *total factor productivity, or TFP,* which is measured by the production parameter A.

TFP uses methods to account for the contribution of both labor and capital to output, so that the residual contribution from A can be computed. The residual captures the contributions other than from the actual input contributions from labor and capital. This residual then gives a sense of how both factors have their productivity raised if A goes up, since A factors the input combination of labor and capital ($l^{0.33}k^{0.67}$).

Figure 4.14 shows the FRED measure of the growth rate of US TFP in blue compared to that of labor productivity in red, post 1951. The series move rather closely together. This enables economists to discuss

[1] In every Cobb-Douglas form, the coefficients on labor and capital add up to one, as in this example: 0.33 + 0.67 = 1.

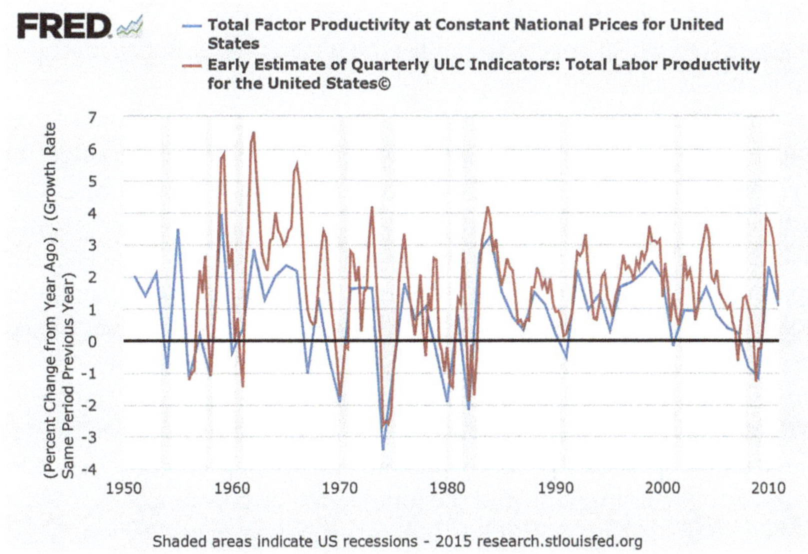

Figure 4.14 US Total Factor Productivity (Blue), and Labor Productivity (Red), 1951–2015

output productivity in broad terms using either labor productivity or total factor productivity. TFP also tends to hit its low point, or trough, during NBER dated recessions.

Shocks to TFP

The RBC theory of Kydland and Prescott argued that using the normal type of production function with shocks upwards and downwards in TFP, or A, are the best way to generate business cycles in theory such that the results of the theory match the actual data. RBC theory uses shocks to A to explain for example the correlation between consumption and output as found in the data for the normal, average, business cycle. Explaining the average correlations between investment and output, and between labor hours and output, are other major examples.

Shocks to TFP have been used to explain not only normal business cycles but also depression type periods and long period of depressed output growth. Explanation for the TFP shocks themselves is then the key next issue in that these TFP shocks are assumed to be exogenous to the model. Using exogenous productivity shocks for normal business cycles seems reasonable. But using exogenous TFP shocks for depressions or long low-growth periods is not as conventional because it leaves a great deal as exogenous.

For example, indicating that there is a depression because productivity has fallen does not help much in formulating policy for stopping a depression. Policy-makers need to know what is causing the drop in production and employment and investment when these changes are very severe. Productivity falling is an explanation that has no policy implications except general ones: increase productivity.

The lack of policy prescription from standard RBC theory based on productivity fluctuations is a limit to its application. It is unclear how the government can increase productivity in business cycle times. Over the long term the government can help increase education and possibly also research and development, and can decrease tax rates so as to increase growth. The question is whether, for example, various types of growth-enhancing expenditure is to be done by the private sector or the public sector. Social insurance expenditure can also be done by either the government or by the private sector if well regulated by the government.

RBC Puzzles

Besides the policy issue, the exogenous TFP shock theory of business cycles has led to many unresolved issues in explaining even normal business cycles. There are a host of *unresolved puzzles* even though there is a large consensus accepting the basis idea of productivity shocks causing business cycles. These are puzzles in the sense that they often can be resolved by further extending the theory.

Such puzzles only become fully resolved when a consensus arises about the resolution. Many such possible answers often get offered which appear to resolve the issue at hand. But such answers can make other related puzzles even harder to solve.

For example, in the standard RBC theory, consumption moves insufficiently relative to output as compared to the data. Many answers have been provided but no one answer is widely accepted. The problem is that a temporary income shock, as occurs with a productivity TFP shock, is treated by a consumer in theory as adding to temporary but not to *permanent income*.

The RBC theory includes within its framework the idea that the representative consumer is forward-looking, and bases consumption on expected permanent income. Therefore current consumption rises some when temporary income rises from a TFP increase, but it does not rise as much as actual consumption in the data rises relative to increases in output. This is called the consumption-output puzzle.

The *consumption-output puzzle* is the most central puzzle in RBC theory. To resolve it a shock from productivity rising needs to induce a significant rise in the consumer's entire expected future stream of income. Then the consumer would be satisfied that future income will support a higher flow of income. This allows the consumer to raise current consumption and the future planned consumption.

The consumer does not want to have consumption jump up and down year by year since it is harder to plan normal life activity. The consumer prefers to *smooth consumption over time*. This means that in RBC theory the consumer only reacts to a current income increase, from a TFP productivity increase, to the degree that the consumer thinks the future stream of income is higher, rather than only the temporary income being higher.

Extensions with Human Capital

One way to resolve the consumption-output puzzle is to have the productivity shock affect not only the current output but also the consumer's ability to have higher future output. Higher future output results if the Education and Research sectors are both 1) included in the total aggregate economy and 2) affected similarly by a productivity shock as is the rest of the economy.

An increase in productivity in the Education and Research sectors allows for higher *human capital accumulation*. A productivity increase causes the entire learning sector to increase its output of knowledge. This does not so much affect current output, but does raise the expected future output.

Considering the economy to be composed of both output production along with Education and Research production does allow for a solution to the consumption-output puzzle. When a total factor productivity shock positively affects output production as well as education and research, then the temporary increase in output in the goods production is buttressed by an additional increase in the whole stream of future output because of the higher human capital that will affect output in the future.

Raising human capital investment for the entire economy causes the permanent income to rise. This increase in output and human capital from a positive TFP productivity shock to both the goods *sector* and the education and research sector causes higher permanent income and so higher current consumption. As compared to only a temporary income increase, the TFP shock causes also a permanent income increase if it affects human capital investment as well.[2]

4.4.2 Growth Theory and Policy

Our understanding of the economic growth process also has its foundation in productivity theory. In particular, by assuming that there exists an exogenous upward trend in productivity, we find that we can explain the basic salient features of our growth trends over time. This growth theory then is closely related to the RBC business cycle theory.

Both the RBC theory and the neoclassical growth theory depend on changes in exogenously specified productivity. In RBC theory, productivity rises and falls relative to some trend. In neoclassical growth theory, the trend of some stable growth rate, such as 2 to 3.5% in recent US history, is explained by an exogenous steady rate of increase in productivity.

[2] See Csabafi et al., 2016, "Tuning In Real Business Cycle Growth Spectra", IMF working paper, forthcoming.

Such growth assumes that productivity rises at a certain rate every year. If real GDP output growth since 1959 was 3.5% (until the Great Recession), then the production function model of the economy implies a specific productivity increase that is implied in turn by parameters of the model in a residual fashion. The implied rate of change in productivity, or the TFP parameter A of the production function, delivers the assumed (or targeted) output growth rate trend.

Again the productivity-based explanation for growth, as for business cycles, is interesting in that it reproduces many features observed in the economy. But it is really a first step. Because the productivity increase is exogenously assumed, we are not fundamentally explaining what causes the productivity trend.

One explanation for the productivity trend again is based on human capital. If the economy invests every year in education and research, then our knowledge base rises. With a stable investment in such human capital, the growth trend can by explained endogenously within the standard neoclassical model, with the one extension of including the human capital sector.

Using human capital investment to explain the productivity trend makes sense in an intuitive way that is widely accepted. It does complicate the standard models. But this human capital explanation also leads to a policy of how to raise productivity.

If human capital accumulation raises productivity, then the government can leave this education and research process entirely to the private sector. In economic theory, we think no government intervention only makes sense if markets are functioning very well. Yet it is broadly accepted that the *human capital market* does not work so seamlessly.

Problems with human capital have to do with many social, political and economic factors. Some groups of people end up without the same access to education as other groups of people. This is true naturally in any market economy since education is costly. But the question is whether there is something the government can do that the private sector cannot do as easily.

Our common solution to government involvement in education goes back a long way to the idea by Henry George (in his 1879 book *Progress and Poverty*) to place taxes on property ownership. We do this in nearly every city, county or municipality in the US, and use some fraction of these taxes to finance the education system in that locality. This means the value of the property, in terms of land and houses, in the locality where the property exists, benefits from having tax revenue to finance education that is available to everyone in that locality.

Many problems still exist since property values in a locality can be depressed as a result of national government or local policy for example with respect to urban blight or natural declines of some industries in favor of others. For example the "rust-belt" of the Midwest from the decline in heavy industry like steel and automobile manufacturing is contrasted by the rise of the sun-belt locations in Texas, Arizona, Florida and California where higher technology industries are thriving.

Governments may need to intervene to ensure that aggregate trends do not adversely affect local education opportunities. Abandoned houses bring down the property value and taxes received on property value in entire neighborhoods. This can be ameliorated by government policy.

Another major example for higher education such as at the tertiary level is that low income groups have less opportunity to pay for such education. Student loans subsidized by the government can help access and enable broader classes of citizens to get higher education. Such local policy as eliminating urban blight and country-wide policy of subsidizing student loans can end up not only ameliorating class discrimination but also can increase economy-wide economy growth.

Policy that leaves large swaths of its citizens out of the human capital growth process is in effect taxing its ability to have strong future economic growth, while at the same time causing inter-class strife that in effect creates additional implicit taxes on the society's ability to grow. The happy coincidence of decreasing internal discord and discrimination while increasing everyone's growth prospects can result from efficacious growth policy. This is possible when we grasp the role of human capital accumulation in fostering higher productivity.

4.4.3 Crisis Theory

Having broader based and better human capital investment in a society helps for trend growth prospects but not so much for business cycle downturns. Especially during crisis periods such as the Great Depression and

Great Recession, human capital investment becomes a much lower priority for the immediate policy focus on how to get out of a crisis depression or recession. Crisis theory instead focuses on immediate actions and near-term consequences.

Until the Great Recession, crisis theory and interest in explaining crises was in remission due to a long period of prosperity in the US since the Great Depression. Other countries around the world continued to have crises and economists have long continued to focus on such international crises. But for domestic US policy, crises management was not the focus until the Great Recession.

The Keynesian theory of using government spending to get out of a recession has been a well-known policy prescription. It was used again during the Great Recession in both national discourse and as justification for some government policy since the 2008 crisis began. However other focuses emerged that were traditionally based in neoclassical *money and banking policy.*

Money and Banking

The 2008–2010 US Great Recession saw the collapse of the *investment bank* Lehman Brothers, through its filing for bankruptcy on September 15, 2008. This led to a *run on banks* in the investment banking sector. In particular the *mutual fund deposits* were withdrawn in a rush, or panic, from investment banks. This led to these investment banks having insufficient reserves to pay out the depositor funds.

The fact that a bank run occurred in the Great Depression, with respect to retail banks, and then reoccurred in 2008 with respect to the investment banks, made it clear to analysts that a bank panic was something that could cause a widespread, international, deep and prolonged economic crisis. Other similarities were examined to try to decide on a policy approach to make the 2008 crisis less costly on the economy and its citizens than was the Great Depression.

One other fact was also clear in making the comparison to the banking collapses in each the Great Depression and Great Recession. The retail banks deposits were not insured by the federal government during the 1929–1933 depression. The investment bank deposits known as mutual fund deposits were also uninsured by the federal government in the US in 2008.

A lack of deposit insurance on investment bank mutual funds arose because these funds were created after the 1980's US financial deregulation. The mutual funds were outside of the Federal Deposit Insurance Corporation, and so were and are still uninsured.

The FDIC was created in March 1933 after a federally declared *banking holiday* and resulted in reopened banks having deposit insurance through the FDIC. Having deposits insured caused currency to be deposited back into banks. Banks then began increasing their lending to private firms for investment, and a recovery ensued.

The response after the mutual fund run on the banks was similar to the Great Depression bank run but a difference is that afterwards the mutual funds did not become FDIC insured. Rather, the US injected massive amounts of new reserves into the banking system to keep it "liquid". This gradually caused the banking system, including both investment and retail banks, to stabilize. Increased lending for investment eventually ensued, and the Great Depression type of consequences were successfully avoided.

The unemployment rate in the Great Recession rose to above 10%, but well below the 25% of the Great Depression. Since unemployment remained high, and real output growth low, the 2008–2010 recession began to be called the Great Recession. But banking policy and monetary policy in combination resulted in averting worse-case scenarios.

Monetary policy took place through the Federal Reserve System (Fed) buying up bad mortgage loans and buying up far more US Treasury debt than it ever had historically. By buying up debt, the Fed injected much money into financial capital markets. This was called increasing the liquidity of the markets. It made the cost of borrowing money low.

The Fed kept its key borrowing rate fixed at 0.025 from 2008 until December 2015, when it was then raised slightly to 0.05 percent. This very low rate has enabled banks to borrow cheaply. This money and banking policy also led to inflation staying near its 2% target rate for most of the period. This averted a big deflation that Irving Fisher and Friedrich Hayek advocated as the key policy needed to avoid a depression.

The real interest rate remained low, and even negative, during the Great Repression. In contrast it was around 10% in the Great Depression. The lack of a large deflation, the ensured solvency of the financial system and the low real interest rates made policy during the Great Recession a relative successful combination of mainly money and banking policy. Keynesian government spending also may have been used during the Great Recession, an area of debate.

Rare Events

One result of the Great Recession on the theory of business cycles is that it was found that the whole business cycle experience could be better explained by allowing for so-called *rare events*. The rare events literature allows for the small possibility of war and bank collapse. Incorporating these possibilities has allowed theory to better incorporate consumer and firm expectations.

For example, when a recession occurs, there is always a possibility of it becoming a Great Depression or a prolonged recession as in the Great Recession. Using this possibility, economists have been better able to explain the effect of productivity shocks on the economy. If a deep or prolonged recession ensues, investment, consumption, and a range of asset prices will all be lower than in a normal recession.

Explaining asset prices in particular creates an entire additional set of business cycle and growth puzzles. Standard RBC and neoclassical growth theory based on exogenous shocks appears unable to explain many aspects about financial markets. Since financial markets determine prices of the marketable assets of the economy, any serious failing of the RBC theory to explain asset prices is taken to be a serious shortcoming. Using rare events has enabled asset price theory to better explain certain financial market features.

4.5 Application: Equity Premium Puzzle

A well-known RBC puzzle is what is called the *equity premium puzzle*. The equity premium is the difference between the historical *return to owning* the *equity shares called stocks* of private companies versus the return to owning *government bonds*. The puzzle is that the neoclassical RBC models predict a smaller difference in these returns than is observed in the data.

The stock market is where shares of ownership in companies are traded. Various countries have different stock markets. Any one country may have more than one stock market or it may not have any. Stock markets trade shares of companies that are registered as public with a particular *stock market exchange*. These so-called exchanges are companies that set up the ability for buyers and sellers to meet in some fashion and trade stocks by buying and selling them. Examples in the US are the two largest, these being New York Stock Exchange (NYSE) and the Nasdaq exchange.

The US government raises money by borrowing from the public. It does this when the US Treasury issues new debt that offers to borrow a specified amount of money at some particular interest rate. Some interest rates on US debt are allowed in effect to vary with inflation. But most US Treasury debt is in terms of a fixed interest rate, to be paid on the debt over its *maturity*. This means an average return, or *yield*, can be computed on the average US Treasury debt over some historical period.

The RBC models predict that the equity return is lower than it actually is found to be within data, and that the return on government debt is higher than is found in the data. This means the difference in the return from holding equity versus holding US government debt is too low in the RBC theory. This result has implications for the *pricing of risk* in theory versus data.

Equity ownership does not guarantee a particular return. Instead the owner receives any level of dividends that the company chooses to be paid out to owners of its stock. The company may go bankrupt and all of the investment in the stock may be lost. Stock ownership is viewed as a risky investment. The theory of risk suggests that the market works so as to provide a higher yield to owners of risky investment in order to compensate them for taking on the greater risk. Stock ownership demands a risk premium that compensates for the risk inherent in each company's business.

In contrast, US government debt is viewed as having very little risk of default. Holding US Treasury debt is therefore viewed as a low risk investment. Treasury debt demands on the market a negligible *risk premium*, since there is little risk of default.

The economic theory of business cycles and growth is used to try to predict correctly the average risk premium that US investors pay for stock versus bond ownership. Since the RBC and growth theory involves an underpricing of stock ownership and overpricing of US Treasury debt, the theory is viewed as insufficiently complete. Its inability to better price risk is a failing of this neoclassical model.

Numerous ways to make the theory better able to predict the equity premium have been put forth. No single extension of the theory has been consensually accepted. Including the possibility of rare events is one way to explain the equity premium.

The basis of the RBC theory of the equity premium is how consumption growth correlates with the equity return. Consumption fluctuations occur in the RBC theory because of shocks to TFP. The comovement of the changes in aggregate consumption with the changes in aggregate firm profit determines the ability of the RBC model to correctly explain the equity premium. Rare events makes consumption move more closely with asset prices and therefore improves the explanation of the equity premium.

The equity premium indicates that basic puzzles in RBC theory, such as the consumption-output puzzle, can spill over and cause problems in explaining financial experience. Many puzzles related to the financial markets exist that continue to challenge neoclassical theory. For example, a focus since the Great Recession has included trying to incorporate debt to equity ratios as an extension of a financial system approach to explaining the equity premium.

4.6 Appendix: Human Capital Over Time

4.6.1 Structural Transformation by Sector

Some of the noticeable trends in GDP shares are due to particular components of GDP. Personal consumption expenditure has trended up by 10% from the mid 1960's to the present. What caused this exactly?

There are four identifiable individual components of personal consumption expenditure: 1) Total Goods which can be divided into 2) Durable Goods and 3) Non-Durable Goods. And there are 4) Services.

Figure 4.15 graphs total "Goods" since 1929. This is the US share of GDP contributed by personal consumption expenditure on "Goods", these being both durable (like washing machines) and non-durable (like food). The share has fallen dramatically and steadily since *WWII*, from 40% in 1947 to 23% in 2013.

Figure 4.16 shows the share in GDP of Services. The postwar shows a rise from 25% in 1947 to 45% in 2013. This marks a steady increase that can explain the overall postwar share increase that is seen in personal consumption expenditure, in Figure 4.4.

Figure 4.15 US Personal Consumption Expenditure on Goods as a Share of GDP, 1929–2014

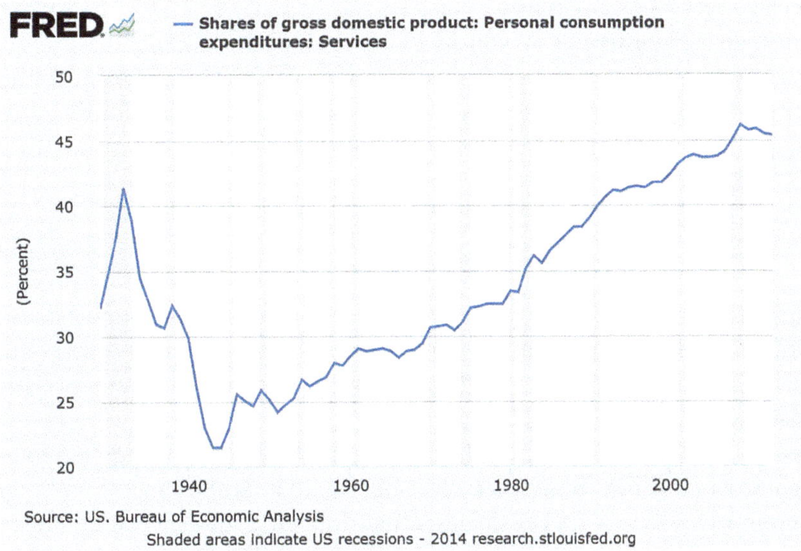

Figure 4.16 US Personal Consumption Expenditures on Services, as share of GDP, 1929–2013

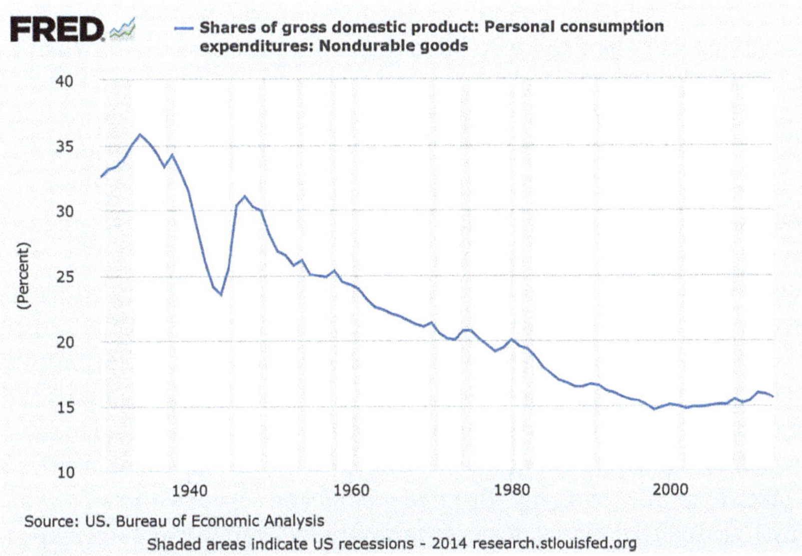

Figure 4.17 US Personal Consumption Expenditures on Non-Durable Goods, as share of GDP, 1929–2013

Figures 4.5 and 4.16 show a remarkable "stylized fact" that there has been a *structural transformation* of the US economy whereby goods consumption is increasingly substituted for by services consumption. In addition, since the Durable goods consumption share of GDP has been steady although cyclic since WWII, as seen in Figure 4.6, this leaves the non-durable goods consumption to be what services are substituting for over time.

Figure 4.17 shows the steady drop in Non-Durable Goods personal consumption as a share of *GDP*, in the US from 1929–2013. From a peak of 36% in 1938, the GDP share of Non-Durable Goods fell to near 15% today, falling by more than half. This was picked up by the Service share increase in Figure 4.16, which increased so much that the overall share of personal consumption in GDP rose over time.

The substitution of Non-Durable Goods for Services and the overall increase in the share of Personal Consumption Expenditure are "stylized facts" of the US economy having to do with its structural transformation. One explanation is that the US economy is transforming from low human capital intensive sectors to high human capital intensive sectors. Many of the industries now classified as services are highly human capital intensive, such as the high tech industries of online services, financial services and aspects of communications.

Efforts are underway to explain in theory how economies gradually transform towards industries with ever-increasing human capital intensities. For example, agriculture was once dominant with a large share of our labor force engaged within it. But now it is viewed as our least human capital sector, and it accounts for less than 1% of our labor force.

4.6.2 Rich to Poor Neighborhoods

Explaining urban blight remains part of the urban policy's main challenges. Support has been found for how public capital amenities such as transportation aides the development of city centers during expansionary periods. Evidence also suggests that prices tend to rise faster in urban city centers than in more outlying areas during expansionary periods.

Taking a hypothesis from macroeconomics, human capital theory can be applied to urban development to explain why blight exists and how business cycles affect it. In a famous article, "Why doesn't capital flow from rich to poor countries?" Lucas (1990) suggests that financial/physical capital does not flow into poor countries because the human capital is insufficient to support such inflows of physical capital. The human capital basis is insufficient to allow a sufficiently high return on capital simply by importing the capital into the less developed country.

The lack of the human capital foundation to support physical or financial capital increases explains why we don't observe rapid capital inflows and rapid development. Instead nations develop slowly. And this slow development may be in line with their ability to build their education systems and their human capital, such that they gradually can absorb new physical capital profitably.

Development based on the return to investing in human capital is an idea put forth in the human capital theory of Nobel Laureate T. W. Schultz's (1964) "Transforming Traditional Agriculture". The Schultz growth theory is formalized in Lucas's (1988) "Mechanics of Economic Growth". The theory says human capital investment only occurs once the return to human capital investment is positive, and then it results that in equilibrium the returns to physical capital and human capital become equal.

The theory of equilibrium capital returns requires that the physical capital to human capital ratio in each of the economy's sectors is proportional, so that both the human capital basis is sufficient to support the physical capital investment and likewise the physical capital investment is sufficient to support the human capital investment. The answer to Lucas's question about why financial capital does not flood into undeveloped economies, or areas of an economy, is that there is insufficient human capital to support the subsequent physical capital development. This feature may also occur with the development of cities, where the blighted neighborhoods are taken to be one "economy" that trades labor and capital with the "rest of the well-developed neighborhoods". Physical/financial capital does not flow rapidly from the well-developed neighborhoods to the blighted neighborhoods because the blighted neighborhoods do not have sufficient human capital to support it. Conversely, the low property values of the blight means the physical capital is insufficient to warrant the investment in human capital, or an inflow of relatively more educated people into the neighborhood.

Blighted areas within urban centers, such as St. Louis, Cleveland and Detroit, show that neighborhood "gentrification" can be held off for generations at a time. During this prolonged period of "lost decades", these neighborhoods continue to be stuck with a low aggregate human capital of their residents. These neighborhoods are unable to support higher quality housing, groceries, and trendy shops typical of the gentrification process that necessarily involves significant physical capital inflow into the neighborhoods. Since education relies to a large extent on property taxes within each neighborhood, the low property values where blight exists keeps grass-roots education funding relatively low and creates a vicious cycle of low education, low human capital levels and low income.

Blighted neighborhoods may tend to have the worst schools because the property value of such neighborhoods is low by definition of blight. Residents of blighted neighborhoods easily can get stuck in a "lost-generations" cycle of growing up and going to school at the worse schools. Then comes the cycle of having low human capital levels, job opportunities, and income levels.

One solution in economics in the face of externalities is to eliminate the source of the externality. In blighted neighborhoods this means eliminating the abandoned commercial and residential buildings. However, many cities allow owners to hold onto such property indefinitely. This creates externalities that property owners of abandoned buildings are imposing upon those residing in the blighted neighborhoods.

A solution is to legislate changes in property laws such that abandoned properties can more easily become city, state, or federal property, and then be torn down and rehabilitated. This could include creation of temporary green spaces, redevelopment or social amenities as in parks. This could break the cycle of low human capital because of low property values that in turn finance the neighborhood schools.

With blight eliminated, development that rushes into city centers during business cycle expansions could encompass the previously blighted neighborhoods rather than leaving them ever further behind. As developed city center prices rise relatively quickly, so can the property values of "un-blighted" neighborhoods, along with the human capital of their residents.[3]

4.7 Summary

The chapter presents facts, theory and application of the comovements of macroeconomic variables. Business cycle features are presented in terms of time series of data for the US economy of certain variables from the National Income and Product Accounts. Correlations of these series are examined.

Consumption, investment and GDP are all highly correlated with each other but pronounced differences exist. Consumption fluctuates by less than does output. Investment fluctuates by more than does output.

Trends also exist in macroeconomic aggregates. Real consumption, investment and output all tend to grow at a common rate that depends upon the time period being examined. A trend growth rate for US long historical periods is often put at 2%. Post-1950's growth had tended to be as high as 3.5% until the Great Recession.

Real business cycle theory explains business cycles through fluctuations in aggregate productivity rather than through government spending as is emphasized in Keynesian economic Cross theory. Instead, exogenous productivity fluctuations are assumed and this enables a standard neoclassical theory to explain normal business cycles.

Crisis times are not explained well by simply assuming a large productivity drop. Instead other forces have been utilized to explain the Great Depression and the recent Great Recession. This direction has seen money and banking as the emphasis for understanding and getting out of depressions or deep recessions.

The most widely accepted explanation for economic growth uses the productivity idea in a way similar to real business cycle theory. This assumes an exogenous upward trend in productivity. While this assumption enables explanation of many basic features of growth, it leaves the explanation of productivity itself as unknown.

Human capital theory tries to explain productivity itself and ensuing economic growth. The basis of economic growth here is due to investment in the ability of people to perform. This investment takes place through education and research and development. Human capital theory has been shown also to help explain some of the RBC puzzles.

Application of the facts and theory is made to one of the RBC puzzles. This is in the area of finance. It concerns the return made in financial markets for taking on the risk of investment in companies that cannot guarantee a particular return. The most well-known of the RBC finance puzzles is the explanation of the so-called equity premium, as introduced here.

The other application is to show the US structural transformation from non-durable goods to services, as a percent of GDP. This indicates a shift in the composition of US industrial output. One explanation is that industry develops in a more human capital intensive fashion over time so as to utilize the rising level of aggregate human capital that characterizes the US economy.

3 Lucas, Robert Jr., 1988. "On the mechanics of economic development," Journal of Monetary Economics, 22(1, July): 3-42. Lucas, Robert E, Jr, 1990. "Why Doesn't Capital Flow from Rich to Poor Countries?," American Economic Review, 80(2, May): 92-96. Schultz, T. W., 1964. Transforming Traditional Agriculture, New Haven: Yale University Press.

4.8 Glossary of Italic Words

acyclic: movement of data series over time that neither positively correlates with general business cycle movements nor negatively correlates with general business cycle movements in a significant way.

asset: a form of holding value such as any capital stock.

banking holiday: closing of private bank sector by the US government during the Great Depression, is an example.

boom: significant or prolonged expansion of the economy during the business cycle.

Cobb-Douglas production function: a type of production function whereby capital and labor are substitutes for each other in producing a certain level of output.

consumption-output puzzle: the problem that real business cycle theory predicts that consumption moves with output by less than actual data series on consumption and output show; consumption is more volatile relative to output in data than in RBC theory.

countercyclic: movement of data series over time that is negatively correlated with general business cycle movements such as in real output.

debt principal: the amount of some currency that is borrowed for a certain period of time, with the promise that interest at some agreed rate will be paid to compensate for the lending of the currency; repaid at end of debt maturity.

depreciation of capital: the degree or percent of capital in use for production that becomes degraded by its use in production; the amount of capital used up in the process of production.

detrended: taking out the trend, or average, movement that occurs within a certain data series so that only fluctuations around that particular trend are left in the data series.

equity premium puzzle: the difficulty in explaining the difference between average equity returns and government bond returns using standard real business cycle theory.

government bonds: borrowing by the government in the form of debt that is sold to the public; each bond is debt of the government and has a certain maturity that marks how long the government is borrowing with the particular bond.

human capital accumulation: the accumulation of knowledge by people through investing time in learning or through any similar means that yields greater knowledge.

human capital market: the buying and selling of means by which to invest in human capital, such as by education institutions, both public and private.

investment bank: a bank that provides wholesale more than retail banking services such as facilitating the buying and selling of private companies, the issuance of corporate debt from corporations to the public, the issuance of new equity in public companies.

isoquant: a diagram that shows how different combinations of inputs can be used to produce a given, constant, level of output.

leading fashion: economic indicators that tend to rise before the real aggregate output growth rate does during a business cycle or tend to fall before the economy's real output growth rate falls.

liquidated: capital stock that is sold off piece by piece after a company becomes insolvent and possibly goes into bankruptcy.

maturity: the length of time that a debt instrument is issued for, such that at the end of that time, the entire *debt principal* that was borrowed must be returned.

money and banking policy: government policy involving changes to the public, governmental, supply of money, usually in terms of the growth rate of money supply, or to the interest rates that the government can affect within financial markets, and including government policy regarding the private bank system.

mutual fund deposits: deposits made in investment banks that typically earn a rate of interest that depends upon what the investment bank in turn invests the mutual funds; government bonds are an investment item for some mutual funds, and these funds are viewed as less risky and tend to earn the lowest returns.

permanent income: the value of the expected future stream of income earned by the consumer, as put on an per period basis such as annual income for the current period.

physical capital **and** *human capital:* value of the stock of tangible plant and equipment and other firm and government assets, and including intangible values such as patent rights, and including the value of the knowledge base and potential skill sets of people.

pricing of risk: the valuation of ventures by markets that involve different degrees of probabilities of corporate or business failure, and different degrees of probable returns.

procyclic: data series that tend to move in tandem with the real GDP growth rate and other series positively correlated with real GDP growth.

Progress and Poverty: the book written by Henry George in 1879 with the subtitle, An Inquiry into the Cause of Industrial Depressions, in which George emphasizes using taxes on property values to finance government expenditure.

rare events: catastrophic events that occur only several times a century, rather than in every business cycle.
real business cycle theory (RBC): postulating that shocks to productivity in the aggregate production function for goods output are responsible for explaining much of the comovement of various economic variables such as consumption, investment and output over the course of the normal business cycle movements of expansion and contraction of the growth rate of real output.
recession: a protracted decrease in the rate of growth of real output and other key economic variables such as employment and investment.
return to owning the equity shares called stocks: the amount of dividend received from profits of a company per unit of capital ownership in the company; amount of income paid out to owners per share of ownership relative to the value of a share of ownership.
risk premium: the difference between the average equity return and the average government bond return.
run on banks: the withdrawal of deposits from banks that is characterized as a contagious withdrawal that is typically based on troubles at certain specific banks; more demand for deposits than can be met by existing bank reserves.
scrap their capital: firms sell off their plant and equipment and land at any price that the market will yield at the current time.
sector: a part of the economy that produces certain broad categories of goods, such as consumption goods, investment goods, or all output; can be for investment that is not readily valued such as human capital.
smooth consumption over time: the normal outcome of an optimizing consumer whereby the consumer has stable consumption over time, for example by borrowing during bad income times and lending during good income times.
stock market exchange: a concern that registers companies and includes certain disclosure requirements by those companies and then allows ownership of those companies to be traded publicly.
structural transformation: the realigning of a nation's economy over time in terms of the nature of its production.
stylized facts: a descriptive set of features.
technological change: an increase in the output from any given combination of inputs results when there is an increase in technological knowledge; a cyclic decrease in technological knowledge and productivity of inputs can happen when physical and human capital is scraped in a recession.
total factor productivity (TFP): the effect yielding output that cannot be accounted for by the value of the inputs alone; a residual after accounting for the contribution to the value of output by known inputs to production.
trend: the average behavior of a data series, with the definition of average defined in different ways including a simple average.
unresolved puzzles: economic behavior as indicated by data series that is not accounted for by theory of the economy.
volatility: a measure of variation such as standard deviation or variance.
written off: capital that is scraped and valued at the low sales value at which they can be sold, rather than at the value the capital can yield when used in production with other inputs in a production process that yields marketable output.
yield: the rate of return on any asset.

4.9 Questions

1. What are business cycles and growth trends in terms of the aggregate economy?
2. What role does real GDP growth play in determining at which point the economy resides in terms of its business cycle?
3. What is the average growth rate of the economy?
4. How do aggregate consumption and investment relate to real GDP over the business cycle?
5. Provide an example of data supporting the idea that government expenditure plays a social insurance role.
6. How do the national income components of compensation, net operating surplus and capital consumption behave over the business cycle?
7. How does real business cycle theory explain business cycles?
8. What are alternative theories of the business cycle other than RBC theory?

9. Define TFP and explain how shocks to TFP can generate a business cycle.
10. Describe an RBC puzzle.
11. How does human capital theory extend RBC models in order to explain productivity change?
12. What is the foundation of neoclassical growth theory and what are some pro-growth policy options?
13. What are some theories of economic crises, how do these differ from RBC theory, and how do these relate to rare events?
14. Explain what is the equity premium puzzle.
15. Describe an example of structural transformation that has taken place in the US since WWII.
16. Why does not capital flow rapidly from high-income neighborhoods to low-income neighborhoods so as to quickly eliminate the income differentials between neighborhoods?
17. Complete the Federal Reserve Bank of St. Louis EconLowdown Course Module "Unemployment".

5 Money, Banking & Policy

5.1 Introduction

The US Federal Reserve System is known as the semi-governmental body that conducts monetary policy for the US, since its inception in 1914. However this monetary policy has been an evolving one, with different regimes at different times. In fact when the Fed was created the US was on the gold standard such that the Fed had very little ability to affect its money supply growth rate and the US inflation rate.

However, the Fed was created when it was likely the gold standard would soon be dropped due to WWI. WWI expenditure was expected to force the US to use inflation and at least temporarily leave the gold standard. Both of these did occur, as the US effectively suspended the gold standard from 1917 to 1919 and the US inflation rate rose rapidly from 3% in 1916 to 20% in 1918.[1]

The evolving nature of the Fed's monetary policy can be seen as it entered the modern era after all links to the gold standard were dropped during 1971–1973, as the *Bretton Woods monetary system* was abandoned. This Bretton Woods system was adopted as part at the end of WWII. It established fixed exchange rates amongst nations, created the International Monetary Fund and the predecessor of the World Bank, and it stipulated that the US was to keep the price of gold fixed at 35 US dollars an ounce.

The modern era after 1971–1973 has had no backing of US dollars by gold, or any tie to gold whatsoever. Money currency was and is not tied in any way to any metallic standard. This has given rise to the era that we are in now, it being that of a *fiat* monetary standard. Fiat money is unbacked, and taken by itself just a worthless piece of paper.

With fiat money, the world economy needed new policies on how to regulate the price level. Eventually the world has begun to settle on what is called *inflation rate targeting.* Inflation targeting advocates for some given low inflation rate to be targeted. This target typically is 2% rather than zero.

The US Fed achieves its inflation target by printing new money at some rate while at the same time targeting the Federal Funds interest rate at some level. The Federal Funds Rate is a target that the Fed changes at will as it sees fit. The growth of the money supply is inferred from data published by the Fed on its monetary aggregates, using its definitions for them.

5.2 Who Made it Happen

The problems of the US private national banking system during the late 1800's and early 1900's led eventually first to the 1908 US Aldrich-Vreeland Act. This required a commission to report on the establishment of a national currency system. It led to the establishment of the Federal Reserve System (Fisher, 1932, p. viii.). Irving Fisher's (1920) *Stabilizing the Dollar* promoted price stability as the goal of monetary policy, which would be what we now call a zero inflation rate target.[2] This "inflation rate targeting", at a low inflation rate level, became the modern monetary policy pursued today.

Keynes (1923) also promoted price stability in his *Tract on Monetary Reform*, as an extension of Fisher's (1911) theory of money demand often called the "quantity theory of money".[3] Keynes (1930) repudiated the quantity theory and Keynes (1936) described a demand for money that depended upon the interest rate.

---

[1]https://fraser.stlouisfed.org/docs/meltzer/craint89.pdf, for gold standardhistory during WWI, and see http://www.multpl.com /inflation/table for USinflation rate data back to the 1800s.

[2]Fisher, I., 1920, Stabilizing the Dollar, Macmillan: New York; and Fisher, I., 1932, Booms and Depressions; New York: Adelphi.

[3]Fisher, I., (1911) The Purchasing Power of Money, 2nd ed. New York, Macmillan.

Keynes was subsequently also closely involved in the establishment of the post WWII Bretton Woods monetary system and its resumption of a gold standard as based on the US dollar, according to Skidelsky (2005), with a system of international fixed exchange rates.[4]

Wicksell (1936) on page 4 of his famous *Interest and Prices: A Study of the Causes Regulating the Value of Money* declares that the "ideal system" of monetary policy would be a perfectly stable aggregate price level.[5]

> "It follows that if it were in our power to regulate completely the price system of the future, the ideal position, affording common advantage to the overwhelming majority of the various groups of interests, would undoubtedly be one in which, without interfering with the inevitable variations in the relative prices of commodities, the general average level of money prices in so far as this conception can be assigned a definite meaning, a point to which we shall return in a moment would be perfectly invariable and stable. And why should not such regulation lie within the scope of practical politics?"

Wicksell (1936) embraced the quantity theory of money. He is perhaps best known for his definition of the concept of a Liquidity effect on interest rates from increasing the supply of money.

Money demand theory was advanced significantly with Cagan's (1956) ability to analyze seven post WWI and WWII hyperinflations around the world as part of a stable money demand function. The Cagan work was included as a chapter in Milton Friedman's (1956) edited book *Studies in the Quantity Theory of Money* (University of Chicago Press, Chicago). This volume also contains Friedman's well-known statement of the quantity theory as a demand for money, in the chapter he contributed called "The Quantity Theory of Money: A Restatement".

John Taylor (1993) proposed the "Taylor rule" of controlling monetary policy by using an interest rate rule. This advocated setting money supply so as to target a certain market interest rate, even while still allowing for inflation rate targeting. The Taylor rule is today the most widely studied rule that has been proposed as a specific way to conduct monetary policy.

5.3 Facts

5.3.1 Public Bank and Private Bank Money

There are two basic types of money. Both come from Banks. One bank is the Federal Reserve Bank (the Fed). This provides money used and issued by the government. These are called *Federal Reserve Notes*. We call this cash, and more formally in government accounting these Notes are called *currency*.

The other bank based money comes from the set of all private commercial banks or related financial institutions. These banks provide money in the form of bank deposits that can be used to make transactions. These bank deposits can be used in exchange for goods through use of a *debit card* that instantly puts a hold on deposits in your bank account.

Or consumers can write a check that debits the bank account when it is deposited by the store. Paper checks are in decline in terms of usage relative to computer linked debit cards. Advances in computer technology have made debit cards increasingly the standard way to pay with private bank deposits.

Both Federal Reserve Notes and bank deposits are used every day to purchase items. Economists consider this purchasing process to be an exchange of money for goods. Money in turn is a means of exchange. Since both cash and bank deposits, typically only in *current accounts*, can be used as a means of exchange, both are considered the main money that is in circulation.

Federal Reserve Notes enter circulation as money for example when the US Treasury Department purchases goods and services as part of the government component of GDP. These purchases are debited from US Treasury accounts at private sector banks. This happens when the sellers of the goods and services deposit

---

[4]Skidelsky, Robert, 2005, "Keynes, Globalisation and the Bretton Woods Institutions in the Light of Changing Ideas about Markets," *World Economy*, Vol 6, No. 1, pp. 15–30.

[5]Knut Wicksell, 1936, *Interest and Prices: A Study of the Causes Regulating the Value of Money*, translated from German by R. F. Kahn, published on behalf of the Royal Economic Society, Macmillan and Company, Ltd., St. Martin's Street, London.

their government checks in their private bank account. These private banks in turn can receive from the government the value of these purchases in the form of cash reserves.

The private banks get the reserves by making deposits of funds into accounts held at the Federal Reserve Bank (Fed). The banks can then ask for cash to be transferred to them in return for debiting this cash from their deposit accounts at the Fed. The Federal Reserve Notes are then transferred from the Fed to the private banks and can be held in their vaults.

Private bank deposits held by the public, or what economists call consumers, are available to consumers in the form of cash or as deposits that can be accessed by bank debit card or by writing a check. Private bank deposits are called *demand deposits* by the Federal Reserve System. This is because the current account deposits can be demanded from the bank to be paid out in full as cash by the consumer at any time the bank is open.

Banks can only lend out a portion of the demand deposits. This is because these demand deposits tend to get used up each period, be it a month, or a quarter of a year. The banks need reserves on hand to pay back the demand deposits when they are spent. Banks tend to offer zero *interest* to those who deposit funds in current accounts. This is because the banks cannot make money by lending out a big fraction of these deposits, since they know they have to repay these deposits usually within the same period that the funds are deposited.

Money Multiplier

If banks lend out all of their reserves except those required by the Fed, then there are zero excess reserves. This gives rise to a multiplier effect on the total private bank money supply when a bank gets more reserves. Say the reserve requirement at the Fed is 10%, then the bank can lend out 90% and keep 10% as reserves held at the Fed. With \$100 in new reserves, a bank would then lend out \$90. The next bank gets the \$90 when it is spent and deposited. It keeps 10% as required reserves, or \$9, and lends out \$81. This continues until 100 + 90 + 81 + 73 + 63 + . . . is lent out.

With rr denoting the reserve requirement of 10%, then $1 - rr = 1 - 0.10$. The total lent out is

$$\begin{aligned}
&100+90+81+73+66+\ldots \\
&=100+(1-0.10)100+(1-0.10)^2\,100+(1-0.10)^3\,100+(1-0.10)^4\,100+\ldots \\
&=100+(1-rr)100+(1-rr)^2\,100+(1-rr)^3\,100+(1-rr)^4\,100+\ldots \\
&=100\left(\frac{1}{rr}\right)=100\left(\frac{1}{0.10}\right)=100(10)=1000.
\end{aligned}$$

The money multiplier is $1/rr$ or in this case $(1/0.10) = 10$. So ten times the initial reserves are added in demand deposits in the private bank money system. This increases the private money supply significantly, under the assumption of zero excess reserves being held.

Some banks may choose to hold more reserves than required by the Fed, and these are called the "excess reserves". As the real interest rate rises, the banks can earn more by lending out the excess reserves. In this case, the lending out of more of the excess reserves as the real interest rate rises implies that the private bank money supply is upward sloping relative to the real interest rate in the so-called money market. This gives an upward sloping supply of money that compares to the downward sloping demand for money, in the market for money.

Savings Accounts, Time Deposits, Credit Cards and Loans

Banks and other financial institutions also offer deposit accounts that are used more for longer term saving than for current exchange purposes. These are typically called *savings accounts*. Since the deposits in savings accounts typically receive some interest on the amount invested, consumers are able to earn a return on their savings in these accounts.

The interest rate on savings accounts sometimes depends on the amount of time that the deposits are held in the bank. This gives rise to another name for certain types of savings deposits as *time deposits*. Generally the longer a consumer is willing to offer savings in an account, the higher will be the interest rate that can be earned on the account.

Consumers typically do not demand back the amount held in their savings accounts every period. Rather consumers hold them for longer periods of time. This allows banks in turn to act as intermediaries and lend out the consumers' savings deposits for the purpose of investment by others. The bank then earns money on the difference between the savings deposit rate and the loan interest rate, minus their cost of supplying the *financial intermediary function.*

Banks can loan out savings deposits to investors without having to hold in reserve the entire amount of the deposits. This is because the consumers tend to keep savings deposited for longer periods of time than their current account deposits. Consumers are induced to keep savings deposited for longer periods by the interest rates offered for the savings.

Investors are induced to borrow the savings through the banks because they think they can earn more in profits than the funds cost to borrow. This creates the demand for loans that the banks intermediate. Banks provide the supply of savings from the consumers to those who want to invest in new capital. This makes the banks intermediaries between savings and investment.

Loans by banks to consumers and firms also can take the form of the issuance of a credit card for small loan amounts. Each credit card typically has some limit to the amount that can be borrowed on the card. These cards typically charge very high interest rates. They are a big source of income to banks, but an expensive way for consumers and firms to get loans.

Credit cards differ from debit cards because purchases using credit cards are not taken out of the spender's demand deposit account. Rather it is added as a debt owed by the spender, in their credit card account at the bank. The credit card involves paying interest on the expenditure unless the credit card is used like a debit card, with the debt repaid within a certain specified short period such as 30 days. Otherwise, the credit card becomes a loan from the bank on which interest must be paid to the bank.

For larger loans, consumers and firms borrow from banks or other financial intermediaries by entering into a contract for the loan. The contract specifies the term of the loan, which is how long the loan can be used before it must be repaid. And the contract specifies the interest rate charged over the term for the loan. Banks do this more on a case by case basis for large loans such as consumer cars and *house mortgages* or for large firm investments.

5.3.2 Monetary Aggregates

When banks loan out the deposits to firms or other consumers, the firms or consumers receiving the loans are given new deposits in their current accounts in the banks. The firms and other consumers that get the loans proceed to spend the money, in what they may view as an investment. This spending of the bank loans by the investors then becomes new deposits in other private banks.

Private banks *create money that enters circulation* by the act of giving new loans to customers in the form of new deposits in their accounts. This is how private bank money gets created. These deposits from new loans meet all the characteristics of money. They are demand deposits that can be used in exchange. They *enter circulation* once the bank loans in the form of new demand deposits are spent by the customers receiving the loans.

The total money supply includes both the public bank money, which are the Federal Reserve Notes in circulation (not held at the Fed) and the demand deposits at banks. These are used each period to buy goods and services. The idea of a *money aggregate* then arises as a way to count the total money supply. Perhaps the most common definition of money is the one that adds together Federal Reserve Notes in circulation and private bank demand deposits.

M1, M2, M3 and the Monetary Base

M1 is a monetary aggregate defined by the Federal Reserve System as currency in circulation plus demand deposits (plus travelers checks and other *checkable deposits*). This is probably the most used of all monetary aggregates. It can be seen to be a combination of Federal Reserve Notes, the government currency we call cash, plus the private bank demand deposits.

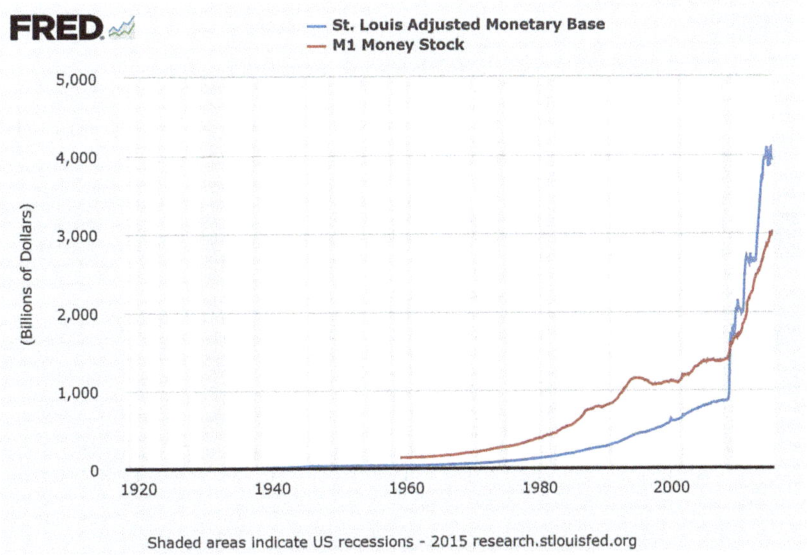

Figure 5.1 US Monetary Base (Blue) and M1 (Red)

M2 includes all of M1 plus savings and small time deposits. This is a broader monetary aggregate. It includes more *monetary instruments.*

M2 is comprised of what we think of money used in exchange, M1, plus the savings and small time deposits. It also includes *money market accounts* such as *mutual fund deposits* at investment banks.[6] These savings and time and mutual fund deposits may act as money that is used in exchange, if consumers routinely use these each month to pay for normal consumption. They may also earn interest and be used as savings that are not used up each period.

M2 combines instruments that include both exchange and savings functions. In this sense it is a broader definition of an aggregate that may include some elements of savings that typically we do not consider money. An aggregate is broader the more interest bearing instruments it includes.

In particular, other aggregates take M2 and add further savings instruments and result in even more broadly defined aggregates. M3 is equal to M2 plus large time deposits, term repurchase agreements, and large money market accounts of institutional investors.

M3 is not really viewed as money in the sense that economists use when we say that money by definition is that used in exchange. The added instruments in M3 are rarely used as a means of exchange. The savings, time deposits and certain money market account instruments of M2 may also rarely be used as a means of exchange.

The broader is the monetary aggregate definition, the more savings that is included. The narrower the monetary aggregate the more it is used for exchange for current consumption. There exists an even more narrow definition than M1.

The *Monetary Base* is the narrowest conventional monetary aggregate. It equals currency in circulation plus cash *reserves* held by private banks (at the Fed). This is meant to capture the total currency, which is the outstanding Federal Reserve Notes in the private domain. It excludes the private bank money in the form of demand deposits and other broader instruments.

The monetary base may be of interest when the focus is on currency, and government money. The base is thought of as the total liabilities of the Fed, which is also often of interest. But when the focus is on all money used in exchange, counting the private bank money is important.

Monetary Data

Figure 5.1 shows the US monetary base and M1 aggregates over time. The base data from the St. Louis Fed Bank goes back to 1918 but the M1 data only back to 1959. Historically M1 has far exceeded the monetary base, as it includes more and broader instruments, in particular the demand deposits.

---

[6]Plus overnight "repos" which are repurchase agreements with a term of one day.

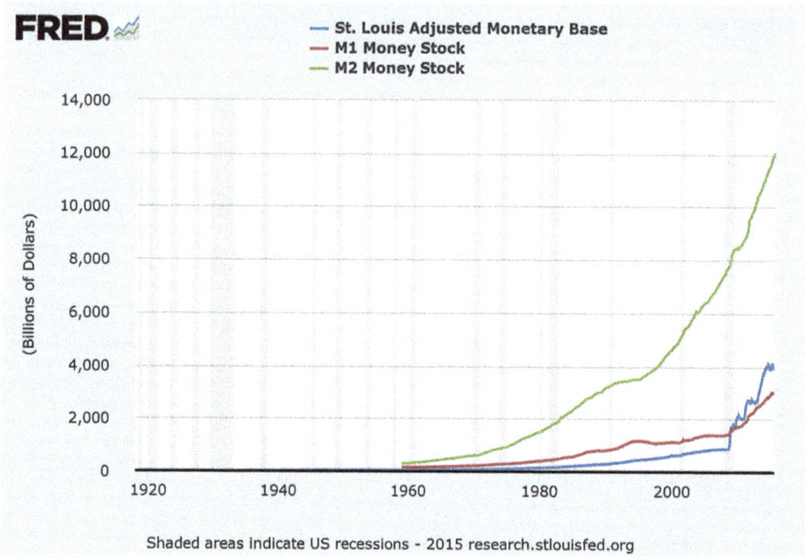

Figure 5.2 US M2, M1, and the Monetary Base

However the Great Recession of 2008 to 2010 saw the monetary base exceed the M1 aggregate for the first time in history. How could it be so? The base includes reserves of banks held at the Fed.

The reserves shot up during the huge expansion of the Fed's monetary supply during the Great Recession. These reserves are money the banks did not want to lend out. Banks did not lend them out because of increased banking restrictions and because for the first time in history the Fed began in 2008 to pay banks interest on reserves they kept at the Fed. As this interest rate paid on excess reserves in fact exceeded the interest rate the banks could earn in the short term money markets, they kept the reserves at the Fed rather than invest them.

Figure 5.2 adds M2 to the previous graph, now in green. The M2 magnitude is much bigger than M1 and the base. The graph shows that these different aggregates differ by non-trivial amounts.

The use of monetary aggregates is varied. For economists studying monetary theory, money demand estimation requires picking a monetary aggregate to use for money. Economists have used all three of the M2, M1 and base aggregates, as well as broader ones for money demand studies.

Lucas and Nicolini (2015) construct a new monetary aggregate that they call NewM1. This includes M1 plus money market deposit accounts (MMDA). MMDA are included in M2, and Lucas and Nicolini add them back to M1 to get a more inclusive measure of currency plus demand deposits. On the basis of this monetary aggregate, they argue that they can find a stable demand for money in the US from 1915 to 2012.

5.3.3 Government's Central Bank

The US Federal Reserve System is what is known as a "central bank", which is the main government bank typically responsible for creating government money and supervising the private bank sector. The US Federal Reserve System comprises a *Board of Governors* that meets in Washington DC plus 12 regional district Federal Reserve Banks. There are subregional Fed banks as well. The 12 regional Feds are more important because they help dictate the monetary policy of the Fed System through their rotating 4 seats on the Federal Open Market Committee of the Board of Governors.

The Chairman of the Board of Governors is known as the head of the US central bank. Now it is chaired by Janet Yellen, while previously it was chaired by Ben Bernanke, Alan Greenspan, Paul Volcker, George Miller and Arthur Burns. The Chair is the main spokesperson for the US on monetary policy, although the 12 regional Bank presidents often present policy discussions.

The Fed is most known for controlling the supply of Federal Reserve Notes in circulation, and in private bank reserves, this being the monetary base. The Fed most directly controls the monetary base. The Fed also conducts banking supervision.

The Fed's control of the monetary base takes place often by targeting interest rates in the capital markets. The main target interest rate traditionally has been the *Federal Funds Rate.* This is the rate paid on federal funds that are traded between banks, where the definition of federal funds are those funds held at the Fed as reserves. Since there exist reserve requirements, there is a supply and demand for federal funds that are held at the Fed as reserves.

The Fed increases the monetary base primarily by buying US Treasury bonds that are held by private financial institutions. When they buy a US bond from the private market, say from a private bank, then the private bank gives up the bond to the Fed in return for reserves being credited to it's reserve account at the Fed. This increases the monetary base by increasing reserves.

The private bank can lend out the new reserves. Then its reserves at the Fed are decreased by the loan amount and its demand deposits are increased by the same amount. If the borrower of the money then spends the new demand deposits, the deposits get transferred to another bank. It is possible that initially only the monetary base would rise, but later also demand deposits rise and so do M1 and M2.

A greater supply of money causes more capital to be supplied in markets. This initially drives down the interest rates. This is how the Fed can target a particular interest rate in the *Federal Funds market.* They can increase the federal funds by buying US bonds or decrease federal funds by selling US bonds.

Open market operations is the name given to the Fed's buying and selling of US bonds in order to change the money supply and interest rates. The open market operations of the Fed are dictated by the Board of Governors and carried out by the New York regional Fed Bank.

While the Federal Reserve System was enacted in 1913 by US Federal law, the Fed Regional Banks are chartered such that they are owned by the private sector. Nonetheless, the Fed System acts as a government entity and controls the government supplied money in the form of Federal Reserve Notes.

Other banking institutions are largely determined by market forces. These financial institutions are heavily regulated however. Federal Deposit Insurance is one feature of the private financial institutions, with all private banks receiving FDIC *deposit insurance* in return for paying a premium to the FDIC for deposits that are insured.

The FDIC insurance works like a bank insurance system. It was the key feature of the March 1933 turnaround of the Great Depression, when the FDIC deposit insurance system was begun. The deposits covered are limited in amount per account. And banks pay different premium fees per deposit covered according to the risk structure of their assets.

5.3.4 Bank Panics Leading to Fed

The US history shows a series of bank panics occurring before the Federal Reserve System was established in 1914. There were seven bank panic periods, as listed below, from 1873 until 1907. These all occurred during the gold standard.

- Panic of 1873: U.S. recession, bank failures; + 4-year depression;
- Panic of 1884: United States & Europe;
- Panic of 1890: UK & Argentina;
- Panic of 1893: U.S. recession, bank failures; Australian bank crisis;
- Panic of 1896: U.S. sharp recession;
- Panic of 1901: U.S. recession;
- Panic of 1907, U.S. recession, bank failures.

Across this pre-Fed era, Figure 5.3.4 shows that the ratio of loans to deposits by US national banks fell during each panic and resulted in a 1.8 ratio of loans to deposits in the 1870's falling steadily down to close to a 1.0 ratio by 1914. This means that less of the deposits were lent out as loans. This means that the efficacy of turning deposits into investment through loans fell steadily and significantly. This declining efficacy

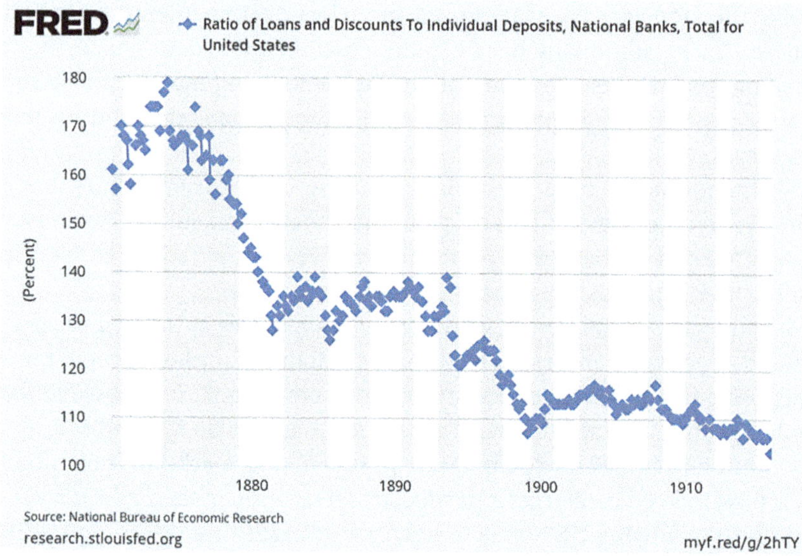

of financial intermediation by the private bank sector is why the Fed was established, albeit without FDIC deposit insurance until the Great Depression.

5.3.5 Private Banking Institutions and Markets

Banks have both assets and liabilities. Assets include loans made, since these are owed back to banks. Assets also include any other form of investment that banks make with their deposits, along with bank reserves held at the Fed.

Bank liabilities include all deposits that the banks owe to the depositors, and any other borrowing by the bank. If assets exceed liabilities, then the banks have a positive equity capital. This bank capital is known as their net worth. Assets can exceed liabilities if banks *leverage up* their liabilities by making for example more loans than they owe in deposited funds.

Banks can loan out more than their total deposits because only a fraction of deposits are demanded back by depositors at any one time. This enables the banks to incur risk by making risky loans and to earn profit by having higher lending interest rates than deposit interest rates. However if there is a sudden demand for deposits, and banks cannot *liquidate* their loans into readily available deposits, the banks can become illiquid and even insolvent.

Insolvency of banks occurs when the net worth is negative. This can happen when loans have to be called in to cover depositor demands, but then the borrowers default on the loans because they cannot repay them. Banks can become remain solvent but become illiquid if their assets still exceed their deposit liabilities, but insufficient reserves prevent banks from being able to meet the demand for deposit withdrawals.

In the case of either illiquidity or insolvency, a bank tends to stop allowing depositors to withdraw their deposits. This can lead to widespread fear of other bank illiquidity or insolvency problems. A run on the bank can ensue whereby large portions of all deposits are demanded back by depositors. This is called a bank panic. It occurred in both the Great Depression and the Great Recession to varying degrees in different countries.

Fractional Reserve Banking

When currency is deposited in the bank, the bank can lend out the currency and only keep in reserve the amount of the deposit that the bank expects to be withdrawn during any given period. This is called *fractional reserve banking* because only a fraction of bank deposits are kept in reserve and the rest are invested in loans or other assets. When loans are made from a new deposit of currency, the total sum of currency plus demand deposits expands as demand deposits across the bank system increase to some degree, up to the limit of where there are zero idle excess reserves in the system.

The leveraging up of assets relative to liabilities yields profit. It also means that the offering of new loans creates new credit for consumers and firms to use. Therefore the fractional reserve banking, which allows for a leveraging up of assets relative to liabilities, creates profit and new credit in the economy at the same time. Sometimes the new credit creation can be explosive and cause economists to research whether the economy overall is borrowing too much. This would mean that it takes on more debt, through the new credit it receives, than it may be able to repay.

Normal swings in credit happen naturally over the business cycle, but also can change unusually during crisis periods. For example, one measure of how GDP moves with respect to money and credit aggregates is called "velocity". It is defined as the ratio of GDP to the monetary aggregate. The velocity of M1 (GDP/M1) accelerated after 2004 up until the 2008 stock market crash and the Great Recession. This jump up in money velocity before 2008 may have been a warning sign of too much credit.

A crash in the value of private sector firms can occur broadly across the economy if the many assets that include loans prove to be unpayable, and so likely to default. Credit swings therefore merit attention as economists study whether large recessions or depressions may result. This was the focus of Irving Fisher's debt-deflation theory of the depressions: that too much credit can lead to a crash in the asset market values and subsequently to a bankruptcy of large segments of the financial intermediation sector.

Financial Markets and Interest Rates

The Federal Funds market is an example of a short term capital market. The supply and demand for the federal funds is based on keeping a certain desired level of reserves overnight at the Fed on any given day. The interest rate in Federal Funds tends to be lower than most other interest rates because there is little investment that can be done with Federal Funds, other than keeping reserves at the Fed.

Capital markets trade many different types of funds. The funds that tend to have the ability to be invested for longer periods tend to have higher interest rates. These longer maturity funds are less liquid by nature of the fact that they are invested for longer periods of time.

Maturity and *liquidity* tend to be inversely related. The longer the maturity of the funds, such as a 10-year US Treasury bond, the less liquid is this investment. With longer maturities, the 10-year Treasury bonds tend to have higher interest rates than the 5-year Treasury bonds.

There are markets for each maturity of US Treasury bonds, and markets for equity stocks, and markets for nearly any kind of financial capital that is easily traded. The interest rates in these markets reflect maturity structures, riskiness of the investment, and liquidity of the investment. Interest rates in each market typically affect interest rates across all of the markets.

For example, a *term structure inversion* occurs when the interest rates on a longer term security such as a 10 year Treasury bond fall below the interest rate of a shorter maturity similar security such as the 1-year Treasury bond. This is unusual but it can happen for example when the demand for 10-year Treasury bonds becomes high enough relative to supply that its interest rate gets pushed down below that of the 1-year bond's level. This inversion of the typical term structure occurred in the years following the Great Recession as the Fed began buying long term Treasury debt in addition to the short term Treasury debt that it usually buys in *open market operations* that are used to increase the monetary base.

Financial analysts focus on a host of features regarding asset prices such as stock prices. Stocks have a dividend payment stream that implies a certain yield on the capital invested while buying the stock. The dividend yield on capital in stock markets is similar to an interest rate for lending money: both give a certain percentage return on the investment. Positive "*capital gains*" occur when the stock is sold at a higher price than was paid when the stock was bought. Positive capital gains increase the effective yield, adding onto the dividend yield for the period the stock was held.

Another financial analyst focus is how a particular industry performs relative to the business cycle. If an industry does well in a recession and poorly in an expansion, then it is a called a *countercyclic industry*. Its stock value will move with a negative correlation compared to the overall market. This gives countercyclic stocks an advantage in smoothing consumption across time, in that there is a demand for them based on offsetting declines in the general stock market during a recession.

Analysts compute so-called "beta-values" that indicate how a particular stock performs relative to the market. Different beta values of stocks, and a mix of stock and bonds, allows for a market portfolio of stocks and bonds to be diversified so that its risk is smoothed out to some degree across expansions and recessions.

5.4 Theory

The US supply of money is provided by the government Federal Reserve Notes and by the private bank system's demand deposits. The theory of money and banking starts with the demand for the money used in exchange. The supply and demand for *real money* give the equilibrium quantity of money and its relative price.

5.4.1 Demand for Real Money

The consumer demands money in order to buy goods and services used for consumption. Firms also demand money to buy items used for investment. Typically the demand for money focuses on the consumer side, but sometimes includes investment sources of money demand.

The quantity of real money being demanded is a real quantity, as in microeconomics. This is because the consumption goods and services being bought are real quantities. Inflation causes the real value of money to depreciate, such that the same amount of nominal dollars of currency cannot buy the same amount of goods after a year of say 5% inflation. As the aggregate price level rises at an accelerated rate, the inflation rate rises and the real money stock buys a lesser amount of goods. This causes real money demand to fall.

Consider first how to compute an empirical measure of the real value of money. Take the nominal stock of a given monetary aggregate and divide by the nominal price of goods, which means dividing by an aggregate price index such as the CPI. If we divide the money stock by the price level, we get the real amount of goods that nominal money is able to buy. This nominal money stock divided by the price level is how the real money supply is defined, since it has been adjusted for inflation that changes the nominal price of goods.

A certain quantity of real money is what consumers need to purchase goods. If goods could be bought without having to exchange for them, there would be no exchange-based demand for money. Money would only be held as an asset that depreciates due to inflation, but this is not the case.

Since money is required for exchange of goods, the demand for consumption goods in large part determines the demand for real money. The close relation between the demand for output and the demand for real money can be seen in Figure 5.3. This graphs the annual percentage change in real M1 money demand (blue), with

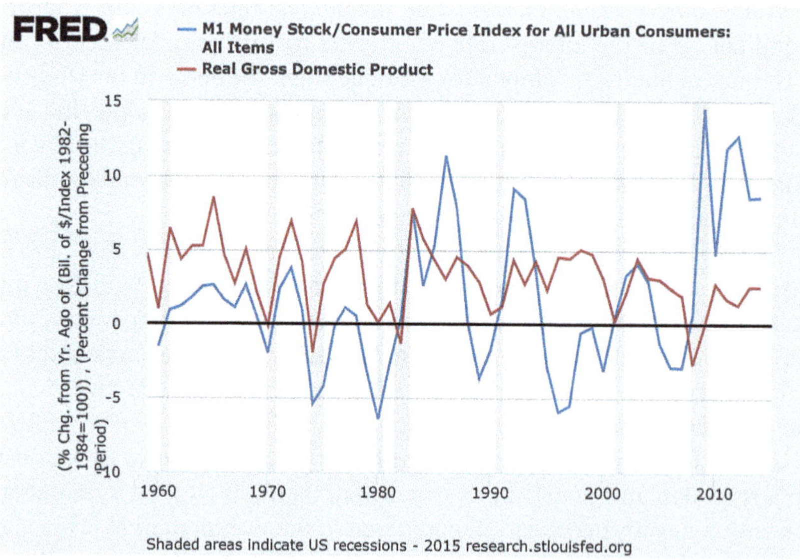

Figure 5.3 Growth Rate of Real M1 Varies with Real GDP Growth, 1979–2013

real money defined as M1 divided by the CPI price index. And the figure graphs (in red) the annual percentage change in real GDP for comparison.

Real M1 and real GDP are fairly closely correlated over the business cycles. This reflects that real money demand rises and falls with income. The first part of the theory of money demand is that its demand follows the level of real income, which is equivalent to real output. Or it can be stated that real money demand follows to a strong degree the demand for real consumption.

When real M1 and real GDP diverge, it is typically because the cost of money, which is mainly the inflation rate, has varied significantly. When real money demand change does not perfectly correlate with real output change, the next focus turns to the relative price of real money. From microeconomics, we find that the demand for any good depends on real income, or real output, and secondly upon the relative price of the good being demanded. Also the relative price of either *substitute* goods or *complement* goods may also be a factor in demand. For real money, the inflation rate is the main component of the relative price of holding real money; higher inflation makes holding money more costly in that it devalues at a faster rate.

Quantity Theory of Real Money Demand

Perhaps the best known theory of real money demand was advocated by Irving Fisher in his 1911 (1st edition) book, the *Purchasing Power of Money.*[7] Here Fisher introduces the *equation of exchange*. This equation is an accounting identity for money and prices and purchases. He then turns this exchange identity into a theory of money demand called the *quantity theory of money*, which itself has several interpretations that are discussed below.

To present this simple equation of exchange, denote the nominal monetary aggregate by M, the aggregate price level by P, the real output by y, and introduce a new term called the income velocity of money that is denoted by V. Here V is defined identically as either the nominal output divided by the nominal money stock, or as the real output divided by the real money stock.

The equation is written as

$$MV = Py. \tag{5.1}$$

And so velocity V is defined as either Py / M, which is in nominal terms, or identically as $y/(M/P)$, which is in real terms. It tells us how many times the money stock circulates in order to pay for the output. Velocity is generally found to always be larger than one.

The equation of exchange can be viewed as a simple accounting of how many times the money stock "circulates" among buyers in order to purchase the aggregate output. As an identity, it is not controversial that velocity can be defined in this fashion. By solving for real money from the equation, a theory of money demand emerges.

Since M/P is how we define real money demand, as the nominal stock of money divided by a measure of the aggregate price level, then the equation of exchange implies that real money equals the inverse of velocity, $1/V$, multiplied by the real output y. Or, dividing equation (5.1) by P and by V, it results that

$$M/P = (1/V) \cdot y.$$

The real money demand from the equation of exchange implies that real money and real output move exactly together if the velocity of money stays the same. Fisher argued that velocity in the early 1900's was stable, so that this is a good way to think of real money demand. The income effect implies that real money changes proportionally with income, and this is verified in much empirical work on real money demand.

Keynes (1923) however suggested that i) velocity changes at times, ii) the changes in velocity represent behavioral changes that are predictable and iii) velocity rises when the nominal interest rate rises since this is the opportunity cost of holding money in order to use it in exchange.

[7] 2nd edition was 1922; see http://www.policonomics.com/wp-content/uploads/The-Purchasing-Power-of-Money.pdf

The idea is that velocity changes when the relative price of money changes. In particular, the relative price of money is viewed as the interest that could have been earned if the money was put in an interest-earning bank account, instead of being held during the period in order to make exchanges for consumption goods. The higher is the interest rate, the less real money the consumer will demand; the consumer will "economize" on holding excess money balances and keep as much as possible in the bank earning interest. The interest rate represents the *opportunity cost* of holding money.

The nominal interest rate tends to equal the inflation rate plus some real rate of interest. This is called the *Fisher equation of interest rates*. This means that increases in the inflation rate increase the nominal interest rate. In turn, a higher nominal interest causes a lower demand for real money. Since velocity is defined as $y/(M/P)$, velocity rises as real money demand falls. So velocity rises and falls as the inflation rate and nominal interest rise and fall, while real money demand falls when the inflation rate and the nominal interest rate rise. Real money demand moves in the opposite direction as its velocity of circulation when the interest rate changes.

Cagan Money Demand

Cagan's (1956) money demand function still is a benchmark for a stable money demand that is used today. It graphs the nominal interest rate, denoted by R, on the vertical axis and the real money demand M/P on the horizontal axis. His money demand is well-defined at $R = 0$, which we consider to be a possible, and typically, the lowest level of nominal interest rates (although negative rates are possible).

Cagan's finds a stable money demand during post-WWI and post-WWII across a wide set of countries that experienced *hyperinflation*. Hyperinflation is defined by a very high rate of inflation, typically more than 50% (at an annual rate). It would appear very difficult to find a stable demand for real money demand during a highly disruptive period such as a hyperinflation, but Cagan managed it.

Cagan is consistent with the format of the quantity theory with $M/P = (1/V)y$, with the focus being on explaining the inflation sensitive term $(1/V)$. Cagan specifies a functional form of how changes in the inflation rate (during hyperinflation the real interest rate is negligible) affect real money demand. Figure 5.4.1 graphs an example of Cagan's money demand function with M/P on the horizontal axis, and R on the vertical axis as the relative price of real money. This type of function has been used to explain money demand internationally and for the US during normal inflation times as well as during extreme hyperinflation periods.[8]

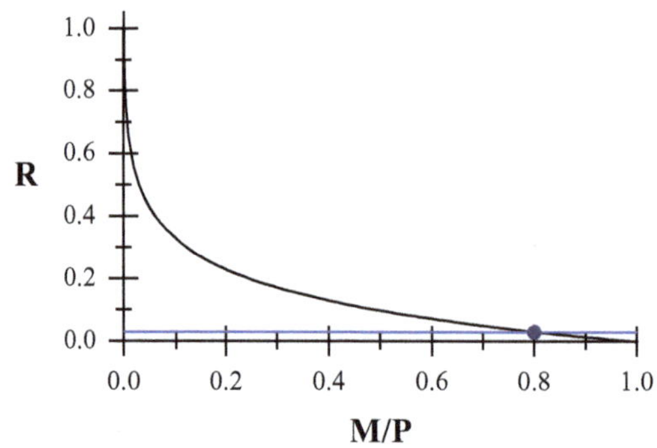

Example of Cagan's (1956) Money Demand Function

As the nominal interest rate rises, real money demand falls. As income rises, the money demand is shifted out to the right. By the Fisher equation of interest rates, with a zero inflation rate, the nominal interest rate R would equal the real interest rate r. Assuming zero inflation and a real interest rate of 3%, or 0.03, the

[8]See Cagan-type stable money demand functions estimated in R.E.Lucas, Jr. (2000) "Inflation and Welfare", *Econometrica*; Nelson C. Mark & Donggyu Sul, 2003. "Cointegration Vector Estimation by Panel DOLS and Long-run Money Demand," *Oxford Bulletin of Economics and Statistics*; Lucas, Robert E. & Nicolini, Juan Pablo, 2015. "On the stability of money demand," *Journal of Monetary Economics*.

Figure 5.4.1 show the equilibrium money demand where the low 3% nominal interest rate intersects the money demand function; here $M/P = 0.8$.

Interest Rates, Money Demand and Velocity

With real money depending on the real interest rate added together with the inflation rate, changes in real money demand react according to the nominal rate. These changes are slight with respect to the real interest rate usually, since it varies only modestly over the business cycle. However inflation can go through long swings upward or even downward, due usually to crisis situations in the economy.

In the 1970's US inflation gradually trended upwards until it reached above 10% in 1980. Nominal interest rates followed the inflation rate, albeit somewhat imperfectly. Theory would predict that real money demand should fall during this inflation rate increase and that velocity should rise.

Figure 5.4 shows the US experience with the 3-Month US Treasury bill (Red). This is called a bill because US debt of less than a year maturity is called a bill, while US Treasury debt with maturities of one year or longer are called US Treasury bonds. This "T-bill" rate, as it is called, is graphed using post-1957 US data from FRED.

Figure 5.4 graphs (in Green) the US inflation rate as defined as the rate of change in the CPI index, since 1929. It is clear that post-1957 the T-bill rate and the inflation rate moved closely together. Figure 5.4 further graphs (in Blue) velocity of currency. Any money aggregate can be chosen with respect to graphing velocity. The velocity perhaps most responsive to interest rate changes is the velocity of currency, which is chosen here.

Figure 5.4 shows evidence of how velocity since 1929 has moved broadly in line with the T-bill rate, moving up and down as the US inflation rose and fell in the 1970's and 1980's. This is why estimating a stable money demand function for the US is possible. Velocity moves in tandem with the inflation rate and nominal interest rate in the way predicted by real money demand theory.

The reason the US Treasury bill rate does not always exceed the inflation rate is that sometimes the increase in inflation is unexpected. This gives rise to an after-the-fact, or *ex-post* rate of real interest that can be negative if it does not cover the actual inflation that occurred during the period. When the inflation rate is highly variable, it becomes hard to predict the inflation rate and this creates uncertainty in financial markets. Financial markets are concerned with the real interest rate, and inflation variability can make this determination of the real rate, *a priori*, before-the-fact, difficult.

Figure 5.4 shows one other graph. The blue line shows the output velocity of currency. Any money aggregate can be chosen with respect to graphing its velocity. The one velocity perhaps most responsive to interest rate changes is the velocity of currency.

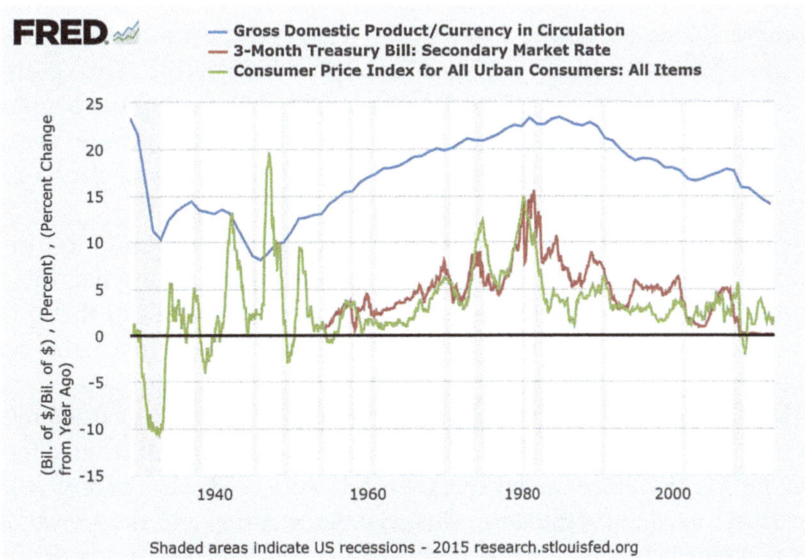

Figure 5.4 US T-Bill Interest Rt.(Red), *GDP*/($Currency) [Blue], Inflation Rt. (Green); 1929 to 2014

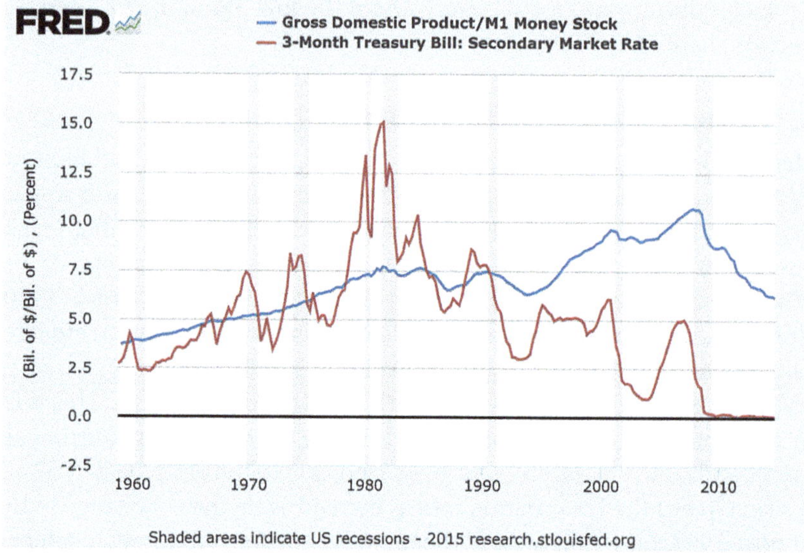

Figure 5.5 US 1959 to 2014: 3-Month Treasury Bill Market Interest Rate (Red) and the (Blue) ratio of *GDP* to the M1 Money Stock (Currency plus Demand Deposits)

Private Bank Money and Financial Deregulation

If we include private bank deposits that earn zero or a very low interest rate by using the M1 aggregate instead of just the currency stock, we get some similar empirical results for the relation between the changes in the velocity of money and the changes in the nominal interest rate. But there is also a big difference. Figure 5.5 graphs the US M1 velocity of money since 1959 in blue and the US 3-Month Treasury bill rate in red.

The difference between Figures 5.4 and 5.5 is that M1 velocity jumped up after 1990 even as the interest rate was falling, while the Currency velocity falls as the interest rate starts falling. Real money demand theory that includes only the relative price of money itself, the nominal interest rate, but not the price of substitutes to money, cannot easily explain these differences.

The answer to this puzzle that many economists have focused on, how interest rates and M1 money velocity did not comove as closely starting around 1980 relative to their historical pattern, is that private bank money that earned interest suddenly emerged in the post-1980 period. This resulted from the major US governmental financial deregulation of the finance sector that created the beginning of non-FDIC insured, interest-earning, "money market funds" at investment banks. These were "checkable" in that they could be withdrawn simply by writing a check, and so they acted like private bank money that could be used for exchange.

Financial deregulation decreased the cost to banks in taking in deposits and in turn in making loans. A low cost substitute, to holding currency and non-interest bearing demand deposits for exchange, was to hold money market funds that bore some interest. Microeconomics tells us that if the price of a close substitute goes down then the demand for the good will also shift down. Financial deregulation is known to have decreased banking costs in general and the emergence of money market funds caused a rapid substitution from demand deposits to money market ("mutual") funds. This caused the velocity of M1 to keep rising even as interest rates fell post-1980: money market funds were substituted for demand deposits, making the demand for M1 fall. Since money market funds were counted as part of M2 but not M1, there was substitution from M1 to M2 in response to financial deregulation and the arrival of interest-earning, "checkable", money market funds.

In a different approach to explaining a stable US real money demand, without recourse to bringing in the cost of substitutes, Nicolini and Lucas (2015) simply devise a new aggregate composed of M1 plus money market funds (which is part of M2). With this "NewM1" aggregate, they find a stable US money demand for periods including during the financial deregulation era of the 1980's.[9]

5.4.2 Money, Quantity Theory & Inflation

The cause of inflation has historically been shown to be strongly correlated with the money supply growth rate. Further research shows strong findings of causation of inflation coming from the money supply growth rate. The money supply growth rate and the inflation rate are strongly positively correlated over time and the causation appears to run from money to inflation.

The theory of money supply growth causing inflation goes all the way back to Irving Fisher's accounting identity in his equation of exchange, $MV = Py$. If velocity of money is stable, along with output being stable, then an increase in the money supply causes the same proportional increase in the aggregate price level. Therefore the quantity theory of money is also interpreted, besides being a theory of real money demand, to be a theory that implies that the growth rate of of the money supply causes a similar growth rate in the aggregate price level. And since the growth rate in the price level is how we define the inflation rate, this means that the quantity theory also implies that the money supply growth rate implies the inflation rate. If the money supply growth rate rises, then so should the inflation rate. This shows the basic money to inflation concept.

For example, the US budget deficit can be financed in part every year by government taxes, new borrowing, and by new money creation by the Federal Reserve Banks. This happens when the US Treasury borrows money to cover the deficit by selling the new bond issues to the Fed rather than to the public. The government (the Fed) is printing new money that the government (the Treasury) uses to pay for expenditures. This money printing fills the government budget gap between expenditures made and tax revenue collected plus new government borrowing. In this way, the money supply growth rate turns into a certain inflation rate, which acts as a tax on the holdings of money.

Money Supply Growth and Revenue for Deficit Spending

Supply and demand analysis predicts that the US is printing money every year to cover deficit spending. For example with a 2% inflation target, as is used now in the US and across many countries in the world, the money supply growth must exceed the money demand growth by 2% each year in order to cause aggregate prices to rise by 2% a year. This money growth means that the US government is printing new money and using it to finance deficit spending.

Consider further the main reason that money demand grows every year. It is needed to buy output. If output growth, say, averages 3%, then the US can increase the money supply by 3% a year and still cause zero inflation. This is because with money demand growing at 3% along with money supply growing at 3%, there is an equality between the growth in supply and demand such that prices would remain stable. Keeping the inflation rate at 0% and printing money at the rate of growth of the economy is called *natural seigniorage*. This is defined as the revenue from printing enough money to satisfy the real growth of the economy while keeping prices stable. This natural seigniorage rate in this example is 3% that the government can "earn" for producing a stable means of exchange that does not change in value: real money. Real money has zero depreciation if the inflation rate is zero.

An inflation rate of 2% in an economy growing by 3% results from a money supply growth rate of some 5% a year. This is a higher inflation than the natural seigniorage rate. The government then can use this 5% money growth to finance a small but significant portion of its budget deficit.

The government revenue from printing new money is often called seigniorage, or simply, the inflation tax. This source of revenue indeed acts as a tax, on real money holdings, which lends credence to the inflation tax nomenclature. The difference of the inflation tax from a normally collected tax is how the inflation tax is collected.

---

[9]Lucas, Robert E. & Nicolini, Juan Pablo, 2015. "On the stability of money demand," Journal of Monetary Economics, 73(C): 48–65.

The Inflation Tax

A normal tax is collected by the government levying a certain tax rate on sales of goods and services and on earned income, both personal and corporate. The government taxes both sides of the national income and product accounts ledger with explicitly known taxes. However the inflation tax is collected only as the money supply is increased. The government collects the inflation tax as soon as the Fed gives it fresh money to use to buy goods and services during the federal government expenditure process.

The inflation tax is collected as soon as the government spends the newly printed money that it gets by selling US Treasury bonds or bills to the Fed. The government gets the goods and services it wants with the fresh money. This is the inflation tax collection process.

Less clear is how the tax becomes imposed upon the economy. It is imposed only once the general price level rises at a certain higher rate than it did before. This does not happen from one-time increases in the money supply. Because a one-time money supply increase causes the price level to rise just once (albeit over time). But the general inflation rate will not increase once the one time price level change takes place.

Rather than from a one-time money supply increase, the inflation rate rises in a prolonged fashion only when an increase in rate of growth of the money supply growth occurs. This causes a prolonged increase in revenue to finance the budget deficit. And the higher inflation rate in turn causes a higher rate of indirect taxation on the value of real money. Put differently, the inflation tax is imposed upon the economy when consumers and firms find that their money purchases less goods and services.

The implicit taxation causes depreciation in the value of money that is imposed upon them by the government. This is the result of the inflation tax. Since the depreciated value is often hard to judge at the time it is occurring, the inflation tax is much more difficult to understand than explicit taxation.

Private bank money creation tends to be cyclical, or to move in a procyclic fashion. It does not typically trend upwards or downwards and so cause inflation or deflation. During crisis periods, the crash of private sector bank deposits can cause significant deflation. In a credit boom, the expansion of deposits can contribute to inflation. This boom of deposits typically results from lending out reserves at a higher rate, causing a higher loan to deposit ratio in booms and a lower such ratio in recessions.

Other than for limited periods during severe contractions or expansions of private sector deposits, or during one-off financial deregulation or re-regulation, the private bank money does not appear to affect inflation in terms of its trend over time. Rather it is the government use of new money creation to finance expenditure that is attributed to the cause of any given trend in the inflation rate. It is in fact the trend inflation rate that the government uses for its target of monetary policy.

5.4.3 Inflation Targeting as Fed Policy

Changing the inflation rate in order to raise taxes temporarily, through money supply printing at an accelerated rate, has come to be seen as a less desirable way to conduct monetary-fiscal policy. Lucas and Stokey (1983) showed how optimal fiscal policy can include the inflation tax as an aspect of fiscal theory, which analyzes how to raise the taxes necessary to finance government expenditure. Lucas and Stokey show how a "smooth" or constant inflation rate is the best policy, as a sub-set of the idea that smooth tax rates generally are the best types of policy for a nation.[10]

Inflation targeting is now conducted in nations across the globe. Some countries have specific inflation targets written into their law, such as New Zealand since 1989.[11] Some have a joint agreement between the executive branch of the government and the central bank to agree on an inflation target, such as Canada. And some countries set an inflation target explicitly such as the UK.

[10] Lucas, Robert E., Jr., and Nancy Stokey, 1983, "Optimal fiscal and monetary policy in an economy without capital," Journal of Monetary Economics, 12(1): 55–93.

[11] "With the passage of the Reserve Bank of New Zealand Act in 1989, New Zealand became the first country to formally embark upon inflation targeting", according to Reserve Bank of New Zealand's official website: http://www.rbnz.govt.nz/research-and-publications/speeches/2006/speech2006-01-18

The United States reportedly does not have an explicit inflation target, but the Fed generally states that its target is a 2% inflation rate. In contrast, by US law in the 1978 Amendments to the 1946 Employment Act, the US is supposed to have a zero inflation rate from 1988 onwards. Surprisingly this law is largely ignored. One reason may be that the 1978 Act provides an escape clause. It says the Fed should achieve zero inflation from 1988 onwards, unless this "conflicts with other goals". To permanently avoid 0 % and instead state 2% as it's target, suggests that the Fed is playing loose with the statutory zero inflation target as set in the 1978 US law.[12]

Many have long argued for price stability, which we would now consider a zero inflation rate target. Irving Fisher was reputed to have first proposed price stability in his 1911 book *The Purchasing Power of Money.* It has even been said that as a result of Fisher's proposal a price level target was put in the US Senate's version of the Federal Reserve authorization act in 1913, but that this clause got dropped in the House version and final bill. As a result, many attribute Fisher's 1920 book *Stabilizing the Dollar* as the place when Fisher first proposed price stability. But it has been convincingly argued by R. Dimand, that this 1920 book was simply a more comprehensive statement of the idea.[13]

Today zero inflation and price stability continue to be promulgated. Orphanides (2014) concludes that

> "The Fed needs a clearer mandate for its second hundred years. What is required is an Act of Congress to make price stability the primary objective of the Federal Reserve."

He suggests that the trade-off, with trying to target some unemployment objective while also targeting price stability, "risks compromising price stability". The current large build-up of excess reserves being held at the Fed provides a realistic warning that echoes Orphanides concern and could be viewed as providing support for a firmer US legal stance on what should be the targeted inflation rate in practice.[14]

5.4.4 The Taylor Rule

Taylor (1993) offered a different view relative to the Fisher equation of interest rates, whereby the nominal rate of interest equals the inflation rate plus the real interest rate. Taylor instead proposed that the market interest rate is determined by a combination of the inflation rate and the economy's output growth rate. The Taylor equation has become a "rule" suggested for use by central banks in the efforts to target a specific inflation rate in a stable fashion.[15]

---

[12]Officially, the Fed target is by 1978 law set at zero, although this is ignored by Fed officials; "In 1978, Congress passed the Full Employment and Balanced Growth Act, better known as the Humphrey-Hawkins Act, which amended the Employment Act of 1946 and was signed into law by President Carter. The Humphrey-Hawkins Act specified explicit unemployment and inflation goals. Within five years, unemployment should not exceed 3 percent for people 20 years or older, and inflation should be reduced to 3 percent or less, provided that its reduction would not interfere with the employment goal. And by 1988, the inflation rate should be zero, again provided that pursuing this goal would not interfere with the employment goal." From the Fed's website at http://www.federalreservehistory.org/Events/DetailView/15

[13]Dimand writes that 'Recent literature on the origins of the Federal Reserve System largely ignores Fisher's 1911 proposal of a price level rule and does not mention that Senator Owen managed to insert such a mandate to target the price level in the Senate version of the Owen-Glass Bill that became the Federal Reserve Act, only to have Representative Carter Glass persuade the House of Representatives to strike it out (see Owen 1919, Fisher 1934). R. H. Timberlake (1993, p. 407) firmly declares that "The first comprehensive proposal for a stable price level policy was made by Irving Fisher in his book Stabilizing the Dollar, published in 1920," and Alan Meltzer (2003), who pays careful attention to discussions in the 1920s about Fisher's compensated dollar plan, also insists that it originated in Fisher (1920), seven years after the passage of the Federal Reserve Act. But Stabilizing the Dollar (1920) was only Fisher's first complete book on his plan, which had already been the subject of the concluding chapter of The Purchasing Power of Money (1911a) and of many journal articles (one reprinted from the March 1913 American Economic Review Supplement as an appendix to the 1913 second edition, pp. 494–502). Similarly, although the economic ideas of Carter Glass have often been minutely examined, Senator Robert L. Owen has largely vanished from the history of the creation of the Federal Reserve apart from the name of the Owen-Glass (or Glass-Owen) Bill.' See: Robert W. Dimandi, "One Hundred Years from Today", manuscript, Department of Economics, Brock University, St. Catharines, Ontario L2S 3A1, Canada; online at https://hope.econ.duke.edu/sites/hope.econ.duke.edu/files/FisherPPM100.pdf

[14]Orphanides, Athanasios, 2014, "The Need for a Price Stability Mandate", Cato Journal, 34(2, Spring/Summer): 265–279.

[15]Taylor, John B. (1993). "Discretion versus Policy Rules in Practice". Carnegie-Rochester Conference Series on Public Policy 39: 195–214.

The difference from the Fisher rule is that the Taylor rule suggests that an increase in the inflation rate causes a even larger increase in the nominal interest rate, while the Fisher rule says the increase is a one-to-one relation between the inflation rate and the nominal interest rate. The consensus view is that both the Fisher equation and the Taylor rule may be correct, with the Fisher relation holding in the "long run", and the Taylor rule being a description of the economy's dynamic path during the business cycle.

Thousands of estimations have been made of the Taylor rule, for different countries and using different variables other than the output growth rate, along with the inflation rate. There is no consensus on how well the Taylor rule is a description of the actual market economy, or of whether central banks such as the Federal Reserve System actually use any type of Taylor rule in making monetary policy. The idea of the Taylor rule as a central bank behavioral equation is strengthened by the fact that the US 1946 Employment Act as amended in 1978 does require the Federal Reserve to consider inflation, employment and the economy's growth rate, in its conduct of monetary policy.

5.4.5 Liquidity Effect of Money on Interest Rates

Money injections into the capital market can temporarily cause an increase in the capital supply and a decrease in the nominal interest rate. After that the market interest rate tends to rise back up and can rise even higher if the money supply increase is part of a sustained increase in the money supply growth rate that causes a higher inflation rate and higher velocity. This is an old idea going back to Ricardo and Wicksell. Consider Knut Wicksell's (1936) version of this in the introduction to his famous *Interest and Prices,* translated by Frank Kahn (italics in original):[16]

> "An excess of money will, according to Ricardo, show itself in two ways - partly through a rise in all prices, partly through a fall in the rate of interest. But the latter, Ricardo emphasizes, can only be a *temporary* phenomenon, for as soon as prices have accommodated themselves to the increased quantity of money, the excess of money no longer exists and the rate of interest must return, other things being equal, to its former level. To bring about a fall in the rate of interest that is in any way *permanent*, the excess of money would have to be constantly renewed and the relative amount of money would have to be continually increasing. Such a result would, therefore, be feasible only with commodity prices constantly rising. This proposition should be capable of general application. Indeed, in the developed credit economy of today it can claim an enhanced significance: for not only does an addition to the amount of material money act as a *cause* of easier credit but an increase (actual or virtual) in the velocity of circulation comes about as an *effect.*"

Wicksell completely states the classical theory of the liquidity effect of money supply increases on the nominal interest rate. This allows him to focus on what is the equilibrium rate of interest in the capital market when no such liquidity infusions from money supply increases are taking place. And from this comes his famous "natural rate" of interest:

> "The rate of interest charged for loans can clearly never be either high or low in itself, but only in relation to the return which can, or is expected to, be obtained by the man who has possession of money. It is not a high or low rate of interest in the absolute sense which must be regarded as influencing the demand for raw materials, labour, and land or other productive resources, and so indirectly as determining the movement of prices. The causative factor is the current rate of interest on loans as compared with what I shall be calling the natural rate of interest on capital. **This natural rate is roughly the same thing as the real interest of actual business. A more accurate, though rather abstract, criterion is obtained by thinking of it as the rate which would be determined by supply and demand if real capital were lent in kind without the intervention of money.**"

Without the intervention of increasing or decreasing the money supply growth rate, and with a zero inflation rate as held approximately under the gold standard when Wicksell wrote, the real interest of

[16]Knut Wicksell, 1936, *Interest and Prices: A Study of the Causes Regulating the Value of Money*, translated from German by R. F. Kahn, published on behalf of the Royal Economic Society, Macmillan and Company, Ltd., St. Martin's Street, London.}

actual business means the real rate of interest that we use as the standard interest rate in a non-monetary economy. With zero inflation, this real interest rate is also the market interest rate , which is the nominal rate of interest. This real rate does not suffer from liquidity effects if the capital market is not subject to temporary infusions of money that cause temporary liquidity effects. Thus the Wickellian view of the world is to consider both monetary factors that temporarily effect interest rates, but also to focus on the capital market when undisturbed, with a "natural rate" of interest prevailing. "Natural" simply means without the liquidity effect of money injections!

5.4.6 Liquidity Effects and Crisis Policy

The economy knows for certain the money supply growth only after the data is published. This makes it hard to predict the inflation rate, which the economy also only knows once the data on the price indices is published. When there is a war, such as WWI, WWII, the Korean War in the early 1950s, and the Vietnam war in the mid 1960's to the mid 1970's, both the money supply growth rate and the inflation rate in the US accelerated.

Acceleration or deceleration in the inflation rate makes it hard to judge the real interest rate that will prevail over the period. In a business cycle, investment demand increases significantly in the expansion and tends to put increasing pressure on the real interest rate. In the contractions, the normal real interest rate falls. But inflation uncertainty can affect the real interest rate because the market may not know if the money supply and/or inflation increase is temporary or permanent.

The immediate drop in the nominal and or real interest rate due to an increase in money supply growth is known as the *liquidity effect on interest rates.* The real interest rate falls at first, as more money hits capital markets. But once the more money is linked to higher inflation, the nominal interest rate rises to reflect that higher inflation rate.

Economic activity can initially be stimulated by the liquidity effect and the lowering of real interest rates. But then economic growth tends to fall once the inflation rate rises since it is a tax. Stimulation by suddenly increasing the money supply growth rate is an option of monetary policymakers such as the Fed. But the future cost of a higher inflation tax always then looms as a consequence.

The still recent extreme growth in the money supply that occurred since the 2008 stock market crash is due to the Fed printing much more money, rather than the private banks making much more loans. This increase in the money supply growth rate has apparently not yet led to higher trend inflation, while it has coincided with a decrease in the real interest rate to low or negative levels as consistent with a liquidity effect. In part economists attribute the lack of ensuing inflation to the fact that since 2008 the Fed pays above market rates on excess private bank reserves that are held at the Fed. This means that excess reserves are being held at the Fed at extreme levels rather than being lent out. For all time before 2008, excess reserves were approximately zero, according to FRED data.

5.5 Application: Ex Post Real Interest Rates

While ex ante few people would agree in normal times to lend their savings at a negative real interest rate, ex post once the actual inflation rate is known it can be seen that certain real interest rates often have been negative historically in the US. The only clear exception to avoiding negative real interest rates may be during times of widespread international bank failure during which safe banks may in effect be paid to borrow money in order to keep the money safe. Some view both the rise in the US dollar exchange rate since the 2008 to 2010 crisis as related to such *safe haven theories*, as well as the recent years of negative real interest rates after the 2008 US bank panic that spread internationally.[17]

Consider how often certain ex post real rates have been negative. The *secondary market* for US Treasury 3-Month bills (T-bills) is where people buy and sell these bills amongst themselves. The primary market is

[17] For example, the UK saw a run on its retail bank Northern Rock in the summer of 2008, with customers lined down the street walkways waiting to withdraw their deposits.

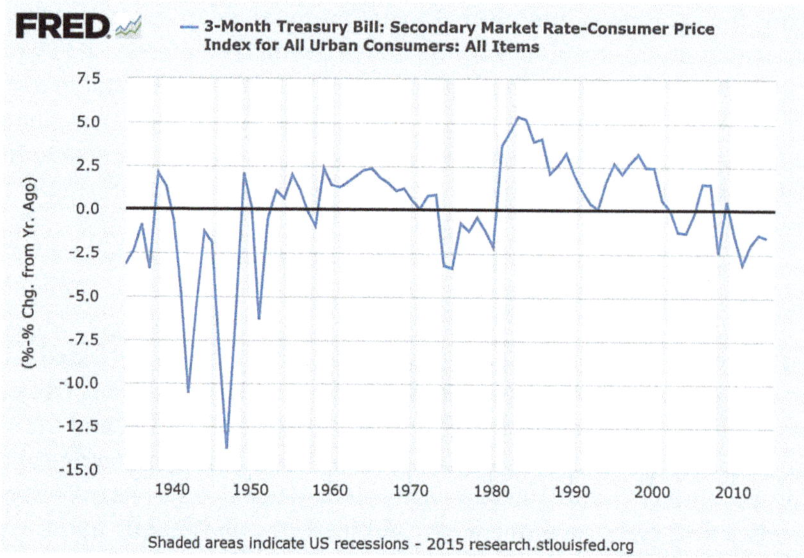

Figure 5.6 Real Interest Rate: Government 3-Month Bill Interest Rate Minus the CPI Inflation Rate, US 1934–2014

where the government buys and sells bills and bonds with certain select banks and large traders in the private sector. The ex post real yield of the 3-Month T-bills is the (ex post, or end-of-period) real interest rate as computed by subtracting the reported inflation rate from the market interest rate.[18]

Figure 5.6 shows the real yield of US 3-Month T-bills since 1934 using the rate of change in the CPI index to measure inflation. It shows very negative real rates in *WWII*, modest real rates of around 2% in the early 1960's, negative real rates in the late 1960s and 1970s, and high real rates in the early 1980s during the a significant US deceleration of the inflation rate. With stable 2.5% rates in the 1990s, during the high US growth period, real rates turn negative again in the early 2000's and during the Great Recession and after it. It may be surprising how often these real rates have been negative historically. For sustained investment growth, these rates should be positive, for example as during the 1990's.

A riskier market interest rate than the US T-bill rate is the private sector's corporate bond rate, the rates at which private corporations borrow money. For high rated firms, with a low risk of default, there is a *AAA* rating, as determined by private bond rating companies such as Moody. The Moody *AAA* bond rate shows the interest rate on debt for the safest companies, but the rate still carries default risk and is higher generally than T-bill rates. However the *AAA* real yield tends to be higher correlated with the US Treasury yield.

Figure 5.7 shows Moody *AAA* rate minus the *CPI* inflation rate, going back to 1918. The *AAA* real interest rate was very high in the Great Depression, when there was high unexpected deflation, and as with the real T-bill rate, it was also high in the early 1980s during that US deceleration of the inflation rate. In the high-growth 1990s, the *AAA* real rate was stable at 5%, well above the real T-Bill rate. For the post 1934 period during which they overlap, the real *AAA* graph resembles a shifting up of the US Treasury real yield graph.

Figures 5.6 and 5.7 indicate that negative real interest rates are not uncommon but tend to be the exception rather than the rule. Periods of negative rates tend to coincide with times of accelerating or decelerating money supply growth rates and inflation rates. Liquidity effects from flooding capital markets with money supply do seem to occur either temporarily or sometimes in a more permanent way as in the post-2008 period for T-bills, and in a way similar to Wicksell's 1936 description.

[18]The Fisher equation implies that the nominal interest rate R equals the real rate r plus the expected inflation rate; the real rate is often computed using the actual inflation rate.

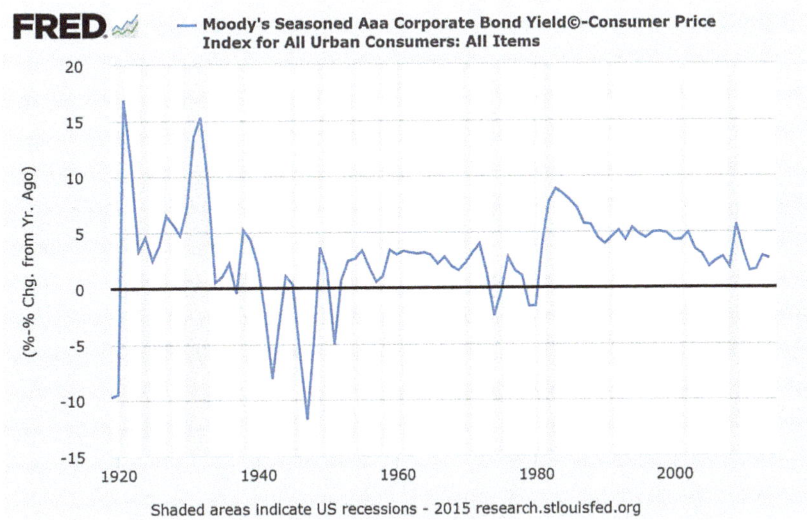

Figure 5.7 Real Interest Rate: Moody's *AAA* Corporate Interest Rate Minus the CPI Inflation Rate, US 1919–2014

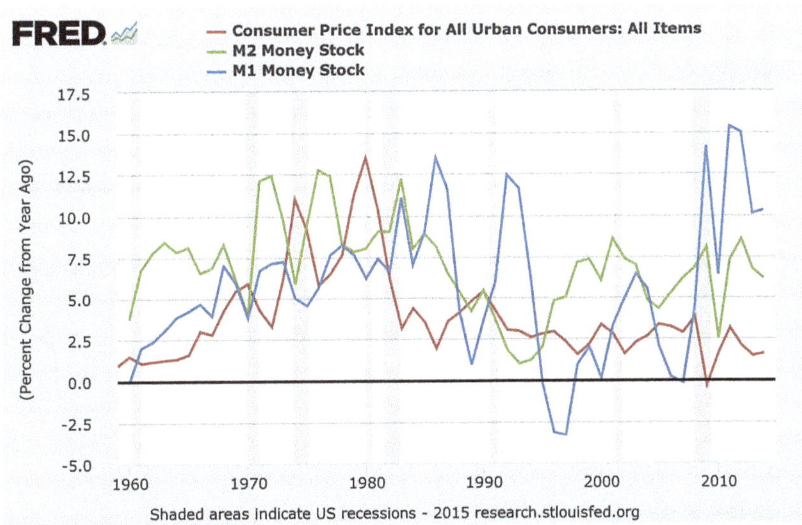

Figure 5.8 Post 1959 US M1, M2 and CPI Growth Rates, Annual Basis

5.6 Appendix: Money, Inflation, Debt, Deficits

Macroeconomic theory related to monetary and fiscal policy tries to explain the US data experience. This is true of trends in historical data, of certain "episodes" in US history, and of recent experience such as the Great Recession and the decade after it.

5.6.1 Elementary US Monetary & Fiscal Data

Figure 5.8 shows the growth rate of US measures of M1 (blue), M2 (green) and the CPI index (red). The money supply growth rates have some close correlation at times and periods of less close correlation. Both M1 and M2 have been shown to cause inflation in a statistical sense known as Granger-causality.[19]

[19]See Alquist, Ron & Kilian, Lutz & Vigfusson, Robert J., 2011. "Forecasting the Price of Oil," CEPR Discussion Papers 8388, C.E.P.R. Discussion Papers; and Haug, A. A., and W. G. Dewald. "Money, Output and Inflation in the Longer Term: Major Industrial Countries, 1880–2001." Economic Inquiry 50 (July 2012), 773–787.

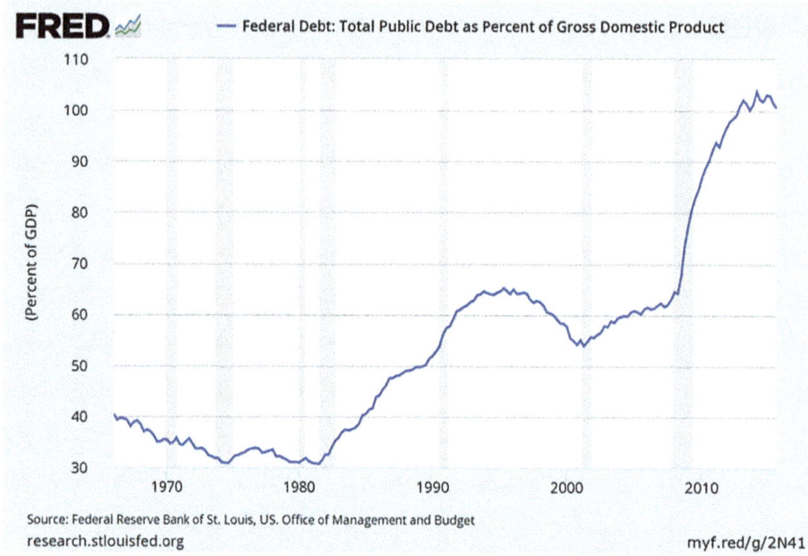

Figure 5.9 US Federal Government Debt to GDP Ratio, 1966–2015

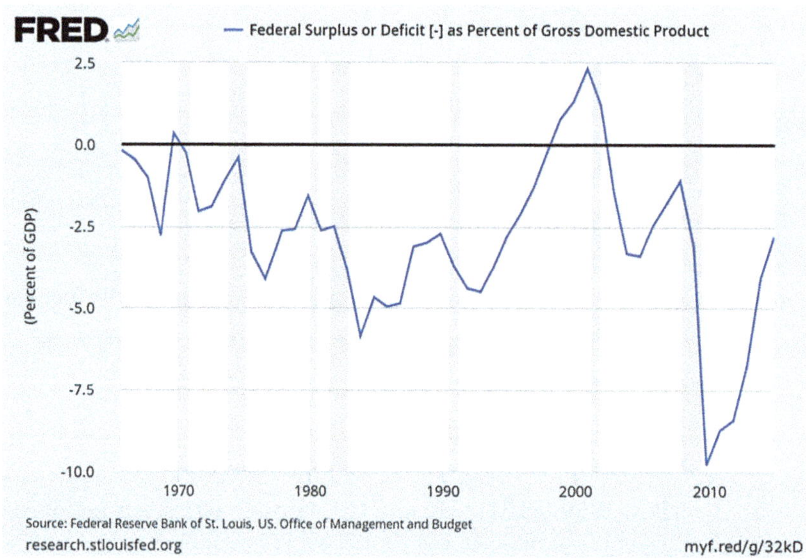

Figure 5.10 US Federal Budget Surplus as a share of GDP, 1965 to 2015

Figure 5.9 shows the US federal government Debt to GDP ratio from January 1966 to July 2015. After staying in the 30 to 40 percent range from 1966 to 1985, the debt to GDP ratio rose substantially. From 30% in 1981, the ratio rose to 64% in 1995, fell back to the mid-50's and then rose above 100% in the last several years.

Since the US can cover its deficits only by borrowing more through issuing more government debt, this rising debt to GDP ratio presumably would coincide with a rising US federal government budget deficit. Figure 5.10 shows that the US federal budget surplus as a percent of GDP went from zero in 1965 to a negative level (indicating deficits) of over -5% of GDP in 1983. The budget deficit gradually was eliminated with a 2.5% surplus relative to GDP in 2000. This was followed by a surplus to GDP as low as -10% in 2010, and a gradually higher (but negative) surplus to GDP ratio after economic recovery began in 2010.

5.6.2 Fiscal Theory of the Price vs. Quantity Theory

The "fiscal theory of the price" argues that the central bank policy is not independent but rather dependent upon the size of the deficits and the build-up of government debt. When the government runs large deficits financed by debt issue rather than by raising taxes, the fiscal theory of the price emphasizes that the inflation rate becomes the residual of the government deficits and debt increases. The central bank gets forced to print money and so finance the deficits, rather than being independent.

During the Great Recession, and the decade occurring post-2008 the inflation rate has not followed the predictions of the fiscal theory in that there have been large increases in the deficits, the government debt, and the money supply growth rate, but inflation has not risen accordingly. This also seemingly contradicts the quantity theory of money that implies that increases in the money supply growth rate lead to higher inflation.

The lack of recent inflation is explained in Chapter 11 below by the fact that the post-2008 expansion of the money supply was largely kept as reserves at the Fed, rather than being lent out by the financial intermediation sector. The Fed's money supply increase was used to finance the government deficits and debt increases post-2008, but then the Fed also induced banks to keep new money supply increases as "excess reserves" held at the Fed. This broke with all previous US history during which virtually zero excess reserves were held. How did this happen? In 2008, for the first time in US history, the Fed paid interest on reserves held at the Fed, and paid the interest at a rate higher than the short term Fed Funds rate, making risk-free excess reserves preferred to the risky loaning out of reserves.[20]

5.7 Summary

The chapter defines public bank money and private bank money. The government-based Federal Reserve System has 12 regional Fed Banks. A Board of Governors resides in Washington, D.C. Rotating sets of Fed Regional Bank Presidents sit on the Board. And the Board is led by a Chairman, now Janet Yellen. Together they form the monetary policy for the US.

Public bank money is the currency issue, or Federal Reserve Notes. Private bank money is created when a bank takes in deposits and opens up deposit accounts. Private banks take in currency and then let the depositor spend it through debits on their demand deposit, or current, account.

Private banks keep some of their currency deposits in reserve in case the depositors demand them. Private banks also lend out the deposits in order to earn profit. They keep a fraction of the original deposit in reserve, in accordance with the banks expectations of the demand for withdrawal of the funds.

Banks leverage up their assets relative to liabilities by making loans and keeping only some fraction of deposits in reserve, giving rise to the name "fractional reserve banking". The leveraging enables the bank to have positive net worth but also opens the bank up to the risk of sudden withdrawals that exceed their reserves. This can cause a so-called liquidity crisis, and can cause insolvency for the bank such that its assets are less than its liabilities.

Deposits in banks can be put in different types of accounts. The current accounts typically earn zero interest, may have fees imposed upon the depositor, and allow the depositor to use these deposits in exchange for goods at any time. The exchange with demand deposits occurs by using a debit card or by paying with a check.

Cash can be obtained by withdrawing funds from the bank, for which the bank must have reserves on had in order to meet such cash withdrawal demands. Depositors may also use credit cards issued by the banks to purchase goods. These act much like demand deposit withdrawals if the credit debt is paid off within the given time period such as a month. Otherwise the credit cards become the same as a loan from the bank which charges relatively high interest payments on credit card debt because of its high default rate.

Adding together the different forms of exchanging for goods creates what economists define as money. There are different monetary aggregates as defined by the Federal Reserve System. The most money-like

[20]A recent conference on the FTPL was held at the Becker-Friedman Institute, with the discussion of the conference video recorded and found at the following link: http://bfi.uchicago.edu/news/feature-story/role-reversal-using-fiscal-policy-manage-inflation

aggregates are public Fed Notes that circulate, called currency in circulation, plus the demand deposits of banks. These are the two main components of the M1 aggregate.

A narrower aggregate than M1 is reserves plus currency, which is called the monetary base. It excludes private bank money and instead represents a measure of public (Fed) bank money. A broader aggregate than M1 is M1 plus deposits that earn more interest, such as time deposits, or savings accounts. These are main components of the M2 aggregate.

The Fed system is the primary institution that comprises the government banking system, while the entire private financial system represents the institutions of private banks and other financial intermediaries. These private institutions create markets for the trading of different forms of assets. The traded instruments include short term and longer term assets.

The shortest term instrument is the one-day overnight deposit held at the Fed, called Federal Funds, which trade at the Federal Funds interest rate. Longer maturity instruments traded include the 3-Month Treasury bills, one year Treasury bonds, 5 year Treasury bonds, 10 year Treasury bonds, and all of the equity stocks of private firms. The equity stocks trade in the stock markets. Firms also issue private debt and this also can be traded on secondary bond markets once it is issued.

The Fed regulates the markets through the Federal Deposit Insurance Corporate that provides deposit insurance to participating banks. Other government regulations affect the banking system, with the goal of making it competitive and less subject to systemic failure. This type of regulation is now called macro-prudential banking regulation.

The theory of the money and banking includes the demand for real money. The quantity theory is that real money demand depends on output, proportionally, and on changes in velocity. Velocity is affected primarily by the relative price of money, which is the nominal interest rate.

The chapter distinguishes between real and nominal interest rates and supplies the theory of how they are linked. The linkage is that the nominal rate equals the real rate plus the expected interest rate. The nominal rate is defined simply as the market interest rate.

The inflation rate ex-post (end-of-period) is measured through the rate of change in a price index such as the CPI. Expected inflation is more difficult to measure. This means we can deduce the ex post real interest rate that prevailed as the residual from subtracting the actual inflation rate at the time from the market interest rates at the time. The real rate can vary from its normal market level when there are unexpected accelerations or decelerations in the inflation rate.

The velocity of money rises when inflation and the nominal interest rate rise because money is more costly to use because of the implicit inflation tax. Velocity can also shift up if the cost of the alternative to money, such as different forms of banking deposits, becomes less expensive such as during financial deregulation.

After the 2008 stock market crash the banking sector was re-regulated. The velocity of money fell both as interest rates fell and as the cost of banking rose due to re-regulation. Changes to banking regulations are a part of money and banking policy.

The more monetary part of money and banking policy is conducted by the Fed as it buys and sells US Treasury debt through what are called open market operations. These were started by the first Fed Chairman Strong, and they allow the Fed to change the quantity of money in circulation.

The growth rate of money is linked causally to the inflation rate by the quantity theory and various types of evidence have supported this historically. The Fed targets the inflation rate by printing money to buy US Treasury debt, and buying and selling such bills and bonds in the secondary markets. They explicitly announce intended targets for the Federal Funds rate along with the inflation rate. Both the Fed's rate of growth of the money supply and the subsequent inflation rate typically rise during wars and crises.

The inflation rate acts as part of an implicit inflation tax on those using money that bears no interest. The government collects the tax when the US Treasury finances spending by selling new debt to the Fed for new money. The private economy bears the burden of the inflation tax when its currency buys less in real terms because the general price level has risen.

A liquidity effect is thought to occur when the Fed suddenly accelerates the money supply growth rate and temporarily drives down either the nominal or real interest rates in markets. If inflation then increases, the interest rates tend to rise back up; the concept is that the real rate will no longer be affected once the money supply growth rate stabilizes at a rate consistent with the Fed's stated inflation rate target. During the Great Recession, much money has been created, real interest rates have been negative, but the Fed has paid interest on reserves held at the Fed so that much of this money has not yet entered circulation and caused the inflation rate to increase above the 2% target.

An application shows the computation of ex post real interest rates for 3-Month Treasury bills and for *AAA*-rated corporate debt. It takes the market interest rates and subtracts the CPI inflation rate to show how the real rates existed over time, including when the real rates ex post were negative. The Appendix shows empirical data on money aggregates growth rates as compared to inflation, and as compared to the growth rates of the Federal budget deficit and the Federal Debt as shares of GDP. It also introduces the fiscal theory of the price level and how this interprets the relation of monetary policy to fiscal policy.

5.8 Glossary of Italic Words

a priori: happens at the start, before subsequent events

Board of Governors: the Federal Reserve System has this board to decide how to set monetary policy through interest rate targets and planned open market operations that affect the aggregate money supply.

Bretton Woods monetary system: a exchange rate and monetary convention agreed to during the later part of WWII and put in place just after the war that fixed a set of countries' exchange rates to the US, while having the US guarantee that it would keep the US dollar value of gold at a fixed rate of $35 per ounce.

capital gain: an income receipt that occurs when an equity share in a firm known as a stock is bought at one price per share and later sold at a higher price per share.

checkable deposits: deposits which the depositor can withdraw by writing a check and paying for goods and services with that check.

complements: a microeconomic concept that an increase in demand for some good causes an increase in demand for a related good.

countercyclic industry: an industry that contracts relatively during an economic expansion in the broader economy, and that expands relatively during an economic contraction in the broader economy.

create money that enters circulation: both the Fed and private banks create money that is used in circulation; the Fed does this when it buys US Treasury debt from the US Treasury, which in turn uses it to finance spending not covered by other taxes or borrowing; the private banks do this when then give more loans out than was originally received as a deposit, and the new loans become new demand deposits that are used to purchase goods and services.

currency: the government's official note that it allows to be used for payments of goods and services and taxes.

current accounts: deposit accounts at banks that can be demanded back in withdrawals of currency at any time, and that usually pay zero interest.

debit card: a bank card that can be used to make purchases at stores such that the purchase sum is immediately debited from the depositors current account.

demand deposits: the name given to current accounts reflecting that the depositor can demand back their deposits in currency at any time.

deposit insurance: a means for banks to insure depositor accounts in the case of bank default, such that the depositors get back their deposits on each account up to some pre-specified dollar limit.

enter circulation: money being spent for the first time, whereby it may be either new Federal Reserve Notes, or new private bank deposits.

equation of exchange: Irving Fisher's 1911 accounting for money and prices whereby $MV = Py$; it can be viewed as a definition of the velocity of money V or it can be viewed in terms of a theory of real money demand, $M/P = (1/V)\,y$.

ex-post: occurs at the end of the period, or after the fact.

Federal Funds market: the market in which federal funds are traded at a certain interest rate called the Federal Funds Rate, where federal funds are overnight deposits by private banks at the Fed.

Federal Funds Rate: the interest rate prevailing in the Federal Funds market.

Federal Reserve Notes: the currency issued by the US government.

financial intermediary function: a business engaged in offering financial services such as intermediating between buyers and sellers of any type of financial capital.

Fisher equation of interest rates: the nominal interest rate equals the (expected) inflation rate plus the real interest rate; the real interest rate is a residual of the known market interest rate (which is the nominal rate) and the known, or expected, inflation rate.

fractional reserve banking: the practice whereby banks keep only a fraction of their deposits in reserve and lend out or buy other assets with the rest in order to earn profit.

house mortgages: a loan used for buying houses.

hyperinflation: a very high rate of inflation; typically defined following Cagan (1956) at 50% or more at an annual rate, during any particular time period within a country.

inflation rate targeting: a monetary policy which aims to keep the economy's inflation rate stable at some specified low level.

interest: what is earned by lending out money, or what is paid when borrowing money; archaically known as usury and something that is outlawed by certain religions such as Muslim still today, and Christian before the Protestant reformation.

leverage up: starting with a certain capital, a firm can leverage up that capital by acquiring additional assets and taking on liabilities to pay for it, such that the liabilities can grow much larger than the firm's net worth; an increase in the debt to equity ratio of a firm.

liquidate: the selling off of assets that were used in the operations of a firm seeking to make profit.

liquidity: the ability to quickly turn assets into forms that are easily traded such as currency.

liquidity effect on interest rates: the idea that an increase of money into capital markets can drive down either the real or nominal interest rate or both; in reverse, the illiquidity effect can increase rates when money is withdrawn from markets.

maturity: the time to which a loan can remain unpaid; at the maturity date of 1 year or 10 years for example the principal that was borrowed needs to be repaid.

money aggregate: a definition of a set of monetary instruments such as currency in circulation plus demand deposits, which is M1.

Monetary Base: currency in circulation plus bank reserves.

monetary instruments: a particular form of financial asset that has a monetary value in a particular currency, such as US dollars.

money market accounts: accounts held at any financial institution that can easily be withdrawn.

mutual fund deposits: money market accounts typically held as deposits at investment banks; the investment banks can declare the type of investment for which each such fund will be used.

natural seigniorage: the goods and services the government can buy with new money printed, whereby its economy is growing and it prints just enough new money so as to keep the inflation rate at zero.

nominal interest rates: market interest rates for any financial asset.

open market operations: the buying and selling of US Treasury bills and bonds by the Fed in the secondary bond market.

opportunity cost: what is given up by using resources to obtain a certain good or service, as typically measured by the closest substitute to that good or service.

Purchasing Power of Money: Irving Fisher's 1911 book that sets out the equation of exchange and the quantity theory of money.

quantity theory of money: the money supply growth rate determines the inflation rate given that the velocity of money and the real output are stable.

real money: the stock of a monetary aggregate put in real terms by dividing by the aggregate price level.

safe haven theories: propositions that some banks or governments are particularly secure during crises as compared to others, such that the lending to these banks by making deposits, or to these governments by buying debt, is viewed as relatively without risk of losing the value of the assets through default of the bank or government.

savings accounts: deposits in accounts at financial institutions that are typically held for longer periods than deposits in current accounts, such that savings accounts can pay more interest than is found for current accounts.

secondary market: a financial market that buys and sells securities such as equity stocks and government bonds that were already initially issued and now are being re-sold and re-bought.

substitutes: goods that can be used in place of other goods.

term structure inversion: when short term maturity debt has higher interest rates than long term maturity debt.

Theory of Interest: Irving Fisher's theory that the market, or nominal, interest rates are determined as the sum of the expected inflation rate and the desired or a priori real interest rate.

time deposits: deposits in banks that only earn a specified interest if they are held at least for a specified amount of time.

5.9 Questions

1. What is the difference between private bank money and public, government, bank money?
2. How do checking accounts, current accounts, and savings accounts differ?
3. How can credit card use be similar to debit card use or be similar to taking out a loan?
4. What is the definition of the monetary base aggregate, the M1 aggregate, and the M2 aggregate?
5. What is the Federal Reserve System, when was it established, and what is its purpose?
6. How do financial markets determine interest rates?
7. Provide a theory of how the demand for money is determined.
8. What is the relative price of money?
9. Describe the difference between the nominal interest rate and the real interest rate.
10. Define the velocity of money and describe what causes it to change.
11. What is the quantity theory of money?
12. In what sense can the money supply growth rate cause the inflation rate to be some particular level?
13. What is the inflation tax; how is it collected; and how is it experienced as a tax in the aggregate economy?
14. Explain how monetary policy is conducted in the US.
15. What is the liquidity effect that can result from increasing the rate of growth of the money supply?
16. In what sense have real interest rates been negative in the US historically?
17. Complete the Federal Reserve Bank of St. Louis EconLowdown Course Module "Capital Markets".
18. Complete the Federal Reserve Bank of St. Louis EconLowdown Course Module "Monetary Policy".

6 Crises and Inflation

6.1 Introduction

The Great Depression of the 1930's and the Great Recession of the 2008–2010 period are marked by major widespread banking sector disruption, panic, and bankruptcies of financial intermediaries. A third major crisis occurred in the 1970's that coincided with the Vietnam war. A fourth crisis during the Korean War of the early 1950's was shorter in duration than the other three crises of the 1930's, the Great Recession and the Vietnam War era.

The banking crisis periods of the Great Depression and the Great Recession did not have high inflation. Inflation was negative in the Great Depression and between zero and 4% in the Great Recession. In contrast, during the 1970's inflation rose steadily towards a peak above 10% in the early 1980's; inflation peaked at 9% during the Korean War.

WWI and WWII were crises based in mass militarization rather than strictly economic factors. These crises did coincide with high inflation, high government deficits and high money supply growth rates. The Korean War also fits this description, and lasted from June 1950 to July 1953.

Economists tend not to focus on war periods. The Vietnam war was viewed as occurring in the 1960's and 1970's but analysis of its effects on the economy are largely ignored. Further, Macroeconomic textbooks have long characterized the post-1953 period as a "peacetime period". Yet the number of US soldiers committed to the Vietnam war was authorized at over 500,000, and the American soldiers killed was reportedly 58,000, larger than the reported 36,000 for the Korean War.

The Vietnam War lasted much longer than the Korean War, with some dating it from November 1955 to April 1975, while US involvement started as far back as 1950 through the first presence of US military advisors. US troop deployment accelerated in 1961 to 1962, and full unit deployment by the US began in 1965. The 1965 to 1975 period is often thereby thought of the US period of the Vietnam War, but economists typically describe this period in terms of "Phillips curves", "cost-push inflation" and "demand-pull inflation" unrelated to the war and the collapse of the Bretton Woods monetary system in 1971–1973.[1]

6.2 Who Made it Happen

Humphrey (1998) claims that the fallacy of a "cost-push" theory of inflation goes back to Sir James Steuart's 1767 *Inquiry into the Principles of Political Oeconomy*. Humphrey contrasts this theory of price determination to the quantity theory of money and other related theories of money demand. "Demand-pull" inflation entered modern macroeconomics textbooks as far back as Samuelson's (1951) *Economics*. In that Samuelson describes how the economy can get inflation if it is already at full employment and aggregate demand increases; both demand-pull and cost-push concepts were non-monetary theories of inflation.[2]

The idea of oil prices causing the 1970's "stagflation" of low growth and high inflation was put forth and remains as a mainstream economic theory of aggregate demand. This stagflation theory was combined with the idea of an exploitable Phillips curve that could be used as a policy tool to lower unemployment by deliberately raising inflation. Hall and Hart (2010) argue that the Solow and Samuelson (1960) idea of exploiting

---

[1]Chinese troop involvement was reportedly 320,000 troops from 1965 to 1971; 3000 Soviet troops are reported to have been in Vietnam during 1964 to 1965, with massive Soviet equipment aid reported throughout the war.

[2]Humphrey, T. M., 1998, "Historical Origins of the Cost-Push Fallacy", *Federal Reserve Bank of Richmond Economic Quarterly*, Vol 84/3, Summer.

a Phillips curve led to this policy option being a part of the US 1962 *Economic Report of the President* by the Council of Economic Advisors.[3]

The cause of the inflation in the 1960's and 1970's that was graphed in terms of a series of shifting Phillips curves over time became widely attributed to oil prices. Hamilton's (1983) finding that no macroeconomic series "Granger-caused" oil prices[4] added fuel to the idea that oil price shocks resulted from a sudden desire for OPEC to exert monopoly power and raise real world oil prices. Barsky and Killian (2002) began an assault on the conventional wisdom by suggesting that oil price increases in the 1970's were caused by the US money supply growth during that Vietnam War era.[5] This was followed up by a finding of Granger causality from US money supply growth to inflation in Gillman and Nakov (2009), as confirmed in Alquist, Kilian and Vigfusson (2013).[6]

Irving Fisher, of quantity theory and interest rate equation fame, apparently provided the modern beginning of the study of the empirical relation between inflation and unemployment in a 1923 journal article.[7] The relation became known as the Phillips curve after Phillips (1958) graphed the relation in a different, perhaps more revealing, way.[8] Theory about the Phillips curve evidence developed when Phelps (1968) proposed the lack of a "long-run" trade-off between inflation and unemployment, in terms of a so-called "vertical Phillips curve". This Phillips curve theory was followed up through Nobel Prize winning contributions by Phelps et al. (1970) and Lucas (1972, 1973) that became known as the expectations theory of the Phillips curve.[9]

Meanwhile, Fisher (1932,1933) had his own theories related to Friedrich Hayek's work that debt and deflation were related in times of banking crises, as during the Great Depression. This was called the "debt-deflation theory" of depressions by Fisher. This theory was revived and a focus of discussion once the Great Recession occurred. It offers an alternative view of Phillips curve experience.

6.3 Facts

6.3.1 The Vietnam War Inflation

Figure 6.1 shows US inflation rates from 1948 to 2014. The Vietnam war period saw continually rising inflation since 1961, but with an acceleration occurring from 1.65% in 1965 to 11% in 1974. Inflation dipped down in 1975, rose back up to 13.5% in 1980, and then fell dramatically to 3.2% in 1983, remarkably close to the 3% inflation rate goal for 1983 that was enacted in the 1978 Full Employment and Balanced Growth Act of US Congress.

The high inflation experience of the Vietnam War was combined with low economic growth in terms of real GDP growth. Recessions followed previous US military wars. After WWI, from 1920 to 1921 there was a

---

[3]Hall, Thomas E. and William R. Hart, 2010, "The Samuelson-Solow "Phillips Curve" and the Great Inflation", Miami University Department of Economics Working Paper; and Samuelson, P.A., and R.M. Solow. 1960. "Analytical Aspects of Anti-Inflation Policy" American Economic Review Papers and Proceedings 50(2), pp. 177–94.

[4]Hamilton, James D., 1983, "Oil and the Macroeconomy since World War II", The Journal of Political Economy, Vol. 91, No. 2 (Apr., 1983), pp. 228–248.

[5]Barsky, Robert B. and Lutz Kilian, 2002, "Do We Really Know that Oil Caused the Great Stagflation? A Monetary Alternative", *NBER Macroeconomics Annual 2001,* Volume 16; MIT Press, Cambridge, MA.

[6]Gillman, Max and Nakov, Anton, 2009. "Monetary effects on nominal oil prices," The North American Journal of Economics and Finance,vol. 20 (3), pages 239–254, December. Alquist, R., Kilian, L., and R.J. Vigfusson (2013), "Forecasting the Price of Oil," Chapter 8 in: G. Elliott and A. Timmermann (eds.), Handbook of Economic Forecasting, 2, Amsterdam: North-Holland.

[7]Reprint or original: Irving Fisher, I Discovered the Phillips Curve: "A Statistical Relation between Unemployment and Price Changes" Journal of Political Economy Vol. 81, No. 2, Part 1 (Mar. - Apr., 1973), pp. 496–502; original was Irving Fisher, 1923, International Labour Review, 13(6, June): 785–792.

[8]Phillips, A. W. "The Relation between Unemployment and the Rate of Change of Money Wage Rates in the United Kingdom, 1861–1957." Economica 25 (November 1958): 283–99. Humphrey (1985) describes "The Early History of the Phillips Curve".

[9]Phelps, Edmund S. (1968). "Money-Wage Dynamics and Labor Market Equilibrium". Journal of Political Economy 76 (S4): 678–711. Phelps, Edmund S.; et al. (1970). Microeconomic Foundations of Employment and Inflation Theory. W. W. Norton, New York. Lucas, R. E. (1972). Expectations and the neutrality of money. Journal of Economic Theory 4: 103–124; Lucas, R. E. (1973). Some international evidence on output-inflation tradeoffs. American Economic Review 63: 326–334.

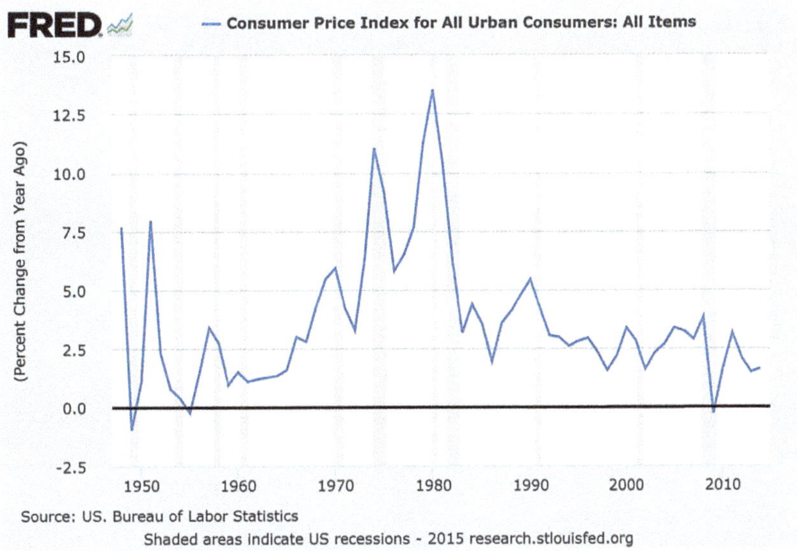

Figure 6.1 US Prolonges, High, Inflation During Vietnam War Era

severe recession with real GDP growth estimated at between –2% to –7%, and with deflation of as high as 18%. There was an apparently more severe –11.6% GDP growth rate in 1946 during a short but severe Post-WWII recession; a short recession is recorded also after the Korean War in 1954 which had a -0.6% GDP growth rate.

The prolonged nature of the Vietnam War more uniquely led to a prolonged period of inflation and an average decade of low growth in the 1970's as compared to a higher average GDP growth rate in the 1960's. Yet at the end of the Vietnam War, as with other wars, there was a sharp recession in 1974 to 1975. GDP growth fell by 6% from 5.6% in 1973 to –0.5 in 1974.[10]

There was also a milder recession recorded in 1970 to 1971, with declining but positive GDP growth. Taken together there was an average low growth period during the 1970s. In combination with the rising, and high average inflation rate of the 1970's, the period was characterized as one of *stagflation*. Stagflation was defined as a prolonged period of low growth plus high inflation. Conventional economic theory could not explain it, within the framework of a "peacetime economy".

Oil Price Shocks?

One way to explain the stagflation period of the Vietnam War era was to ignore the effects of the War. Typically wars, the end of wars, and subsequent recessions came in sequence. But the modern era introduced what was a prolonged war experience for Vietnam as compared to WWI, WWII and Korea.

The prolonged nature of the Vietnam War made it harder to associate recessionary periods during the Vietnam War era with the War itself. Instead the war was largely ignored in economic discourse. Instead a direct link between high inflation and low economic growth was sought.

The main event motivating explanations of stagflation was the series of oil price increases that occurred in the 1970's. The monthly average of the oil prices (West Texas Intermediate Crude) jumped first in July 1973 from $3.56 a barrel to $4.31 in August 1973. Then in December 1973, prices jumped from $4.31 to $10.11 in January 1974, a 235% increase. This latter jump is often called the first "*oil price shock*".

Oil prices continued to edge up steadily. By April 1979 they were up about 50% at $15.85. The West Texas Intermediate (WTI) Crude oil US dollar price per barrel was the most watched oil price. Figure 6.2 shows this price from 1973 to 1980, with the jump up in 1973 and the subsequent 50% additional climb going into the Spring of 1979.

[10]"Finally, in January 1973, representatives of the United States, North and South Vietnam, and the Vietcong signed a peace agreement in Paris, ending the direct U.S. military involvement in the Vietnam War"; "the last American troops departed on March 29" of 1974 although the war persisted for the Vietnam nation until 1975; see http://www.history.com/this-day-in-history/u-s-withdraws-from-vietnam

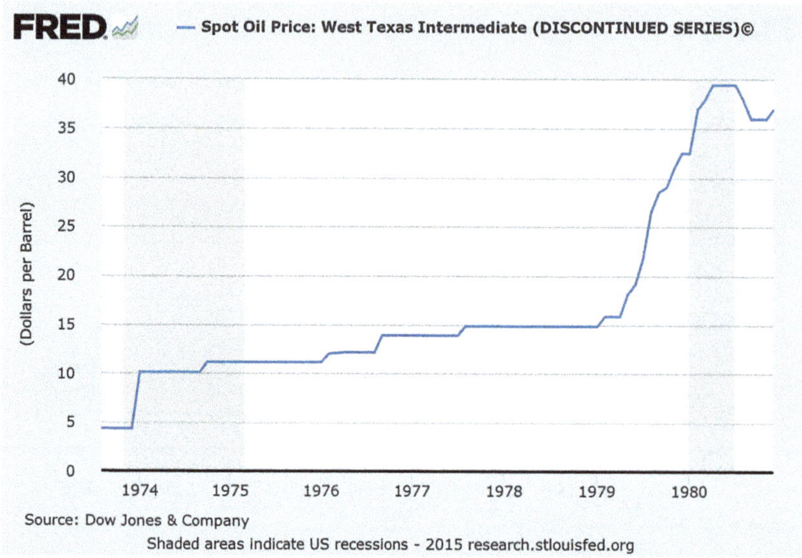

Figure 6.2 Spot Oil Prices: West Texas Intermediate Crude, US Dollars per barrel, August 1973 to December, 1980

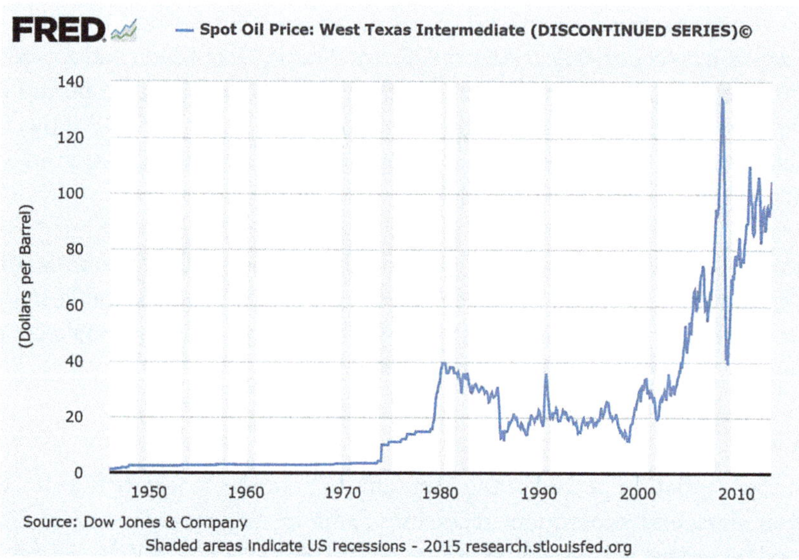

Figure 6.3 WTI Oil Prices, January 1946 to July 2013, US Dollars per barrel

The so-called second "oil price shock" rise is dated as occurring in 1979. It occurred over the course of a year from April 1979 to April 1980, when the WTI oil price rose from 15.85 to 39.50. This was a rise of 250%, similar to the first "oil price shock".

Figure 6.3 shows the WTI oil price going back to January 1946, and up until July 2013, after which FRED discontinued updates of this series. After the early 1980's, oil prices fell back down to 15.44 in February 1986. The 1980's and 1990's were characterized by fluctuations around $15. A large climb upwards followed after the 2001 recession.

Taken in historical context the oil shocks of the 1970's may appear more as historical curiosities than foundations for a basis for a theory of oil shocks causing stagflation. But it remains true to this day that oil shocks continue to be debated as to their underlying cause, and as to what constitutes an oil shock. In addition, it remains a controversy as to how they affect the economy, and "stagflation" times.

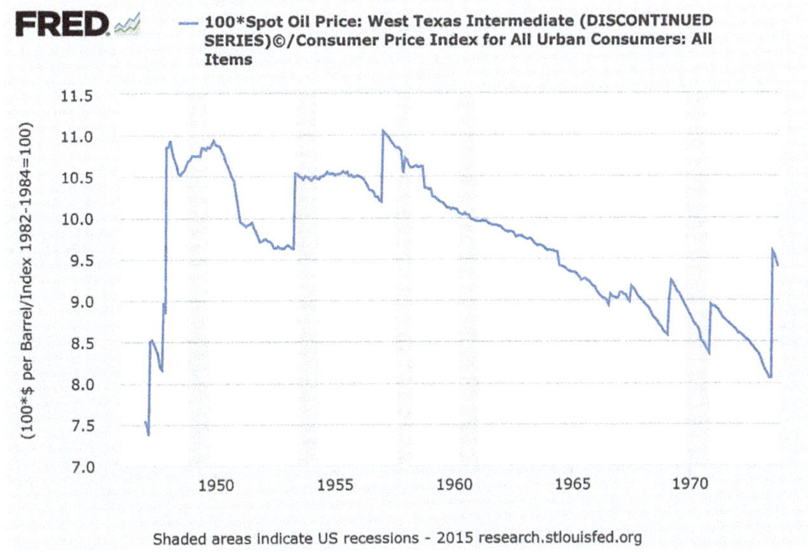

Figure 6.4 Real WTI Oil Prices, from Jan. 1947 to Dec. 1973: WTI US$ per barrel divided by US CPI index, in 1982 Constant Dollars

A simple factual view of oil prices is to consider them in real terms rather than nominal, US dollar, terms. Figure 6.4 graphs real oil prices by dividing the WTI price by the CPI price index with 1982 as the base year. This puts the oil prices in 1982 constant dollar units.

Real oil prices were relatively stable for the decade from January 1948 to November 1958. From November 1958 until July 1973 real oil prices steadily trended downwards. Real prices in 1982 dollars fell from $11 in 1958 to $8 in 1973, a 27% decrease. When the first oil jump came it was from July to August of 1973 when the real oil price rose from $8.05 to $9.58 (in 1982 prices), a 19% increase that left it still below the real 1958 level.

From December 1973 to January 1974, the real price rose to $21.6 in 1982 dollars, almost double the 1958 levels of 11. But if real prices have been increasing by 5% every year smoothly from 1958 to 1973, they would also have doubled from 11 in 1958 to 22 in 1973. This means the huge increase in December 1973 that is known as the first oil shock was in effect making up for a long trend down in the real price of oil, by establishing a price consistent with a steady 5% upwards trend in the real oil price. A 5% real price increase might be consistent with a normal return on oil capital.[11]

Figure 6.5 shows the 1947 to 2016 real oil price view, in 1982 US dollars. Clearly the second oil price shock of 1979 to 1980 also significantly raised real oil prices. But after 1983, real oil prices remained stable until 2001. As seen in the nominal prices, the real oil price rose significantly from 2001 to 2014. But real prices have since fallen back down to the level of early 2004. These facts about real oil prices raise questions of why the 1970's "oil shocks" occurred and what was their effect on the economy. For example, if the 1970's oil shocks cause stagflation, then did the post-2014 downward oil shock cause lower inflation and higher economic growth?

US Inflation and Growth Experience

Figure 6.6 shows for 1954 to 2000 that the CPI inflation rate (in blue) and the Real GDP growth rate (in red) have almost mirror images. The negative correlation is striking. When the inflation rate rises, real GDP growth tends to fall; when inflation falls, real GDP growth tends to rise.

[11]The WTI price of oil became the world standard; it is based oriiginally on the West Texas oil called "Texas light sweet". West Texas includes most of the Permian Basin which is a main source of oil-bearing rock that is being used to produce oil by "fracking" production methods. See "Where Oil is Booming: West Texas", Russell Gold, Wall Street Journal, p.B1, October 31, 2016. "One of the state's oldest oil fields, the Permian Basin in West Texas, is booming again, thanks to advanced technologies such as hydraulic fracturing and horizontal drilling. And Permian oil output shows no signs of stopping at its current 1.7 million barrels a day"; Wall Street Journal, "Permian Basin in Texas to Drive Down Oil Prices", Russell Gold, Sept. 1, 2014.

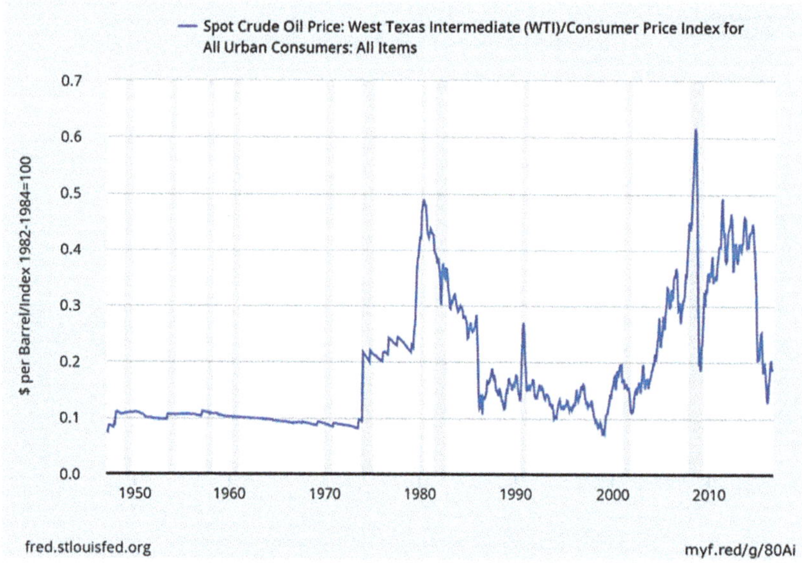

Figure 6.5 Real Oil Prices in 1982 US Dollars, 1947–2016

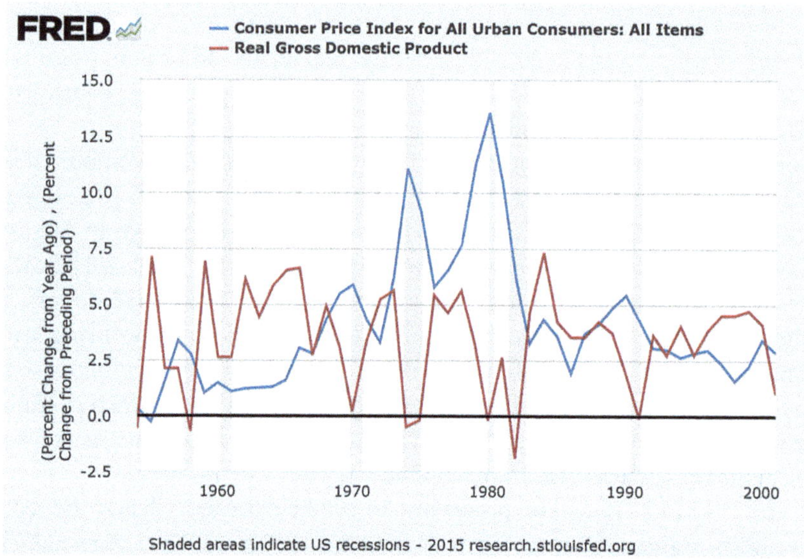

Figure 6.6 US CPI Inflation Rate (Blue) and Real GDP Growth Rate (Red), 1954 to 2000

Instead of an oil shock explanation of the Vietnam War era of "stagflation", this suggests a long term negative effect of the inflation tax on growth, similar to how higher corporate and personal income tax rates have been found to decrease real GDP growth. But then what caused the high peak of US inflation in the 1970's and early 1980's if not oil shocks? During the post-2000 period, the inflation rate and real GDP growth rate move closely together. This may be evidence supporting debt-deflation theories that are put forth for crisis periods. After examining money supply evidence as a possible basis of historic US inflation experience, including the 1970's, the debt-deflation theory is considered as a hypothesis for Phillips curve episodes such as occurred during the Great Recession.

Money Supply Growth, Inflation and Oil Prices

Evidence has found that the money supply growth rate causes inflation in US data, as well as in a broad set of international historical studies. More recently, studies have found that both money supply and inflation have *Granger-caused* oil prices. This evidence includes the period of the 1970 oil price "shocks".

Lutz Kilian of the University of Michigan is one the US's most well-regarded oil study experts. He has written numerous articles explaining how the price of oil is determined. Kilian and coauthors are known for suggesting that monetary factors can cause oil prices to rise.

Gillman and Nakov (2009) build on their suggestions by supplying theory and evidence for this relation. They show how increases in money supply growth can "Granger-cause" both the inflation rate and the US Dollar oil price to rise. Alquist, Kilian and Vigfusson (2011) extend this work on Granger causality of nominal oil prices by money and inflation, with emphasis on including the experience during the 1970's.[12]

6.3.2 Granger-Causality of Oil Prices

Clive Granger received the Nobel prize in economics for work on showing "causality" in economic data. Granger-causality is a relation between two data series whereby changes in one data series systematically are correlated with subsequent changes in another series. This preceding movement of one series gives the impression of "causality" by that series of changes in the other series.

Alquist, Kilian and Vigfussion (2011, pp.11–12) explain first the inflation causality findings:

> "There are several reasons to expect the dollar-denominated nominal price of oil to respond to changes in nominal U.S. macroeconomic aggregates. One channel of transmission is purely monetary and operates through U.S. inflation. For example, Gillman and Nakov (2009) stress that changes in the nominal price of oil must occur in equilibrium just to offset persistent shifts in U.S. inflation, given that the price of oil is denominated in dollars. Indeed, the Granger-causality tests in Table 1a indicate highly significant lagged feedback from U.S. headline CPI inflation to the percent change in the nominal WTI price of oil for the full sample, consistent with the findings in Gillman and Nakov (2009)."

They then report the monetary causality found:

> "Gillman and Nakov view changes in inflation in the post-1973 period as rooted in persistent changes in the growth rate of money. Thus, an alternative approach of testing the hypothesis of Gillman and Nakov (2009) is to focus on Granger causality from monetary aggregates to the nominal price of oil. Given the general instability in the link from changes in monetary aggregates to inflation, one would not necessarily expect changes in monetary aggregates to have much predictive power for the price of oil, except perhaps in the 1970s (see Barsky and Kilian 2002). Table 1 a nevertheless shows that there is considerable lagged feedback from narrow measures of money such as M1 for the refiners' acquisition cost and the WTI price of oil based on the 1975.2–2009.12 evaluation period."

6.4 Theory

6.4.1 Oil Price Shock Theory

Alquist, Kilian and Vigfusson 2011, p. 6–7, then explain that monetary caused oil price changes should not be confused with real oil shocks, in an application of the difference between nominal and real:

> "If the U.S. money supply unexpectedly doubles, for example, then, according to standard macroeconomic models, so will all nominal prices denominated in dollars (including the nominal price of oil), leaving the relative price or real price of crude oil unaffected (see Gillman and Nakov 2009). Clearly, one would not want to interpret such an episode as an oil price shock involving a doubling of the nominal price of oil. Indeed, economic models of the impact of the price of oil on the U.S. economy correctly predict that such a nominal oil price shock should have no effect on the U.S. economy because theoretical models inevitably are specified in terms of the real price of oil, which has not changed in this example."

[12]"Forecasting the Price of Oil", (2011), by Alquist, Kilian and Vigfusson, International Finance Discussion Paper Number 1022, The Federal Reserve Board of Governors; also published in the 2013 book, *The Economics of Forecasting*, Volume 2, Chapter 8, by North-Holland. See: http://www.federalreserve.gov/pubs/ifdp/2011/1022/ifdp1022.pdf for the Board of Governors version.

Oil price shocks nonetheless long have been made a foundation of so-called "*supply-side shocks*" that are used to explain the US Vietnam War era of stagflation. Recent research into the identification of oil shocks finds that the two famous oil shocks of the 1970's were largely monetary based shocks. If true, then the jump in nominal and real prices was to catch up for past inflation, as a result of money supply increases.

If inflation caused the 1970's oil shocks, then oil shocks did not cause inflation. Oil shocks causing high inflation in the 1970's is exactly the basis of the supply-side *oil shock theory* of economic stagflation during the Vietnam War era. Research debunking this view leaves a monetary explanation as the primary cause of both the oil shocks and the inflation.

Metallic Standards and the End of *Bretton Woods Gold Standard*

The monetary causation of oil prices leaves the question of what caused the US money supply increase and subsequent inflation and oil prices during the Vietnam War. US historical evidence shows how high inflation coincides with wartime. This typically is caused by printing money to pay for wartime government deficits without having to raise this tax revenue for example through increases in the corporate income and personal income tax rates.

The money supply growth and subsequent inflation by the early 1970's was so high as to drive the US off the gold standard, which it had been on since 1834 except for temporary departures, in a way that now appears to be permanent. The permanent end of a gold standard is significant since the US had its currency backed by a metallic standard since its inception in 1776 via the US Declaration of Independence. This metallic backing of its currency saw many changes over time, but always re-emerged until 1971–1973 when the last vestiges of the gold standard was abandoned in a series of steps.

The Coinage Act of 1792 created the US dollar through free US coinage into silver and gold at a set ratio per dollar (15 silver grains to 1 gold grain). From 1792 to 1834 silver was the main circulating currency. The Coinage Act of 1834 changed the *conversion ratio* to 16 to 1, causing gold to instead be the main circulating currency. From 1834 to 1971 the US remained on a gold standard except for brief suspensions during and after the Civil War (until 1879), and during WWI and WWII. During these wars, money was printed to cover deficits from wartime spending and inflation was high; hyperinflation plagued the Confederate US states during the Civil War.

The *Bretton Woods agreement* at the end of WWII set the US dollar as being redeemable in gold, although only for international central banks, at $35 dollars per gold ounce. The Vietnam War expenditure pushed up the US government budget deficit.[13] This deficit was apparently financed by the US Treasury selling dept that was bought by the fed. This created new money that caused inflation pressure in the US.

Other countries linked to the US by the *fixed exchange rates* of Bretton Woods in effect had to buy up US dollars with their own currencies in order to keep their underlying exchange rate values from departing from the fixed rates of Bretton Woods. In this way the US *exported inflation* of the Vietnam War to the Bretton Woods nations. With international inflation then rising, US President Nixon even tried to control US inflation by instituting wage and *price controls* through an executive action in August 15, 1971, for the first time since the price controls of WWII; these controls failed to stem inflation.

The controls of 1971 included suspension of currency into gold, initially for 90 days. This violated the Bretton Woods agreement, which had started the International Monetary Fund (IMF), and ended the gold standard.[14] Although administered during the height of US involvement in the Vietnam War, these US price controls were said to be "unprecedented in peacetime"[15] and they lasted until 1974. But by 1973 the countries

[13]The federal deficit suddenly shows a surplus in 1969 because President Johnson included on-budget for the first time in US history the surplus-accumulating Social Security Trust Funds, which acted effectively to mask the growing federal budget deficit; no general Treasury revenues could be used for the Social Security system and in turn the system could not transfer funds to the general Treasury even if the system was currently running a surplus as it was then.

[14]See the IMF website description at https://www.imf.org/external/about/histend.htm

[15]See the website: http://www.econreview.com/events/wageprice1971b.htm, or "Wage and price controls: Nixon's imposition of controls on wages, prices and rents was an unprecedented U.S. government intrusion into a peacetime economy. The initial 90-day freeze

of the Bretton Woods system adopted floating exchange rates with respect to each other so that the other gold standard remnant of fixed exchange rates was eliminated.

Confluence: Inflation, War End, Gold Standard End, Recession

President Nixon resigned as President on August 9, 1974 and Vice-President Gerald Ford was inaugurated President. The same month the US cut military aid to Vietnam. The US Dow Jones Industrial average lost 45% of value from January 1973 to December 1974, the biggest stock market crash since the Great Depression. Real GDP growth declined every quarter for two years from the first quarter 1973 to the first quarter of 1975.

The explanation for this crisis period's confluence of a 45% value stock market crash, the end of US Vietnam military involvement, the deepest recession since the Great Depression at the time, the end of the Bretton Woods monetary system and rising inflation was generally taught in macroeconomic theory to be the result of oil shocks, starting with the Arab *oil embargo* of 1973. In short, the theory is that supply side increases in aggregate average cost of production caused this set of events. Supply side oil shocks still are taught today as the reason for the 1970's inflation, including by the bestselling ones. Mankiw (2015) writes that

> "Some of the largest economic fluctuations in the US economy since 1970 have originated in the oil fields of the Middles East."... "Firms in the United States ...experience rising costs, and they find it less profitable to supply their output of goods and services at any given price level. **The result is a leftward shift in the aggregate-supply curve, which in turn leads to stagflation.**" (p. 450–451, Seventh Edition, N. Gregory Mankiw, Principles of Macroeconomics).

Blaming the oil exporters for their breaking the fixed price oil sales contracts, which were agreements made during the Bretton Woods gold standard, is like blaming friends for trusting you. It ignores the havoc that the US Vietnam War imposed on markets, including the US dollar priced international oil market.

6.4.2 Oil Shock Theory of Stagflation

According to the oil shock theory of stagflation, the Organization of Petroleum Exporting Countries (OPEC) were a group that acted like a monopolist who could at any time suddenly exert monopoly power over price. Ignoring the long term contracts made by US affiliated energy countries with OPEC member countries that were based on a fixed price of $35 per ounce of gold in US dollars, the OPEC monopoly theory is that suddenly for no known reason to this date, OPEC decided to exert monopoly power, refuse to export oil under previously contracted prices during the Arab oil embargo of October 1973, and then raise oil prices.

The two monopolistic oil price shocks of the 1970's are said to be the cause of the 1970's stagflation. This is despite the fact that in August 1972, the US raised the dollar price of gold to $38, thereby devaluing the US dollar.

> "In March 1973, the G–10 approved an arrangement wherein six members of the European Community tied their currencies together and jointly floated against the U.S. dollar, a decision that effectively signaled the abandonment of the Bretton Woods fixed exchange rate system in favor of the current system of floating exchange rates."[16]

In May 1973, the US devalued again by raising the official price to $42.22 dollars per gold ounce. Meanwhile market prices of gold left $35 an ounce after 1967, rising from $44 in 1971 to $106 in 1973, about a

initially worked, as the vast majority of Americans cooperated and inflation was temporarily stemmed. But Nixon later abandoned the controls amid growing inflationary pressures–including those created by the 1973 oil embargo. In 1974–75, the nation endured its deepest recession since the 1930s, following the worst inflation in the postwar era." from the 1994 LA Times, found at http://articles.latimes.com/1994-04-27/business/fi-50976_1_nixon-administration/2

[16]From the official website of the US Department of State: https://history.state.gov/milestones/1969–1976/nixon-shock

240% rise. This is very close to an accounting of the 235% increase of the "first oil shock" at the end of 1973. Nominal, US dollar "world" oil prices had to rise as fast as the gold price in order to by the same amount of gold, or what we could call real goods and services. Gold prices in return are thought to have built in actual and expected inflation rates.

On December 31, 1974, US citizens were allowed to own gold for the first time in some 40 years and the US Treasury began the sale of gold stock in 1975, and in 1976 the International Monetary Fund began a 5-year gold sales plan. The free market for an unregulated gold price became established.

From March 1979 to March 1980 gold prices rose from $260 per ounce to $650, a 250% increase, quickly followed by a 250% increase in the US dollar price of oil from April 1979 to April 1980. This was the so-called second oil shock. It can be seen once again to be well accounted for by the change in the world price of gold.

OPEC's real profits suffered as their fixed dollar price contracts, based on a fixed dollar price of gold, became worth increasingly less. The Arab oil embargo is perhaps viewed fairly as a contract renegotiation of long-term, fixed-price, oil contracts, in the face of the collapse of value of the US dollar in terms of gold, once the international monetary system collapsed. The US 1974 to 1975 recession, happening once US military engagement ended, is perhaps better viewed as a typical postwar recession. And the rise in the US inflation rate during the 1970's is perhaps best viewed as a result of the money supply financing of the Vietnam war, as was typical of the other three US wars of the twentieth century.

Supply Shocks, Aggregate Demand & Supply in Nominal Prices

Not surprisingly, construction of the full oil shock theory of stagflation requires quite a large set of assumptions. Exploration of the assumptions behind this theory helps consideration of its plausibility, which is useful if the above scenario of its implausibility is still unconvincing. First assume that the long run supply of output is vertical. This is an awkward assumption in that in the long run, economic growth shows that output expands along some sort of positive trend in the US history, implying an ever larger supply of output every year. A vertical aggregate supply (*AS*) curve is an odd Keynesian concept not found in the modern Ramsey-based models that now underlie Neoclassical and New-Keynesian economics.

If we said the *short run supply of output* was fixed, it would seem a bit more plausible, since at any one moment of time we cannot increase the aggregate output. But the *long run aggregate supply of output* in economics means what can be supplied over some appropriately longish time period. Long run is actually not strictly defined in economics, in terms of any consensus of a time period. The language of long and short run dates back to classical and neoclassical economists, including Adam Smith and Alfred Marshall, but in Marshall it is the short run supply that is fixed not the long run.

Nonetheless, assume the long run supply of aggregate output is fixed and cannot be raised regardless of price. Second assume that the price is the US dollar price of goods and services. In other words, the price is a nominal price, not a relative one as in all microeconomic theory. This makes the theory a uniquely nominal theory of macroeconomic supply and demand, combined with a fixed level of real output, inconsistent with micro foundations of using only a real relative price.

Third assume that the short run aggregate output supply and demand curves (*AS* and *AD*) are appropriately upward and downward sloping respectively, as in microeconomic theory. That seems logical, although no definition of short run exists here. The main idea seems to be that the equilibrium output can be any level, as supply and demand change; this level may fall short of the fixed long run level.

A trick used here is that output can only fall below the fixed long run level. It cannot rise above it. No extra *capacity utilization*, no added manufacturing plants, and no higher employment rates are allowed once the economy is at its *fixed long run level of output,* for which there is no empirical support.

Now assume that the equilibrium between the short run supply and demand naturally somehow coincides with the fixed long run level of output. This means there is a coincidence of short run and long run equilibrium supply, at some given nominal price that we will call the equilibrium price. The jargon used is that this coinciding point is called the "full-employment level of output", a concept that was used in the Keynesian Cross analysis of the 1950's, and once again is used in this analysis.

Figure 6.4.2 illustrates this Keynesian nominal price theory of *AS–AD*. The vertical long run supply is at $y = 2.5$ and the short run upward sloping black aggregate supply (*AS*) curve and the black downward sloping aggregate demand (*AD*) curve intersect coincidentally at $y = 2.5$. An oil price shock is said to raise the cost of production and shift back the *AS* curve to the red *AS* curve, with lower output (of 2) and a higher price level (of 3).

Now consider that if aggregate demand is instead given initially by the blue *AD* curve, then an increase in demand such as from government spending, in the typical story, can shift the *AD* curve out to the black *AD*, with a higher output (going from 2 to 2.5) and a higher price (going from 2 to 2.5). This would "return" the economy to full output but further shifts out in the *AD* would cause only a higher price and no more output since 2.5 is the maximum output given by the vertical long run supply curve. Note that unlike Keynes's (1930) business cycle theory that gave rise to the Keynesian Cross analysis, here there is no automatic equilibrating mechanism and apparently the economy could forever remain at below full employment.

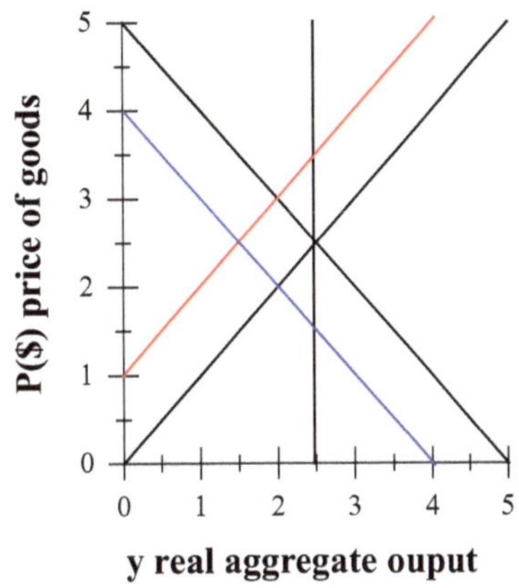

The idea in the analysis is that the nice coincidence of short run and long run supply at an output of 2.5 and price of 2.5 is somehow disturbed. Either a "*supply-side shock*" (higher cost of production) or a "*demand-side shock*" ("insufficient" or "too much" aggregate demand) is supposed to be able to shift the short run supply or demand respectively. But output can only fall from its long run level; it cannot increase.

Take an oil supply shock that causes an increase in the cost of production in the US of its aggregate output. In this theory, the oil shock causes the short run supply curve to shifts upwards and backwards. The new short run equilibrium occurs where it crosses short run demand, in a movement upwards along the demand curve. The new output is lower, below the *"full-employment" long run level of output*. And the nominal price in the economy is higher, which is called "*cost-push inflation*".

The comparative statics actually only tell us that an oil shock causes a higher price level and a lower level of output. That is the end of the analysis. It explains only a one time rise in the nominal aggregate output price level and a one time fall in real output. If there are two "oil supply-side shocks", as is claimed for the 1970's, then there are two of these like events.

Even accepting all these assumptions, a big problem with this analysis is that stagflation is defined by a low growth rate of output and high rate of inflation over a prolonged period. The above analysis only gives a single price level increase and a single drop in output. Prolonged inflation is caused by prolonged price level increases at a certain rate over a number of years; similarly with a lower real GDP growth rate.

One or two price level jumps do not satisfy the definition of prolonged inflation, as far as any evidence has ever been found. Second, output dropping from one level to another two times in a decade does not satisfy the definition of a prolonged lower growth rate of output. Rather the real output level would fall twice, but its growth rate may be little affected over time. The other key criticism is that supply and demand for real output do not depend on the nominal price of output.

Demand Management Theory as Demand Side Shock

The demand side shock that causes a higher price but no output increase is typically said to be caused by the government spending programs that cause the economy to "overheat", like a car running without enough oil. The economy has higher aggregate demand from higher spending. But if starting from the nice equilibrium with a coincidence of long run and short run supply, then higher demand cannot cause the usual movement up the aggregate supply curve to a higher output level in this story; instead it only raises the price level.

When output is already at its full employment level, it cannot rise when demand shifts out. Only a higher price level results. The shift up in demand keeps the fixed long run level of output. The higher price level is said to explain what is called "*demand-pull inflation*".

The problems of demand pull inflation are several: 1) what happens to short run supply? It must shift back as well to keep the coincidence of the short run *AS* and *AD* with the new long run level of output, but now with a higher price. 2) A price level increase again does not cause prolonged inflation, just a one-time price level increase. And again, 3) supply and demand for real output do not depend on nominal prices.

Using Cost-Push Shocks to Justify Government Spending

The supply side oil shock theory and demand side government shock theory is nonetheless another chapter in the writing of so-called stabilization theory. This claims that the government can increase spending in order to increase aggregate output, for example after an oil caused supply shock, but has to be careful not to push output past its fixed long run level. If the government does push output too far, it results in higher inflation, but no higher output.

Further, if the government is subject to unscrupulous price gauging by powerful international cartels acting in conjunction as a monopolist, then aggregate cost can be pushed up suddenly at any unknown time. Problems with the oil shock theory of stagflation include that it apparently never happened at any other time in US history except after the breaking down of the 200 year old international gold standard system of fixed exchange rates; that it is based on non-economic theories of equilibrium using nominal instead of real prices; that it is put forth as a peacetime consequence of demand management policy even during a major US War. This theory is promulgated despite the fact that tens of thousands of US soldiers died, the Bretton Woods monetary system collapsed, US inflation was exported worldwide, and as the US involvement in the Vietnam War came to an end the US experienced both a stock market collapse and severe recession, similar to the experience at the end of previous wars.

6.4.3 Relative Price of Output and Real Oil Shocks

There is a simple way to show oil shocks in aggregate supply and demand analysis that is consistent with our model (Ramsey, 1928) that form the basis of modern macroeconomics. In short, the price of output is always a relative price. This is developed more fully in the subsequent Chapters 8–10 (and in Gillman, 2011, *Advanced Modern Macroeconomics*).

Let the nominal price of output be the nominal price of goods and services (GDP) as denoted by *P*. And let this goods nominal price be relative to the nominal price of labor, as denoted by *W*, which stands for the nominal wage rate. And let this relative price of goods to labor be stated as *P*/*W*. Now plot the *AS* and *AD* curves with this relative price *P*/*W* in a way consistent with the mainstream (Ramsey, 1928) micro-based macro-economy. A detail for now is that each of these *AS* and *AD* sets of curves is for the given equilibrium capital stock that is attained at the equilibrium relative price at which the *AS* and *AD* intersect.

Now redraw Figure 6.4.2 as Figure 6.7 below. Since the equilibrium capital stock is given there is no such thing as a "longer run" than these supply and demand curves so that we can delete the fiction of a vertical long run supply curve. Now should an oil shock be such that the dollar price of goods (and services) rises but the dollar price of wages remains the same for some unknown reason, then indeed, output supply would shift back to the red supply curve from the black one. The relative price *P*/*W* would rise and output would fall. This makes sense in that the real wage, which of course is simply *W*/*P*, has fallen and less labor is offered at the equilibrium price (since the wage *W* did not rise by the same proportion as the price of goods *P*).

It is unclear if in a Keynesian usage of nominal *AS* and *AD* drawn against only the nominal price *P*, it would be argued that the meaning really is that the wage rate did not keep up with the output price level

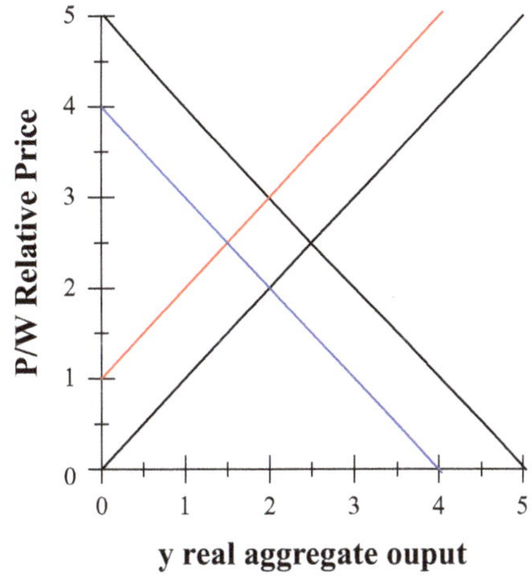

Figure 6.7 "Cost-Push" Shift back in (red) AS as P/W rises

when oil prices were increased in the 1970's. But this would be needed in order to have a consistent theory of aggregate supply and demand as based on the standard (Ramsey, 1928) optimization economy. Such a result would occur if in fact the oil price rise represented a relative price increase in goods relative to labor, which is a plausible analytic approach.

Or a shift within the relative price framework might be postulated to occur only on the demand side. For example a shift down from black to blue *AD* curves in Figure 6.7 would result in the price of goods falling relative to the price of labor, and less equilibrium output. This shift back in the *AD* curve is shown in Chapter 8 below to result during business cycle recessions (although the *AS* curve shifts back as well such that output falls and *P/W* actually rises).

6.4.4 Long Run Inflation and Growth Theory

Neoclassical growth theory gives a credible theory of the effect of inflation on output growth that is unrelated to theories of government demand-managed inflation or monopolist oil-price caused inflation. Such growth theory uses monetary economies as based on the Ramsey model extended to endogenous growth. It combines how money supply growth causes inflation, and how inflation in turn acts as a tax that lowers output growth.

Modern neoclassical growth theory has evolved steadily from Lucas's (1988) explanation of economic growth using human capital investment to explain growth endogenously, within the model, instead of through exogenous technological change. Complementary theory uses the firm side more, such as McGrattan and Prescott's (2012) emphasis of intangible capital as explaining technological change. Gomme (1993) and others combined the monetary side to show how inflation acts like other taxes on income and causes a lower growth rate of real aggregate output.

The growth theories that explain technological change and include monetary factors including inflation provide a straightforward basis to explain the data of Figure 6.6. There inflation and growth appear to be systematically negatively correlated. Growth theory allows for shocks to the money supply growth rate as required for example to finance the demand of wars. Changes in the money supply growth rate in turn cause inflation. The inflation taxes the economy so as to lower the return to human and physical capital. This lower return on capital causes a lower growth rate. As the inflation rate rises and fall, this growth theory predicts that the growth rate of output should move in the opposite direction as the inflation rate. This effect is suggested by the negative correlation of real GDP growth and the inflation rate as seen strikingly in Figure 6.6.[17]

[17]Gillman (2009) provides a Routledge published book collection of journal articles that include the theory and evidence for the effect of inflation on growth, using the Lucas endogenous growth theory (Gillman, Max, 2009, Inflation Theory in Economics: Welfare, Velocity, Growth and Business Cycles, Routledge, Oxon UK and New York, USA).

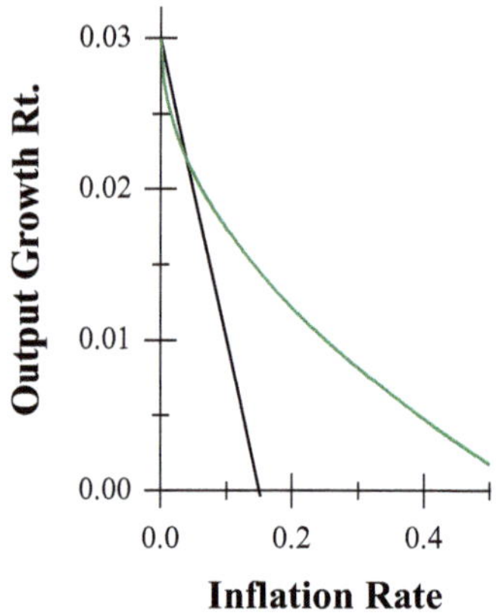

Figure 6.8 Theory: how Inflation Tax Lowers the Output Growth Rate

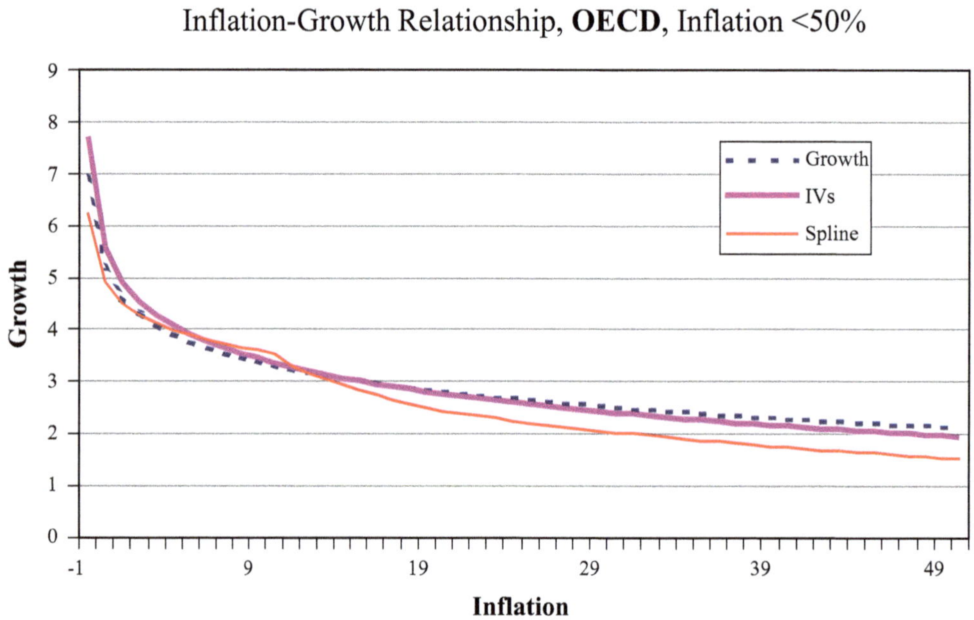

Figure 6.9: Effect of inflation on real GDP Growth rate, OECD developed country sample set; panel data estimation

Figure 6.8 shows possible theoretic effects of the inflation rate on the long term growth rate. The straight black line indicates that as the inflation rate rises the growth rate falls at a constant rate. A more nuanced theory is that as the inflation rate rises, the growth rate indeed falls but at a decreasing rate as in the green line. This curved type of inflation-growth profile is backed by empirical evidence and theory (Gillman et al., 2004). As the inflation rate rises, the usage of fiat money (cash) is subject to higher tax rates, causing consumers to increasingly substitute to other costly means of exchange through the use of banking, rather than the use of cash. The avoidance of the inflation tax gives a valve by which the consumer can escape the tax such that there is not as much of a decrease in employment and in the output growth rate, as the inflation rate gets ever higher.

Empirical evidence is reported by Gillman, Harris and Matyas (2004) for both OECD developed countries and less developed countries. Figure 6.8 shows the estimated effect for a panel of OECD developed countries in Gillman et al. (2004); similar results are found for a panel of Less Developed countries. Consistent with the Gillman and Kejak (2005a, 2005b) theory, growth is the dependent variable explained by inflation (and other variables) such that as inflation rises the growth rate of real GDP falls strongly at first, and then at an ever-diminishing rate (as in green line of Figure 6.8). See also evidence of Granger-causality from inflation to unemployment in Shadman-Mehta (2001).[18]

6.4.5 Phillips Curve, Inflation and Unemployment

A misconception results when supply and demand are viewed in terms of aggregate output as the quantity and the nominal aggregate price level as the price. This ignores the microeconomic perspective that all prices are relative prices.

Nonetheless it is common to graph aggregate output this way and argue that supply and demand shocks can cause inflation. This reasoning is that an increase in either marginal cost, such as an "oil shock" from the supply side, or in aggregate demand, such as from a government spending increase, cause a shift up in either supply or demand and cause a higher price level. The movement from one nominal price level to a higher one is said to define an increase in the inflation rate.

A rise in the price level from one period to another would amount to a one period increase in inflation that would die out thereafter. A one period inflation increase is very temporary and not generally a focus of policy. The reason is that one period shifts do not provide for an explanation of the underlying inflation rate. *Sustained inflation* is not caused by nominal output rising from a one period shock.

Theories of *cost-push inflation* and demand-pull inflation can be illustrated by using theories of the nominal value of output. But these theories are based on one period shocks in the price level and a temporary inflation rate increase. The theoretical concept of clearly identifying cost-push and demand-pull shocks that cause temporary inflation is not backed up by evidence.

The use of a nominal price level also goes against the tradition in economics of using real quantities and relative prices. It is necessary to focus on the change in nominal prices to understand inflation. As a result, what has emerged from this historical evolution of macroeconomics is an investigation of how the real economy can be affected by inflation over time.

The *Phillips Curve* involves both statistical and theoretical concepts that capture a relation between changes in the inflation rate and the performance of the real economy. Apparently the evidence was first discovered by Irving Fisher's published statistical work in 1923. Fisher (1923) graphed a positive correlation between inflation rates and unemployment rates over time, with time on the horizontal axis.[19]

Figure 6.10 shows some elements of a Fisher type of relation of the US Civilian Unemployment Rate in blue and the CPI inflation rate in red for the years 1948 to 2015. During the periods when the two data series move opposite of each other, a type of Fisher/Phillips relation is seen with the negative correlation. For example, in the 1960's, when the US involvement in the Vietnam war was just starting to accelerate, the inflation rate rose and the unemployment rate fell. Counterexamples of a strong positive correlation also exist such as during the 1970's and early 1980's when both inflation and unemployment were high. This mixed experience led to theories of when the negative correlation would exist and when it would not. This theoretical development is usefully framed using the style of graphs that Phillips (1958) pioneered.

Phillips (1958) graphed the *inflation - unemployment statistical relation* in a different way than Fisher (1923). Phillips used United Kingdom data to graph the rate of change in nominal wages as the vertical axis and the unemployment rate as the horizontal axis of the graph. He then plotted the pairs of the wage percentage change

---

[18]Gillman, M, Mark N. Harris and László Mátyás, 2004. "Inflation and growth: Explaining a negative effect," *Empirical Economics*, 29(1, January): 149–167. Gillman, M. and Michal Kejak, 2005a. "Inflation and Balanced-Path Growth with Alternative Payment Mechanisms," *Economic Journal*, 115(500): 247–270; Gillman, Max and Michal Kejak, 2005b,"Contrasting Models of the Effect of Inflation on Growth, "*Journal of Economic Surveys*, 19(1): 113–136. Shadman-Mehta F., 2001, "A re-evaluation between wages and unemployment in the United Kingdom." *Economica* 68: 567–606.

[19]Reprint: Irving Fisher, 'I Discovered the Phillips Curve': "A Statistical Relation between Unemployment and Price Changes" Journal of Political Economy Vol. 81, No. 2, Part 1 (Mar. – Apr., 1973), pp. 496–502; original: Irving Fisher, 1923, ibid., International Labour Review, 13(6, June): 785–792.

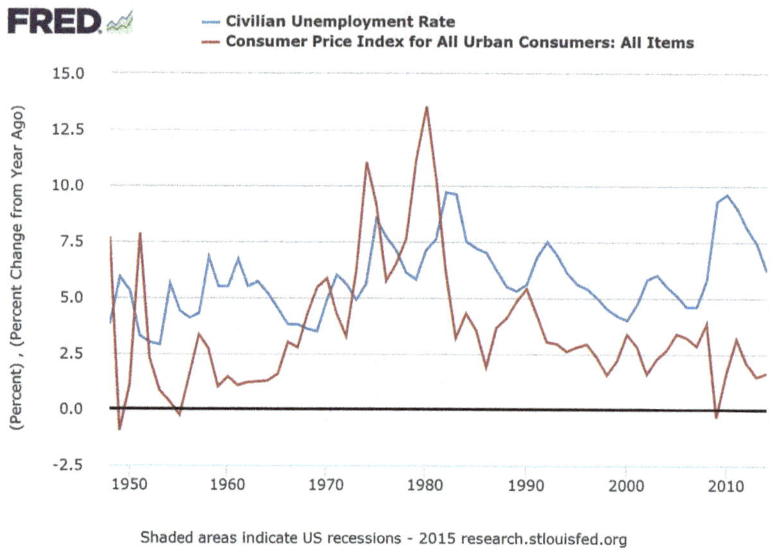

Figure 6.10 US CPI Inflation and Unemployment Rates

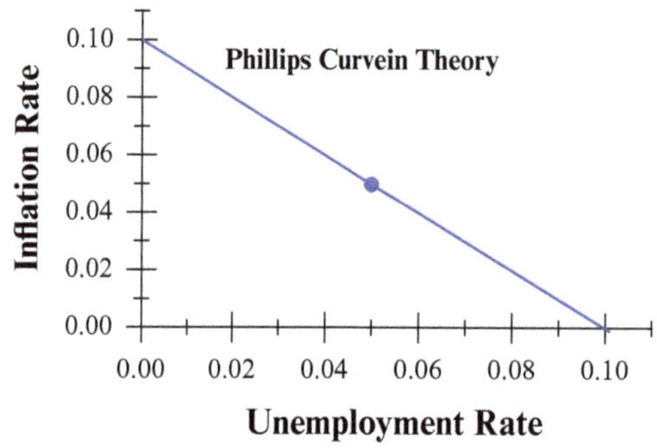

Figure 6.11 Phillips Curve: Example Short Run Statistical Trade-Off of Unemployment Rate and Inflation Rate, where each point on line represents a particular year

and the unemployment rate for each year as a point on the graph. For his data period, this gave a downward slope, indicating statistically that higher wage inflation was linked to lower unemployment.[20]

The Phillips curve is purely a statistical relation, and can be shown in different ways. Instead of nominal wage rates, the CPI inflation rate is typically used in modern Phillips curve graphs. Thus many standard Phillips curves simply graph each point as representing the inflation rate and unemployment rate of a given year, in a given country.

The problem is that the Phillips curve relation breaks down over and over again, while holding for some very limited periods. To illustrate this, consider the theoretical rendering of the Phillips curve graph. Figure 6.11 shows a single Phillips curve, with a negative or what we can call an *inverse relation between unemployment and inflation.*

The actual Phillips Curve for US data can be graphed for the US using the FRED data base.[21] This data runs from 1948 to 2009, on a monthly basis. Defining each data point for inflation as the percentage change

[20]Phillips, A. W., 1958, "The Relation between Unemployment and the Rate of Change of Money Wage Rates in the United Kingdom, 1861–1957," *Economica*, 25 (100, Nov.): 283–299. Original article online at http://people.virginia.edu/~lc7p/202/Phillips58.pdf

[21]https://research.stlouisfed.org/pdl/258?pageID=1&ob=&od=asc&filter[0]=0&filtergo=Filter

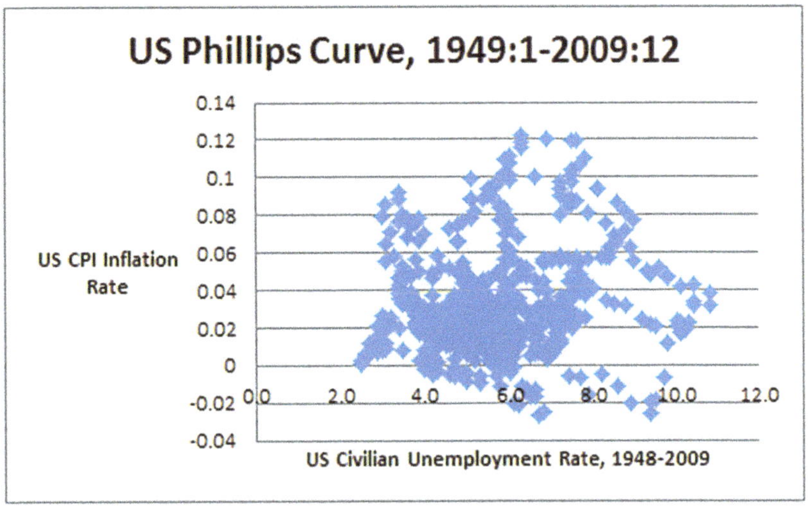

Figure 6.12 FRED data for Phillips Curve, 1948–2009

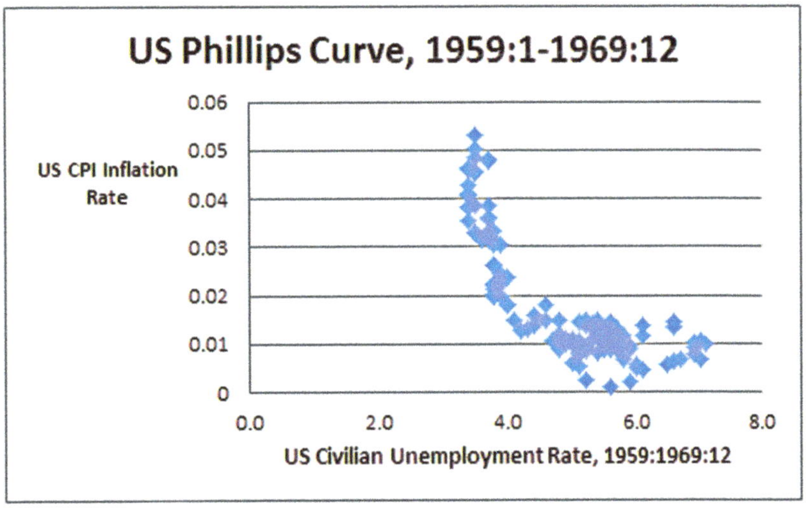

Figure 6.13 US Phillips Data with Negative Slope

from one year before, for each month, provides a full data series of inflation rates. These are then graphed with the monthly unemployment rate data series, in Figure 6.12.

It is clear in Figure 6.12 that there is not a negatively sloped curve, as in Figure 6.11, for the full data set. However, the US data that is perhaps most often used is the decade of the 1960's, as the US became more engaged in the Vietnam war. Figure 6.13 graphs the data from 1959:1 to 1969:12. There appears to be the expected inverse relation between US inflation and unemployment, as in a Phillips curve. Note that during the exact same time period, the Russell 3000 stock market index rose 66%, an average of 6% per year.

Figure 6.14 graphs the monthly US Phillips curve data for 1981:7 to 1983:11. Here a Phillips curve emerges as the US Federal Reserve reduced money supply growth rapidly in the early 1980's, while the unemployment rose and the inflation rate fell. This was a reverse movement down a Phillips curve. Paul Volcker was Chairmen of the Federal Reserve System when this *Volcker deflation* occurred. At the same time, the Russell 3000 stock index fell 21% in the year from August 11, 1981 to August 12, 1982, from 169 to 134, corresponding closely to the main part of the downward portion of the Phillips curve in Figure 6.14. This asset price drop is shown in Figure 6.15.

From January 1983 to June 1983, inflation fell while the unemployment rate remained the same, with inflation hitting a low point of 1.74% in June 1983. From July 1983, inflation began rising again and unemployment began falling. Figure 6.14 shows that this apparently began a new Phillips curve, which appears shifted

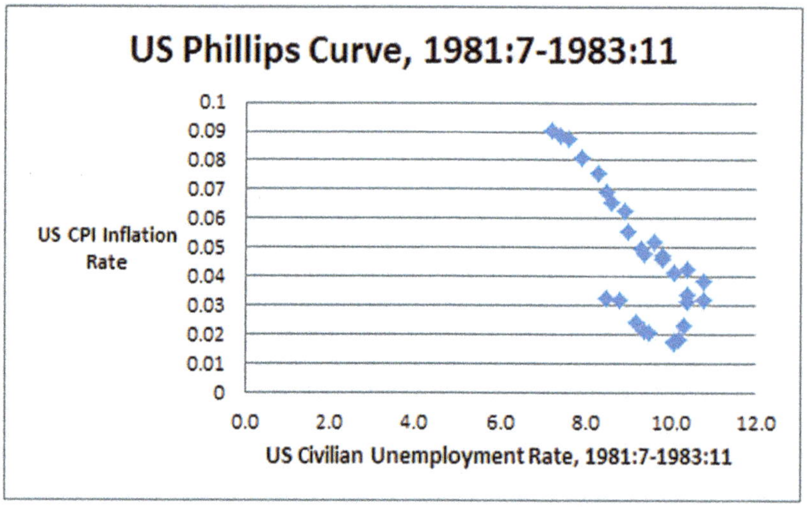

Figure 6.14 US Phillips Curve is Shifted Out During Volcker Deflation

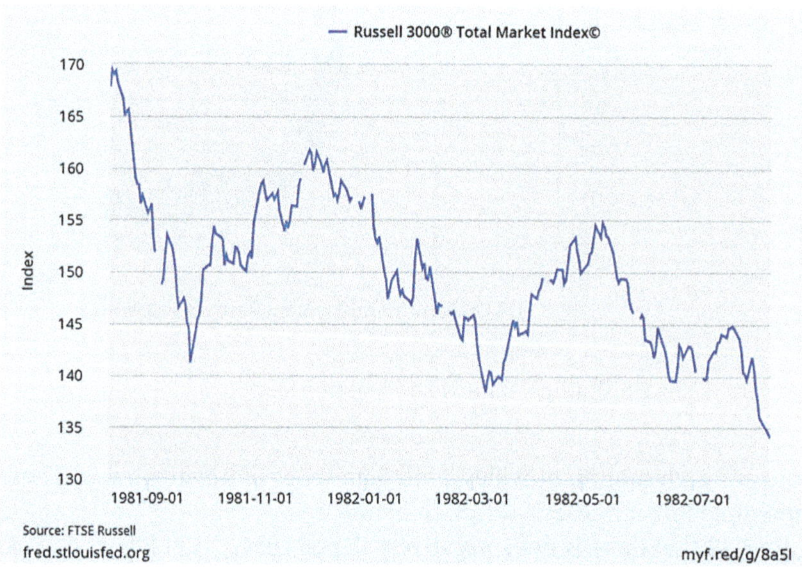

Figure 6.15 Russell 3000 Asset Decline by 21%: 08/11/1981-08/12/1982

inwards relative to the Phillips curve relation of July 1981 to January 1983. During this upward swing of the Phillips curve, the Russell 3000 had begun rising already and from August 12, 1918 to October 11, 1983, it rose from 134 on August 12, 1981 to 240 on October 11, 1983, a 79% increase in asset prices. This stock boom overlaps the period of the 1983 upward turn of the Phillips curve until October 1983.

Expectations Theory of Phillips Curve

One theory of the shifting of the empirical Phillips curves over time, when they exist at all, is that they occur because the inflation rate accelerates or decelerates unexpectedly. This theory explain the existence of Phillips curves because of differences between expected inflation rate and the actual inflation rate. It became known as the *Expectations Theory of the Phillips curve.*

In particular, if the inflation rate accelerates unexpectedly, the unemployment rate is expected in theory to fall. Conversely if the inflation rate decelerates unexpectedly, the unemployment rate is expected to rise. When inflation stays in the range that is expected, no Phillips curve exists in theory.

The expectations theory may explain why in the 1960's there was a movement up a Phillips curve when inflation accelerated, and in the early 1980's a movement down another Phillips curve.`

The other part of the Expectations Theory is that over time as people adjust their expectations to the actual inflation rate, the Phillips curve relation either shifts outwards or inwards. It shifts outwards as inflation expectations increase and inwards as inflation expectations decrease. The movement out in the Phillips curves, from that of Figure 6.13 to that of Figure 6.14, would be explained as an increase in the expected inflation rate. The shift inwards in Figure 6.14 during the later part of 1983 would be explained as a decrease in the expected inflation rate, as people began to realize the extent of the Volcker deflation as being of a permanent nature.

The concept behind the Expectations Theory is that there is confusion between real demand for output and a change in the nominal value of output. When inflation accelerates unexpectedly, firms see the nominal value of demand rising. At first they raise their nominal price for output and at the same time raise output supply, thinking that in part the nominal price increase is due to an increase in the real demand for their goods. They do not realize the full extent to which the general price level is rising at a faster rate, and so partly confuse the nominal price increases with real price increases, the latter of which induces a greater supply of goods.

If firms expect the inflation rate to be the same as it was previously, and yet see prices for their products increasing, then they think that the current price increase is a real one. This leads them to supply more output at a higher price, as they think they are moving up their real supply curve. But if in fact the real price (in *constant dollars*) is actually not higher because the aggregate inflation rate has accelerated beyond their expected inflation rate, then their nominal price rise may be just keeping pace with the new higher inflation rate and no new supply of output is warranted.

This means that if they mistake part of what is only a nominal price increase for a real price increase, they mistakenly increase output and employment so that the unemployment rate falls. This is the theory for why the inverse relation exists between inflation and unemployment. Expected inflation is less than the actual inflation rate, and firms increase output because they think the nominal demand increase is a real demand increase.

Once firms realize that the inflation rate is higher, they adjust their expectations to the actual inflation rate. They then reduce output and employment and the unemployment rate rises. Once expected and actual inflation rates become equal again, the *trade-off between inflation and unemployment* no longer exists. Inflation can remain higher while unemployment goes back to its previous level as expectations adjust to a new higher inflation rate.

Figure 6.16 provides the Expectations Theory extension of the simple Phillips graph. Along the original Blue line, inflation and unemployment both are 5% when the expected inflation rate is also 5% and so equal to the actual inflation rate. Everywhere along the blue line, the expected inflation rate is 5%, but to the right of the 5% unemployment rate, along the blue line, the actual inflation rate is lower than the expected 5%. To the left of the 5% unemployment rate, along the blue line, the actual inflation rate is higher than the expected inflation rate.

When actual inflation rises from 5% to 8%, in an unexpected fashion, the economy moves upwards and backwards along the Blue line to a new equilibrium (as in the 1960's Phillips curve). The unemployment rate falls to 2% while actual inflation is 8%. Once the economy realizes the actual inflation rate is 8%, so that the expected inflation rate also equals 8%, unemployment rises back up to 5%. The economy then shifts its position onto the Green Phillips curve along which the expected inflation rate is 8%. In the process of moving from the Blue to the Green Phillips curves, they move from a lower point on the Black vertical line to a higher point on the Black line. This Black line is called the *Vertical "Long Run Phillips Curve"*, to which the economy must return, at a 5% unemployment rate. The 5% unemployment rate is then called the natural rate of unemployment, which occurs when there is *no Money Illusion* as defined by when the actual inflation rate equals the expected inflation rate.

Figure 6.16 also shows that if inflation decelerates from an expected 5% to 2%, the economy shifts from the Blue Phillips Curve to the Red Phillips Curve. The economy may first move downwards along the Blue

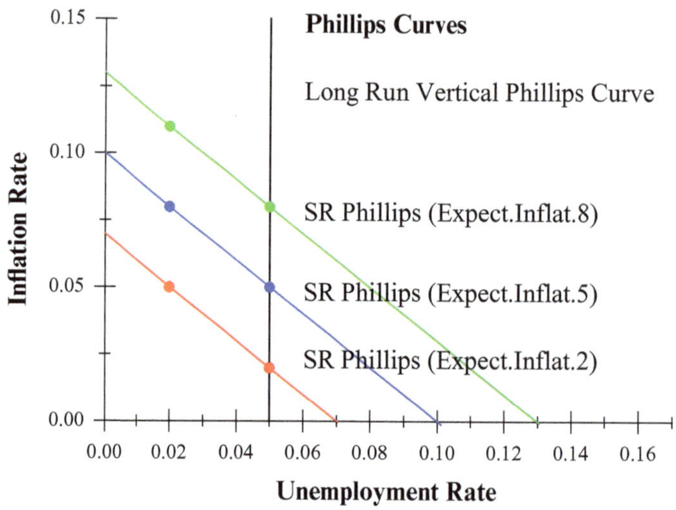

Figure 6.16 Phillips Curve: Short Run Statistical Trade-Off Versus Long Run No-Tradeoff; Unemployment Rate Unaffected by Inflation Rate at "Natural Rate of Unemployment"

line (as in the 1981 actual Phillips curve) if the expected inflation rate is lower than the actual one, because the nominal price decline is thought to be a real decline in the demand for goods. The economy shifts back to the Red Phillips curve once expectations adjust to the actual inflation rate being 2%. So the economy once again is on a point along the vertical Black long run Phillips curve.

The Green, Blue and Red Phillips curves are known as *short run Phillips curves,* each of which intersects the *vertical long run Phillips curve* at the natural rate of unemployment of 5%. The long run vertical feature expresses the idea that there is no long run trade-off between unemployment and inflation, once actual inflation equals expected inflation. Edmund Phelps and Robert E. Lucas, Jr., won Nobel prizes for characterizing this long run Phillips curve and the temporary nature of the short run Phillips curve. Both Nobel Laureates reasoned that the opposite movement between the inflation rate and the unemployment rate is a temporary trade-off that only occurs when expectations of inflation are incorrect.

Expectations can shift anytime, so movement up or down a short run Phillips curve is not necessary when the inflation rate changes as long as the change is an expected one. This is partly why the Federal Reserve announces their inflation target and tries to avoid unnecessary, inefficient, short run Phillips types of tradeoffs. See Sargent for more on how a short run Phillips curve can be avoided when changing the inflation rate.[22]

Banking Theory of Crises and Debt-Deflation

The so-called stagflation era of the Vietnam war was a *low growth "crisis"* in US economic history. Rather than exhibiting a decade long Phillps curve, the 1970's was characterized more in line with a mix of negatively and positively sloped Phillips curve periods. For example, inflation and unemployment went in the same direction monthly from 1973:9 - 1974:11, and 1975:1 - 1976: 11.

There was no broad financial sector collapse in the 1970's , but banks were implicitly taxed when the inflation rate rose above the maximum interest rate they were allow to offer under Regulation Q of the 1933 Banking Act. After the inflation rate rose above the Regulation Q interest rate ceilings, in the early 1980's a major bank deregulation began in legislative and regulatory steps from 1981 until 1994. The deregulation of the finance sector during the 1980's and 1990's is thought to have caused higher productivity in the bank sector. This in turn is thought to have led to lower costs of financial intermediation across an array of its

[22]Sargent, T.J., 1982, "The Ends of Four Big Inflations", in *Inflation: Causes and Effects,* editor, R. E. Hall, p. 41–98, NBER and the University of Chicago Press; online at http://www.nber.org/chapters/c11452.pdf

services. The high growth period of the US during the mid-1980's throughout the 1990's may have been facilitated by this national *bank deregulation.*

The bank industry deregulation allowed interstate branching by banks, a fuller range of banking services offered by investment banks, and a general decrease in restrictions on what type of firm could offer financial intermediation within and across States. In contrast, during the Great Depression and Great Recession, a reversal of bank deregulation in essence occurred. More regulations were imposed in both cases because the finance sector was viewed as subject to system-wide failure.

The failure of a broad part of the finance sector is often called *systemic financial failure.* It becomes of utmost concern to policymakers because a collapse of the bank sector can cause a collapse of investment in the economy. This in turn can lead to lower real GDP growth and higher unemployment rates.

The crises of the Great Depression and the Great Recession both saw major banking crises, unlike the stagflation Vietnam war era or more typical US recessions. This gives rise to theories of why the bank sector collapses and how this can lead to a collapse of the economy. Irving Fisher characterized a bank collapse as coming from a "*Debt-Deflation downwards spiral*". As the economy fell, asset values fell, and the repayment of loans became more difficult. Bank balance sheets began showing a negative equity, so that they became insolvent, and many closed during both the Great Depression and Great Recession. The insolvency of banks made the financial intermediation of investment difficult, so investment and output fell, with the result of a deep recession or depression.

A bit of the debt-deflation theory can be seen with the deflation that occurred recently in the US. Figure 6.17 graphs the Phillips curve from July 2008 to May 2009 for the US. The Dow Jones Industrial Average fell from 11,555 on August 1, 2008 to 7063 on February 1, 2009, a 39% fall. Asset prices fell dramatically by this measure, as the unemployment rate rose and inflation fell.

For the same period of July 2008 to May 2009, Figure 6.18 shows the S & P 500 price index decline that correlates highly with the Phillips curve. The Standard and Poor's 500 is an index of a collection of companies in the US with listed shares on the stock exchange, similar to the Russell 3000 or the Dow Jones Industrial Average. It illustrates how asset price decreases may be a key factor in explaining Phillips curves during crises.

Fisher's debt-deflation theory does not contradict the Expectations Theory, but his banking theory explains a similar experience as in a Phillips curve. The computed inflation rate also includes the cost of capital goods. As the price of capital falls, so does the price index. For example the CPI price index and the GDP deflation price index provide very similar measures of the inflation rate. The GDP deflator includes an investment component that a capital asset price crash will affect. Such a decline of the cost of investment goods relative to labor gets reflected in a decrease in the calculated inflation rate that occurred during the Great Recession.

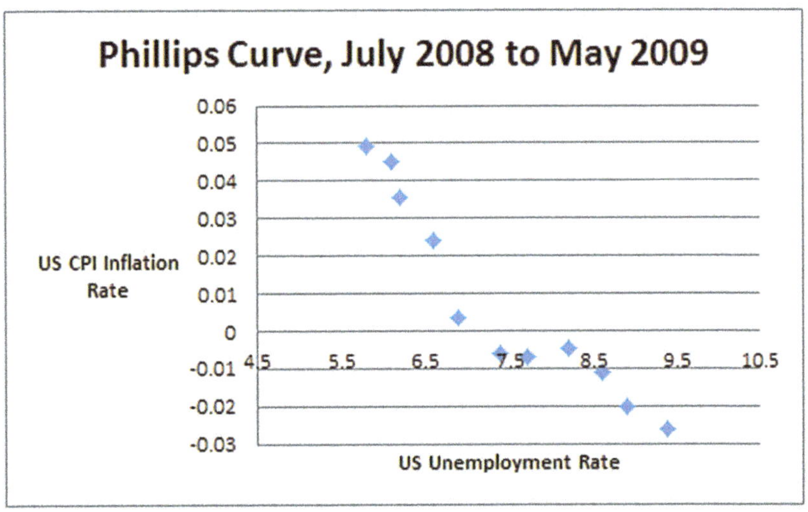

Figure 6.17 Phillips Curve During US Stock Market Crash and the Great Recession

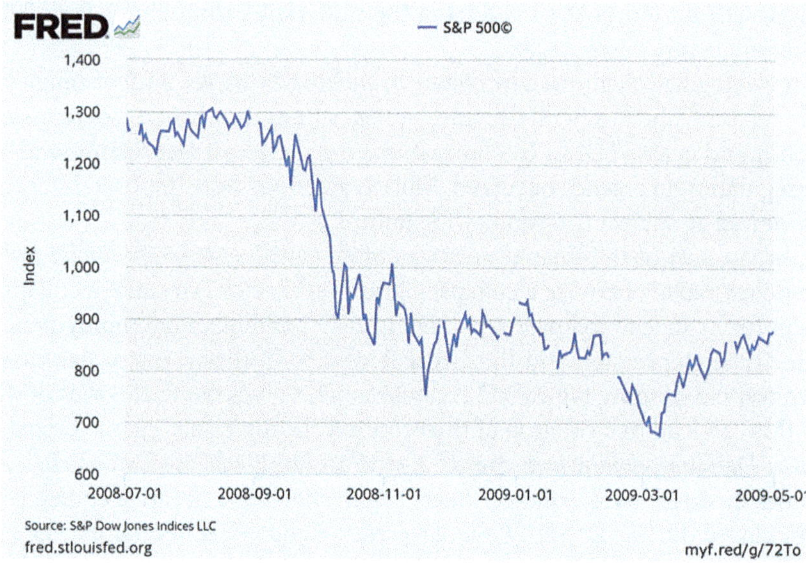

Figure 6.18 Standards & Poors 500 Stock Price in Great Recession

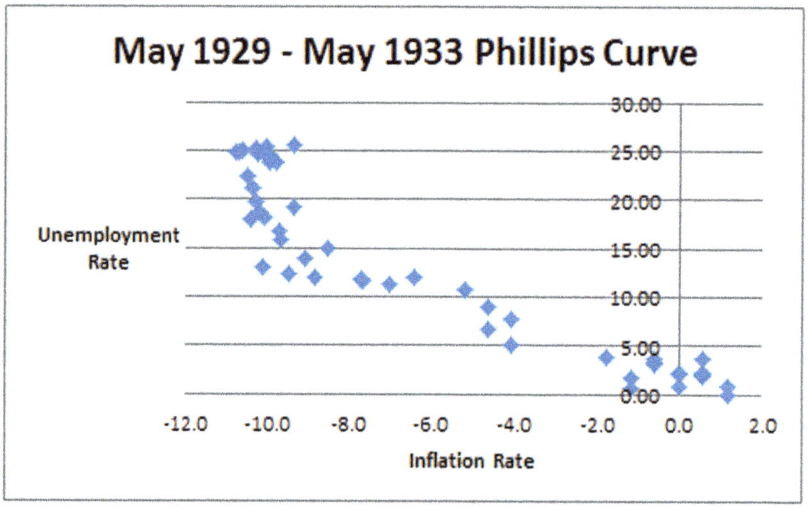

Figure 6.19 US Phillips Curve During Great Depression

Further study might indicate the degree to which sharp Phillips curve periods coincide with large swings in asset prices that explain part of the inflation rate changes. This may help disentangle the Fisher debt-deflation theory from the Expectations Theory of the Phillips curve experiences. Both may be consistent, but there may also be an asset value story that is not fully recounted with only the Expectations Theory of the Phillips curve.

Rare Events & Lost Decades

The US Great Depression is sometimes called a "*rare event*", and the inclusive decade from 1929 to 1939 classifies as what is termed a " *lost decade*" because of the length of time for GDP to recover to its 1929 level. Figure 6.18 shows that the Great Depression exhibits a striking Phillips curve, here shown from May 1929 to May 1933.

Figure 6.20 shows for the exact same period the Dow Jones Stock average in terms of its percentage change from a year ago. The strong negative correlation between the Depression's Phillips Curve and its asset price

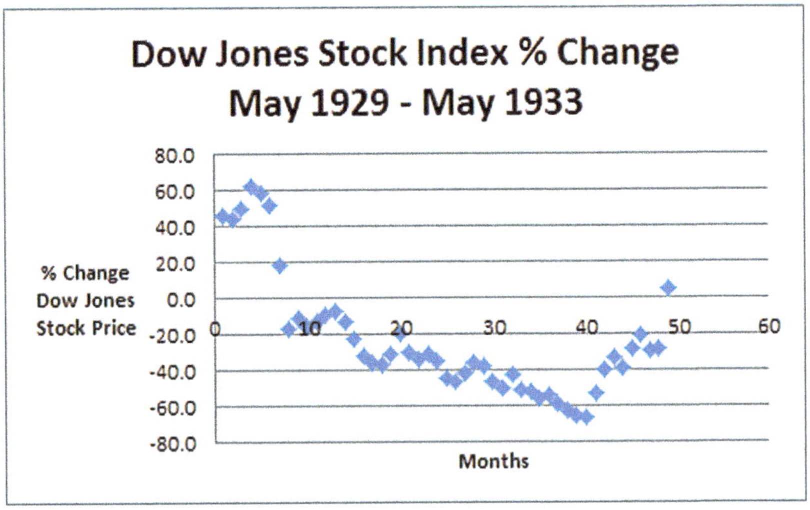

Figure 6.20 Dow Jones Industrial Average Percentage Change in Great Depression

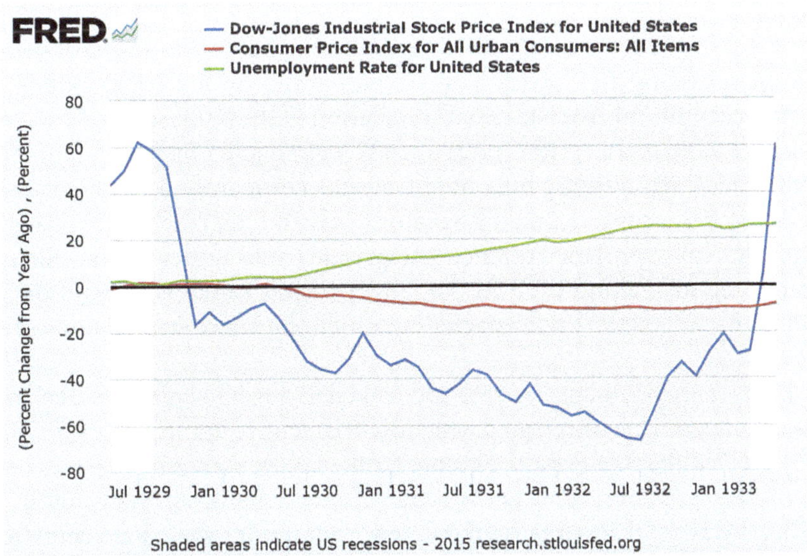

Figure 6.21 Inflation, Unemployment and Stock Prices in Great Depression

change suggests that part of the decline in the inflation rate may have been caused by the decline in asset values, as is consistent with Irving Fisher's theory of debt-deflation. Asset price deflation can lead to aggregate price level deflation.

With time on the horizontal axis, from May 1929 to May 1933, Figure 6.20 shows the three series of the previous two graphs over time. Until July 1932, the unemployment rate in green rises as the CPI inflation rate in red falls, and as the percentage change in the Dow Jones Stock price average in blue falls.

In a fashion consistent with the debt-deflation theory, it may be that as capital prices fall the price of goods and services falls relative to the price of labor, making the relative price of labor higher, and unemployment greater. While the bankruptcy of firms also makes the unemployment rate higher, there may be a viable relative price component of the explanation for the empirical correlations not only of unemployment and inflation, but also of asset prices.

"Lost decades" refer to long periods of low growth in real output, for a given country, such as during the Great Depression. The low growth period after the US Great Recession has given rise to the post-2008 years as being called a lost decade as well. The Vietnam war period was called one of stagflation. It might qualify equally as a "lost decade" because of the low growth experienced.

Japan experienced low growth in the 1990's that led to the coining of the term "*lost decade*" by Hayashi and Prescott (2002). It is interesting that this also coincided with an asset price crash and bank system difficulties. It also had low inflation as in the US 2008–2016 period. Banking explanations of the Japan lost decade have been given, but there is no consensus on the relation between asset values, inflation, the health of the banking system and low growth periods. [23]

6.5 Application: Great Depression Turn-Point

The Depression started when President Hoover promoted and eventually passed the Tariff Act of 1930, also called the Smoot–Hawley Tariff Act. It raised excise taxes on imports (called tariffs) to 59.1% of their value on about one third of imports. Then Hoover attempted to "balance the federal government budget", which saw a large and growing deficit in 1931 and 1932, with the Revenue Act of 1932 as passed June 6, 1932. In particular it raised the top marginal personal income tax rate to 63% from 25%, while doubling the estate tax and slightly raising the corporate tax rate.

6.5.1 US Bank Collapse and Government Response

Besides the Revenue Act of 1932, the focus of US legislation in 1932–33 may have been more on money and banking than on spending and taxes. The US embarked on a radical extension of the federal government in its support and "macroprudential" regulation of the bank sector. On January 22, 1932, the Reconstruction Finance Corporation (RFC) Act of 1932 was enacted by which federal loans were made available to the entire banking industry plus life insurance companies and railroads. On February 27, 1932, the Banking Act of 1932, cosponsored by Senator Glass and Representative Steagall, allowed for the Federal Reserve Bank System to provided financing to private banks under "extraordinary circumstances". This has been interpreted as making the Fed the lender of last resort role. And on July 22, 1932, the Federal Home Loan Bank Act of 1932 was enacted by which the US chartered and regulated the savings and loan industry.

Nonetheless, by 1933, unemployment was 25% and real GDP down to half of its level in 1929. And during 1933 the bank crisis continued. This culminated with the US Executive branch of government being informed on March 1, 1933 by the Fed that the Federal Reserve Bank of New York gold reserves had fallen below the 40% required ratio of gold reserves relative to the Federal Reserve Bank currency notes.

On March 3, 1933, the Federal Reserve Bank of New York, under their President George L. Harrison, adopted a resolution recommending action to the Federal Reserve Board. The action recommended was the imposition of a nationwide bank holiday to stop the panic and the outflow of gold reserves as people cashed in their currency for gold (under the gold standard that held at the time). President-elect Roosevelt was reportedly unwilling to consider this.

On March 4, 1933, the Federal Reserve's 12 Regional Banks took the decision in their own hands. That day saw the "Fed" lock their 12 Regional Bank doors. And they closed or restricted operations of private banks in 37 US States.

Bank Holiday of March 1933

On the same day of March 4, 1933, President-elect Franklin Roosevelt was sworn into the Office of the President of the US. In his inaugural address that day, Roosevelt emphasized reducing unemployment and strictly regulating the bank sector. On the next working day, at 1a.m., Monday March 6, Roosevelt declared the suspension of all banking transactions, to last until March 9, 1933.

[23]See Fumio Hayashi and Edward C Prescott, 2002, "The 1990s in Japan: A Lost Decade", Review of Economic Dynamics, 5(1, Jan.): 206–235.

Meanwhile, the Federal Reserve Board managed to classify private banks into three categories, A, B, and C, with A being solvent and able to be reopened now, B being possibly able to be reopened with some restructuring, and C being insolvent and unable to be reopened. On March 9, 1933, Congress passed and the President signed the Emergency Banking Act of 1933. This retroactively approved the nationwide bank holiday and set out how the government could strictly regulate the bank re-openings.

On March 13, 1933, the twelve regional Federal Reserve Banks were allowed to reopen. By March 15, more than 90% of private banks reopened and deposits poured in much faster than withdrawals. Some 4000 commercial banks and 1700 savings and loan banks did not reopen as they were declared failed and closed.

Gold and Money

After the bank reopenings in March 1933, the US under Roosevelt's executive proclamation on April 5, 1933 required that gold coins and notes be returned to the Federal Reserve Bank system by May 1, 1933, in exchange for Federal Reserve notes. Since the Gold Act of 1900, the price of gold was $20.67 per ounce. Roosevelt prohibited the export of gold on April 19, 1933, and the US officially violated terms of the gold standard as of that day.[24]

Reportedly the same day, on April 19, 1933, Senator Elmer Thomas met with the President and staff and drafted what became called the Thomas Amendment. The amendment was known as the Inflation Bill before its enactment into law via the Agricultural Adjustment Act. Under the Thomas Amendment the US was given permission to reduce the gold content of its dollar by 50%. In addition it required the Federal Reserve System to purchase $3 billion worth of US Treasury debt using Federal Reserve Notes (later, the Fed would get back the $3 billion).

By May 10 some $800 million in gold coins and notes had been accumulated by the Federal Reserve Bank system. On May 12, The Agricultural Adjustment Act was signed into law with the Thomas Amendment added. This meant that the gold value of the dollar was now one-half of its original level.

On June 5, 1933 the US link to the gold standard, started in 1879 under the Resumption Act and reinforced by the Gold Standard Act of 1900, was completely broken under Roosevelt. On that day he signed the Congressional Joint Resolution to Suspend the Gold Standard and Abrogate the Gold Clause, which eliminated the right to claim payment on any debt in gold note or coin.[25]

The Day After Gold: Deposit Insurance Enacted

The day after the US gold standard ended, on June 6, 1933, the Banking Act of 1933 was enacted. As sponsored by Senator Carter Glass (D-VA) and Representative Henry Steagall (D-AL), this act introduced formal regulations on the banking industry, such as on within-state and interstate branching, and speculative investment by banks. These effectively restricted bank branching and created the division between commercial and investment banking; regulations gave banking institutions one year to decide whether they were commercial or investment banks.

However another key ingredient was drafted within the Banking Act of 1933 before it was passed. Reportedly Senator Glass only agreed to the bill after an amendment was added to permit federal bank deposit insurance. And despite reported threats by President Roosevelt to veto the Act because of this provision it was added to the Congressional Bill and passed within the Banking Act of 1933. It established the Federal Deposit Insurance Corporation (FDIC) on a temporary basis with the authority to provide deposit insurance to banks that became members of the FDIC system of insurance, and gave the FDIC regulatory power over non-FDIC-member banks. Further the FDIC deposit insurance fund was capitalized by an initial US Treasury loan of $289 million.

The FDIC came into effect on January 1, 1934, and it provided insurance for up to $2500 per deposit account. The Banking Act of 1933 also prohibited the paying of interest on checking accounts (later known as Regulation Q). This set of banking laws, from the Reconstruction Finance Corporation (RFC) Act of 1932

---

[24]https://fraser.stlouisfed.org/docs/meltzer/craint89.pdf

[25]http://freedom-school.com/h-j-r-192.pdf

to the March banking holiday and the Emergency Banking Act of 1933, followed closely by the Banking Act of 1933, coincide with the trough of the US Great Depression being reached in the first quarter of 1933. And they set the structure for Federal and private banking that is used to this day, with significant amendment having occurred over time.

For example, the Banking Act of 1935 amended the 1933 Act so as to establish the Federal Open Market Committee, which included voting rights by the Federal Reserve Bank. Follow-up banking reform continued throughout the 1930's, as this chapter's Appendix shows. The Appendix also notes specific legislation enacted immediately after the 2008 Great Recession that was designed to begin banking reform once again.

6.5.2 Irving Fisher with the Last Word

After rising and then falling again, the DJIA stock index started rising ever upwards in March 1933, and never reached its Depression levels again. National output also started upwards in March 1933. And the unemployment rate turned downwards.

Fisher (1933) argues that the way out of a severe debt-deflation type of depression is to "reflate" the price level. He stresses that the primary way to reverse the sequence of events is to increase the money supply so the deflation does not cycle ever downwards. And he argues that this is exactly what President Roosevelt accomplished with the series of legislative and executive actions starting in March 1933.

Fisher emphasizes March 1933 as the turning point that would not have happened without the "reflation" banking policy. This view considers the banking collapse the key to the Great Depression. And it makes the ending of the Depression hinge on the resuscitation of the bank system by various banking Acts starting in March 1933.[26]

6.6 Appendix: Great Depression & Recent Policy

6.6.1 Other 1930's US Banking Acts

On May 12, 1933, the Emergency Farm Mortgage Act was signed which enabled the US government to extend loans to farms who were behind on loans, and so delinquent on them. This was followed on May 27 by an Executive order of Roosevelt creating the Farm Credit Administration (FCA) to supervise all farm credit institutions.[27]

Also on May 27, 1933, The Securities Act of 1933 was enacted. This act regulated and enforced information disclosure by companies and corporations about their operations. On June 6, 1934, the Securities Exchange Act of 1934 was enacted so as to establish the Securities and Exchange Commission. This commission regulated companies and provided oversight of the securities markets in which shares of private company stocks are traded. This was a matter of providing oversight of the actual market-place in which financial capital was exchanged, and so it was closely associated with the regulation of the financial intermediary industry.

On June 13, 1933, The Home Owners Loan Act provided emergency relief for home loan indebtedness. Then on June 16, 1933 by The Farm Credit Act of 1933 was passed which strengthened the system of Federal Land Banks and Federal Intermediate Credit Banks, for farmers, as well as creating Banks for Cooperatives and a Central Bank for Cooperatives, all aimed at farming and rural development.[28] On June 26, 1934, the Federal Credit Union Act was passed, according to the Act's written preface, in order "to establish a Federal Credit Union System, to establish a further market for securities of the United States, and to make more available to people of small means credit for provident purposes through a national system of cooperative

[26]Point 39. Those who imagine that Roosevelt's avowed reflation is not the cause of our recovery but that we had "reached the bottom anyway" are very much mistaken' (Fisher, 1933, p. 346).

[27]http://www.fca.gov/about/history/historyFCA_FCS.html

[28]Twelve Federal Land Banks were started across the US in 12 regional districts, in 1916, through the Federal Farm Loan Act of 1916, with the aim of providing long term credit to farmers and rural citizens. The Agricultural Credits Act of 1923 likewise started twelve regional Federal Intermediate Credit Banks, with the aim of providing short term credit to the farm sector.

credit, thereby helping to stabilize the credit structure of the United States" (http://research.archives.gov/description/299841). This allowed the FCA to charter all federal credit unions, leading to more than 4000 by 1942, when the FDIC took over oversight of the credit unions.

US banking legislation continued to ensure the soundness of the banking system with additional deposit insurance. On June 28, 1934, the National Housing Act of 1934 was enacted and it created the Federal Savings and Loan Insurance Corporation (FSLIC) as the means of providing deposit insurance to the "savings and loans" banks. This was later (in 1989) absorbed into the FDIC with a separate insurance fund for these banks.

The Banking Act of 1935 made the FDIC permanent and increased the amount of deposits covered for each account to $5000. Thus federal deposit insurance, after starting as an amendment in the bottom of the trough of the Great Depression, became fully enacted as a permanent institution that remains in this banking insurance role today.

The US Treasury gold depository at Fort Knox, Kentucky, was built in 1936 to hold the huge stock of US government gold reserves that had by then accumulated. This book-marked one sense in which the loss of gold reserves during the banking panic of 1933 was stopped and fully reversed through this sequence of bank Acts. It was the loss of gold reserves that led to the recommendation to shut down the bank system in March 1933, and this accumulation of gold by 1936 showed how successful the banking reforms with deposit insurance turned out to be.

Lessons appeared to have been learned about the role of banking policy, as seen when the US bank panic of 2008 occurred and policy focused on the bank sector. And in contrast, opposite types of policy were taken elsewhere that show fragility of the market system. This contrast in policy mirrored the Great Depression.

6.6.2 Great Depression Federal Spending

Just as fast and furious as were the banking and money laws was the pace of government spending laws that were enacted. The Emergency Relief and Construction Act of 1932 of July 21, 1932, signed by President Hoover established the Reconstruction Finance Corporation (RFC). The Act's three main provisions according to Hoover are that it provided $300 million in temporary loans to States, $1.5 billion in loans for public works construction, and could assist agriculture.[29] Hoover also signed the Economy Act of 1932 that enabled the federal government to make purchases from federal agencies.

Roosevelt started his government spending acts on March 20, 1933, with the Government Economy Act. This cut government spending through a 15% reduction in pay to federal employees and a reduction in war veterans benefits. It reduced rather than increased spending.

On March 22, Roosevelt signed a law that began the end of prohibition, and instead the taxing of alcohol with the Beer-Wine Revenue Act (prohibition formally end in December 1933 with passage of the 21st Amendment to the US Constitution).

On March 31, Roosevelt signed into law The Emergency Conservation Work Act that created the Civilian Conservation Corps (CCC). The CCC for nine years provided jobs for those otherwise unemployed. The work was initially organized in conjunction with the Army and involved road building, telephone wiring, tree planting, national park development, and went on to many other activities using camps across all of the US States and using over 1 million people in the jobs and supervision.[30]

Following up on Hoover's July 1932 Emergency Relief Act, that gave grants to state and local governments, Roosevelt extended this on May 12, 1933 with the Federal Emergency Relief Act of 1933. This Act addressed unemployment related hardships, through the Reconstruction Finance Corporation, and later the Federal Emergency Relief Administration.[31]

Also on May 12, 1933, the Agricultural Adjustment Act was enacted. It is seen as the first of the modern farm bills. Production was restricted by paying farmers not to grow food. It was declared unconstitutional in 1936 but replaced by a government subsidy program for agricultural produce in 1938.

---

[29] http://www.presidency.ucsb.edu/ws/?pid=23170

[30] http://www.ccclegacy.org/CCC_Brief_History.html

[31] http://www.socialwelfarehistory.com/eras/federal-emergency-relief-act-of-1933

On May 18 came the Tennessee Valley Authority Act which invigorated an area of Appalachia through public works that go on to this day through the TVA.[32] On June 16, 1933, the National Industrial Recovery Act of 1933 was passed and existed for two years. It helped engender fair competition, while introducing a minimum wage and allowed union bargaining, in addition to creating another public works program. Also on June 16, 1933, The Emergency Railroad Transportation Act established a Federal Coordinator of Transportation who was directed to allow for anti-trust exceptions in helping the railroad industry consolidate.

The National Labor Relations Act of 1935 and The Social Security Act (SSA) of 1935 were also major initiatives that strengthened unions ability to bargain and that set up the Social Security trust fund for an old age federal pension plan financed by taxes. The SSA also provided for federal grants to States for state-run unemployment insurance programs, grants for state-run aid to dependent mothers with children, and grants to states for disabilities. Also it instituted vocational training and family health programs.[33]

6.6.3 International Policy Contrast

In Europe, parallel in time to F. D. Roosevelt's election and the subsequent revival of the United States, was Hitler's rise to power and the subsequent devastation of the German nation. In Germany an opposite strategy to Roosevelt's buttressing of US democracy was taken: Majority Party Chancellor Hitler dissolved the parliament's ability to pass legislation and turned the Nazi Third Reich into an unopposed platform for making laws that expropriated capital from huge swathes of its population. A tyrannical form of government began that killed its citizens, expropriated their wealth and ultimately attempted to expand this systemic repression across all of Europe. As democracy began its march to annihilation in Europe, the Roosevelt banking reforms and his Civilian Conservation Corps volunteer work camp sites across the country helped turn around the US economy and allowed the US to keep markets and political and social systems democratic in form.

On February 25, 1932, when Roosevelt was Governor of New York, Hitler became a German citizen. In 1932 elections, while Roosevelt won the US Presidential vote, Hitler's Nazi party came in second to President Hindenburg's Social Democratic Party in the German national vote. On January 30, 1933, Hitler was made Chancellor of Germany by President Hindenburg, while Roosevelt was inaugurated as US President on March 4, 1933.

Hitler, like Roosevelt, began a flurry of activity starting in March 1933. Roosevelt's was legislative, designed to reinvigorate the US economy. Hitler took a different approach. On March 21, 1933, Hitler had decrees signed by Hindenburg that released Nazis from prison, allowed for the arrest of anyone criticizing the Nazi party, and secretly established special courts and summary judgement and execution for political offenders. On March 23, 1933, the new German parliament, despite the Nazi party not having a majority, passed Hitler's "Enabling Act" that allowed him to make law without parliament approval. This ended democracy in effect and began a dictatorship. Before the voting that day, Hitler persuaded another major party to join the Nazi Party in a coalition majority that would guarantee passage of the Enabling Act. Since parties opposing the Nazis could now be imprisoned, a huge majority then voted for the Act.

In March 1933, instead of Roosevelt's CCC camps, Hitler established the first political prisoner concentration camp, Dachau. It served as a prototype for subsequent concentration camps. On April 26, 1933, Interior Minister Goring established the Gestapo from the political and intelligence departments of the police. On August 2, 1934, President Hindenburg died and Hitler abolished the office of President and made himself "Fuehrer and Reich Chancellor". Instead of putting people to work in public works, in March 1935 Hitler announced that the German army would expand to 600,000 men, thus violating the Treaty of Versailles that ended WWI. On September 15, 1935, Hitler established laws stripping Jews of citizenship and forbidding marriage by Germans with Jews, in laws known as the Nuremberg laws. In 1936 Hitler established the Sachsenhausen concentration camp, and in July 1937 the Buchenwald concentration camp. On September 30, 1938, Hitler negotiated the Munich Agreement by which he annexed to Germany the part of Czechoslovakia called the Sudetenland. The Neuengamme concentration camp was created

[32]http://www.tva.com/abouttva/history.htm

[33]http://www.ssa.gov/history/35act.html

in December 1938 and Poland was occupied by Germany and Russia starting in 1939. The UK declared war on Germany. WWII followed into which the US under Roosevelt ultimately entered and declared war on Germany after getting bombed by Japan in Pearl harbor. The opposing strides towards strengthening democracy by the US and weakening democracy by Germany finally collided in WWII, and Germany was defeated. [34]

Redux during the Great Recession, it is striking that during the bank crisis and stock market crash of 2008 President Bush's flurry of legislative activity in 2008 contrasted with Russian Putin's flurry of isolationalist military activity, in a way evocative of Roosevelt versus Hitler. Bush signed into law the February 13 Economic Stimulus Act of 2008, the June 30 Supplemental Appropriations Act of 2008, the July 30 Housing and Economic Recovery Act of 2008, and the October 3 Emergency Economic Stabilization Act of 2008. These acted to give additional federal unemployment insurance, to shore up housing loans and to recapitalize the US banking system (albeit a large military expenditure for Iraq and Afghanistan was also approved). Bush left government at the end of his term in January 2009.

Vladimir Putin on March 6, 2008, lifted the Commonwealth of Independent States sanctions previously imposed on the Abkhazia region of Georgia. Two days later on March 8, Abkhazia declared independence. On March 21, the Russian parliament (Duma) adopted a resolution asking the Russian President Putin to recognize both Abkhazia and South Ossetia as independent nations. On April 3, during a NATO summit in Romania, Putin sent letters to the "Presidents" of Abkhazia and South Ossetia offering "practical" support. On April 8, the Russian Foreign Minister was reported as stating publicly that Russia would do everything possible to keep Abkhazia and South Ossetia from joining NATO. On May 8, Putin exchanged the Russian Presidency for a term (his second) as Prime Minister. After a series of military clashes, in August war broke out between South Ossetia and Georgia and it included Russian military involvement. On August 26, Russia formerly recognized Abkhazia and South Ossetia as independent states. Effective December 31, 2008, exactly eight years to the day after Yeltsin's last day as the first Russian Federation President, during which Putin was already the Prime Minister, the 1993 Russian Constitution was amended to allow six year instead of four year terms for both President and Prime Minister, and an unlimited number of terms in each office.[35]

An eerie comparison of Russia's 2008 Constitution change to Hitler's "Enabling Act" may occur naturally given the commonality of these events. In 2014 Putin's Russian military additionally took over part of Ukraine; the US dollar value of the Russian ruble fell in half from 23 Rubles per US dollar on July 16, 2008 to 46 Rubles per US dollar on November 20, 2014;[36] and the Russian stock market RTSI index fell by half from about 2000 on March 1, 2011 to 1000 on November 20, 2014. In December 2014, the Russian central bank began buying rubles to stop their slide in value and began loaning vast amounts to Russian private banks to stem a run on deposits at some banks. Russia also announced plans to build a bridge from Russia to the Crimea, just as Hitler declared such a bridge plan when trying to conquer Russia.

Meanwhile, since 2008, the US instituted many bank reforms and the unemployment rate fell back to the 5% level; the US dollar appreciated more than 20%, going from its low of 1.6 US dollars per Euro on April 15, 2008 to 1.25 US dollars per Euro on November 20, 2014; and the US Dow Jones Industrial stock market index rose 46% from 12058 on March 1, 2009 to 17686 on November 20, 2014.[37] This appears to be another set of divergent paths between a major democracy and a major tyranny as a result of different policy approaches during crisis periods.

---

[34]Although some suggest that if it were not for Britain's wartime double-agent spy Joan Pujol Garcia, known as Garbo, Hitler may not have been defeated, either at all or not as quickly. See Talty's (2012) non-fiction book *Agent Garbo: The Brilliant, Eccentric Secret Agent Who Tricked Hitler and Saved D-Day.*

[35]Article 81 of the Russian Constitution now reads: "One and the same person may not be elected President of the Russian Federation for more than two terms running". The word "running" meant "in a row", and so allowed Putin to embark on a third Presidential term in 2012, such that he may remain President for a fourth term (of another six years) through 2024, afterwhich he could again become Prime Minister.

[36]54 rubles to US dollar as of 12-29-2014.

[37]The Dow Jones Industrial average troughed at 6547 on March 9, 2009.

6.7 Summary

The chapter focused on different crisis periods in US history: the 1930's Great Depression, the 2008–2010 Great Recession, and the 1970's period including the Vietnam war and stagflation. Facts were presented about possible oil shocks causing the high inflation of the 1970's. Evidence suggests that money supply growth and inflation Granger-cause oil price increases, rather than the reverse causality.

The oil shock theory of stagflation is then discussed in terms of supply-side, cost-based, shifts back in aggregate supply. Demand side shocks were discussed in theory in terms of "*demand-side management*" of the economy, through which too much government spending can cause inflation. This body of theory uses a nominal aggregate price of output, in contrast to microeconomic foundations in which supply and demand depend on relative prices rather than nominal prices.

An alternative theory to explain stagflation is presented. Here increased money supply growth causes inflation that acts as a tax that lowers the return on capital and the real GDP growth rate. The inflation tax theory explains low output growth and evidence is presented for this.

The relation to inflation and unemployment is then discussed in terms of the Phillips curve. Using both evidence and theory, the concept of the Phillips curve is developed. It started out as an empirical description of how the inflation rate and the unemployment rate are negatively correlated during certain time sequences of periods in US history, and in other countries like the UK. Then the idea arose that this created an empirical "trade-off" whereby the government could increase the inflation rate and so lower the unemployment rate.

The ability to exploit the Phillips curve trade-off and so lower unemployment with higher inflation was cast in doubt with the Expectations theory of the Phillips curve. In this theory, there is a long run "vertical" Phillips curve to which the economy returns after departures from it in the short run. The theory maintains that the curve is vertical at the so-called "natural rate of unemployment", which inflation cannot alter once expectations adjust to the actual inflation rate.

Crisis periods of the Great Depression, Great Recession and the Vietnam war era are examined in terms of Phillips curves that existed at times during these crisis periods. Correlation of the Phillips curves with changes in asset market values also occurred during these periods. This evidence may explain part of the inflation effect seen in the Phillips curve. This correlation is consistent with debt-deflation of Irving Fisher that arose to describe the Great Depression and it has been used during the Great Recession. A connection between bank crashes, stock market crashes and inflation rate declines may present an complimentary narrative of Phillips curve behavior that does not preclude the Expectations theory of the Phillips curve.

An application of the crisis analysis is made to the Great Depression in terms of the importance of banking law changes. The Appendix presents other Great Depression policy components. It also compares these to Great Recession policy and presents opposite policy approaches used in Europe during each the Great Depression and Great Recession that repressed democracy and market-based economies.

6.8 Glossary of Italic Words

bank deregulation: a change in legislation, or regulation, that decreases the legal constraints on operating a financial intermediary.

blaming the oil exporters: a theory holding that Middle East oil producers under the guise of OPEC raised prices suddenly in unexpected monopolistic fashion such that profits rose and oil buyers suffered a real higher cost; this occurred supposedly just after the US went off the gold standard in 1973 and again in 1979, during which time international US dollar oil prices and US dollar gold prices moved in tandem.

Bretton Woods agreement: International agreement, similar to a treaty, which was established in 1944 in Bretton Woods, Connecticut, and which set forth an agreement to establish a system of fixed exchange rates among a group of advanced industrial countries such that all of the countries' exchange rates were fixed in relation to each other and to the US; the US exchange rate was further fixed in terms of US dollars per ounce of gold, thus making the exchange rate system a continuation of the gold standard via US fixing of the price of gold in terms of US dollars; reportedly influenced in significant part by attendees John Maynard Keynes and the US economist Harry Dexter White.

Bretton Woods Gold Standard: see above.

capacity utilization: the usage by firms of their capital invested in plant and equipment; can be expressed in terms of a rate that varies for example between 70% and 95% during the business cycle.

conversion ratio: the usage here is in terms of the paper currency issued by a country's government and its redeemability from paper into a given metallic standard, historically either gold or silver, but also including copper and possible bronze.

cost-push inflation: an increase in the rate of change of the aggregate price level caused by an increase in the nominal cost of producing aggregate output.

deflation: a decrease in the inflation rate which may include a negative level of the inflation rate.

debt-deflation downwards spiral: a defaulting on debt that leads to a selling off of assets at relatively low prices, as then followed by a declining aggregate price level and a possibly negative inflation rate.

demand-pull inflation: an increase in the rate of change of the aggregate price level caused by an increase in the demand for aggregate output.

demand-side management: a government policy so as to increase or decrease aggregate output demand by changing the amount of government spending, with the general aim of reducing the swings in the business cycle, but mostly focused on getting out of a recession.

demand-side shock: a sudden unexpected change in aggregate demand, coming from some source of market demand that is external to the market economy.

expectations theory of the Phillips curve: the theory which claims that a short run regular inverse relation may exist between the inflation rate and unemployment rate, but this relation holds only when expectations of inflation are different from the actual inflation rate; once expectations adjust to the actual inflation rate, there is no trade-off.

exported inflation: the transition of inflation existing in one country to it also existing in another country; this happens for example when one country prints money to pay for a war, drives up domestic inflation, and another country wants to keep the exchange rate between the two countries unchanged, so that second country also inflates its domestic currency; also happens when exchange rates are fixed and one country initiates an increase in inflation.

fixed exchange rates: a system whereby a group of countries agree to keep their exchange rates for their currency, in terms of other currencies, at a fixed rate that almost always differs with respect to each country in the group.

fixed long run level of output: the theory that over an unstated but presumably "long" period, output is fixed at some level.

full-employment long run level of output: the level of output in theory that is consistent with a full employment rate; assumes that full employment can be identified, which is controversial, and assumes a level of output, as opposed to a growth rate of output that would be more appropriate for an economy that is growing over time.

Granger-causality: a statistical relation whereby certain variables appear to change before other variables change, such that the relation is sufficiently systematic to conclude that the change in the earlier changing variable appears to cause the later-changing variable to move over time; it is not a proof of causality in general but only of causality in the certain sense as defined by Clive Granger, who won the Nobel Economic prize.

inflation - unemployment statistical relation: the statistical correlation between the inflation rate and the unemployment rate, first identified rigorously by Irving Fisher.

inverse relation between unemployment and inflation: the concept that when the inflation rate rises, the unemployment rate falls; or when the inflation rate falls, the unemployment rate rises.

long run supply of output: the theory that there is some level of output in the long run, where the time period of the long run is not rigorously defined.

lost decade: low economic growth, in terms of the rate of change of real GDP, for a long period of time such as ten years, in a certain country, during a certain era.

low growth "crisis": an episode during which macroeconomic policy may focus on low growth as being too low for too long; examples are: the Vietnam War period of "stagflation", the low average growth era after 2008, and the 1990's in Japan.

oil embargo: a cutting off of the supply of oil, by ending a contract to supply oil at a certain price; was said to occur in the early 1970's.

oil price shock: a sudden increase or decrease in the price of oil; can be in real or nominal terms and there is research on both nominal and real oil price shocks.

oil shock theory: aggregate macroeconomic theory in which changes in the price of oil, either nominal or real, have a significant impact on the economy.

Phillips Curve: a graph with the inflation rate typically on the vertical axis and the unemployment rate on the horizontal axis, with each point on the graph representing the particular inflation rate and unemployment rate for a particular country in a particular period, such as a year; are periods when downward sloping curves have been historically identified.

price controls: the regulating or fixing of prices typically by a government.

rare events: the concept that unusual factors can significantly affect a nation's economy, and that these factors only occur infrequently; examples are wars and bank crises.

short run Phillips curve: the inflation rate relation to the unemployment rate during a period in which the two are inversely related.

short run supply of output: the aggregate output supply curve of the economy that holds in some undefined "short run" period; it is usually said to be upward-sloping, and contrasted with a long-run "vertical" supply of output curve.

stagflation: a prolonged period of low growth plus high inflation.

supply-side shocks: a change in the aggregate cost of production of output that causes a shift in the aggregate output supply curve.

Sustained inflation: a rate of low, moderate or high inflation that is relatively unchanged over a span of years; not to be confused with a one-time change in the aggregate price level that causes a temporary change in the inflation rate that does not persist.

systemic financial failure: an occurrence of bankruptcy, or insolvency, or illiquidity across a broad swath of the financial intermediation sector; for example it includes times when depositors temporarily cannot withdraw their deposits from financial firms, or when depositors cannot reclaim deposits in a financial firm.

trade-off between inflation and unemployment: the theory that an increase in inflation can bring about a decrease in unemployment, in a way exploitable by policy; or simply a statistical relation found in data.

Vertical Long Run Supply Curve: the aggregate output supply curve of the economy that holds in the some undefined "long run" period; it is usually said to be a "vertical" supply of output curve such that output does not change regardless of the price of output; it is typically contrasted with a "short-run" upward sloping supply of output curve.

Volcker deflation: Paul Volcker was Chairman of the Board of Governors of the Federal Reserve System during the early 1980's when the US inflation rate was lowered dramatically and quickly from over 10% at an annual rate, to about 2 to 3% annually; it coincided with an economic recession and a type of statistical movement down along a Phillips curve.

6.9 Questions

1. Name three economic crisis periods in US history and characterize each in terms of key economic factors such as real GDP growth, inflation, and unemployment.
2. How would you define an oil price shock, and how do such shocks enter theories of economic crisis and inflation?
3. What factors have been shown empirically to be determinants of oil price movements, and what kind of empirical evidence has been used in this regard?
4. What evidence is there on the effect of inflation on the real GDP growth rate in the long run, and what is the theory that explains such evidence?
5. Explain the theory of how oil price shocks affect aggregate output and inflation, as based on a nominal theory of the aggregate price of output; critique this theory.
6. What is the oil price shock theory of stagflation?
7. What was the Bretton Woods monetary system, and how does its ending relate to the oil price shock theory of stagflation?
8. What is a Phillips curve?
9. Explain the expectations theory of the Phillips curve?
10. What relation exists in evidence between periods in which Phillips curves are found and periods in which stock market crashes occur?

11. Describe and explain a banking based theory of economic crises?
12. How are rare events and lost decades sometimes related in theories of economic crisis?
13. What role did banking legislation play in the 1930's Great Depression?
14. Complete the Federal Reserve Bank of St. Louis EconLowdown Course Module "Great Inflation".
15. Complete the Federal Reserve Bank of St. Louis EconLowdown Course Module "The Great Depression 3".
16. Complete the Federal Reserve Bank of St. Louis EconLowdown Course Module "The Great Depression 4".

PART III

Cycles and Growth

7 Savings, Investment & Interest

7.1 Introduction

Investment that leads to capital accumulation is known to have generated wealth in Western societies. It works primarily through the functioning of capital markets in which market interest rates determine how the capital is allocated. In contrast, in societies banning interest on capital, capital accumulation tends to be much less.

For example religion-led governments which ban interest on capital have been prevalent throughout history. Christian religion banned "*usury*", or charging interest on capital loans, well into the 14th century. Muslim religion still bans usury and instead through "*Islamic banking*" constructs all interest payments on loans as equity dividend payments. An interest rate and dividend yield rate can be equal but the former is a *debt contract* and the latter an *equity ownership arrangement*.

The advent of the acceptance of charging a price for capital, in particular either an interest rate on lent capital or in terms of a price for an equity stake in capital, led to the market system known as "capitalism". Globalization of the economy has meant the worldwide use of capital markets to intermediate savings towards investment. Intermediation of capital involves the broad use of all of the institutions that comprise capital markets, such as stock markets, banks and the finance industry which is the largest percent of GDP in the US of any industry (at 12% of GDP in 2014).

7.2 Who Made it Happen

Adam Smith's (1776) Wealth of Nations included persuasive economic grounds for allowing interest on capital, just as the industrial revolution was beginning in Great Britain (England, Wales and Scotland) and as American Independence was declared. The market for capital became a staple of economics.

Keynes (1936) described the market for capital using special assumptions that he believed to be valid during the crisis of the Great Depression. This evolved through J. R. Hicks (1937) and Alvin Hansen (1950) into what became known as IS-LM analysis. This Keynesian theory emphasizes the role of government and it continues to be a foundation for Keynesian discourse today.

The American Irving Fisher brought this study of capital and interest to a rigorous level in Neoclassical terms. Fisher published (1896, 1907, 1930) succeeding versions of his Theory of Interest. And he developed apparently the first mathematical economic *optimization theory of consumption smoothing over time* through savings and investment. This implies a theory of capital markets that forms the basis of Neoclassical capital theory still widespread today.

7.3 Facts

When the bank sector collapses during a crisis period, savings by consumers and investment by firms tends to fall. This is a key characteristic of a big recession or depression. This makes *current period output* lower as well as decreasing the ability of the economy to *accumulate capital* that will increase output in the future.

Explaining crisis behavior has occupied both Neoclassical and Keynesian economists. They tend to view the solution differently. The former focuses on fixing the private bank sector so that private investment can resume. The latter focuses more on the government doing the investment in place of the private sector. The two approaches can be complimentary for example when the government investment serves a social insurance objective.

7.3.1 Income as the Flow from Wealth

As interest became common in use, wealth accumulated more easily. The OECD publishes annual figures of average household income and wealth across the OECD member nations, as part of its "Life Satisfaction Index".[1] Income and wealth very widely across the OECD countries. In some wealth is greater than income and in some the reverse holds.

Nations with high *wealth to income ratios* are led by the US and Switzerland, with the highest wealth to income ratios at around 4. Canada, Sweden, Italy and the United Kingdom have such ratios around 2. Similarly, other developed countries such as Germany, France, Austria, Luxembourg, Denmark, and Israel have lower wealth to income ratios, but ones still above 1. Czech Republic, Spain and Ireland have ratios near one, perhaps as characteristic of less developed economies.

Turkey, Hungary and Greece rank at the bottom of *life satisfaction*, have relatively low income levels, and have less wealth than income, so their wealth to income ratios are less than one. Similarly the Slovak Republic, Russia, Poland, Estonia, and Slovenia also have less wealth than income. Only Brazil and New Zealand rank high in life satisfaction and have less wealth than income, perhaps because of their natural environmental resources that are not easily captured in wealth estimates.

Another way to look at wealth and income is to consider income the flow from the given amount of a country's wealth. This is why the wealth tends to be larger than the income flow. It is not always true since many forms of wealth are not counted in measures of a country's wealth, even though they may contribute to the income flow of the country.

For example if W is the amount of wealth, and r is the real interest rate earned on the wealth, then rW is the income earned on the wealth. Suppose that the real interest rate may be of the order of magnitude of 0.05 for 5%. Then write income as the interest flow:

$$Income = r \cdot (Wealth) = 0.05(Wealth).$$

Income is just a fraction of wealth. With all wealth accounted for, a country's natural average income would be just a fraction of its wealth, with the fraction being the real interest rate. In this example the wealth to income ratio in turn is $(Wealth)/Income = 1/r = (1/0.05) = 20$.

If $r = 0.10$, this would give a Wealth to Income ratio of $1/(0.10)$, which is equal to 10; the wealth to income ratio is 1 divided by the interest rate expressed in fractions of one (eg. 0.10). Rearranging the terms in equation (7.1), we have that

$$(Wealth)/(Income) = 1/r. \tag{7.1}$$

The US and Switzerland have a wealth to income ratio of 4 such that the implied interest flow on wealth is $r = 0.25$, since $4 = 1/\ (0.25)$. This means 25% of Wealth is yielded each year as the flow of income from the wealth. This is too high of a yield relative to interest rates seen in capital markets, which are typically lower in most types of capital markets.

So the analysis here shows that most likely much of the wealth that is yielding the actual income flow is not fully accounted for in the OECD wealth accounting. Rather it is likely that the wealth level is actually even higher for all countries than that which is reported in OECD accounts. But we might surmise from the OECD data that countries in which the reported wealth is high also have sophisticated financial markets and this apparently coincides with high income levels found in countries with high wealth levels. In addition, it appears that the most financially sophisticated countries have both the highest wealth to income ratios and the highest wealth and income levels, each taken separately.

The Application at the end of this chapter shows how wealth is calculated as a permanent income stream divided by the interest rate. This application shows how individuals can earn an income stream on their wealth. The income stream can be from either labor or capital income, from both their "human capital" and their financial capital wealth in the form of "savings". And in fact, in the Ramsey (1928) World of the next

[1] See http://stats.oecd.org/index.aspx?DataSetCode=BLI

chapter, consumption is a fraction of the permanent income stream, which in turn is the flow from the value of human and physical capital that is accumulated over time.

7.3.2 Savings & Investment: Accounting & Data Trends

Figure 7.1 shows data for the post-WWII US with a distinct pattern in which the NIPA definition of the "Personal Saving Rate" moves consistently in the opposite direction to the Gross Private Domestic Investment as a share of GDP. We have seen the share of investment before, in Chapter 2. We liken this share to the share of investment in GDP, where Y = C + I + G + NX, and the investment share is I/Y.

The NIPA Personal Saving Rate is defined as the ratio of "personal saving to the disposable personal income (DPI)". Personal savings in the National Income and Product Accounts (NIPA; Account 4: Personal Income and Outlay Account) is explained as the "net acquisition of assets minus the net acquisition of liabilities" in the NIPA description.[2]

Figure 7.1 shows the marked opposite movement between the Investment share (Red) and the Savings share (Blue), which indicates a strong negative correlation between the two series. This is as high as a -0.35 correlation, depending on the exact large subsample used. It means for example that there is a tendency of the net savings of the household, in this NIPA definition of assets minus liabilities, to fall when private investment goes up. In other words, the decrease in personal savings becomes an increase in investment for when they are negatively correlated.

Taken as the whole economy, the negative correlation is saying that the representative agent reduces the saved income when this personal savings is used for investment. In this way, as a representative agent combining both the private firm and the household (but excluding here the government), we should get the sum of the investment and saving equal to a constant over time. It is possible that Savings and Investment may differ somewhat because of net exports, a fact of economies engaging in trade that is described in texts dating back at least to Keynes's (1030) *Treatise on Money*. In the Appendix it is shown how investment and savings add up to a constant, when including net exports, although it requires a serious focus on the untangling the details of the NIPA definitions of Savings and Investment, which is a bit tedious but interesting that the constant results from their sum.

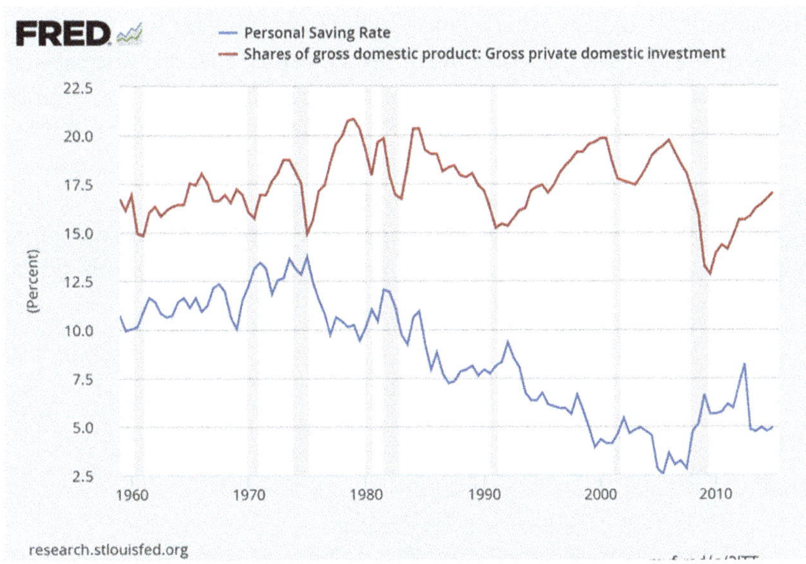

Figure 7.1 Personal Saving Rate: Personal saving as a percentage of disposable personal income (DPI), frequently referred to as "the personal saving rate," is calculated as the ratio of personal saving to DPI. Personal savings can be viewed as the net acquisition of assets minus the net acquisition of liabilities

[2]Available at http://www.bea.gov/national/pdf/nipaguid.pdf

7.4 Theory

Capital market theory starts with supply and demand for capital. It typically calls the supply of capital "*savings*" and the demand for capital "*investment*". This market theory describes the equilibrium in the capital market as occurring at a certain equilibrium real interest rate at which the quantity of capital supplied (Savings) equals the quantity of capital demanded (Investment).

7.4.1 IS-LM Analysis

Keynes's (1930) idea of unused savings during crises evolved into Keynes's (1936) use of the supply and demand theory of capital markets. In Keynes's (1936) *General Theory,* his proposal could be described in microeconomic terms as simply assuming that the price of capital, the real interest rate, becomes fixed at an above-market level such that this "price floor" led to an excess supply of capital at which the quantity supplied of capital exceeds the quantity demanded; see Figure 7.20 below.

However Keynes (1936) instead departed from common usage of excess capital supply from a fixed price. Instead he described Great Depression events by shifting the supply of capital out by more than the demand for capital. This causes the real interest rate to be driven down.

Recall that the first Keynesian theory of aggregate demand management originated from Keynes' (1930) Treatise on Money, took the form of the "Keynesian Cross" and uses the National Income and Product Account identity between aggregate income (GDI) and aggregate output (GDP). It also adds a consumption function with particular assumptions added. Its policy analysis was designed to show how government spending can increase aggregate output.

Now arises a second Keynesian analysis as devised by extending Keynes (1936). This ends up showing how both government spending and money supply increases boost aggregate output. This uses the capital market with the consumer's aggregate supply of savings rather than the Keynes (1930) focus on the consumer's aggregate consumption function. The first was called the Cross analysis and the second is called *IS-LM analysis.*

IS Curve

The IS stands for Investment (I) and Savings (S) and the IS curve is meant to show the equilibrium interest rate and output level corresponding to the equilibrium in the capital market. The capital market is here defined as the demand for capital by firms (Investment) and the supply of capital by consumers (Savings). It is assumed that each Investment and Savings depend of the given level of output, and that the equilibrium in the capital market occurs at a certain equilibrium real interest rate at which the quantity of capital supplied (Savings) equals the quantity of capital demanded (Investment).

The main assumption of IS analysis is that when aggregate income increases, the aggregate supply of capital shifts out by more than the aggregate demand for capital shifts out. If supply shifts out by more when

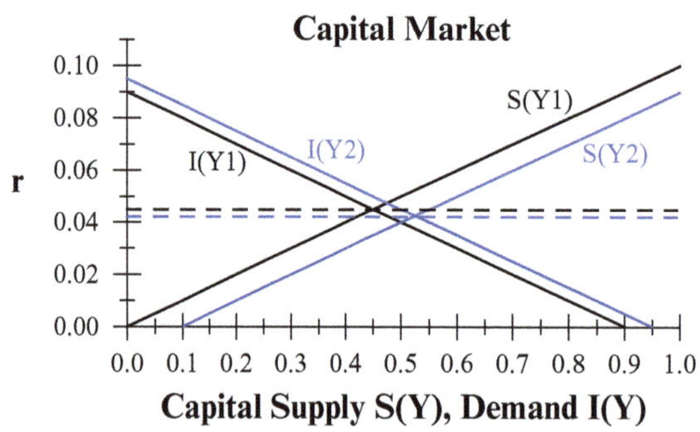

Figure 7.2 Keynes's (1936) Graph: Supply and Demand for Capital Shift Out When Income Y Rises (Black to Blue) ; Interest rate r falls as Y rises

aggregate income rises, as is always implicitly assumed in IS-LM analysis, then the interest rate falls. Relating the falling interest rate to a rising income level provides a negative relation between interest rates and income.

Consider Figure 7.2's representation of the one graph in Keynes' (1936) *General Theory*. It shows initial supply and demand for capital at the income level of Y1. S(Y1) is the savings curve, and so the supply of capital; I(Y1) is the investment curve and so the demand for capital. When income rises from Y1 to Y2, the savings curve S(Y2) shifts out by more as compared to the investment curve I(Y2), which also shifts out but by less. As a result, the interest rate drops.

If savings always shifts out by more than investment, and if both *demand and supply for capital* depend upon the level of output, then when output rises, the interest rate falls. So the various *equilibria* of the I and S lines can be plotted using all of these assumptions in the space of *Y* and *r*. Figure 7.3 shows this resulting so-called "*IS curve*" that slopes down, when plotted in (*r*, *Y*) graphical dimensions.

The shifting out of S by more I when income/output rises is a very special assumption. It generally does not hold. In fact, the most normal association would be that savings and investment shift out together with income, by the same amount and the result would be that the real interest rate stays the same. This is consistent with *stylized facts of economic growth*, known as Solow growth facts: the interest rate stays constant over time as output grows at some trend rate (See Chapter 9 below for the focus on the economy's *growth facts*).

However Keynes was concerned with "*excess savings*" during the Great Depression. His argument of a downward sloping IS curve is what could be viewed as a reformulation of his Keynes (1930) idea that there is more savings than investment in a recession. In this supply and demand framework, which Keynes (1936) shows graphically for the first time, he makes savings supply shift out by more than investment demand when income goes up, in order to make his point of a fall in the real interest rate. This special case may or may not have held during the Depression, or even a normal recession. But it is a way to present a reason for why the real interest rate falls, which is a stylized fact of a recession. One possible internal contradiction here is that Keynes assumes income is rising when the real interest rate falls, while we expect the opposite in a recession: that income falls.

What the student may find surprising is that when IS curves are used today they are always assumed to be downwards sloping, without regard to whether the assumptions necessary to get this result actually hold. And because IS-LM is used for policy analysis at any time, and not just during crisis periods, this can be even more surprising to the student.

The reason that the downward sloping IS curve is still used today is that it allows a graphical description of the concept of how government intervention through greater spending can increase output. This remains attractive to economists. It is a step up from the Keynesian Cross's similar analysis, of how government spending can increase output, because now the analysis uses the micro-founded concepts of the supply and demand for capital and the capital market equilibrium. The Cross only uses a Keynes proposed consumption function and the NIPA accounting whereby GDP equals GDI.

Both the consumption function approach and the market for the supply and demand for savings can be derived from the optimization techniques of Keynes's famous student Ramsey. But Keynes just makes

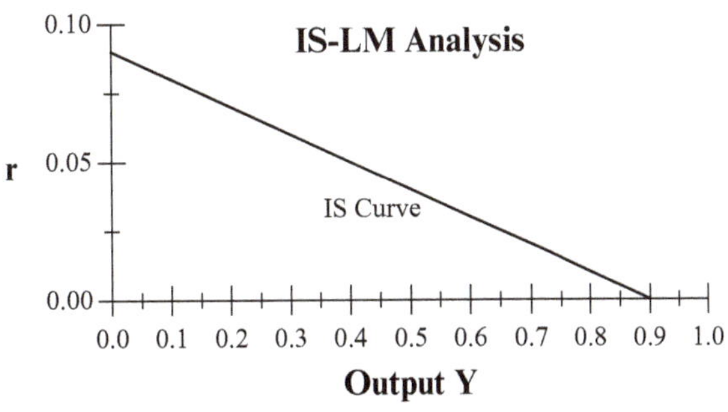

Figure 7.3 Downward Sloping IS Curve of Keynes, Hansen

assumptions on how curves shift around. This above gave the Cross analysis, and below new assumptions give the IS-LM analysis.

Liquidity Preference for Money: LM Curve

To see this policy implication of IS-LM analysis, we need the "LM" part of the analysis. The full IS-LM was constructed by Hicks (1937), in a publication that appeared the year after Keynes's (1936) *General Theory.* Thus the full IS-LM analysis was put in the economic sphere almost immediately after Keynes outlined his theory.

The *LM curve* is named for what Keynes (1936) called the *demand for real money*. He also called this demand the *"liquidity preference for money"*, since Keynes viewed money as the most "liquid" of all assets. The name "liquidity preference" stuck, rather than for example just DM, the demand for money.

The liquidity idea is that money can be immediately used in exchange, as opposed to less liquid assets such as bonds. Bonds are less liquid because first they have to be sold and put into money form before they can be used in exchange. The LM curve then is derived from the so-called money market.

In the money market, there is a supply and demand for money. The interest rate is again the price of money, which is a form of capital. To make this presentation of the LM curve simplest, assume zero inflation, so that the aggregate price level is unchanged.

Zero inflation allows us to think of real money as being the same as nominal money, which in turn is just the amount of dollars held. It also allows us to think of the nominal interest rate as being the same as the real interest rate, since inflation is zero. This is because Fisher's equation of interest rates says that the nominal interest rate R (which is the normal market rate) equals the real interest rate r plus the inflation rate.

Why do we now use the money market in combination with the capital market? One sound reason is that the consumer divides income into savings and consumption. So either the consumer saves the income, or uses it for consumption for which the consumer needs money in order to exchange for consumption. The consumer savings become part of the supply of capital that is available for investment. The consumer consumption requires spending money that is assumed to create the demand for money.

Turning to the money market now, again there are special assumptions used to do the IS-LM policy analysis. The idea is to see how the supply and demand for money changes when income goes up. This will tell us the theoretical effect on the real interest rate in the money market when income goes up. If for example demand shifts out by more than supply, when income goes up, then any supply and demand graph of money will result in the interest rate going up.

In fact a greater shift out in the demand for money than in the supply of money, when income rises, is the precise assumption that the LM analysis always makes. This implies that in the money market the interest rate rises as income goes up, as demand rises by more than supply. So the relation between interest rates and income in the money market is that the two move in the same direction. This gives what is called an upward sloping LM curve.

Figure 7.4 shows a money market with a *fixed government supply of money*. This ignores the *private bank supply of money*, which when added would make the supply of money curve a normal upward sloping function that also depends upon income. But if we assume that the money supply is fixed, as supplied only by the Fed in a way that does not depend on income, and we then assume that money demand shifts out when the income level Y rises, say from Y1 to Y2, then naturally the interest rate must rise in Figure 7.4.

IS and LM Together

Graphing all possible interest rates in such a money market as in Figure 7.4 results in an LM curve, as always graphed using the (r, Y) dimensions, that is upward sloping. This LM is illustrated in Figure 7.5, along with the previously *"derived" IS curve* that is downward sloping. The idea is that this gives a unique equilibrium level of interest and output where the IS and LM curves intersect.

In general, if both money supply and money demand shift out equally with income along the growth path of the economy, then the interest rate remains unchanged. The LM curve is a flat, horizontal line, just as is the IS curve along the growth path of the economy. So this *upward sloping LM curve* is again a result of many special assumptions.

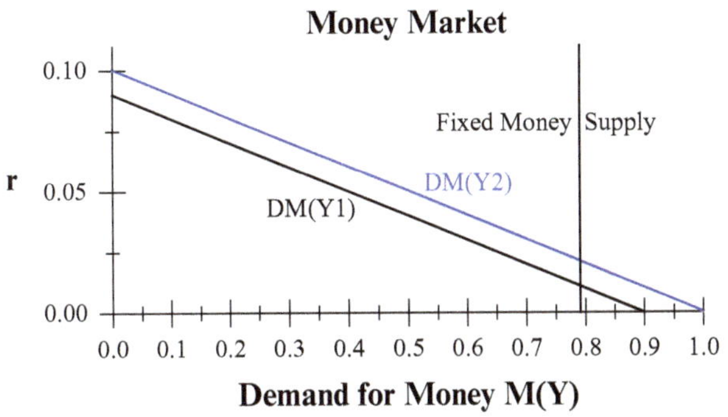

Figure 7.4 Downward Sloping Demand for Money that Depends on Y (DMY1-Black) and Shifts Out When Y Increases (DMY2-Blue)

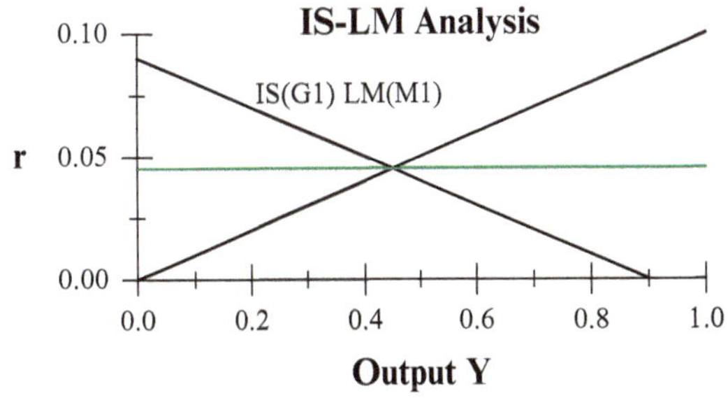

Figure 7.5 Downward Sloping *IS* Curve and *LM* Curve from Money Market, Giving "Equilibrium" Y and r

Especially the standard LM graph completely ignores the private bank money supply which is the largest component (demand deposits) of the so-called M1 monetary aggregate (the sum of currency plus demand deposits at banks). In general, as the real interest rate rises, more loans are made, demand deposits rise, and the M1 supply of money is then an upward sloping supply curve that rises with the interest rate. It is not a straight vertical line as assumed in IS-LM analysis.

7.4.2 IS-LM Policy

The special cases of IS-LM analysis are set up for a reason. They can be used to show how 1) an increase in government spending increases output and raises the interest rate. To do this, it is assumed that the government spending does not have to be paid for by taxes, that this spending is the same as an exogenous increase in investment demand that shifts out investment demand in the capital market, and that the supply of capital is not affected so the demand shift moves the equilibrium up along the original supply curve. The result is that the equilibrium quantity of capital invested increases, as the real interest rate rises, from an increase in government spending.

Such an increase in government spending in turn causes the IS curve as graphed in (r, Y) dimensions to shift out, and reach a new higher equilibrium real interest rate and higher output level, as the IS shifts out along the unchanged LM curve. This is why in Figure 7.5, the IS curve is written as IS(G1), indicating that it depends on the level of government spending. If government spending rises from G1 to G2, then the *IS curve shifts out*; the LM does not shift.

The other policy in the IS-LM set of assumptions is 2) that a shift out in the fixed money supply by the Fed causes an increase in the money supply in the money market, while the money demand curve is unchanged. This supply of money increase drives down the real interest rate.

The increased Fed money in turn causes the LM curve to shift outwards This gives a new intersection with the existing IS curve at which the real interest rate is lower and the output level is higher. The idea here is that only the government controls the money supply, so it is "exogenous" to the economy; we ignore the private bank supply of money. Then we say the LM curve depends on the current money supply; say it is M1. If M1 rises to M2, then one can see in the money market Figure 7.4 that indeed the interest rate would fall.

Combining the LM curve with the IS curve, an increase in the government money supply causes the LM curve to shift out and down. This means that the new LM curve intersects the IS curve at a new equilibrium point (moving down the IS curve) at which the interest rate is lower and the income level is higher.

Now we have sketched the key policy moves by the government within IS-LM analysis. An increase in either government spending or in the government money supply increases output. In the former case the interest rate rises. In the latter case the interest rate falls. But in both cases, output rises. So the government comes out quite nicely here in being able to increase output by doing either of two changes, which actually can be related. If the increase in government spending is financed by printing more money, then both policy changes occur at once. Note that such policy analysis never worries about or includes how there may be future inflation from continually printing money to pay for government spending.

Graphical IS-LM Policy

The IS-LM idea is that an increase in either government spending G or an increase by the central bank in the fixed money supply $\bar{M}$ both cause output to go up. It was argued by Keynes that the government spending can have a larger impact on output Y than the increase in the money supply. After showing each policy, the stronger impact of government spending is shown for the "liquidity trap" case.

Assume a shift out of investment demand for capital in the capital market occurs because of a government spending increase. This is shown in Figure 7.6 by the shift out in capital demand from the downward sloping Black line to the downward sloping Blue line. The interest rate *r* rises while the output *Y* is the same.

When transferred to the (*r*, *Y*) dimensions of the *IS* line, this increase in Investment causes the *IS* line to have a higher interest rate at every *Y*. So it shifts out the *IS* curve. Figure 7.7 shows the how the *IS curve shifts out* as a result of a higher *G*.

If the fixed central money supply $\bar{M}$ is increased, from M1 to M2, then in the money market the interest rate *r* falls. The output level *Y* has not changed. Figure 7.8 shows this shift out of the fixed money supply and the decrease in the real interest rate.

The increase in the fixed money supply causes the interest rate to fall. This means that the *LM* line, or curve, which depends on the given fixed level of money supply, shifts out and to the right. Figure 7.9 illustrates how the *LM curve shifts* out when the money supply increases.

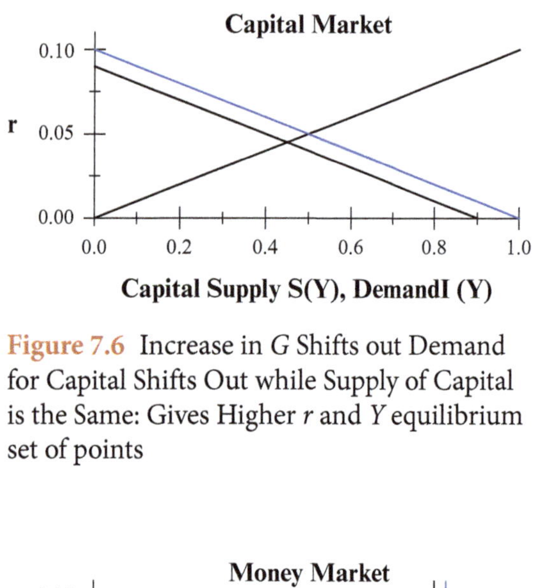

Figure 7.6 Increase in *G* Shifts out Demand for Capital Shifts Out while Supply of Capital is the Same: Gives Higher *r* and *Y* equilibrium set of points

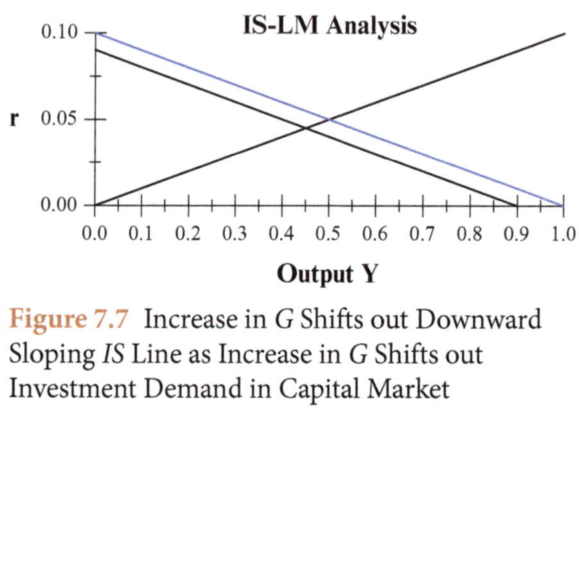

Figure 7.7 Increase in *G* Shifts out Downward Sloping *IS* Line as Increase in *G* Shifts out Investment Demand in Capital Market

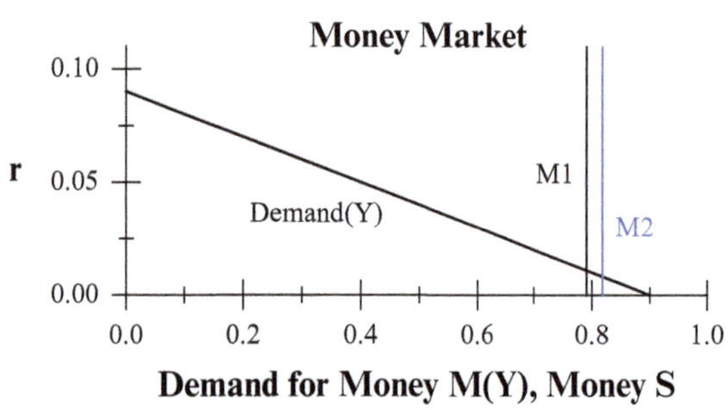

Figure 7.8 Downward Sloping Demand for Money and Fixed Supply of Money, with Fixed Supply of Money Shifting to the Right

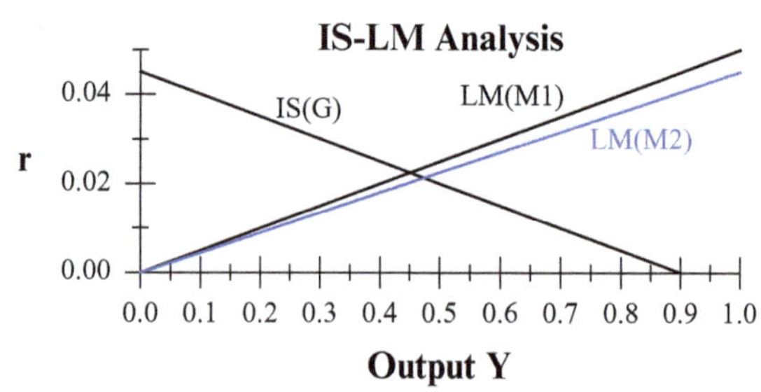

Figure 7.9 *LM* line shifts out when Fixed Money Supply Increases Causing Output *Y* to Rise

The final part of the original analysis of Keynes (1936) is that government spending is more powerful than monetary policy because monetary policy only works if increasing the money supply can lower interest rates. If real interest rates are at a "bottom level" and cannot be decreased then monetary policy is supposedly ineffective and this is called a "*liquidity trap*" in which more money (liquidity) has no effect.

Writers since Keynes put this in the *IS-LM* analysis by assuming that money demand in the money market is flat at the current fixed money supply. Increasing the money supply leaves the interest rate unchanged as a result. Then the *LM* line is actually a curve that flattens out at the current interest rate.

If the *LM* curve is flat where it intersects with the *IS* curve, then shifting it out only extends a flat line rather than shifting it. The interest rate cannot fall, and output cannot rise. So monetary policy is "ineffective" in raising aggregate output. Figures 7.10 and 7.11 illustrate this *monetary policy "ineffectiveness"* relative to government spending increases. An increase in government spending can increase output even if the economy is in a liquidity trap.

Keynes (1936) writes that he does not believe the economy in the Great Depression was in a liquidity trap, and writes that he does not think a liquidity trap has ever existed, although he does emphasize this idea. And so it lives on in IS-LM analysis, today being called the *"zero lower bound" of interest rates.*

The upshot is that in times of a zero interest rate, the IS-LM advice is that only government spending can raise output. Monetary policy will not work. And there is nothing else is in the basic Keynesian theoretical arsenal. Reforming the private bank sector so that it is operational is the Neoclassical solution to this, rather than increased government spending by itself (it may require government spending to reform banking but not necessarily).

Critique of IS-LM Policy Analysis

Of course if the government increased spending, it would need to raise taxes or debt to do this. If the money supply is increased at an accelerated rate to pay for the spending, then the so-called inflation tax would rise. In other words, continually financing government deficit spending by printing money would raise the rate of growth of the money supply and cause inflation. Inflation is assumed to be zero in the IS-LM analysis.

So the IS-LM policy analysis has an internal contradiction in practice: there is almost never just a one-time increase in spending and one-time increase in the money supply. Rather spending programs are started that continually increase the amount of deficit spending. If no other taxes are used to finance this spending, and instead money is printed, then the money supply has to be continually augmented each period, and the growth rate of the money supply will rise.

The *Neoclassical monetary theory of Fisher's* (1922) book, *The Purchasing Power of Money*, implies that inflation results when the money supply growth rate is increased. This explains inflation which the IS-LM analysis is not set up to do. It implicitly assumes zero inflation and only looks at one-time changes in the money supply and in the price level.

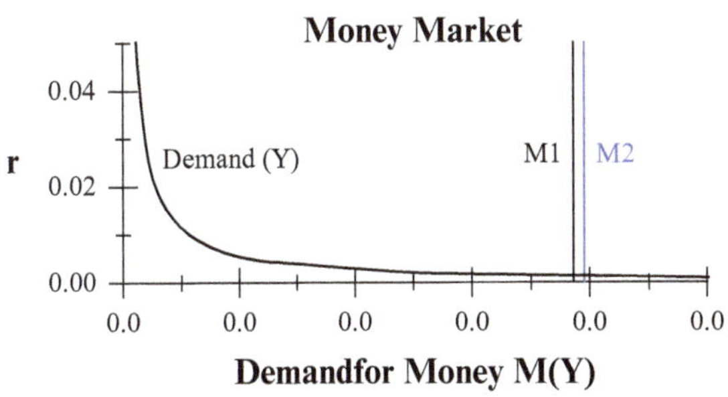

Figure 7.10 Liquidity Trap: Downward Sloping Demand for Money is flat at intersection with Fixed Money Supply $\bar{M}^1$, so an Increase in Money to $\bar{M}^2$ Does not Decrease *r*

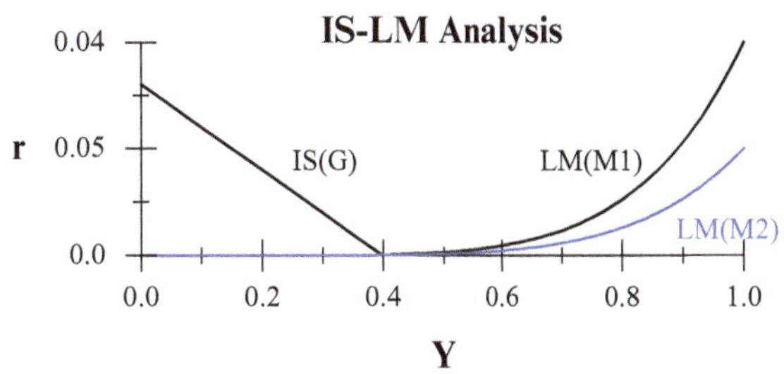

Figure 7.11 *IS* and *LM* curves intersect at flat Portion of *LM*. When *LM* shifts out From Money Supply Increase, *Y* output does not change

Keynesian IS-LM analysis is subject to a host of criticism: there is no attempt to study how the economy changes over the normal business cycle using IS-LM; the analysis ignores that along the trend growth path the IS and LM are flat, horizontal, coinciding lines; it ignores that private bank money exists and creates an upward sloping supply of money that depends on output. Money supply is therefore not fixed by the government. And the analysis ignores that inflation results when an persistent increase in deficit government spending is financed by printing money at a faster rate. Neoclassical policy, instead of focusing on government spending and printing money, focuses in on what is wrong with the private sector, if anything, in the first place, such as a collapse in the bank sector's intermediation of savings into investment.

7.4.3 Neoclassical Model of Savings and Investment

Irving Fisher's (1907) book *The Rate of Interest* and its 1930 revision, *The Theory of Interest*, gave us what appears to be the first macroeconomic diagram of the economy over time with capital accumulation. Fisher does this by focusing the "intertemporal" choice over just two periods, the current period and the next period.

The representative agent maximizes the *utility function of consumption in the current period and consumption in the next period.* This utility is maximized subject to a production function that turns current period output into next period output through capital investment. Equilibrium occurs at the tangency of the indifference curve with the production possibilities curve, thereby giving the equilibrium amount of consumption in each of the two periods.

Fisher's diagram is given in Figure 7.12. It shows a production possibilities curve (blue) in which a decrease in current period consumption C0 enables more *future period consumption* C1. The indifference curve (red) shows a constant utility level for different combinations of consumption in period 0 and consumption in period 1. The equilibrium occurs where the two curves are tangent.

On the horizontal axis, for the consumer, at time 0, the equilibrium consumption is the difference between the current income level and the amount of savings. For the firm the amount of savings provided by the consumer is turned into investment, at time 0, allowing production of output for the next period, at time 1. The firm produces the output using the investment, or capital. This figure holds the labor supply constant.

Figure 7.13 turns the graph around so that it looks like a *production function for future period consumption.* The only difference is that instead of consumption being the horizontal axis variable, now it is capital in the form of either savings (from consumer) or investment (by firm). The vertical dashed line shows the income level in period 0; it is given here as 100. And the difference between the income and the consumer's consumption in period 0 is capital saving. This difference is also equal to the firm's investment in period 0, which is used to yield the output in period 1. The slope of the tangency point is the real interest rate.

The *Fisher two-period diagram* and analysis translates into the Neoclassical supply and demand for capital. Figure 7.14 graphs the supply and demand for capital from this framework, including the interest rate that is the slope in Figure 7.13.

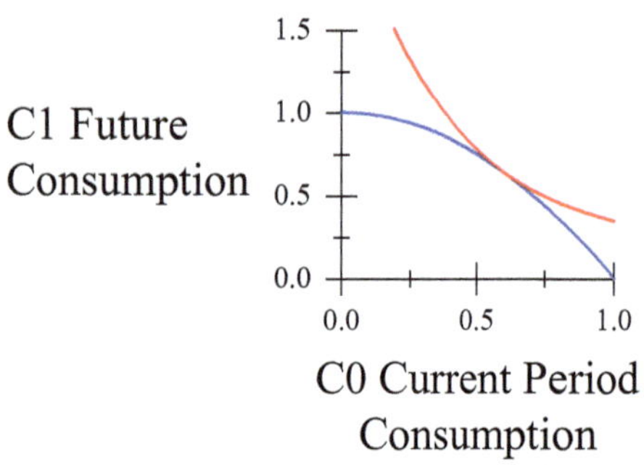

Figure 7.12: Production Possibility Curve Between Current and Next Period Consumption (Blue) and Equilibrium Utility Level Indifference Curve (Red)

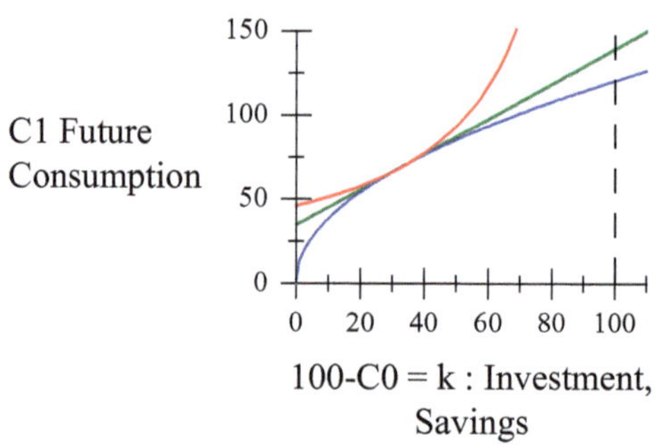

Figure 7.13 Production Function for Next Period Consumption (Blue), Equilibrium Utility Indifference Curve (Red), and Budget Line (Green)

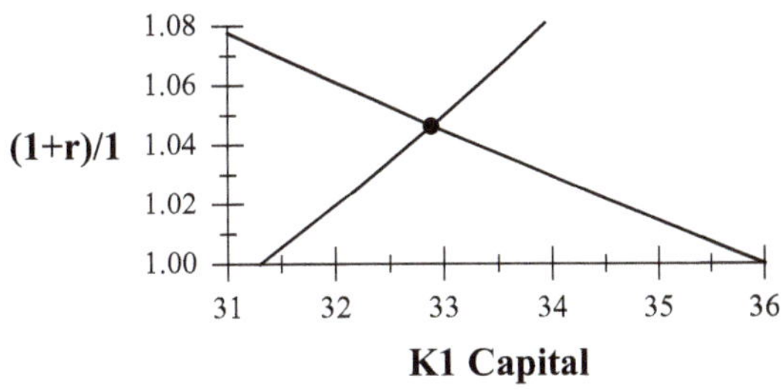

Figure 7.14 Savings and Investment: Aggregate Supply and Demand for Capital *k* in Example Economy

The supply of savings is derived directly from the slope of the indifference curve and demand for investment is derived directly from the slope of the production function. Doing this derivation implicitly, the resulting supply and demand curves together give the *"market" in capital*, a market which is a different way to represent the "general equilibrium" of Figure 7.13. In the supply curve, the price of saving one dollar is 1 plus the interest you get back, or $1 + r$, relative to the value of the dollar today, which is 1. So the relative price of capital is $(1 + r)/1$.

Of course, we could have just written that the price is r, but we want to emphasize the opportunity cost of consuming 1 dollar today versus savings and receiving $1 + r$ dollars tomorrow. This is the relative price of capital, or the "gross" interest rate $1 + r$.

The savings and investment today implies the supply and demand for future consumption. The cost of one dollar of future consumption in economic terms is $1/(1 + r)$. Figure 7.15 which shows the *supply and demand for future consumption* C1, with a relative price of $1/(1 + r)$.

In a simple two-period model, the consumer cannot save and have the firm invest again since there is no third period. So period 1 consumption, C1, also equals period 1 output Y1. In a model with an infinite future horizon, and not just two periods, the consumer would keep saving and the firm keep investing each period out into the future.

The capital market is derived implicitly from optimization unlike the diagram Keynes drew in his 1936 General Theory. There he simply draws the supply and demand for capital in a similar diagram, without using a general optimization model such as the one that his student Ramsey pioneered. The Fisher model here is a two-period special case of Ramsey's more general model.

Keynes then makes assumptions about how these shift when income goes up. We can do similar comparative static exercises. But now the precise optimization framework of Fisher can be used as in modern economics.

Increase in Productivity of Capital

The main comparative static change used in modern analysis is to assume a change in the firm's productivity of producing output with the given amount of inputs. When productivity increases, as happens in the

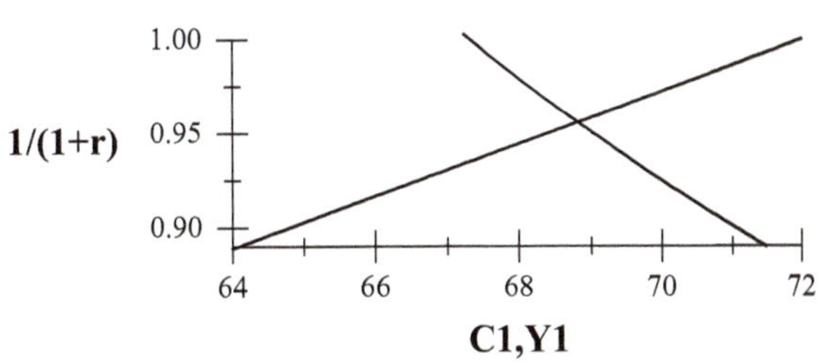

Figure 7.15 Market for Future Period Consumption

upswing of the business cycle and over time with growth, the demand and supply curves for both capital and next period consumption are affected. Here the productivity increase means that the parameter factoring the production function (A) increases, while we are holding labor constant.

Figure 7.16 shows how the *increase in productivity of capital* causes the demand for capital to shift out from the Red Baseline to the Black new demand curve. And the Red Baseline supply of capital curve shifts back from the Red Baseline to the new Black curve, due to the income effect of having more profit on the production of output using capital investment. As a result of the shifting demand and supply for capital, the *equilibrium capital invested* remains unchanged, while the interest rate rises.[3]

The relative price rises as the interest rate goes up. We expect this result in a business cycle expansion, which is typically explained in part by a productivity rise. The real interest rate rises in expansion and falls in contractions, as productivity rises and falls. But capital investment remains unchanged with the *productivity increase*, which is inconsistent with a business cycle expansion in which investment typically rises. This means the model is not quite rich enough to capture both that the real interest rate rises and that investment is higher in the normal business cycle expansion.

Increase in Current Period Income Endowment

The problem with the two period model and having only an *increase in capital productivity* is that the initial period income is left unaffected by the productivity increase. In reality current income also rises in a business expansion as more labor is hired. Labor is abstracted from in the *Fisher savings-investment analysis*. But we can include its effect on output by simply *increasing the given, assumed, current income* at the same time as we increase productivity.

Increasing only the current income acts to shift out the supply in capital, but not the demand. Figure 7.17 shows that this causes the interest rate to fall and the equilibrium quantity of capital saved and demanded to rise. However a rise in current income that occurs during a business cycle expansion usually coincides with a rise in the interest rate, not a fall.

It is interesting that this comparative experiment of changing only the current income resembles Keynes' (1936) version of how the capital market reacts as income goes up. So this particular analysis supports part of Keynes: there exists a fall in the real interest rate when the endowed income increases. Of course in the Great Depression income was falling rather than rising.

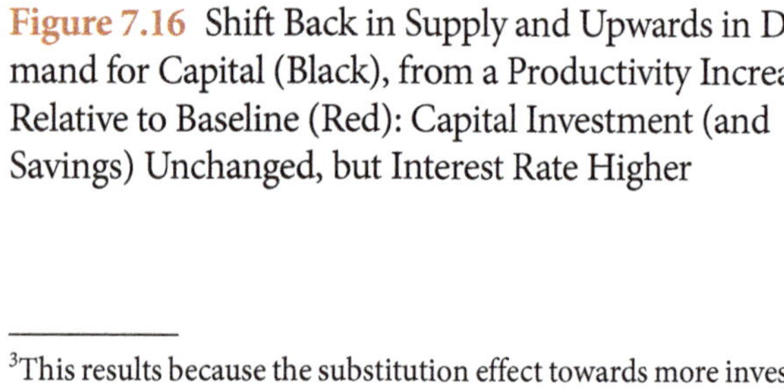

Figure 7.16 Shift Back in Supply and Upwards in Demand for Capital (Black), from a Productivity Increase Relative to Baseline (Red): Capital Investment (and Savings) Unchanged, but Interest Rate Higher

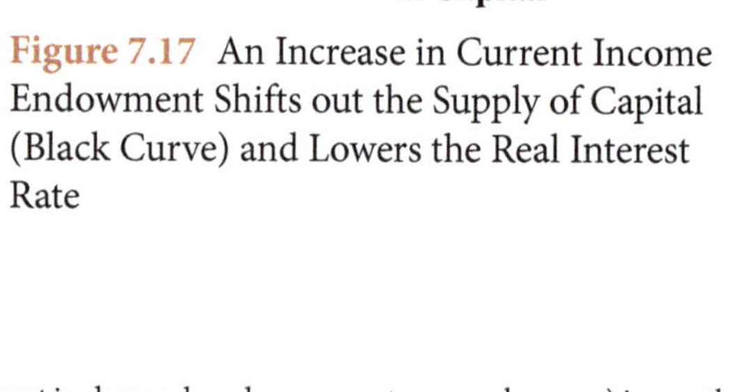

Figure 7.17 An Increase in Current Income Endowment Shifts out the Supply of Capital (Black Curve) and Lowers the Real Interest Rate

[3]This results because the substitution effect towards more investment (shift out in demand, and movement up supply curve) is exactly offset by the income effect of less investment (shift back in supply, and movement up demand curve).

7.4.4 Business Cycle Explanation with 2-Period Model

In a typical business cycle, both interest rates and the equilibrium quantity of capital savings and investment rise. Achieve this by combining a productivity increase with a current income increase. Figure 7.18 shows that with an *equi-proportional increase in both productivity and current income* (up by 5% each here), the supply and demand for capital shift out in such a fashion that demand shifts out by more than supply. The interest rate rises, and so does investment, thus reproducing the basic features of a business cycle expansion.

Show a contraction here by reducing productivity and current income by an equal percent. Figure 7.19 shows the resulting shift back in demand by more than supply shifts back. The interest rate and equilibrium capital supplied and demanded falls.

Fixed Interest Rates and Excess Supply of Capital

Figure 7.20 shows what happens when a recession as in Figure 7.19 occurs when at the same time the interest rate is fixed, and cannot adjust downwards. Then a normal recession becomes a severe recession, in that the equilibrium amount of capital demanded is much lower. So there is much less investment.

The *fixed interest rate* captures Keynes' idea of how an *excess supply of capital* might result. Here, at the fixed, above natural market rate of interest (which would have fallen if it was not fixed), there is an excess supply of capital. This type of excess supply always occurs when a price is fixed above its equilibrium level, as discussed in Chapter 1.2.6. In general, prices are not fixed and so this is just a way to express Keynes's concept of an excess supply of capital by assuming fixed real interest rates.

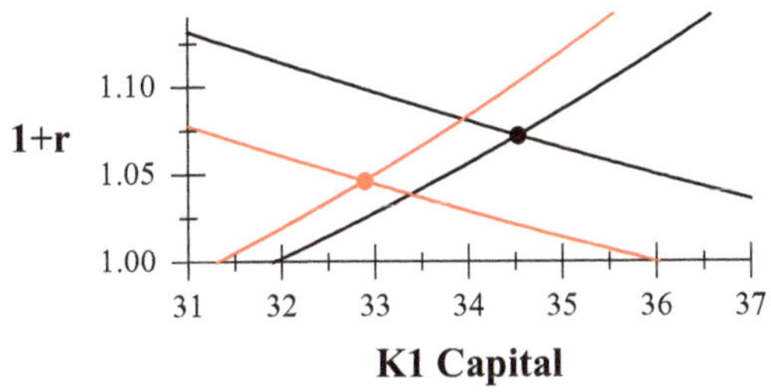

Figure 7.18 Capital Market with 5% Increase in Goods Productivity and Income Endowment (Black) versus Baseline (Red)

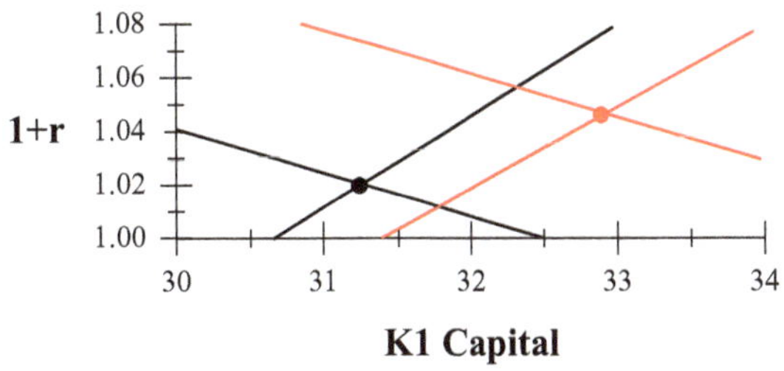

Figure 7.19 Capital Market with 5% Decrease in Goods Productivity and Income Endowment (Black) in versus the Baseline (Red)

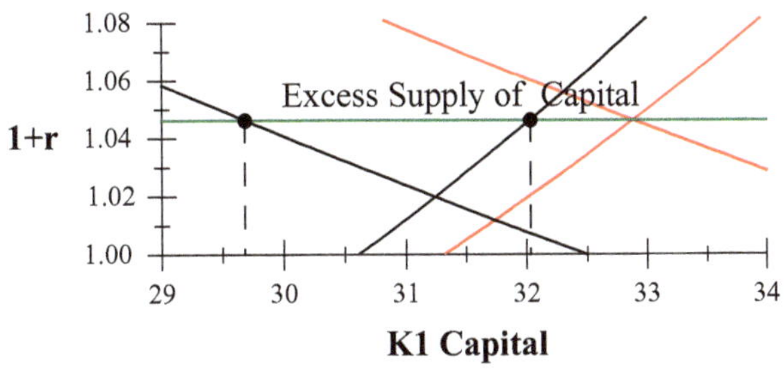

Figure 7.20 Excess Capital Supply Indicated by Horizontal Distance between Vertical Dotted Lines

Alternative Theory with Banking

A fixed interest rate did not actually occur during the Great Depression as the real interest rate rose to around 10%, which is a very high level. So the fixed interest rate theory is in terms of the real interest rate and rarely can this be held fixed, even if the nominal interest can be fixed by the government (Federal Reserve System).

An alternative theory to a fixed real interest rate for explaining a very low investment level during a crisis is a *collapse in the private bank sector*. Then the Neoclassical solution would be to fix the problem that the banking sector has, and so revive private savings and investment. This focus on banking problems was seen in policy during the Great Recession in the US during the 2008 to 2010 period. Such a decrease in bank productivity is shown in Neoclassical *AS-AD* terms in the next chapter, Section 8.6.

A fixed nominal interest rate can be maintained by a central bank through heavy intervention in the capital markets. In particular, for the US the Fed can maintain a near constant Federal Funds short term interest rate by buying and selling US government debt. At any fixed interest rate, the real interest rate may be any value, such as positive ten percent in the Great Depression, or a negative one to two percent as occurred during and after the Great Recession of 2008–2010.

The real interest rate matters for capital markets, but capital markets determine rates in the unit of currency of the particular capital market. By nature, this means that all market interest rates are nominal interest rates. Nonetheless, market participants care only about real interest rates. And Fisher's two-period case of Ramsey's (1928) model can tell the story of the capital market during a business cycle.

7.5 Application: Present Discounted Value

Fisher's (1896) *Appreciation and Interest* apparently first showed systematically the economic idea of *discounting the value of future income* in order to put it in *present value terms*.[4] Fisher provides a definition and clarification (p. 19):

"The ordinary definition of the present value of a given sum due at a future date is that sum which put at interest today will 'amount' to the given sum at that future date . . . The literal meaning of present value implies that it is the actual market price today of a future sum due."

Within a two-period setting restricted to only the current period and the next period, we can show what could be earned on income if it was saved. This income is the interest. This interest earning then is used to show how much income a saver would have next period including the original amount that was saved.

For example the next period value of 1 dollar is 1 + r dollars next period if r is the (real) interest rate. This means that the future value of one dollar held today, given that the interest rate is r, is given by 1 plus the interest rate r, or 1 + r. The 1 + r exactly equals the economic future value of 1 dollar today.

Once future value is understood, the converse of this is easier to grasp: present discounted value. Suppose you know you will have 1 + r dollars next period. Then what is the current period value of that 1 + r dollars owned next period? The answer is that you need 1 dollar to generate 1 + r dollars next period. So the value of 1 + r dollars next period is 1 dollar today.

Having figured out that 1 + r dollars tomorrow is worth 1 dollar today, we have now computed the *"present discounted value"* of 1 + r dollars held next period. The present discounted value is 1 dollar. Therefore this implies a method of discounting that uses the interest rate in the discounting process.

In particular, consider how much we would need today to invest in order to have 1 dollar tomorrow. The answer would be that if we have 1/(1 + r) today, or 1/(1 + r), and we invest it, then we will have the 1/(1 + r) tomorrow plus interest earned on it.

The interest earned on one dollar invested is found by taking 1 dollar and multiplying it by 1 + r, and getting the result of $1 \cdot (1 + r) = 1 + r$. So if we have $\frac{1}{1+r}$ today and we save it and earn an interest rate of r, then we get next period the amount invested $\left(\frac{1}{1+r}\right)$ multiplied by 1 + r. This means we get $\frac{1}{1+r} \cdot (1+r) = \frac{1+r}{1+r} = 1$. In other words we get 1 dollar next period if we invest $\frac{1}{1+r}$ today.

[4] Irving Fisher, 1896, Appreciation and Interest, published for the American Economic Association by the Macmillan Company, New York (75 cents price in paper).

Now we have the way to discount the value of future income. One dollar next period is worth $\frac{1}{1+r}$ today, as just established. Therefore, any income next period has a present discounted value that is found by multiplying the next period income by $\frac{1}{1+r}$.

For example 100 dollars next period is worth $\frac{1}{1+r}(100)$. Assume an interest rate of 5%. In fraction terms, a 5% interest rate is written as a rate of 0.05. So the present discounted value of 100 dollars next period, when $r = 0.05$, is $\frac{100}{1+0.05}$. This can be written as $\frac{100}{1.05} = 95.24$. The reason 100 dollars next period is worth only about 95 dollars today is that we can save and invest 95 dollars today and earn interest so that we get back 100 dollars tomorrow.

The present discounted value of next period income is thereby found by multiplying next period income by $\frac{1}{1+r}$. This is the same as *computing present value* by dividing the next period income by $1 + r$. And the next period future value of current income is found by multiplying current income by $1 + r$.

For example if ownership of a share of a company's stock means that it earns a dividend of 100 dollars every period, and the interest rate is 5%, then the current value of the next period dividend is $\frac{100}{1.05} = 95.24$. Now extend the concept in order to value in present terms the entire future stream of dividends.

Start with two periods. If income, say d, was received and invested for two periods, then after one period the income would be $d(1 + r)$, as it would be augmented by the interest. Then that income $d(1 + r)$ would again be invested at the rate r, for another period. Interest would be earned on $d(1 + r)$, which is $rd(1 + r)$, plus the principal $d(1 + r)$ would be returned at the end of the second period. This means that $d(1 + r) + rd(1 + r) = d(1 + r)(1 + r)$ would be earned, or $d(1 + r)^2$. The interest is "*compounded*" in that interest is earned in the second on interest that was earned in the first period.

Similarly if the income d was received two periods in the future, then the present discounted value would be $\frac{d}{(1+r)(1+r)}$, or $\frac{d}{(1+r)^2}$. This is true because if $\frac{d}{(1+r)^2}$ were invested now and earned interest for two periods, then the future value of $\frac{d}{(1+r)^2}$ would be $\frac{d}{(1+r)^2}(1+r)(1+r) = d$. The two-period future value of $\frac{d}{(1+r)(1+r)}$ is d. This makes the present value of a dividend d received in each of the next two future periods equal to $\frac{d}{(1+r)} + \frac{d}{(1+r)^2}$.

Any savings that earns a positive real interest rate has a higher future value of income because it earns interest, and this interest gets componded. The future "*compound interest*" value is higher than the present value of the savings. It also makes the present discounted value of any income to be received in the future less than the amount of income received in the future without any discounting.

The value of a constant stream of dividend dollar payments d can be computed, for three periods or longer, including an infinite dividend stream. Making the assumptions 1) that the dividend starts being paid in the next period, 2) that the dividend is constant and 3) that the interest rate stays constant, then the present discounted value of the *infinite dividend stream* is

$$\frac{d}{1+r} + \frac{d}{(1+r)^2} + \frac{d}{(1+r)^3} + \quad = \frac{d}{r}.$$

The simple algebraic sum results in a final value of d/r.[5] The permanent dividend d as divided by the interest rate gives the present discounted value its infinite stream. Let p denote the present discounted value, then consider the "price" p for a stock yielding d as given by $p = d/r$. This is the simplest basis for understanding how prices of stocks of companies are determined in actual capital markets. Compute a company's hypothetical price-earnings ratio from the formula $p = d/r$; dividends are "earnings" and so $(p/d) = 1/r$ is the price-earnings ratio.

The price divided by the earnings of the company is like the Wealth to Income ratios introduced in the beginning of the chapter (in Section 3.1). This analogy is true in that an individual's ownership of a share in a company gives that individual wealth equal to the price of the share. And the income earned on that wealth is indeed equal to the dividends paid out by the company on that share. Each company then has its own "internal" r as implied by the market, just as for the US the implied r for its Wealth/income ratio was 0.25.

Generationally, while people are young and earning money from labor, they tend to have little financial wealth in terms of ownership of equity shares. Then the income earned is the flow of "interest" on their "human capital". As people retire, their savings is invested so as to give them a flow of interest income on their financial capital saved. With no labor income, as when fully retired, then their income earned is equal only to the interest flow on their wealth that has been saved.

7.6 Appendix: Savings & Investment Shares

Figure 7.21 graphs again the NIPA definition of the Personal Savings Rate as a percent of disposable income (in blue) and the NIPA definition of the investment share (in red), for 1947 to 2015, quarterly. Net exports as a share of GDP are added in the green line, this being a stable amount around zero until 1991 when the net export share of GDP started trending downwards. In purple in Figure 7.21, is the sum of the saving rate and the investment share minus the net exports share of GDP (NX) and finally also subtracting the trend total of 27(percent). This line trends around zero as expected if domestic investment equals savings.

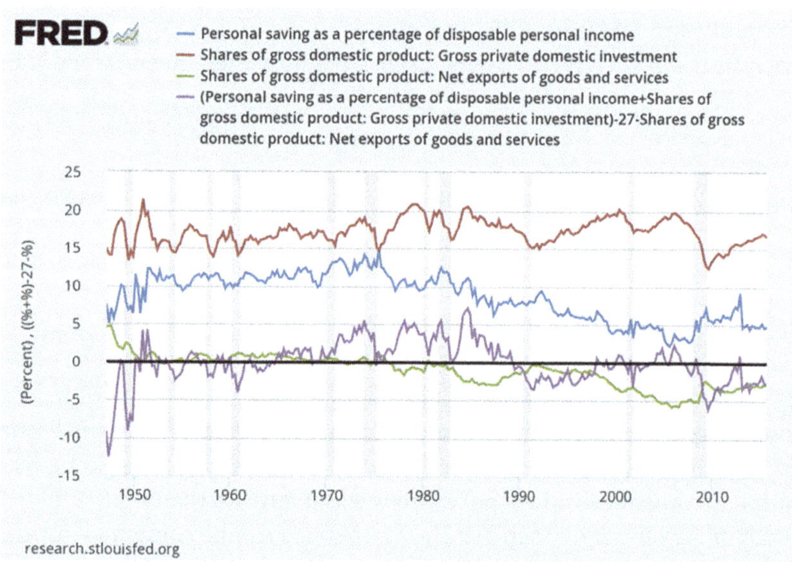

Figure 7.21 Adjusted Personal Savings Rate Plus Investment Rate Minus Net Exports

---

[5] $1 + a + a^2 + a^3 \quad = \dfrac{1}{1-a}$; here define a as $a \equiv \dfrac{1}{1+r}$; then $\dfrac{1}{1+r} + \left(\dfrac{1}{1+r}\right)^2 + \left(\dfrac{1}{1+r}\right)^3 =$

$$\frac{1}{1+r}\left[1 + \frac{1}{1+r} + \left(\frac{1}{1+r}\right)^2 + \quad\right] = \frac{1}{1+r}\left[\frac{1}{1-a}\right] = \frac{1}{1+r}\left[\frac{1}{1-\frac{1}{1+r}}\right] = \frac{1}{1+r}\left[\frac{1+r}{r}\right] = \frac{1}{r}.$$

Note that there is another way to view whether investment equals savings. To see this, note that by the NIPA accounts that Y = C + I + G + NX. Solve for I as I = Y−C−G−NX. Use the concept that domestic investment equals domestic savings, or I = S, and it follows that I = Y−C−G−NX = S. Now compare S = Y−C−G−NX to the definition of the "Personal Savings Rate".

NIPA defines personal savings as disposable income minus consumption. Using S^p for the personal savings, this would be symbolically represented as $S^p = Y-T-C$. Disposable income is the after tax income, or symbolically written as Y-T. Taking the disposable income Y−T and subtracting consumption C gives the personal savings definition of $S^p = Y-T-C$.

Now assume a balanced government budget, such that government spending equals tax revenue. This balanced budget means symbolically that G = T. Subtract consumption C from disposable income Y−T while assuming that G = T, we get our personal savings Y−T−C is equal to Y−G−C. Part of income is accounted for in terms of what is sent abroad as net exports. So subtract net exports NX from Y-C-G to get savings equal to Y−C−G−NX. So starting with the "personal savings" definition and assuming that G = T, it results that S = Y−C−G−NX, as above, as in Figure 7.21.

Accounting for federal budget deficits and surpluses, consider an exact reconstruction of the Savings share of GDP as in I = S = Y−C−G−NX using the "personal savings rate". Since the latter is (Y−T−C)/(Y−T), it can be put in terms of GDP by factoring it by (Y-T)/Y. Then we have $\frac{Y-T-C}{Y-T}\frac{Y-T}{Y}=\frac{Y-T-C}{Y}$, which gives the savings as a share of GDP. Use FRED data for Taxes as a share of GDI (from NIPA) to obtain the data corresponding to T/Y, which forms part of $\frac{Y-T}{Y}=\frac{Y}{Y}-\frac{T}{Y}=1-\frac{T}{Y}$. Factoring $\frac{Y-T}{Y}$ by $\frac{Y-T-C}{Y-T}$ gives $\frac{Y-T-C}{Y}$. Now add government budget surplus of T-G as a share of GDP by adding $\frac{T-G}{Y}$ to the normalized personal savings rate of $\frac{Y-T-C}{Y}$. This gives us $\frac{Y-T-C}{Y}+\frac{T-G}{Y}=\frac{Y-T-C+T-G}{Y}=\frac{Y-G-C}{Y}$. Subtract net exports as a share of GDP to get: $\frac{Y-G-C}{Y}-\frac{NX}{Y}=\frac{Y-G-C-NX}{Y}$. This gives exactly the definition of total savings as a share of GDP when I = Y-C-G-NX, and S = I.

Figure 7.22 graphs the refinement of the purple line above in Figure 7.21 that now considers that the federal budget surplus is not always zero. After adjustment, it shows similar results, with far off the normal trend for

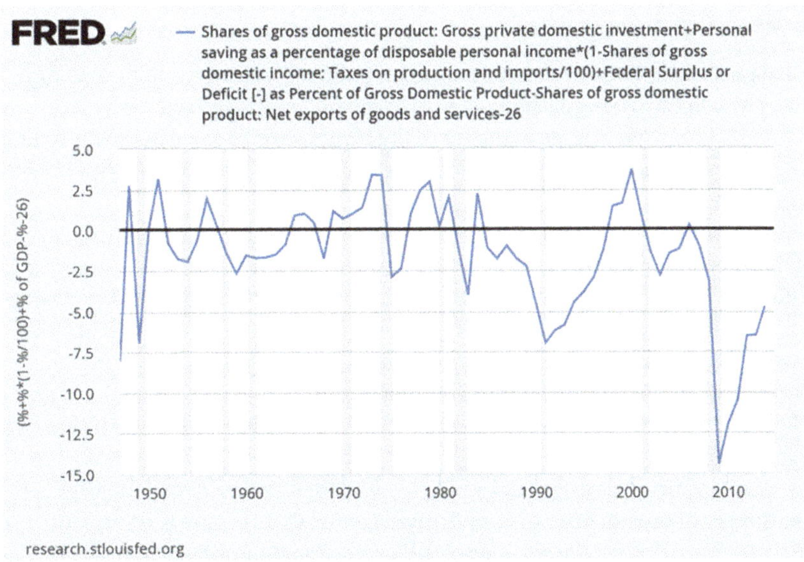

Figure 7.22 Adjusted Residual of US Investment Plus Savings: Seemingly Procyclic Behavior

the period since 2001. The Federal Funds interest rate was fixed below the inflation rate for the 2002 into 2005 and from 2008 until 2015, leading to negative real interest rates for much of this 2001 to 2015 period. Low investment appears to be the main contributor to this result, also the factor Keynes (1930,1936) emphasizes in explaining the Great Depression.

7.7 Summary

The chapter shows the market for capital in terms of the supply and demand for capital from both the original Keynesian view and the original Neoclassical view of Fisher. The Keynes (1936) graph and analysis led to IS-LM analysis. The chapter describes the special assumptions required to graph the IS and LM curves with their assumed downward and upward slopes, respectively. These assumptions are quite fragile and do not hold generally in the Fisher analysis.

The IS-LM framework remains useful because it "motivates" the idea of strong government intervention in order to ameliorate a recession. The concept is that an increase in government spending acts as a private investment shift out in demand that causes higher output and interest rates. Government increases in the money supply acts to cause also higher output, but with lower interest rates; inflation is ignored in this analysis of monetary policy.

The Neoclassical optimization approach of Fisher's two-period model is also represented graphically in terms of an optimization-derived supply and demand. Keynes's (1936) special case that is the only graph in his *General Theory* is reproduced qualitatively in the Fisher supply and demand for capital by assuming an exogenous increase in current income.

The real business cycle movement in investment, interest rates and consumption growth is reproduced with Fisher's model by assuming both an output productivity increase and an increase in the exogenous current income endowment. This is a simplified version of Ramsey's (1928) model covered in the next Chapter 8.

Capital theory fundamentals are presented in the Application. These also originated in Fisher's first work on interest rates. The resulting analysis shows how the relative price of future income is less than one, because we have to wait to receive it. This relative price is the so-called discount factor, and for a one period ahead income this discount factor, or price of the one-period ahead income, is $1/(1 + r)$ where r is the one-period interest rate. The Appendix shows the sense of how savings tends to equal investment in the NIPA, in the first case when the federal budget surplus or deficit is assumed to be zero and second when it is fully accounted for.

7.8 Glossary of Words

accumulate capital: the process of keeping and continuing to build any form of wealth over time.

Appreciation and Interest: book by Irving Fisher, 1896, Macmillan Company, New York.

collapse in the private bank sector: when large segments of the bank sector become insolvent or illiquid; when depositor payments of the bank are suspended; when there is a bank panic and depositors attempt to withdraw more deposits than banks have on reserve.

compound interest: the amount of interest that gets paid on past interest already earned; this causes the interest on interest result that is called compounding.

compounded: this is another way to say the we take into account that interest will be earned on past interest already earned.

computing present value: this is done by assuming some level of an interest rate that will hold over time and using this rate to find what would be the current market value of some amount of given future income.

current period output: output or income given in the current period.

debt contract: an obligation to borrow money and then pay it back at some point in the future, typically with a set rate of interest on the money borrowed.

demand and supply for capital: firms invest capital which leads to their demand for capital and consumers save income which leads to their supply of capital; here it is implicitly assumed that income is transformed costlessly into capital.

demand for real money: the use of money for exchange leads to a demand for money in real terms, or real money; money can also be held as an asset but it yields zero interest and typically is not as good as holding "risk-free" government bonds.

derived IS curve: the derivation of the IS curve comes from first showing the supply and demand for capital as a function of the real interest rate; an increase in current income causes the investment demand for capital curve to shift out by less than does the savings supply of capital, leading to a lower interest rate with income; this gives a downward sloping relation between (exogenous) income and the equilibrium real interest rate which is called the IS curve, graphed with r on the vertical axis and Y on the horizontal.

discounting the value of future income: determining the present value of income received in the future by using the interest rate; note that the present value of a future income is less than the future value itself if the interest rate is positive.

equi-proportional increase in both productivity and current income: when both exogenous parameters for the level of productivity and the level of income are increased by the same percent.

equilibria: more than one equilibrium.

equilibrium capital invested: the market quantity of capital that is demanded at the market price of the real interest rate.

equity ownership arrangement: a contract by which some fraction of a company is owned by a party to the agreement.

excess savings: the quantity of capital that is supplied, at a fixed real interest rate, that exceeds the quantity of capital that is demanded at that fixed real interest rate.

excess supply of capital: the same as excess savings.

Fisher savings-investment analysis: the use of two periods to focus in on the savings by the consumer and investment by the firm in a simple optimization analysis involving time and the decision on capital usage.

fixed government supply of money: the usual assumption in the IS-LM analysis is that there is no private bank money supply; there is only the government money supply and it is assumed to be a set exogenous amount; because it is exogenous, it does not change when income changes.

fixed interest rate: an interest rate somehow set at a certain level in the market, typically by the government; note that some believe that the real rate of interest cannot be set, even though the nominal interest rate can be fixed.

future period consumption: the amount of output consumed in the second period; as a two-period model, there is no further investment and all second-period output is consumed.

General Theory: of Employment, Interest and Money, by John Maynard Keynes, published in 1936; famous book suggesting the subsequent IS-LM analysis, the possible existence of liquidity traps, and the consumption function used in the subsequent Keynesian Cross analysis.

increase in productivity of capital, or, increase in capital productivity: when the productivity parameter of the production function for output, holding labor constant, is increased, causing more output per any given amount of capital input.

increasing the given, assumed, current income: an increase in the exogenous current income level that is given in the two-period Fisher savings-investment model.

infinite dividend stream: a dividend payment that is paid every period, for the indefinite future.

investment: the quantity of capital that is inputted into the production function in the two-period Fisher savings-investment model, or the quantity of capital that is demand in Keynes's IS-LM capital market.

IS curve: the equilibrium interest rate that corresponds to different levels of the exogenous income level, using the way in which shifts in savings supply and investment demand are assumed to react when income exogenously increases; is downward sloping by the restrictive assumptions made.

IS curve shifts out: this occurs typically when government spending is increased under the assumption that the government spending acts as a shift out in investment demand; the assumption here also is that there is no initial increase of exogenous income as a result of government spending rising.

IS-LM analysis: The determination of the "equilibrium" level of output and the real interest rate at the same time as equilibrium in both the capital market and the money market also occurs.

Islamic banking: a contractual way to turn all debt-based interest payments into equity-based dividend payments, as a result of religious law banning the payment of interest.

Keynes' IS-LM analysis: a set of specialized assumptions that indicates how both government spending and money supply increases can raise output.

life satisfaction: a basis in which to measure well-being that includes income and wealth as two factors of many factors.

liquidity preference for money: the demand for money as named by Keynes and his followers.

liquidity trap: a market equilibrium in which the interest rate cannot fall by more; see zero lower bound for its modern incarnation.

LM curve: the locus of equilibrium interest rates and income that are consistent with such equilibria in the Keynesian money market; is upward sloping by the restrictive assumptions made.

LM curve shifts: shows how the LM curve moves when the exogenous government money supply is assumed to change.

market in capital: the supply and demand for capital, and their equilibrium.

monetary policy ineffectiveness: in a liquidity trap in IS-LM analysis, it is not possible to raise output by increasing the money supply, making monetary policy have no effect on output.

Neoclassical monetary theory of Fisher's: the relation showing that the money supply and aggregate price level move together when real output and money velocity are stable; the demand for money as a function of output and the inverse of the velocity of money circulation.

optimization theory of consumption smoothing over time: gives the equilibrium amount of savings and investment out of current income that provides for the highest utility level and relatively equal consumption amount in both current and future periods.

present discounted value: the current, or market, value of income to be received in the future; uses the interest rate to discount the future value to the present value.

present value terms: putting the future income stream in dollar amounts that reflect what its market value would be in the present.

private bank supply of money: the supply of money created by banks when they increase the demand deposits in their accounts, for example by making new loans to depositors; this supply tends to rise as the real interest rate rises, giving an upward sloping supply curve.

production function for future period consumption: the ability to provide output in the next period by investing in capital during the current period, holding labor constant.

savings: the amount of income offered to those who want to use it for investment and in return offer interest on the amount borrowed, in addition to returning the amount borrowed.

stylized facts of economic growth: the normal trends such as a steady real output growth rate, a rising wage rate, and rising income per person; also includes a stable, unchanging real interest rate.

supply and demand for future consumption: the production of output for the next period provides the supply of future consumption, since all output is consumed in the second period, while the demand for future consumption results from the current period savings decision of how much to save and to consume in the current period; the demand for next period consumption is a residual of the savings decision in the first period.

The Purchasing Power of Money: a book published by Irving Fisher in 1922 that sets out the "quantity theory of money" and the "equation of exchange."

The Rate of Interest: a book published by Irving Fisher in 1907 that sets out the Fisher equation of interest rates whereby the nominal interest rate equals the sum of the real interest rate and the expected inflation rate.

upward sloping LM curve: the result of specialized assumptions in the money market; does not hold in general.

usury: interest on capital lent out.

utility function of consumption in the current period and consumption in the next period: a hypothetical concept that attributes a certain amount of benefits called utility to different combinations of current and future consumption levels.

wealth to income ratios: the amount of wealth divided by the amount of income; income divided by wealth conversely can be considered a measure of the wealth productivity, or the rate of income flow from capital wealth.

zero lower bound of interest rates: Fisher (1896, p. 30, equation 12) asserts that nominal interest rates cannot fall below zero, or in our notation, that $R \geq 0$; this zero is commonly called the lowest that nominal rates can go although there are a few historical claims of the existence of negative nominal interest rates.

7.9 Questions

1. Describe what is usury, Islamic banking, and explain how the recognition of the role of interest changed the market economy's ability to create wealth.
2. What is the relation between wealth and income levels that is found internationally, how does this relate to life satisfaction, and how can a flow of income be generated by a certain stock of wealth?
3. Explain how Keynes (1936) used a capital market to lay the foundation for the construction of an IS curve, and indicate the assumptions required to make the IS curve slope downwards.
4. How is the LM curve constructed from the money market?; and what assumptions are necessary to ensure that the LM curve is upward sloping?
5. What is the IS-LM analysis used for in terms of ways to increase aggregate output?
6. How does a critique of the IS-LM analysis involve the role of inflation?

7. How does the Fisher two-period analysis use optimization theory to determine the equilibrium quantity of the savings and investment of capital?
8. The Fisher two-period analysis uses a production function to transform invested capital into output next period; what choices by the consumer and firm are involved in this production process, and how does the production determine the consumption in the second period?
9. Describe the market for capital in Fisher's two-period model.
10. Describe the market for future period consumption in Fisher's two-period model.
11. What happens in the markets for capital and future period output when the productivity of capital is exogenously increased?
12. What happens in the markets for capital and future period output when the current income endowment is exogenously increased?
13. What happens in the markets for capital and future period output when both the productivity of capital and the current income endowment are exogenously increased by the same percent, and in what sense is this consistent with a business cycle expansion?
14. How can an excess supply of capital result when the interest rate is fixed?
15. How can an explanation based in the banking sector explain a depression in aggregate activity?
16. What is the future value of 100 dollars received two periods from today, when the full capital is saved and it earns an interest rate of 10 percent each of the two periods?
17. Complete the Federal Reserve Bank of St. Louis EconLowdown Course Module "Time Value of Money".
18. Complete the Federal Reserve Bank of St. Louis EconLowdown Course Module "Soar to Savings".

8 AS – AD & Business Cycles

8.1 Introduction

The basis of both Neoclassical and Keynesian models has evolved to include the dynamic theory of capital accumulation, as seen in Fisher's two-period theory of capital, but extended now to the full future (infinite) horizon. Ramsey (1928) along with the 1965 independent extensions of Ramsey by David Cass and T.C Koopmans created what is often called the Ramsey-Cass-Koopmans (RCK) model of Neoclassical economics. This model, which here is called "Ramsey's World" (or RCK, equivalently) is presented graphically below in this and subsequent chapters. The Ramsey model underlies both Neoclassical and New-Keynesian economics.

The Ramsey model uses the consumer utility maximization subject to the aggregate output production function, with savings behavior that is endogenous. Here the Ramsey model is also spelled out using the exact aggregate supply and demand graphs that are implied by the model. These graphs can be used to show the market for aggregate output, and the market for each the labor and capital inputs.[1]

A key feature of using aggregate supply and demand in the Ramsey model and its graphs is to use a relative price for output. Here the relative price is the real price of goods in terms of the amount of labor hours necessary to produce a good, given the equilibrium amount of the capital stock. This contrasts with instead using the interest rate as in IS-LM analysis as the "price" of output, in a rather loose way not derived from utility maximization.[2]

The interest rate in the Ramsey model is tied by optimization to the growth rate of the economy, which is constant and is initially assumed to be zero. As a consequence, the interest rate is also constant in the Ramsey model. But the wage rate steps in to be the variable that allows the full display of the supply and demand in both output and input markets.

The data for the real price of labor, and for capital, is available and is shown in this chapter. From these data series, the cyclical fluctuations in such data can be surmised. The Ramsey economy is then used to figure out the least amount of changes in the economy we need to assume in order to mimic the stylized facts of the business cycle. This is done in a way consistent with the Real Business Cycle theory outlined in Chapter 4. This analysis uses productivity and time endowment changes and it is set out using supply and demand, the corresponding relative price, and the markets for output of goods, and inputs of labor and capital.

8.2 Who Made it Happen

Macroeconomics arising out of the Great Depression of the 1930s was called "Depression Economics" by Paul A. Samuelson with in his second edition of his *Economics* textbook in 1951 (his final 19th edition was in 2009). This analysis became what we now call the Keynesian Cross analysis. However Samuelson famously extended the Keynesian Cross by using it to describe what he called aggregate supply and aggregate demand for output, even though no utility maximization was employed (only the Keynesian consumption function and national income accounting). To this day, some will use the Cross to "derive" aggregate output demand and supply even though this is not consistent with our accepted microeconomic foundations of using utility maximization subject to the production function technology.

[1]The text assumes log-utility in goods and leisure and Cobb-Douglas production with labor and capital as inputs.

[2]The capital stock at time t is given in the recursive equilibrium model and so $AS - AD$ can be graphed at time t knowing this equilibrium capital stock at time t; see Gillman (2011) *Advanced Modern Macroeconomics* for details.

Keynes (1930, 1936) already was aware of the utility maximization approach as applied to Macroeconomics when he developed his main theories, but he chose not to use it. Instead Keynes simply postulated various economic relations rather than deriving them from what we think of as economic fundaments like utility and production. Samuelson continued this practice by saying that Keynes's Cross analysis determined aggregate demand and aggregate supply.

That Keynes was aware of the alternative "utility maximization" approach is clear because it was Keynes's own brilliant student Frank Ramsey that developed it in his 1928 "Mathematical Theory of Savings", published in the renown *Economic Journal* of which Keynes was editor. Ramsey died in 1930 at age 26, and Keynes then wrote about Ramsey's famous 1928 article in Keynes's 1933 book, *Essays in Biography,* in the last chapter on Ramsey called "Ramsey as an Economist". Keynes writes

> "But he has left behind him in print (apart from his philosophical papers) only two witnesses to his powers - his papers published in the *Economic Journal* on "A Contribution to the Theory of Taxation" in March 1927, and on "A Mathematical Theory of Saving" in December 1928. The latter of these is, I think, one of the most remarkable contributions to mathematical economics ever make, both in respect of the intrinsic importance and difficulty of its subject, the power and elegance of the technical methods employed, and the clear purity of illumination with which the writer's mind is felt by the reader to play about its subject. The article is terribly difficult reading for an economist, but it is not difficult to appreciate how scientific and aesthetic qualities are combined in it together (p. 295, original edition, Harcourt, Brace and Company, New York)."

Ramsey (1928) in turn gives credit to his teacher. In his Theory of Savings he states that "Mr. Keynes has shown me that the rule governing the amount to be saved can be determined at once from these considerations." So Ramsey works out what Keynes suggested to him, with a greater mathematical precision than what may have been imagined by Keynes. This Ramsey work extends Irving Fisher's consumption and savings approach from two periods to the complete future horizon.

Ramsey uses the standard Cobb-Douglas production function with labor and capital as inputs into producing output, with diminishing marginal products of each labor and capital. Being the first to set out this capital theory, Ramsey also includes labor time, and so his approach implies that there is some limit, or constraint, to our time use as well as to our goods usage. This sets out what is still the basis of the modern macroeconomic economy, both Neoclassical and New-Keynesian. It allows for modern aggregate supply and demand analysis as derived from utility maximization subject to production technology, for graphing the goods market, the capital market and the labor market.[3]

Understanding time usage plays a big part in modern Macroeconomics. Gary S Becker (Nobel Laureate 1992) made prominent the theory of the allocation of time, in his 1965 article "The Allocation of Time" (in *Economic Journal).* Becker made clear how all of our time is valued "at the margin" at the same rate as our work time. This makes both the "shadow value" of leisure and all other uses of time a part of the decision of economic analysis.

Besides the so-called "leisure" time, Becker describes other uses of time that can take away from our labor force participation. For example, time usage could also include time spent studying in school, or on-the-job training, or for fertility and child-raising. Becker details such analysis in his books: *Human Capital, The Economic Approach to Human Behavior* and *A Treatise on the Family.*

Considering the full value of time allows for us to account for time not spent in the labor force or simply in leisure. Consider Becker's 2005 *American Economic Review* article: there he and coauthors use the full income value of time to study the worldwide distribution of income. The authors find that by counting the rising human capital that was resulting from the world population's increasing health as a source of their non-market (shadow) income, the worldwide distribution of this fuller income measure was getting more equal rather than less equal, as some argue on the basis of financial income alone.

[3]See Gillman (2011) where this AS – AD graphical analysis is set out for the first time for the output market.

8.3 Facts

8.3.1 Monetary Prices Versus Relative Prices

The price of goods in nominal terms indeed can be well-represented by an aggregate price index such as the Consumer Price Index (CPI). This does not represent the real price of goods, upon which decisions are made. A real price in microeconomics can only be what we call a *relative price*, or the opportunity cost of the purchase of the good.

The problem with discussing nominal, real and relative prices in Macroeconomics is that we use these terms in different ways. The "real" price of a particular good can be put in a "constant US dollar basis" by dividing the nominal price of the good by an aggregate price index such as the CPI index, as was done for gasoline prices in the Application in Chapter 1. This is a "real" price in the sense that it takes out the inflation factor.

Standard Microeconomic analysis typically starts without money, or currency. Applying the same tradition to Macroeconomics reflects what is called the Classical "dichotomy" where the economy has a real side and a nominal side, each of which does not affect the other. However, since the inflation tax affects real decisions, it is recognized that there is never a pure separation of the real and nominal factors of the economy. Nonetheless, macroeconomics based on micro foundations uses real prices of the output of goods and services and of the input of labor and capital. For example, the CPI tells us about inflationary increase in the price of the aggregate basket of goods, which is a fact about the nominal side, although it may affect the real side.

In real terms without recourse to using money, a key main choice is how much goods to purchase in exchange for time spent working. This brings to the forefront the value of time as part of the relative price of output that Macroeconomists focus on in a way consistent with microeconomics (in which there is no money).

Real Price of Goods Relative to Time

The nominal wage rate is not a real price, or a relative price, since it also includes the inflationary increase in the wage rate as well as any possible real change in the price of time. This means that both the goods nominal price in terms of the CPI index and the working time nominal price in terms of the market wage rate include a similar inflationary component. This leads immediately to the concept of the relative price between the two main items that enter the consumer's utility: a relative price that shows the real value of aggregate goods relative to that of the aggregate labor required to produce the good, given the equilibrium capital stock of the aggregate economy.

Dividing the nominal price of goods, call it P, by the nominal wage rate, call it W, gives the result of P/W. Dividing one by the other cancels out the nominal dollar aspect contained within each nominal price. The relative price of goods to labor (working time) can therefore be represented for example by the CPI index divided by the market wage rate, using the notation of P/W. The demand for goods can be expressed therefore as being dependent on this real price of goods relative to the price of time. Dividing the nominal price of goods by the nominal price of time gives us the *real price of goods relative to time.*

FRED has US Data on the price of goods relative to the price of time via their real wage series. Starting in the beginning of 1979, FRED publishes the index of the average weekly wages and salaries of full time employees aged 16 and over. Give the notation W to this nominal wage data. This is given in real terms by dividing the wage by the CPI price index. Give the CPI the notation of P. Then the price of goods relative to the price of time can be expressed as P/W, or $1/w$, where w is the real wage (W/P), and so $1/w$ is simply the inverse of the real wage rate.

Should we expect that goods become more expensive over time relative to wages or less expensive over time less to wages? FRED's longest data series, quarterly data from 1979:1 to 2015:3, of the CPI divided by the nominal wage rate is given in Figure 8.1. It shows large swings upward and downwards, and a significant trend downwards. With a focus on the trend, it implies that the answer to the question is that the price of goods falls relative to the price of labor over time.

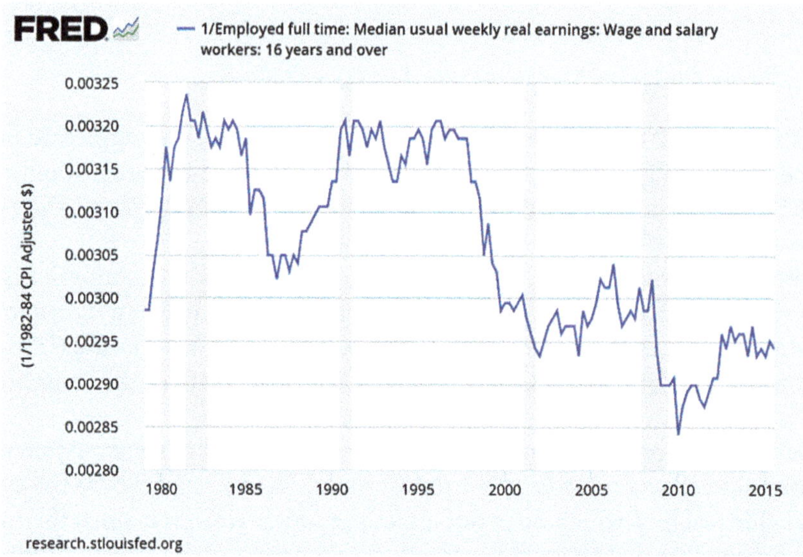

Figure 8.1 US Nominal Price of Goods (CPI) Divided by the Nominal Wage Rate (average weekly wage and salary, full time, 16 and over): P/W, 1979 to 2015

A falling relative price of goods, and conversely a rising relative price of labor, makes sense in that it means that our real wage, relative to the average goods price, is rising over time. In other words, the inverse of a falling price of goods relative to labor is a rising price of labor relative to goods. This rising real wage means that our real income rises and we can buy more goods and experience economic growth.

Over time, the relative price of goods to labor then should cycle around a downward trend. It should fall in expansions and rise in recessions. Put differently, the real wage should rise in expansions and fall in recessions.

Cyclical evidence of the price of goods relative to the price of time is mixed. After the short but deep 1981 recession, Figure 8.1 shows that the price of goods fell relative to wages, as the real wage increased. This real wage rise is typical of an expansion, and consistent with real business cycle theory.

Following the US stock market crash of some 22% of the Dow Jones Stock index on October 19, 1987, Figure 8.1 shows the US price of goods relative to labor rising, as consistent with a recession. This means the real wage began falling, which it started to do before the 1991 recession and continued through the 1991 recession. From 1998 to 2001, the price of goods relative to labor was falling and the real wage was rising, both as consistent with an expansion. Post 2001 evidence is mixed, during the Great Recession and its era as a potential "lost decade", which is the subject of Chapter 11 below.

Real Wage and GDP Growth

Figure 8.2 shows another dimension of the procylic nature of the real wage. It graphs the *nominal wage growth rate minus the inflation rate* for US data from 1966 to 2014; the result is the growth rate of the real wage, as graphed in Blue.[4] The real GDP growth is graphed in Red. It is clear that the real wage growth rate matches the detrended real GDP growth rate during much of the period, almost from 1966 right up until 2000.

After 2001, the Figure 8.2 series move inversely, apparently part of the pathology induced during the Great Recession. The real wage did rise substantially during the Great Recession, as well as during the fixed, below inflation rate, nominal interest rate period from 2001 to 2004. These two fixed nominal interest rate

[4]Note that if the real wage is written as W/P, then the percentage change in the real wage equals the percentage change in W minus the percentage change in P. The latter percentage change in P is the CPI-based inflation rate in this FRED graph.

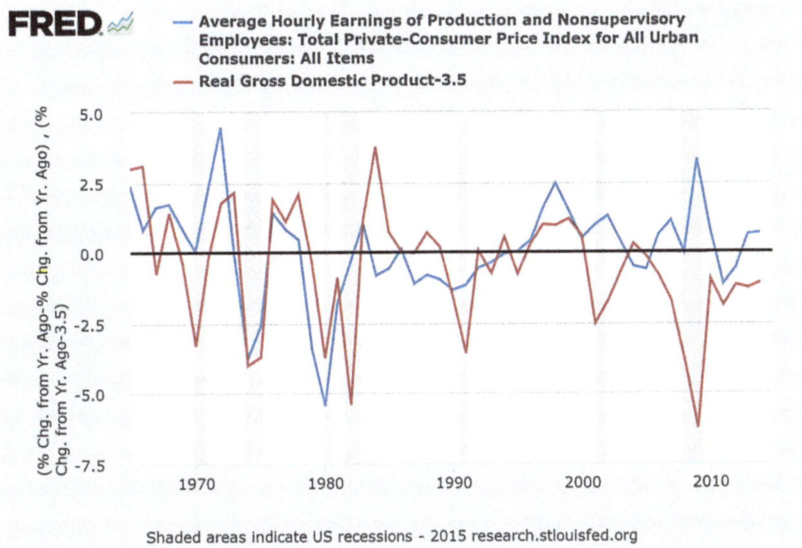

Figure 8.2 Annual Growth Rate of Real Wage Rate and Trend-Adjusted Real GDP, US 1965:6–2014

periods induced a negative real interest rate that may have been behind the *countercyclic movement in wages* in these atypical recent episodes. Excluding the post 2001 period for now, as one heavily distorted by Fed policy that induced negative real interest rates, the rest of the time the stylized facts confirm a *procyclic real wage growth.*

Labor Force Participation Rate and Real GDP

Another aspect of the wage rate is whether people are working or not, as reflected in the labor force participation rate. If this participation rate is procyclic, the real wage becomes more procyclic. This is confirmed in recent studies.

Chodorow-Reich and Karabarbounis (2016), in "The Cyclicality of the Opportunity Cost of Employment",[5] describe how the "opportunity cost" of employment includes both the actual wage earned in employment and the opportunity cost of switching from non-labor market participation to working in the labor market. Non-labor market participation includes an "earnings" of all of the various social insurance benefits received when unemployed: these benefits are generally lower than the wage rate earned while working and these benefits are generally earned in a recession. This makes the overall wage rate more procyclic by including the low benefits received in recessions as part of the effective real wage rate:

> "We consider both unemployment insurance (UI) benefits, which are directly related to unemployment status, and non-UI benefits such as supplemental nutritional assistance (SNAP),welfare assistance (AFDC/TANF), and health care (Medicaid). The latter belong in the opportunity cost to the extent that receipt of these benefits changes with unemployment status".

Non-wage factors help determine how procyclic is the total opportunity cost of working, which is usually thought of as only the real wage rate. These factors make more cyclical the whole opportunity cost (meaning the "effective" wage rate, or what is called the "shadow" wage rate): "The opportunity cost is procyclical and volatile over the business cycle." This procyclic "shadow" wage rate (opportunity cost) of labor is consistent with explaining why the labor force participation rate is so procyclic.

Figure 8.3 shows the Civilian Labor Force Participation Rate from 1958 to 2014, in Blue, compared to the detrended Real GDP growth rate in Red. It shows that the annual average growth rate of the US Civilian

[5]Gabriel Chodorow-Reich and Loukas Karabarbounis, 2016, *Journal of Political Economy,* vol. 124, no. 6.

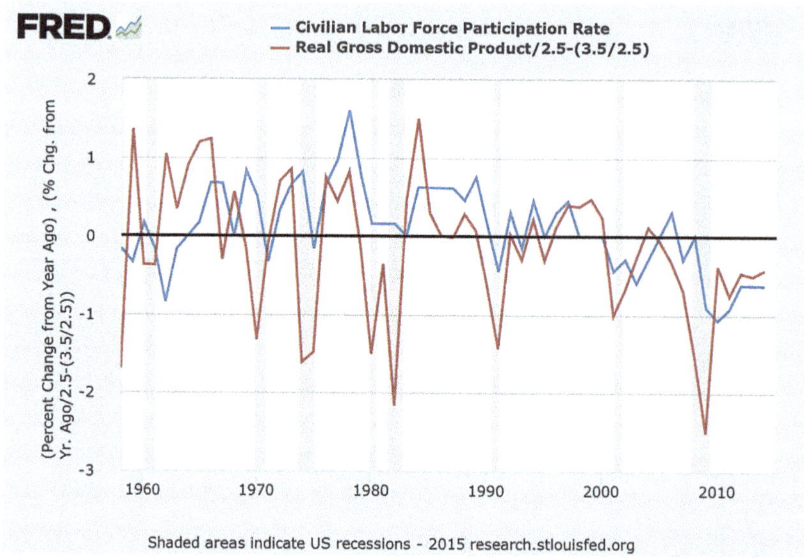

Figure 8.3 US Labor Force Participation Rate (Blue); Real GDP (Red); 1957:7–2015.14

Labor Force Participation Rate is regularly procyclic. The *Labor force participation growth rate* generally is positively correlated with real *GDP* growth rate, rising with business expansions and falling (relative to its trend) in business contractions. Here *GDP* growth is normalized by dividing it by 2.5, and then a subtracting by 1.4 so that it is comparable in magnitude to the labor force participation growth rate. This measure, unlike the real wage growth in Figure 8.2, is procyclic also in the post 2001 period, thereby giving evidence that the total "shadow" wage rate is procyclic for the entire post 1965 period.

8.3.2 Capital to Goods Price & Debt-Deflation

Data on the *nominal price of capital relative to the nominal price of goods* presents data on the *real price of capital relative to goods*. Consider that a major recession often coincides with a real asset decline. Figure 8.4 shows a real asset price series (in Blue), as measured by the *Russell 3000* index, plus the CPI based inflation rate (in Red) for 1979 to 2015. The two series show that during recessions a positive correlation tends to result.

A question raised by the "debt-deflation" theories of Fisher and Hayek is whether the real decline in asset prices can cause, in part, a decrease in the inflation rate since the price index includes components reflecting the cost of capital. Figure 8.4 shows that the inflation rate (red line) fell severely during the 1981 recession's real asset price decline, and fell significantly during both the 2001 and 2008–2010 recessions and real asset price declines. The asset price declines would have caused part of the lower measured inflation rate.

For example, GDP includes residential investment that on average has been 5% of GDP while durable goods consumption has been about 8% of GDP for a total of 13%. These are capital intensive goods and will decrease in real price relative to labor when capital values fall. This can cause the measured inflation rate to fall, even if the fall is due to a real decline in capital relative to goods or labor.

The 2001 and 2008–2010 "debt-deflation" episodes can be seen from the corresponding real asset market value crashes along with the decline in the inflation rate. This correlation is also visible in the 1981 to 1982 deep recession and in the 1991 recession, when there were also deflations and big asset price declines.

Another way to view the relation of capital value to real GDP growth is graphed in Figure 8.5. This shows how during the post-2000 period the *real price of capital relative to goods*, in Blue, is especially

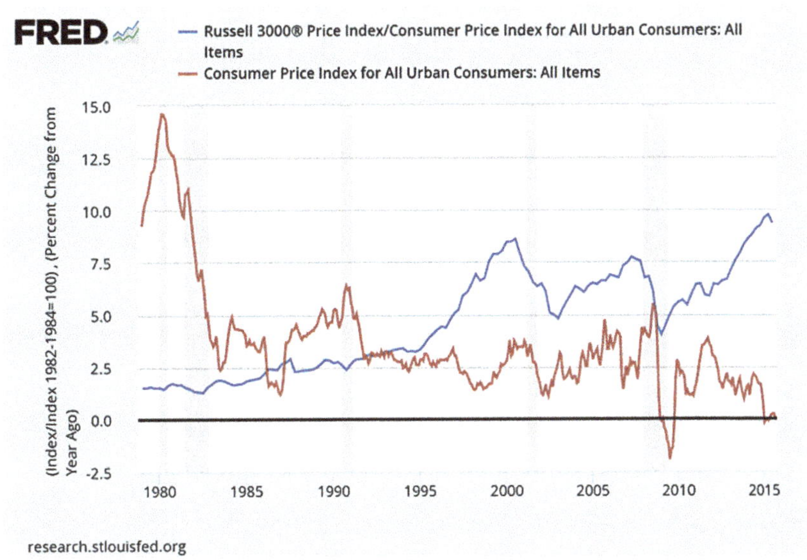

Figure 8.4 Real Price of Capital (Blue) and CPI Inflation Rate (Red)

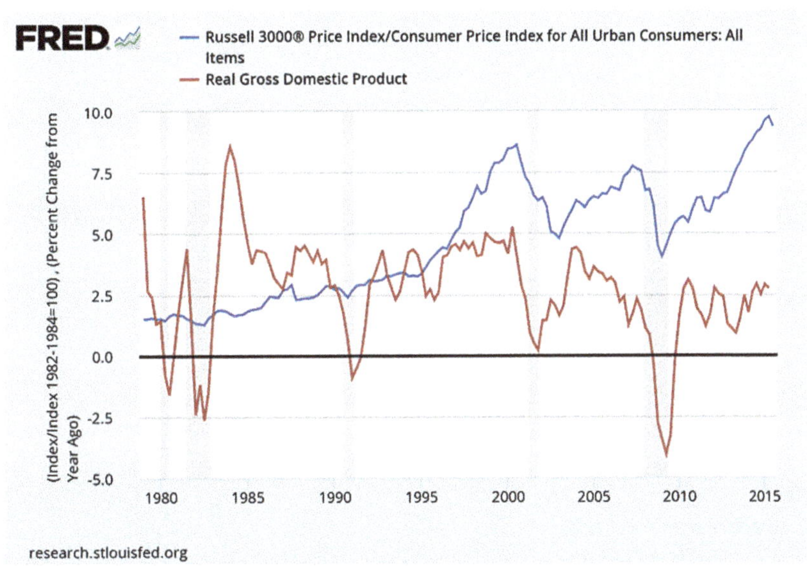

Figure 8.5 Real Price of Capital (Blue) and Real GDP Growth Rate (Red)

procyclic as compared to the growth rate of real GDP in Red. The real price of capital relative to goods is systematically procyclic with declines in the real price of capital relative to goods coinciding to some degree with recession since 1978.

A procyclic movement in real asset prices is consistent with real business cycle theory which says that the real interest rate should be procyclic in this theory. This is because procyclic real asset prices imply a procyclic "equity return" to capital, which is one measure of the real interest rate. So both real interest rates and real wages appear to be somewhat procyclic.

Asset prices relative to wage rates also appear procyclic. Figure 8.6 shows that asset prices relative to wage rates, as graphed in blue, are procyclic in a way similar to asset prices relative to goods prices in Figure 8.5 In comparison, graphed in red are a normalized goods prices relative to wage rates. This can help explain why investment is more volatile than consumption over the business cycle.

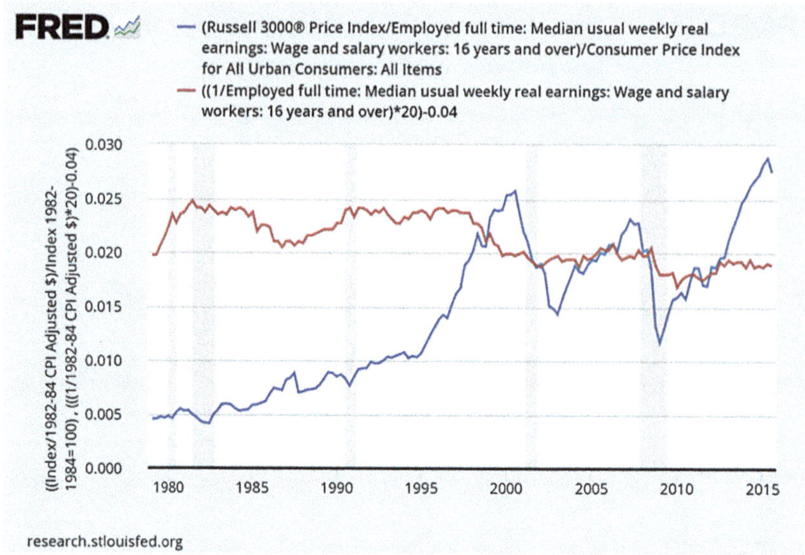

Figure 8.6 Asset Prices Relative to Wage Rates

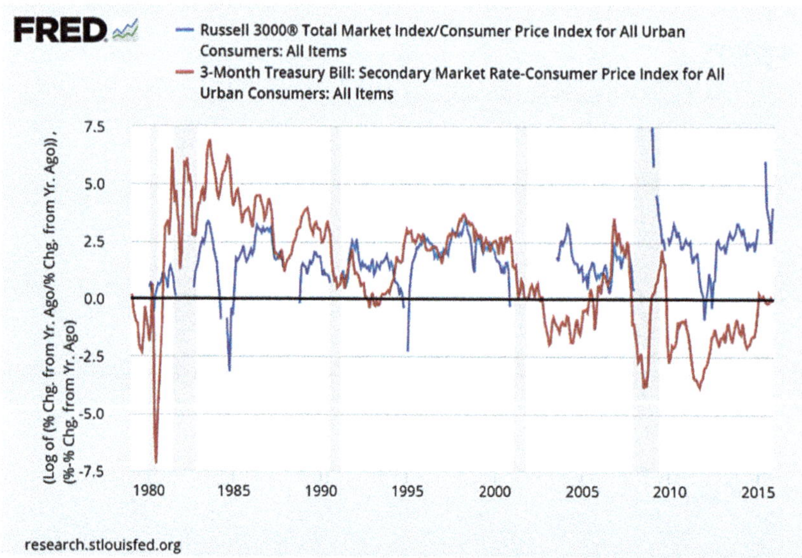

Figure 8.7 Equity Premium as Difference Between Blue line of Annual Percentage Change in Russell 3000 Index Minus Red line of Annual Real Yield of Treasury 3-month Bill (found by substracting the CPI annual Inflation Rate)

Finally, consider evidence on the "equity premium". The equity premium is defined as the difference between the average risky equity return and the average "risk-free" government bond return. Figure 8.7 shows the annual percentage change in the real price of capital in blue as measured by the FRED's Russell 3000 equity index versus the real interest rate on 3-month Treasury bills in red. One notable result is that the equity premium is relatively very high in the post 2007 period.

It may be that the Federal Reserve kept real interest rates negative for much of the Great Recession, which led to more holding of risky equity than would be normal in a business cycle. Holding more risky equity would allow investors in part to make up the "lost return" of the "lost decade" of the Great Recession in terms of the negative return that was earned from holding "risk-free" Treasury debt.

The *portfolio balance between risky equity and risk-free debt* appears to have been tilted by Fed policy so as to induce more demand for risky equity. This acts to subsidize and therefore raise the real value of capital, perhaps beyond what is fundamentally supportable by the future profit and dividend yields of the Russell 3000 and other capital markets. If so, then a decrease in the real value of equity value would be expected once the Fed stops "flooding" capital markets with excess reserves and thereby continues to keep the "riskfree" interest rates artificially low.

8.4 Theory

8.4.1 Stylized Facts Of Cycles

Stylized facts from the theory of business cycles can be explained with *aggregate supply for output (AS) and aggregate demand (AD)*. Over business cycles, output, the employment rate, the investment rate, the real wage rate and the real interest rate are procyclic: rising in expansions and falling in contractions.

Evidence on the two factor input prices can be mixed during such "rare events" as lost decades and Great Recessions, when "unconventional" macroeconomic policies can distort input prices. For example, the Fed driving down the real interest rate to negative levels during the Great Recession can act to subsidize capital inputs while acting as a tax to labor inputs that raises the wage rate and lowers the labor force participation.

8.4.2 *Ramsey's World* with AS – AD

Aggregate demand and supply (*AS – AD*) for goods and labor in the "Ramsey World" allows for capital accumulation, which brings in the "dynamic" time element. Frank Ramsey (1928) created the modern framework for capital accumulation over time with goods and labor. Ramsey apparently attended John Maynard Keynes's graduate lectures. Soon after this, Ramsey published his 1928 article in the Economic Journal when Keynes was Editor (from 1911 until 1945).

Ramsey (1928) built the mathematical structure of modern dynamic economics by extending Fisher's two-period model to an infinite future horizon, while adding in the labor decision. This uses a standard production function for output with both capital and labor inputs, and initially assumes zero economic growth. The equilibrium capital stock results from investment made in past periods. Since the equilibrium capital stock is known to the representative agent in the current period, the *AS – AD* analysis can be graphed as a function of the equilibrium capital stock. Not only can the output market be graphed in this way but so can the labor and capital markets.

To graph *AS – AD* in the Ramsey World, the critical departure point is to establish the real price of goods relative to a different real economic activity. Both goods and time are consumed by the representative agent acting as consumer, with time consumed in the form of leisure when not working. A starting point for the relative price is the real price of goods relative to leisure.

The real interest rate is used in IS-LM analysis. But in the Ramsey World that underlies modern macroeconomics, the real interest rate is fixed by the "exogenous growth rate" assumed for the economy. The real interest rate therefore cannot change when comparative static exercises are used to explain the stylized facts of the business cycle. The real interest rate is constant in Ramsey (1928) and in Solow's explanation of growth.

In contrast, the price of leisure is what economists call a "shadow price": its price is its value as spent in its next best alternative activity, which here is time spent working. The price of labor is the wage rate, making the *shadow price of leisure* also the wage rate. Therefore the price of goods relative to leisure is the price of goods divided by the wage rate.

Real Price of Goods Relative to Labor

The nominal price of goods can be represented by the CPI index, since this is the cost of a representative basket of consumption goods. It may be "normalized" to be 100 in the base year. Or consider simply a normalization of the nominal price of one good to be 1.

Divide the nominal price of 1 dollar for one good by the nominal wage rate, being the dollars received per hour. This gives dollars per good divided by dollars per hour. The dollars cancel out. We are left then with the hours required per good. This is a *real price of goods. The real price of output is the amount of time required to produce one good.*

The real price can also be seen in terms of the units of measurement for the prices. Notationally, \$1 per one good can be written as $\frac{\$1}{good}$. And the nominal wage rate is some number of dollars, say X, per one hour. This can be represented as $\frac{\$X}{hour}$. Then the relative price of goods to labor is the ratio of the two prices. This ratio is $\frac{\frac{\$1}{good}}{\frac{\$X}{hour}}$. The nominal part is the dollar sign \$ and this cancels out, leaving $\frac{1}{X}\frac{hours}{good}$. This means that 1/X hours is required to produce one good. If X = 2, then real price of one unit of goods is half an hour of labor time.

The relative price of goods is the nominal price of goods P divided by the nominal price of labor W. This P/W is a relative price of goods for labor. It is the same as the inverse of the real wage, or $1/w$, where the real wage is defined by the nominal price of labor divided by the nominal price of goods, or W/P, and where we use the notation that W/P is the real wage w $(W / P \equiv w)$. Inversely, the real price of labor relative to the price of goods is $w/1$ which just equals w, the real wage.

How does the real interest rate enter the Ramsey analysis? It is part of the relative price for current consumption versus future consumption, which is one plus the real interest rate, or $1+r$, as in the Fisher two-period model. Also as in Fisher, the capital market in the Ramsey World sees the equilibrium real interest rate determine the equilibrium quantity of capital that is supplied and demanded. The difference is that the depreciation rate of capital in the Ramsey World is less than the one that was implicitly assumed in the Fisher two-period model, a detail that will remain in the background of the graphs.

Production, Utility, & Supply and Demand

With both labor and capital variable at the same time in the production function for output, the stylized facts of business cycles and growth, and even a bank-led economic crisis, can be graphically presented. With aggregate output production expressed as $y = f(l, k)$, the aggregate output y is a function f of labor l and capital k, with both labor and capital optimally chosen by the consumer and firm simultaneously over the entire future expected horizon.

The time dimension enters explicitly when there is positive economic growth instead of zero economic growth as will be assumed for the analysis of the business cycle. Time subscripts allow a generalization that allows for positive economic growth as in the next Chapter 9. Let t indicate the time period of output and inputs, with $y_t = f(l_t, k_t)$. The other notation to be used are superscripts for supply (s) and demand (d).

On the firm side, the representative agent acting as the firm maximizes profit subject to the production technology $y_t^s = f(l_t^d, k_t^d)$. The result of firm profit maximization is three key components of supply and demand in output and input markets: the firm's equilibrium 1) supply of output y_t^s, 2) demand for labor l_t^d and 3) demand for capital k_s^d.

On the consumer side, the representative agent acting as the consumer *maximizes utility* over goods and leisure subject to *budget constraints on goods allocation and on time allocation.* This gives the other three key components output and input supply and demand: 1) the demand for consumption goods, denoted by c_t^d, 2) the demand for leisure, denoted by x_t, which also implies the supply of labor l_t^s, and 3) the supply of capital

k_t^s. Symbolically, at time t, utility is a function u of goods c_t^d and leisure x_t [or $u_t = u(c_t^d, x_t)$]; the explicit firm and consumer optimization problems are only presented as footnotes, and mentioned here for intuition as to how supply and demand are derived in the full Ramsey World model.

The aggregate output is representative of what is consistent with the National Income and Product Accounts (NIPA) (Y = C + I + G + NX). It is assumed that there is no government spending and no trade (G = 0 and NX = 0). This makes it a "closed economy". Aggregate demand is y_t^d. Investment comes from the net increase in capital, arising from the firm's demand for capital k_t^d. Denote real investment as i_t. With the consumer demand for goods c_t^d and the investment in capital i_t, it follows that the goods resource constraint of the economy is [6]

$$y_t^d = c_t^d + i_t.$$

In equilibrium markets "clear", meaning that the *quantity demanded equals the quantity supplied at the equilibrium price in each market.* The quantity supplied of output, labor and capital will equal the quantity demanded of output, labor and capital, respectively. This means that once *markets clear*, it is true that $y_t^d = y_t^s$, $l_t^d = l_t^s$, and $k_t^d = k_t^d$ allowing a dropping of the supply and demand notation and simply stating that

$$y_t = c_t + i_t.$$

Note that here that the capital market clears and so the equilibrium quantity of investment i_t depends on the equilibrium quantity of capital stock that we can call k_t.

The societal resource constraint on time simply says that the agent splits the total time between working and taking leisure. Notationally (and dropping time t subscipts) total time endowment of the consumer (such as 24 hours a day) can be denoted by T. This total time is split between leisure time x and working time l (or $T = x + l$).

Production of output can be graphed in two dimensions with the input on the horizontal axis by either letting labor be variable and capital be fixed, or by letting capital be variable and labor fixed. At the same time the production function can be "turned around" along the horizontal axis by making leisure instead of labor the variable on the horizontal axis. This because once the consumer chooses either leisure, or labor, the other is residually implied (since $T = x + l$).

Dropping time subscripts t for the rest of the Chapter, Figure 8.8 shows goods output that is consumed, c, on the vertical axis and the input of labor l on the horizontal axis; capital is held constant at its equilibrium level. The production function is in Blue; the utility function indifference curve between goods and labor is in Red. These curves in turn imply the supply and demand functions presented below.

Conversely, Figure 8.9 "turns around" the production function and makes it a production possibility curve. The indifference curve between goods and leisure is in Red, and the production possibility curve is in Blue, both with capital held constant at its equilibrium level. Here $T = 1$

AD-AS Construction

Aggregate demand for goods depends upon the relative price $1/w$, which is the relative price for goods to labor (or equivalently the goods to leisure price). This relative price and the equilibrium quantity of consumption c is found directly from the slope of the Red indifference curve in either Figure 8.8 or Figure 8.9, given the equilibrium capital stock k.

Consider Figure 8.8. The slope of the blue production function is the marginal product of labor, which equals in turn the real wage w. At a zero quantity of labor, the slope is steep and the marginal product high.

[6] $i_t = k_{t+1} - k_t + \delta_k k_t$ is the accumulation of capital condition; δ_k is the depreciation rate and $\delta_k k_t$ is the depreciated capital that are most closely related to the the NIPA measure called "Fixed Capital Consumption" introduced in Chapter 2. $k_{t+1} - k_t$ is the change in the capital stock over time; so if investment is greater than just maintenance of depreciated capital $(\delta_k k_t)$,then the stock k rises over time.

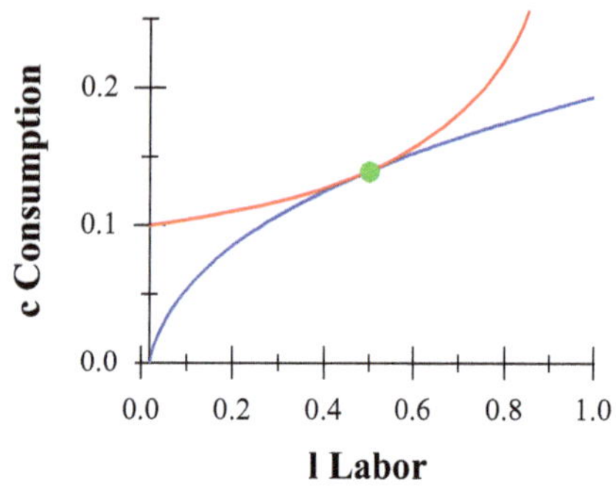

Figure 8.8 Production & Utility Indifference Curve in Ramsey World

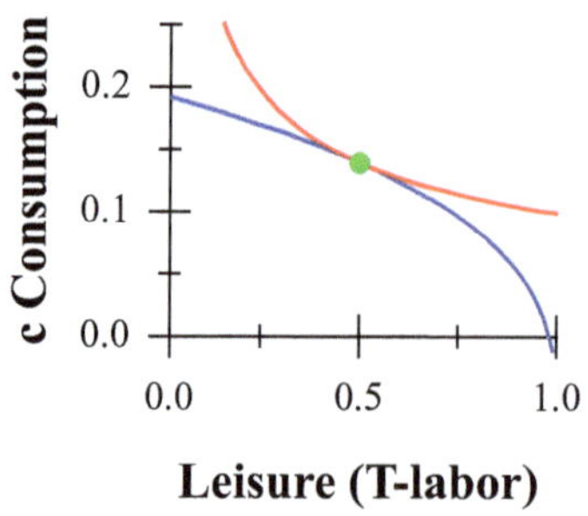

Figure 8.9 Alternative Production & Utility Indifference in Ramsey World

As more labor is employed, move up along the production function. The slope gets flatter as the marginal product goes down. This means the wage w is lower at higher quantities of labor demanded by the producer of goods. As labor demanded, l^d, increases, w decreases. As l^d increases, more output y^s is supplied. So as $1/w$ increases, the wage gets smaller, more labor l^d is demanded and more output y^s is supplied. Result: as $1/w$ increases, the supply of goods y^s increases. This gives the basic upward sloping aggregate supply of goods relation (*AS*) as a function of the relative price of goods $1/w$.

From the red indifference curve of Figure 8.8, the relation between aggregate demand for consumption goods and the relative price of goods, $1/w$, is established. Along any one indifference curve, including the red one here, different combinations of consumption goods and labor yield the same constant level of utility. The slope of the indifference curve, as with the production function, equals the real wage. This is because the real wage is the marginal rate of substitution between labor (or leisure) and goods.

At low levels of labor supplied by the consumer, the slope of the indifference is relatively flat. This means the real wage w is low when the consumer supplies little labor and demands few goods for consumption. The slope gets higher as more labor is supplied and more goods demanded for consumption. This means that as w rises, the consumer supplies more labor and demands more consumption goods. At a low labor supply, w is low and so $1/w$ is high. At a high $1/w$, little labor is supplied and few goods demanded for consumption. At a low $1/w$, much labor is supplied and more goods are demanded. Result: as $1/w$ increases, the demand for consumption goods decreases. This gives the basic downward sloping aggregate demand for consumption goods as a function of the relative price of goods $1/w$.

Aggregate demand (*AD*) for output, denoted by y^d, is the sum of consumption demand and investment. So far only the consumption demand was discussed. Investment is only the maintenance required to keep the capital stock constant, in an economy with zero growth as is first assumed in this Chapter. This maintenance investment is necessary because capital depreciates at some rate. Maintenance keeps the capital depreciation in check, and it is a simple multiple of the depreciation rate of capital as multiplied by the capital stock. It does not depend on the relative price of output $1/w$. So once consumption demand is determined, and investment is added to this total demand for output, the resulting downward function of *AD* on the relative price $1/w$ follows from the consumption part of total output demand.

Therefore *AD* is a downward sloping function of the relative price of goods to labor $1/w$, given the equilibrium capital stock k $\left[y_t^d = AD(1/w_t, k_t)\right]$. Aggregate supply (*AS*) of output is an upward sloping function of the relative price of goods to labor $1/w$, given the equilibrium capital stock k_t $\left[y_t^s = AS(1/w_t, k_t)\right]$. So *AD* is a "normal" downward sloping demand function. And *AS* is a "normal" upward sloping supply function. Both demand and supply for output shift outwards (are positively affected) when the equilibrium capital stock k_t increases.

Equilibrium output y_t is then determined at point where the quantity supplied of output equals the quantity demanded, as measured along the horizontal axis. This occurs graphically where the *AS* and *AD* curves intersect. We get the equilibrium relative price $1/w_t$, as measured along the vertical axis, from this intersection of the *AS* and *AD* curves.

Comparative Static Change In Equilibrium: *AS – AD* vs IS-LM

The Keynesian IS-LM analysis assumes that both the supply and demand for capital depend positively on the *exogenously* given level of income. An exogenous increase in income shifts out both the supply and demand for capital there. Here, in contrast, the capital stock is the equilibrium capital of the full Ramsey dynamic World, so k_t is determined within the model, *endogenously* as we say.

Here an increase in k_t could occur if some parameter such as the *productivity parameter* should change. This would be a part of a "*comparative static*" experiment that would show the new equilibrium after a change in one of the model's important assumed parameters. If a higher equilibrium capital stock results from a change in one of the economy's fundamental production or utility parameters, this k increase is endogenously determined within the optimization model. If k rises as a result of a parameter change, it causes shifts out in both the aggregate supply *AS* and the aggregate demand *AD* curves in a precise way as determined exactly within the model. Note that there cannot be just an exogenous increase in the equilibrium capital stock in the Ramsey World.

If it were indeed the productivity parameter that went up, then there are other possible repercussions to the *AS* and *AD* curves as well, because they are a function of the underlying technology and utility parameters of the model. In the example of an increase in the productivity parameter, it results the *AS* curve shifts out because of the direct effect of the productivity parameter upon the *AS* function, as well as from the increase in k. For the *AD* curve in this example of a productivity increase, it would only be affected by the *change in the capital stock.*

The result that we would see in the example of a productivity increase is that the aggregate supply curve ends up shifting out by more than aggregate demand. The relative price $1/w_t$ falls. The equilibrium quantity of output y_t rises.

There is a sharp methodological difference here in the Ramsey World relative to IS-LM analysis. Since the IS-LM analysis is not a utility and profit maximization model, any statement of supply and demand is simply a hypothetical possibility. There is no derivation of the slope in any textbook IS-LM graph that is based on *optimization*.

In contrast, supply and demand in the Ramsey World are exactly equal to the *equilibrium conditions that are derived from the optimization problem* (maximization subject to constraints). Since any IS-LM model that is written down does not come from optimization, the IS-LM analysis can only resort to an argument of what would happen if output rises *by assumption, whereby exogenously this change is assumed to occur.* The latter IS-LM is an argument of what might be. The Ramsey World is a precise statement of what exists, given the abstractions of the World that are included.[7]

In the Ramsey World, only fundamental parameter assumptions of the model can be changed by assumption. And there is a broad consensus in the economics profession of what parameters should be the focus of change: productivity of goods production and the time allocated to the market sector. The equilibrium decision variables such as output and income (these are equal as in NIPA accounting), the amount of time spent working, and the amount of capital used in production *cannot be assumed to be changed exogenously.* This is because these variables result from the equilibrium conditions of supply and demand.

Besides the output productivity parameter, the other parameter that will be changed here is the total amount of time being devoted to work and leisure. This can be changed by allowing it to rise or fall according to how much time is spent in other activities besides work and leisure. For example education time and child-raising take away time from work and leisure.

Education and useful household activity make up a huge portion of time allocation, and are not what we think of as work or leisure. Changes in *time allocation for work and leisure* are thereby plausible indicators of such alternative activity. In economic data, the Labor Force Participation Rate is a main indicator of when more or less time is being made available for work and leisure.

[7]Fisher's 2-Period World is also as precise as is Ramsey's but it is a special 2-period case of Ramsey's world that lacks continuous capital accumulation.

8.4.3 Ramsey Markets for Output, Labor and Capital

First the basic Ramsey World markets for goods, labor and capital are set out in graphs, assuming a *zero growth rate*, in a conventionally accepted standard utility and production economy.[8] With zero economic growth, variables do not change, making it a good place to start. It allows a focus on the business cycle. Time subscripts can be and so are dropped. By conducting comparative static changes in the firm's productivity and in the consumers time endowment, business cycles are then explained in terms of supply and demand and the stylized Real Business Cycle Facts.

With zero growth, all variables are unchanged, or *"stationary", over time*, for any given equilibrium. The constant capital stock k is maintained by enough investment every period just to cover the capital depreciation. Symbolically the maintenance quantity is given by δk where δ is the depreciation rate. The *depreciation of capital* is part of what is measured at "Fixed Capital Consumption" in NIPA accounts.

Figure 8.10 graphs the Ramsey downward-sloping demand for consumption c^d in Green, as derived from optimization. It then adds investment required to maintain the capital stock. Reading along the horizontal axis, this gives the sum of $c^d + i = y^d$, as in the NIPA accounting (with zero government spending and zero net exports assumed), where the difference between the total aggregate demand (AD) and consumption is investment, which can be measured along the horizontal axis. The constant amount of investment for maintenance, given the equilibrium capital stock k, means that the investment simply shifts out the consumption demand, by a constant horizontally measured amount on the graph, so as to aggregate demand for output.[9]

To restate, the Green curve is the equilibrium consumption demand function, which depends negatively on the relative price $1/w$, and positively upon the equilibrium capital stock k. The Black curve is the sum of this consumption demand and the constant amount of equilibrium investment needed to maintain the capital stock at a constant level. This Black curve is the AD curve. The horizontal difference between the lines is the investment amount that is equal to the capital maintenance ($\delta\, k$).

Figure 8.11 graphs the corresponding AS curve for the same example economy as used to derive the AD curve. The representative agent firm's aggregate supply of output AS is a function of certain technology parameters assumed (in the production function), including productivity, and of the relative price $1/w$, given

Figure 8.10 Ramsey Aggregate Output Demand *AD* (Black) & Consumption Demand (Green)

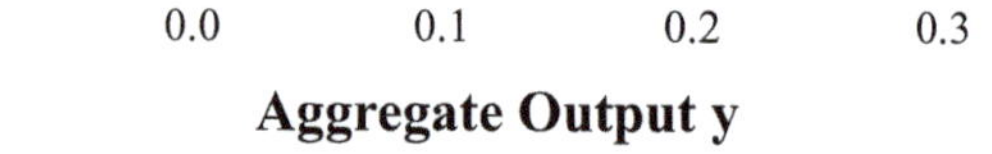

Figure 8.11 Ramsey Aggregate Output Supply *AS*

[8]Log utility over goods and leisure and Cobb-Douglas production using labor and capital.

[9]The baseline example is to assume $u = \ln c + \alpha \ln x, y = Al^{\gamma}k^{1-\gamma}$, with $\gamma = \frac{1}{3}$, $\alpha = 0.5$, and T=1, along with ρ =0.03, A = 0.15 and $\delta_k = 0.03$. Note that with $r = \rho + \delta_k$, where ρ is the rate of time preference used by the consumer to discount future utility; the example implies that r = 0.03 + 0.03 = 0.06 and an equilibrium value of k = 2.3148.

the equilibrium capital stock k. Graphing this *AS* curve gives an upward sloping aggregate supply curve of output y relative to the relative price $1/w$ (vertical axis), given the capital stock.[10]

Consider the flexibility of the Ramsey World. If one really wanted to derive a vertical long run *AS* curve in the Ramsey World, then this can be done by making couterfactual assumptions. Similarly the opposite of a nearly horizontal *AS* also results from counterfactual assumptions. For example, a near horizontal *AS* curve results in the very special case when the share of labor costs in output approaches *1*, which is counterfactual since it ignores the share of capital in output cost which "economic accounting" finds to be significant.[11]

The other counterfactual example of a vertical *AS* curve is used in the stagflation theory of low growth during the Vietnam war era in Keynesian analysis. Figure 8.12 illustrates this case with a near vertical *AS* curve that results only if the share of labor costs in output approaches zero.[12] Such a *vertical AS curve* is counterfactual as well since labor accounts for a significant share of output cost. Assumptions of either a near one or near zero labor cost share in output are at odds with the data, from which economists typically put the labor share between one-third and two-thirds.[13]

Going back to the standard Ramsey World, Figures 8.10 and 8.11 are graphed together in Figure 8.13. The intersection of *AS* and *AD* gives the relative price of output equal to $1/w = 7.2$, as shown by the dashed horizontal line. Conversely, the equilibrium wage rate is $w = 0.14 = 1/(7.2)$. The equilibrium aggregate output y can be read off the graph; it is 0.21. Here the equilibrium capital stock, upon which both *AS* and *AD* depend, is $k = 2.3$.

Figure 8.14 graphs, for the same standard Ramsey World that gives the above *AS - AD*, the implied equilibrium supply of labor and demand for labor. The labor supply l^s is an upward sloping function of the relative price of labor to goods, or $w/1$, which is equivalent to the real wage rate w. The firm's labor demand l^d is a downward sloping function of w. Both labor supply and demand depend (positively) on the equilibrium capital stock k. At their intersection, the equilibrium labor time is 0.5, and the wage is 0.14, consistent with the Figure 8.13 *AS - AD* graph.[14]

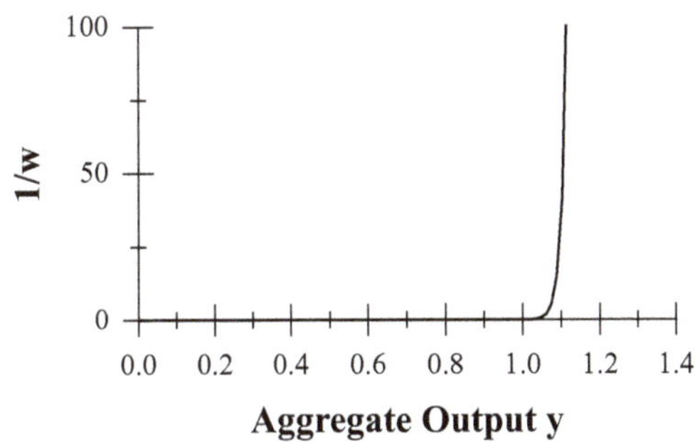

Figure 8.12 *AS* Curve: Near Zero Labor Share in Output

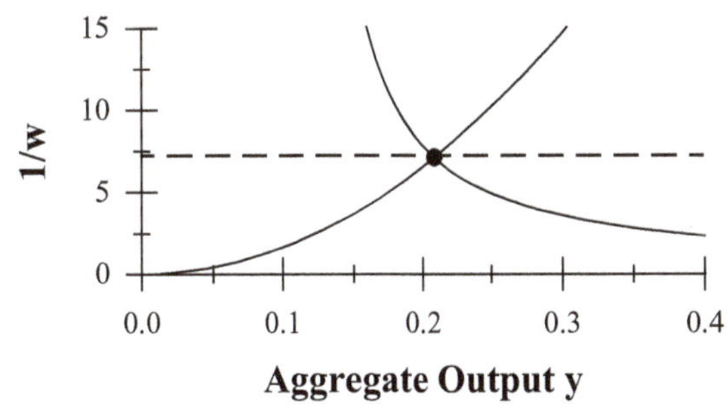

Figure 8.13 Ramsey *AS - AD* Equilibrium

---

[10]For the mathematically inclined advanced inquirer, the *AS* derived function is $y^s = A(k)^{1-\gamma}\left(\frac{\gamma A}{\omega}\right)^{\frac{\gamma}{1-\gamma}}(k)^{\gamma} = A^{\frac{1}{1-\gamma}}\left(\frac{\gamma}{\omega}\right)^{\frac{\gamma}{1-\gamma}}k$. Solving for the relative price $\frac{1}{w}$, it is equally written as $\frac{1}{w} = \frac{\left(y^s\right)^{\frac{1-\gamma}{\gamma}}}{\gamma A^{\frac{1}{\gamma}}(k)^{\frac{1-\gamma}{\gamma}}}$, which can be graphed.

[11]This occurs when the Cobb-Douglas production parameter γ approaches 1.

[12]This occurs when the Cobb-Douglas production parameter γ approaches 0; in the figure the labor cost share is $\gamma = 0.0\ 12$, or 1.2%.

[13]If the labor share, which notationally is γ is assumed to be $\gamma = 0.67$, as is usually assumed, then the AS curve is concave with a decreasing marginal cost as output rises. The example here instead assumes $\gamma = 0.33$ in Figure 8.10, giving a rising marginal cost as output rises; alternatively if $\gamma = 0.5$ the *AS* curve is linear. $\gamma = 0.33$ is in line with the Mankiw, Romer and Weil (1992) argument that the labor share is smaller than typically assumed because much of labor is in the form of human capital and this is accounted for as part of the share of capital costs in production.

[14]Mathematical inquirers can find that for the example given that labor supply is $l^s = T - \frac{\alpha}{1+\alpha}\left[T + \left(\frac{\rho}{w}\right)k\right]$, and labor demand is $l^d = \left(\frac{\gamma A}{w}\right)^{\frac{1}{1-\gamma}}k$. Solved in terms of the price w, labor supply is $w = \frac{\alpha\rho k}{T-(1+\alpha)l^s}$, and labor demand is $w = \gamma A\left(\frac{k}{l^d}\right)^{1-\gamma}$.

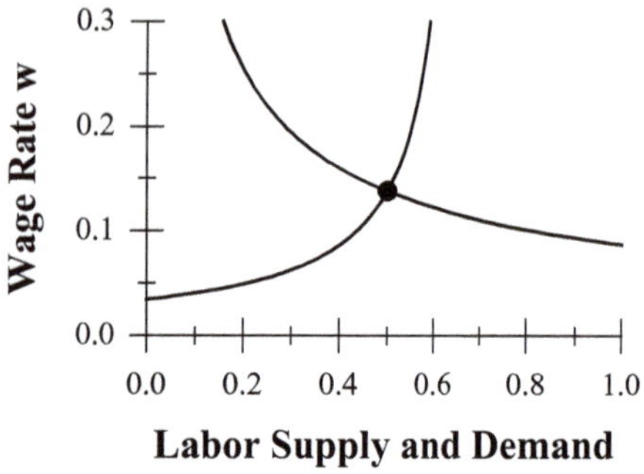

Figure 8.14 Labor Market in Example Ramsey Model

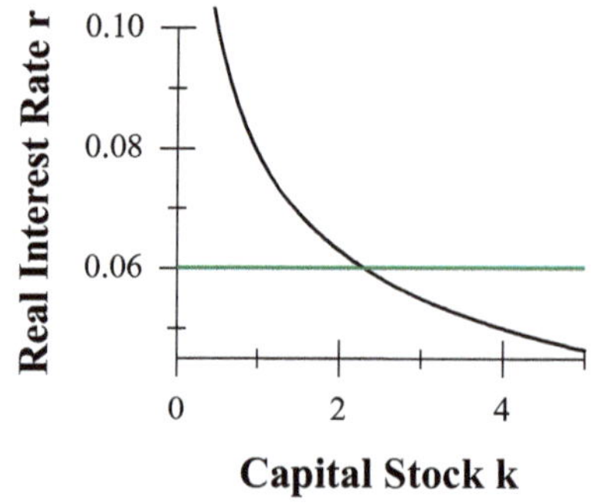

Figure 8.15 Capital Market with Downward Sloping Demand for Capital that equals the Marginal Product of Capital, Holding Labor Constant, Plus Fixed Interest Rate

Figure 8.15 graphs the corresponding Ramsey World capital market. The demand for capital is downward sloping and equal to the marginal product of capital, which is diminishing as the capital employed increases. The supply is horizontal at the interest rate r because in the Ramsey Model the growth rate is "exogenous" and set at zero; the real interest rate is 6% in the example, or $r = 0.06$.[15] The Ramsey model can be extended to make the growth rate and the real interest rate *endogenous* by adding human capital.[16]

Figure 8.16 graphs the same equilibrium, now using the production function (in Blue), with labor on the horizontal axis and goods consumption on the vertical axis; the indifference curve (in Red)is tangent to the production function at the equilibrium consumption level and labor quantity; $c = 0.14$ and $l = 0.5$. Added in Green is the consumer's budget line, which is also equal to the firm's profit line, and which has a slope equal to the equilibrium real wage w, or 0.14. Here the equilibrium consumption exactly equals the equilibrium wage rate (of 0.14). The production function and utility level *indifference curve* gives a overall perspective of both goods and labor markets simultaneously, which enrichens the analysis of looking at each market, one at a time.[17]

Another overview results by looking at the input market. Figure 8.17 graphs the equilibrium "*input markets*" through the "*isoquants and isocost lines*", as in microeconomics with labor on the horizontal axis and capital on the vertical axis. Similar in nature to an indifference curve, the Blue isoquant curve gives the constant equilibrium level of output y (of 2.3) which can be obtained by different combinations of labor and capital.

The Red negatively sloped line is the isocost line, similar in nature to the Green budget line in Figure 8.16; it shows that the real cost equals the real output level at the tangency point between the Blue isoquant and Red isocost line (zero profit results as in competitive equilibrium). The slope of the isoquant is negative. So consider the absolute value of the slope, so that it is a positive number, Then the slope exactly equals the equilibrium relative price of labor to capital, or w/r, which equals $0.14/0.06 = 2.3$ (this slope in turn equals the equilibrium capital stock k in this example).

---

[15]The real interest rate net of depreciation equals the rate of time preference as in Ramsey (1928). Alternatively, write that $r = \rho + \delta = 0.06$, in the example. Note: Figure 8.15 graphs the capital demand from the marginal product of capital such that $r = (1-\gamma)A\left(\frac{0.5}{k}\right)^{\gamma}$, where $l = 0.5$.

[16]See Gillman, 2011, Advanced Modern Macroeconomics, Pearson Financial Times Press, Chapters 12, 13, 14, 19 and 20.

[17]Mathematical inquirers: The production function as graphed is $c^d = 0.26248\left(l^d\right)^{\frac{1}{3}} - 0.069$, where the latter 0.69 is investment of capital depreciation; the utility level curve is $c = \frac{e^{-2.3206}}{(1-l)^{0.5}}$; and the budget line is $c^d = (0.13889)l^s + (0.03)(2.3148)$.

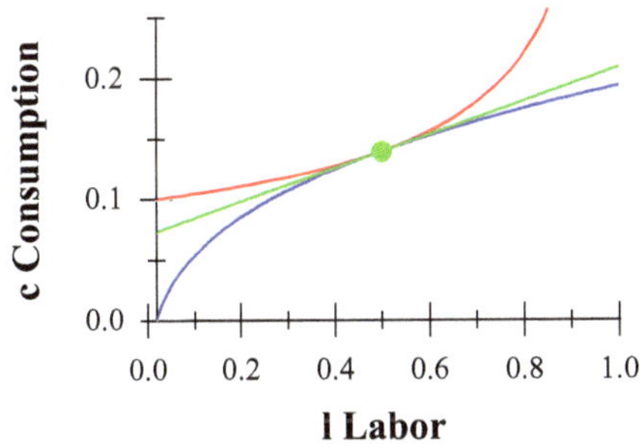

Figure 8.16 Production & Utility Levels in Ramsey World, with Budget Line (Green) Added

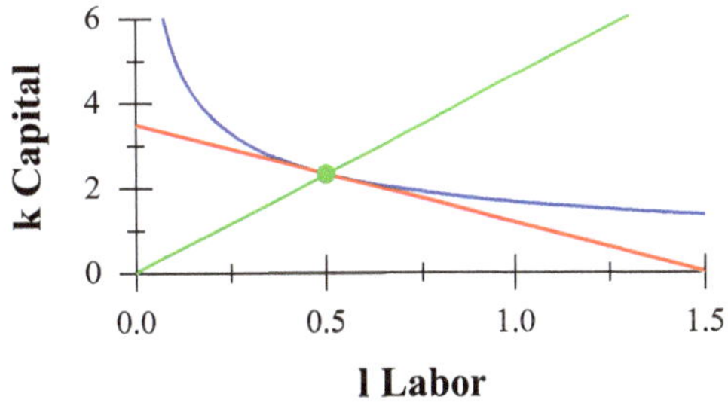

Figure 8.17 Factor Market Equilibrium in Ramsey World

Finally the analysis shows the equilibrium ratio of capital to labor, or k/l. This is called the *factor input ratio.* The equilibrium factor ratio equals the slope of the Green ray going out from the origin; here the slope of this Green ray is $2.3/0.5 = 4.6$.[18]

"Supply Side Economics": Productivity Increase

An increase in goods productivity through the increase in the productivity parameter A (where $y = Al^{1/3}k^{2/3}$) causes the relative price of aggregate output, $1/w$, to fall because the *AS* shifts out more than the *AD* curve. This is sometimes called "*supply-side economics*". It is used in describing real business cycle (*RBC*) theory. In *RBC* theory productivity rises in expansions and causes a net increase in aggregate supply. This net *AS* shift out results in an increase in equilibrium aggregate output y.

To illustrate this *comparative static* change, let there be a 5% increase in the production function productivity parameter (A). The marginal cost of producing goods falls as a result and the *AS* curve ends up shifting out by more than *AD*. The increase in productivity causes the marginal productivity of both labor and capital to increase, and so affects not only the goods market but also the labor and capital markets.

Figure 8.18 graphs the original *AS* – *AD* equilibrium in Red and the new shifted-out *AS* – *AD* equilibrium in Black after productivity A rises by 5%. Both *AS* and *AD* shift out; the *AS* curve shifts out by more; and so the relative price of goods $1/w$ falls in the new equilibrium as the real wage w rises. This means the real price of goods to leisure, or its marginal cost, falls, while output expands.[19]

Figure 8.19 shows that the firm's labor demand shifts out because of a higher marginal productivity of labor, while the consumer's labor supply shifts back because of a higher equilibrium capital stock that creates an "income effect" such that they do not want to work as much at the now higher wage rate. The net effect on the equilibrium quantity of labor is zero: the consumer ends up working the same amount of time, while the real wage is pushed upwards to a higher wage because of both demand shifting out and supply shifting back. Here the real wage rises 16%.[20]

Figure 8.20 graphs the shift out in the demand for capital from the original Red curve to the new Black curve, with the capital stock rising by 16% from $k = 2.3.$ to $k = 2.7$. The marginal product of capital rises which causes the demand for capital to shift out, while the interest rate remains fixed (at 6%, with zero economic growth). Maintenance cost on the higher capital also rises, so investment rises.

---

[18]The isoquant curve as graphed is $k = \frac{1.64}{\left(l^d\right)^{\frac{1}{2}}}$; the isocost line is $k = 3.47 - 2.3l$. And the factor input ratio is $k/l = \frac{2.315}{0.50} = 4.6$.

[19]Mathematical inquirers can find that the new *AS* – *AD* equations are $\frac{1}{w} = \frac{1}{y^d(1.5) - 2.6797(0.03 + (1.5)0.03)}$; and $\frac{1}{w} = \frac{\left(y^s\right)^2}{\left(\frac{1}{3}\right)(0.1575)^3(2.6797)^2}$.

[20]Mathematical inquirers can find that the new labor supply and labor demand equations after the productivity increase are

$w = \frac{(0.03)2.6797}{1-(1.5)l^s}$ and $w = \frac{1}{3}(0.1575)\left(\frac{2.6797}{l^d}\right)^{\frac{2}{3}}$.

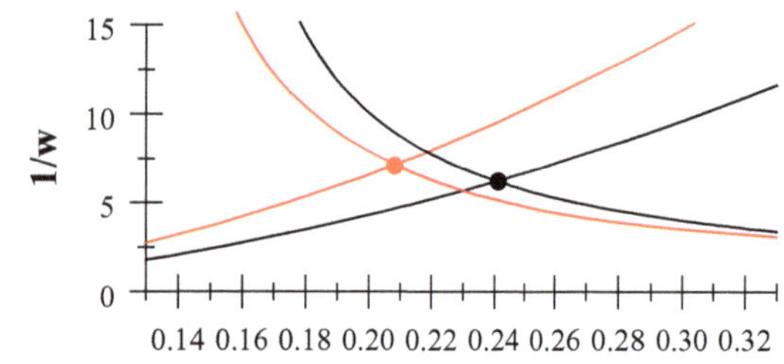

Figure 8.18 Productivity Increases 5%; new AS - AD Equilibrium (in Black)

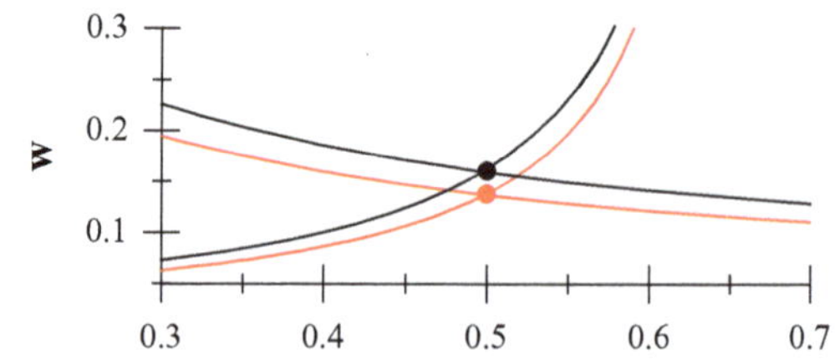

Figure 8.19 Productivity Increases 5% (in Black); Raises w, Employment Unchanged

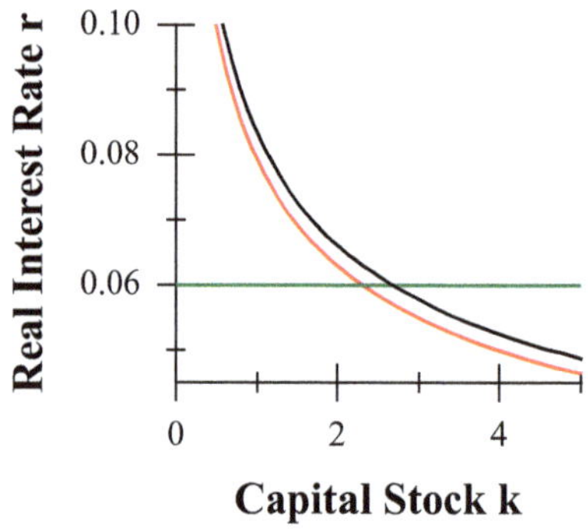

Figure 8.20 Productivity Increases 5%; Shifts Out of Demand for Capital (in Black)

The fall in relative price, which here is $1/w$, is not emphasized in supply-side economics descriptions as much as the increase in output that results. The rise in the real wage is an important part of this analysis. It implies why the relative price of goods to labor, $1/w$, must fall.

A productivity increase causes a rise in the real wage as a standard result in *RBC* theory, along with the rise in output, both reproduced here. There is a net *AS* shift out and a fall in the relative price of output. These latter two results are typically not discussed in *RBC* theory, but with the *AS* - *AD* analysis, they are exactly found to be the result (derived fully in Gillman, 2011).

8.4.4 RBC Analysis: Goods & Time Endowment Changes

Business cycles are explained in the first instance by shocking the productivity of the production function for goods output. The problem with using only the goods output productivity increase is that time spent working does not change, as in Figure 8.19. This is comparable to the employment rate not changing. In contrast we think of an employment rate that rises in an expansion and falls in a contraction. Or, in terms of the unemployment rate, which is highly correlated with the employment rate, we think of unemployment as falling in expansions and rising in contractions.

The inability of a productivity change alone to affect sufficiently the employment rate, which is procyclic in business cycle facts, is a well-known problem. However a solution to the problem is straightforward. It comes by adding one more comparative static change that is used in combination with the productivity change.

In particular, consider that when productivity increases, we get more output from our given amounts of inputs. This results in an increase in our *endowment of goods*, given out production function and input levels. Thinking of an increase in productivity as increasing our goods endowment directs logic towards the second important endowment in the economy that also can be changed: the time endowment devoted to work and leisure.

The time endowment is fixed at some amount here denoted by T. During the business cycle expansion, more time is taken from the education and household sector and devoted in work and leisure as the real wage rises. The wage increase during an expansion induces a higher "labor force participation rate", which provides more time for work and leisure. An increase in the time endowment T is thereby a change in what is called the "*external margin*" *of time use,* which the consumer uses to decide how much time is available for work and leisure. By exogenously increasing the time endowment T, the external margin for time usage is changed for the consumer. A more complex analysis can make this change in the external margin endogenous, through the decision of how much time to spend in education. But here, consider simply changing T to capture this movement in and out of the labor force.

The increase in the time endowment works initially by shifting out the consumer's supply of labor and demand for goods such that the employment rate goes up. This time increase also causes a higher capital stock that in turn causes a shift out in the firm's demand for labor, while at the same time inducing some shift back in the consumer's supply of labor. The net effect on labor supply is for it to shift out, giving an equilibrium higher rate of employment. In a contraction, a decrease in this time T is comparable to a reduction in the labor force participation rate as found in the data, and a net shift back in labor supply.

Combining an increase in the time endowment with the increase in goods productivity can explain the basic stylized facts of business cycles, for all but the real interest rate, which stays constant in the zero growth model. This is because the problem of employment not rising from only a goods productivity increased is solved by adding the time endowment increase, so that employment ends up rising.

Assume that both the productivity factor A and the time endowment T increase by five percent, or 5%. This then combines two changes in parameters into one comparative static analysis of the resulting change in equilibrium. Figure 8.21 shows the the supply and demand for aggregate output, or AS and AD curves, both shift out. The AS shifts out by more so that the relative price of output $1/w$ falls. This means that output rises, as does the real wage, both as in a business cycle. Here the capital stock has risen by 21%, as shown below in the capital market graph.[21]

Figure 8.22 shows that the firm's labor demand shifts out, both because of the increase in goods productivity and the increase in the capital stock. The consumer's labor supply pivots slightly, as the labor supply shift out caused by higher time T is offset by the labor supply shift back caused by a higher goods productivity. It leaves labor supply in roughly the same place, with the result that equilibrium employment rises as in business cycle stylized facts. The labor supply rises 5% from 0.5 to 0.525. The wage rate rises by 16%, from 0.014 to 0.16.[22]

The capital market sees capital investment rise, as in a RBC expansion, because the marginal product of capital increases for two reasons. Employment of labor increases and this provides more labor for each level

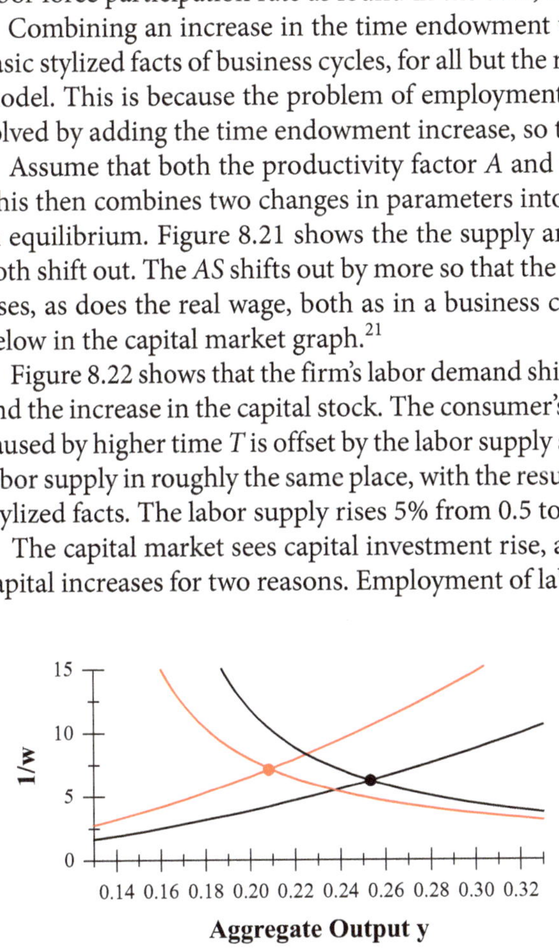

Figure 8.21 Business Cycle Expansion in Goods Market: AS – AD Equilibrium with 5% Increase (in Black) in Both Productivity A and Time T as Compared to the Original (in Red)

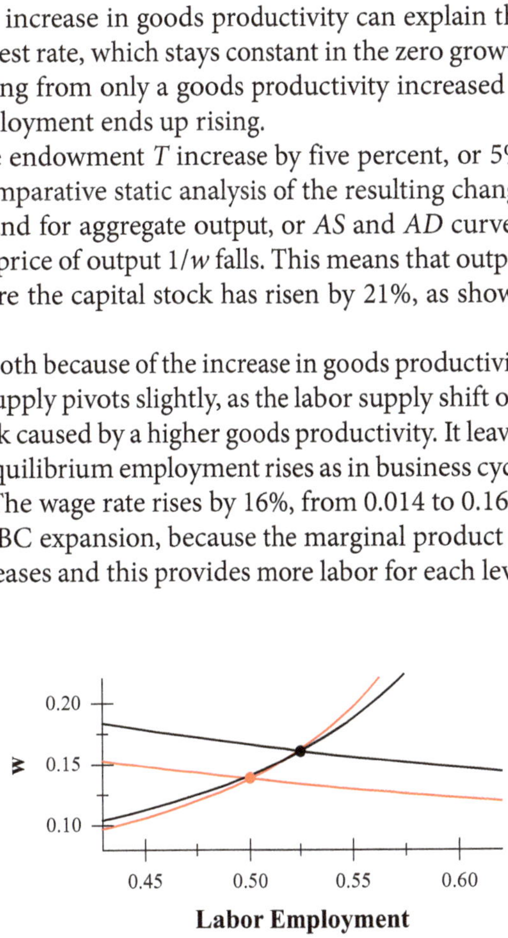

Figure 8.22 Business Cycle Expansion: Labor Market has a Shift out in Demand (Black) and Pivoting of Supply (Black) as Compared to Original (Red)

[21]Mathematical inquirers can find that the new AD curve is $\frac{1}{w}=\frac{1.05}{y(1.5)-2.81(0.03+(1.5)0.03)}$. The AS curve is $\frac{1}{w}=\frac{(y^s)^2}{\left(\frac{1}{3}\right)(0.1575)^3(2.81)^2}$.

[22]Mathematical inquirers can find that the new labor supply is $w=\frac{\alpha\rho k}{1.05-(1+\alpha)l^s}=\frac{0.5(0.052632)2.8137}{1.05-(1.5)l^s}$, and the labor demand is $w=\gamma A\left(\frac{k}{l^d}\right)^{1-\gamma}=\frac{1}{3}(0.1575)\left(\frac{2.8137}{l^d}\right)^{1-\frac{1}{3}}$.

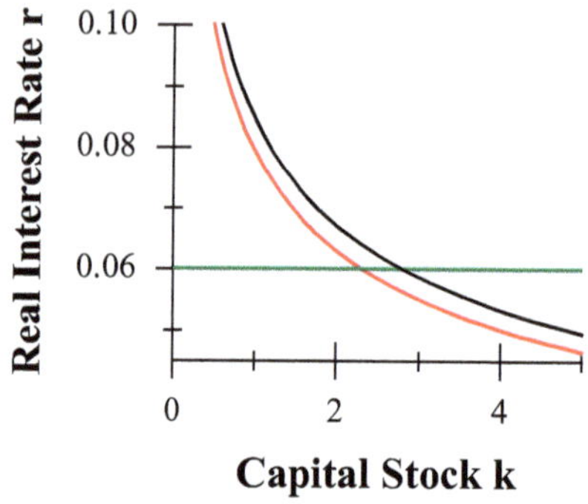

Figure 8.23 Capital Market Shows Shift Out of Demand for Capital (Black Curve) When both Factor Productivity *A* and Time Endowments *T* Increase by 5% relative to the Original Example Equilibrium (Red Curve)

of capital. This raises the marginal product of capital. In addition, the productivity of both labor and capital rise because the productivity factor *A* rises. A shift out in the demand for capital results since the demand for capital is the value of the marginal product of capital curve. The supply of capital remains unchanged as the horizontal supply curve at the equilibrium rate of interest implied by assumed zero growth rate economy.

Figure 8.23 shows that the capital demand shifts out (Black) relative to the Baseline (Red). The interest rate remains at 0.06; the capital stock rises from 2.3 to 2.8, a 21% increase. [23]

The goods, capital and labor markets all show facts consistent with a business cycle expansion: an increase in the real wage rate *w*, in the equilibrium capital stock *k*, in labor employment *l*, and in consumption *c* and output *y*. For a business cycle contraction, or recession, a decrease in both the goods and time endowments by 5% causes decreases in the same variables that increased in the expansion. Only the real interest rate and output growth rate do not rise and fall in an expansion as business cycle facts suggest.

A procyclic real interest rate and growth rate of output can be reproduced by endogenizing the rate of technological progress in terms of *human capital* accumulation. This is provided in the Appendix to Chapter 9 (See Gillman, 2011). It uses what is called "endogenous growth" theory.

8.5 Application: Crisis from Fixed Wage

An analytic description used by Keynes (1936) to explain severe business cycle downturns, such as a depression, is to assume that the real wage is fixed at is normal level during good times. When a recession hits, the real wage is assumed to be unable to adjust downwards, as in the Ramsey World. This gives rise to an excess supply of labor at the fixed wage rate, and results in less employment that with flexible wage rates that can adjust downwards in a recession. The fixed real wage makes possible "Unemployed Labor", or "surplus labor", during a Great Depression or Great Recession as Keynes (1936) suggested.

Alternatively, with normal flexible prices, a Depression can be explained in the Ramsey World through a crash in bank productivity. This is shown in the following Appendix, making use of a bank sector to intermediate consumer savings into firm investment.

For now, consider the short-cut assumption of a fixed wage. Figure 8.24 shows the original example equilibrium labor supply and demand curves, in Red. Suppose a contraction occurs as above through occurs

[23]Mathematical inquirers can find the capital demand curve is $r = \left(1-\frac{1}{3}\right)0.15\left(\frac{0.5}{k}\right)^{\frac{1}{3}}$ at the original example and $r = \left(1-\frac{1}{3}\right)0.1575\left(\frac{0.525}{k}\right)^{\frac{1}{3}}$ in the cyclic Expansion.

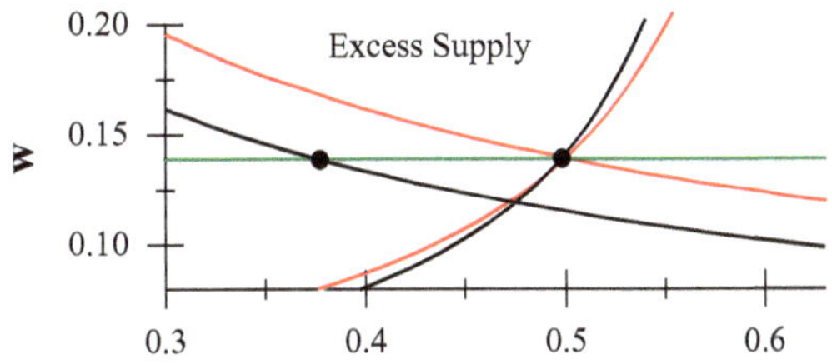

Figure 8.24 Excess Labor Supply with a Fixed Wage During Contraction (in Black) relative to the original example equilibrium (in Red)

through a 5% decrease in both the productivity parameter A and the time endowment T. Assume the wage rate remains fixed at its pre-recession level of 0.14. With the capital stock allowed to adjust and with a flexible real wage rate, the normal equilibrium would be given by the equilibrium in the labor market supply and demand as graphed in Black.

With the wage "stuck" at 0.14, an *excess supply of labor* at the equilibrium is given by the horizontal distance between the quantity demanded in the Black demand curve at $w = 0.14$, and the quantity supplied in the Black supply curve at $w = 0.14$. A greater quantity of labor is supplied, at that "*non-market clearing fixed wage*", than is demanded. The excess supply of labor equals 0.12. This 0.12 is about 24% of the total labor supplied (a bit less than 0.5) at the fixed wage of $w = 0.139$. This could be compared to a 24% unemployment rate, which did occur during the Great Depression.

Keynes (1936) has passages in which he describes how the wage rate may be unable to adjust downwards, where he calls this excess labor supply "involuntary" unemployment. Modern New-Keynesian models make this very assumption of either wage or price rigidity as a centerpiece of the model,[24] even though it is very difficult to "fix" a real wage rate. The idea of assuming different degrees of wage or price rigidity seems to be that labor or goods markets do not adjust as fully as the Ramsey competitive equilibrium suggests.

8.6 Appendix: Crisis from Banks

A Depression story using a fixed wage ignores the role of banking. Consider instead modeling the bank crisis by letting a bank sector supply the intermediary service of collecting the savings by the consumer and lending this to the firm for investment. Now let the productivity factor for this bank sector fall by 26%.[25]

For example, the FRED data as sourced from the Chicago Federal Reserve Bank shows a computation of the National Financial Condition Leverage Sub-Index. This is a measure of aggregate consumer and firm leverage, which may be a striking indicator of the productivity in financial intermediation of savings into investment. Figure 8.25 presents this FRED data for the US post-1973. The index falls dramatically at the start of the Great Recession and recovers slowly, staying below trend.

A 26% bank productivity decline within the bank-augmented Ramsey World simulates a Great Recession type crisis, in that the result is a 34% decline in the capital stock. A drop of 34% in the value of equity stock value occurred in the US from May 2, 2008 to January 9, 2009 when the U.S. Dow Jones Industrial (DJIA) stock average dropped from 13,058 to 8599. It occurred during the banking crisis of the Great Recession which included the insolvency of Lehman Brothers investment bank in September 15, 2008, when Lehmans filed for Chapter 11 bankruptcy.

---

[24]Most typical is "Calvo pricing" in which the firm can only occasional change prices.

[25]See Gillman, 2011, Advanced Modern Macroeconomics, Chapter 16.

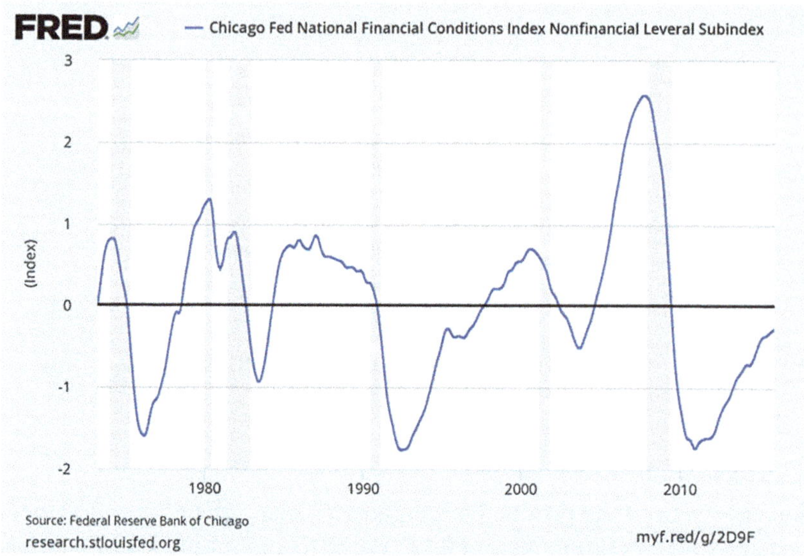

Figure 8.25 Chicago Fed National Financial Conditions Leverage Sub-Index

The Great Recession crash of stocks and its run on investment banks is modeled in the Ramsey World by changing one, single, parameter: the productivity of the bank production function in providing savings to investment intermediation. In particular, a 26% decline in bank productivity results in a loss of the economy's capital stock by 34%.

Figure 8.26 shows the initial *AS* – *AD* equilibrium in Red and the new equilibrium in Black after a 26% decrease in *productivity of the bank intermediation sector*. The *AS* – *AD* curves shift back from the Red curves to the Black curves. This happens exactly because the effect of this bank productivity decline is to decrease the capital stock by 34%, which in turn then shifts back both aggregate supply and demand for output. Output falls and the relative price of goods to labor $\frac{1}{w}$ rises.[26]

Figure 8.27 shows that the equilibrium supply and demand for labor change from the Red curves to the Black curves such that employment and the real wage fall. Employment falls from 0.44 to 0.40, a 9% decrease in the employment rate. The labor market shows how the bank productivity decrease causes significantly lower employment. [27]

Figure 8.28 graphs the isoquant, isocost and factor input ratios in blue, red and green respectively, with the darker colors representing the example economy bank crisis. The bank crisis causes the isocost line to pivot down, as the wage rate to real interest rate ratio falls, and the isoquant to shift down, while the capital to labor ratio also pivots down and the employment level falls.

Figure 8.29 graphs the production function, utility level and budget line in blue, red and green respectively, with the darker colors representing the bank crisis. It shows that the bank crisis causes the production function to pivot down, and the levels of utility, consumption, and employment all to fall.

The banking crisis model of reduced bank productivity therefore extends the Ramsey World to provide a way to endogenously generate a crisis type drop in employment without the need to impose fixed prices of labor or capital. The banking extension allows the bank sector to be modeled directly, with a plausible result that the cost of investment rises, employment, output, and capital all fall significantly.

---

[26]Mathematical inquirers can note that here $y_t = \frac{1}{1+\alpha}(w_t + \rho k_t) + \delta_k k_t$, which in the example is $y_t = \frac{1}{1.5}(0.00893 + (0.0526)0.0552) + (0.05)(0.0552)$.

[27]Mathematical inquirers can find the Red curves graphed as $w_t = 0.333(0.1)\left(\frac{0.0552}{l_t^d}\right)^{1-0.333}$, and $w_t = \frac{(0.5)(0.0526)(0.0552)}{(1.5)\left(1 - l_t^s - \frac{(0.0552)}{(0.7)^{\frac{1}{0.333}}}\right) - 0.5}$.

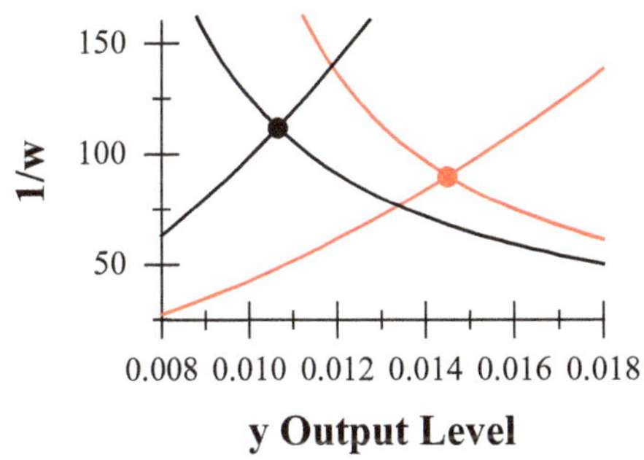

Figure 8.26 *AS* - *AD* Shift after Bank Crisis Fall in Bank Productivity

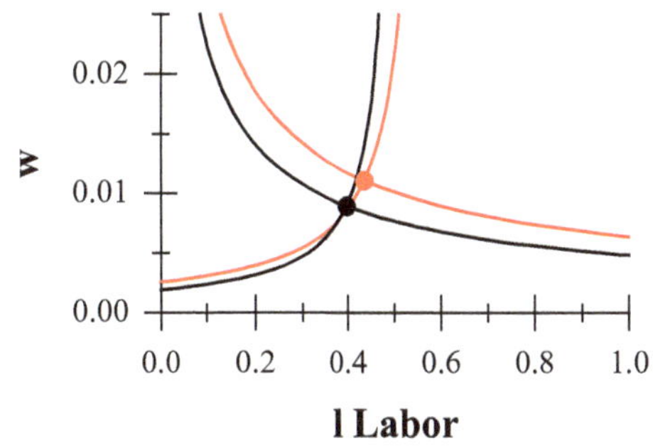

Figure 8.27 Lower Employment & Wage Rate during Bank Crisis

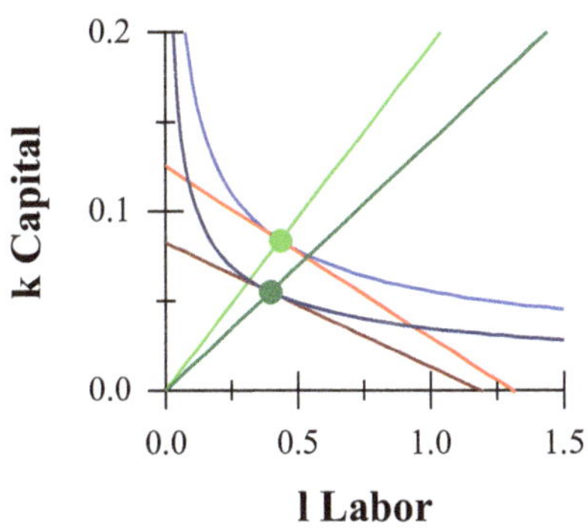

Figure 8.28 Factor Market During Bank Crisis (Darker Colors)

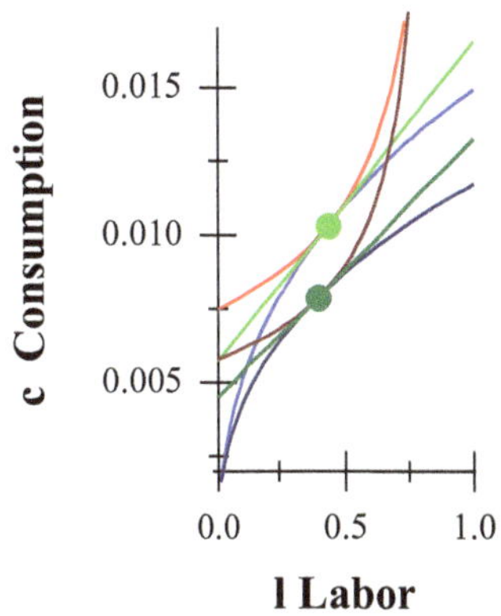

Figure 8.29 Consumption & Utility Falls during Bank Crisis

However the analysis does not fully capture the Great Recession or the post-2000 US period well because the bank productivity decline implies that the real wage falls, while in the 2008 to 2010 the real wage rose. This can be easily addressed by adding in the experience of the large drop in the labor force participation rate that accompanied the post–2000 and 2008–2010 periods. Analytically, by decreasing the time endowment for work and leisure, *T*, the real wage is pushed up. With a large enough decrease in the time endowment, this pressure upwards on the wage would offset the decline due to a lower capital stock as a result of both the bank crisis and the decrease in *T*, causing the real wage to rise. The employment fall would be greater with such a decrease in *T*.

8.7 Summary

The chapter presents facts and theory about real business cycles and crises. After discussing how microeconomic theory uses relative prices, it sets out a relative price for goods relative to labor. This is shown to be typically countercyclic in FRED data, and is equivalent to the inverse of the real wage. The typical procyclic nature of the real wage growth is shown relative to real GDP growth for US data up until 2000, after which the relation becomes inverted. However, the labor force participation rate remains procyclic after 2000 and as a result reflects aspects that support a procyclic real wage overall.

In the post 2000 two asset value crashes, it appears that the decline in real capital value coincides closely with the decreased inflation rate. This supports the Debt-Deflation crisis theory of Fisher and Hayek. Some equity premium evidence is suggested in terms of the appearance of a possibly "too-big" of an increase in this premium during the post 2000 period.

Thus there is evidence of both normal business cycles and more extreme bank-related crises that can be used in comparison to the Ramsey World theory. The business cycle theory is presented with the aggregate output supply and demand of the Ramsey model, using the $AS - AD$ notation. The Ramsey World AS and AD are dependent upon the relative price of goods to labor and upon the equilibrium level of the capital stock k. Using supply and demand, the Ramsey World with capital accumulation sets out the market for output, labor and capital.

First a comparative static increase in productivity is conducted. The AS and AD both shift out with AS shifting out by more and the relative price of goods to labor falling. This is consistent with a fall in the relative price of goods as input productivity rises. Here the productivity increase is viewed as increasing the endowment of goods. In the labor market, the wage rate rises but employment is unchanged because of offsetting shifts in the supply and demand for labor.

To more fully explain business cycle facts, a time endowment increase is added to the goods productivity increase, with each rising by 5% simultaneously. An economic expansion is shown through the equal increase in both the productivity parameter and the endowment of time for work and leisure. Employment time increases, the real wage rises, output rises and investment rises, while the relative price of goods to labor falls. An economic contraction is described similarly with an equi-proportional decrease in both the goods and time endowment.

An application to a depression is shown by assuming the same conditions for a contraction, of an equal proportional decrease in the goods and time endowments, while also holding the real wage rate fixed. This causes an excess supply of labor. Output falls by more and the employment rate is substantially lower, similar to depression-like conditions. Alternatively, the Appendix shows how a large decline in bank productivity, such as during a bank crisis, causes Great Recession type declines in employment and asset values. This uses the Ramsey World as extended to include bank intermediation of consumer savings into firm investment.

8.8 Glossary

AS - AD: aggregate supply of output (AS) and aggregate demand for output (AD): the Ramsey World derivation of output supply and demand based on optimization, with a relative price of $1/w$ and given the equilibrium capital stock of k.

budget constraints on goods allocation and on time allocation: conditions under which the firm and consumer maximize their profit and utility respectively; goods allocation is output given technology and input levels; time allocation is total time available for work and leisure.

change in the capital stock: the capital stock changes with any change in the given parameters of the model from one equilibrium level to a new equilibrium level.

comparative static experiment: a change in a given parameter and the study of how this change causes the economy to go from one equilibrium to another.

countercyclic movement in wages: real wages moving in the opposite direction of the change in GDP growth, such as if real wages rise during a recession.

debt-deflation theories of Fisher and Hayek: how a bank crisis can lead to depression and a plummeting inflation rate.

decrease in the goods and time endowment: a decrease in the productivity parameter for goods production or in the time available for work and leisure.

depreciation of capital: the amount of capital used up during the period.

endogenous: explained within the model economy.

endowment of goods: amount of output from a given technology of production and level of inputs.

endowment of time: amount of time available for work and leisure.

equilibrium capital stock: amount of capital such that the quantity demanded equals the quantity supplied at a particular price of capital as given by the real interest rate.

equilibrium conditions that are derived from the optimization problem: marginal cost equal marginal benefit is a general characterization of all optimally derived equilibrium conditions; from these supply and demand are in turn established.

excess supply of labor: a higher quantity of labor that is supplied than is demanded at the particular price of labor, the real wage.
exogenous: determined by assumption outside of the model economy.
external margin of time use: where the consumer decides how much time to set aside for work and leisure; contrasts with internal margin of how much to work and how much to take in leisure; to enter or exit the labor force.
factor input ratio: quantity of capital divided by quantity of labor.
inflationary increase in the price of the aggregate basket of goods: an increase due to monetary factors rather than to real factors.
involuntary unemployment: excess supply of labor.
human capital: accumulation of skills and education over time that raises lifetime wage stream, treated in output production similar to physical capital.
indifference curve: a constant level of utility produced by different combinations of goods and leisure.
input markets: the markets for capital and labor.
isoquants and isocost lines: like indifference curve, isoquant shows the constant level of output with different levels of inputs; like budget line, isocost shows constant level of production costs with fixed input prices and different levels of inputs.
Labor force participation growth rate: the rate of change in the total population that is actively seeking work in the labor force.
markets clear: when the quantity supplied equals the quantity demanded at the equilibrium price.
maximizes utility: the representative consumer does this when making choices subject to the budget constraint.
nominal price of capital relative to the nominal price of goods: the real price of capital as found by taking a nominal price of a capital data series and dividing by the CPI index.
nominal wage growth rate minus the inflation rate: real wage growth rate.
non-market clearing fixed wage: a wage rate that does not clear the market so that there is excess supply or excess demand for labor at that fixed wage.
optimization: maximizing utility subject to income by the consumer or maximizing profit subject to production technology for the firm.
portfolio balance between risky equity and risk-free debt: investors choose the riskiness of their overall market investment according to their desire to take on risky investment.
procyclic real wage growth: when real wages rise in business cycle expansions and fall in contractions.
productivity of the bank intermediation sector: the amount of output produced given the bank production technology and quantity of inputs.
productivity parameter: the flow of output from the level of the inputs as combined by the production technology.
quantity demanded equals the quantity supplied at the equilibrium price in each market: implies all markets clear.
Ramsey's World: the model economy that Frank Ramsey created in 1928; has zero growth of output in equilibrium.
Ramsey vertical AS curve: this is possible only as the share of labor in output costs goes to zero, which contradicts evidence in the long run and short run.
real asset price series: found for example by dividing a market asset price series by the CPI index.
real price of capital relative to goods: same as a *real asset price series.*
real price of goods: found relative to another series such as wages.
real price of goods relative to time: the nominal price of goods such as the CPI index divided by the market (nominal) wage rate.
relative price: price of any good in terms of another; units always used in microeconomics.
Russell 1000, 2000, and 3000: different examples of average prices of capital for collections of companies.
shadow price of leisure: the real wage rate
shift the aggregate demand and aggregate supply curves: the whole demand or supply schedule pivots or moves in a graph due to a change in a given exogenous parameter of the model.
stationary over time: a variable that is relatively constant over the long run.
steady technological progress: a continuous or constant rate of growth of the production productivity parameter.
stylized facts from the theory of business cycles: facts of business cycles that are accepted to some wide degree of consensus.
supply-side economics: a focus on the supply curve of aggregate output shifting out, such as from productivity increases.
time allocation for work and leisure: total time set aside for these two purposes.
zero growth rate: the output growth rate is zero.

8.9 Questions

1. Describe a statistical definition of the relative price of goods to labor.
2. Characterize the variation over the business cycle and trend over time in the empirical measure of the real price of goods relative to labor.
3. Describe how the real wage rate changes relative to the changes in real output growth.
4. Identify a measure of the value of equity capital and describe how this has changed over time.
5. Describe a sense in which the value of equity correlates with the inflation rate in recent US history, and how this relates to the debt-deflation explanation of crises.
6. How has the labor force participation rate changed over time both cyclically and in terms of its long run trend?
7. What is the relative price of goods to labor in the aggregate demand and aggregate supply analysis, or $AS - AD$, of Ramsey's World?
8. How does the equilibrium capital stock affect the aggregate demand and aggregate supply analysis of Ramsey's World?
9. What is the real price of labor relative to goods in the labor market's supply and demand for time spent working in Ramsey's World (it is the inverse of the real price of goods relative to labor)?
10. Explain a business cycle expansion in Ramsey's World using graphs and a description of the graphs. What variables change in ways that are consistent with the evidence presented in the Chapter?
11. How do aggregate supply and demand shift during a contraction, or recession, in Ramsey's World?
12. How does the labor market change when there is a recession in Ramsey's World?
13. Describe how an excess supply of labor can exist and can potentially be consistent with certain aspects of a depression.
14. Explain how a banking crisis can be modeled in the Ramsey World using goods and labor markets.
15. Complete the Federal Reserve Bank of St. Louis EconLowdown Course Module "The Great Depression 5".

9 Growth, Progress & AS-AD

9.1 Introduction

In the Ramsey (1928) World, economic growth is assumed to be zero, in the sense that real GDP, consumption and investment are all *"stationary" in the equilibrium.* This zero growth of the economy was consistent with Classical Economic assumptions. But zero growth did not seem to be consistent with the steady growth in output seen during the Industrial Revolution that started in the 1700's in the United Kingdom.

During the 1700's, "Classical" economists such as David Ricardo, John Stuart Mill, and Karl Marx all tended to describe the economy as having a zero growth rate on average per person in the economy. A zero growth World was prominently discussed in particular by the British economist Thomas Malthus in his (1798) book, *An Essay on the Principle of Population.* There he puts forth that evidence implies that as output grows, population will grow so as to keep per-capita, or per-person, output constant. This means the growth rate of real GDP per-capita growth stays at zero. This became the Classical economic view of certain historical evidence: zero growth. Therefore Ramsey's (1928) embodiment of a zero growth World was in line with this typical reading of the trend growth rate experience.

The *industrial revolution* that started in Great Britain is dated typically as beginning in the 1750's, although this is just a commonly used date and some put the beginning in the 1600's. From the beginning of the industrial revolution to today, economists have identified a rising growth rate trend. By the time of the mid-twentieth century a positive growth rate in real GDP had been identified as having existed throughout most of the time since the industrial revolution.

The assumption that the growth trend was positive in modern times rather than zero as in the Classical Economics period brought about a rethinking of how to explain the facts of the economy. With growth in real GDP taking place, growth in real consumption and real investment had to keep pace with the growth in real GDP. Otherwise either the share of consumption in GDP would rise steadily or fall steadily, as would the share of investment in GDP tend towards a limit of zero or one.

The idea of all variables other than time allocations growing at a steady rate, gave rise to the idea of a "*balanced growth economy.*" A stable share of consumption and of investment in GDP therefore continues to be part of the stylized facts of the growth experience. Explaining a stable growth rate in the economy became a challenge that was met successfully in the mid-twentieth century.

9.2 Who Made it Happen

Robert Solow won the Nobel Prize in Economics in 1987 for summarizing the key stylized growth facts that we want our standard production theory to be able to explain. His 1956 article outlined an approach in theory to explaining these facts.[1]

The facts are thereby known as the *stylized Solow growth facts.* Solow emphasized how a steady productivity increase could explain several growth facts. Solow's assumption of a steady productivity increase was later embodied in the *Ramsey-Cass-Koopmans economy* so that the full utility maximization framework could explain Solow's facts in the standard micro-founded approach.

[1]Solow, Robert M., "Contribution to the Theory of Economic Growth." The Quarterly Journal of Economics, Vol. 70, No. 1. (Feb., 1956), pp. 65–94.

Arnold Harberger (1998), when head of the American Economic Association, emphasized in his Presidential Address how Solow's stylized growth facts could be extended. He argued that as productivity rises the real cost of goods falls over time due to this technological progress that allows for less labor time to produce output. The fall in average and marginal cost was said to occur naturally as output went up.[2] A falling marginal cost curve was described as the same as an aggregate supply curve shifting out, steadily over time. This falling price became a result that could indeed be graphically illustrated using Ramsey's AS-AD economy when using the proper relative price of goods to labor, as shown below.

Uzawa (1965) and Lucas (1988) made the growth process dependent on investment in human capital. This explained the assumed technological change of Solow as an outcome of human capital growing over time. This meant that it was no longer necessary to assume that productivity increases, because the productivity increase became a choice of the representative consumer as part of the decision of how much human capital to accumulate. The Lucas growth theory became known as *"endogenous growth theory"*, since the growth process relied on the decision to invest in human capital.

9.3 Facts

9.3.1 Stylized Growth Rate Facts

The first stylized growth fact is that real output grows at some steady rate. Second, all variables that grow over time appear to grow at the same average rate as real GDP output. In particular, output y, consumption c, investment i, as well as the capital stock k and the wage rate, all appear to grow at the same rate. This positive, common, growth rate of these economic variables is considered to be the *trend growth rate* of the economy. Note that this does not explain a rising real growth rate as during the industrial revolution, a topic of much current research.

The trend growth rate of the economy is specific to whatever period of time and whatever country is being examined. For example a post-1950's US real GDP growth rate as high as 3.5% can be identified. Typically we use the 2% trend growth rate for describing the US economy. This is based on a more historical average such as post-WW2 or some use the last 100 years for the time period. We will use a 2% trend growth rate for the US as our main description of the US trend growth rate.

A positive growth rate is typical for developed economies. Near zero growth can still be seen in countries which have not started along a steady growth path. African countries are often pointed out as having had no growth. Other economies that are developing very rapidly, such as China and India, apparently have much higher growth rates than the 2% seen in developed economies.

Figure 9.1 shows the real GDP growth rate for the US (blue), European currency (Euro) area (green), Japan (purple), Switzerland (green-blue), and the United Kingdom (orange). These are all now considered to be developed countries. The US and UK generally have the most reliable, and accessible, data going back the longest in time. The FRED-sourced graph shows a moderate average rate near the 2% mark. Note that the green Euro-zone recent growth average appears higher than 2% because Germany has had high growth that dominated this post-1995 Euro-zone data.

9.3.2 Solow's Stylized Growth Facts

Solow starts with a constant growth rate, such as 2%. This constancy of the growth rate is not true in fact. But it is true that on average for any historical period of any country there does exist an average growth. The 2% rate is taken as a reasonable representation of modern developed economies.

[2]Harberger, Arnold C, 1998. "A Vision of the Growth Process," American Economic Review, American Economic Association, vol. 88(1), pages 1–32, March. Harberger writes "that it would be perfectly fair to represent my presentation today as a paean in praise of 'real cost reduction' as a standard label" for the measured technological productivity change that contributes to sustained output growth. Harberger uses the term "real cost reduction" sixty-nine times in his article, by my count, including diagrams but not appendices.

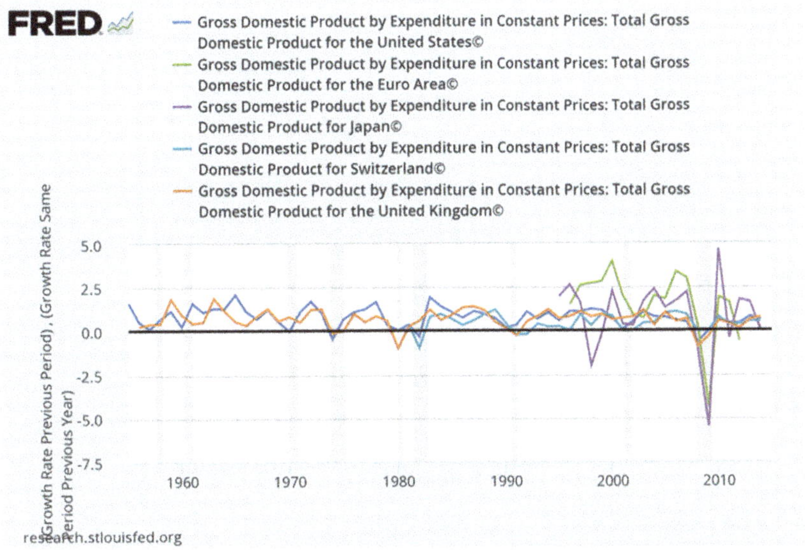

Figure 9.1 Real GDP Growth Rate, annual basis, for Four Industrial Nations Plus the Euro-zone Countries

The persistent growth means that there should be growth in real aggregate output over time. Then the other growth facts follow from Solow's theory. First, the real wage should grow over time. Second, the real interest rate, however measured, is stable over time. Third, going with a rising real wage is that the per capita income rises. Fourth, going with a stable real interest rate, the output to capital ratio is constant over time.

With the constant output growth rate, these facts are:

1. The real wage w rises steadily over time with an average growth rate equal to the constant output growth rate.
2. The real interest rate r remains constant on average over time.
3. The per capita income, which is defined as output divided by the total labor supply, rises at the same constant average growth rate.
4. The *output to capital stock ratio* remains constant on average over time.

9.3.3 Solow Plus Growth Facts

We herein add four additional facts to the stylized Solow growth facts. We call these the "Solow Plus" growth facts. Consider that the cost of goods and new capital is the same in the Ramsey-Solow World, which we normalize to one. Harberger describes that real cost reduction lowers the percent of real GDP that is used in production. A way to capture this is by comparing the Ramsey-Solow cost of goods (and capital) relative to labor. This ends up being a consistent way to show all of the other Solow Growth Facts at the same time.

Steady technological progress makes the real price of goods relative to labor lower over time (Harberger, 1998). The CPI index, the nominal price of goods, divided by the nominal wage rate, gives the real relative price of goods to labor and this means that this should fall over time. As this relative price is the inverse of the real wage, the rise of the real wage over time is equivalent to the fall of the real price of goods relative to labor over time.

Therefore the first *Solow Plus growth fact* is that

1. The relative price of output to labor falls over time. This is our real price of output relative to labor, $1/w$, so we would expect this to fall over time. Indeed this fact is satisfied if the Solow Growth Facts are met, as they include that the wage rate w rises over time. The other Plus facts are:

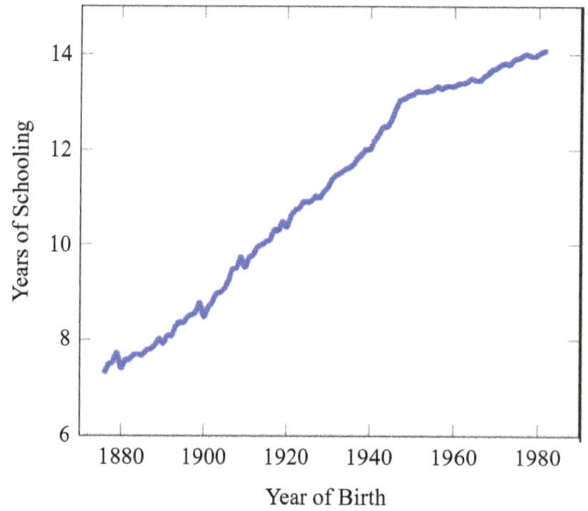

Figure 9.2 US Years of Education by Birth Cohort

2. Empirical stylized facts are well-known to include that the average hours worked per week has very gradually decreased over a time period such as the beginning of the industrial revolution to today. View this in the Ramsey-Solow World as the time spent working each period very gradually falling and trending downward. This is the second Solow Plus growth fact to be explained.
3. Empirical stylized facts also strongly support that time spent in education has steadily rises over time, since the industrial revolution began. The average degree earned and years of schooling continue to steadily, very gradually, rise over time. Consider this rise in education time relative to total time as the third Solow Plus growth fact to be explained.
4. Certain evidence has been presented arguing that share of time spent for leisure has also been falling over time. For an anecdotal example, the US economy arguably has one of the highest *human capital level per capita*. Similarly it is a standard in the US to allow two weeks of vacation time per year, one of the lowest vacation periods seen internationally. It is significantly less than the vacation time allowed in developed economies of Europe such as the UK, France or Germany in which four tends to be the minimum. A trend down in leisure time will be taken to be the fourth and final Solow Plus growth fact to be explained, and its explanation relates to number 3 above.

Consider Fact number 3 above. The years of education in the US has been documented as steadily increasing over time. Figure 9.2 shows the trend increase upwards for more than a century from 1876 to 1982.[3]

9.4 Theory

9.4.1 Zero Growth to Positive, Constant, Growth

The Solow theory of sustained growth assumes that there is *exogenous technological progress*. This is stated in terms of a productivity parameter of the output production function that increases at a constant rate over time. This causes variables to grow at a constant growth rate.

Given the "exogeneity" of the productivity parameter increase, this assumption gives a theory explaining the growth facts, but not one explaining how the productivity trends up. This productivity rise is defined as

[3]"Balanced Growth Despite Uzawa", 2016, Gene M. Grossman, Elhanan Helpman, Ezra Oberfield, Thomas Sampson, Working Paper 21861, page 3, January. Original data therein cited as: "Source: Goldin and Katz (2007) and additional data from Lawrence Katz." See: http://www.nber.org/papers/w21861

technological progress since it changes the technology of production so as to require fewer quantities of the inputs in order to produce the same amount of output. It may be true that this progress is due to research and development or to human capital or to "knowledge", but the theory is silent on what causes technological progress.

Because the technological progress is assumed, the theory is known as an *exogenous growth theory*. It is in fact a simple extension to go from the Ramsey World of Chapter 8 to a Ramsey-Solow World here. The difference is that the constant productivity parameter A of the Ramsey World now instead is assumed to rise at a constant rate in the Ramsey-Solow World.

The equilibrium output growth rate in the Ramsey-Solow World (also called the Ramsey-Cass-Koopmans model) is a simple function of the assumed rate of growth of the productivity factor. Real output grows at a certain well-defined rate. This growth theory is known as Solow Growth theory. It accounts for the four basic stylized Solow growth facts.

9.4.2 Facts along a Balanced Growth Path Equilibrium

Consider first that economic growth typically is meant to be equivalent to real output growth. Second, all variables that can grow, will grow at the same rate as output growth, along the balanced growth path of the Ramsey-Solow World. This growth equilibrium is called a *"balanced growth path" equilibrium*. It means real output, consumption goods, and capital all grow at the same rate.

To explain business cycles in Chapter 8, changes in two parameters, output productivity and the time endowment, were used. These change the two main resources of the macroeconomy: goods and time endowments. Think of the representative agent acting as firm and experiencing the output productivity change and acting as the consumer and experiencing the time endowment changes.

Apply these same two *"comparative static"* changes in order to explain the process of continuous economic growth over time, along the balanced growth path equilibrium. First, the productivity increase alone is used to explain the first four Solow growth facts. The time endowment change is added to the productivity increase in order to explain the additional four Solow Plus growth facts, while at the same time keeping intact the original four Solow growth facts.

9.4.3 Growth Puzzle that Solow Solved

The idea that all variables that can grow continuously over time will in fact grow at the same rate raises the question of how output can grow if labor cannot. Labor is a time allocation that is constrained by a stationary, or constant, time endowment that is unchanging over time. If the labor share of time were to continually grow, there would be no leisure time. The consumer would not choose to allow this, so the time allocation shares are instead stationary, unchanging along the balanced growth path.

If capital alone grows, while labor is constant, then the marginal product of capital would get increasingly small. This follows from the diminishing product of capital property that characterizes the production process. Adding more capital causes smaller and smaller increases in output. And the real interest rate equals the marginal product of capital and in turn would have to go towards zero as more capital was used, with constant labor.

A diminishing marginal product does not allow for a constant marginal product of capital if capital keeps growing. Or, if capital grows faster than output, this is also inconsistent with a balanced growth equilibrium along which all variables grow at the same rate. It is also inconsistent with Solow Growth fact number four of a constant output to capital ratio over time, which seems to hold empirically.

A constant labor employment rate, as combined with the concept of a rate of growth of capital equal to the rate of growth of output, creates a puzzling problem for the economy to have sustained, and balanced, growth. Robert Solow solved this basic problem. He shows that if labor is somehow "augmented", then both "augmented-labor" and capital inputs can grow at the same rate, with the result that output will also grow at this common rate. So the question became: how to augment labor when labor time is fixed?

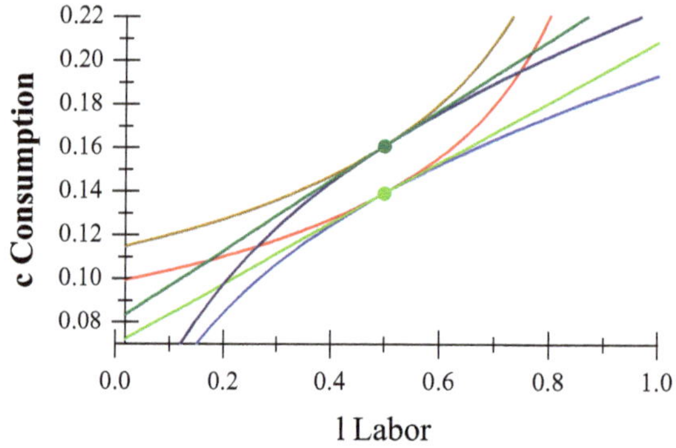

Figure 9.3 General Equilibrium Production, Utility Levels and Budget Lines with Goods Productivity Increase (Darker Curves) Compared to Baseline (Lighter Curves)

Solow's answer is simple in retrospect: allow for *technological progress* that in effect "augments", or supplements, the labor input, so that both the augmented labor and the capital grow at the same rate as output. Then the balanced growth path equilibrium is achieved, along with the four Solow stylized growth facts.

The output productivity factor used to explain business cycles is now applied to the theory of economic growth. Solow said that productivity, which can be represented by a parameter A (in the output production function $y = Al^{1/3}k^{2/3}$), rises at a certain rate every period so that A now rises over time and is so denoted with a time subscript, by A_t. With a rising productivity factor, labor is in effect augmented by the productivity. The augmented labor rises at the same constant growth rate as output and capital. Any constant increase over time in A causes augmented-labor, capital, output, investment and consumption goods to all grow at the same rate. Choosing the growth rate in A_t then results in hitting a particular economic growth rate such as 2%.

This is a simple but powerful theory. As a slight extension of the Ramsey model in Chapter 8, the Ramsey-Solow World also is presented with supply and demand analysis. First just the four Solow facts are explained. Then, the additional Solow Plus growth facts are explained by taking a cue from the business cycle analysis. There adding a time endowment change resolved the business cycle problem of there being no change in employment from just changing productivity. Here adding the continuous change in the *time endowment* allows explanation of the Solow Plus facts.

9.4.4. A Comparative Static Productivity Increase

The *comparative static* change behind Solow's Growth theory is an increase in productivity. For a one-time increase in productivity, this was described and illustrated in Chapter 8, in goods, labor and capital markets, using Figures 8.21-8.23. Consider in addition how the one-time productivity change affects the production function, indifference curves, and the factor market diagram.

Figure 9.3 graphs the production function along with the equilibrium utility function both for the original equilibrium, in lighter colors, and after the 5% increase in productivity, in darker colors. The productivity increase pivots up the production function from the origin, equilibrium utility level indifference curve shifts up, and the budget line pivots up as its slope rises. Its slope is the relative factor input price rate of the real wage rate divided by the real interest rate, or w/r; here w rises, and r stays the same, as in the Ramsey World. As the real wage rises, so does consumption and output, while labor employment is unchanged at 0.5.[4]

---

[4]Mathematical inquirers can graph the production function at its new position as $c_t^d = 0.30386\left(l_t^d\right)^{\frac{1}{3}} - 0.0803913$ the utility level curve shifts to $c_t = \dfrac{e^{-2.1743}}{\left(1 - l_t\right)^{0.5}}$ and new budget line is $c_t^d = (0.16078)l_t^s + (0.03)(2.6797)$.

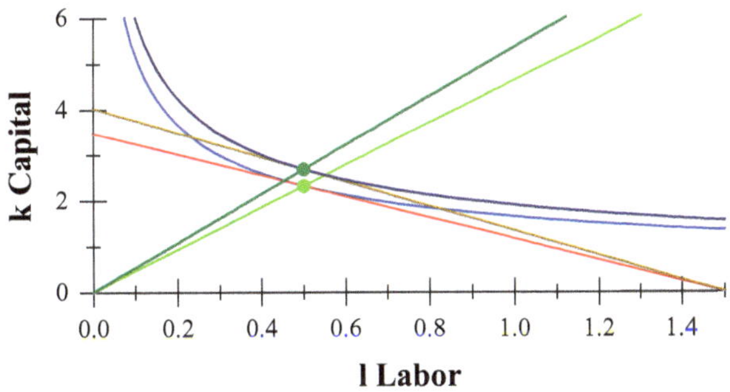

Figure 9.4 Factor Market Equilibrium with Goods Productivity Increase (Darker Curves) Compared to Original (Lighter Curves)

Figure 9.4 graphs the factor input market's equilibrium isoquant and isocost lines, along with the factor input ratios, both at the original equilibrium and after the 5% productivity increase. The darker color lines show the new equilibrium, with the isoquant level curve (Blue) shifting up as the level of output increases, the isocost line (Red) pivoting up as its slope of w/r increases, and the factor input ratio of k/l (Green) rising as the capital stock increases and labor is unchanged.[5]

9.4.5 AS-AD with Solow Growth

Now extend the analysis by assuming a continual increase over time in the productivity parameter A so as to get a targeted constant growth rate of output such as 2%. The growth process is then illustrated over four periods of time in both the goods and the labor market, using the Ramsey-Solow *AS–AD* in the goods market and supply and demand in the labor market. These graphs shows how the equilibrium output and the wage rate rise, while the labor employment remains unchanged. Also graphed is the production function and indifference curve, as well as the factor input market. These graphs show how the production function shifts up due to technological progress, and how the ratio of the wage rate to the real interest rate rises, and the capital to labor ratio rises.

The use of markets to represent *Ramsey-Solow growth theory* means that the optimization methods of Ramsey are combined with the technological progress of Solow. However Solow (1956) presented his model only from the firm side, while leaving the consumer's savings rate exogenous: or outside of the explanation of the model. He did not include full utility maximization by the representative agent acting as both consumer and firm.

The full Ramsey-Solow optimization World was put forth in 1965 by each David Cass and T.C Koopmans independently. They extended the Ramsey model to include Solow's features of economic growth. This means that the so-called Solow growth model is also known as the Ramsey-Cass-Koopmans (RCK) model of neoclassical growth. Koopmans became the 1975 Nobel Laureate for related work.

Call the Ramsey extension, with productivity rising at a constant rate, the Ramsey-Solow World for simplicity. It is the basis for the *AS-AD* graphs using the same utility and production function example as previously in Chapter 8. The productivity parameter A now is dependent on time and is written A_t. The graphs are made by computing the output and wage rate at each time period, while assuming that the productivity factor A_t rises at a steady rate over time.

[5]Mathematical inquirers can find that the new isoquant curve is now $k = \frac{1.8948}{(l^d)^{\frac{1}{2}}}$; the isocost line is now $k = 4.0195 - 2.6797l$; and the factor input ratio is now higher at $\frac{k}{l} = \frac{2.6797}{0.50} = 5.36$.

9.4.6 Solow Growth from Ramsey World

The production function remains the same (Cobb-Douglas) form, but now add in time subscripts to clarify that these variables can change over time.[6] Typically, target a constant growth rate of 2%. The assumption that productivity A grows over time at a certain implied constant rate then implies that output rises by 2%.[7]

The productivity growth implies the Solow Growth facts, as well as the declining real price of output relative to labor, a Solow Plus fact. In particular, over time the real wage w_t rises; the output to capital ratio (y_t/k_t) is constant since both output y_t and capital k_t grow at the rate; and the output to labor ratio that we call labor productivity, or per-capital income as denoted by y_t/l_t, grows since output y_t is growing and the time allocation to labor l_t is constant in equilibrium.

9.4.7 AS-AD with Continual Technological Progress

Use the same example economy as in Chapter 8 but now allow for *continual technological progress*.[8] Let the productivity parameter increase from its initial value at a constant rate with the result that aggregate supply continually shifts out by more than aggregate demand each period. This is consistent with the one-time increase in productivity that we examined to explain a business cycle expansion in Chapter 8: *AS* shifts out by more than *AD* and so the real price of goods relative to labor $1/w$ falls.

Figure 9.5 shows that the *AS–AD* curves shift over time, with output rising and the relative price of goods to labor falling, as the equilibrium *AS–AD* moves from Red to Purple to Blue to Black equilibria. Both consumption and output rise at a 2% rate, as does investment and the capital stock.[9]

Figure 9.6 shows how the labor supply and labor demand shift over time, in a similar fashion to the *AS-AD* goods market in terms of showing three productivity increases after starting at the initial period (Red). As in Figure 8.19, the labor demand shift out and labor supply shifts back so as to labor employment unchanged and the wage rate rising. The equilibrium shifts from the Red to Purple to Blue to the Black curves over 4 periods (such as years).[10]

---

[6]The production function for output is $y_t = A_t(l_t)^{\gamma}(k_t)^{1-\gamma}$, with γ between 0 and 1.

[7]The productivity parameter growth rate (μ) depends on this 2% value for output growth and on the gamma parameter (γ). In our particular example it results that productivity growth is 0.0067. This is a 0.67% productivity parameter growth rate that corresponds to a 2% output growth rate, when $\gamma = 1/3$. The productivity growth rate is residually found as being equal to the growth rate of 2% factored by the labor share in output cost, γ; or (0.02) (1/3) =0.0067. Therefore $A_{t+1}=A_t(1+0.0067)$, and A rises by 0.67% each year.

[8]The example assumes that $\gamma = \frac{1}{3}$, $\alpha = 0.5$, and $T = 1$, along with $\rho = 0.03$, and $\delta_k = 0.03$. Since $r = \rho + \delta_k$, this implies $r = 0.03 + 0.03 = 0.06$. The initial $A_t = 0.15$ and $k_t = 2.3$ as in the previous example; A_t grows over time, by assumption, and k_t grows over time as a solution to the optimization.

[9]Mathematical inquirers may note that the graphed *AS–AD* curves are given by

$$\frac{1}{w_{t+1}} = \frac{1}{y^d_{t+1}(1.5) - 2.8331[(0.0098039)(1.02) + (0.05)(1.5)]};\ \frac{1}{w_{t+1}} = \frac{3(y^s_{t+1})^2}{(0.15099)^3(2.8331)^2};$$

$$\frac{1}{w_{t+2}} = \frac{1}{y^d_{t+2}(1.5) - 2.8898[(0.0098039)(1.02) + (0.05)(1.5)]};\ \frac{1}{w_{t+2}} = \frac{3(y^s_{t+2})^2}{(0.15199)^3(2.8898)^2};$$

$$\frac{1}{w_{t+3}} = \frac{1}{y^d_{t+3}(1.5) - 2.9478[(0.0098039)(1.02) + (0.05)(1.5)]};\ \frac{1}{w_{t+3}} = \frac{1}{y^d_{t+3}(1.5) - 2.9478[(0.0098039)(1.02) + (0.05)(1.5)]},$$

$$\frac{1}{w_{t+3}} = \frac{3(y^s_{t+3})^2}{(0.153)^3(2.9478)^2}.$$

[10]Mathematical inquirers note the graphed labor supply and demand curves are: $w_{t+1} = \frac{(0.5)(2.8331)(0.0098039)(1.02)}{1-(1.5)l^s_{t+1}}$,

$$w_{t+1} = \frac{1}{3}(0.15099)\left(\frac{(2.8331)}{l^d_{t+1}}\right)^{\frac{2}{3}};\ w_{t+2} = \frac{(0.5)(2.8898)(0.0098039)(1.02)}{1-(1.5)l^s_{t+2}},\ w_{t+2} = \frac{1}{3}(0.15199)\left(\frac{(2.8898)}{l^d_{t+2}}\right)^{\frac{2}{3}};$$

$$w_{t+3} = \frac{(0.5)(2.9478)(0.0098039)(1.02)}{1-(1.5)l^s_{t+3}},\ w_{t+2} = \frac{1}{3}(0.153)\left(\frac{(2.9478)}{l^d_{t+3}}\right)^{\frac{2}{3}}$$

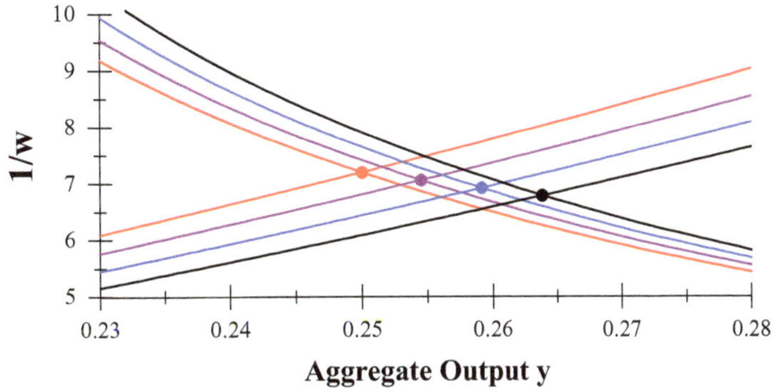

Figure 9.5 *AS-AD* Equilibria Over Time With 2% Exogenous Growth Example; Moving From Red to Black Curves over 4 years

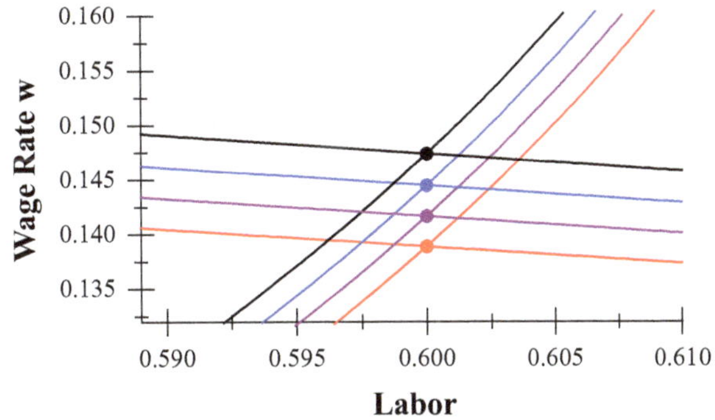

Figure 9.6 Labor Market with 2% Exogenous Growth and Rising Real Wage, Constant Employment, Over Time

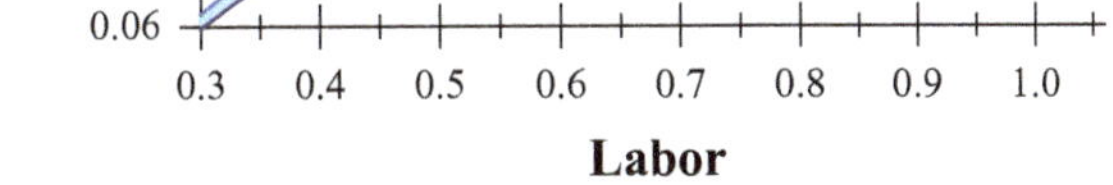

Figure 9.7 Exogenous Growth with Rising Production, Consumption and Utility Levels and Constant Employment

Figure 9.7 shows the production function and utility indifference curves, along with the budget lines, as Ramsey-Solow growth occurs. Consumption rises, and labor is unchanged, as the production function pivots up over time from Blue to Dark Blue. The utility level given within each indifference curve rises over time so that the indifference curves shift up from Red to Brown. Income rises for the consumer over time so the budget line shifts up from light Green to Green, while its slope is given by w_t and this rises over time as well.

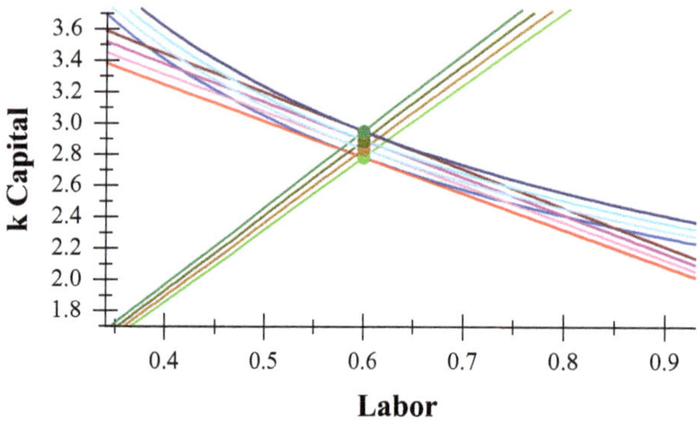

Figure 9.8 Factor Market Equilibrium with 2% Exogenous Growth, rising Capital to Labor Ratios, Real Wages and Output Levels, and a Constant Employment Rate and Real Interest Rate

The Solow-Ramsey growth in factor markets can be seen in the isoquant-isocost factor diagram. Figure 9.8 shows that labor l_t is unchanged as capital k_t rises by 2% a year, so that the Light Green ray from the origin, with a slope equal to the capital to labor ratio k_t/l_t, pivots up from the origin over time from Light Green to Sienna to Brown to Green. Consequently the factor input ratio of capital to labor k_t/l_t rises as do the slopes of the rays from the origin.

The curved isoquant shifts up (from Blue to Dark Blue) as the level of output rises at the 2% rate, since each isoquant shows how to combine labor and capital for a given output level. As the output level increases, and the isoquant shifts upwards, likewise the isocost budget line pivots up (from Red to Brown). The slope of each isocost line is $-w_t/r_t$. This slope gets steeper as the real wage w_t rises and r_t is constant over time, so that w_t/r_t rises over time at a 2% rate.

Figures 9.5 to 9.7 show different micro-founded perspectives over time of the rising wage rate w_t, the constant real interest rate r_t, the rising output y_t and the constant labor l_t. These comprise three of Solow's growth facts: of the wage rate rising, the interest rate being constant, and the output per labor rising.

The fourth Solow growth fact is subtle but it can be seen clearly in Figure 9.8 with careful inspection. Since the isoquant gives the level of output, its increase shows the increase over time in y_t. Since the factor input ray from the origin shows the increase in the capital stock k_t, while l_t is constant, the degree of increase in the factor input ray shows how k_t rises. Since the isoquant and the ray from the origin intersect at the equilibrium tangency point between the isoquant curve and the isocost line, both y_t and k_t rise at the exact same rate. This means that y_t/k_t is constant. This is the fourth Solow Growth fact and it is broadly accepted as holding true in empirical evidence. Since both output and capital grow at a 2% rate, all of the four Solow growth facts are met, as well as there being a balanced growth rate path along which all increasing variables do so at the same 2% rate.

In addition, in Figure 9.5, there is a falling relative price of output $1/\ w_t$. This illustrates the Harberger (1998) claim of a falling real cost of goods along the balanced growth path. It results directly since the wage rate is rising. And it is called here a Solow-Plus Growth fact.

9.5 Application: Trend Down in Time

A trend downwards in the time endowment available for goods and leisure is added here to the productivity trend upwards in order to capture the rest of the Solow-Plus Growth facts. A rising time path of education time is a stylized fact of developed economies. This increase in education time (including child rearing time) takes away time from work and leisure. Adding a downward trend in T_t, with a time subscript added to the time endowment for work and leisure, in the Ramsey-Solow World, captures this trend. Combining this downward trend in T_t with the trend upwards in productivity A_t, explains the standard Solow Growth facts plus the rest of the Solow-Plus Growth facts.

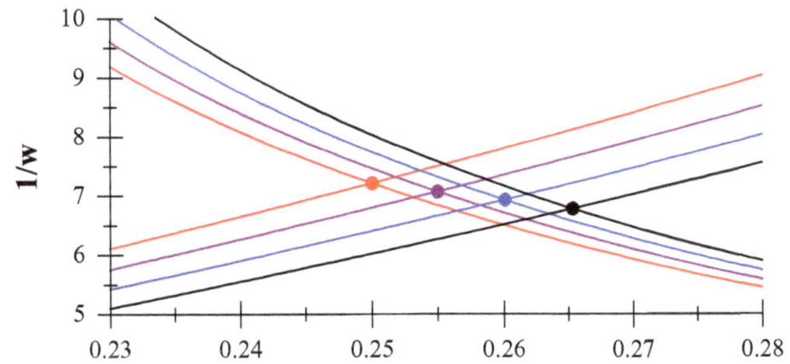

Figure 9.9 *AS-AD* Equilibria With Productivity *A* Trending Up and Time *T* Trending Down

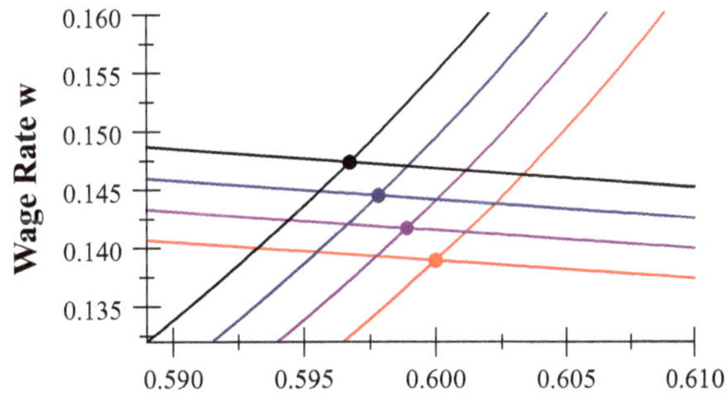

Figure 9.10 Labor Market with *A* Trending Up and *T* Trending Down

So add the second *comparative static* exercise during each time period during which there is also the constant productivity increase. Here let the time endowment T_t fall very slightly (by 0.18% a year). This slow decline in our example Ramsey-Solow World implies a decline in work time by 12% over 40 years, an estimate of the decrease in the US work week found by Mark Aguiar and Erik Hurst (2009).

The continual decrease in T_t explains the very slowly falling hours of work per week experienced in developed countries, the second Solow-Plus growth fact. Combined with the rising productivity, it leaves the real wage rising and inversely the real price of goods to labor falling over time, which is the first Solow-Plus Growth fact.

The decline in the time for work and leisure is explained by the rise in education time, which is the third Solow Plus growth fact of a well-known trend upward in education time. Finally, with T_t declining, the Ramsey-Solow World also implies that leisure time falls over time, which is the fourth Solow-Plus Growth fact. This leisure time decline is plausible if education time and the human capital stock are rising, so that leisure time has a higher opportunity cost.

Figure 9.9 assumes that at the same time the goods productivity factor A_t grows at 0.67% a year, the time endowment T_t falls by 0.18% a year. It shows the combined effect on the *AS–AD* curves. The equilibria move from the Red to the Black curves over time. Qualitatively, the graph is similar to Figure 9.5 in which only productivity is rising: output rises, the relative price of output falls, as both *AS* and *AD* shift out over time, with *AS* shifting out by more. So the Solow-Plus Growth fact of a decline in the relative price of goods to labor is unaffected qualitatively. Note that now the balanced path growth rate is 1.8%, lower than the initial 2%, because of the effect of the time endowment falling.

Figure 9.10 shows the labor market with both a rising productivity A_t and a falling time T_t. Now the graph looks qualitatively different from Figure 9.6 above in that the labor employment l_t now falls slightly over time; the wage rate w_t still is rising in both graphs. The falling employment time represents the second Solow-Plus

Growth fact of a slightly falling working hour week over time. The decrease in T_t represents the rise in education time, the third Solow-Plus Growth fact. Leisure time also falls, although this is not shown here, but this is the fourth Solow-Plus Growth fact. Education time can explicitly rise in an extended Solow-Ramsey World if a human capital investment sector is included; this is explained in the following Appendix which adds human capital investment.

9.6 Appendix: Growth with Human Capital

Consider extension of the Ramsey-Solow World by including human capital accumulation. This replaces the need to have exogenous technological change. Instead as the human capital h_t rises over time, the *effective wage rate* rises over time. A high enough return to human capital accumulation creates "endogenous growth" over time.

The human capital model solves for the economy's balanced path growth rate endogenously within the model. The growth depends on parameters such as the productivity in the human capital sector. But, amazingly, no parameters change over time as in the Solow-Ramsey World yet there still is a constant sustained balanced growth path.

Lucas (1988) extended the Ramsey-Solow World by including a sector producing human capital investment. Call this the human capital extension the "*Ramsey-Lucas World*", in that Lucas (1988) took the Uzawa (1965) model with a goods sector and a human capital investment sector and made it fully dynamic as in Ramsey (1928).[11] The "effective wages" are the wages received per hour of time in accordance with, or augmented by, the representative agent's human capital. These wages can be thought of as the "rental time value of human capital". This is given notationally as the product of the wage rate and the human capital stock, or $w_t h_t$.

The implied *AS–AD* of the Ramsey-Lucas World are graphed here with output y_t on the horizontal axis again and now $w_t h_t$ on the vertical axis. Note that now the "raw" labor time l_t, which is not augmented by human capital, receives a wage rate w_t that is stationary and unchanging over time. However it is the effective wage $w_t h_t$ that is actually earned by each unit of labor time l_t since the l_t is augmented by its human capital stock. The effective wage $w_t h_t$ rises over time since the human capital stock h_t that augments raw labor rises at the balanced growth path rate.

The Ramsey-Lucas World in the graphs of *AS–AD* and the labor market thereby include one big change as compared to the "exogenous growth" Ramsey-Solow World. Now the wage rate w_t is constant. But the wages received as indexed by the human capital stock h_t rise over time, as does w_t in the Ramsey-Solow World.

Using an example economy, Figure 9.11 graphs the output y_t and the effective wage rate $w_t h_t$ over four periods of time as is done above for the Ramsey-Solow World. The real price of goods relative to the labor l_t is one divided by the effective wage rate, or $\frac{1}{w_t h_t}$. The *AS* and *AD* curves shift out at a balanced growth path rate of 2%. This results since there is a positive return from investing in human capital, which is a result of assuming a particular, specified, level of productivity in the human capital sector, just as a particular value of goods productivity, A_t, is assumed in the Ramsey-Solow World. There is also an assumed value of A_t in the Ramsey-Lucas World, but A_t does not change here, in contrast to the Ramsey-Solow World.

It is notable that Figure 9.11 looks qualitatively identical to the Ramsey-Solow Figure 9.5 except that now the price of labor is the effective wage $w_t h_t$, where the raw wage rate w_t is constant. This replicates the first Solow-Plus growth fact of a falling relative price of goods to labor, which is here $1/(w_t h_t)$ (instead of w_t in Ramsey-Solow), during economic growth. As in Ramsey-Solow, the *AS* curve as before shifts out by more than the *AD* curve. But: no parameter of the economy is changing to produce this result. The human capital stock is an endogenous variable that is changing and it therefore explains the Solow-type growth of the economy. Except now growth occurs because of rising endogenous human capital h_t, rather than exogenously rising productivity A_t.

[11]Uzawa, Hirofumi, 1965. "Optimal Technical Change in an Aggregate Model of Economic Growth," International Economic Review 6(1): 18–31.

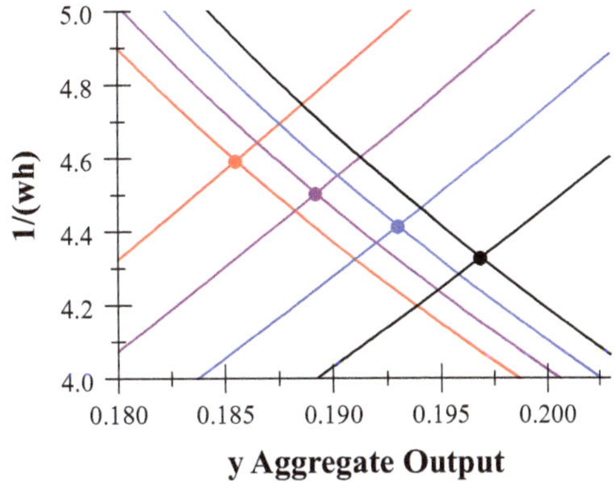

Figure 9.11 Endogenous Growth shifts in *AS-AD* over Four Time Periods.

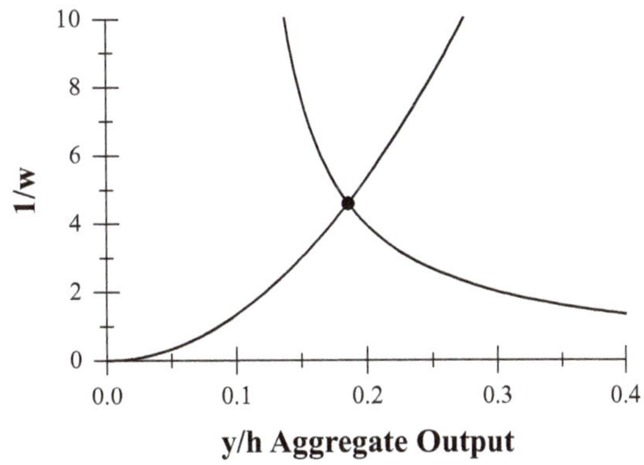

Figure 9.12 *AS–AD* with Human Capital and Endogenous Growth with the Raw Real Wage *w* on the Vertical Axis and Output/ Human-Capital on the Horizontal Axis

Alternatively consider the stationary version of the above Figure 9.11. Figure 9.12 shows the stationary wage w_t as graphed against the stationary output to human capital ratio of y_t/h_t. Nothing moves over time in this version of the graph. But it is the exact analogue of the Figure 9.11, except that the *AS* and *AD* functions are multiplied through by h_t. Figure 9.12 is drawn with the raw wage rate on the vertical axis, which is stationary, and with the output to human capital ratio on the horizontal axis, which is also stationary along the balanced growth path.

The endogenous growth world within the labor market can also be demonstrated. If graphed as in Figure 9.12, in terms of w_t, then over time there is no change in the equilibrium labor market, as both the wage rate w_t and employment time l_t are stationary. However if graphed with the effective wage $w_t h_t$ and the employment time l_t, the resulting graph replicates the Ramsey-Solow labor market graph of Figure 9.6. Figure 9.13 graphs the example economy's supply and demand for labor over four time periods with the effective wage $w_t h_t$ on the horizontal axis and labor l_t on the vertical axis.

Figure 9.13 appears identical to the Ramsey-Solow Figure 9.6, but again in the Ramsey-Lucas Figure 9.13, no parameter is changing, as is A_t (rising) in Figure 9.6. Since the human capital stock h_t is growing at the economy's constant growth rate, the effective wage rises over time while labor employment l_t is stationary.

The equilibrium in Figure 9.13 moves up from the intersection of the Red curves to that of the Black curves as time passes. This replicates the exogenous growth Solow facts of a rising wage rate but now in terms of the effective wage rate rising as human capital rises. And now the economy's growth rate is determined by how much time is spent in human capital accumulation, which depends on the productivity of the human capital investment sector.

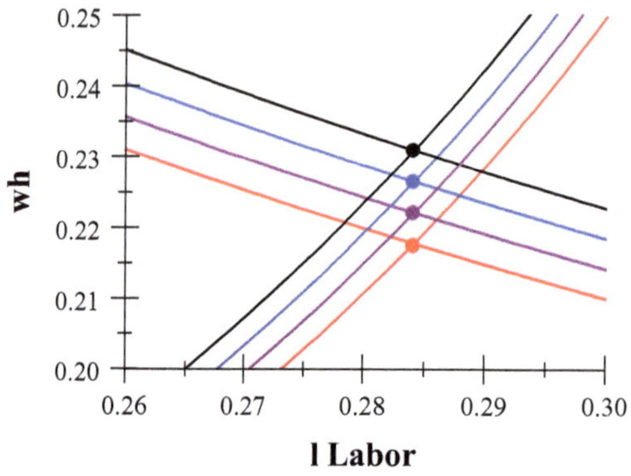

Figure 9.13 Labor Market with Endogenous Growth as Graphed with the Effective Wage on the Vertical Axis.

Should the productivity in the human capital sector be allowed to rise (exogenously) very slowly over time, this would be consistent with evidence of a rising productivity in the US human capital investment sector over time. Adding in such a trend up in human capital productivity would result in a replication of the rest of the Solow-Plus growth facts. The time spent working would fall very gradually. The time spent in education would rise equally gradually. And the time spent in leisure would fall slightly at the same rate. One difference from showing this as in the Appendix above using Ramsey-Solow Growth and an exogenous downward trend in the time endowment T_t: allowing human capital productivity to rise slightly over time in Ramsey-Lucas also means that the growth rate of the economy will very gradually rise over time. This extension then also succinctly captures the slow transformation of society from a zero growth one, as in the *Classical, Malthusian-Marxian economy,* to a high growth, Neoclassical, developed economy.

9.7 Summary

The stylized growth facts are set out in terms of the real wage rising, the per capita income level rising, the real interest rate being constant and the output to capital ratio being constant. Robert Solow's theory explained these facts. Ramsey's World was extended to include Solow's steady rise in the productivity parameter in order to explain these facts using aggregate supply and demand analysis.

The comparative static increase in productivity, as in Chapter 8, now occurs during each consecutive time period; a continuous productivity increase is assumed. The *AS* and *AD* both shift out over time with *AS* shifting out by more during each period of time, causing the relative price of goods to labor to fall over time. This is consistent with a fall in the relative price of goods to labor as productivity rises.

A productivity increase affects the labor market through a higher real wage and an unchanged employment rate. As productivity rises over time, labor demand shifts out each period and labor supply shifts back each period so as to leave employment unaffected. The continual productivity increase causes the real wage rate to rise, with employment time unchanged.

Using *AS-AD* graphs and labor market graphs, as well as production function and input market graphs, the Solow Growth facts are demonstrated. These also produces the Solow Plus growth fact of a falling relative price of goods to labor.

The Application adds a downward trend in time endowment within the Ramsey-Solow World. This enables an explanation of the other Solow Plus growth facts. The time spent working each week falls very slowly over time. The time in education can be interpreted as rising slowly over time. And the time in leisure falls slowly over time.

The Appendix shows that with an extension of the Ramsey World to include human capital, the Ramsey-Lucas World of endogenous growth results. Here, instead of assuming a rising productivity trend, there is a sector that uses time to produce human capital. The choice of education time endogenously leads to the economy's growth rate. A similar representation of growth, as in the Ramsey-Solow World, is shown using *AS-AD* and the labor market, where now the wage rate is the human capital augmented wage rate; the raw wage rate is stationary.

Also adding a very small but steady rise in the productivity of the human capital (education) sector's productivity, the economy's growth rate rises over time, the education time rises over time, the working time per week falls over time, and the leisure time falls over time. This implies that the Ramsey-Lucas World can explain the Solow Growth facts with no parameter change, unlike the Ramsey-Solow World, and can explain the Solow-Plus growth facts with only one parameter change: a small steady rise in education sector productivity. In contrast, the Ramsey-Solow World required two parameter changes to get the Solow-Plus Growth facts, these being the change in output productivity and in the time endowment.

9.8 Glossary

balanced growth economy: all of the variables which change over time in an economy grow at the same rate, such as output, capital, and consumption.

balanced growth path equilibrium: this is the name for an equilibrium in which there is balanced growth.

Classical Malthusian-Marxian economy: an economy in which there is zero economic growth, as was envisioned back in Great Britain before the industrial revolution began raising the economy's growth rate above zero.

comparative static: a change in one exogenous parameter, while holding all other parameters the same, and finding the new equilibrium that results.

continual technological progress: occurs when productivity in production occurs not just once, but rather every period at the same rate, indefinitely.

effective wage rate: the raw wage rate (w) multiplied by the human capital stock (h); gives the total wage income received per hour given the stock of human capital that the labor contains.

endogenous growth theory: a body of analysis which explains the growth rate as being a result of the choices made by the representative agent, such as time spent accumulating human capital.

exogenous technological progress: productivity advances that occur at some specified rate; imposed exogenously on an economy to achieve some desired balanced growth rate.

exogenous growth model: A model for example that allows for technological progress to be assumed at a certain rate, such that all variables grow at the same rate on the balanced growth path.

human capital levels per capita: the amount of human capital, such as education and training, held on average by each person in an economy.

industrial revolution: A time from around 1750 to 2000, depending on how one wants to date it, when industrialization occurred at a newly rapid pace; typically thought to have started in England, and then to have spread across the Western world.

output to capital stock ratio: a measure of the value of the economy's real output divided by a measure of the value of its capital stock.

Ramsey-Cass-Koopmans (RCK) economy: the representative agent economy with capital accumulation, with exogenous technological progress and so exogenous growth, and with utility maximization subject to the production function.

Ramsey-Lucas World: the extension of the RCK economy to incorporate endogenous growth by adding a human capital investment sector in which the agent decides upon the amount of resources to devote to such human capital investment.

Ramsey-Solow growth theory: this is a way to describe the RCK economy in which there is the Ramsey feature of capital accumulation with utility optimization and the Solow feature of assumed technological progress that causes a positive growth rate for the economy.

Solow-Plus Growth fact: this is a feature of the economy, or stylized fact, that has been found to be characteristic of the growth process over time but which was not a focus of Solow's original work.

stationary in the equilibrium: all variables are at their equilibrium level and stay constant or stay growing at the constant growth rate of the balanced growth path.

steady technological progress: an assumed increase in productivity of the goods production sector such that this continues at the same rate over time, so that each and every input become more productive at a constant rate, in producing output.

stylized Solow Growth facts: facets of evidence that appears to hold over time as an economy grows, and that appear as fundamental aspects of the growth process.

technological progress: a continual improvement in productivity in producing the aggregate output good.

time endowment: the amount of time that the representative agent is assumed to be given each period for work and leisure.

trend growth rate: the rate of real output increase over the long term.

9.9 Questions

1. Explain the stylized facts of economic growth known as the Solow Growth facts.
2. What additional facts are the "Solow-Plus" Growth facts that we also are able to explain?
3. Explain what happens to labor employment over time with the only change being that goods productivity steadily rises.
4. Explain what happens to output and consumption over time with the only change being that goods productivity steadily rises.
5. What variables move together on a balanced growth path equilibrium and what variables do not change?
6. What happens to output and labor employment if both the goods productivity factor rises over time and the time endowment falls slightly over time?
7. Offer an explanation of why hours per week trend down over the long historical period in developed economies while at the same time the time spent in education trends upwards.
8. Graph the labor market when both goods productivity rises and the time endowment falls over time, both at a constant rate.
9. How does endogenous human capital accumulation change the explanation of any of the Solow Growth facts?
10. How does endogenous human capital accumulation change the explanation of any of the Solow-Plus Growth facts?
11. Complete the Federal Reserve Bank of St. Louis EconLowdown Course Module "Economic Growth".

PART IV

Policy

10 Policy as Social Insurance

10.1 Who Made it Happen

From Karl Marx's and Charles Dicken's criticism of 19th century working conditions to Henry George and George Bernard Shaw's conception of "*socialism*" based on property taxes, the advent of modern democracies with extensive *social insurance* resulted from personalities including the British Winston Churchill and William Beverage and the American President F.D. Roosevelt and President Johnson.

Consider President Johnson's first description of a Great Society in his University of Michigan speech:[1]

> "For in your time we have the opportunity to move not only toward the rich society and the powerful society, but upward to the Great Society. The Great Society rests on abundance and liberty for all. It demands an end to poverty and racial injustice, to which we are totally committed in our time. But that is just the beginning. The Great Society is a place where every child can find knowledge to enrich his mind and to enlarge his talents. It is a place where leisure is a welcome chance to build and reflect, not a feared cause of boredom and restlessness. It is a place where the city of man serves not only the needs of the body and the demands of commerce but the desire for beauty and the hunger for community. It is a place where man can renew contact with nature. It is a place which honors creation for its own sake and for what it adds to the understanding of the race. It is a place where men are more concerned with the quality of their goals than the quantity of their goods. But most of all, the Great Society is not a safe harbor, a resting place, a final objective, a finished work. It is a challenge constantly renewed, beckoning us toward a destiny where the meaning of our lives matches the marvelous products of our labor."

A profound statement of noble goals motivated much legislative activity. At the same time many in Western democracies worried about loss of freedom through too much government. This included Friedrich Hayek's description of the corruption of autocratic political power in his prescient 1944 cautionary book called *The Road to Serfdom*. The Chicago School of Economics formed around the time of Hayek and Milton Friedman after their post-WWII founding of the Mt. Pelerin Society.

Hayek joined the University of Chicago in 1950, along with Frank Knight, in the university's Committee on Social Thought. Other early Chicago economists of the "original" Chicago School besides Knight included Jacob Viner, Henry Simons, and Lloyd Mints, according to Blaug (1980, 1992).[2] George Stigler (1988) also mentions Paul Douglas, Henry Schultz and Oskar Lange, who Stigler describes as a "socialist".[3] The next generation included the so-called "*libertarian*" perspective of Milton Friedman, along with George Stigler, Gary Becker, Arnold Harberger and then Robert E. Lucas, Jr., the latter of which lifetime's work is credited for providing the advanced Ramsey (1928)-basis that now forms the foundation for much of modern Macroeconomics. For example the Stokey and Lucas (1989) foundations of modern Macroeconomics are put forth and extended in textbook fashion by Ljungqvist and Sargent (2004).[4]

---

[1]President Johnson proposed the concept of a Great Society at a 1964 University of Michigan Commencement Address. The address is given in full in the Heritage Society archives at http://www.heritage.org/initiatives/first-principles/primary-sources/lbj-launches-the-great-society

[2]Blaug, Mark, 1992, The Methodology of Economics, 2nd edition, Cambridge University Press: Cambridge; 1980 1st edition.

[3]Stigler, G. 1988, "The Chicago School", Chapter 10 of *Memoirs of an Unregulated Economist*, The University of Chicago Press, Chicago.

[4]Nancy Stokey and Robert E. Lucas, Jr., 1898, with Edward C. Prescott, Recursive Methods in Economic Dynamics, Harvard University Press. Cambridge, Massachusetts, and London, England; Lars Ljungqvist and Thomas J. Sargent, 2004, *Recursive Macroeconomic Theory*, Second Edition, MIT Press. See also for example: De Vroey, Michel, 2016, *A History of Macroeconomics from Keynes to Lucas and Beyond*. Cambridge University Press, January. See also Robert E. Lucas, Jr., 2013, *Collected Papers on Monetary Theory*, Harvard University Press, edited by M. Gillman, Cambridge, MA; and Sargent, Thomas J. 2015. "Robert E. Lucas Jr.'s Collected Papers on Monetary Theory." Journal of Economic Literature, 53(1): 43–64.

Ayn Rand's 1936 *We the Living*, 1943 *The Fountainhead* and 1957 *Atlas Shrugged* provided a philosophical counterpoint to an all-encompassing social entitlement of the U.K.'s Beverage Report and the U.S.'s "Great Society" concepts of government. George Stigler in his 1975 *The Citizen and the State: Essays on Regulation* presented a Rand-related view in terms of how government regulation acts perversely to protect industry from competition, rather than promoting healthy markets. The US and UK government "welfare programs" provided a large encompassing role for government that was counterpointed by arguments for a much more limited role of government, although even Hayek wrote in favor of a government social insurance policy with the caveat that it not stifle competition or lead to establishment of a totalitarian state.[5]

The economic presentation of this philosophical, political economy, debate on the role of government became centered around Keynes (1930,1936) and the Neoclassical basis formed by Keynes's student Frank Ramsey (1928). The consumption theories of each Keynes and Ramsey led to alternative ways to view the economic utility-maximizing goal of *consumption smoothing over time*. Keynes's consumption function, as based on Ernst Engel (1857), was used to suggest more government involvement as based on income inequality while the consumption function contained within Ramsey's economy, and promulgated by Milton Friedman (1957) 100 years after Engel, suggested the prominent goal of strengthening the consumer's permanent income. Smoothing consumption can be aided substantially by optimal social insurance policy.[6]

James Meade of the United Kingdom won the Nobel Prize in 1977 for his international trade theory. However Meade was already an esteemed economist during the 1930's Great Depression era and wrote a textbook called Economic Policy and Analysis in 1936 (first edition) and 1937 (second edition). This opened up with a Part I called "Unemployment", and then it includes subsequent Parts on "Competition and Monopoly", "The Distribution of Income", "The Supply of the Primary Factors of Production", and finally "International Problems" which included international trade. This made a full standard textbook with a topical focus on the great unemployment of the day.

In surmising policy to implement for the unemployment problem, he wrote how the current, limited-time, unemployment insurance program could be modified.[7] Rather than continuing the strict program of paying out insurance payments only as based on how much had been paid in, for each worker's particular case, and for a limited period, Meade suggested expanding the program to give unlimited payouts as long as people were unemployed, regardless of what they paid into the *unemployment insurance fund*.

Meade's unemployment insurance expansion program was simply justified by Meade. During an expansion, workers naturally would pay into the insurance fund through the corresponding taxes in place for this funding, and during the recessions the workers would naturally draw down these funds when unemployed. The idea was born that the aggregate system could be devised so that the economic downturn's payouts could be balanced by the economic upturn's payments into the insurance fund. Therefore strict limits on individual payouts were not necessary.

---

[5]In a radio broadcast transcript of the NBC at the University of Chicago Round Table discussion, Professor Maynard C. Krueger asks Hayek "Is a comprehensive system of social insurance a violation of your definition of good planning?" In the subsequent sequence of question and answers, Hayek is quoted as saying "The only point where the problem can arise is how far to make it compulsory and how far, incidentally, it is used to strengthen the monopolistic actions of trade unions, because that is one way in which it may well eliminate competition."..."I have always said I am in favor of a minimum income for every person in the country.".. "I mean to secure a minimum income upon which everyone can fall back. You have it, of course, very largely in the form of unemployment insurance." (p. 101, 1994: from *Hayek on Hayek: An Autobiographical Dialogue*, by F. A. Hayek, Edited by Stephen Kresge and Leif Wenar, The Univesity of Chicago Press.)

[6]Friedman, M., 1957, *A Theory of the Consumption Function*, Princeton University Press: Princeton.

For a modern perspective of Keynesian versus the Friedman consumption function see the work of Christopher D. Carroll, for eg. Caroll, 2001, "A Theory of the Consumption Function, With and Without Liquidity Constraints (Expanded Version)." NBER Working Paper No. 8387.

[7]The National Insurance Act of 1911; it also provided health insurance.

10.2 Facts

10.2.1 The Beverage Report

The unlimited unemployment insurance became instituted in the UK following WWII after Winston Churchill asked for a commission to study the social insurance issues. The Beverage report of 1942 recommended a broad social insurance system to stabilize the income of UK citizens over time and in adverse situations.[8] As the report put it,[9]

> "The second principle is that organisation of social insurance should be treated as one part only of a comprehensive policy of social progress. Social insurance fully developed may provide income security; it is an attack upon Want . . . The third principle is that social security must be achieved by co-operation between the State and the individual".

Subsequently the UK legislated the National Insurance Act in 1945, an obligatory unemployment insurance system with unlimited-over-time benefits, as well as the Family Allowances Act for large families, the Industrial Injuries Act of 1946 for work injuries, the 1948 National Health Act for free universal health insurance, along with the 1948 National Assistance Act for other aid and the Education Act of 1944. This established Britain's "welfare state".

The Beverage Report quote above succinctly summarizes an over-riding goal of a government policy of providing social insurance that is designed to smooth income over time. This income-smoothing idea is consistent with the Fisher and Ramsey analysis when the income-smoothing is replaced instead by the term "consumption-smoothing". Another difference from Fisher and Ramsey analysis is that the government does not have a role initially; advanced analysis bringing in shocks into the analysis and externalities could potentially justify government intervention. Of course such shocks were the rule not the exception during the Great Depression and WWII in Britain, and distinction between a government role and the private sector in providing for the means of consumption smoothing was not emphasized perhaps as much.

10.2.2 British and American "Welfare States"

The British welfare state could be said to have spread across Australia, New Zealand, and indeed to the US. In the US, broad government social insurance began with President Franklin Delano Roosevelt's "New Deal" policies of the 1933 Social Security Act and the 1933 Banking Act that provided federal deposit insurance for bank deposits, and a host of legislation through the 1930's. The US social insurance coverage expanded broadly into its modern form in the 1960's with President Johnson's "Great Society" policies.

President Johnson proposed the concept of a Great Society in 1964. His follow-up to some of President Kennedy's initiatives, at which time Johnson was Vice-President, resulted ultimately in a host of acts, namely: The Food Stamp Act of 1964, the Economic Opportunity Act of 1964, the Voting Rights Act of 1965, the Social Security Act of 1965 and the Social Security Amendments of 1967, the Elementary and Secondary Education Act of 1965 which established "Head Start", the Higher Education Act of 1965, the Immigration and Nationality Services Act of 1965, the National Foundation on the Arts and Humanities Act of 1965 and the Civil Rights Act of 1968.

The US established some decades later what Britain began after WWII. The term social insurance in the US brings to mind mainly the Social Security System, last reformed in 1983, which provides retirement income, health insurance, and disability insurance. Yet the US actually has a federal government -sponsored full "social insurance" policy similar in spirit to what the Beverage Report made as a primary goal.

[8] "Social insurance and allied services." Report by Sir William Beveridge. London, HMSO, 1942.

[9] The Beverage Report is reprinted in part in the *Bulletin of the World Health Organization*, 2000, 78 (6), pp. 847–855.

10.3 Theory

10.3.1 Moral Hazard Danger of Social Insurance

The goal of social insurance is unimpeachable as an honorable objective of modern society. The question is what role the government should have in this as opposed to institutions that arise naturally in a free market to fill the demand for such insurance. The central problem that James Meade (1937) ignored has become the key problem that economists focus on in helping to design public policy that the government may be able to provide in the sense of broad social insurance.

The problem is called "*moral hazard*". In short, if a government policy has the effect of increasing the probability of the "bad state" occurring, then the policy has created "moral hazard". For example, suppose that the policy increases the probability that social insurance will be needed, so that citizens find themselves more likely to be in the "bad" situation of either being unemployed, or needing medical care, or being no longer able to work, or being too old to be able to work. Then this increase in the probability of the "bad" situation occurring is called the "moral hazard" of providing government social insurance. Examples make this crucial policy concept more clear.

Unemployment Insurance

A simple, well-studied, example is unemployment insurance. Once the "duration" of unemployment payments becomes unlimited in time, previously working citizens have less incentive to find a new job. This means that the probability of unemployment for the economy as a whole goes up if even one worker decides to just stay unemployed and continue to receive benefits.

The design of unemployment insurance is not to subsidize being unemployed: it is to provide temporary income while being "forcibly", or what some call "involuntarily", being unemployed. But when the incentive to find new work is decreased by the unemployment insurance benefit being of unlimited duration, so that it might continue to be paid forever, then the worker's probability of being unemployed becomes higher. The policy has in effect subsidized the "bad state" of being unemployed, making that situation more likely.

The US enacted the The Personal Responsibility and Work Opportunity Reconciliation Act of 1996 (PRWORA), also known as the "Welfare Reform Act". This ended welfare benefits in the US as unlimited time payments, or what is often called an "entitlement" program. Instead, federal income beneficiaries were required to find work within two years and federal payments were cut-off after five years. This addressed the problem of moral hazard in the sense that an unlimited time duration of unemployment benefits simply acts as a subsidy to not-working. Incentives for finding work would seem to have been improved under PRWORA. The "Welfare-to-Work initiative" that is in the 1996 reform was revised in the next, 2003, welfare reform act called the Welfare Reform Extension Act of 2003, and possibly weakened, an issue still being discussed; currently US States are allowed leeway in devising implementation of this aspect of the program.[10]

[10] "The Welfare-to-Work initiative, which required work in exchange for time limited financial assistance. Recipients of TANF, or Temporary Assistance to Needy Families, were required to work at least 20 hours per week, and the reform statute listed 12 authorized activities accepted to meet this requirement. According to reports, within 3 years of the reforms enactment, millions of Americans had moved from being dependent on welfare to being self-sufficient. In addition, agencies reported a reduction in the number of social welfare cases." Quote from http://www.welfareinfo.org/reform/. The 1996 Act "dramatically reshaped cash and food welfare programs and helped reduce federal welfare spending. It replaced the Depression-born program of Aid to Families with Dependent Children (AFDC) with fixed annual grants to states for Temporary Assistance to Needy Families (TANF) for six years, ending on September 30, 2002" (from Vee Burke, "The 1996 Welfare Reform Law", Congressional Research Service, Welfare Reform Briefing Book, Call 7-5700). "That the 1996 welfare reform was a success, in overall terms and on average, is almost universally accepted by policy analysts and researchers" (See Robert Moffitt, 2008, "A Primar on US Welfare Reform,"University of Wisconsin IRP working paper; http://www.irp.wisc.edu/publications/dps/dplist.htm). See also the US government summary at https://archive.opm.gov/wtw/.

Bank Insurance

A second example is bank deposit insurance provided by the US government through the Federal Deposit Insurance Corporation (FDIC). If the government guarantees repayment of customer deposits, this can encourage banks to make riskier loans and investments. The higher risk of the asset portfolio the more likely that a bank becomes insolvent and that the "bad" situation occurs with bank bankruptcy and the FDIC having to pay out money from its insurance fund.

A government policy that induces moral hazard by decreasing incentives for achieving the good outcome acts to increase the probability of the bad outcome. This increases the "insurance fund" needed to cover payments during the "bad times". Economists have found therefore that for unemployment insurance, benefits must be paid out with limited duration so as to decrease moral hazard. For bank insurance, the US altered the FDIC so as to charge premiums from banks for the deposit insurance that are based on the riskiness of their loan and investment portfolio

Policies that are well-designed attempt to be "*incentive compatible*" through a social insurance scheme that will not increase the probability of the bad situation occurring. Limited duration of unemployment benefits and risk-based premiums for deposit insurance are examples of improved government social insurance with less moral hazard. The role of the government in "redistributing income" then can more sensibly be termed in the sense of how to provide assistance when necessary without changing incentives to achieve the good state of affairs. As of 2006, all FDIC deposit insurance premiums are risk-based, with a higher premium per dollar of deposits insured for a more risky class of assets and liabilities that a bank may hold. While, a detailed examination of the FDIC is given in the Application of this Chapter below, consider how the FDIC phrases it:[11]

> "Federal Deposit Insurance Reform Act of 2005 passed by Congress earlier this year to create a stronger and more stable insurance system. Among the final regulations is a new rule on the risk-based assessment system that will enable the FDIC to more closely tie each bank's premiums to the risk it poses to the deposit insurance fund. In addition, the FDIC has new flexibility to manage the deposit insurance fund's reserve ratio within a range, which in turn will help prevent sharp swings in assessment rates that were possible under the design of the former system."

Fringe Benefits and Tax Law

The need to keep healthy the incentives for achievement extends beyond legislatively enacted programs to all of the ways that the government engages in a social insurance policy. For example *government regulation* is not enacted by Congress but rather constructed by agencies of the government. These regulations can "over-reach" their primary objective if they change incentives in a negative way.

For example "fringe benefit" regulations by the Internal Revenue Service were long viewed by Congress as being overly-oppressive and led to a succession of two-year moratoriums on the IRS issuing regulations on what employer-provided benefits were taxable as income and what were "tax-free". The inability of the federal government to agree on how to define fringe benefits left the income base of the US tax system in disarray such that increasingly more income escaped taxation through classification as a fringe benefit, thus "narrowing" the income tax base of the US.

Incentives are an important part of national policy. The fringe benefit regulatory morass was finally overcome with the US Congress enacting a law that instructed the IRS on how fringe benefits should be taxed in IRS issued regulations, in the Tax Reform Act of 1984. The Act created incentives for the proper use of fringe benefits as part of enhancing the workplace environment rather than as a means of evading income tax.[12]

Once the *income tax base* was well-defined, this led to the opening up of reform of income tax law that emerged in the Tax Reform Act of 1986 that lowered both corporate and personal income taxes while eliminating special preferences in the tax code that caused implicit subsidization. For example the bias for short

[11]FDIC Press Release, November 2, 2006; found at https://www.fdic.gov/news/news/press/2006/pr06101.html

[12]For descriptions of the fringe benefits aspect of the 1984 Tax Reform Act, see: Ken Kies, 1984, "Analysis of the New Rules Governing the Taxation of Fringe Benefits," Tax Notes, September 3, p. 981; Wendy Gerzog Shaller, 1985 "The New Fringe Benefit Legislation: A Codification of Historical Inequities", *Catholic University Law Review* Vol. 34, No. 2, Winter, Article 7.

term investment over long term investment was decreased by eliminating the 10% investment tax credit (ITC) that was thought to bias investment in this way towards the short term horizon. It was the biggest tax increase provision of the 1986 Act that was aimed at simplification and incentive enhancement of productive activity. The ITC elimination was important in allowing the 1986 Act reductions in the personal and corporate income tax rates to be considered at the time as "revenue-neutral".

After the Economic Recovery Tax Act of 1981, with its reduction in income tax marginal rates, the 1984 and 1986 subsequent tax reform Acts soon contributed to the US economy's unprecedented ten year expansion in the 1990's. This included a stock market boom and high economic real output growth that did not end until the 2000 "dot com bubble" burst of US stock markets and the subsequent 2001 recession. And these tax reforms just preceded the fall of the Soviet Union (on December 25th, 1991) and the subsequent enlargement of global markets to include Eastern Europe and greater parts of Asia.

10.3.2 Inequality and Consumption

Consider the consumption functions of both Keynes (1936) and the Ramsey-Friedman one. The Keynesian consumption function is used in Chapter 3 to construct the Keynesian Cross analysis. The basis of that Cross analysis lies in one particular aspect of the consumption function.

In particular, in the *Keynesian consumption function*, as income grows the share of income that is spent on consumption falls. In turn, this means that the share of savings rises as income goes up. This implies that low income consumers spend most of their income and high income consumers save most of their income, when the economy is viewed with extension to many representative agents rather than just one. With consumers having the same Keynesian consumption function and difference incomes, low income consumers have a relatively high share of consumption in income and high income consumers have a lower share of consumption in income.

One implication might be just to redistribute income from low income consumers to high income consumers in order to raise aggregate consumption. Consider the detail of where this idea comes from. For low income consumers the consumption share of income can be 100% in the Keynesian model. As income rises, the spending share of income approaches a set fraction. Over time, as income rises in a society, this also means that all of the shares of consumption and savings out of income level out at constant shares that add to one. The constant shares both come from the b in the Keynesian consumption function that is written as $C = a + bY$ in the Keynesian Cross of Chapter 3 above.

Write the consumption share by dividing consumption C by income Y. Then use that $C = a + bY$, and write $C/Y = (a + bY)/Y$, or $\frac{a}{Y} + b$. The consumption share is $\frac{a}{Y} + b$ and so it depends on the income level. This Keynesian consumption share of income can be close one (or even above one) when the income level is low. This is because with a low Y, then $\frac{a}{Y}$ is high. One can think of $\frac{a}{Y}$ as being "capped" at one unless the consumer is able to borrow or get income transfers from the government.[13]

However as income gets high, then $\frac{a}{Y}$ goes towards zero. This means the consumption share of income goes towards b as Y gets high. When Y is low, then $\frac{a}{Y}$ is relatively high, and the share is higher than just b. As Y rises, $\frac{a}{Y}$ falls, and the share becomes lower and so approaches the level of b.[14]

When income inequality exists, the Keynesian consumption function suggest that different consumption shares might be equalized simply by redistributing income. For example, Figure 10.1 shows the Keynesian consumption as a fraction of income $\left(C/Y \text{ or } \frac{a}{Y} + b\right)$, when $A = 0.10$ and $B = 0.67$. The consumption share starts very high and falls as income Y rises until it approaches two-thirds at high income levels. This graph shows that consumption is higher as a fraction of income the lower is the level of income.

---

[13]A fraction for C/Y greater than one implies that the consumer must borrow income, or be given income for example by the government, in order to consume some "minimum" level of income.

[14]The limit of $\left(\frac{a}{Y} + b\right)$ as Y goes to infinity is b.

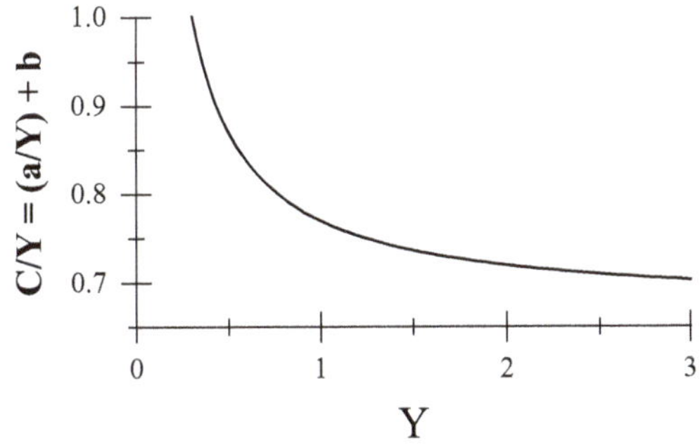

Figure 10.1 Consumption as a Fraction of Income: in the Keynesian Theory of Consumption $C = a + bY$

As income rises, the first constant a becomes unimportant and the consumption share approaches the constant b. In turn, the savings share of income approaches $1 - b$, since $1 - (C/Y) = 1 - b$ for large income Y. A constant consumption and savings share is similar to the Ramsey-Friedman consumption function. However in the Ramsey World, the consumption share is a constant out of permanent income rather than current income. And Ramsey World savings is the constant residual share of permanent income. And in the Ramsey world, the constant b is in fact determined by the behavioral preferences of the representative agent.[15]

Some evidence supports the notion that of the Keynesian consumption function that consumption shares out of current income are high and can be close to one. Other evidence supports the Friedman permanent income hypothesis, in which consumption is a constant share of permanent income. Surprisingly the Ramsey type consumption theory actually can be stated in a fashion that can be viewed as spanning both the Keynesian and the Friedman views of the consumption function.

10.3.3 Permanent Income Consumption

Milton Friedman's (1957) *permanent income hypothesis of consumption* states that consumption follows current income in part. But the difference that Friedman argues is that consumption is determined by the consumer's expectations of the entire discounted value of the whole future stream of income and not just the current income. Permanent income is defined typically as the whole expected future income stream to be earned, with a *present value discounting* of the income stream.[16] Friedman in brief specified that consumption is a fraction of permanent income, where y_p denotes permanent income, and the real consumption goods demand is $c = a\, y_p$; a is fraction such as two-thirds.

In general, think of permanent income as a fraction of the flow from both human and physical capital. It is the wage flow on human capital (or whT in the notation of Chapter 9) plus the interest flow on physical capital (or rk in notation). In the Ramsey World, or the Ramsey-Lucas World extension, it turns out that the fraction of this permanent income consumed depends simply on how much leisure time is preferred.[17]

Figure 10.2 shows consumption in the Ramsey World as a constant two-thirds of permanent income. If the representative consumer faced "perfect capital markets" then it would be possible to borrow and accumulate both human capital and physical capital. Then this capital accumulation would enable the consumer to perfectly smooth consumption across time, and consume a set fraction of permanent income (y_Perm).

---

15 See Gillman (2011) to see that the preference for leisure determines the rate of consumption out of permanent income in a simple Ramsey (1928) (homothetic) economy.

16 Friedman, Milton, 1957,.*A Theory of the Consumption Function*. Princeton University Press; Princeton.

17 Ramsey-Lucas consumption is $c = \frac{rk + whT}{1+\alpha}$, where $\alpha = 0.5$ is a leisure preference parameter that gives that consumption is two-thirds of permanent income; h=1 in Ramsey without human capital and T is the time endowment which can be set to one (see Gillman, 2011); as leisure preference α rises, c consumption demand falls.

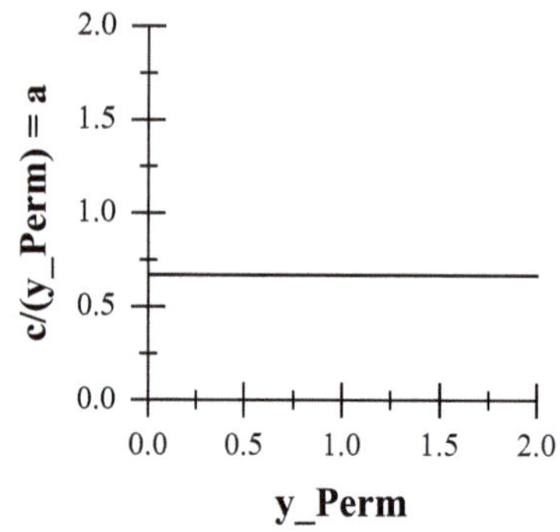

Figure 10.2 Consumption as a Fraction of Permanent Income: Ramsey-Friedman Theory

Perfect consumption smoothing over time is the heart of Friedman's *permanent income hypothesis* of consumption. And surprisingly this is also what the Ramsey World delivers: a constant share of permanent income is consumed. That this constant share depends on leisure preference is a facet that Friedman did not include.

Friedman omitted how the fraction is derived because he used a Fisher two-period framework to form his hypothesis rather than the full dynamic optimization that the Ramsey World uses. Using the Ramsey World with goods and leisure, the constant share of permanent income that is consumed indeed does depend only on leisure preference, and it falls as leisure preference rises.

In practice many obstacles exist which make the future income uncertain and which lead to an inability to save and accumulate either human or physical capital. This makes the actual consumption share of income perhaps somewhere in between Figures 10.1 and 10.2. As a result a need to help the consumer smooth income over time becomes the key macroeconomic policy consideration of a government. Such policy can be a main component of the provision of "social insurance", as outlined in the UK Beverage Report or by US President Johnson's Great Society speech.

10.3.4 Ramsey World's Keynesian Cross

Remarkably, the Ramsey World can reproduce its version of the "Keynesian Cross" by increasing goods sector productivity (A in the last two Chapters) rather than by increasing government spending as in the Keynesian version. Start by writing the Ramsey consumption in terms of wage income (or human capital income) plus the capital income. This re-writing is possible since consumption is a fraction of permanent income, which in turn is comprised of the flow of income from each human capital and physical capital.

Often consumption is thought of as being a function of wages, while wealth is ignored. In contrast, in the Ramsey World, the capital stock k plays a key part in the equilibrium and in the consumption function itself. Consider writing the Ramsey consumption demand in a form comparable to the Keynesian consumption function. This can be done by writing Ramsey World consumption (which is given by $c = \frac{whT + r'k}{1+\alpha}$) as $c = a' + b'w$, where w is the wage rate, and a' and b' are so-called parameters. But actually a' is equal to the fraction consumed out of physical capital. In particular, $a = \frac{r'k}{1+\alpha}$, where r' is the real interest rate net of depreciation $(r - \delta_k)$, k the capital stock, and α is leisure preference. And the "parameter" b' is actually the share of permanent income coming from human capital, whereby $b' = \frac{Th}{1+\alpha}$, where T is the time endowment for work and leisure, and h is the human capital stock. The human capital h is equal simply to one in the standard Ramsey World of exogenous growth, but can be a variable h in the Ramsey-Lucas World that includes human capital.[18]

[18]Mathematical inquirers: The example economy implies that $a = \frac{(r-\delta_k)k}{1+\alpha} = \frac{0.03(1)}{1+0.5}$ and $b = \frac{T}{1+a} = \frac{1}{1+0.5} = 0.67$.

What changes occur that can alter the a' and b' of the Ramsey consumption function? For example, the two key changes examined in Chapters 8 and 9 are the change in the productivity parameter (A) and in the time endowment T. If productivity rises, so does the capital stock k. This increases the a' parameter. If T increases, the b' parameter increases.

The graph of the Ramsey consumption function relative to wages is presented in Figure 10.3.[19] Two lines are graphed. One is presented in a version similar to Keynes's consumption function, with $c = a' + b'w$. The other is an economic national income accounting identity that emerges within the Ramsey World and gives us a 45 degree line as is used in the Keynesian Cross analysis.

In particular, in the example Ramsey World it also results that consumption can be written equivalently as $c = wT$, for all values of the productivity parameter A. Figure 10.3 graphs c on the vertical axis and wT on the horizontal axis. So $c = wT$ gives a 45% line. The interpretation of this is that along this line consumption expenditure equals the "full" wage income that results as if all time value contributes to "full income" (if $T = 1$ then $wT = w$). Becker (1965) introduced this "full income" concept, where it is here defined as being equal to the value of all of the time endowment, or wT.

Figure 10.3 adds the second line of $c = a' + b'w$. Both equations are representations of consumption in the Ramsey World, with a different view than is provided in the graph in Figure 8.10 in Chapter 8, in which the AD aggregate demand function is constructed. Instead here is reproduced the well-viewed Ramsey World version of where the equilibrium consumption is determined at the intersection of the 45% line and the upward sloping consumption function that has a positive constant and a slope less than one. The intersection of the black 45% line and the black $c = a' + b'w$ occurs at the equilibrium c and w which both equal 0.06 in the example.

Let productivity A rise 5% as in Chapter 8.[20] This does not affect the 45% line or the slope coefficient b' $\left(b' = \frac{Th}{1+\alpha}\right)$ of the $c = a'+b'w$ representation of consumption. However, the capital stock k rises 16% causing the vertical-axis intercept a' to increase by 16%. This causes in Figure 10.3 the consumption function to shift upwards in a parallel slope-preserving fashion, as represented by the Blue line. The new equilibrium occurs where the Blue consumption function intersects the 45% line, at the new higher consumption level of $c = w = 0.695$.

The comparative static exercise of Figure 10.3 in the Ramsey World model replicates what looks like a "Keynesian Cross" shift up in equilibrium output through increased government expenditure, as in Chapter 3. But here the "Ramsey Cross" occurs from the most standard Real Business Cycle theory change in parameters, this being an increase in goods sector productivity. Permanent income in the private non-government

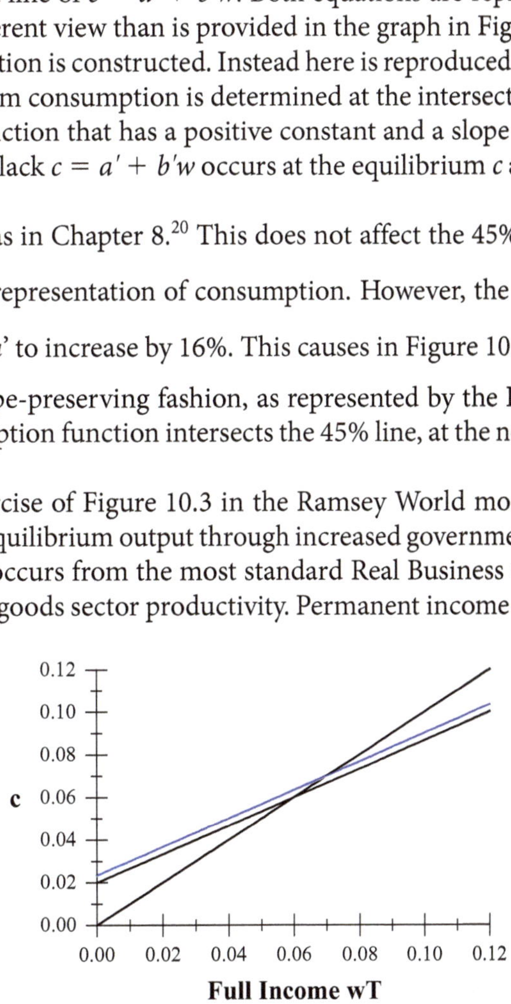

Figure 10.3 Ramsey Consumption Theory and Busines Cycles: Change in A

[19]Mathematical inquirers: Here the example economy is $\gamma = \frac{1}{3}$, $\alpha = 0.5$, $\rho = 0.03$, $T=1$, $\delta_k=0.03$ and $A=0.1134$. Then $k=1.00$, with $c = w = 0.06 = \frac{2}{3}y$ investment i is one-third of output $y=0.09$, and employment is $l=0.5$.

[20]Starting from the baseline value to $A=0.11$.

sector rises as the capital stock k rises because of increased productivity, as opposed to the Keynesian theory of moving to a higher consumption level as a result of the government increasing expenditure. The productivity increase causes a rise in permanent income and consumption by the Friedman permanent income hypothesis that lives in the Ramsey World. This implies that government policy may want to induce private sector productivity to rise.

10.3.5 Spanning Keynesian & Friedman Consumption

In Keynesian parlance the shift upwards in Figure 10.3 might be accomplished by the government. The Keynesian idea of this shift up is that the government turns unused savings during a recession into investment by government spending, for example on infrastructure. But here the shift up is simply due to the goods sector productivity rising as in a business cycle expansion with the result that the Ramsey World capital stock k increases. Private sector investment increases and causes the shift up in the consumption function in Figure 10.3. In the Ramsey World expansion, the shift up in the consumption function includes no change in the " *propensity to consume*" in that b' does not change. What matters is the economy's capital stock. The government does not change this in the Ramsey World but the private sector does.

Figure 10.3 constructs an example Ramsey World version of the Keynesian Cross without government intervention using a parameter involved with the real business cycle expansion theory. Further it remains consistent with the fact that the representative agent in the Ramsey World is consuming a constant fraction out of permanent income as in Friedman's permanent income consumption function. Indeed the slope of the consumption function in the Ramsey Cross diagram, b', is identical to the fraction of permanent income that is consumed in the Ramsey-Friedman World (with $h=1$).

The diagramming of the Ramsey World as a Ramsey Cross simply shows a decomposition of the income into its labor and capital components. The capital component makes up the vertical axis intercept a' in Figure 10.3. The implication is that what determines the share of consumption out of current income of wages is one's leisure preference. And what determines the level of consumption is one's human and physical capital. Policy that has the end result of increasing society's human and physical capital, or its wealth, leads to higher consumption.

Note that the time endowment T can also be increased as in a business cycle expansion of Chapter 8. This would increase the capital stock k, increase a', and shift up the consumption line $c=a'+b'w$. Thus a business cycle can be diagrammed using this "Cross" view within the Ramsey World.

10.3.6 Policy in the Ramsey World

A Keynesian Cross diagram is not a basis for income redistribution in the actual economy. Indeed, we can reproduce a version of it in the Ramsey World that includes no role for government. This leaves the question of what role government policy has in the Ramsey World. We ask this since it is the Ramsey World that can well-describe business cycles and economic growth.

Changing the distribution of income in the Ramsey World, or the *Ramsey-Lucas World* with human capital, would involve most importantly changing the human and physical capital of different targeted groups in society. Government spending financed by taxes has no ability to do this in the Ramsey World simply by transferring income. Rather government spending can mainly alter income distribution in the Ramsey World if it efficaciously eliminates some barrier that exists to the accumulation of human and physical capital. A general statement of efficacious government policy is that it increases consumption-smoothing and wealth by providing social insurance that was otherwise unable to be provided by the private economy.

A direct policy alternative taken by more centrally planned economies than the United States has sometimes been to spend government money financed by taxes so as to try to increase output productivity, or A. This so-called industrial policy has been cited for an explanation of some of Japan's practices in the 1980's and 1990's. It might be claimed that the Soviet Union historically tried to "industrialize" its economy by decreasing consumption goods and subsidizing certain manufacturing goods through government investment aimed at increasing the productivity of manufacturing output.

There is little evidence in favor of such national industrial policies aimed at higher productivity. The US apparently also indirectly engages in a type of productivity enhancement through eventual commercialization of its military and NASA space production and research. But that is more of a consequence rather than the aim of its military and NASA space expenditure.

In order to include income equality in the Ramsey Model, the simple representative agent economy has to be extended to different agents who have different characteristics. Then it becomes a matter always, in the end, of increasing consumption-smoothing and wealth of some agents with a possible trade-off involving the cost of such programs to other agents. This is perfectly consistent with President's Johnson description of the *Great Society*.

10.3.7 Income Transfers Financed Through Taxes

First consider what happens with a simple tax and transfer in the representative agent Ramsey World. This analysis carries over to when there are two different agents, one more productive than the other. When the tax is leveled on the more productive agent and the income transfer is given to the less productive agent, the same qualitative results for the overall economy result as in the following single agent economy. This shows the problem with simple taxing and transferring, a main focus of actual macroeconomic policy across the world.

An employment policy of a tax-financed income transfer, with the tax on either goods purchases or labor income, causes the labor supply to shift back and employment to fall. A perfect insurance system with no moral hazard in contrast would not result in such a shift back in labor supply on a permanent basis. It is the income effect of the transfer that causes the labor to shift back, and this disincentive to work would not exist with a perfect insurance system.

Benefits of all types that are permanent transfers from the government to the consumer have the same effect of shifting back the supply of labor. Thus the broader interpretation of the tax and transfer analysis is that a wide variety of programs within a country's social welfare system can have the disincentive effect on the supply of labor.

A country with a large welfare system such as Sweden does not necessarily have a larger disincentive to work in that it may be more efficient at eliminating moral hazard type problems. Therefore an efficient social welfare system may have less disincentive to work than a less efficient social welfare system even if the efficient one is bigger in terms of the magnitude of the taxes and the transfer. The important aspect of the benefit program is not just its size but its efficiency in terms of decreasing uninsured risk and in inducing less moral hazard.

The effect of a tax on labor income that is used to finance a transfer payment shows how the incentive to work can be decreased. Assuming capital constant for the most simple view of this in a special case of the Ramsey World, Figure 10.4 shows how consumption demand shifts back from the Red curve to the Black curve because of a tax on labor income, when the tax proceeds are redistributed back to the consumer. The tax causes a lower relative price of goods, $\frac{1}{w}$, a lower equilibrium goods demand c^d, and a higher real wage w. The *tax wedge* is created as the difference between the price of output paid by consumers (along the Red

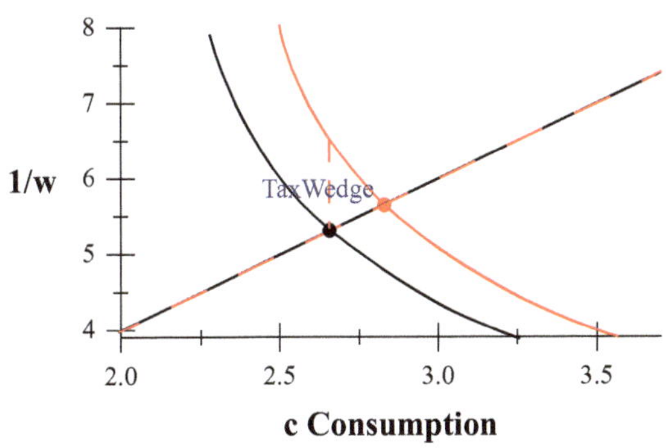

Figure 10.4 Ramsey World Goods Market: 20% Tax on Goods with Income Transfer

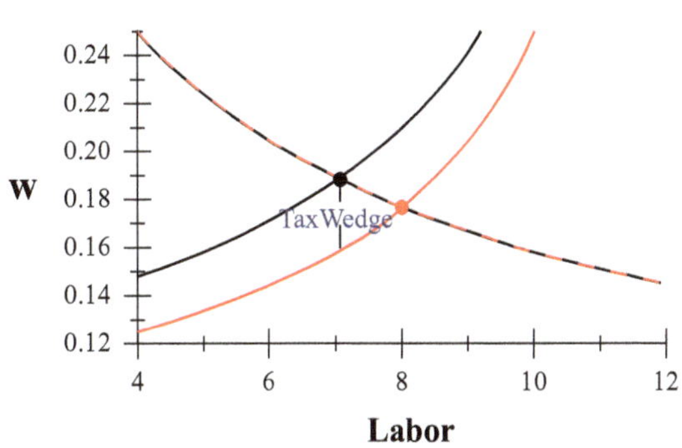

Figure 10.5 Ramsey Labor Market: Goods Tax of 20% with Income Transfer

consumption demand curve) and the price received by suppliers at the intersection of the black supply and demand curves for output. The tax wedge here is the cost of the tax in time per unit of goods.

In the labor market, Figure 10.5 shows how imposing the income tax and giving the tax proceeds back to the consumer causes a shift back in the supply of labor and less employment. The tax wedge in the labor market is the difference between that paid by firms for labor, at the intersection of the Black curves, minus that received by the consumer supplying labor (along the red supply curve). The tax wedge here is the cost of the tax in goods per unit of time.

10.3.8 Ricardian Equivalence, Taxes & Moral Hazard

Government programs have to be paid for with taxes. Ricardian equivalence is a statement of this paradigm. It says that the discounted value of the expected future government tax revenue needs to be sufficient to pay for the expected future stream of government spending.

The government budget constraint says what happens to government spending each period. Either $G>T$ and there is a government budget deficit or $G < T$ and there is a government budget surplus. Deficits are financed by government borrowing. If the Federal Reserve System buys the debt, the government is typically using the inflation tax to finance the deficit. Other debt sold to the public simply adds to the government's total outstanding debt in circulation.

The idea that the borrowing and spending today must inevitably be paid off by taxes in the future is called "*Ricardian equivalence*", after David Ricardo's treatise on *The Principles of Political Economy and Taxation*, with the last (3rd) edition of 1821. It is based on the economy's respect for the government budget constraint every period, now and into the future: anything spent now must be paid for later by some source of government revenue, typically taxes.

The *government wealth constraint* can be computed by adding up of the government budget constraints at each period over time, as discounted to the present with an interest rate. This simple concept can be applied to a variety of financial elements. For example, deficit and debt limits of the European Union can be interpreted as to whether or not a certain deficit to GDP ratio or debt to GDP ratio is sustainable over time in terms of the expected future tax revenue of the government (see Gillman, 2011, Chapter 19).

When government spending each period is high relative to revenue sources, the debt to output ratio will be high. A high ratio can result in a high risk premium on government debt that increases the cost of the debt even by more. To reduce this ratio the government must either lower government spending or raise taxes. The best route is to institute policies that raise economic growth while lowering deficits and debt to GDP ratios.

Another application of Ricardian tax theory is to find the expected increase in output that results from an increase in government spending. If the economy does not increase output after an increase in government spending, the spending program fails to revive an economy. This can happen for example if a government income transfer today is viewed as being paid off by future taxes. The consumer's permanent income may fall by an amount such that it negates the boost in current income from the transfer today.

The uncertain impact of such policy also applies to temporary tax cuts, for which there have been numerous examples in actual economies such as the US. "Non-Ricardian" theories suggest that government spending can be financed by borrowing such that the *"multiplier" of government spending* is large, and the net effect on the economy is positive. In contrast a neoclassical perspective in terms of Ricardian equivalence can suggest a possibly zero "multiplier effect" as opposed to a Keynesian approach that would argue for "non-Ricardian" equivalence and a strong multiplier effect.

Getting out of recessions by a Keynesian type of government borrowing and spending, without raising taxes immediately, is a possibility to help bring about a recovery. Ricardian theory reminds us that this approach can be seen as a short term solution that burdens future generations with its cost. Other approaches use taxation, with historical examples both of increasing tax rates (Hoover's 1932 Tax Revenue Act) and decreasing tax rates (Reagan's 1981 and 1986 Tax Revenue Acts).

Sometimes during an economic contraction the government seeks to lower tax rates as a way to induce long term expansion that can offset the contraction. Decreasing tax rates can increase the equilibrium employment and output growth. But this may be difficult to enact during a recession when the demand for government spending can increase.

For example, the financing of government unemployment systems require raising revenue through taxation. For an unemployment system that has adequate funds to cover payouts during a recession, there is no unfunded government expenditure that needs to be financed. But for large drops in employment, the unemployment insurance fund may be inadequate and additional government spending may be required that needs to be financed by new taxes either now or in the future.

Perhaps more important than cyclical changes in the tax rates as a means of fighting recessions, which is used only infrequently as government policy, is how tax rates affect long run employment, output and economic growth. And so the total level of government spending and taxation to cover the spending becomes an issue of the efficacity of the government policy in a broad sense. Generally, the higher is government taxation as a share of aggregate output, the greater will be the disincentives to productive activity.

Spending has to be financed by some form of taxation. And in practice, there is no such availability of a "perfect" tax that does not distort the incentives of the representative agent. Arguably, all taxation is distortionary. There is a distortion to incentives from either a tax on goods purchases, or on labor income, or on capital income.

Distortions also result from the nature of the spending. With a perfect unemployment system, with no "moral hazard", there is no distortion from the transfer of the unemployment benefits to those unemployed. Moral hazard here is defined as the decrease in the incentive to work that is caused by the government payment and taxpayer receipt of unemployment benefits. When there is no moral hazard, there is no bigger incentive to avoid work.

An unemployment benefit payout ideally covers missing income when not employed, as in a perfect insurance system. But with the income benefits being treated in part by potential workers as a permanent benefit, the transfer itself is also distortionary in that the extra income shifts back the supply of labor. People on a permanent income subsidy are being subsidized to not work, with the resulting "moral hazard" of a higher probability of unemployment for workers in the aggregate economy.

10.3.9 Social Insurance Examples

Monetary Policy as Social Insurance

The US Federal Reserve System has a mandate to conduct monetary policy by controlling inflation and by taking into account employment and economic growth. The 1946 Employment Act directed Congress to promote "maximum employment, production and purchasing power". This is a weak mandate that was enacted for the Fed during the Bretton Woods gold standard era. However it does show the combination of employment and monetary policy through its inclusion of "purchasing power".

After the high inflation period of the Vietnam war, in 1975 Congress adopted Resolution 133 which mandated "the goals of maximum employment, stable prices, and moderate long term interest rates." This was made an amendment to the Federal Reserve Act in 1977. By adding "moderate" long term interest rates, it takes into account the goal of having low long term expected inflation, in that this gets reflected directly into long term interest rates via the Fisher equation of interest (that the nominal interest rate equals the expected inflation rate plus the real interest rate).

With the Vietnam era inflation continuing, in 1978 Congress enacted the Full Employment and Balanced Growth Act (or Humphrey-Hawkins Act) which amended the 1946 Employment Act. This actually specifies in law that our current inflation rate should be zero! How? It says the Fed is to bring down the inflation rate in steps to 3% and then down to zero by 1988, given that other goals can also be met. The other goals are most typically taken to be the maximum employment goal.

Therefore the 1946 Employment Act as amended says the US has an inflation target and that it is zero. This is contrary to stated Fed policy discussion of the Federal Open Market Committee as stated in the minutes of its meetings. There a 2% inflation target is typically mentioned. The idea apparently seems to be that we can help achieve the employment goal by a permanent inflation tax.

The operation of the Fed is thereby an implicit type of social insurance scheme of balancing employment with price stability. Many argue that some inflation is good for the economy, with the corresponding belief that this is sufficient to permanently try to have inflation at 2%. Others argue that any inflation acts as a tax that lowers long term growth and employment.

The Act also now advocates as a goal "steady economy growth", as Senator Hubert Humphrey remarked in Congressional Record "Remarks" upon the signing of the legislation. Higher inflation apparently brings lower economic growth. Debate exists on whether this is true for low rates of inflation. Believing that some inflation is good for growth, the Fed then is also weighing economic growth prospects against the detractions of paying an inflation tax.[21]

The balancing of unemployment through the conduct of monetary policy remains an issue of considerable debate. If the Fed systematically can stimulate output through accelerating the money supply growth rate, then it is engaged it a type of business cycle means of social insurance. If however such policy causes distortions to capital markets through "liquidity effects", then the social insurance may come with a certain degree of moral hazard in that it can make the possibility of a financial market crash more likely in the future.

Macroprudential Policy

Bank insurance is provided by the Federal Deposit Insurance Corporation, under the Federal Reserve System supervision as part of "Macroprudential" policy. Risk-based deposit premiums are charged for banks that are members of the FDIC in return for the guarantee of a certain specified dollar amount of each depositor's funds in the bank. The risk-based premiums have only been used since 2006; before that the premiums were not based on the riskiness of the bank.

Deposit insurance premiums were linked to the riskiness of the asset structure of the bank in order to avoid "moral hazard" in the insurance scheme. Here this would mean that the banks invest in a riskier portfolio of loans because they know depositors will be insured no matter how great is the risk of default by the bank. If a bank does take on additional risk because of the non-risk based insurance, then the bank increases the probability of a bank insolvency. This is the meaning of moral hazard in the bank sector: that deposit insurance increases the overall riskiness of the sector because the price of the insurance does not take into account the risk of each bank.

Bank crises can arise for a variety of reasons, including industry specific risk but more likely from aggregate risk components. For example the bank crisis of 2007–2009 came about after huge debt was undertaken in the US during wartime activity on two fronts in Iraq and Afghanistan. Debt acceleration poses the threat of higher future taxes that generally cause lower growth and so lower asset prices. This can cause asset prices to fall.

An unexpected asset price fall can lead to a bank crisis if it includes the prices of assets that serve as collateral for loans. In 2007–2009, housing prices fell after rising continuously for a long period of time. When interest rates rose as well, and so loan fees increased, consumers who found the new loan repayments too high could not sell the house and pay back the debt since the house prices fell. This caused bankruptcy and bank failure since many such loans were spread across banks all across the US and Europe.

Both the 1930s and the 2007–2009 crises were characterized by a lack of insurance against so-called aggregate risk arising from the banking sector. The lack of effective insurance in the banking industry in effect can be interpreted as causing a large drop in bank productivity (see the Appendix to Chapter 8). The difference in the response to the crises was that the governments acted to supply insurance in banking only in 1933 for the US, through the establishment of the Federal Deposit Insurance Corporation, while international governments acted much more quickly in the 2007–2009 crisis, through a variety of measures designed to insure the liabilities of banks, ex post after the crisis occurred. The ad hoc insurance supplied during the modern crisis enabled the recession to be much less pronounced than the 1930s depression, but perhaps just as prolonged.

The use of *ad hoc* bank insurance after the fact results in an inefficient banking insurance system. Such insurance, after the 2008 US bank panic, covered all types of financial intermediation, from commercial banking to investment banking, to insurance (the company AIG was rescued by US government action) to car financing in the form of automobile company aid from governments, especially in the US, and the government financing of new car purchases through a subsidization of old car "scrapage" schemes internationally. But because the initial shock to the investment banking system was not insured by the normal bank insurance

[21]Gillman et al. (2004) find that inflation decreases economic growth even at low levels of inflation; debate on this still continues; see Max Gillman & Mark N. Harris & László Mátyás, 2004. "Inflation and growth: Explaining a negative effect," Empirical Economics, vol. 29(1), pages 149–167, January.

elements already in place, since investment banks are not members of the FDIC, the shock ended up acting as aggregate risk that was uninsured.

Other Social Insurance Policy Examples

Most government policy can be viewed as social insurance: police, military and laws for insurance against property and wealth theft or loss. Federal disaster insurance, bank insurance, and health insurance (Medicare) are clear cases. Other important State-based programs are State-based unemployment insurance, insurance company insurance funds that exist in all fifty US States, and State-based health insurance (Medicaid).

All government expenditure might be put in terms of social insurance. Federally funded roads, ports, rail, air and other transportation infrastructure supplement States and public-private projects that may prove unable to supply the cycles of demand for normal service and for emergency times.[22] Education, research and training support by local, state and federal government helps insure progress in the market for human capital.

Low income support programs are all a form of insurance for the event that human capital and work opportunities are sufficiently low in terms of the income stream that results. They are not designed as permanent transfers, although they inefficiently may act in that fashion. Fiscal and monetary policy of government is designed to try to smooth out income streams of citizens across time. Such an ultimate objective of social insurance policy is consistent with consumption smoothing.

10.4 Application: FDIC Post-2010 Dodd-Frank

The FDIC is an "independent" US government agency established by the Banking Act of 1933 that manages what is now called the Deposit Insurance Fund (DIF). It is run by a Board of five Governors selected by the US President, and approved by the Senate, with no more than 3 from one political party. For example one of these directors is currently Thomas M. Hoenig, an Economics PhD and former head of the Federal Reserve Bank of Kansas City.

The FDIC is designed to insure stability of that part of the financial system which it overseas. It pays back depositors on insured deposits, for failed banks that are members of the FDIC, in amounts limited to be up to $250,000 across an array of different bank type funds. Banks have to be members of the FDIC and these banks then pay a *deposit insurance premium* per unit of deposit covered.

The idea is that the expected payouts for insured deposits of failed banks by the FDIC equal the expected premium payments from member banks into the FDIC. Making the deposit insurance system have a zero expected profit could be said to be the aim of such a government run insurance system. However this is a difficult task in that it requires forming reasonable expectations about future bank failures.

How much each bank pays for deposit insurance has changed over time. It depends first on each bank's "assessment base". This base has changed from being the amount of deposits of the banks to becoming instead the amount of net liabilities. Then an "*assessment rate*" is charged for each member bank, depending on the FDIC defined risk-class into which each bank the FDIC assigns them.

In particular the 2010 Dodd-Frank banking act changed the terms of the payment that each bank makes. As stated in this FDIC online website,

> "From the beginning of the FDIC until 2010, a bank's assessment base was about equal to its total domestic deposits. As required by the Dodd-Frank Act, however, the FDIC amended its regulations effective April 2011 to define a bank's assessment base as its average consolidated total assets minus its average tangible equity."[23]

The assets net of equity are equal to a bank's net liabilities. So the assessment base is exactly this, the net liabilities of the bank. This is the revision to the previous historical basis of just the amount of insured

---

[22]Part of the motivation of the US national highway scheme authorized in the 1950's by President Eisenhower was a means of facile emergency military mobilization; this system is called the Dwight D. Eisenhower National System of Interstate and Defense Highways.
[23]Consider that the FDIC website is an excellent source of the various details, and this quote is from one of their many online pages: https://www.fdic.gov/deposit/insurance/.

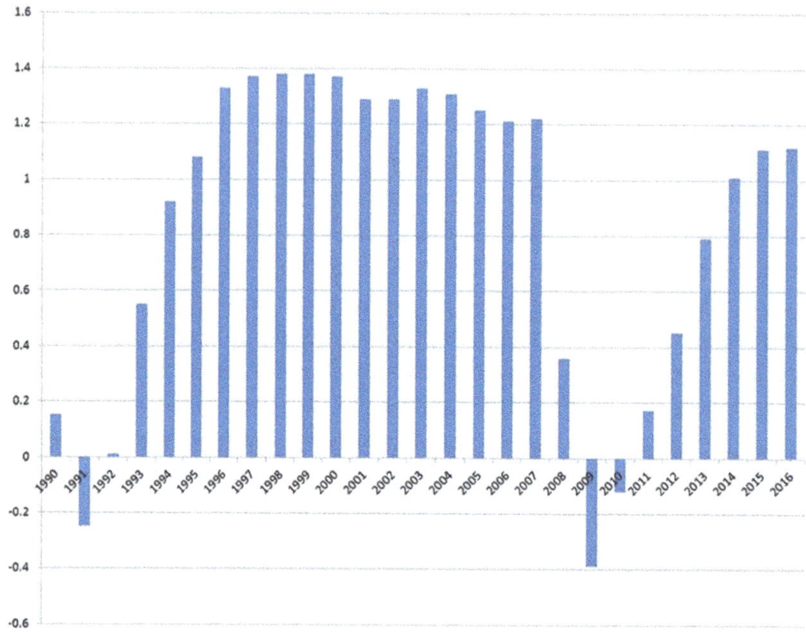

Figure 10.6 FDIC Ratio of Reserves to Insured Deposits, 1990 to 2016 (year to date, August), in percent

deposits. Given this net liability assessment base, then different assessment rates apply. This makes sense in that any set of net liabilities can be more or less risky than another, and so should pay an insurance premium that rises with the riskiness of what is being insured.

Current reserves in the FDIC *Deposit Insurance Fund* (DIF) are around 1.15 but scheduled to rise to 1.35 by 2020 according to new rules now finalized as a result of the Dodd-Frank Act:

> "Congress in the Dodd-Frank Wall Street Reform and Consumer Protection Act increased the minimum for the DIF reserve ratio, the ratio of the amount in the fund to insured deposits, from 1.15 percent to 1.35 percent and required that the ratio reach that level by September 30, 2020. Further, the Dodd-Frank Act also made banks with $10 billion or more in total assets responsible for the increase from 1.15 percent to 1.35 percent."[24]

Figure 10.6 shows the ratio of reserves in the fund to insured deposits historically on an annual basis since 1990, using FDIC's data. The ratio has risen back up to its targeted range after falling during the 2008 US bank crash.

10.4.1 Auto Insurance versus Bank Insurance

For example, a driver of a $15,000 car, would have the assessment base be the $15000 that is insured and lower premiums the safer the individual's driving history appears to be. This would be consistent with the FDIC practice of using the deposits insured as the assessment basis, and the nature of the bank's riskiness within the net liabilities as the basis of the assessment rate.

But the 2010 US banking act changed the FDIC to require that instead it directly use the net liabilities as the assessment base, since these vary depending upon the size and riskiness of the bank. And then further examining the bank in terms of the nature of the net liabilities, it determines the assessment rate, or the

[24]From official FDIC "Press Releases": "FDIC Board Adopts Final Rule to Increase Deposit Insurance Fund to Statutorily Required Level;" March 15, 2016. At: https://www.fdic.gov/news/news/press/2016/pr16021.html

premium per unit of deposits that the bank must pay, which can therefore differ across each and every FDIC insured bank.

Small banks are classified as being either Grade A, B, or C, and either "Well Capitalized", "Adequately Capitalized" or "Under Capitalized", with this matrix ending with a bank rated between 1 and 4 in its risk-classification, with 1 the best and 4 the worse. The assessment rate then is set for each classification, and is lowest for "1" banks, and highest for "4" banks. Large banks are individually analyzed using a risk scorecard and their assessment rate is then set as a result of their assigned "score". The assessment rates vary from 2.5 to 45 basis points for each dollar of their "assessment base"; these rates are multiplied by their "base" of net liabilities to give the annual deposit insurance premium that each bank must pay.

In its operating the fund, the FDIC also determines a Designated Reserve Ratio (DDR) for the system, different from the DIF reserve ratio. This DDR is simply the total amount collected in the Deposit Insurance Fund, equivalent to the insurance premiums collected from banks, divided by the total amount of insured deposits of the FDIC member banks. Since the 2010 banking act, the FDIC has set this DDR rate at 2%. This means that the FDIC has on-hand, in its Deposit Insurance Fund, 2% of the amount of total deposits insured. They reached this 2% figure by determining that since 1935 this DDR ratio was at most 2% (around 1940), and post-WWII at levels has been around 1.2 to 1.5% during non-crisis times.[25] So setting it at its highest historical peak since 1935 seems to be the FDIC way of insuring that the fund has sufficient reserves.

10.4.2 Bagehot and More Equity for Stability?

Walter Bagehot in his 1873 book *Lombard Street: A Description of the Money Market* argues that capital reserves need only be kept in the central bank, at some minimum ratio of the liabilities of the total banking system. Bagehot argued that having the Bank of England hold the reserves for the system allowed individual banks to hold minimal to no reserves except for everyday cash demands, and as a result made London the financial center of the world. With banks holding close to no reserves, Bagehot said the British system was the most efficient and so dominated the financial markets. Today, now on a fiat money standard (unbacked currency) rather than the gold system, the FDIC performs a related reserve task in today's US financial markets. But, alarmingly, this reserve insurance fund is only for FDIC member banks. It excludes huge portions of the financial intermediation system of *"non-bank" banks* and other financial intermediaries.

In a talk in May 2016, Thomas Hoenig seemingly argued against the Bagehot Lombard Street argument of minimal reserves for each individual bank. Hoenig stated "I will cite research that shows the banking industry and the economy do better in the long run with more---not less---equity capital."[26] Now an important qualification is that the equity capital of a bank is its net worth. This is not the same as reserves held by the bank or banking system. The reserves held by the banking system are each bank's own reserves plus the FDIC Deposit Insurance Fund's quantity of dollars.

It may well be that banks have a higher net worth (equity capital) when the economy is strong and growing. That makes sense, but the causality can certainly be from the strong economy to a high net worth for a bank. Possibly the causality works the other way as well. Banks will always leverage up their net worth by having high ratios of liabilities to net worth, because in this way they make more profit. The degree and riskiness of the leveraging ultimately determines the riskiness of the financial intermediation system. And an efficient reserve system minimizes the lost opportunity for economic growth from unnecessary reserves and regulations.

[25]See "Toward a Long-Term Strategy for Deposit Insurance Fund Management", FDIC Quarterly, 2010, 4(4): 29–39.

[26]"A Capital Conflict"—Remarks by FDIC Vice Chairman Hoenig to the National Association for Business Economics (NABE) and the Organization for Economic Cooperation and Development (OECD) Global Economic Symposium, Paris, France, May 23, 2016. https://www.fdic.gov/news/news/speeches/spmay2316.html

10.4.3 Investment Banks Still Outside FDIC

According to the FDIC website, on "What Is Not Insured?":[27]

> "Increasingly, institutions are also offering consumers a broad array of investment products that are not deposits, such as mutual funds, annuities, life insurance policies, stocks and bonds. Unlike the traditional checking or savings account, however, these non-deposit investment products are not insured by the FDIC."

The mutual funds that triggered the Great Recession are still uninsured by the FDIC. Yet economists typically consider these funds as part of the money supply just like FDIC demand deposits. Nicolini and Lucas (2015) include these mutual funds in their definition of the money supply, when finding evidence in support for a stable US demand for real money.[28]

When there was a "run", or bank panic, on the mutual fund deposits at investment banks during 2008, the liquidity in the finance system was insufficient. Traditionally famous investment banks failed such as the 85 year-old Bear Sterns on March 16th, 2008. As the Wall Street Journal put it in their 2009 article headlined "Inside the Fall of Bear Stearns": "In 72 nail-biting hours, an investment bank turned from healthy to nearly insolvent".[29]

There were also insurance companies that were bailed out by the Fed such as AIG. AIG was the world's largest insurance company at the time. In September 2008, the US Treasury summarizes that all of the following occurred:[30]

1. Fannie Mae/Freddie Mac conservatorship
2. Lehman Brothers bankruptcy
3. AIG stabilization effort

A Wall Street Journal headline on September 16th, 2008 was: "U.S. to Take Over AIG in $85 Billion Bailout; Central Banks Inject Cash as Credit Dries Up: Emergency Loan Effectively Gives Government Control of Insurer; Historic Move Would Cap 10 Days That Reshaped U.S. Finance"[31]

The article continues:

> "the Fed will lend up to $85 billion to AIG, and the U.S. government will effectively get a 79.9% equity stake in the insurer in the form of warrants called equity participation notes."

Insurance schemes for insurance companies actually exist in all 50 US states. These are similar to the federal FDIC insurance fund except they vary in nature state by state, across the entire US. These funds were not brought within the FDIC after the financial crisis despite the Fed actively giving money to keep the insurance market from collapsing in the wake of an AIG collapse.

Pensions have a US government sponsored insurance fund that is also not part of the FDIC, or of any comprehensive financial intermediary industry government deposit insurance fund. The Pension Benefit Guaranty Corporation (PBGC) is a US agency that [32]

> "protects the retirement incomes of more than 40 million American workers in nearly 24,000 private-sector defined benefit pension plans. A defined benefit plan provides a specified monthly benefit at retirement, often based on a combination of salary and years of service. PBGC was created by the Employee Retirement Income Security Act of 1974 to encourage the continuation and maintenance of private-sector defined

---

[27]Found at https://www.fdic.gov/consumers/consumer/information/fdiciorn.html

[28]Lucas and Nicolini, 2015. "On the stability of money demand," Journal of Monetary Economics, 73(C): 48–65.

[29]See http://www.wsj.com/articles/SB124182740622102431

[30]www.treasury.gov/resource-center/data-chart-center/Documents/20120413_FinancialCrisisResponse.pdf

[31]http://www.wsj.com/articles/SB122156561931242905

[32]http://www.pbgc.gov/about/who-we-are.html

> benefit pension plans, provide timely and uninterrupted payment of pension benefits, and keep pension insurance premiums at a minimum."

Yet this remains a separate system subject to systemic failure during economic crises. As Franzen (2010) puts it in an OECD working paper, pensions use the same risk management tools as the rest of the financial intermediary sector, yet their risk still may not be adequately gauged.

> "Risk management has stayed at the above-cited fore-front of the pension industry. The perfect pension storm [of 2008] set the stage for the risk management revolution to reach the doorsteps of pension funds. Modern risk management tools analogous to those which are used in other sectors of the financial industry such as securities firms and banks are increasingly applied by pension funds. Nowadays, pension funds in many jurisdictions calculate Value-at-Risk (VaR), apply risk budgeting concepts and analyse fat tails. Asset-Liability-Management (ALM) is routinely applied as strategic risk management tool, albeit the quality of the models and the rigour in its application still vary. But it is questionable if the risk management approaches now being applied by Defined Benefit [annuities] pension funds are in all cases well suited to their needs. More fundamentally, the perception of risk appears to be currently in a state of flux. Unlike securities firms, banks or insurance companies, there is no consensus between pension funds, their sponsors, regulators and accountants on the significance of the different risk factors facing pension funds. "

Financial intermediaries that administer and thereby privately ensure pension fund solvency, such as Prudential Financial, Inc. and PGBGC, were not brought into the FDIC after the 2008 crisis. Thus the FDIC still only insures commercial banks, and not the rest of the financial intermediation industry, specifically excluding: Investment banks, Insurance companies, and Pension companies. All of these could be brought within an efficient deposit insurance system for the entire financial intermediation industry with premiums per deposit based on the assessed risk of the funds being insured.

10.4.4 FDIC Across All Financial Intermediaries

One answer to the global *"contagion" risk* of the international financial system is to devise a FDIC type institution to insure all of the financial intermediaries both within the US and including all international financial industry components that want to participate. Then each bank and "non-bank" bank of each country could choose to be a member of the world deposit insurance system. And a good degree of financial stability would be established across the global financial sector with well-calculated risk-based premiums.

As described in Gillman (2009), a type of International Deposit Fund (IDF) could be established and possibly run by an institution such as the International Monetary Fund (IMF) or other such group such as the Bank for International Settlements. "The central component of such an international deposit insurance system is that banks would have the incentive fully to reveal information on the nature of the structure of their assets and liabilities. This would enable the IMF-IDF to give them the lowest possible deposit insurance premium for their balance sheet structure. Uncertainty of what is really on the balance sheets of a bank, due to incomplete disclosure, would require the IMF-IDF to charge a higher deposit premium."[33]

The European Union already is putting in place an FDIC type risk-based bank deposit insurance system on an international basis. According to the EU, "As a further step to a fully-fledged Banking Union, in November 2015, the [EU] Commission put forward a proposal for a European Deposit Insurance Scheme (EDIS), which would provide a stronger and more uniform degree of insurance cover for all retail depositors in the banking union."[34]. The EDIS would insure deposits up to 100,000 Euro for EU member banks. Importantly, the EDIS would also allow membership by non-EU banks in non-EU countries that choose to join the insurance scheme. This would be run by the Single Supervisory Mechanism (SSM), now already established by the EU, and by its already-established Single Resolution Mechanism for banks. The EU sets

[33]Gillman, Max, 2009, "International Deposit Insurance", Economic Affairs, 29(3), p.103.

[34]http://ec.europa.eu/finance/general-policy/banking-union/index_en.htm

out that the European Central Bank would be the "central prudential supervisor" of the SSM and the EDIS member banks.[35]

The lack of an internationally based, efficient, risk-based premium deposit insurance system is inducing banks to create their own self-insurance in what could create a significantly less efficient international financial system. The 2010 Dodd-Frank legislation requires major banks to create "living wills" under which the companies may keep operating even in the face of insolvency of the parent holding companies. This requirement is being met by effected banks proposing to create an additional subsidiary to which they could transfer funds in times of crisis and avoid their capital being depleted by international claims to their assets. As Karen Petrou is quoted about "living wills":[36]

> "The best and most transparent way to deal with this would be an international agreement among regulators . . . Regulators can't agree. Each...wants to protect the interests and financial system of their home country . . . We're just lurching from one idea to the next, creating a jerry-built system of financial regulation".

Creating more layers of self-insurance continues to move away from Bagehot's conclusions as to why the British financial system was leading the world in the late 1800's: because each bank kept minimal reserves and basically all reserves for the system were held by the Bank of England. Now FDIC risk-based premiums can serve this role if spread to the whole international financial intermediation system in an efficient way, while stopping the ad hoc self-insurance process. This Bagehot-inspired approach could create an efficient macroprudential system for the global finance network.

10.5 Appendix: Taxes, Public Goods, Insurance

The theory of government expenditure is separated traditionally from the theory of government finance of its expenditure. The optimal theory of taxation traditionally is called *"public finance" theory* and it dates back to Frank Ramsey's (1927) theory of balancing out the marginal distortions of different sources of taxation. Different items that can be taxed, such as personal income, corporate income, and sales of goods, have different price elasticities of demand.[37]

As the price of income and goods go up due to tax increases, consumers avoid the tax increase by substituting towards a different sources of income or different goods not subject to the tax increase. The more substitution induced by the tax increase, the greater is the economic distortion of the tax. The distortion is more when the substitution induced by the tax is more, because the more avoidance that the tax induces, the greater is the divergence of the reallocation of resources from its equilibrium amount before the tax increase.

The optimal financing then involves making the marginal *"deadweight loss" triangle* the same at every margin upon which taxes are imposed. This balances out the marginal distortion caused by the system of taxes, so that each dollar of taxes raised has the same marginal distortion regardless of source. This is known as the Ramsey system of optimal taxation used by a government to finance expenditure.

An example is the typically high tax on cigarettes and alcohol and gasoline. Each of these has a relatively low elasticity of demand, so that little substitution takes place in the face of a tax, and high taxes then induce a relatively low marginal distortion. Second, these items are associated with public "bads". Public "bads" are the opposite, perhaps, of public goods.

Public bads are goods that cause negative externalities to be imposed upon others when they are consumed. Cigarettes cause cancer, second-hand smoke cancer, and stresses to the health care system that could be avoided if cigarettes were not smoked. Alcohol causes externalities such as road deaths to innocent people, and stresses on the health care system. Gasoline causes pollution and stresses to the climate's disposal of carbon dioxide.

---

[35]For an example of optimal social insurance with full information revelation by those insured: See Golosov, Mikhail, and Luigi Iovino, 2014, "Social Insurance, Information Revelation, and Lack of Commitment", NBER Working Paper No. 20633; October.

[36]John Carney, "Big US Banks Plan to Bail Themselves Out", Wall Street Journal, 13 October 2016; pp. C1–C2.

[37]Ramsey, Frank. "A Contribution to the Theory of Taxation." Economic Journal. 37, March 1927: 47–61. See also Mulligan, 2004 at http://home.uchicago.edu/~cbm4/econ260/E203rams.pdf

These bads are associated with costs, or "externalities", to those not consuming directly them. Public goods present a contrast. "*Public goods*" are defined most famously by Samuelson in 1954 as goods that are produced and that are consumed jointly in some fashion by a host of consumers.[38] The theory of government expenditure is not terribly far advanced from Samuelson's original description. Distinctions are made between government consumption goods and government investment goods, but the theory is simply that public goods provide benefits to a host of households. Typical examples given are parks, efficient transportation systems, and government low income "transfers".

However, efficient government provided insurance given incomplete information of individual behavior has become increasingly important in public discourse as the goal government spending programs. Is welfare aid for food stamps, low income housing, and low income health insurance (Medicaid) expenditure on a public goods or expenditure on social insurance programs? What public good is there that is not subject to consumption by only a certain special set of consumers? Parks are only good for those who visit them. And many charge admission now. But clearly parks typically present positive externalities in terms of preserving animal and plant species, and in decreasing stress of the population for example, in the event that bad times occur.

The pricing of public goods is a key question. Such pricing needs to include the "*marginal social cost*" as well as the "*marginal private cost*". The marginal social cost net of marginal private cost is positive if consumption of the good includes a negative externality that imposes cost on others. The marginal social cost net of marginal private cost is negative if consumption of the good includes a positive *externality* that decreases the cost of goods to others.

Goods can be priced accurately by including both private and social cost. For example a private property price can include the benefit of being next to a public park. If goods are priced accurately in this broad sense, then public goods can be supplied efficiently.

It may be that all public goods can be viewed in terms of providing insurance in some fashion. If so, then like public goods the pricing of such social insurance becomes key to its efficient provision. For example, parks provide some degree of insurance also to future generations, which current generations value, in terms of ecosystem survival and all of the unknown benefits that such survival entails.

The most well-known social cost measure in macroeconomic policy discussion recently is "*aggregate risk*". The term aggregate risk comes mainly from finance theory in which some business cycle risk to a firm's profit can be eliminated by diversifying the portfolio of shares being held (eliminating firm-specific idiosyncratic risk), but the rest of the risk to asset markets from the business cycle cannot be eliminated. This is an example of aggregate risk associated with asset prices and the business cycle.

During the Great Recession, the aggregate risk imposed by the banking system's potential failure became a key focus of policy discussion. In particular, a financial system failure puts at risk the normal intermediation of savings to investment. Thus optimal bank insurance that provides coverage of systematic risk that banks individually add to the total systematic risk of the bank systems has been a focus. The US Fed has even picked out certain US banks as "systematically important" and levied greater capital requirements upon them, in order to somehow compensate for the systemic risk that large banks individually add.

In banking, greater capital restrictions have not occurred as part of a systematic optimal insurance system for the financial sector. Rather they have been a piecemeal approach engendered by the 2010 "Dodd--Frank Wall Street Reform and Consumer Protection Act". The efficiencies of the FDIC system's approach of risk-based premiums could be extended to try to include the systematic risk induced by any one bank, through a higher premium for deposit insurance.

An efficient risk-based premium system could be extended across the entire financial intermediation system, going beyond commercial and retail banks to investment banks, insurance companies and pension funds. Price based solutions that build the aggregate riskiness into premiums paid into a deposit insurance fund can efficiently insure failed financial intermediaries. Rather than this approach, instead "quantity restrictions" on financial intermediaries through higher reserve requirements has been followed in an "ad hoc", or piecemeal, fashion. Along with greater quantity restrictions on banking, has come the problem

[38]Paul A. Samuelson, 1954, "The Pure Theory of Public Expenditure", The Review of Economics and Statistics, 36 (4, Nov.): 87–389.

of an unending subsidization of the banking sector during what is known as the Great Recession that may still be enveloping the world economy today, as set out in the next Chapter 11.

10.6 Summary

The chapter reviews the beginning of "social welfare" systems in the US and UK. It then provides the theory of moral hazard, which is when a policy causes an increase of the probability of the "bad state" occurring. It provides examples of moral hazard in historic US policy.

Then the chapter examines the consumption functions that underlie the Keynesian Cross theory of Chapter 3. It compares this to the Ramsey World consumption function of Chapters 8 and 9. A "Cross" actually emerges in the Ramsey World, whereby the shift up in the consumption line comes from the normal increases in productivity and in time endowment, the components used to explain business cycles and growth in Chapters 8 and 9.

The Keynesian consumption function suggests that income inequality might be aided by simple transfers from high to low income citizens. The Ramsey World instead makes the task improving the permanent income stream of the consumer. Here this happens for example through economic growth that raises the capital stock including human capital.

Social insurance policies outside the realm of "fiscal policy" are also discussed, especially banking insurance. An Application is made to detail the US banking insurance system and the FDIC. And an Appendix discusses the broad issues of public goods, externalities and social insurance, and aggregate risk.

10.7 Glossary

ad hoc: a change which is made extemporaneously, or without being part of an internally consistent plan, or that is done just to address a single issue without considering the full; its Latin meaning is "to this" or "for this".

aggregate risk: a risk that affects the entire economy rather than just a set of firms or consumers; by nature it is hard to insure against using private markets alone; example: a business cycle.

consumption smoothing over time: using the expected income stream over the full horizon to choose consumption each period so that it is for example smoothly growing or constant each period; may require borrowing and saving.

deadweight loss triangle: the lost consumer surplus and producer surplus resulting from a tax or regulation that forces the competitive equilibrium price to a different level.

Deposit Insurance Fund (DIF): a collection of payments kept in a well-defined location to be used in the event that an insured member of the fund undergoes any sort of bankruptcy or insolvency that makes payment of the owed deposits infeasible; the US DIF is run by the FDIC to pay depositors of insured banks should the bank become insolvent or otherwise unable to meet obligations.

deposit insurance premium: the fee charged by the deposit insurance regulatory agency, or by the private group of firms in the case of private deposit insurance (called Clearinghouses for banks before the Fed started in 1914); the aim is to make the sum of the payments into the fund equal to the expected payments out of the fund over time.

externality: an effect on the marginal benefit or marginal cost of consuming any good that is not built into the price paid for the good; can be positive, or an amenity, or negative such as congestion or pollution; typically exists only because of a lack of perfectly defined property rights.

government regulation: any code of the legal system that acts to restrict or otherwise control aspects of the economy, or society more broadly; typically created by executive bodies of federal state and local governments such as Internal Revenue Service guidance, or local zoning ordinances; the US Congress does not pass legislation that is regulation per se, but it can pass legislation that directs a government agency to create codes of a specific interest to the Congress.

government wealth constraint: the expected discounted future revenue stream of the government equals its expected discounted future expenditure stream.

Great Society: a vision of programs put forth by President Lyndon B. Johnson in the 1960's to provide a fuller support system for those being kept out of full engagement with the market economy and/or social system of the US that was emerging at the time.

incentive compatible: contracts, including government policy that affects its citizens, that induces the affected people to act in a way that enables the contract, or policy, to be implemented as was designed; in contrast, a lack of incentive compatibility induces behavior that defeats the stated purpose of the contract.

income tax base: the aggregate amount of income upon which any given income tax falls; for example, a tax base can be larger if the tax rate is lower because people hide their income to a lesser degree and instead more fully declare the amount of income to be subject to the tax.

Keynesian consumption function: the aggregate consumption rises as aggregate income rises, but consumption rises at a decreasing rate; an implication is that income transfers to low income people cause a greater increase in consumption than do income transfers to high income people.

libertarian: a political philosophy based on free market economies.

marginal private cost: the cost of one additional unit to the consumer buying the product; may not include the full social cost at the margin.

moral hazard: an unintended consequence of a policy or action that induces people to undertake behavior that makes such policy or action inefficient; an increase in the probability of the bad state of nature occurring for any given policy or action; lack of moral hazard for example means the government unemployment benefits do not induce more people to stay or become unemployed.

multiplier of government spending: the amount of increased national output divided by the magnitude of the increased government spending; this is argued to be positive in Keynesian economics, but can be negative in Neoclassical economics.

non-bank banks: financial intermediaries that take on activities typically performed by commercial or retail banks, such as collecting deposits; investment banks and credit unions made up a big proportion of non-bank banks after the financial sector deregulation in the 1980's eliminated the interest ceiling on deposit accounts; not members of the FDIC and so not covered by FDIC insurance.

permanent income hypothesis: consumption follows the expected permanent stream of income coming from the expected discounted future wealth of human and physical and financial capital, rather than just following current income.

permanent income hypothesis of consumption: the hypothesis of consumption as a fraction of expected wealth, or that consumption depends on the present value of expected future income.

propensity to consume: the fraction of current income that is consumed; can be expressed as a marginal propensity such that it is the increase in consumption from an increase in income as that increase in income gets arbitrarily small as in a mathematical derivative.

public finance theory: a body of economy analysis that is based originally in the work of Frank Ramsey saying that the optimal distribution of tax rates equates the marginal distortion of the tax rate across the different sources of taxation; updated with new perspectives found in the Diamond-Mirrlees theories that are based on individualization of tax rates.

Public goods: a good that is consumed by any arbitrary group of consumers, either for free or at a cost that does not reflect the actual price.

Ramsey-Lucas World: an economy with optimization of utility subject to a goods production sector as well as a human capital investment sector such that the growth rate of the economy is endogenous to the decisions made by the representative agent.

Ricardian equivalence: the government respects its budget constraint that the expected present discounted value of expenditures equals the expected present discounted value of revenue; interpreted to imply that consumers understand for example that current deficit spending financed by government borrowing must be paid back to future taxes that increase by an equivalent amount in present value terms.

socialism: the political philosophy of using government taxes and expenditure to redistribute income.

tax wedge: the difference between the after-tax price received by suppliers and the tax-inclusive price paid by demanders; typically equal to the explicit tax rate or an imputed rate.

unemployment insurance program: a government, or other group, for example a union, system of paying income to those who become unemployed; sometimes payments made out to members corresponding to what payments have been paid in by those members.

10.8 Questions

1. How did the modern "welfare state" begin in the United Kingdom?
2. How did the modern "welfare state" begin in the United States?
3. Describe how moral hazard can arise in the implementation of programs designed to supply a "social security net" to low income households.
4. How does the Keynesian consumption function imply that income redistribution may be beneficial?

5. How can an analogue to the Keynesian Cross be constructed in the Ramsey World?
6. What shifts the consumption function in the Ramsey World analogue of the Keynesian Cross diagram?
7. How does the Ramsey consumption function imply that the effect of income redistribution depends on how the program for this is run?
8. Explain how "Ricardian equivalence" implies limits on the effects of government redistributions of income.
9. In what sense are certain examples of government policy in effect the same as social insurance schemes?
10. How does the FDIC work to insure against bank runs and panics? What changes to the FDIC policy resulted from 2010 Dodd-Frank legislation?
11. How could an international financial intermediary insurance system be set up so as to contain or limit global financial crises?
12. What is the relation among public goods, externalities, and social insurance?
13. Complete the Federal Reserve Bank of St. Louis EconLowdown Course Module "Government Budgets".
14. Complete the Federal Reserve Bank of St. Louis EconLowdown Course Module "Fiscal Policy".

11 Great Recession & Lost Decade

The period of 2008 to 2009 marks the official National Bureau of Economic Research (NBER) designation of the time during which the US economy was in recession. However this period and the subsequent years are typically called the "Great Recession". The reason is that the US in 2008 entered a near decade of low growth, low employment relative to the population, and a high degree of US federal participation in banking and financial markets not seen since the Great Depression of the 1930's. Many aspects of the Great Recession are consistent with a "*lost decade*", as also happened after the 1929 stock market crash of the Great Depression.

This chapter will conclude the book by applying some basic principles to explain the Great Recession experience. Facts, tools and analysis developed throughout the book are employed in this task. There are alternative explanations and many debates about the subject material herein contained. References to this debate are offered throughout.

11.1 Who Made it Happen

11.1.1 Fed Regulation of Capital Markets: 2001 to 2006

The terrorist attacks on New York in 2001 induced the Federal Reserve System to flood the capital markets with loans on September 12, 2001, by an amount equal to $45.6 billion, as compared to $0.19 billion on September 5th the week before.[1] These emergency loans were just a fraction of the additional open market operations conducted by the Federal Reserve Bank of New York's trading desk. On September 12th the Fed increased the monetary base by $38 billion, on September 13th, by another $70 billion, and on September 14th by another $81 billion (these were done with "repurchase agreements, or as "repos").

Alan Greenspan was Governor of the Federal Reserve System. The Federal Funds interest rate (FFR) had been falling from 6.5 percent in December 2000 to 3.5 percent on September 12th, 2001. This occurred as stock market asset values fell: for example, the Russell 3000 stock index went from 3127 at the end of August, 2000, down to 2361 at the end of August, 2001, a near 25 percent decline in asset values. The interest rate drops and stock market asset value decreases could be considered as part of a normal recessionary environment.

The big change, besides the initial burst of money supply increases in the days following the 9/11 attacks, was that Greenspan began fixing the *Federal Funds rates* (FFR) at near-constant very low levels for three years. By January 2th 2002, the FFR was down to 1.62 percent, having been reduced rapidly from 3.5 percent on September 12th, 2001. From January 9th, 2002, to October 30th, 2002, the FFR was kept very close to 1.75 percent, basically being constant. Meanwhile the Consumer Price Index inflation rate remained slightly below the FFR until August 2002, after which the inflation rate rose above the FFR causing negative interest rates.

After being held at 1.75 percent until October 2002, when the real interest rate was already in negative territory, the Fed lowered the FFR to a constant rate of about 1.25 percent from November 2002 to June 2003. Even as the inflation rate continued to stay around 2 percent, the Fed then stepped down the FFR to a third, even lower, fixed FFR interest rate of 1 percent for nearly a year from July 2003 to June of 2004.

From August, 2002, until May, 2005, the CPI inflation rate was above the FFR. This made the real interest rate effectively negative throughout this period. This is notable because this marked the Fed's first experiment in fixing the nominal interest rate at a constant level, mostly below the inflation rate.

The CPI inflation rate was up to 3 percent in June, 2004, when the Fed finally started raising the FFR rate, thus ending three steps of fixed interest rates for two and a half years, from January 2002 until June 2004,

[1]Federal Reserve Bank of Chicago 2001 Annual Report, p. 14; these were secured loans to commercial banks.

at or below 1.75 percent. But then another year of fixed FFR interest rates followed: at 5.25 percent from July 2005 to July 2006.

The rapid rise in the FFR means that the Fed raised the real interest rate from a level as low as a negative 2 percent in May 2004 to a positive real interest rate of about 2.75 percent for the fixed FFR year from July 2005 to July 2006. This is a nearly 5 percent increase in the real interest rate within a two year period.

The 2006 to 2007 level of interest rates appeared to be a "normalization" of the Federal Funds market by letting the interest rate reflect the inflation rate and a positive real rate of interest. But the problem is that this "normalization" came after unprecedented control and suppression of the real interest rate in negative territory. Meanwhile the mortgage market was subsidized through loan guarantees for market rates at very low levels for quite a few years, such as when the FFR was fixed at a low rate. Much of these were adjustable rate mortgages on which the interest rate was tied to a market rate such as the FFR rate.

The Fed's interest rate fixing of the FFR for three and a half years of the four and a half years, from January 2002 to July 2006, marks an unprecedented control of an asset market. It occurred at the same time of high subsidization of the mortgage loan market. The heavy FFR market control, or "regulation", was the background for similar FFR market control by the Fed during and after the Great Recession. After the stock market 2008 collapse, the Fed also became heavily involved in intervention in the mortgage loan market after mortgage defaults occurred because of the sudden surge of real interest rates from 2004 to 2006.

11.1.2 Fed Regulation of Capital Markets: 2008 to 2016

Figure 11.1 shows that from January to December 2008 the Fed reversed course. It lowered the FFR, graphed in Blue, rapidly so as to induce once again a negative real interest rate as graphed in Green, compared to the CPI inflation rate as graphed in Red, for a year-long period. From November 2008 until December 2015, the Fed kept the FFR at 0.25, or a quarter of one percent, or less. The real interest rate, ex post, as a result was negative most of this time, except from January 2009 until October 2009 when the CPI inflation rate was negative.

From November 2009 until October 2014, the CPI inflation rate remained about 2 percent, as compared to the fixed FFR of near zero percent, for a negative real interest rate of about 2 percent for nearly 5 years. This experience is similar to when there was a negative real interest rate during 2002 to 2005. Figure 11.1 shows in Green more than seven years of negative real interest rates caused by fixed FFR policy of the Fed in the post 9/11 period.

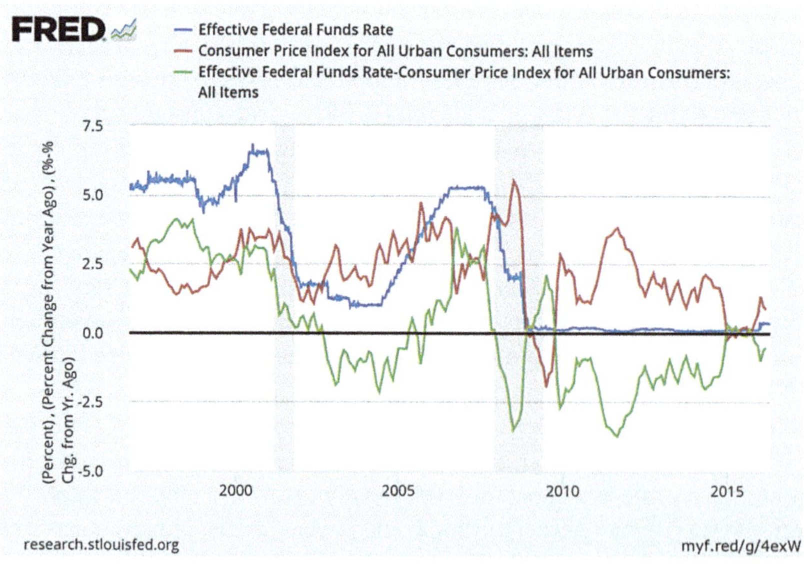

Figure 11.1 Great Recession and Post 9/11 Negative Real Interest Rates (Green) vs. FFR (Blue) and CPI inflation at a monthly frequency (Red)

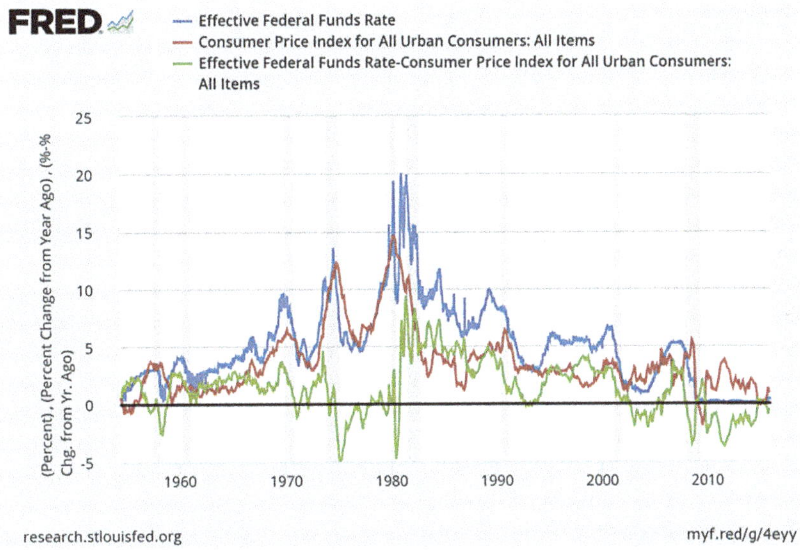

Figure 11.2 Post 1954 to 2002, the Green Real Interest Rate was Positive as the Norm

It appears that the Fed acted as if this fixed FFR policy and subsequent negative real interest rates was a successful policy that worked once, and so would work again. But did negative real interest rates, and the volatile Fed policy compared to its history post- Bretton Woods (the gold standard ended in 1971–1973), help or hurt capital markets and the economy? Figure 11.2 shows that using a fully flexible FFR, the Fed had kept the real interest rate, as computed by subtracting the CPI inflation rate from the FFR, in a positive range for more than twenty years from October 1980 until July 2002, when the first of their three steps down in the fixed FFR rate occurred.

In fact, going back to September 1954, the *real interest rate* by this calculation fell below zero only a few times before 2002. Studying the data, it does not appear that the Fed actually intended the FFR to be below the inflation rate, at any time, as they stayed as close as possible to the inflation rate during the acceleration and deceleration of the CPI inflation rate during the tumultuous interest rate decade of the 1970s. If anything, a near zero real rate in the 1970's seems to have been the norm, but certainly not a steady negative real interest rate.

The post September 11, 2001, US Fed policy was markedly different from the previous, long, postwar period after the March 4, 1951, Fed Accord with the US Treasury.[2] Positive real interest rates were the norm, rather than the exception, during 1954–2002, but negative real interest rates became the norm rather than the exception in the 2002 to 2016 period, as in Figure 11.2. This is the same period that marked the era of the Fed keeping constant the level of the FFR, with occasional shifts, and excepting during the rise from 2004–2006, and the fall from 2007–2009. The new, post-2001, fixed, Fed control of the FFR capital market became associated with negative real interest rates.

11.1.3 The US Treasury: Who Won the War?

The United States launched the war in Afghanistan on October 7th, 2001. This war is said to have lasted until 2014, although US troops have continued fighting there until the present 2016. During this period, there is also the war in Iraq and in Syria. Beginning with the 2008 Emergency Economic Stabilization Act, there were also federal outlays for various banking assets and other US companies through the Troubled Asset Relief Program (TARP). According to Phil Gramm and M. Solon (2016), 954 financial institutions received assistance from the TARP fund.[3]

---

[2]https://www.richmondfed.org/publications/research/special_reports/treasury_fed_accord

[3]"The Great Recession Blame Game", Wall Street Journal, April 16–17, 2016; page A11; Opinion page.

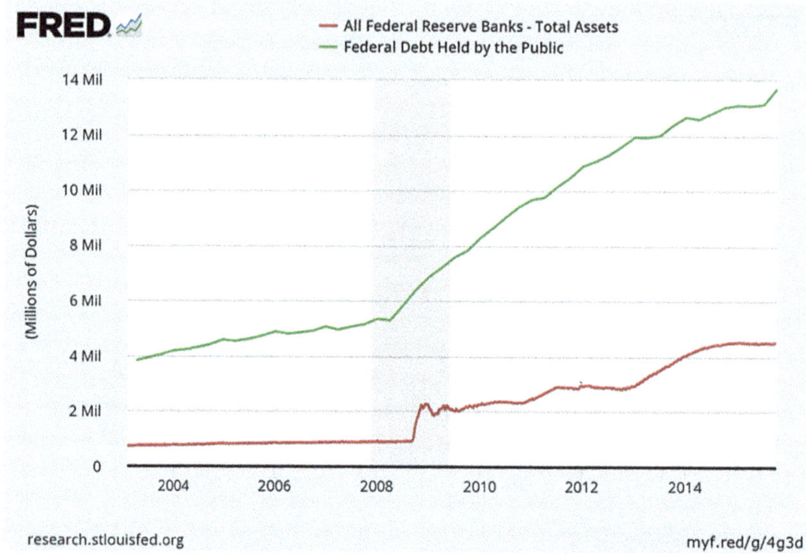

Figure 11.3 US Federal Debt Held by Public and US Federal Reserve Total Assets

As seen in the Table below, from surpluses of $124 billion in the Fiscal Year (FY) 1999, $237 in FY 2000 and $127 billion in FY 2001, ending in September 2001, the US Treasury budget achieved significant steady surpluses for three years.[4] Surpluses turned to deficits starting in FY 2002 and every year after to date, with a significant surge in deficits after 2008. The budget deficits were $157 billion in 2002, $374 billion in 2003; $413 billion in 2004; $319 billion in 2005; $248 billion in 2006; $161 billion in 2007; and $454 billion in 2008. The 2009 to 2012 surge followed with large deficits of $1,416 billion in 2009; $1,294 billion in 2010; $1297 billion in 2011; $1089 billion in 2012; $680 billion in 2013; $483 billion in 2014; and $439 billion in 2015%. This gives a sum of $8.8 trillion in *federal budget deficits* from a steady sequence of deficits for the fourteen fiscal years from 2002 to 2015. This is an average deficit per year over the 14 years of $630 billion versus an average surplus of $167 billion for the three previous years. [5]

The table summarizes the 1999–2015 US federal government FY budget totals:

FY	1999	00	01	02	03	04	05	06	07	08
Surplus	124	237	127	−157	−374	−413	−319	−248	−161	−454
Average	1999–2001:		167	09	10	11	12	13	14	15
	2002–2015:		−630	−1416	−1294	−1297	−1089	−680	−483	−439

Figure 11.3 compares the increase in Federal debt held by the public as compared to the increase in Federal Reserve System assets. Both trended up at a faster rate since 2008, while federal debt rose at a faster rate than Total Assets of the Fed. As the Fed assets grew from $0.9 Trillion on September 10th, 2008, to $4.5 Trillion on September 9th, 2015, the Treasury debt held by the public rose from $6.4 trillion in the fourth quarter of 2008 to $13.7 trillion in the fourth quarter of 2015, a $7.3 trillion increase compared to the total Fed debt increase of $8.8 for the entire FY 2002 to FY 2015 period.

Some of the federal debt increase is from increased borrowing unrelated to its budget deficits and some results directly from its deficits. From October 2008 to September 2012, the federal budget deficits were all over a trillion, for a four year total of over $5 trillion (1416+1294+1297+1089=5096). From September 2008 to September 2012, the Fed increased its assets to by $1 trillion to $2.8 trillion, a $1.8 trillion increase. This

[4]See https://www.fiscal.treasury.gov/fsreports

[5]157+374+413+319+248+161+454+1416+1294+1297+1089+680+483+439 = 8824.

could be interpreted in essence as the Fed financing 36% (1.8/5.01=0.36) of Treasury spending by "printing money" from 2008 to 2014. During all of the twentieth century US international wars, such an increase in the Fed purchase of Treasury debt has typically coincided with large increases in Treasury debt.

11.1.4 The Banking System

A near doubling of Fed assets occurred from October 2012 to September 2014, when the Fed increased its assets from $2.8 trillion to $5.5 trillion, a $2.7 trillion increase. The following Figures show that this increase was composed almost entirely of just two classes of assets: Fed purchases of mortgage backed securities and excess reserves held by private banks at the Fed.

Consistent with the increase in excess reserves since 2008, Figure 11.4 shows how M1 rose at a steadily accelerated rate path after 2008. The steady trend upwards from 1975 to 2008 is replaced by a much higher trend growth in M1 after 2008.

The new reserves to the private banking system resulted from the banks buying US Treasury debt and in turn the Fed buying back the Treasury debt from the banks. The banks then may have been lent out the reserves to some extent, but kept huge quantities of them "parked" in the Fed as excess reserves. Figure 11.5 shows that the private bank accumulation of excess reserves, rather than lending them out for private sector investment, is unparalleled in US history. Before 2008, excess reserves were historically always zero.

Figure 11.5 shows that the total Fed assets (Blue) minus the total *Mortgage Backed Securities* (MBS) (Green) give a Purple line that shadows the Excess Reserves (Red) line. This exercise is taking the Fed holdings of mortgage backed securities, which rose from 0 in Jan. 2009 to 1.7 trillion in Sept. 2014, and then subtracting the MBS from the total Fed assets. The result is that essentially all that is left on the Fed balance sheet is excess reserves.

First, what this shows is that the total amount of reserves that were lent out, and not kept as excess reserves, very closely follows the total MBS holdings. This means that private banks in essence got rid of their holdings of loans in the form of MBS and swapped them for new loans. The Fed purchase of the MBS would help banks indirectly, even if the Fed's MBS were of good quality, since the entire market value of mortgage loans was depressed as a result of the wave of mortgage bankruptcies.

Figure 11.6 shows the new Purple line when also subtracting the excess reserves, as well as MBS purchases. This Purple residual, after subtracting MBS and excess reserves, fluctuates somewhat while staying near zero.

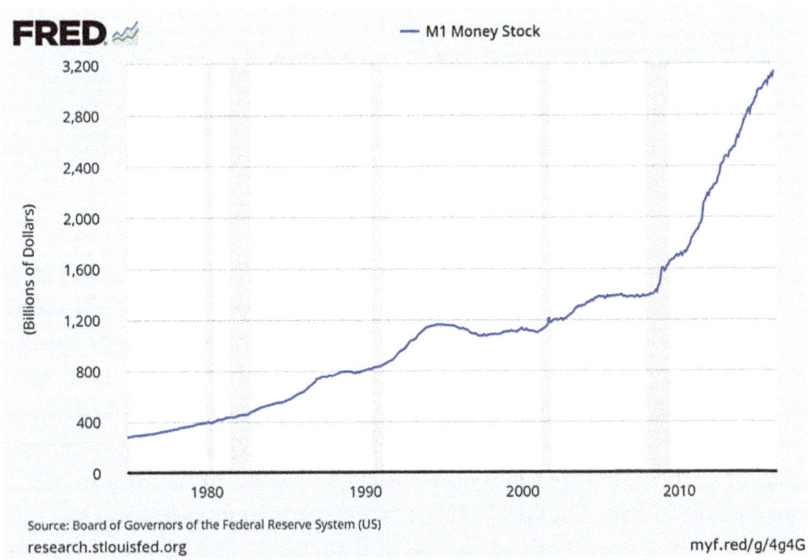

Figure 11.4 Historic Acceleration of the M1 monetary aggregate following 2008

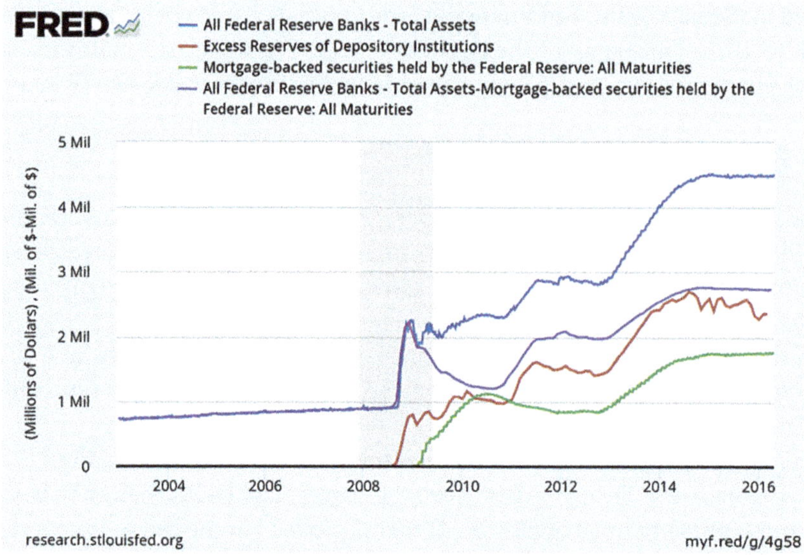

Figure 11.5 Total Fed Assets (Blue) Minus Mortgage Backed Securities (Green) shows Line (Purple) following Excess Reserves (Red)

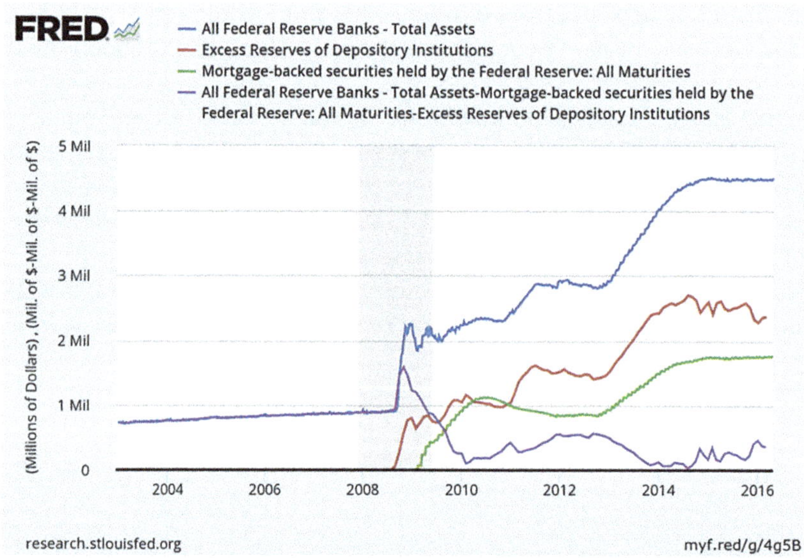

Figure 11.6 Purple Line shows (Fed Assets) Minus (MBS) and (Excess Reserves) = Zero

Second, this means in essence that only the reserves created from the MBS purchases were lent out. Everything else besides the MBS reserves, which the private bank system received from Fed purchases of securities, has since been held in as excess reserves kept at the bank. These are not lent out. Third this suggests that the excess reserve increase alone would largely explain the increase in the M1 money supply.

Why did this unprecedented holding of excess reserves occur? There is no mystery here. The Fed began paying interest on excess reserves in 2008 for the first time in history. And the excess reserves interest rate has been a steady quarter of a percentage point above the rate earned in the FFR market

The higher rate on excess reserves than on FFR is a facet that is in violation of the Congressional law that allowed interest to be paid on reserves. The old idea behind paying interest on reserves was that private banks were "taxed" by having to keep idle reserves at the Fed, equal to 10% of deposits. Of course banks would choose to keep reserves on deposits anyway, earning no interest. So if they chose 7% to be held, the Fed requirement of 10% would impose a tax on the additional 3% reserves that the banks had to hold. The Fed payment of interest on the entire required reserves, at the FFR rate, would eliminate any such tax.

But the intent of the law was greatly subverted by Fed action. It was The Financial Services Regulatory Relief Act of 2006 that authorized the Fed to pay interest on reserves held at the Fed, to be effective October 1, 2011. Then at Fed request this effective date was then moved up to 2008 in the middle of the Great Recession crisis. And further, despite the intent of just paying interest on required reserves, the policy was formulated by the Fed to allow an above FFR interest rate to be paid on all reserves.

The result was the inducement of the private banks to keep the excess reserves parked in the Fed, and earning above market interest rates on them. The private banks were in essence subsidized to not lend out the reserves. If the reserves were fully lent out, with effectively zero excess reserves as in all of previous US history since the Fed was established, then the money "multiplier" would have occurred as new loans were made and made again.

What would a normal money multiplier of the lending out of all non-required reserves have led to? An huge acceleration in the demand deposit component of M1, and so in M1 itself. Most expected that this would have caused the inflation rate to rise above the Fed target, and so the Fed would lose credibility in keeping inflation at its target. How did the Fed stop this: a policy of subsidizing banks which induced less lending and new investment. And almost all of these excess reserves still are sitting in the Fed today.

The interest on excess reserves is a direct subsidization of the banking system that did not exist before 2008. It would certainly classify as a subsidy since it has been kept above the Federal Funds rate by design since its inception in 2008. And the normal acceleration of M1 that would lead markets to expect higher inflation was averted at the cost on an ongoing distortion to capital markets. The Fed is causing Moral Hazard: increasing the probability of the bad state, which in the case of a Great Recession, is the state of below-normal investment.

11.2 Facts

Congressional legislation and government policy during the Great Recession is a complex web that has caused a complex set of distortions in capital markets.

11.2.1 Fed "Bailout" of US Bank System?

The amount of loans made by the banking system, as a result of the massive Fed increase in purchases in US Treasuries and MBS, amounts to the level of the MBS that the Fed bought, as in Figures 11.5 and 11.6. The banks lent out an amount equivalent approximately to the MBS that was bought from them, while keeping all the rest of the Fed's assets, being mainly Fed purchases of US Treasury debt from the banks, as reserves held by and at the Fed. These were the excess reserves of the private banks that were allowed starting in 2008 to earn from the Fed a special newly introduced interest rate on reserves. The interest on excess reserves ended up going primarily to a small number (10) of the US banks categorized as "systematically important", making these banks the main beneficiaries of the excess reserve interest payments.[6] The entire bank sector benefited from the increased demand for the MBS as this lifted the value of this class of loans broadly.

In effect, the Fed allowed the US banking system to exchange MBS for "better" new loans. The problem with the MBS that the Fed purchased is that the entire MBS market was depressed in value because of the failure or the *"sub-prime" mortgages* during the Great Recession. So even if the Fed purchased "good" MBS as the Fed assets, rather the sub-prime ones, their purchases raised the value of all MBS in the market at a time when the banks desperately needed higher asset values to avoid insolvency.

Thus the banking system was "bailed out" by the Fed propping up of the value of MBS by massive purchases, and by the interest paid for the excess reserves at a rate above the Federal Funds rate since 2008 and still continuing today. The Fed's MBS mortgage loan purchases were in essence taken off the balance sheets

[6]See Daniel L. Thornton, 2016, "Another Unintended Consequence of QE", Common Sense Economics Perspective, No. 13.

of the financial intermediation system, for one big part of the money supply increase. And much of the Fed's US Treasury securities purchases were in effect immediately transferred back to the Fed as excess reserves earning more than the Federal Funds interest rate.

The Fed's post-2008 MBS purchases included MBS guaranteed by the *US government sponsored "enterprises"*, in particular, Fannie Mae, Freddie Mac, and Ginnie Mae, with such holdings equaling $1.6 trillion in March 2014. These agencies find their roots going back to the 1930s Great Depression bank legislation designed to subsidize mortgage loans (See the Chapter 6 Appendix on these laws). The Fed's Federal Open Market Committee (FOMC) was allowed to buy such debt by an authorization made permanent in 1968, but with the condition that the purchases not favor any one market or type of asset. Under the 1968 authorization, these purchases

> "are not designed to support individual sectors of the market or to channel funds into issues of particular agencies."

However supporting the housing sector was the clearly stated intent of the Fed. The Fed November 2008 FOMC minutes included language that the MBC purchases were designed

> "to reduce the cost and increase the availability of credit for the purchases of houses, which in turn should support housing markets and foster improved conditions in financial markets more generally."

Since this language was in contradiction of their original authority with respect to government sponsored enterprises (GSE), as Richmond Fed President Lacker pointed out, the Fed FOMC suspended the guidelines "indefinitely" in January 2009.[7]

The complex policy combination saw the Fed succeed in avoiding a banking panic amongst the banks that were not insured under the FDIC (Federal Deposit Insurance System). The uninsured deposits include all of the mutual fund accounts of the Investment bank sector. That sector arose essentially during the late 1970's and early 1980's so as to get around the law that put a ceiling on interest rates that could be paid for deposits in commercial banks. During the high inflation of the 1970's and into the 1980's, it became worthwhile for consumers to move their deposits into the mutual funds and so try to get an interest rate that at least included the inflation rate. This enabled them to avoid the inflation tax partly or in whole.

But the problem of the creation of the *Non-Bank Banks*, such as investment banks with "checkable deposits" in the form of mutual funds, is that these banks were created after the FDIC structure was put in place. Deposit insurance therefore only covered retail/commercial banks of the standard variety and not the new investment bank deposits that were similar in nature to commercial bank deposits, except that they did not have FDIC insurance.

There was a run on the mutual banks after the Leyman Brothers bankruptcy in September 2008. In the UK, this run on the banks spilled over to retail banks since the UK did not have as well-defined a system of deposit insurance. The Northern Rock bank in the UK was a retail/commercial bank that saw people lining up in the street to take out their deposits in the summer of 2008, on television news and media outlets. Thus there really was a run on banks, both investment banks in the US and commercial banks in the UK.[8]

The Fed successfully stopped this run, as did the Bank of England, by adding liquidity to the system with lending to investment banks through their "discount window" (through "Primary Dealer Facilities"), massive purchases of short term debt, and by suddenly adding deposit insurance in the UK case. If the Fed had stopped its unusual interventions after the 2008–2009 crisis, in terms of adding more money into the bank system, then the crisis-induced subsidy to the US banking system would have effectively stopped.

---

[7]Please see "The First Time the Fed Bought GSE Debt", by Renee Haltom and Robert Sharp, Economic Brief, Federal Reserve Bank of Richmond, April 2014. On web at https://www.richmondfed.org/-/media/richmondfedorg/publications/research/economic_brief/2014/pdf/eb_14-04.pdf

[8]I was attending a Bank of England conference the day of the run on Northern Rock. Charles Goodhart sat next to me at the conference dinner as we awaited Mervyn King, Governor of the Bank of England, to give the conference dinner address; the Governor did not show up, as the Northern Rock panic exploded into his governance.

So it is adverse that the Fed chose the path of a long-running bank subsidization that has not ended. This path certainly relates to the other key component of how the bank system has been subsidized and taxed. The US Dodd-Frank 2010 Act significantly increased private bank asset requirements. This led to regulatory factors of an economic "taxation" nature that ostensibly have decreased the productivity of the banking system, with the idea that the legislation has made the banking system safer.

The policy debate and confusing mix of simultaneously both subsidizing and taxing the US bank system therefore entangles what caused the Great Recession and the mortgage loan collapse: was it the bank system that was to blame? Was it the Federal Reserve that was to blame? Was it the US Congress running huge government deficits that was to blame? Or was it simply the US sponsored mortgage agencies that issued government-guaranteed debt to borrowers that had a high risk of default should interest rates have risen (which they did)? The answers to these questions bear upon why the post- Great Recession recovery has been anemic, yielding what some call a US "lost decade" as also occurred during the 1930's.

11.2.2 Banking Legislation: Deregulation, Re-regulation

The high inflation of the Vietnam war era led to a 1978 US Supreme Court decision that allowed nationally chartered banks to use their own state's interest rate law ("usury" laws) in other states. This allowed banks to offer a higher interest rate in certain US states. And it led to "competitive deregulation" which saw US states such that Delaware and South Dakota effectively eliminate the interest rate ceilings of the 1933 *Regulation Q* era.

After the 1978 Court decision, statutory US laws followed that continued breaking up the 1933 Banking Acts regulation of the bank sector. This caused a step-by-step deregulation of the bank sector.

1. The 1980 Depository Institutions Deregulation and Monetary Control Act phased out interest rate ceilings.
2. The 1982 Garn-St. Germain Depository Institutions Act allowed "thrift" institutions, or "savings and loans" banks, to act as full banks by allowing commercial lending. After a mid-1980's run on Ohio's savings and loans institutions, all savings and loans were required to acquire deposit insurance under the Federal Savings and Loan Insurance Corporation (FSLIC); subsequently the FSLIC was dissolved and merged into the FDIC.
3. 1989 Financial Institutions Reform and Recovery Act. This act created an Office of Thrift Supervision that oversaw, for example, American Insurance Group (AIG), Washington Mutual, and IndyMac: these are three of the "headline" large financial intermediaries that became insolvent during the 2008 crisis and helped ushered in its bank panic.
4. The 1994 Riegle-Neal Interstate Banking and Branching Efficiency Act allowed for banks to branch across states freely. This had been previously restricted but was being subverted by bank holding companies that would in effect branch across state and so elude the restriction from the 1933 Banking Act known as Glass-Steagall.
5. The 1999 Gramm-Leach-Bliley Act (GLBA) allowed financial services companies to engage in banking, insurance and the securities business of investment banks, with the stipulations that these each remain separate and subject to the original Glass-Steagall regulations. Note that according to former Senator Glass, "A bank operating within a holding company was still subject to Glass-Steagall (which was not repealed by GLBA)".[9]
6. The 2000 Commodity Futures Modernization Act prohibited the Commodity Futures Trading Commission from regulating derivatives such as "credit swaps" that played a big role in the illiquidity crisis in 2008. These "derivatives" were devices by which the risk of Mortgage-Backed Securities (MBS) was "stripped-off" and sold internationally to financial firms across the world. The default on a large number of the MBS caused firms holding these derivative "risk strips" to suffer major losses. The international holding of defaulted

[9] "The Great Recession Blame Game", by Phil Gramm and Michael Solon, Wall Street Journal, 15 August 2016; op-ed page.

MBS derivatives decreased the solvency of many of the financial firms holding these, especially the MBS that were based on "sub-prime", or high-risk, borrowers. The sub-prime market included those who had low income levels and who would have had difficulty making their mortgage payments if the interest rates rose, as many were on a variable interest rate mortgage loan. So when the Fed suddenly increased interest rates from 1% to 5.5%, many such mortgage loans went into default.

Re-regulation Acts included

1. the 1987 Competitive Equality Banking Act that was enacted "to regulate nonbank banks, impose a moratorium on certain securities and insurance activities by banks", and other provisions. How much this affected financial markets is not clear; it was not a major re-regulation.
2. The 1989, Financial Institutions Reform and Recovery Act gets mentioned under deregulation and re-regulation. It did create the Resolution Trust Corporation to wind up defaulted thrift institutions.
3. Similarly the 1991 Federal Deposit Insurance Corporation Improvement Act aimed to provide a lower cost winding-up of failed insured banks.
4. The 2002 Sarbanes-Oxley took an accounting approach and required the Securities Exchange Commission to issue regulations that brought about more accurate and clear accounting by all public companies, resulting in new reporting requirements.
5. Most restrictive of all, the 2010 Dodd-Frank Wall Street Reform and Consumer Protection Act has a rather "blame game" official name to it, suggesting it was the fault of banks for the 2008 financial crisis. Its preamble states that it is "To promote the financial stability of the United States by improving accountability and transparency in the financial system, to end "too big to fail", to protect the American taxpayer by ending bailouts, to protect consumers from abusive financial services practices, and for other purposes."[10] It ends up increasing capital reserves most of all, while also leading to the designation of "*systemically important financial institutions*" with increased capital reserves. In addition, there are also now at least nine US "globally systemically important banks" (GLIB), under the Basel Committee on Banking Supervision (Basel III). And so the "too big to fail" concept, despite stated intent, entered US law and international law, and increased capital requirements have resulted.
6. The Financial Services Regulatory Relief Act (FSRRA) of 2006, authorized the Fed to pay interest on reserves held at the Fed, to be effective October 1, 2011. The rate to be paid on reserves was supposed to be the same as that paid on Federal Funds.
7. The 2008 Emergency Economic Stabilization Act moved up the effective date of the 2006 (FSRRA) law to October 1, 2008. The date was advanced apparently in order to subsidize the "too big to fail" banks by the payment of interest on reserves. This has led to the payment of interest on excess reserves, at a rate steadily a quarter of percent higher than the Federal Funds rate, since its inception in 2008 and during its subsequent continuous use.

Interestingly, continued payment of interest on excess reserves ever since 2008 goes mainly to the "US's systemically important banks", meaning a small group of banks gets the bulk of interest on reserves, so that they get subsidized even as they are taxed through higher capital reserve requirements. The continual subsidization part was originally not the plan. In fact, according to the Fed FOMC minutes of December 2007, Fed officials

> "recognized that, as economic activity recovered and financial conditions normalized, the use of certain policy tools would need to be scaled back, the size of the balance sheet and level of excess reserves would need to be reduced, and the committee's policy framework would return to focus on the level of the federal funds rate."[11]

---

[10]http://www.cftc.gov/idc/groups/public/@swaps/documents/file/hr4173% _enrolledbill.pdf

[11]"Fed Expects Weak Economy, Fears 'Prolonged Retraction'", By Neil Irwin, Washington Post, January 7, 2009.

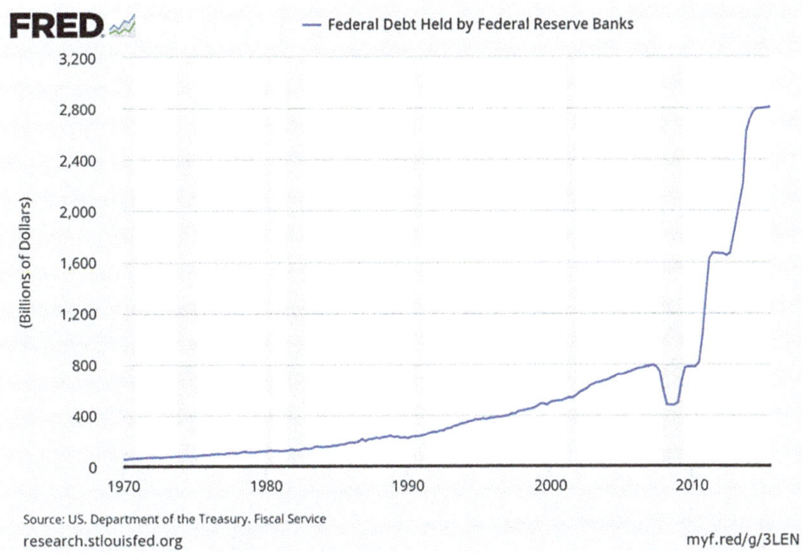

Figure 11.7 Federal Debt Held by Fed Rose Dramatically from 2009 to 2015, up by $2 trillion

Another eight years after the date of this Fed FOMC meeting, no normalization of this type has yet to happen. So was there a "monetary finance" of the large US Treasury deficits and if so how did the Fed's abnormal banking policy lead to a lack of inflation? And can this low inflation be sustained?

11.2.3 Deficit Increase, Debt, and "Monetary Finance"

The facts show two facets that are consistent with a "monetary finance" of the US Treasury deficits. One, the Fed's purchases of US Treasury debt rose dramatically during the years of 2008–2016. Two during these same years the US Treasury's deficits were also far above past historical averages. This implies that the Fed purchased a significant portion of US Treasury debt which therefore in effect financed the US Treasury deficit by printing money. "Printing money" occurs when the Fed buy US Treasury debt that occurs when deficits occur. This printing of money to pay part of the US Treasury deficit is called "monetary finance" of the US Treasury deficit.

Figure 11.7 shows the Federal Debt held by the Federal Reserve System from the first quarter of 1970 to the fourth quarter of 2015. There is an increase from $0.8 trillion, just before and after the NBER dated Great Recession, up to $2.8 trillion in 2015. This is a $2 trillion increase in the Fed's holding of this federal debt. It is a dramatic, a-historical, acceleration of US Treasury debt held by the Fed.

At the same time, from FY 2009 to FY 2015 the US Treasury annual deficits summed up to a $6.7 trillion increase that was financed by issued new US Treasury debt. So for 2009 to 2015, roughly 30% of the US Treasury deficits can in fact be described as being "*monetarily financed*", that is by printing money.

Meanwhile the US Treasury also borrowed from the public. Figure 11.8 shows for the same period that the Federal debt held by the public dramatically increased relative to the historical average dating from 1970. For the third quarter of 2009 to the fourth quarter of 2015, debt held by the public rose from $7.6 trillion to 13.7 trillion, a $6.1 trillion increase. This total US debt increase was $6.1 trillion held by the public, plus $2 trillion more held by the Fed, for a total increase of roughly $8.1 trillion. Of this $8.1, $6.7 of it is directly from US Treasury deficits. The remaining roughly $1.4 trillion by the estimates given here, would have been the result of additional US Treasury borrowing that in effect was not reflected in the US Congressional federal budget totals.

The fact overview creates two puzzling aspects within capital markets. Most of the US debt increase, or roughly 83% of it, was from US federal budget deficits. And some one third of this was financed by the Fed buying the debt, which is called in common terms "monetary finance". The result of these two events, the

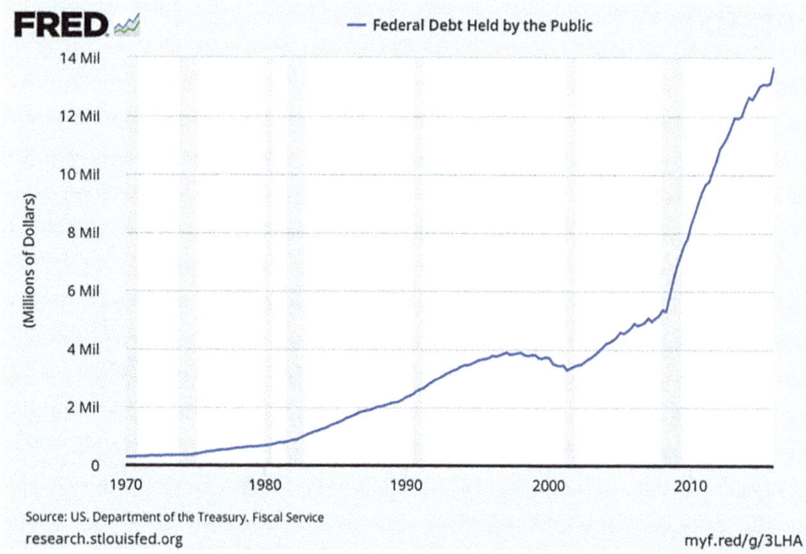

Figure 11.8 Federal Debt Held by the Public increased by $8.1 trillion after the NBER Dated End of the Great Recession, from 2009:3 to 2015:4

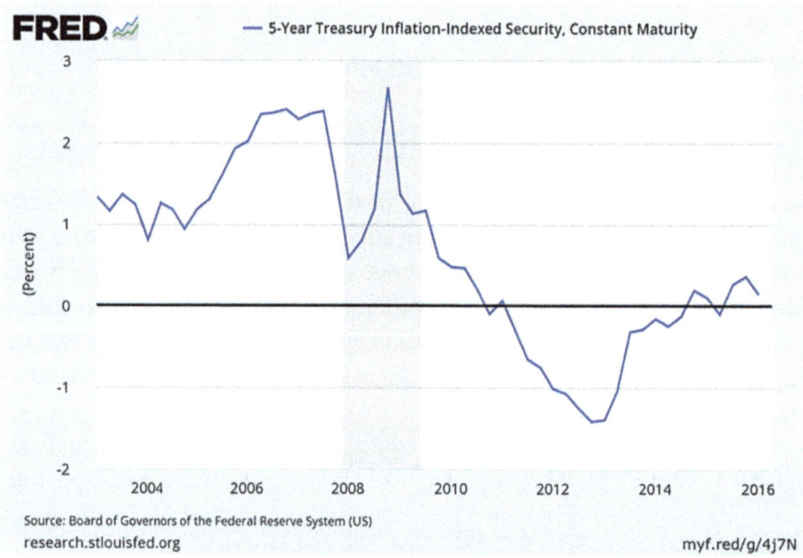

Figure 11.9 Real Interest Rate of post- 2003 period as Measured by Inflation-Indexed US Treasury 5-Year Maturity Debt

increase in debt held by the public, and the monetary finance of debt by the Fed, historically have been seen to each cause, by themselves, significant upward pressure on the markets nominal interest rates.

First, the increase of US debt held by the public typically raises the real interest rate in capital markets. Second, the monetary finance of debt typically raises the inflation rate. Neither of these events appear to have happened post 2009.

11.2.4 Real Interest Rates and the Inflation Rate

Figure 11.9 shows a measure of the real interest rate before, during and after the Great Recession. Using inflation-indexed US Treasury debt with a 5-year maturity, real interest rates were rising from 1% to about

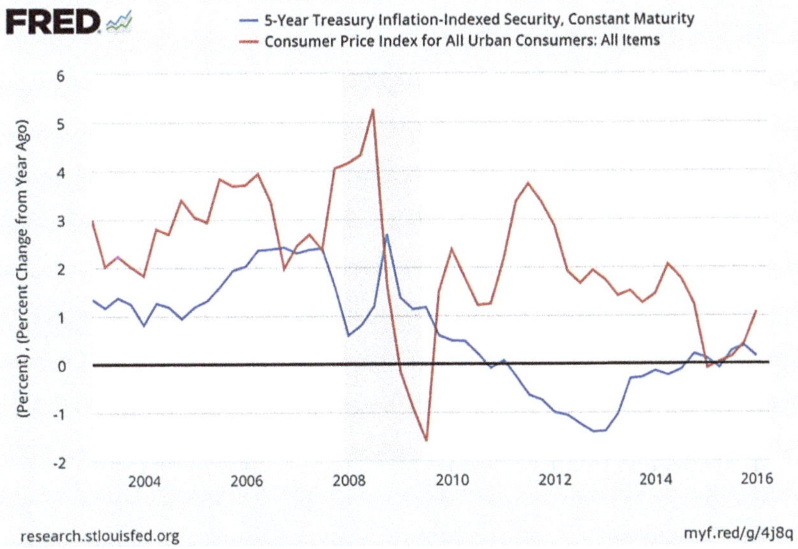

Figure 11.10 CPI Inflation Rate moves Opposite of Real Rate, at times, during 2003–2016

2.3% during the expansion years from the fourth quarter of 2004 to the third quarter of 2007. Then the real rate fell suddenly from 2.3% to 0.6% from the third quarter of 2007 to the first quarter of 2008.

Real interest rates rose sharply back up to 2.5% during the NBER-dated Great Recession, and then back down to 1% at the end of the NBER-dated Great Recession. After that, the real rate falls steadily down to a negative 1.4% in the fourth quarter of 2012 (2012:4). It then climbs up to near zero starting in 2013:3 and stays near zero (with a slight rising trend) for the two and half years ending in 2016:1.

Figure 11.10 shows that the annual CPI inflation rate moves somewhat as a mirror image of real interest rates, in that the two data series seem to move directly opposite of each other for extended periods. This may imply that even the 5-year Inflation-Indexed Treasury debt does not perfectly capture the actual inflation rate. When it does not capture the inflation rate, this may mean that the change in inflation was somewhat unexpected. Unexpected inflation, when rising, is known to cause lower ex-post real interest rates. For example, the real rate was negative for almost all of four years, from 2010:3 to 2014:3, during which time the inflation rate rose to as high as 3.7% in 2011:3.

Unexpected deflation, when the inflation rate is falling by more than expected, can cause higher real interest rates. From annual rates of 5.2 to 1.6%, the CPI inflation rate fell from 2008:3 to 2008:4, a very sharp decrease. This could have caused the real rate to spike up in 2008:4, since market forces were no longer allowed to affect the Federal Funds rate. The FFR was controlled strictly by the Fed to remain at between 0 and 0.2% until December 2015. Then the FFR was increased by the Fed by to 0.4%, while the interest rate on excess reserves was increased to 0.5% so as to remain above the FFR.

11.2.5 Loan Rates Follow Real Interest Rates

Increasing bank capital reserves, as required under US post-2008 law, makes it harder to intermediate deposits into loans. This can show up as a decrease in the loan to deposit ratio. Forcing down the market interest rate on short term assets to near zero, with negative real interest rates ensuing, can also induce less savings by the private sector to be intermediated through banks into investment. A low real interest rate decreases the cost of current consumption relative to future consumption. More current consumption ensues with less savings of income. Less private savings then is offered to banks for intermediation into investment by firms.

Meanwhile an unusual excess of the Fed purchases of the bank holdings of Treasury debt means that these bank investments come from their private sector deposits. This forces the household portfolio of investments to include a large portion of the public sector debt. This in turn leaves less of the private sector bank deposits

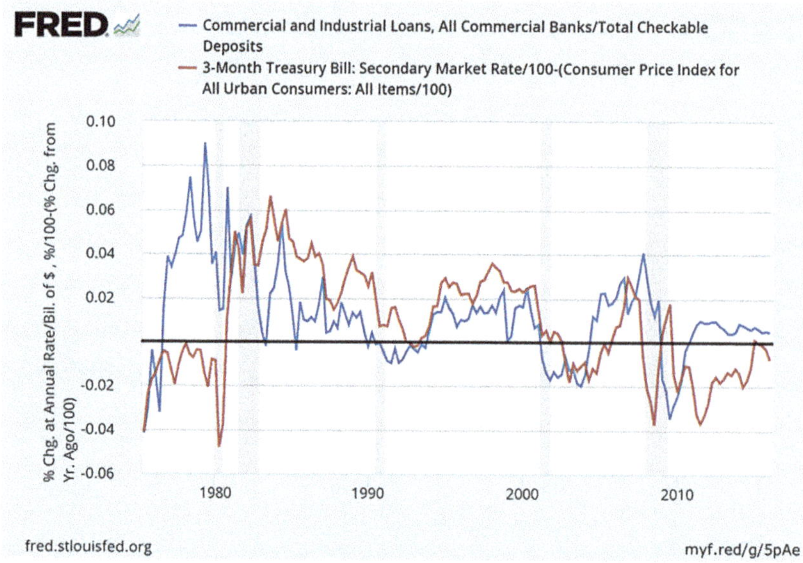

Figure 11.11 Commercial and Industrial Loans from Commercial Banks Divided by All Checkable Deposits

to be directed into private firms. This private sector investment that is directed into private firms is typically either in the form of loans by banks to firms or direct holdings of firm securities (stocks) or holdings of firm corporate debt.

Less savings being available for private investment means that the loan to deposit ratio will be lower. It also means that with relatively more in low interest public debt, private investment tends to go into riskier ventures that have the potential of a higher yield. This is called "*seeking return*" in the jargon of the Great Recession, a side effect that means that stock investments might be overly tilted towards riskier returns.

The simplest way to see some of this picture is to look at the private sector loan to deposit ratios. The loan to deposit ratios can be examined with different measures. And these can be compared to different market residuals such as real interest rate.

Take a first example of a measure of total loans from FRED. This is all "Commercial and Industrial Loans from all Commercial Banks". This basically captures all loans made by the commercial bank sector to both consumers and firms. Divide this by "Total Checkable Deposits", to get a ratio of loans to deposits. Total Checkable Deposits includes standard demand deposits plus other "checkable" funds, such as money market mutual funds on which one can write a check and pay for purchases. So it is probably the broadest measure of deposits.[12]

Figure 11.11 presents in the Blue line the loan to deposit ratio as just defined, in terms of "Commercial and Industrial Loans, from all Commercial Banks, divided by Total Checkable Deposits. It is graphed for the period of May 1975 to June 2016. Mainly the loan ratio is high and rising during business cycle expansions, and low and falling in business cycle contractions (or recessions). The ratio has been falling since 2011, and is well below the levels reached before 2008. This is evidence of how investment, through loans relative to deposits, remains low and is a feature helping to explain why the Great Recession is dragging on with continual very low real GDP growth.

A remarkable fact that helps explain loan to deposit ratio movement within Figure 11.11 is the real interest rate. The Red line is the second graphed relation in Figure 11.11, the real interest rate as given by the 3-month Treasury Bill rate minus the percentage change in the CPI price index. From around 1981 until 2010 there is a rather close correlation, or comovement, of the two data series. This means that as the real interest rate rises, the percent of loans made out of deposits also rises; similarly for declines in the real interest rate. This means that the loan to deposit ratio tends to rise and fall with the real interest rate.

[12] I thank Dan Thornton for emphasizing this point to me.

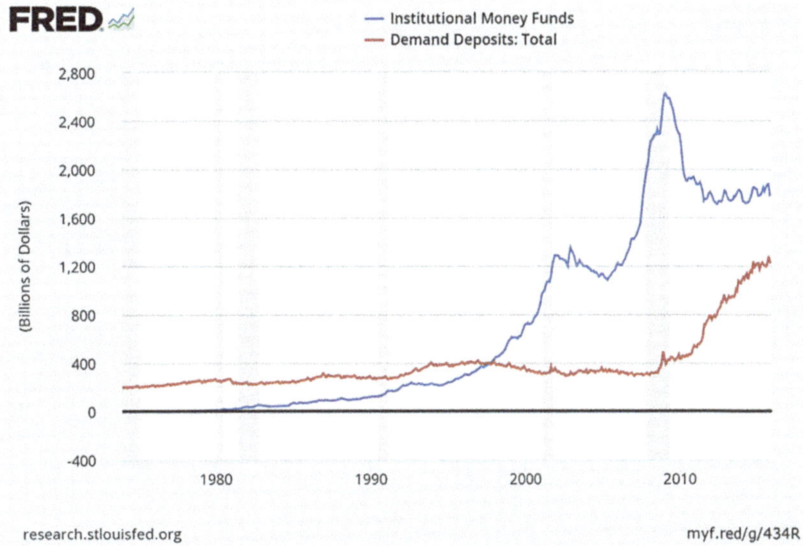

Figure 11.12 Institutional Money Funds (Blue) and Demand Deposits (Red)

Special attention in Figure 11.11 can be given to the periods when the real interest rate is negative for a prolonged period. This occurred in the 1975 to 1980 period, and in the 2010 to 2016 period. During these "awkward", or "unconventional" times, we see that the loan to deposit ratio is significantly and consistently higher than the real interest rate. This means that the normal relation between the two data series seems to break down at the same time that capital markets are shocked by unusual, possibly distortive, and continual negative real interest rates.

11.2.6 Loan to Deposit Ratios

The loan to deposit ratio can be measured in other ways. For example, an important question is how did the nature of deposits change during the Great Recession? Figure 11.12 graphs two data series that are different types of deposits by savers. In Blue is graphed the Institutional Money Funds, which are the investment bank mutual funds. These are very similar to demand deposits at commercial banks, except that instead they are deposits of savings funds offered for investment by the "non-bank banks", and in particular the investment banks such as Goldman Sachs, JP Morgan, and Merrill Lynch. Merrill Lynch was one of the most famous investment banks (founded in the same year as the US Federal Reserve System, 1914) until the Great Recession. Under duress, it was bought by Bank of America in 2009, and now "Merrill Lynch Wealth Management" is the current corporate form of its predecessor Merrill Lynch and Co.

What the Figure 11.12 indicates is that as the level of Demand Deposits at banks was relatively constant from the 1970's until 2009, the Institutional Money Funds gradually took off in popularity, starting in 1981. This was at the same time as the major 1980's bank deregulation that included the elimination of the "Regulation Q" interest ceiling on what banks could pay in interest. This means there was a huge shift from using only demand deposits to what became higher interest earning Institutional Money Funds of investment banks.

The popularity of the Institutional Money Funds was reversed in 2009, after a run on such money market funds occurred during the financial *panic* during 2008–2009. Instead the funds were shifted to the more standard demand deposits at commercial banks. Such commercial bank deposits were insured by the FDIC; the Institutional Money Funds were not (and are not) FDIC insured, as various investment banks went insolvent during the financial panic.

Figure 11.13 shows two alternative data series for the US loan to deposit ratios. These are the Consumer Loans to Demand Deposit ratio, in Red, and the Commercial and Industrial Loans to Demand Deposit ratio, in Blue. These show that starting in 2008, just as funds were starting to be shifted from institutional non-bank Money Funds to commercial bank demand deposits, that both loan ratios fell steadily right up until 2015.

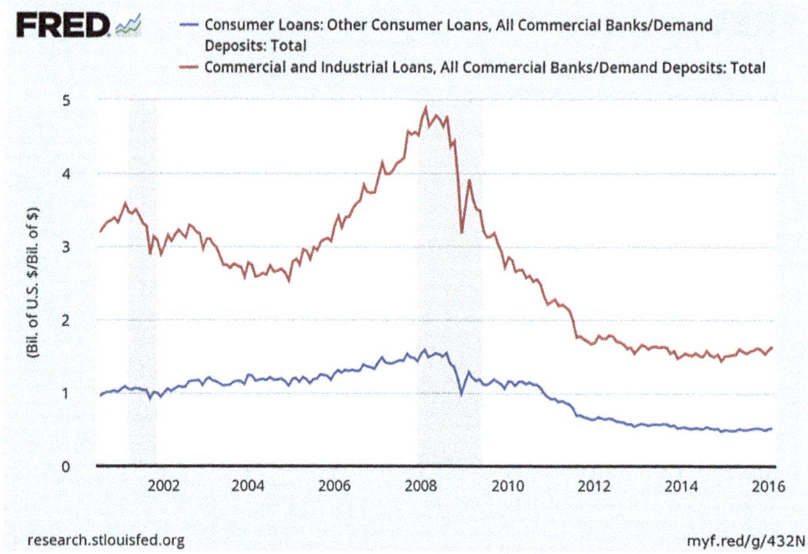

Figure 11.13 Loan to Demand Deposit Ratios: Consumer Loans Ratio in Red; Commercial and Industrial Loans Ratio in Blue

It appears the Commercial and Industrial Loans to Demand Deposit ratio is just starting to turn up in 2016, while the Consumer Loan to Demand Deposit Ratio keeps falling even to date. The Figure also shows that these loan to deposit ratios are far below their levels since 2000. This is direct evidence on how the Great Recession is still not finished in that it appears to be not just a 2008–2010, NBER-dated, recession but also a "lost decade" of poor economic performance, since 2007.

Figure 11.13 can be viewed in terms of the "*utilization rate*" of financial capital. It shows the fraction of savers deposits that are turned into loans for investment (either household investment or firm investment). This financial capital utilization rate has fallen dramatically and steadily since 2008, with the Consumer Loan to Deposit ratio still continuing to fall in 2016. The recent slight uptick in the Commercial and Industrial Loan to Deposit ratio may be indicative hopefully of a turn upwards in this aspect of the economy.

11.2.7 Financial, Physical, Human Capital Utilization

As the economy expands gradually over time, with continuous real GDP growth, the demand for money for use in circulation also expands. However the US use of Demand Deposits was shown in Figure 11.12 to be nearly constant since the 1970's. Figure 11.14 shows since February 1984 the natural log of each the Currency in Circulation, in Red, and the total Demand Deposits, in Blue. By using the natural log, the slope of each line indicates the growth rate of the data series. The Blue line for Demand Deposits has a slope fluctuating near zero on average for the most part until 2008. The Red line for Currency in Circulation shows a near constant, and positive, slope, and so a near constant growth rate of Currrency in Circulation, for the whole period.

Figure 11.15 shows that the result is that the currency to demand deposit ratio rose steadily until 2008. The steady currency positive growth and near zero demand deposit growth meant that investment and correlated currency use were rising until 2008. Then after 2008 demand deposits grew because deposits were moved from investment banks to commercial banks, while currency grew at about the same rate. So the ratio of currency to currency plus demand deposits fell.

But looking at currency divided by all demand deposits and mutual funds, a different view emerges. This currency to funds ratio remained below 0.5 from 1980 to 2001. Then it rose above 0.7 in 2005, fell to 0.6, and rose back to 0.7 from 2011 onwards. This shows a fundamental shift down in the utilization rate of funds into investment just as the currency to deposit ratio rose until March 1933 as disintermediation occurred.

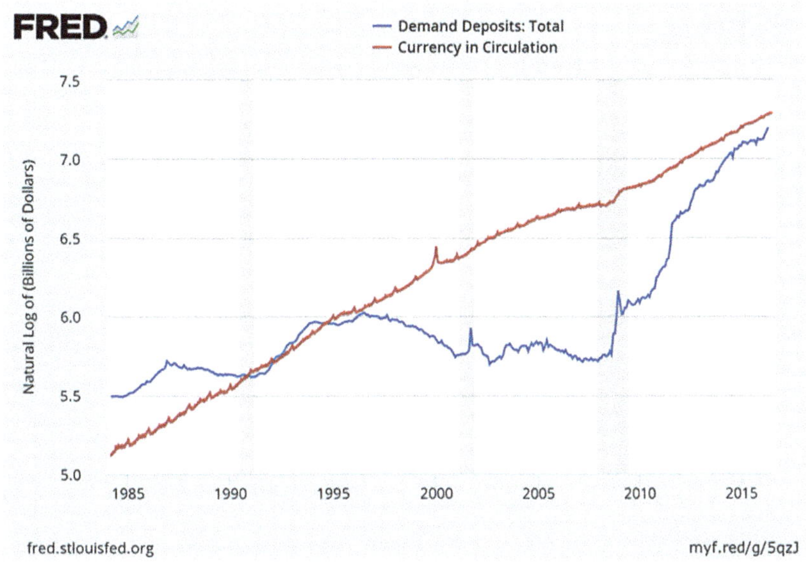

Figure 11.14 Natural Log of Currency in Circulation and Natural Log of Demand Deposits: Slope of Graphs Equals Growth Rate of Each Series

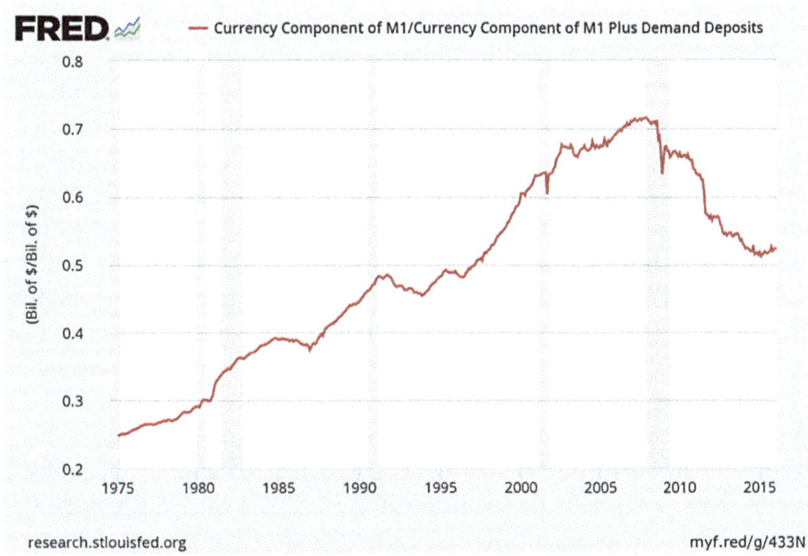

Figure 11.15 Ratio of Currency in Circulation to the Sum of Currency in Circulation and Demand Deposits

The US human capital utilization rate also could be viewed as having peaked around 2000. This can be seen using one measure: the US Civilian Labor Force Participation Rate. Figure 3.11 shows that the labor force participation rate rose steadily since the early 1960's and reversed steadily down around 2000. This evidence is a subject of much debate. Theory for this is given below, but regardless of the theory, it indicates that the US used its "human capital" in work effort at a decreasing rate since 2000, except from 2004 to 2008 when the rate was steadying at around 66%.

Another indicator of a lower capital utilization rate during the Great Recession and up to the present is the Figure 3.12 of the US home ownership rate from 1965 until 2016. This rate rose continually from 1965 to 2004 and then turned down and has continued to fall ever since. This is a lower capital utilization rate of residential investment (houses). Or it can be viewed as a lower investment rate by consumer households in houses.

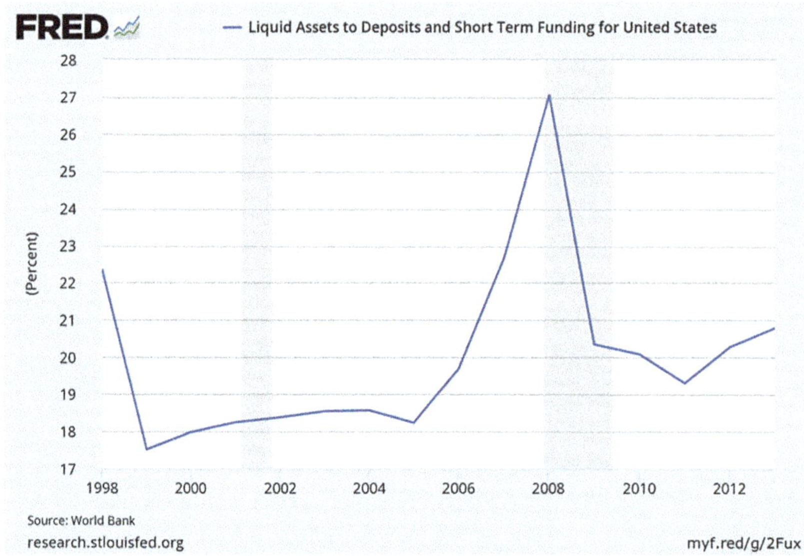

Figure 11.16 Ratio of US Liquid Assets to Deposits plus Short Term Funding

11.2.8 Why Fed Acted: Run on Mutual Funds

The last evidence presented here on what the Fed did during the Great Recession Bank Crisis is one showing why the Fed began its action to increase the money supply in 2008. Figure 11.16 shows the ratio of US "*Liquid Assets*" to Deposits and Short Term Funding. Here the definition from FRED is that "Liquid Assets consist of Cash and Balances with Central Bank, Due from Other Financial Institutions, Trading securities, Available-for-Sale Securities, Other Securities, and Unearned Income from Securities.

During the lead up to the 2008 crisis, the liquid assets were rising relative to deposits. This indicates a lot of "liquidity" in the financial system by which banks can meet demands for deposit withdrawals, or increased "*Disintermediation*". The very heart of the nature of the 2008–2009 bank crisis is that these liquid assets suddenly fell dramatically relative to deposits. This is because deposits were removed from the Institutional Money Funds, of the investment banks. These banks struggled to come up with the assets needed to allow depositors in such money funds to "cash-out" their deposits and then move them elsewhere out of potentially failing investment banks.

In order to keep off a total collapse of the financial system of intermediation, the Fed had to step in and provide the liquidity as funds were shifted out of investment banks to commercial banks. This kept the entire investment bank sector from potentially falling into insolvency. But this was just the beginning of the Fed action, in which it did succeed, by dramatically expanding its asset holdings as it bought assets with liquid funds that investment banks desperately needed. This Fed action drove the Federal Funds Rate (FFR) quickly down to zero as in Figure 11.1 above. But did the Fed have to subsequently keep the FFR at zero or near zero as it has done continuously since 2009?

11.3 Theory

11.3.1 Bagehot's law of financial efficiency

Walter Bagehot wrote *Lombard Street: A Description of the Money Market* in 1873. He argues first that England's London had become the center of finance in Europe at the time, in the mid 1800's.[13] This occurred, according

[13]"therefore, the reserve in the Banking Department of the Bank of England is the banking reserve not only of the Bank of England, but of all London and not only of all London, but of all England, Ireland, and Scotland too" (W. Bagehot, Lombard Street, reprint

to Bagehot, as a result of the Bank of England evolving into a central bank from a private bank that in turn provided sufficient reserves for the entire Great Britain financial system. As a result of this Bank of England reserve role, the rest of the British financial system was able to hold virtually zero reserves, according to Bagehot. This made for a highly efficient intermediation of savers deposits into loans that led to the accelerating British wealth accumulation that occurred at the time. This high finance efficiency was apparently key in Britain's continued leadership in the so-called "*industrial revolution*" as it was maturing in the 19th century.

Bagehot's law of financial efficiency can be stated as holding the minimum amount of reserves in a centralized, government-run entity, sufficient to provide liquidity for the entire financial system while at the same time not imposing reserve requirements on the rest of the private financial intermediation system. Bagehot recommended 1) Allowing private financial intermediaries to keep all reserves at the central authority, such as the Bank of England, and 2) having access to additional reserves through private bank borrowing from such authority at increased interest rates when needed, and 3) allowing the central authority to add additional reserves as it deemed sufficient, was how the financial system could stay "slimmed-down" in keeping a minimum of uninvested capital aside as reserves in case of emergencies.

In modern times, an International Monetary Fund Working Paper, number WP/14/118 by Demirgüc-Kunt et al. estimates that 100% of countries in all regions of the world have either implicit or explicit bank deposit insurance schemes.[14] That means: every country in the world has a governmental bank deposit insurance scheme. In the modern world of fiat (unbacked) money instead of the previous gold standard, deposit insurance and its funding takes the place of holding gold reserves.

In Bagehot's world, in contrast the central bank simply had to choose what percent of the money supply, which was convertible to gold, to keep as gold reserves at the central bank. Bagehot suggested 40% was sufficient. In the US, on March 3, 1933, when the Federal Reserve System shut down, for the first and only time in its history, the stated reason was that its reserves were less than the legally required level: this percent of US required reserves (in gold) was the exact same percent, 40%, that Bagehot (1873) recommended.

When the Fed reopened in 1933, *deposit insurance law* was simultaneously enacted in the US within the 1933 Banking Act with the establishment of the FDIC and its explicit system for providing a fund for bank failures so as to avoid a system-wide panic. This created an historical "bend-point" whereby future history became that of a deposit insurance system existing even while the gold standard remained tenuously alive. The US gold standard system was watered down significantly in 1945 with only central banks able to redeem US dollars for gold. The complete end of the gold standard came in 1971 under President Nixon. All the while, during the gradual demise of the gold standard, the FDIC and the US government deposit insurance system was in place.

The FDIC in turn is financed by banks paying premiums for the customer deposits that the FDIC insures. The FDIC insurance premium paid by banks differs according to which risk class the FDIC has placed each bank, with riskier classes of banks paying a higher premium per dollar of deposits that are insured. Using different premiums based on risk class of bank assets actually was not enacted in the years from 1933 to 2005.[15] Based on a 2005 FDIC US law, it was only in 2006 that the FDIC first started using risk-bases to allow for differential premium classes, as it still does today.

The theory behind the ubiquity of governmental bank deposit insurance across the world is that an efficient deposit insurance system serves exactly as the Lombard Street -envisioned minimal central government quantity of reserves that is sufficient to prevent bank panics. Such efficiency in a bank reserve system allows for more intermediation of savings into loans and investment, and greater wealth accumulation.

2010, p.19, by Greenbook Publications, llc.). Wales is oddly omitted here, but is often lumped together with England due in part to the 1297 Magna Carta "constitution" of the UK having applied to both England and Wales; 3 articles of the Magna Carta apparently are still statutory law in only England and Wales.

[14]https://www.imf.org/external/pubs/ft/wp/2014/wp14118.pdf

[15]"The FDIC merged the Bank Insurance Fund (BIF) and the Savings Association Insurance Fund (SAIF) to form the Deposit Insurance Fund (DIF) on March 31, 2006 in accordance with the Federal Deposit Insurance Reform Act of 2005. FDIC maintains the DIF by assessing depository institutions an insurance premium. The amount each institution is assessed is based upon statutory factors that include the balance of insured deposits as well as the degree of risk the institution poses to the insurance fund" (FDIC online statement of risk-based premium history. at https://www.fdic.gov/deposit/insurance/risk/)

11.3.2 Debt-Deflation & Credit Booms

Since 2008, part of the justification for the ad hoc, piecemeal, bailout of the bank sector that has been ongoing internationally, instead of a comprehensive reform using the risk-based deposit insurance model of the FDIC, is that there was such a deep crisis in 2008 that anything was justifiable. Any policy was perhaps thought to be acceptable as long as a Great Depression experience was avoided. But has it been necessary to have a prolonging of the Great Recession into a Lost Decade?

The crash of capital asset markets, such as the Dow Jones Industrial stock average in 2008, coincided with the crash of the banking system in terms of investment banks. This caused a serious "Debt-Deflation" consistent with Irving Fisher's original definition: a downwards cycle of firms and banks going bankrupt and of increasing unemployment and of ever decreasing asset values. These coinciding asset crashes and Phillips curves for both the 1929 and 2008 period in Chapter 6 above (Figures 6.16 to 6.19).

The coincidence of high unemployment and falling inflation rates that occur in these debt-deflation periods naturally give rise to temporary Phillips curves, lasting mainly for just the time of the stock market crash (or boom). While here it is offered that these periods are characteristic of bank crisis periods, most view the exact timing of the occurrence of Phillips curves as an unaddressed and unexplained phenomena. Taking the latter point of view, one could say: look, here in the Great Recession is a Phillips curve behavior and so let's just somehow increase the inflation rate. The corollary of this logic is that it does not matter how we increase the inflation rate; just increase it.

Taking the other point of view, this being that Phillips curves tend to happen either when bank productivity crashes or advances significantly, gives a different view of how to avoid a big deflation. Rather the answer is to efficiently reform the bank sector, in the Great Recession case through efficient, encompassing, financial sector deposit insurance with risk-based premiums. This would enable the private sector lending and private money supply (demand deposits) from making loans expand and keep inflation from declining. Then the burden of increasing the public, government, Federal Reserve money supply component (currency) would be largely eliminated.

Therefore the idea that Phillips curves during crisis periods, or high growth periods, are due to financial sector decline or advance in productivity is an important concept. It turns the theoretical policy prescription into one of reforming financial intermediation through extension of the FDIC blueprint. This is instead of the current indiscriminate, unending, distortionary bank sector subsidization through interest on excess reserves, increased bank asset reserve regulation, plus large expansion of the government money supply, a policy that has now occurred continuously since 2008.

The graphs of the Great Depression and Great Recession show a coincidence of Phillips curve behavior with asset price collapse, during a time of bank collapse. Consider evidence to exemplify the reverse: a Phillips curve that is coincident with a huge advance in bank productivity and in the value of asset prices. For this there is the famous modern US textbook example of Phillips curves: the decade from 1959 to 1969.

Figure 6.12 shows the famous US Phillips curve existing markedly for January 1959 to December 1969, almost an eleven year period. Note first: the economy was moving up the Phillips curve in this example over time, starting at the bottom part of the graph and moving up and to the left as the inflation rate increased and the unemployment rate decreased. This is the opposite of how the economy moved down the Phillips curves in the Great Depression and Great Recession.

So is the 1960s decade consistent with the banking explanation of the Phillips curve? This is a big question as previous literature ignores the banking element in this period. Yet the banking productivity advance during the 1960's has been called the beginning of the international financial system's use of multinational corporate finance.[16] And coincident with the 1960's Phillips curve was a decade-long US asset price boom.

---

[16]"UMNBs [universal multinational banks] are the most important financial intermediaries in the international markets." (p.22) "Broadly speaking, the present structure of the domestic banking industry was established in the late- 1950s and early-1960s, which period saw significant New York merges leading the creation of Chase Manhattan, Chemical Bank and Manufacturers Hanover. "[which together later became JP Morgan Chase]. "This period also saw the banks develop the idea of full-service banking including leasing, installment credit, factoring, mortgage banking, and so on. Credit cards were introduced and became an important mode of consumer payments and credit. . . . The 1960s also saw the remarkable growth in international banking activities of the major

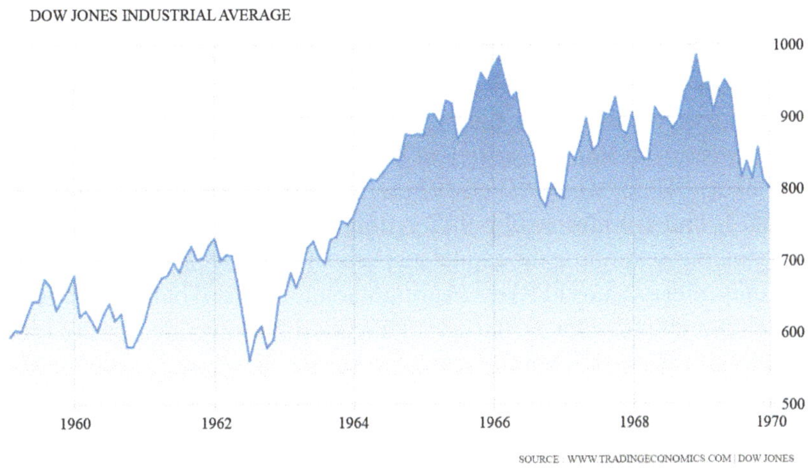

Figure 11.17 Dow Jones Industrial Average during the 1960's

Figure 11.17 shows that the Dow Jones Industrial Average rose from 600 to 1000, a 66% increase over 10 years of 1959 to 1969, or 6.6% average increase per year. Meanwhile inflation was measured as rising about one-half of a percent per year on average. This is a marked advance in real asset values and the cost of capital.

Altogether, the suggestion emerges that deficit-debt downward spirals are linked to banking collapse during Phillips curve eras such as the Great Depression and Great Recession. Conversely, credit booms likewise can be linked to major banking technological advance and asset price jumps during Phillips curve eras such as the 1960's decade. The credit booms during banking advance constitute the flip-side of credit crashes ("debt-deflation") during banking collapses, both being accompanied by and perhaps generating the Phillips curves during these periods.

The Phillips curves during banking crashes or banking advances lead to a type of deflation or inflation that appears to be characterized by an aggregate price level that is driven by a relative price change in capital asset values relative to labor costs. Such a relative price change driving a measured inflation decrease or increase may argue for action to re-balance the relative price change if prudent, rather than simply supplying more or less government money supply. The private money supply is what is crashing or booming during these banking crashes or advances. This suggests a focus on the government in helping banking during a collapse, with the most efficient reforms such as the FDIC. And it may suggest regulating banking prudentially during a dramatic expansion of banking that stems from technological advance, or even from financial deregulation.

11.3.3 Tax on Capital Markets and Welfare Loss

In contrast, if the government and its central bank view a banking crisis led recession as causing deflation that is excessive and that they want to avoid, then the government may focus on the easy path of just printing central bank money rapidly rather than focusing on the more difficult task of reforming the financial sector. Efficiently reforming the financial sector can quickly bring it out of crisis and "reflate" the economy, as happened immediately following the US 1933 Banking Act, and its establishment of the FDIC. Inflation went from a negative 10% to a positive 5% in less than a year.

The 1930's banking legislation amounted to a *"normalization" of the banking sector* and the economy that effectively ended the Great Depression. And it was done without dramatically increasing the government money supply of currency. Instead the "reflation" was done by private banks intermediating savings to investment, causing demand deposits and loans to grow.

banks. In 1956 US banks operated 123 branches abroad. Between 1960 and 1970 the number of foreign branches increased from 124 to over 500 . . . The post-War international banking boom is closely linked to the spread of US multinational enterprises in the aftermath of the Marshall plan, and to the emergence of the Eurodollar markets . . ." (Neil Coulbeck, 1984, The Multinational Banking Industry, pp. 181–183, Routeledge). The 1960s constituted "the second era of dynamic growth for multinational banking . . ." (p. 30, The globalization of banking, in Handbook of International Banking edited by A. W. Mullineux, Victor Murinde, Edward Elgar Publishing, 2003).

During the 1960's similarly there was a bevy of banking regulations and legislation to regulate the tremendous growth in US banking both within the US and in the international capital markets. Again, here during the 1960's inflation, the use of the government to decrease the inflation rate by reducing the government supply of money was not resorted to. Rather the regulation of the growing bank sector was the policy focus.

During the Great Recession, seemingly inefficient banking reform and bank sector subsidization has occurred while also dramatically increasing the government money supply (in terms of the monetary base of "reserves plus currency"). This is a jumble of policy action that may not have been well-designed.

For example, by continuously flooding the capital markets with newly printed money, the Fed has managed to keep the Federal Funds interest rate (FFR) on overnight loans between banks near zero. This has occurred by a continual flood of money into capital markets. This flood has not only lowered the nominal, market, FFR, but also has continually pushed down the real interest rate. The flood has created low real interest rate "swamp", where return on savings is so low as to be not worth offering much savings for intermediation.

Wicksell in his (1898 p.4) *Interest & Prices: A Study of the Causes Regulating the Value of Money* describes how real interest rates can be driven down both temporarily and permanently. The accelerated rate of growth of the US Monetary Base since 2008 allows according to Wicksell for the real rate to be driven down in a "permanent" way because of the Fed providing persistent liquidity to capital markets. But Wicksell's prediction of higher inflation has not yet occurred. Instead reserves are earning interest from the Fed and not being lent out. This defers the normal money creation process whereby excess reserves are completely lent out, demand deposits are created, and the money supply accelerates in a money multiplier fashion.

The Fed-created capital market "swamp" from persistent liquidity is a distortion that implies a certain tax and subsidization scheme is in effect. In particular, a continual use of the Fed to distort capital markets by providing unending liquidity acts as a subsidy to investment but a tax to savers. Investors are happy to get money for a near zero real interest rate but savers are not willing to supply much at a near zero interest rate.

Enforcing a near zero or negative real interest rate, not just a near zero nominal interest rate, acts as the imposition of an effective ceiling on real interest rates that distorts capital markets away from their *natural "Wicksellian" real interest rate equilibrium* (which would likely be in the range of 2 to 4+%, given US history). Consider Figure 11.18 as a representation of the capital market supply and demand for capital, which are savings and investment respectively. The relative price of capital is $(1+r)/1$, or simply $1+r$. This $1+r$ is called the "gross" real interest rate (the net interest rate r could instead be used).

Figure 11.18 includes an real interest ceiling at around 0.5%. Post–2008 the actual real interest rate has actually been lower and in fact at negative rates almost the entire period, so the graph abstracts from the exact level of the real interest rate. It also abstracts from the fact that the real interest rate fluctuated at mostly negative levels as the inflation rate fluctuated around positive levels almost the entire post-2008 period.

In Figure 11.18 the example equilibrium rate is at a level somewhat above 4%. The real interest rate ceiling at 0.5% causes the quantity supplied (the savings) to be less than the quantity demanded (the investment). This causes an excess demand for capital at the enforced ceiling.

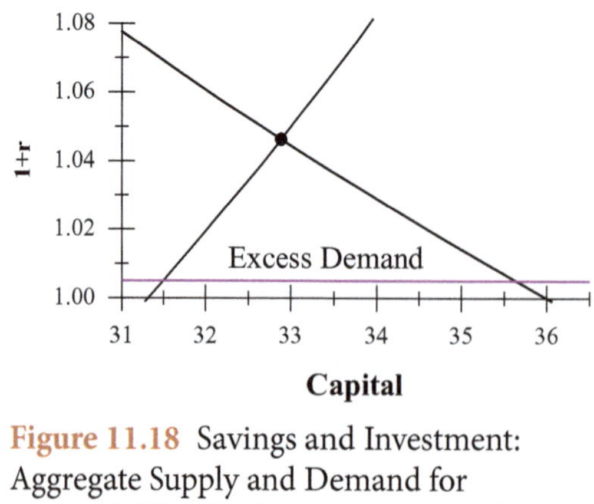

Figure 11.18 Savings and Investment: Aggregate Supply and Demand for Capital k With Real Interest Rate Ceiling

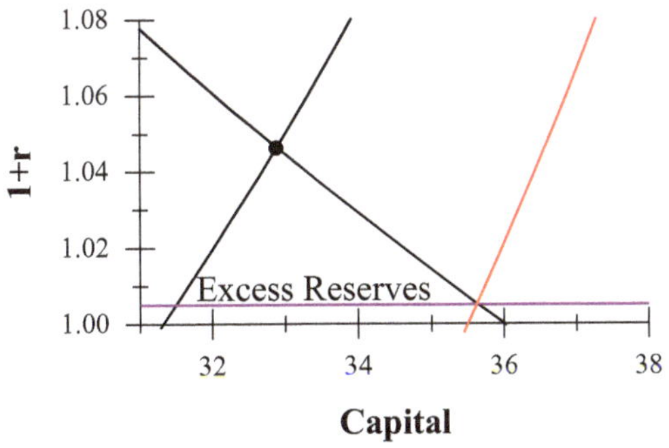

Figure 11.19 Fed's Shift out of Supply of Capital through the Open Market Purchases of US Treasury or Treasury backed Securities: Creating the Bank System's Excess Reserves

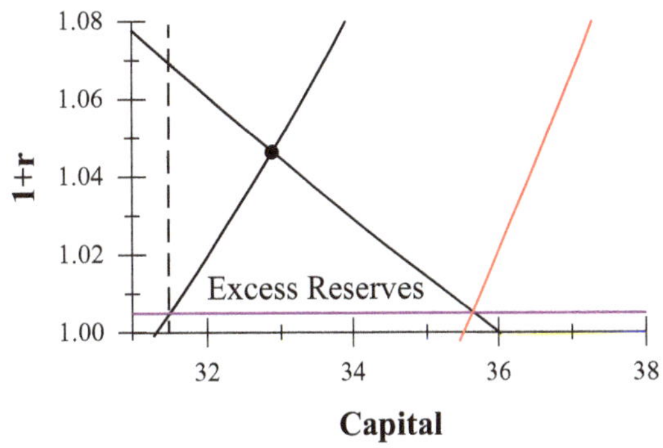

Figure 11.20 High *r* for Private Investors, Low *r* for Private Savers, and the "Deadweight Loss Triangle"

Figure 11.19 shows how the ceiling is effectively imposed. There is a large additional supply of capital, as given by the red supply line in the graph. This is due to the central bank increase of the monetary base. In particular, since interest is paid on reserves in the US since 2008 at a rate higher than the Federal Funds rate, the excess supply of capital is exactly analogous to the US banking system's excess reserves.

The excess reserves, which were effectively zero throughout US history before 2008, have been caused by the Fed's massive open market purchases of US Treasury debt since 2008, as well as purchases of mortgage backed securities (MBS). The MBS consist of loans guaranteed by the US Treasury, so these MBS are effectively US Treasury liabilities, or debt, as well. This means that the black supply and demand lines in Figure 11.19 are the private sector supply and demand for capital while the excess reserves are the US government's excess supply of capital that enforces the real interest rate ceiling.

Figure 11.20 shows the implicit tax that is imposed by an effective real interest rate ceiling. The dotted vertical line shows the quantity of capital that is saved and invested by the private economy. The Savers receive a very low real interest rate, at the 0.5% level of the ceiling. And because of an artificially, Fed policy-induced, low supply of capital for the private sector, the real interest rate for the private investment is effectively very high, near 7% in the graph. The "triangle" in Figure 11.20, marked by the dotted vertical line and the supply and demand curves, is what microeconomics calls the "dead-weight loss" of "lost consumer and producer surplus". This surplus is welfare that would not be lost if instead the natural Wicksellian real interest rate prevailed, where the black supply and demand curves intersect. Economists sometimes call this the Harberger triangle, because of his study of welfare loss from tax and subsidization.[17]

As George Selgin of the Cato Institute put it in a Wall Street Journal editorial called "A Legal Barrier to Higher Interest Rates", [18]

> To set a floor on how far the rate could go, the Fed started paying interest on banks' reserve balances with the Fed, taking advantage of the 2006 Financial Services Regulatory Relief Act giving it permission to do so. Alas, it did not work. Government sponsored enterprises . . . which . . . weren't eligible for interest on reserves (IOR), started making overnight loans to banks at rates below the IOR rate. In effect, this turned what the Fed hoped would be a floor on the fed-funds rate into a ceiling. To raise rates now the Fed increases the rate on reserves.

Selgin's quote is about the nominal interest rate, which has been kept almost exactly constant. But since the inflation rate has been above the nominal interest rate on excess reserves for almost the entire post-2008 period, the ceiling on nominal interest rates translates into a ceiling on real interest rates that is at a mostly

[17]The Harberger triangle work is brought together in Harberger's 1974 book, Taxation and Welfare, published by Little, Brown.
[18]George Selgin, "A Legal Barrier to Higher Interest Rates", the Wall Street Journal, September 27, 2016; Op-Ed page.

negative level that fluctuates somewhat with the inflation rate (rather than staying exactly constant as in the above figures).

11.3.4 Financial "Repression"

The forcing down of real interest rates has been called a part of the US government's "financial repression" of the financial intermediary sector. It is part of distorting the flow of savings towards the government sector's spending and away from the private sector's investment.[19] As the Wall Street Journal (WSJ) puts it:

> "This time, though, the signs of stress are a result of something else: The campaign by governments to direct financing to themselves, limiting access by the private sector. In the U.S., there are legal changes under way in the money markets, which is prompting money to shift from `prime' funds, which buy short-term debts issued by companies, to instead buy short-term debt issued by the U.S. Treasury. This is merely the latest example of what academics call financial repression, a broad category of government policy adopted to require savings to be lent cheaply to the government. Repressive policies were the norm in Western markets for decades following World War II. That was until the financial liberalization was begun by Margaret Thatcher in the U.K. and then-President Ronald Reagan in the U.S. New rules since the Lehman Brothers failure [in 2008] have again tightened the screws on lending to the private sector, while favoring government financing in multiple ways, most obviously through exempting banks from holding capital against government debt".[20]

Banks typically have to hold reserves against loans they make, but apparently not for government debt. This increases the distortion towards savings going into "risk-free" government debt rather than into risky private sector investment.

11.3.5 "Seeking Yield": Capital Market Distortion

Figure 11.20 shows how an effective real interest rate ceiling distorts capital markets, causing a higher real interest rate in effect for investors in the private sector. How has this played out in the facts of the Great Recession? Many economists have described the post-2008 period right up to the present as one in which investors have been forced to "seek yield". This means that the traditional *portfolio balance* between holding a certain amount of low yield government debt and higher yielding private sector investments has been distorted towards holding more government debt.[21]

The pushing down of the real interest return on government debt has forced the private sector to find higher yielding private investment in order to try to balance out the return on the whole portfolio with the desired amount of overall riskiness. With banks forced to hold so much government debt, this means the rest of private savings deposits get directed more towards higher yielding private sector investment. This is the "seeking yield" part of the consequences of the Great Recession government flooding of capital markets with money (held as reserves). But it is accepted in finance theory, in terms of what is called the capital asset pricing model of optimal market portfolio holdings, that higher yield in private investment comes with higher risk. This higher risk in the private investment, during this seeking-yield post-2008 period, is balanced by large holdings of low risk, low yield government debt.

The high interest rate in Figure 11.20 in this way represents the high yield, but also higher risk, that occurs in a capital market that is induced into "seeking yield" in order to compensate for the low return and large holdings of government debt. Put differently, the private sector investment as a whole is riskier than it would be otherwise. Figure 11.21 captures this "tilting" of the average portfolio's holding of risky private sector investment.

---

[19]See also V. V. Chari, Alessandro Dovis and Patrick J. Kehoe, 2016, "On the Optimality of Financial Repression", Federal Reserve Bank of Minneapolis Research Department Staff Report XXX, January.

[20]James Mackintosh, Streetwise (column), WSJ, August 2, 2016; p. C1–C2.

[21]See Parantap Basu and William T. Gavin (2010), What Explains the Growth in Commodity Derivatives? Federal Reserve Bank of St. Louis Review, January/February 2011, 93(1), pp. 37–48.

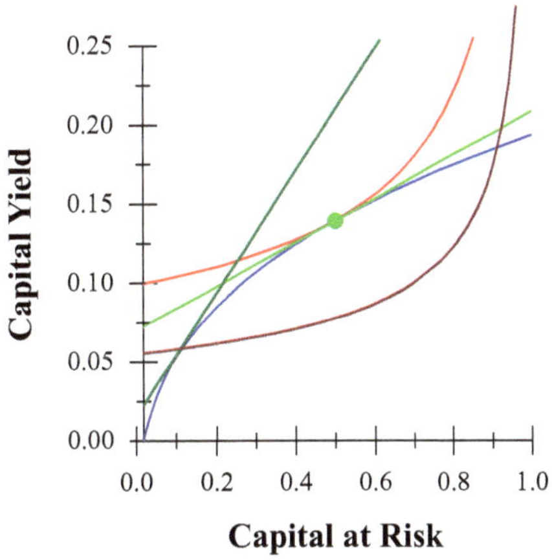

Figure 11.21 Optimal Portfolio Diversification between Market Portfolio (Tangency) and "Risk-free" Government Debt

Figure 11.21 graphs the portfolio yield on the vertical axis and the share of the portfolio invested in risky private capital on the horizontal axis, as is done in the capital asset pricing model graphs. The blue production possibility curve is the "efficiency frontier" of the total risk and yield of investment in the private sector economy. This frontier was developed by Sharpe (1964) and Lintner (1965), and allows for the individual "idiosyncratic risk" of each firm to be pooled together (and so eliminated) so that only "systemic risk" remains and is graphed on the horizontal axis.[22]

The indifference curves in the graph, the red and brown (convex) curves are typically attributed to Tobin (1958).[23] They show the representative household-saver preference for diversifying between the risky portfolio of private sector investment and the so-called *"riskless" portfolio of government debt.* In Figure 11.21 the natural tangency between the production possibility curve of the "efficiency frontier" of private investment and the red indifference curve of the representative saver is the undistorted equilibrium amount of the share of capital that is invested privately, with the rest invested in "risk-free" government debt.

When the real return on the private sector is pushed up by policy distortions that cause the "seeking of yield", the investors see a higher price of risk relative to yield while the savers face a lower price of risk relative to yield. Figure 11.21 represents this policy induced new equilibrium by the intersection of the brown indifference curve with the blue production possibility curve. This shows a "wedge" between the interest cost of investment in the private sector and interest return to savers in households. This intersection thereby corresponds to the ceiling induced wedge between the return to savers and to private investors in Figure 11.20.

The distorted equilibrium is seen with a steeper slope along the blue production possibility curve at the point of the intersection relative to the tangency point as in the natural equilibrium. This indicates a higher price of risk relative to yield. For the saver, the intersection of the utility curve with the production possibility curve indicates a lower price of risk per yield, as seen by the flatter slope of the indifference curve upon which the saver equilibrium resides.

Figure 11.21 exaggerates possibly the degree to which the equilibrium has changed during the Great Recession, using this standard risk-yield diagram of the capital asset pricing model. But it maintains the two different equilibrium in such a way that they are consistent with the same preferences of the representative agent, who is both investor and saver in the aggregate economy. To see this, note that the degree of diversification between the risk free government bonds and the risky private capital changes as the share in risky capital falls

[22]Lintner, John, 1965, "The valuation of risk assets and the selection of risky investments in stock portfolios and capital budgets," *Review of Economics and Statistics*, 47 (1): 13–37; Sharpe, William F. ,1964,. "Capital asset prices: A theory of market equilibrium under conditions of risk," *Journal of Finance*, 19 (3): 425–442.

[23]Tobin, James, 1958, "Liquidity Preference as Behavior Towards Risk," *Review of Economic Studies* 25.1: 65–86.

from 50% to 10% of total capital investment, as given by the vertical axis of Figure 11.21. This is certainly an exaggeration of the decreased share of the portfolio in private capital.

The preferences still can remain constant as given by a set preference map of utility curves. The two equilibria have the same share of the risk-premium in the total interest yield of the portfolio. The total yield is the government risk-free rate plus the risk-premium from private sector investment. The ratio of the risk-premium to the total yield in the Figure 11.21 example starts at the original tangency equilibrium of a risk-premium to yield ratio of a total yield around 13.5% minus a risk-free rate of around 7.5%, for a risk-premium of 6%. Relative to the total interest yield, 6% is 58% of 13.5%.

In the new distorted equilibrium, the total yield changes to around 6% minus a risk-free yield of 2.5%, or a 3.5% risk-premium, relative to a total yield of 6%. This gives a risk premium (3.5) that is an identical 58% of the total yield (6.0). So the preference for a certain percent of risk relative to yield is maintained in the new equilibrium, despite the degree of diversification changing from 50% in private investment to 10%.

The purpose of Figure 11.21 is to illustrate the theory of how the real interest rate ceiling distorts capital markets in terms of not just a lower quantity of private sector investment than in the natural undistorted equilibrium, but also a riskier overall portfolio for investors but a less risky one for savers. Many have explained the Great Recession in these terms of seeking risk. Here the concept is related to the finance theory standard of the "capital asset price model" and its yield-risk graphical presentation. It shows that not only are quantities distorted but so is the quality of private sector investment distorted, towards riskier investment.

The manifestation of a riskier private sector portfolio can be a so-called "bubble" in asset prices, such as in the Dow Jones Industrial Average, the Standard and Poor 500, or the Russell 3000. Given the policy distortion, such a bubble is fully rational, many would argue. But if the policy distortion is eliminated, it may well be that the fundamentals of the return on the investments end up yielding less than is promised by current asset stock prices. This means the stock market might "crash" if the policy distortion of the interest ceiling on real interest rates is eliminated, and so prices return to "fundamental values". If so, in retrospect we would call current stock price levels a bubble. But at the current time of the high prices in stock markets, such as in 2016 when the Dow once again rose above 2007 levels to record highs, it is never clear that there exists a bubble that must pop. Or put differently, it is unclear that the price of overall portfolio risk to yield (the slope in Figure 11.21) is being pushed higher only by government policy that is unsustainable in the long term.

Figure 11.22 shows that real asset prices, here seen as the Russell 3000 stock index divided by the CPI price index, have trended significantly upwards since 2010 without real GDP trending upwards. This also

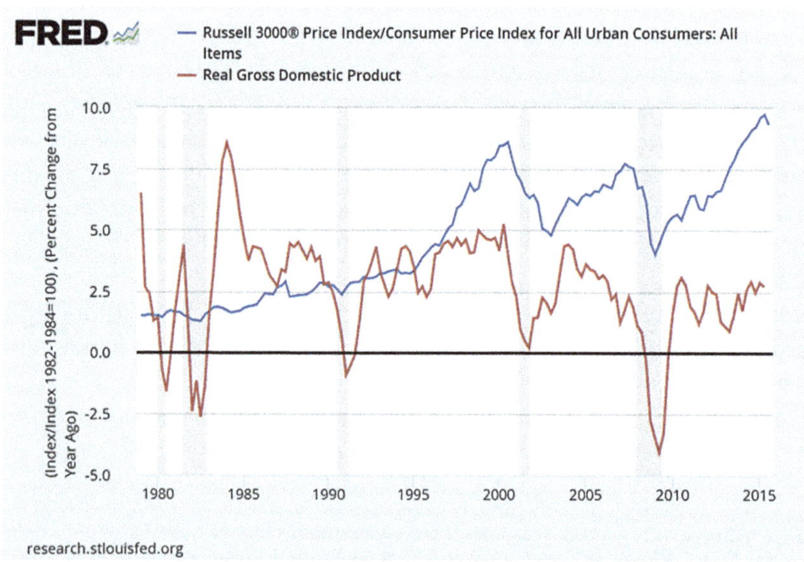

Figure 11.22 Real Capital Asset Prices (Russell 300/CPI) relative to Real GDP Growth

happened in the 1996 to 2000 period. It simply indicates that there may be a significant asset price reversal if real interest rates start moving back to "historically normal" levels. If there is risk seeking because of too low real interest rates, then allowing higher, more normal, or "natural", rates of interest can cause a short term reversal in asset price levels.

11.3.6 Government Capital Flooding

Consider that in Figure 11.21 when the private sector "capital at risk" becomes less, this means that the fraction of the portfolio invested in the private sector falls relative to that invested in risk-free government debt. So even as the risky interest rate on private investment rises, the decrease in the government risk-free rate, and the increase in the fraction of the portfolio held in risk-free debt, means that the average overall return on capital may actually be falling, including both risky and risk-free capital investment.

Meanwhile a smaller fraction of capital investment going into private sector investment means that the real wage gets pushed upwards. Indeed, the real wage markedly rose during 2008 to 2009, as well as during 2001–2003, in opposite movement relative to detrended real GDP growth, as shown in Figure 8.2, when real interest rates were unusually low or negative during these periods. Overall this can induce a rise in the price of human capital relative to physical capital.

The result would be seen as an increase in the wage to real interest rate ratio, or w/r. In the economic theory of firm production, such a rise in relative factor prices induces substitution from labor (human capital) to capital. This would be consistent with a falling labor force participation rate, a falling employment rate, and lower growth due to less human capital investment. All of these phenomena have been a feature of the Great Recession and the almost "lost decade" of 2007 to 2016.

Figure 11.23 shows the blue isoquant which is a constant level of output for different combination of human and physical capital inputs. The light green isocost line shows the natural equilibrium tangency point that determines the Human to Physical capital ratio in an undistorted market. The slope of the isocost line is the wage rate w divided by the real interest rate r, or w/r. When w is pushed up while r is pushed down by policy, then for the same level of production (same isoquant) the equilibrium would move to the left where the dark green isocost is tangent to the blue isoquant. The human capital to physical capital ratio become lower as w/r becomes higher. Of course the isoquant could be shifted in as well to a lower level of output as representative of the Great Recession (when the output growth rate was negative). Relatively less human capital is consistent with a lower economic growth rate; this can be seen when the Ramsey model is extended to explain growth endogenously through addition of a human capital investment sector (as in Chapter 9 Appendix).

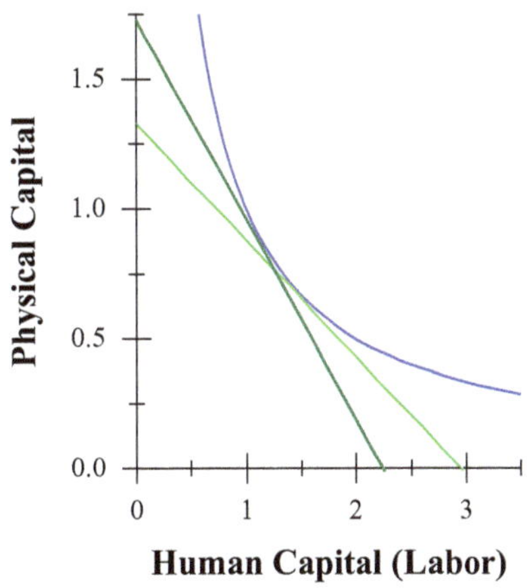

Figure 11.23 Policy Induced Substitution from Human Capital to Physical Capital, from Light Green Tangency to Dark Green Tangency

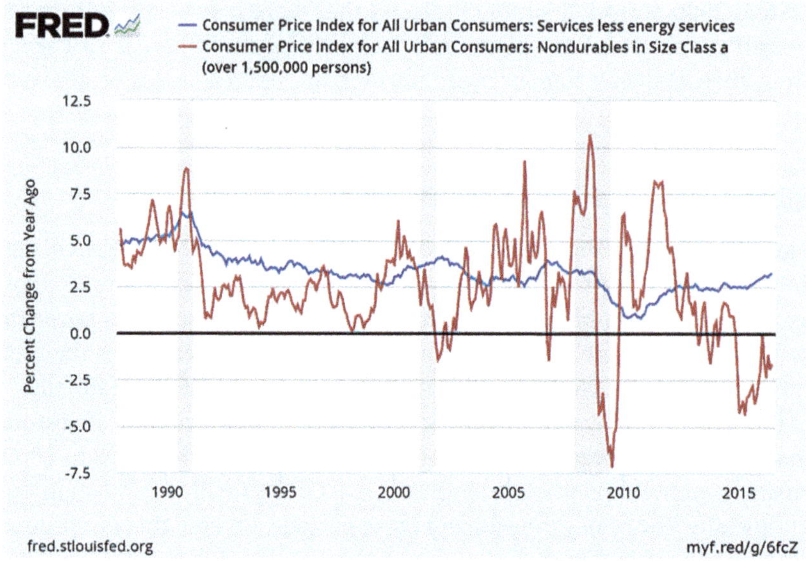

Figure 11.24 Large Decline in the Percentage Change in the CPI price index for Non-Durables (Red) relative to Services (Blue), in 2009 and since 2012

A way that this theoretical relative price change of inputs can be seen in the data of output prices is through the CPI for services, which are human capital intensive, versus the CPI for non-durables goods, which are more physical capital intensive. Figure 11.24 shows that in the percentage change in a CPI price index for Non-Durables relative to Services fell in 2009 and continually after 2012 to the present, as the gap between the Blue and the Red data series is positive. Relatively cheaper capital prices make the cost of more capital-intensive non-durable goods less expensive relative to the cost of more labor- (or human capital) intensive Services. Post 2012, this difference in the CPI components has been large in historical (post-1987) terms.

The second related effect is that government investment has pushed out private investment. This is seen by the low loan to deposit ratios. And it is seen by the massive holdings of government investment in Mortgage Backed Securities and in Treasury debt. This is manifestly enforced by the massive quantities of excess reserves held by Fed for private banks. The total capital input may rise, as in Figure 11.23, even as private investment falls, given the US government's massive increase in debt during the Great Recession.

Private banks get paid interest on the excess reserves above the Federal Funds rate, and so give the reserves back to the Fed. Without the interest paid on excess reserves, the interest ceiling on the real interest rate would collapse as the excess reserves would gradually be lent out. With the interest paid on excess reserves capital markets remain distorted here and internationally.

11.3.7 Internationally Inefficient Bank Subsidization

The globalization of financial intermediation that developed significantly starting in the 1960's meant that capital funds could move across country to take advantage of differentials in real interest rates found internationally. If the US real rate is relatively low, US funds can move to another country, buy up that other country's currency, and receive a higher return on capital.

The buying up of another country's currency, say using US dollars, leads to an appreciation of that country's exchange rate relative to the US dollar. The demand for the foreign currency increases its price relative to US dollars, and this price is the exchange rate. The rise in the exchange rate in turn makes exports of that foreign country more expensive relative to US demand for their products as imports. This is the way that international exchange rates move, reflecting the supply and demand of a country's currency relative to another country's currency.

Artificially low real interest rates in the US, in the sense that they are being forced down by US government policy, can induce in effect similarly artificially low real interest rates in other nations that trade with the US. The reason is that governments of other countries may not wish to see their exchange rates appreciate relative to the US dollar as this would increase the price of exports in terms of US dollars. Therefore they increase their money supply enough to push down their own real interest rate through repeated, accelerated, rates of money supply growth.

Worldwide the Great Recession has seen the term *"quantitative easing"* applied post -2008 to US money supply accelerated growth policy, to the United Kingdom's money supply accelerated growth policy and to the European Central Bank's money supply accelerated growth policy. This has led to low real interest rates in the US, UK and Eurozone (including 19 of the 28 EU economies). Other international governments have also followed suit in order to avoid appreciation against the currencies of such a large trading block as the US, UK and Eurozone represent.

For example, Switzerland for several years post -2008 refused to follow this accelerated money supply growth policy and the result was an historic appreciation of its currency relative to the US dollar, UK pound, and EU's Euro. One Swiss franc went from being worth $0.78 US in October 2006 to $1.30 in August 2011, a two-thirds increase in value. Finally Switzerland began to supply more money and steadily drove the US $ value of one Swiss franc back down to $1.02 in July 2012, and was near this $1.02 level four years later in July 2016. Interestingly, the Swiss National Bank had no large Swiss government debt increases to buy, so the began buying a portfolio of the Swiss private business sector. This could be said to be in effect a partial nationalization of Swiss private industry as an consequence of their keeping level with the US real interest rate.

Should the US real interest rate really be around zero, or is it policy induced? And then the question is should the international exchange rates of some of the most developed countries be such as to imply near zero real interest rates internationally or is this phenomena policy induced? There are different points of view on this and it is a lively debate.

Some believe that world economic growth is permanently low for now and will stay low and that the near zero real interest rates reflect this correctly. Others argue that the internationally near zero real interest rates are a result of US monetary policy designed to bail out the financial sector in an inefficient fashion, thereby forcing other nations to follow suit or else see their exchange rates appreciate. The argument has been put forth in this chapter that these low real interest rates are not endemic of long term low international real GDP growth rates but rather a result of misguided monetary and banking prudential policy that taxes international capital markets. Thus the question is whether the "lost decade" of post -2007 has been policy induced or some sort of difficult-to-explain sudden drop in real developed world economic growth as in a permanent "secular stagnation".[24]

11.3.8 Deconstructing 3-Equation Central Bank Model

The IS-LM analysis of Keynesian economics from the 1930's has persisted within modern textbooks today. This IS-LM construct has been buttressed by the use of IS and LM terms in modern dynamic general equilibrium analysis, much of which is built upon Ramsey's foundation. The new modern IS and LM equations are even sometimes designated as aggregate supply and demand equations.

The three equation New Keynesian model is the most famous of the modern Keynesian models. This one is typically called a central bank model. There are many alternative version of this model now being promulgated. The central bank model is also called the "dynamic New Keynesian model".[25] It is purportedly a model of the dynamic equilibrium rather than the balanced growth path equilibrium that we studied in the Ramsey World Chapters. This makes it advanced relative to the material covered, but still an important model to discuss because of its wide usage in macroeconomics today.

---

[24]Lawrence Summers takes the "secular stagnation" view in several often referenced blogs; see http://larrysummers.com/category/secular-stagnation/

[25]A good exposition can be found in Matteo Iacoviello's course lecture notes, Chapter 4, "The Dynamic New Keynesian Model"; at: https://www2.bc.edu/~iacoviel/teach/0809/EC751_files/dnk.pdf

The most standard of the New Keynesian three- equation "central bank model" includes a so-called IS curve, sometimes called the aggregate demand equation. The second equation is a version of the Phillips curve typically with a permanent Phillips trade-off whereby higher inflation implies a lower unemployment rate. And the third equation is an interest rate equation that the central bank supposedly follows in its control of the money supply. This third equation is some version of the so-called Taylor (1993) rule of nominal interest rates that links them to inflation and real output.

The first IS equation is known from the long run, balanced growth solution of the Ramsey World "intertemporal" equation that results from choosing the optimal capital investment. This is known typically as the "Euler" equation because Euler's 1757 thermodynamics analysis included the equation that Ramsey built into the basis of dynamic macroeconomic theory. It links the growth rate in a variable like consumption, in the Ramsey World, to the real rate of interest.

On the balanced growth path, during what is essentially the "long run", the growth rate of all growing variables converge to dependence on the real interest rate, including real GDP output growth. In the New Keynesian IS equation, real output growth is linked to the real interest rate in a version that is similar to the balanced growth path equilibrium of the Ramsey World. It is justified as a "dynamic" current period equation because this New Keynesian model has no physical capital accumulation, the key addition of the Ramsey (1928) contribution.

Having zero capital accumulation means that capital investment is zero, so that $Y = C + I$ becomes simply $Y = C$. Therefore the New Keynesian 3-equation model claims that using output in the IS-called Euler equation is a current period, dynamic, equation showing departures from the balanced growth path equilibrium. This is not consistent with the Ramsey World in which capital investment is included, and output only enters the Euler equation per se as a balanced growth equilibrium solution.

The New Keynesian IS equation also extends the real analysis of the Ramsey World to include some monetary features, using the Fisher relation of interest rates. In particular the real interest rate is equal to the nominal interest rate minus the inflation rate, as in the Fisher equation. This brings inflation into the analysis by using what typically is thought of as a long run relation: that the real interest rate is just the residual of the nominal rate minus the inflation rate. This is a long run feature in that evidence and conventional wisdom supports the idea that the Fisher equation of interest rates holds in the long run but may not in the short run dynamic transition of the economy as it encounters various "shocks".

The second Phillips curve equation comes in various forms but the consensus version is that the inflation rate rises with the output level. This then is a permanent Phillips trade-off, even though it is just postulated for the current period, as a dynamic event. But while earlier Phillips curve versions ended the trade-off when the expected inflation rate equaled the actual inflation rate, current versions as derived from a full New Keynesian dynamic optimization model simply make the inflation rate move up when the output level moves up, as a permanent feature that holds for all time, including the "long run".[26]

The third equation postulates a separate "Taylor rule" that is not derived from their original utility maximization model but is simply assumed to result from some sort of central bank calculation outside of the utility maximization model. Here the nominal interest rate is "set" by the central bank according to a combination of the level of the inflation rate and the level of output. Either inflation or output might be deemed as having more importance in determining inflation, but inflation typically has more. Further, it is postulated that if inflation goes up the nominal interest rate rises by even more than does the inflation rate. This last feature is known as the Taylor (1993) principle of how the central bank reacts to inflation rate increases in terms of setting the nominal interest rate while conducting its monetary policy, as discussed in Chapter 5.

In contrast, Davies et al. (2016) show how a Taylor type rule can be viewed instead simply as the asset behavior in an equilibrium economy with money supplied by the central bank. The "Taylor principle" holds in Davies et al. (in an observationally equivalent way to the Taylor rule), as long as the nominal interest rate is above zero, as it has been throughout US history. The Taylor rule in Davies et al. is actually the Euler

[26]See a recent New Keynesian 3-equation model as applied to long run growth rates, with a long run Phillips curve, in Laubach and Williams, 2015, "Measuring the Natural Rate of Interest Redux", Working Paper 2015–16, Federal Reserve Bank of San Francisco.

equation of the economy. In the "long run", Davies et al. show how this Euler equation transforms into a Fisher equation of interest rates.[27]

Further critiquing the New Keynesian three equation model, there is a combination of a having no money in the final model and yet having inflation. The inflation in this model is somewhat disguised relative to historical discussion of how the money supply growth rate causes inflation. Instead, the inflation here is always a relative price change due to a change in marginal costs of production relative to the price of labor, the wage rate. The wage rate is eliminated in the final 3 equation form, but the relative price rises because it is assumed there is monopoly power of the firm and that there are shocks to the monopoly power, and the resulting "mark-up" on price.

The lack of any inflation except relative price -caused inflation is a large departure from Fisher's monetary theory that indicates how money supply changes lead to inflation rate changes. So this New Keynesian 3-equation model is used explain high inflation periods such as the 1970's Vietnam war era by saying that there were large monopolistic relative price increases, in particular due to the OPEC price increases that occurred after the complete demise of the remnants of the Bretton Woods gold standard in 1973.

The lack of money supply based inflation within the model makes the model consistent only with periods dominated by relative price changes. And its use of the long run relation between the real interest rate and output growth, in the IS curve, mean that it postulates the relative price changes as part of a long run equilibrium that holds all of the time. The Phillips curve equation implies that increases in relative prices cause higher output. And then, in combination with the central bank equation, this means that the Fed would raise nominal interest rates in accordance to the relative price increases and so cause output to increase.

The 3-equation model includes that the Phillips curve relation is exploitable for central bank policy purposes. At least two Nobel Prizes were given out for the theory that Phillips curves are not so-exploitable (Lucas, 1996, citing his 1972 Phillips curve model; Phelps, 2006, for his book edition emphasizing non-exploitability). But taking the 3 equation model as it is, if the central bank can cause a relative price increase of goods and capital relative to labor, they can as a result cause output to rise. And then they can raise nominal interest rates after they get the relative price increase to cause higher measured inflation. This appears to present a good way to get out of recessions: cause a relative price increase in goods relative to labor. However the 3 equation model is interpreted simply as raising the inflation rate in any way, including by increasing the Fed's money supply growth rate, which is not the basis of the model at all. This is a contradictory use of the model relative to its designed content.

During the Great Recession, the 3 equation model did not much help policy discussion. To take it literally as in the model, the Fed's goal would have been to cause a relative price increase in goods relative to labor. This would have had to happen during a crash in the banking sector's productivity in intermediating funds, as occurred in the 2008 to 2010 period. But in contrast, this period was characterized by a decrease in the inflation rate that induced a relative price decline in the price of goods and capital relative to labor.

To reverse the relative price decline of the Great Recession, one might want to focus on the immediate cause in terms of the bank sector crash. But, using only the 3 equation New Keynesian model, the Fed would not be doing anything with respect to banking. All they would be doing is setting market interest rates, in particular the Federal Funds rate. And apparently, the idea would be to raise the Federal Funds rate (FFR) and so induce more relative price increases and a higher measured inflation. The Fed did the opposite and kept the FFR prolongedly low at near zero for eight years, still counting.

The Great Recession's market economy did not cooperate with this model apparently and neither did actual US government policy. Rather a great focus was put on subsidizing the bank sector, and lowering the FFR. In addition, with the payment of interest on reserves for the first time in US history, and at a higher rate than the FFR, the main FFR determination was a result of what interest rate was paid on excess reserves. This Fed payment of interest on excess reserves increased bank earnings directly, at the cost of general Treasury revenues which receives the "profit" that the central bank makes from its job of supplying the nation's money supply.

Laubach and Williams (2015, ibid, above footnote) use the 3-equation model as extended to the long run to argue that the US has been in a 65 year downwards trend in its long run economic growth. The implication

[27]Davies, C., M. Gillman, M. Kejak, 2016, "Euler Equations and Interest Rates Rules", working paper revision, July 12.

is that this is due to bad luck and not bad policy. So continuing a near-zero interest rate policy appears to them a potentially good idea.

The long run Phillips curve used in Laubach and Williams (2015) to generate such results is arguably distorting the picture. They estimate a positive relation between the inflation rate and output growth and then apply this relation to the whole post 1960 period. This forces down their estimate of the real output growth rate, making it seemingly biased, since the inflation rate fell dramatically (following the 1978 US law which directed the Fed to lower the inflation rate towards zero) throughout the 1980's and into the 1990's during which time real GDP was high.

If in fact growth was high and sustained in the 1960's, 1980's and 1990's, then the decrease in US statutory tax rates during those eras, in terms of the personal and corporate income tax, as well as the decrease in the inflation tax and in broad degrees of economic regulation, may have helped cause the high growth rates of those decades. This would be what is called good macroeconomic policy, not good luck. Laubach and Williams present the bad luck idea for why real interest rates have been low, or negative, during the post-Great Depression period: it's just a result of a long swing towards international GDP stagnation, is their proposition. But rather than bad luck, the current Lost Decade may well be a result of the bad policy from the Fed implicitly taxing world capital markets though its unprecedented control of capital prices.

11.4 Application: Normalizing Policy

The policy take-away during the period after the Great Recession of 2008 to 2010, during what might well be called a lost decade of low growth, is that belief in the 3-equation New Keynesian model means that the US is in a new era of low growth, given the long run linkage of the first, IS, equation of the model. Belief in the 3-equation model makes this a natural conclusion. And then the result is that there is nothing that government policy can do to reverse this. Negative or low real interest rates are simply the fundamental "secular" trend now facing the US for the indefinite future, and near zero nominal interest rates are therefore justified.[28]

Alternatively, consider the results of the analysis presented in this chapter. The Phillips curve trade-off was temporary and held only during the crash in bank intermediation and in asset prices. Once banking was stabilized, since 2010, there is little discernible Phillips curve behavior in the data. Economic growth resumed, with no Phillips curve relation, but nominal interest rates were still forced to near zero. The second equation of the 3 equation model, the Phillips curve, does not hold now and has not held apparently since a brief 2008–2009 appearance during the simultaneous bank crisis and asset market crash.

Second, the money supply has dramatically been increased by the Fed, but inflation has not occurred as Fisher's quantity theory model suggests. But that is because the money is in the form of reserves that as of 2008 receive interest above the market rate of the Federal Funds rate, thereby encouraging keeping the reserves while discouraging using the reserves to instead make loans. Turning all of the current excess reserves into loans would dramatically increase private bank demand deposits and the money supply in turn. Inflation would then rise undoubtedly.

Paying interest on excess reserves is an example of what economists term Moral Hazard. The government policy is paying banks not to lend out reserves and create new investment, thereby increasing the probability of the "bad state" of insufficient private investment. Increasing the probability of the bad state is the very essence of a policy-induced increase in Moral Hazard. It may have been deemed to be a good idea to give banks emergency revenue during the crisis, with the clearly stated intent in Fed minutes of ending this interest payment. This then is a limited duration ad hoc form of providing deposit insurance coverage to the banks. But the indefinite continuation of the interest payments simply has induced banks to lend out less reserves and so has created the moral hazard of a "lost decade" state of affairs with less investment relative to savers deposited funds.

Were interest payment on excess reserves ended, and the reserves were lent out, then as inflation rises, the Fed would see increasing pressure to raise nominal interest rates. This is exactly what occurred in 2005

[28]As in Lawrence Summer's "stagnation" blogs.

after holding the FFR below the inflation rate for nearly three years: high inflation induced the Fed to end its fixing of the FFR interest rate below the inflation rate. Currently, negative or zero, or very low, real interest rates cause less savings to be intermediated to private investment, as in an implicit tax on savings caused by an effective ceiling on real interest rates. If the Fed is creating an effective ceiling on real interest rates, this makes it seem that "stagnation" is endemic to the economy when instead it is an outcome of the paying of interest on bank reserves at a fixed interest rate above the FFR while keeping the FFR near zero. The FFR market has become dominated by paying a higher interest rate on reserves. This gives banks a "risk-free" bonanza of interest on reserves that they normally would only receive once they lent out the reserves for investment.[29]

Of the New Keynesian three equation model, the Taylor equation has been deemed irrelevant to actual interest rates. The IS equation indicates stagnation. And the Phillips curve no longer holds or is relevant post- bank crisis. So the only take-away is the IS equation indicating stagnation. Does the conclusion that the economy is in a fundamentally long term stagnation follow when the rest of the model is apparently invalid during the Great Recession's lost decade?[30]

Excess reserves are not being fully lent out as loans, as in all previous pre-2008 history, and the stagnating growth does indeed continue. The proper policy path that leads to a normalization of the economy is to stop paying interest on excess reserves and raise the FFR so that the real interest rate is positive. There would be a resulting bump up in the inflation rate, perhaps over 5 to 10 years, but more likely over just a few years, as the excess reserves are lent out and the money supply expands. The nominal interest rate would be allowed to rise with the inflation rate and the real interest rate would be kept positive and procyclic as reflecting supply and demand in the capital market over the normal business cycle. That normalization would take care of the purely monetary policy part of the government policy path to full policy normalization.

The answer to full normalization is not heavily regulating banks through higher reserve requirements. The answer is a Bagehot goal of minimal reserves and the most efficient intermediation as is possible. This is done by having all financial intermediaries join the FDIC and pay premiums that insure their depositor funds. The premium rate paid would depend on the riskiness of the intermediary's portfolio, as with current FDIC policy. And if an intermediary chooses to have relative large reserve levels, that intermediary would tend to pay a lower risk premium, depending on the riskiness of the rest of the intermediary's asset portfolio. That would take care of the so-called "macro-prudential" side of regulating the financial intermediary sector. Spreading this risk-based deposit insurance premium system to the international finance sector would stabilize global financial markets.

Finally, the fiscal aspect is that the US federal government has to respect its budget constraint in the sense of moving from a continuing, unending bank sector bailout, and wartime economy, to a more normal federal government role of financing normal social insurance systems. This need include the cost of international military activity; but this is a small fraction of the federal budget relative to past military activity during major wars. Normalizing the federal budget expenditures, which in all fairness could have happened once the financial sector collapse was over, is imperative in keeping the Fed from printing money at the historically accelerated rate it chose since 2008. The Fed would not have to buy so much Treasury debt if the Treasury did not have to borrow so much to cover its deficit.

The Ramsey World as extended to including money may well explain the current economy, once all of the implicit taxes and subsidizations taking place in the capital market are included. This can be from the New Monetarist perspective of Williamson (http://newmonetarism.blogspot.com/), that views money as the most liquid asset, or from the neoclassical models that includes money simply as a means of exchange.

The neoclassical approach emphasizes liquidity only in terms of the classic Wicksellian liquidity effect of driving down the real interest rate by accelerating the rate of growth of the money supply. This liquidity effect can explain the long stream of low real interest rates through a repeated application of accelerated money supply growth: This money growth is apparent in the Fed's near continuous huge asset build-up since 2008,

[29]The original idea of paying interest on bank reserves goes back historically and in recent literature but there it was apparently never linked to the idea of paying interest at a rate permanently above the Federal Funds Rate. See Guzman, Mark G., 2008, "The Impact Of Paying Interest On Reserves In The Presence Of Government Deficit Financing," Economic Inquiry, 46(October, 4): 624–642.

[30]As Summers argues in his blog: http://larrysummers.com/category/secular-stagnation/

Figure 11.25 US Economy's Python Digestion of Prickly Porkupine-Inflation

which in turn reflect the path of excess reserves. Once these reserves get loaned back out, the neoclassical Ramsey world with money would predict Figure 11.25: a lump of inflation over time to be gradually digested by the US economy.

11.5 Appendix: Being Earnest on Banking

Why was interest paid on reserves in 2008? The Fed says it was just to stop penalizing banks from having to hold required reserves, an old concept dating back to economists such as Milton Friedman. Banks need to hold reserves in the normal course of business. The Fed requires this to be about 10%. To the extent that this amount of reserves is more than what banks would normally hold, the Fed is "taxing" banks by requiring more non-interest bearing reserves than banks would have chosen on their own. So the idea was to pay interest on all of the required reserves: this would actually subsidize banks by paying interest not only on the additional reserves required by the Fed compared to what they would normally hold, but also on the usual reserves the banks would normally hold.

Then the idea of paying interest was allowed to morph unexpectedly in terms of economic theory behind the idea. Instead of paying interest only on required reserves, in 2008 the Fed allowed interest to be paid on all reserves held at the Fed including excess reserves. Now, historically before 2008 in the US, excess reserves were zero, always. Now suddenly with interest paid on excess reserves as well as required reserves, excess reserves began piling up as the Treasury issued debt and sold it to banks, the Fed bought the debt from the banks, and the banks kept the proceeds as excess reserves at the Fed. This enabled risk-free income at a rate above the Federal Funds Rate (FFR), since the FFR was one-quarter of a percent less than the rate paid on excess reserves. This essentially eliminated the Federal Funds market and replaced the setting of FFR interest rates by the Fed to the setting of the interest rate on excess reserves.

The truth is that discussion at the Fed explicitly emphasized the amount of money this would send to the main, small, group of US banks that accounted for most of the reserve holdings. This money would shore up their balance sheets. And so it did. The average amount of excess reserves on which interest was paid since from 2014 to 2016 is about $2.4 trillion. At an interest rate currently of 0.25% on excess reserves, as from 2008 until November of 2015, these reserves were paying (2,400,000,000,000) (0.0025) = 6,000,000,000. This is $6 billion a year being paid to the 10 "systematically important" banks that hold the bulk of the excess reserves. For each of the 10 banks on average this is a guaranteed source of $600 million a year, a sizeable part of any corporation's annual revenue.[31] Figure 11.26 shows the FRED graph for the required reserves interest rate (Blue) interest on excess reserves (Purple and Green) and Federal Funds rate (Red) from 2009–2015.[32]

[31] Thornton, D. "Another Unintended Consequence of QE", Common Sense Economics Perspective, No. 13.

[32] See same graph in Timothy S. Fuerst, 2015, Comment on: "Speculative runs on interest rate pegs" by Marco Bassetto and Christopher Phelan, Journal of Monetary Economics, 73(July): 115–118.

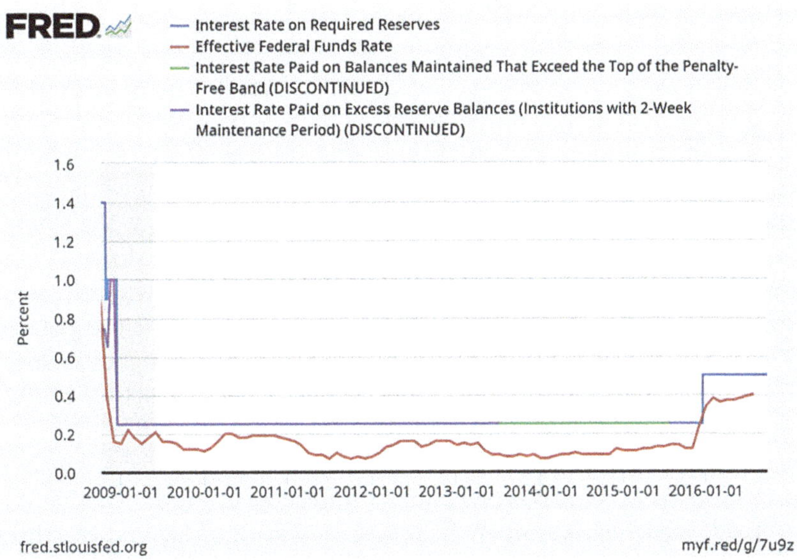

Figure 11.26 Interest on Excess Reserves vs. Federal Funds Rate, 2009–2015

In December 2015, the interest rate on excess reserves was raised by a quarter of a percent to 0.5%. This means that for the year of 2016, double the amount will have gone to the 10 banks, or $12 billion. This is an average of $1.2 billion per bank for the year, a huge source of revenue.

Excess reserves finally showed signs of starting to decline during 2016. So the average interest paid to each of these private banks may continue to decline: but even $1 billion is a lot of risk-free revenue for a bank to receive from the Fed each year. Normally, as in historically in the US, any such direct subsidy to private sector banks would need to be authorized by Congress according to the budget reconciliation laws of the federal budget process. The Fed has essentially skirted the US Congressional budget process by directly paying banks money for any given level of reserves.

The Fed also broke its own "law", of not specifically benefiting any one sector by its purchases of assets when it bought up the mass of mortgage-backed securities (MBS). So they abruptly changed their policy to explicitly drop the language of not supporting any one sector. This support of a sector through asset purchases normally is done through the Treasury, as it was under President Bush in 2008. Then the Treasury purchases of MBS had to be budgeted through the Congressional budget process according to the expected loss incurred from buying risky debt. In particular, the expected loss on mortgage purchases, via MBS holdings, would have to have been approved by the Congressional budget for the fiscal year.[33]

So the Fed skirted the US Congress budget process a second time with MBS purchases, along with the excess reserve interest payments, leading various members of US Congress to call on re-writing the statue governing the Fed. Of course the Fed Presidents oppose that; for example Jeffrey Lacker testified to the US Congress Subcommittee on Monetary Policy and Trade, of the House Financial Services Committee, arguing delicately for no changes to the Fed, as in his conclusion:[34]

> "Many aspects of the Fed and our financial system have changed since the Fed's founding, and some claim that the Federal Reserve's governance structure is a historical anachronism. Nevertheless, our core function–providing stable monetary conditions to facilitate economic activity–remains unchanged. And the continued relevance of the trade-offs taken into account by the authors of the Federal Reserve Act argues for the continued utility of the finely balanced arrangements they crafted."

[33]Passed into law in 1974, The Congressional Budget and Impoundment Control Act requires Congress to make a budget each year and enact laws required to attain the budget that they agree upon; sometimes this takes the form of a Budget Reconciliation Act that adjusts programs so as to meet the Congressional budget target. Such an Act then must be signed into law by the President or vetoed.

[34]See https://www.richmondfed.org/press_room/speeches/president_jeff%lacker/2016/lacker_testimony_20160907

Meanwhile regulations, through "stress tests" that the Fed has imposed, require higher reserve requirements on what the Fed has deemed as "systematically important" banks. So the Fed pays interest on these reserves at the same time that it demands more reserves. This skews the bank portfolio towards holding more excess reserves and making less loans. In itself it would be expected to cause a decrease in lending activity.

What bank policy was the real smoking gun of the 2008 bank panic? Can there be any regulatory cause of the bank panic as a result of distortions in the capital market induced by the regulation itself? It might be said that there are five main sets of regulation, policy changes and legal aspects that contribution to the 2008 bank panic. And these five all involve the indirect subsidization of mortgage loans.

The first is the Fed purchase of a large portfolio of MBS. The second is the federal tax-based subsidization of house mortgages, from a long-standing policy of allowing the income tax deduction of interest paid on housing loans. Third, housing loans have been federally guaranteed for high-risk, low-income, mortgage loans since the 1930's, but these guaranteed loans accelerating since 1999 when the Federal National Mortgage Association (Fannie Mae) began easing requirements for loans.

Fannie Mae is an acronym for a strange subsidization entity for mortgage loans, which has switched ownership between the government and the private sector over time, depending on whether it ran losses or profits on its loan portfolio. The US federal government had privatized Fannie Mae in stages through 1954 and 1968 legislation that made its operations no longer appear within the US federal budget process. After 1970, it acted as a private corporation that was "government sponsored", or a "government sponsored entity" (GSE).

The government sponsorship was the federal guarantee of the repayment of the mortgage loans made by Fannie Mae. It became listed and traded publicly on the New York stock exchange in 1970. The first mortgage backed securities trading also began in 1970, according to Jaffee and Quigley[35]

From $3 billion in 2003, Fannie Mae's purchases of new mortgage loans rose steadily to $20 billion in 2006. This is the period that overlaps with the Fed's strict control of the FFR interest rate, between 1% and 2%, that created negative real interest rates that are good for borrowers. Fannie Mae was found by the Office of Federal Housing Enterprise Oversight (OFHEO) in May of 2006 to have reported profits that were overstated by $11 billion, hiding the extent to which the "sub-prime" loans were under-performing, with a $350 million penalty imposed on Fannie Mae by the Security and Exchange Commission. Fannie Mae became bankrupt in September 2008 after the Fed suddenly raised interest rates in 2005–2006. This agency was then "de-chartered", or placed into federal "conservatorship", and so taken over by the Federal government.

The fourth factor is that the US Commodity Futures Modernization Act of 2000 (CFMA) allowed over-the-counter trading of derivatives to not be classified as futures or securities, and thus Credit Default Swaps based on mortgages were able to avoid regulation. According to Matthew Sherman (2009), "The bill prevented the Commodity Futures Trading Commission from regulating most over-the-counter derivative contracts, including credit default swaps." As a result, "derivatives trading expanded quickly, increasing from a total outstanding nominal value of $106 trillion in 2001, to a value of $531 trillion in 2008."[36]

The trading of MBS became more unregulated. The FDIC had been in the practice of giving first precedence to Credit Default Swaps (CDS) when winding up a defaulted bank. In this way, the liquid assets associated with CDS could be resolved quickly rather than waiting months for their resolution in courts. And the FDIC could then reorganize and sell the bank's assets and keep it an ongoing concern under different ownership so that the bank system was not disrupted.

The 2000 CFMA allowed the same first-claim-on-assets prioritization of CDS traded, on the over-the-counter market by private financial intermediaries, that the FDIC was using when a bank became insolvent. The prioritization of CDS that were based on MBS meant that these CDS's became guarantees that mortgage loan losses would be repaid first out of assets by any financial institution that went into default. This gave a subsidy to the value of MBS-based CDS that made them more profitable for financial intermediaries to hold relative to other assets. This prioritization of MBS-based CDS occurred at the same time as when the mortgage

[35]"The Future of the Government Sponsored Enterprises: The Role for the Government in the US Mortgage Market", by Dwight Jaffee and John M. Quigley, Working Paper 17685. http://www.nber.org/papers/w17685

[36]Pages 2, 11, respectively; Matthew Sherman, 2009, "A Short History of Financial Deregulation in the United States", July, Center for Economic and Policy Research, Washington, D.C.

market subprime loans were encouraged by federal government policy. And many of these loans could not be repaid once the Fed stopped fixing interest rates in 2005 and instead raised interest rates dramatically.[37]

When the MBS went into default and the CDS insurance went to be cashed in at a host of insolvent investment banks, there were insufficient liquid assets that could be used to pay off the insurance against mortgage risk paid for by the CDS's. This caused a flood of CDS's that could not be paid back, as in a default on the contract's ensuing payment, and this amplified the bank crisis among investment banks. It resulted in a run on the deposits, or money market funds, of the investment banks leading to several bankruptcies.[38]

"Un-prudential" federal subsidization of housing loans through government sponsored enterprises, and imprudent financial regulation that allowed CDS's of private investment banks the same prioritization that the federal government FDIC used in the special case of banks becoming bankrupt, plus the statutory income tax deduction allowed for interest on mortgage loans, led to a triple subsidization of the use of financial instruments that drained the liquid assets of the financial system once the housing prices collapsed starting in 2007. This occurred only starting in 2007 because the drop in housing prices then meant that the collateral value of the mortgage loans became less than what was owed. The loans then had negative value, so the investment demand for mortgage backed securities began to tumult.

The fifth factor is the Fed fixing of nominal interest rates. Had the Fed not fixed nominal interest rates for nearly three years from 2002 to 2005, at levels below the inflation rate, thereby subsidizing borrowing with negative real interest rates, and then dramatically raised them from 2005 to 2007, the mortgage crisis would have likely not have occurred. For example, if the market interest rates fell to 1% in 2001, and then were allowed to rise back up so as to keep the real interest rate positive and at levels of the real interest rate consistent with an expansion in the economy, then the Fed's role in subsidizing borrowing would not have occurred. As it happened, the Fed contributed the fifth subsidy to mortgage borrowing by creating negative real interest rates that significantly lowered the interest rates on mortgage loans for a sustained multi-year period by its fixing of the FFR below the CPI inflation rate.

11.6 Summary

The Federal Reserve Bank System's (the Fed's) response to the terrorist attacks on the US on September 11, 2001, began an era of highly unusual control of capital markets by the Fed. Interest rates in terms of the Federal Funds Rate (FFR) were held fixed for years at a time, unlike any previous period in US history since the Fed was established in 1914.

Fixed interest rates occurred in three steps from 2002 to 2005, and at a single fixed rate from 2008 until the end of 2015. This capital market control, through maintaining a fixed FFR for a year or more at a time, accounts for about 11 of the last 14 years. During this time the real interest rate was forced into negative ranges for much of the time as the CPI inflation rate fluctuated at rates above the FFR.

The US Treasury ran continual high deficits ever since fiscal year 2002. They borrowed by issuing new Treasury debt, which private markets bought. The Fed bought back a large fraction of the total new Treasury debt borrowing since 2002. This typically is called monetizing the debt by printing money to buy it up with the result of higher inflation.

That the higher inflation did not result left markets to ponder when the inflation rate would rise or if the dramatic increase in the monetary base would ever even translate into higher inflation. The inflation did not result since much of the Fed's purchase of Treasury debt from private banks ended up back in the Fed as excess reserves held by the private banks at the Fed.

---

[37] See William T. Gavin, 2015, "Bankruptcy Rules for Derivatives: How Have They Changed and Why Do They Matter?", manuscript, December.

[38] "The CMFA made a change in bankruptcy law for derivatives that contributed to crises at Enron and WorldCom. It made it profitable for banks to create and trade the collateralized debt obligations (CDO) and the credit default swaps (CDS) that exploded in use between 2004 and 2008. These instruments, which derived their value from subprime mortgages, fell sharply in price during 2008 and were the immediate cause of the insolvencies at Bear Stearns and Lehman Brothers." W. T. Gavin, ibid, above footnote, p. 1.

Before the Fed began paying interest on excess reserves in 2008, essentially zero excess reserves had always previously been held at the Fed. Indeed the Federal Funds market was just a market through which banks borrowed from each other in order to meet the weekly required reserve level that they were obligated to meet under Fed regulations. Once the Fed paid interest on excess reserves, those reserves grew to about \$2.5 trillion, today now somewhat lower.

The interest paid of reserves was a quarter of one percent from 2008 until December 2015, at which time it rose to a half of a percentage point. This generated interest paid by the Fed to private banks of some \$6 billion a year in 2015 and double that, to \$12 billion, in 2016. Moreover, Fed minutes show that almost all of this interest on excess reserves has been going to a group of only 10 banks. This amounts to \$1.2 billion in 2016 on average being paid to each of the banks, completely "off-budget" and skirting the US Congressional budget process.

The Fed also directly aided the bank industry during the Great Recession and afterwards by buying and holding a large portfolio of mortgage backed securities (MBS). Historically Fed regulation prohibited the Fed from buying assets that favored any one industry; this language was dropped from Fed rules during the Great Recession. Again, if the US Treasury had bought these MBS as they did at the end of President George W. Bush's second term as President, then any expected losses on the purchases would have to have gone through the Congressional budget process. The Fed purchases of MBS, for the first time in US history, again allowed the propping up of the bank industry, while evading the approval of the required appropriations that normally would have to be approved through the US Congressional budget reconciliation acts that are signed into law by the President.

The effect of the setting of the FFR below the inflation rate for so many years since 2001 forced negative real interest rates onto capital markets while the Fed flooded capital markets with purchases of US Treasury debt. This in effect put a "ceiling" on the real rate of interest at a level below the "natural" real rate of interest that would exist were the Fed not intervening persistently in capital markets.

Wicksell and Friedman had long discussed how any such long-term, persistent, or semi-permanent, lowering of the real interest rate by increasing the rate of growth of the money supply would lead to sustained higher inflation. This higher inflation did not result yet because the huge amounts of the reserves have not been lent out and have been kept instead as "excess" reserves back at the Fed, as a result of the Fed paying interest on the reserves.

The distortions to capital markets have resulted because at low real interest rates a lower private savings rate results. In essence Fed policy has forced up the risky private investment real interest rate while lowering the "risk-free" government interest rate paid on US Treasury debt. A lower loan to deposit rate has resulted because this investment gauge, by various measures, tends to follow the real interest rate. A low real interest rate leads to less loans and private investment relative to total bank deposits.

Policy debates center around what the Fed should do henceforth. One proposal is to continue to keep the FFR low since the low GDP growth rate of the "lost decade" following the Great Recession has been just the bad luck of a long-stagnating world economy. In contrast is the option to raise the FFR, and eliminate the interest on excess reserves, so as to end a bad policy regime of implicitly taxing capital markets by imposing a low real interest rate ceiling on them through persistent liquidity injections. If the latter international capital market tax effect of Fed policy is a valid hypothesis, and if the interest payment on reserves is ended, it is very likely the US and possibly world economy will experience a burst of sustained inflation well above the Fed target of 2% a year. Risky capital market returns in terms of "high" stock market valuations would also be expected to fall, just as the risk-free real interest rate would be expected to rise.

The good part of a complete capital market deregulation in terms of ending the Fed's "price-of-capital controls" is that capital markets would likely become reinvigorated towards "fundamentals" and normal real GDP growth would likely be able to resume worldwide. Higher inflation for a time would simply be part of the tax imposed to pay for the decade-long spree of a sustained high level of deficit spending. That is how Ricardian equivalence works: everything spent by the government eventually has to be paid for through taxes.

11.7 Glossary

deposit insurance law: starting with the FDIC in 1933, bank deposits up to a certain limit were insured by the US federal government; such insurance schemes exist internationally; insurance companies and pension companies can be part of such insurance systems.

disintermediation: when consumers take their savings out of the private financial intermediation industry.

Federal Funds rates: the rate charged on overnight deposits at the Fed by private banks to private banks, as the banks seek to meet their weekly reserve requirements at the Fed.

financial panic: when savers distrust the solvency of banks they try to take out their savings immediately, causing typically an inability of banks to meet demands, leading to greater efforts to get back deposits, in a ever-crescendoing bank panic.

industrial revolution: when manufacturing progress occurred in the 1700's and 1800's and a shift away from agriculture occurred towards more manufacturing.

lost decade: a era of low, stagnating, real output growth.

Liquid Assets: assets used for example in inter-bank markets to clear immediate demand on their deposits.

monetarily financed: typically a deficit and debt financed time of government spending during which the central bank buys up a substantial portion of government debt so as to increase the rate of growth of the money supply in the process; can be an increase in the reserves that do not get lent out as in the aftermath of the Great Recession.

Mortgage Backed Securities (MBS): bundles of loans made to buy houses that are sold in capital markets.

natural "Wicksellian" real interest rate equilibrium: the rate of interest that Wicksell and Ricardo advocated as being consistent with the natural supply and demand in capital markets, while not be affected by central bank actions.

non-bank banks: the non-commercial or non-retail banks that began arising in the late 1970's and 1980's that paid interest on deposit accounts at rates that exceeded the restrictions of Regulation Q interest ceilings on what FDIC insured banks could pay on deposits; included investment banks.

normalization of the banking sector: eliminating Federal Reserve Bank heavy control of the pricing of capital markets; having zero excess reserves at the Fed as in all previous US history since 1914 and before 2008; not allowing the Fed to pay interest on excess reserves.

quantitative easing: the policy of increasing the money supply through an increase in the central bank buying of its government's debt since 2008; resulted in excess reserves in the US where interest was paid on excess reserves.

real interest rate: nominal or market interest rate minus the inflation rate or expected inflation rate.

riskless portfolio of government debt: holdings of US Treasury debt, or an ownership in funds that invest in such debt.

seeking return: private investor or investment bank trying to increase the overall return on a portfolio already heavily weighted towards a large amount of risk-free debt, paying a "below-normal" interest rate, by buying increasingly risky equity shares in private corporations that also have a "higher than normal" return.

systematically important: banks judged by US banking regulation as ones that can induce aggregate risk should they fail.

sub-prime mortgages: loans for houses made to those who may be unlikely to repay the loans should interest rates rise and housing prices fall; housing loans made to low income households with future interest payments that can easily exceed the ability to pay.

US government sponsored "enterprises: these are agencies created by the federal government in order to carry out a particular US government policy, such as through making direct loans or federally guaranteeing loans.

utilization rate: the rate at which human, physical or financial capital is used productively relative to the entire stock of such capital.

11.8 Questions

1. What interest rates did the Fed set from 2001 until the present time?
2. What evidence is there that the Fed increased the rate of growth of the money supply since 2008?
3. What was the composition of the Fed's assets in the period since 2008?
4. How much excess reserves has the Fed held in the years since 2008?
5. How large were US Treasury deficits in the period following the terrorist attacks on September 11th, 2011?

6. In what sense could it be argued that the Fed "bailed out" the US bank system after 2008?
7. Describe at least two US bank acts that regulated banks more severely and two US bank acts that deregulated banking requirements.
8. How did financial capital and human capital utilization rates change in the post-2000 period?
9. What is Bagehot's theory for the financial success of Britain in the late 1800's as a center for international banking?
10. In what evidence can it be found that Phillips curve behavior was associated with correlated asset price booms or crashes?
11. How can a fixed low interest rate that is paid on excess reserves held at the Fed act to impose a ceiling on the real interest rate in capital markets?
12. How can an effective ceiling on real interest act to impose a tax on capital markets that 1) distorts investment towards more risk-free government debt, 2) induces a lesser percentage of portfolio investment in the private sector, and 3) induces investment in the private sector that is riskier than without the tax but also higher yielding that without the tax.
13. What are potential international consequences of a policy that forces down real interest rates in worldwide capital markets?
14. Give an example of how the New Keynesian model has been used to justify continued use of extremely low market interest rates as controlled by the Fed?
15. How might monetary policy be "normalized" so that capital markets are no longer under a fixed-price regime?
16. Approximately how much revenue has gone to the private bank sector from the Fed as interest on excess reserves? Does this policy evade the US Congressional budget process? Does the purchase of MBS by the Fed evade the US Congressional budget process?
17. Complete the Federal Reserve Bank of St. Louis EconLowdown Course Module "The Great Depression 6".

Index

D

E

R

S

www.ingramcontent.com/pod-product-compliance
Ingram Content Group UK Ltd.
Pitfield, Milton Keynes, MK11 3LW, UK
UKHW052010041026
15590UKWH00008B/2260

9 781524 916756